# THE GOVERNMENT

OF

# THE UNITED STATES

NATIONAL, STATE, AND LOCAL

BY

WILLIAM BENNETT MUNRO, Ph.D., LL.B.
PROFESSOR OF MUNICIPAL GOVERNMENT
IN HARVARD UNIVERSITY

New York
THE MACMILLAN COMPANY
1919

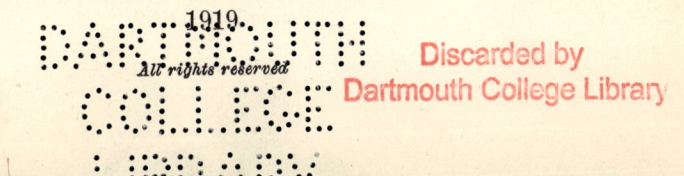

*All rights reserved*

COPYRIGHT, 1919,
BY THE MACMILLAN COMPANY.

Set up and electrotyped. Published February, 1919.

Norwood Press
J. S. Cushing Co. — Berwick & Smith Co.
Norwood, Mass., U.S.A.

To

**Samuel Walker McCall**

in token of my
homage and gratitude

# PREFACE

My aim in the preparation of this book has been to provide a general survey of the principles and practice of American government as exemplified in the nation, in the states, and in the several areas of local administration. I have endeavored, so far as the limits of a single volume would permit, not only to explain the form and functions of the American political system, but to indicate the origin and purpose of the various institutions, to show how they have been developed by law or by usage, to discuss their present-day workings, merits, and defects, and to contrast the political institutions of the United States with analogous institutions in other lands. Surprisingly little has been written on the history of American political institutions, and not much more on the principles which these institutions are assumed to exemplify. Text-books, in the main, have emphasized the practical workings of governmental agencies to the neglect of these other things.

The plan, scope, content, and temper of this book are in large measure the outgrowth of my experience as a teacher. My students, by the drift of their questions and discussions, have moulded my ideas of what a text-book ought to contain. This book is theirs as much as it is mine. That fact may help to explain why some features of American government are dilated upon at considerable length, while others are left as self-evident propositions to the perception of the reader. It explains, moreover, why the same problem is occasionally discussed from different angles, even though this has involved some degree of repetition. And if the general tone of the book betrays an optimist, my sufficient answer is that no man can be for many years associated with the American undergraduate and remain anything else.

I am under obligations to Professor John A. Fairlie of the University of Illinois, to Professor A. N. Holcombe of Harvard University, and to Congressman F. W. Dallinger of Cambridge for many helpful suggestions. Miss Alice Holden of Wellesley College has given me much-appreciated assistance in reading the proofs and in preparing the index.

WILLIAM BENNETT MUNRO.

January 5, 1919.

# CONTENTS

| CHAPTER | | PAGE |
|---|---|---|
| I. | English and Colonial Origins | 1 |
| II. | Preliminaries of National Government | 14 |
| III. | The Constitution and Its Makers | 26 |
| IV. | "The Supreme Law of the Land" | 44 |
| V. | How the Constitution Has Developed | 57 |
| VI. | The Citizen and His Rights | 71 |
| VII. | The President | 88 |
| VIII. | Presidential Powers and Functions | 105 |
| IX. | The Cabinet and National Administration | 126 |
| X. | The Senate: Its Organization | 146 |
| XI. | The Senate: Its Functions | 162 |
| XII. | The House of Representatives: Its Composition | 176 |
| XIII. | The House of Representatives: Organization and Procedure | 191 |
| XIV. | The General Powers of Congress | 208 |
| XV. | The Taxing Power | 219 |
| XVI. | The Borrowing Power, the National Debt, and the National Banking System | 233 |
| XVII. | The Power to Regulate Commerce | 246 |
| XVIII. | The War Powers | 265 |
| XIX. | Miscellaneous Powers of Congress | 277 |
| XX. | Constitutional Limitations on the Powers of Congress | 288 |
| XXI. | The Workings of Congressional Government | 299 |
| XXII. | Political Parties in National Government: Their History and Functions | 312 |
| XXIII. | Political Parties in National Government: Their Organization and Methods | 330 |
| XXIV. | The Judicial Power of the United States | 342 |
| XXV. | The Supreme Court and the Subordinate Courts | 357 |
| XXVI. | The Government of Territories | 372 |
| XXVII. | The Place of the States in the Nation | 389 |
| XXVIII. | The State Constitutions | 404 |

## CONTENTS

| CHAPTER | | PAGE |
|---|---|---|
| XXIX. | THE STATE LEGISLATURE | 415 |
| XXX. | THE GOVERNOR | 431 |
| XXXI. | STATE ADMINISTRATION | 445 |
| XXXII. | STATE FINANCE | 460 |
| XXXIII. | STATE PARTIES AND PRACTICAL POLITICS | 473 |
| XXXIV. | THE STATE COURTS | 489 |
| XXXV. | DIRECT LEGISLATION AND THE RECALL | 501 |
| XXXVI. | THE RECONSTRUCTION OF STATE GOVERNMENT | 522 |
| XXXVII. | THE HISTORY OF LOCAL GOVERNMENT | 535 |
| XXXVIII. | COUNTY GOVERNMENT | 546 |
| XXXIX. | TOWNS, TOWNSHIPS, AND VILLAGES | 560 |
| XL. | THE AMERICAN CITY | 572 |
| XLI. | MUNICIPAL ORGANIZATION | 588 |
| XLII. | MUNICIPAL ADMINISTRATION | 602 |
| XLIII. | COMMISSION AND CITY MANAGER GOVERNMENT | 619 |
| INDEX | | 637 |

# THE GOVERNMENT
OF THE UNITED STATES

# THE GOVERNMENT OF THE UNITED STATES

## CHAPTER I

### ENGLISH AND COLONIAL ORIGINS

IN the political history of the American people the most notable achievement has been the welding of many commonwealths into one great federal state. For this accomplishment the main credit has usually been given to the group of fifty-five men who sweltered through the summer of 1787 in the convention hall at Philadelphia and forged at white heat what Gladstone generously called "the most wonderful work ever struck off at a given time by the brain and purpose of man." But the thirteen colonies which they welded into an enduring union had already been brought by more than one hundred and fifty years of historical development into a close political kinship. That was what made any sort of organic union possible. The American Revolution was merely the culmination of colonial growth, and the constitution was the logical outcome of conditions which the Revolution brought into being. *The indebtedness of the United States to English and colonial experience.*

In one sense the American Revolution was not a revolution at all. It was not a cataclysm like the French Revolution of the eighteenth century; it did not sweep away fundamental institutions, or transform political ideals, or shift the weight of political power from one class among the people to another. It merely changed the resting-place of sovereignty. The sovereign power had hitherto been vested in the crown. It had been exercised by the grant of charters or through instructions sent by the home authorities to the colonial governors. Henceforth it was to vest *The continuity of American political history.*

in the people of the thirteen commonwealths, to be exercised by them through their own constitutions and laws. In the continuity of American political institutions, therefore, the Revolution marks a break of no great violence. It guided political evolution into new channels, and set the political ideals of the New World more clearly before its people.

American constitutional history, therefore, does not begin with the Declaration of Independence in 1776 nor yet with the founding of the first seaboard colonies more than a century and a half previously. Its beginnings go back to the days of the Saxon folk-mote and the Curia Regis of Norman England. The principles of civil liberty as established by Magna Carta, the Bill of Rights, by the Habeas Corpus Acts, and by the whole fabric of the Common Law were the patrimony of the American colonists from the outset. By migrating to America they lost none of the rights and liberties which they had possessed at home. They did not therefore create anew but brought with them the political traditions upon which a free government could be set up. The right to a share in the making of laws, the right of self-taxation, the right to trial by jury, the right of petition, the right of all men to be dealt with equally before the law — these rights did not originate in America. They are the heritage of the whole Anglo-Saxon race. The American Revolution preserved them at a time when they were in danger of being trodden under foot and the American constitutions, both state and national, merely asserted them anew.

Unity of the colonies.

The thirteen colonies which formed the nucleus of the United States were the outgrowth of small communities planted along the Atlantic seaboard during the course of the seventeenth century.[1] When the first settlers came, it was not with the idea of founding new states; hence they were organized as trading companies with charters similar to those given to such corporations in other parts of the world. But the colonists soon found that something more than this was necessary. Hence the company charters

[1] For a narrative of this political development, see Professor Edward Channing, *History of the United States*, Vols. i–ii (N. Y., 1905–1908).

gave way in some cases to colony charters; or where no such charters were forthcoming, the people went ahead without the formal authority, establishing their own local and general governments. But the lines of this political development were not everywhere parallel. Differences in the occupations of the people and to some extent in the temper of the colonists themselves led to a departure from uniformity throughout the various communities. These political differences were not, however, of great importance. If the general and local governments of Virginia and Massachusetts, for example, appear in colonial days to have been quite dissimilar, that is only because contrasts always appear more sharply than similarities when one takes only a superficial view of two governments. In their political ideals and institutions all the colonies were fundamentally alike; the differences among them are of slight account when weighed in the balance with the broad and deep resemblances. All the colonies had been founded by Englishmen or had passed under English control. The population everywhere was overwhelmingly of one religious faith and nearly all claimed the English language as their mother tongue. The common law of England formed the basis of the legal system everywhere. There was a substantial unity in language, in religion, and in law, and these in all ages are the great bonds which have drawn neighboring communities together.

It was because of this unity in race, language, religion, and law that there was a substantial similarity in political institutions.[1] To begin with, the basis of colonial government was in each colony the same. Alike in all of them it was the supremacy of the crown. Explorers went out under royal auspices; they took possession of new lands in the sovereign's name; the territories which they gained became royal property. The crown gave the first company charters; it also gave the colonial charters which replaced these earlier grants. When a colony had no charter, its

The basis of colonial government — royal supremacy.

---

[1] The best general outlines of political organization in the colonies as a whole are those given in C. M. Andrews, *Colonial Self-Government, 1652–1689* (N. Y., 1904), and in Evarts B. Greene, *Provincial America, 1690–1740* (N. Y., 1905).

government existed only by royal recognition. In theory, therefore, the crown was supreme as respects the colonies, and in America this doctrine lived on and was recognized until the Revolution. Not until the closing years of the colonial period did parliament ever assume to interfere with the forms of colonial government, and at no time did the colonists concede its claim to do so.

*Decay of this basis in England.* But in England the doctrine of royal supremacy lost ground. Parliament was able to bring the crown under its influence, and though it left the royal prerogative in outer form unimpaired, parliament steadily arrogated the real power to itself. At the middle of the eighteenth century, accordingly, Englishmen on both sides of the Atlantic were living under the same sovereign but under different notions as to the true rôle of the crown in matters of government. In England the virtual supremacy of parliament was established and recognized; in America the colonists knew and admitted no sovereignty but that of the crown. This point should be made clear, otherwise the attitude of the colonists in the days before the Revolution is not easy to understand. The thirteen colonies were alike in their subjection to the crown; they were also alike in their disregard of the fact that in the home land the old royal powers had passed under the sway of parliament.

*The forms of colonial government — charter, royal, and proprietary.* It has been customary to divide the thirteen colonies into three groups, namely, charter, royal, and proprietary. Connecticut and Rhode Island had charters and elected their own governors. Massachusetts after 1691 had a charter with an appointive governor.[1] Pennsylvania, Delaware, and Maryland belonged to proprietors, and these proprietors appointed the governors; the remaining seven colonies had neither charters nor proprietors, hence they were directly under the control of the crown, and by the crown their governors were appointed. But this differentiation in colonial status is not of any great importance, for all of the colonies were under relatively the same degree of control by the crown and its officers, and all of them, whether with charters or without, had much the same degree

[1] These various charters are printed in William MacDonald, *Select Charters Illustrative of American History, 1606–1775* (N. Y., 1899).

of freedom in managing their own affairs. For the present-day student of colonial institutions it would have greatly simplified matters if the English crown, in early days, had made all these things outwardly uniform, — if it had given all the colonies the same charter or given them all no charters at all. But that has never been the English way of doing things. The fact is that at no time was there any serious effort to make clear, beyond any chance of future dispute, just what autonomy a colony was to have and what final powers it was not to have. The general attitude on both sides, until just before the Revolution, was to refrain from any quarrel over theories or fundamentals of government, to deal with each problem as it arose, one or other side giving way as the circumstances seemed to dictate. This, indeed, has been a characteristic of English colonial policy at all stages of its development and in all parts of the world.

Through what channels did the crown exercise its supervision over the American colonies? The agencies of control were not the same at all periods, but broadly speaking it was the practice to leave to the Board of Trade in England all matters relating to trade with the colonies, while political questions, including the making of appointments, were placed in the hands of the Privy Council. This latter body acted, as a rule, on the advice of a standing committee known as the Committee for Plantation Affairs. But the jurisdiction of the Board of Trade was never strictly defined, and the royal ministers, either directly or through the board, frequently interfered. All instructions went directly to the colonial governors in the name of the crown. As for parliament, it had no way of controlling colonial affairs except in so far as it could influence the Lords of Trade or the Privy Council. Acts of parliament did not apply to the colonies unless they made express stipulation to that effect, and in very few was such provision made until after 1760. Then, when parliament began its practice of enacting special revenue laws for the colonies, the question of its right to do so was openly denied by the colonists. On the whole the system of home control was not well organized or efficient. There was always room for divided counsels, inaction, and delay. Hence the colonies, often at variance

*How England controlled the colonies.*

with one another, were let alone when a strongly centralized colonial office in London might have interfered to good advantage. When the home authorities did finally show vigor and determination, it was in behalf of a cause which united the colonies in their opposition.

*Framework of colonial government: the governor.*

Each of the thirteen colonies had a governor as its chief executive; in eight of them this official was appointed by the crown, in the others he was either elected by the people or named (as in Pennsylvania) by the proprietor of the colony.[1] The position of the colonial governor was something like that of the king at home; he summoned the colonial parliament or assembly and could dissolve it when he willed. In some respects his authority was far more extensive than that of the crown, for he had the right to veto the assembly's acts, while in England the crown had lost this power in relation to acts of parliament. The appointing authority of the colonial governor was also extensive, and he was the head of the militia in each of the colonies. The governors were of various types, but occasionally of high caliber. Their work was not easy; on the one hand they were supposed to carry out instructions from London issued by men who frequently knew next to nothing about colonial conditions; on the other hand they were the pivots of local administration, responsible for the efficient management of affairs yet dependent upon the colonial legislatures for money and support. The colonial governor had to serve two masters, one who gave him his appointment and the other who gave him his pay. From the nature of things he could rarely serve both well.

*The colonial legislature.*

In each colony there was also a legislature, usually composed of two branches. The lower chamber was in all cases elected by the people, but each colony had its own qualifications for voting and in most of them these requirements were strict. The ownership of property was usually required as a prerequisite for voting, and often religious tests were imposed as well.[2] The members of this elective chamber

---

[1] A discussion of his powers may be found in E. B. Greene, *Provincial Governor in the English Colonies of North America* (N. Y., 1898).

[2] For a full survey see A. E. McKinley, *The Suffrage Franchise in the Thirteen English Colonies* (Philadelphia, 1905).

were chosen by towns in New England or by the counties in the southern colonies, usually for short terms. The upper chambers were primarily executive bodies; in most cases the members were named either by the royal governor or by the proprietor. In addition to being the upper house of the colonial legislature, this body was also, in a few colonies, the governor's council, advising him and sometimes controlling his appointments. These colonial legislatures passed laws and claimed the sole right to legislate on any matter which concerned the colony's internal affairs. They alone could authorize the levy of taxes, and this control of the purse gave the colonial legislatures an indirect but nevertheless a strong hold upon the course of executive policy. In most of the colonies, however, all legislation was subject to the governor's veto and subject also to disallowance by the English authorities if they saw fit. The powers of these colonial legislatures were growing steadily when the eve of the Revolution approached.[1]

In all the colonies the groundwork of jurisprudence was the common law. It was not established in the colonies by any definite enactment, but like other Anglo-Saxon institutions it migrated with the flag. In addition, the colonial legislatures (subject to the governor's veto and to the power of disallowance by the home authorities) had the right to make laws so far as these were not repugnant to the laws of England. In recognition of the fact that new countries present new legislative requirements, the colonial assemblies were given a fair degree of freedom in law-making; but governor's vetoes were not rare, and colonial laws were occasionally disallowed when copies reached the law officers of the crown of England. The colonists thus became familiar with two political ideas which have continued orthodox in America to the present day, first, the idea of an executive veto and, second, the idea that a law may be invalid because of its repugnance to usages or statutes more fundamental than the law itself; in other words the conception of unconstitutionality. *Laws and the disallowance of laws.*

In one great field the colonial legislatures were virtually

[1] E. B. Russell, *The Review of American Colonial Legislation by the King in Council* (N. Y., 1915).

8    THE GOVERNMENT OF THE UNITED STATES

<small>The control of taxation.</small>

supreme, namely, in the matter of raising revenue. From time to time they formally declared their exclusive right to determine what taxes should be levied, and on the whole they managed to make good their claims in this domain of government. The legislatures also controlled the appropriations, but there were numerous disputes as to whether this control gave the legislatures full power to fix all executive and judicial salaries, including the salary of the governor himself. As a rule, however, the colonial legislatures had their way on this point as well.

<small>The judiciary.</small>

As for the judicial organization some differences existed among the several colonies, but here again the general lines were uniform. All of the colonies had local courts, usually presided over by justices of the peace who were appointed by the governor. Above these came, in most cases, the courts of quarter sessions made up of the justices in each county. And finally, each colony had a higher court which in some cases consisted of the governor and his council but which in others was a separate body made up of regularly appointed judges. From these highest colonial courts appeals might be carried to England where they were decided by the Privy Council. The Privy Council was not a court in the ordinary sense; its right to confirm or quash the judgments of the colonial courts was merely one phase of its authority to advise the king, who in turn was the final arbiter in all matters affecting the colonies. Until the years preceding the Revolution appeals to the Privy Council were not frequent, but they steadily became more common after 1750. All of the colonial courts followed English judicial procedure; the right of trial by jury and the other privileges which Blackstone calls "the liberties of Englishmen" were everywhere given full recognition. The colonists were thus by actual experience well schooled in the doctrine that men had inalienable rights.

<small>Local government.</small>

It was in the field of local government that the greatest differences in the form if not in the spirit of colonial government appeared.[1] In all the New England colonies the unit of local administration was the town, with its town

[1] A further discussion of local government in colonial times is included below, ch. xxxvii.

meeting of all the citizens and its elective local officers. The town raised its own taxes and spent them, made its own by-laws, and sent its representative each year to the colonial legislature. It was a miniature republic, rarely interfered with from above. This splendid and enduring type of local government was the joint product of racial temperament and geographical environment, and great importance should be attached to the training in self-government which the men of colonial New England secured through a simple and democratic plan of handling their neighborhood affairs. It had a considerable part in determining the common attitude on public questions in later days. The southern colonies, on the other hand, established the county as their chief unit of local administration. County officers were appointed by the governor, and there was no general meeting of all the inhabitants to vote the taxes or to determine matters of local policy. Finally, in the middle colonies, particularly in New York and Pennsylvania, there was a mixed type of local government, a combination of the town and county systems, which bridged the gap between the extremes of New England and the South. Yet the differences in the frame of local government throughout the thirteen colonies were not greater than those which one can find among the several states to-day. They did not impair the political homogeneity of the people. The principle of local autonomy was everywhere strongly upheld and asserted.

With such general approach to uniformity in race, religion, language, and law, with such marked similarities in political organization and development, with common problems arising from the pressure of outside enemies, it might be expected that the various colonies would steadily draw more closely together and develop in time some form of federal union. There were some steps in that direction. As early as 1643 the four New England colonies of Plymouth, Massachusetts Bay, Connecticut, and New Haven united in a league of friendship, particularly for mutual support against Indian attacks. It was arranged that each of these colonies should send two delegates to a joint conference each year. For many years this New England

*Early attempts to federate the colonies.*

**(1) The New England Confederation of 1643.**

confederation proved a useful agent of inter-colonial action, but it was at best a weak and incomplete arrangement. There was, moreover, a great deal of jealousy among its four members, and its existence ceased after the Indian dangers, against which it had been organized, had passed away.

**(2) Penn's suggestion, 1696.**

From time to time during the next hundred years other proposals for confederation were made. William Penn made such a suggestion in 1696, and at various dates conferences representing several colonies were called to discuss the possibilities. But the clash of diverse local interests always proved to be a stumbling-block, and it required a serious common danger to impress on all the colonies their essential unity and their need of coöperation. Something of this sort came into view when the French wars demonstrated to all the New England and middle colonies their weakness as isolated units in the face of an aggressive and united enemy.

**(3) The Albany Congress, 1754.**

At the suggestion of the Lords of Trade a congress was called at Albany in 1754 with a view to forming a confederation for mutual defence, and especially to devise a plan for keeping the Iroquois from joining with the French. Seven colonies were represented; the southern ones did not send delegates, as the immediate danger seemed to be far from their own doors. Benjamin Franklin brought forward a plan of union, and the congress, after making some changes, adopted it unanimously. Franklin's plan, commonly known as the Albany Plan of Union, contemplated a conference or congress made up of one delegate from each colony, this conference to determine the means of common defence, the number of troops to be supplied by each colony, and the amount of money to be contributed by each. The crown was to appoint a president-general, who should command the united forces and have the spending of the money so raised. But although the delegates at Albany approved this plan, it was rejected by the several colonies when it went before them for approval. The Albany Plan, accordingly, came to naught. But it did have its influence in paving the way for the first Continental Congress of the Revolutionary War.

One further meeting of colonial delegates before the actual outbreak deserves a word, namely, the so-called Stamp-Act Congress. In 1765 the representatives of nine colonies met at New York to draw up petitions to the home government on colonial grievances, particularly with reference to the Stamp Act. No project of union was at this time broached, but the incident showed that when any matter clearly affected their interests, most of the colonies could readily get together and take a common action. Why was it, in view of the manifest advantages of coöperation, that the thirteen colonies did not come into some sort of working federation long before the actual outbreak of troubles with England? Local jealousies afford one reason. A failure to realize that, in a broad sense, all their chief interests were alike, is another. The home government, moreover, was never favorable to any scheme of union such as would give the colonies a solidarity of action in all matters. It was ready to have them join for the common defence, provided the carrying out of such plan were intrusted to officers sent out from England. In a word, the colonies never realized their essential unity until the acute controversy with the mother country made it clear to them. Then, and then only, did any real union become practicable. (4) The Stamp-Act Congress, 1765.

This is not the place to narrate the events which led to the breach with England. It should be pointed out, however, that there was no general dissatisfaction with the type of existing government in the various colonies. The revolution did not come because all the colonies wanted charters or elective governors or manhood suffrage. Its underlying causes were economic; they concerned questions of trade and taxation. But once the spirit of resistance was aroused, it found, as it always does, new and broader grievances. The colonists soon came to a realization of the fact that democracy, especially in New England, had been forging ahead more rapidly than at home, and in the Declaration of Independence new ideals of democracy, unknown at this period in England, found vigorous expression. It was the events of 1773–1774, including the imposition of the new taxes and the four repressive acts of parliament suspending the charter of Massachusetts and institut- (5) The first Continental Congress, 1774.

ing other drastic measures of coercion, which supplied the inspiration to union hitherto lacking among the colonies. One of their number was now in danger of having its liberties curtailed: what of the others, each in turn? Singly the thirteen colonies might easily be brought one after another to comply with the demands of parliament. The danger was not now confined to north or south; it was common to all. Hence the calling of the first Continental Congress, which met at Philadelphia in the autumn of 1774 with delegates present from all the colonies except Georgia. These representatives were chosen in a variety of ways, some by the colonial legislatures, some by conventions, and some by the committees of correspondence or informal committees of townsmen such as had been established in Massachusetts to unify popular action in case the legislature should be dissolved. The object of this Congress was to ward off an impending common peril by showing a united front. Its members adopted various addresses to the home authorities; pledged the coöperation of all the colonies in resistance to oppressive demands, and, finally, agreed that a similar congress should be called in the following year.

(6) The second Continental Congress, 1775.

Before the early summer of 1775, when this second Continental Congress assembled, once again at Philadelphia, the situation had rapidly gone from bad to worse. The open clash of arms had come at Lexington and Concord, and the fate of Massachusetts seemed to be sealed unless the other colonies should quickly and loyally come to her aid. There was now no hanging back. All the colonies without exception sent their delegates to the Continental Congress of 1775, and this body at once assumed general direction of the whole colonial cause. Without any quibbles as to the source or scope of its powers the Congress appointed Washington to the chief command, called upon all the colonies for assignments of troops and supplies, and took upon itself the right to issue paper money on the joint credit. Its powers were usurped out of the necessities of the situation; the legal questions were left to be discussed and settled later. The only sanction of its acts was the acquiescence of the people, but in the last analysis is not this the only effective sanction that any public authority can have?

It was not possible, however, that a situation so anomalous should long be maintained. The colonies were still subject to the king although in active resistance to the royal authority. They had tacitly assumed the attributes of sovereignty without declaring themselves sovereign states. This situation, however, came to an end with the Declaration of Independence in 1776. On July fourth of that year the colonies became states, each independent of the crown and independent of each other. This action made it even more imperative that the Continental Congress should rest on a firmer and more stable basis than that of a body brought into being by Revolution with no clear definition of its powers or duties. Accordingly, on November 15, 1777, the Continental Congress sought to gain for itself the forms of legality by adopting the "Articles of Confederation and Perpetual Union," which had been in process of preparation by one of its committees for some months previously. This step was the culmination of the long process by which the thirteen communities had been brought to a full realization of their political kinship; it was at the same time the starting point from which, ten years later, a far stronger and more lasting union was evolved.

(7) The Declaration of Independence, 1776, and the Articles of Confederation, 1777.

# CHAPTER II

## PRELIMINARIES OF NATIONAL GOVERNMENT

*Constitutional importance of the Articles.*

THE action of the Continental Congress in preparing and adopting the Articles of Confederation represented a step of profound importance in the evolution of the American political system. Now, for the first time, a group of delegates representing all the colonies were ready to set up a union which would be something more than a mere alliance for the common defence, which would be "perpetual" in character and thus endure in peace as well as in war. That, of itself, is enough to designate the adoption of the Articles as a milestone in the march towards a real federation. But even more deserving of attention is the fact that the various provisions of the Articles had a dominant influence upon the minds and actions of those who formed the national constitution ten years later. Some of these provisions worked out well, and they were perpetuated in the new constitution; others worked so badly that they were discarded without much regret or hesitation; while still a few others, not having clearly demonstrated their full possibilities for either good or ill, were either dropped altogether or retained in modified form. The experience of the states under the Articles of Confederation was of the greatest value in this way, subjecting various political theories, as it did, to the test of actual operation under difficult conditions. The student of political institutions should not pass lightly over the ten critical years in which the Articles of Confederation embodied, somewhat crudely perhaps, the principles and practice of New World federalism. These were formative years of the greatest importance, and the American people probably learned more

# PRELIMINARIES OF NATIONAL GOVERNMENT 15

about the science of government in this decade, 1777–1787, than in any other.[1]

The Articles of Confederation and Perpetual Union were adopted by the Continental Congress after a good deal of discussion, which served to show that no one among the delegates had much enthusiasm for the system of joint government which they established. They were then sent to the legislatures of the thirteen states for ratification. By the provisions of the Articles the several states entered into a firm league of amity; but each state retained its sovereignty, freedom, and independence. Every right not expressly delegated to the confederation remained with the states. The organ of the confederation, as provided by the Articles, was to be a Congress made up of delegates from all the states, each state to send not fewer than two nor more than seven. But whether a state sent the minimum or the maximum number of delegates, it was in any case to have one vote only. The legal equality of all the states was thus recognized, although there were already great differences among them in area and in population. Virginia and Massachusetts each had, at this time, eight or ten times the population of either Georgia or Delaware or Rhode Island. The union was thus a loose confederation, as distinguished from a close or organic federation of states.[2] *Their general provisions.*

As for powers, the Congress of the new confederation was given relatively few. It was to manage the war and to handle foreign relations. It might call upon the several states for contributions of money or men, but it had no way of compelling them to respond. It had various internal powers such as those of establishing a postal service and managing Indian affairs. With nine of the states assenting, it could make treaties, borrow on the joint credit, coin money or issue bills of credit, and it did issue paper money *Powers of Congress under the Articles of Confederation.*

---

[1] A. C. McLaughlin, *The Confederation and the Constitution* (N. Y., 1905), is the most useful single volume on this period. John Fiske's *Critical Period of American History* (13th ed., Boston, 1898), is an extremely interesting book, but not always accurate.

[2] For the exact text of the Articles see William MacDonald, *Select Documents Illustrative of the History of the United States, 1776–1861* (N. Y., 1903).

in large quantities to pay the expenses of the war. But it had no power to tax, no power to regulate trade, and no effective authority to settle disputes among the various states themselves. The powers lodged in the Congress by the Articles were not extensive when judged in the light of later events, nevertheless they represented substantial concessions on the part of the states. Public opinion was not at the time prepared to go much further. National self-consciousness, even under the stress of a war for existence, had not yet developed to the point of rendering a stronger union possible.

Little attention was bestowed upon the executive branch of the government. It was apparently assumed that the Congress, while in session, would itself perform all necessary executive functions, but provision was made for a committee of the states to sit and act when the Congress was not in session. No mention was made of executive officers, but it was taken for granted that the Congress might appoint such as were needed, and it did so appoint a superintendent of finance, a secretary of war, a foreign secretary, and other officials. In this action is foreshadowed the "heads of departments" who later became an integral part of the federal executive under the constitution of 1787.

Ratification of the Articles.  Even as it was, the various states were slow in ratifying the Articles of Confederation, and it was not until 1781 that all had given their assent. Consequently the main dangers of the war were over before the confederation completed all its legal formalities. So long as the issue of the war hung in the balance the instinct of self-preservation moved all the states to give the Congress of the Confederation a varying degree of support. Some responded to every call for men, supplies, and money; others lagged behind. Each state's compliance depended partly upon its own native spirit of loyalty and partly upon whether the state lay within the zone of immediate war dangers. The Congress had no coercive power; it had no means of compelling any state to bear its due share of the war burden. During the years 1782–1786 it called upon the several states for contributions amounting to six million dollars but received only one million in all. The wonder is that it did so well, in view of its limited resources. The problems with which it had to deal, moreover, were extremely difficult, for the strain of the war bore heavily upon all the states. Each was inclined to magnify its own sacrifices. The common peril did not suffice to extinguish all interstate jealousies. These things as well as the inherent defects of the articles account for the unsatisfactory workings of central government under the confederation. At the best, the whole arrangement was a makeshift, and after the conclusion of peace in 1783 none of the states appeared to have any interest in it. Hard times came with the close of the war; the country was deluged with paper money, and in several of the states there was much economic confusion. This kept them from giving serious attention to the workings of central government. Each state was too intent upon the solution of its own problems.

Turn for a moment from the affairs of the confederation and see what the states themselves had been doing during the war and after. As the hostilities spread from one colony to another in the early months of the war, the various royal governors and officials left the country, thus breaking down, in part, the existing governments. In consequence of this the Continental Congress, even before it adopted the Declaration of Independence, advised that each colony should reconstruct its government to suit its own needs. Some of them lost no time in following this advice. Virginia at once elected a convention which, under Jefferson's leadership, adopted a constitution with a bill of rights and provision for a new frame of state government. One after another the remaining states followed, until Massachusetts, the last of the thirteen, adopted its first state constitution in 1780. *The first state constitutions.*

While these constitutions differed considerably in their detailed arrangements they all present a marked similarity.[1] In every case provision was made for a governor, to be chosen by the legislature or by the voters; in nearly every instance *Their chief provisions.*

[1] A conspectus, showing the main features of these several state constitutions, may be found in Edward Channing, *History of the United States*, Vol. iii, pp. 459–462.

there was provision for a legislature of two chambers; and in each for a judiciary, appointed either by the governor or by the legislature or by a branch of the legislature. The colonial governor's right to veto legislation was abolished in all but two states, and in every one of them the governor's appointing authority as it had existed in colonial times was taken away or curtailed. Greatly increased powers were everywhere allotted to the state legislatures. The principle of the separation of powers, that is, of keeping the executive, legislative, and judicial powers separate, gained recognition in only a few of these state constitutions; but in one of them it was stated plainly, namely, in the Massachusetts constitution, which set forth the doctrine as follows: "In the government of this commonwealth, the legislative department shall never exercise the executive and judicial powers, or either of them: the judicial shall never exercise the legislative and executive powers, or either of them: to the end that it may be a government of laws and not of men." From this unequivocal statement in one of the new state constitutions, however, it is not to be concluded that the doctrine of separation of powers was already finding general favor. Most of the states did not at the outset seem afraid of making the state legislature supreme.

*The principle of separation of powers.*

Another characteristic of the earliest state constitutions was the emphasis which most of them placed upon securities for individual liberty. Many of these guarantees already existed at common law, but the events which preceded and accompanied the Revolution convinced the framers of the various state constitutions that it would be well to have them incorporated into these organic documents. Freedom of speech and of assembly, the right of trial by jury, the privilege of the writ of habeas corpus, — these and many other so-termed inalienable rights now found their way to definite expression in terms of constitutional guarantees. Yet on the whole the new constitutions did not establish governments that were radically different in form from those which existed in colonial days. Little or nothing was borrowed from outside. The new state constitutions embodied the results of a liberal overhauling

*Emphasis upon securities for individual liberty.*

of what had long existed in the several colonies. Indeed the colonies which had possessed charters before the Revolution found very little overhauling necessary. So far as the frame of government in each of these thirteen communities is concerned, the Revolution and the subsequent adoption of new state constitutions made no violent changes. There were, however, great changes in the spirit of government, in the responsiveness of officials to public opinion, in the attitude of the people towards those in authority, and in possibilities afforded for future political development.

The framing of these state constitutions, moreover, had an important educative influence. While they were in process men turned their thoughts to the fundamentals of government. They examined anew a multitude of questions relating to the state and the social order. They talked of Locke and Montesquieu, of social compacts, checks and balances, popular sovereignty and the natural rights of the citizen. Hence there were available in all the states, groups of men who, when the time arrived, could be called upon to help in the larger work of framing a constitution for the nation as a whole. Without the preliminary work done in the endeavor to make federalism efficient under the Articles of Confederation and in the making of these state constitutions, the task set before the federal convention of 1787 would have been infinitely harder to perform. The whole people, moreover, became familiar with the idea of a constitution or fundamental law as the basis of government, a written document emanating from the people, ordained into force by them either directly or through their representatives, and guaranteeing them against abuses of power. This was something that as Englishmen they had never learned. *The revived interest in political fundamentals.*

Such was the situation which existed in the years immediately following 1783 when peace once more came upon the land. At Philadelphia there was a Congress made up of delegates from the several states as provided for by the Articles of Confederation. Its meetings were still held, although rarely were all the states represented. Each of these states had adopted its own new constitution; each was turning attentively to the settlement of its own problems. *The critical period — drifting toward anarchy.*

Economic conditions everywhere were disorganized, for business had been neglected during the war and the mass of private debts was very large. There was a great scarcity of real money although the land was flooded with paper notes, some issued by the confederation and some by the states. Each state was seeking to relieve its own necessities by pressing its own advantages, grasping at everything within reach. So avaricious indeed were some in asserting their claims that interstate ill-feeling rapidly developed. In some cases the boundaries between the colonies had never been authoritatively fixed; now that the colonies had become states they were coming close to blows over disputed claims to border territory. Likewise there were commercial jealousies. Each state was hurrying to build up its own trade at the expense of its neighbors. Those which had natural advantages tried to exclude others from the use of them. The initial skirmishing in a war of hostile tariffs and trade discriminations began as early as 1785, when New York imposed fees upon all vessels entering its ports from Connecticut or New Jersey. Virginia and Maryland were at swords' points over the navigation of the Potomac. Trouble was impending all along the line.

Weaknesses of the Confederation:

Why did not the Congress at Philadelphia intervene to prevent this drift towards federal anarchy? Its members no doubt would gladly have done so had they only possessed the power. But the Congress, no longer supported with any enthusiasm by the states, had become an almost negligible factor in public affairs. It had no rights of taxation and hence no revenues. Yet money was urgently needed to pay interest on loans made in France and Holland as well as in America during the war; also to pay the ordinary expenses of government. To make matters worse, the officers and soldiers of the revolution had in many cases served without pay other than certificates of indebtedness, and they were now clamoring for what they had fully earned.[1] The enormous quantities of paper money which had been issued became so depreciated that notes finally ceased to pass as currency at all, although they were sometimes

1. Its lack of revenues.

[1] L. C. Hatch, *The Administration of the American Revolutionary Army* (N. Y., 1904).

bought and sold in bundles by speculators who hoped that some day they might perhaps get one cent on the dollar for them. The Congress, it is true, still possessed its power to call on the several states for money contributions and did so frequently; but it encountered evasion more often than response. Some states quietly ignored the requests; others gave a small part of what was asked and grumbled loudly at that; only in rare instances were calls complied with promptly and in full. In the later years of the confederation only two states, New York and Pennsylvania, were making any serious attempt to fulfil their financial obligations to congress. Without funds the confederation was impotent.[1] It could neither pay off the old army nor raise a new one. It could not meet the interest payments on the national debt. It could not provide ships to protect the commerce of the states against the Barbary pirates who were seizing American seamen in the Mediterranean and holding them for ransom. It could not provide for proper diplomatic representation of the United States abroad. The entire income of the confederation during its later days was less than two hundred thousand dollars a year.

By the Articles of Confederation the Congress had authority to borrow on the common credit (provided nine states assented), and some loans were secured under this authority. But with no regular revenues to insure prompt payment of interest or the repayment of principal at maturity it was not possible to obtain funds except on onerous terms either at home or abroad. John Adams in 1784 was sent to Europe on a borrowing expedition, but all he could obtain was about three hundred thousand dollars, and for even this relatively small sum it was necessary to promise an exorbitant rate of interest. The public credit was down to bed rock. Yet any new country, particularly after an exhausting struggle, needs large sums for upbuilding, and this was America's situation. The need, however, was not so much for larger borrowing powers as for a national credit supported by a national income as a basis for borrowing.

2. Lack of credit for borrowing.

Equally important among the specific weaknesses of the

[1] C. J. Bullock, *The Finances of the United States, 1775–1789; with Especial Reference to the Budget* (Madison, 1895).

3. Its lack of power to regulate commerce.

Confederation was the lack of any power to regulate trade, either with foreign nations or among the several states or with the Indian tribes of the great hinterland. The regulation of trade involves, as a rule, the making of tariffs and the congress could impose no duties on imports or exports. Each state was already making its own tariff, and each was doing its best to attract commerce to its own ports. The common good counted for next to nothing in their respective policies. Commercial rivalry among neighboring states was rapidly engendering bad feeling, and a spirit of avarice and retaliation was in the air. The central government could do nothing but sit in silence while this interplay went on. Meanwhile, moreover, the opportunity to make favorable commercial treaties with various European nations was slipping rapidly away. It was obviously desirable that in such matters all thirteen states should act together. Yet under the existing conditions no such common action could be hoped for. "We are one nation to-day and thirteen to-morrow," said Washington. "Who will treat with us on such terms?"

4. Its military impotence.

Most ominous of all was the outlook in international relations. England was still intrenched in Canada to the north, while Spain possessed the southwest. The American colonies had won their independence with the aid of France, but who could tell how long the tottering Bourbon monarchy would stay friendly or continue in a position to render aid? Two powerful nations of Europe were on the confederation's flanks: what if they should some day join hands to raid the land and divide the spoils? Nor was such an eventuality altogether beyond the range of possibilities, particularly if the states should fall to quarrelling among themselves. Even if all should make common cause, stand united, and prepare for this danger, it would continue to present a serious aspect; but without preparation or unity, with the states split into rival factions, one faction perhaps calling in outside assistance, the peril would be overwhelming. Seventy-five years later, when a much larger group of American states engaged in civil strife over the issue of slavery, the danger of foreign intervention, and with it the probable disruption of the Union for all time, was still serious. Yet by that time both France and Spain had practically withdrawn from the Western Hemisphere. How much more vividly the danger must have appeared to sagacious men in the last decades of the eighteenth century!

The shortcomings of the confederation are well summarized in what Washington called "the absence of coercive power." "I do not conceive," he wrote, "that we can exist long as a nation without having lodged somewhere a power which will pervade the whole Union in as energetic a manner as the authority of the state governments extends over the several states." In other words the Congress of the Confederation could deal only with the states and not directly with the people as the legislatures of the various states could do. Specifically it was impotent because it lacked four things which every strong national government must possess: ability to raise revenues by taxation, to borrow money, to regulate commerce, and to provide adequately for the common defence by raising and supporting armies. And these, rather significantly, were the four greatest powers given to the Congress of the United States by the constitution which in 1787 replaced the old Articles of Confederation. *General defects of the confederation.*

Notwithstanding its meagre authority, however, the achievements of the old Congress were highly creditable. It kept the armies in the field until peace was assured, and in the face of stupendous difficulties furnished them with supplies. Despite its cumbrous and imperfect executive machinery it negotiated the Peace of 1783 whereby the independence of the thirteen states was given full recognition by Great Britain. During these years the Congress was the sole embodiment of federal authority in America, the one centripetal force that held thirteen jealous communities to a policy of reasonably united effort. What it lacked in formal powers was counterbalanced in part by its patience and its patriotism. *What the confederation accomplished.*

During these years there were thoughtful men both in the Congress and outside of it who realized that things were heading in the wrong direction. The confederation, they urged, must be strengthened or it would go to pieces *Attempts to strengthen the confederation.*

for lack of funds. As early as 1781 the Congress had made a request to the several states that it be allowed to lay a five per cent tax on certain imports. Nearly all the states were willing, but Rhode Island refused. Two years later a different proposition was put forth, namely, that the several states should collect certain import duties and apply all the proceeds to paying off the debt incurred by the confederation during the war. But this suggestion was declined by four states. In 1786 matters came to a crux when the Congress plainly put the whole matter before the nation. "A crisis has arrived," it declared, "when the people of the United States, by whose will and for whose benefit the federal government was instituted, must decide whether they will support their rank as a nation by maintaining the public faith at home and abroad, or whether, for the want of a timely exertion in establishing a general revenue and thereby giving strength to the Confederacy, they will hazard not only the existence of the Union but of those great and invaluable privileges for which they have so arduously and so honorably contended."

The Annapolis convention, 1786. Now it happened about this time (1785) that Maryland and Virginia were endeavoring to reach an agreement concerning the navigation of the Potomac. Commissioners from these two states, having reached an understanding, proposed that Pennsylvania and Delaware be also asked to assent to the arrangement. Thus the project enlarged until in the end all the states were asked to send delegates to a convention to be held at Annapolis in 1786 to consider the trade interests of the confederation and "how far a uniform system in their commercial regulations may be necessary to their common interest and their permanent harmony." The response, however, was disappointing, for when the convention met, only five states were represented.[1] The others did not seem to be sufficiently interested. Consequently the Annapolis convention did not feel that it would be worth while to take up the task for which it had been called together. Alexander Hamilton of New York, however, suggested that another attempt

[1] The states represented were Virginia, New York, New Jersey, Pennsylvania, and Delaware.

be made and resolutions were adopted pointing out the critical condition of affairs and asking all the states to send representatives, not less than three or more than seven, to a convention to be held in Philadelphia the next summer.

The purpose of this convention, as stated in the resolution, was "to take into consideration the situation of the United States, to devise such further provisions as shall appear to them necessary to render the constitution of the federal government adequate to the exigencies of the Union and to report such an Act for that purpose to the United States in Congress assembled, as, when agreed to by them, and afterwards confirmed by the legislatures of every state, will effectually provide for the same." Copies of the resolution were sent to the Congress and to all the state legislatures. Congress indorsed the idea and it found favor in most of the states, chiefly because Washington, Hamilton, Madison, Franklin, and others lent their personal influence in support of it. No one openly proposed that the convention should be authorized to draft a new constitution. The ostensible purpose was to supplement and strengthen the Articles of Confederation. All of the states except Rhode Island responded to this call and appointed their delegates. In some states the appointments were made directly by the state legislature; in others the legislature authorized the governor to appoint the delegates. All were summoned to meet at Philadelphia in May, 1787.

*The convention of 1787.*

# CHAPTER III

## THE CONSTITUTION AND ITS MAKERS

*The convention's allies.*

MUCH has been written about the difficulties which had to be surmounted in getting the states to send delegates to Philadelphia in 1787, and even more, perhaps, about the obstacles which faced these delegates when they came together. Yet the convention of 1787 met under fortunate auspices. It represented a people who had already shown their capacity for drawing together in the face of outside pressure and of staying united as long at least as danger threatened. All had passed through the trials of a long and bitter war; all loved their new freedom because they had been through such sacrifices to make it their own. Practically all were believers in the merits of republican government, for those who did not so believe, the Tories, had been harried out of the land. There were some monarchists at heart, no doubt, but they were not proclaiming their sentiments aloud. The convention of 1787, moreover, represented a people who already had acquired a considerable round of experience in the making of new governments, thirteen of them, and had seen these fruits of their own handiwork gain in power. The states themselves were forging ahead, even if the confederation was not. The public mind had been tuned up by political discussion. And, most vital of all, every one now felt that something needed to be done.

*Obstacles to its success.*

On the other hand, despite those various motives and forces which made for a closer union and a stronger central government, there were great and real obstacles in the convention's way. The northern and southern states were already becoming quite unlike in their economic and social environment. In every state the local patriotism was intense. There was everywhere a dread of external authority, a conviction that all good government must come from within not without, from below not from above. The very distances which separated the states one from another, the absence of good roads, the infrequency with which men travelled from one part of the country to the other — all these things helped to accentuate provincialism. Liberty had been won; equality there always had been; but of fraternity there was as yet little or none at all. Georgia and Massachusetts, for example, had much in common, but among their people there was no ready realization of this identity in ideals or in interests. Taking it all in all, however, it was the fundamental sense of kindred that counted; the minor elements of unlikeness among the states did not, in the end, prove to be as great obstacles as might have been expected.

The convention was summoned to meet on the second Monday in May, 1787, but when that date arrived many of the delegates had not reached Philadelphia and more than a fortnight was lost in getting started. At length, a sufficient number being on hand, the convention unanimously chose Washington as its president, decided that its deliberations should be secret, and plunged right into its work. The meetings were held in the old brick State House in Philadelphia, the building in which the Declaration of Independence had been signed.[1] *Organization of the convention.*

Who were the men assembled here to wrestle with the problem of welding thirteen restless and sensitive communities into a strong nation? There is a popular notion that they embodied most of the wisdom and resourcefulness in the land, that the Fathers of the Republic formed a galaxy of New World Solons and Ciceros. In truth, however, and very fortunately, that was not the case. The convention of 1787 was a gathering of very diverse types. It contained many men of great political wisdom. It also in- *Who composed it?*

---

[1] The *Records of the Federal Convention of 1787*, by Max Farrand (3 vols., New Haven, 1911), afford the best source for a careful study of the convention's work. The same author's *Framing of the Constitution of the United States* (New Haven, 1913) gives an excellent summary of the larger compilation. Mention should also be made of Edward Elliott, *Biographical Story of the Constitution* (N. Y., 1910).

cluded in its membership some men whom nature had endowed with neither ability nor good temper, as the proceedings disclose. All that can truly be said of the convention's make-up is that it included men of widely different ability, temperament, and experience; and therein lay its real strength. It contained, as has been so often pointed out, a few men of rare political genius, such as George Washington, Alexander Hamilton, and James Madison; likewise some judicially-minded spirits, such as Benjamin Franklin, James Wilson, John Dickinson, Robert Morris, and Roger Sherman; some thoroughly well-meaning men of moderate attainments, such as William Paterson, John Rutledge, and the two Pinckneys; a few long-winded obstructionists, like Luther Martin, who did little but clog the wheels; and two score of others who rarely had much to say but who listened attentively and voted right when important issues arose. The men in this last group were the ones whom William Pierce in his contemporary pen-picture of his fellow delegates termed the "respectable characters" of the convention, and they outnumbered all others.[1]

There were fifty-five men in the constitutional convention, representing twelve states. Pennsylvania sent her full quota of seven; while New York, on the other hand, sent only three, and these were absent a large part of the time. More than half the delegates were college graduates; a majority of them had held public offices of one sort or another, some of them posts of high importance. Not a few were men of large business interests, while as many others were in very modest worldly circumstances. Every shade of opinion and political belief was represented: from Alexander Hamilton, who would have created a thoroughly centralized and aristocratic union, to Luther Martin of Maryland, who wanted the old confederation left as it was, weaknesses and all. Its variety of ideas and attitudes, not its omniscience, was the great asset of this convention. Many wiser groups of men at vari-

*Variety of the opinions and interests represented.*

---

[1] William Pierce of the Georgia delegation diverted some of his time from the serious work of the convention to write and leave for posterity an interesting though somewhat facetious sketch of his colleagues. It is printed in the *American Historical Review*, iii, pp. 310-334.

ous times in human history have set their minds to the work of law-making, but never has there been a body more evenly balanced, or more willing to compromise for the sake of progress, or more intent on creating a frame of government able to meet the strain that might be put upon it.

Washington presided throughout the convention's deliberations. As presiding officer he felt himself debarred from a prominent part in the debates and is only once on record as a participant; but he rendered great service in quieting the occasional storms of personal animosity, and his commanding influence was on many occasions unobtrusively exercised in the right direction. Benjamin Franklin, who headed the Pennsylvania group, was the greatest savant of them all, but he was now eighty-one years old and his voice would no longer rise above a whisper. But his mature judgment and his quiet optimism were steadying factors of great value. Some of the wisest suggestions came from him. In point of political genius, imagination, and eloquence, none of the delegates equalled Alexander Hamilton of New York. He was still a young man, only thirty, well educated, and with intense political convictions. He distrusted popular government and wanted the ship of state to be well ballasted. It is often said that he was at heart a monarchist, but he was hardly that. It is fairer to speak of him as a friend of centralized republicanism such as exists to-day in France but for which there were no precedents in his time. Hamilton, unfortunately, was absent from meetings a great deal, owing to personal business of an urgent nature, but when present, he always had ideas to put forward. The convention did not often fall in with his views, and while the delegates applauded his oratory they regularly voted his proposals down.

*Leaders of the convention: Washington, Franklin, and Hamilton.*

Then there was James Madison of Virginia. He is often called the "Father of the Constitution," and if the attribute of paternity must go to some one man, he is entitled to it. Less brilliant than Hamilton, he was far more widely read, more discriminating in his opinions, less aggressive and more patient in the advocacy of his own views. Every

*James Madison.*

one, in the words of the chronicler Pierce, acknowledged his greatness. From early days an industrious student of past politics and present history, he knew what had brought about the rise and fall of every federation from the Achæan League to his own day. In preparation for the convention he had prepared some elaborate "Notes on Ancient and Modern Confederacies," and this manuscript furnished him with ammunition for his part in the debates. He was no orator, but his sound and sure knowledge of historical precedents made him what Pierce termed "the best-informed man" in the convention. Madison was from first to last the most influential member of the convention, and he owed this to his untiring industry as a student, his unfailing readiness to work in harmony with men whose opinions differed from his own, and his unquestioned personal integrity. Much of what we now know about the proceedings of the convention is due to Madison's methodical industry, for day by day he entered in his private journal a résumé of what went on. The constitution as finally drafted was not a mirror of his own political ideas, but it included the things he had most strongly contended for.

*The rank and file.* There were others among the members whose prominence almost gave them rank as leaders. Luther Martin of Maryland was one of these, if the frequency and prolixity of his speeches in the convention may be taken as indications of prominence. James Wilson and Gouverneur Morris of Pennsylvania, Roger Sherman and Oliver Ellsworth of Connecticut, Elbridge Gerry of Massachusetts, William Paterson of New Jersey, the two Pinckneys of South Carolina, were all active in the proceedings. It is hard to tell just how much real influence each exercised, for in the constitutional convention of 1787, as in all other deliberative bodies, the men most frequently on their feet are not necessarily the ones whose opinions counted heavily with their colleagues.

While the convention contained men of all ages, from Mercer of Virginia, who was only twenty-eight, to Franklin, who was almost eighty-two, one is impressed with the fact that much of the best work was done by the younger members. James Madison, who contributed most to the daily labors, was thirty-six; Alexander Hamilton, who made the greatest single argument of the whole summer, was only thirty; and Gouverneur Morris, who put the fine finishing touches to the document, was just thirty-five. The constitution, accordingly, reflected the zeal and optimism of these young men, chastened to moderation by the mature judgment of their older colleagues. Much youthful courage was gathered within these four walls during the summer of 1787, but there was also enough conservatism to keep it in bounds.

In organizing, the convention adopted its own rules. On all questions the vote was taken by states, each state having one vote. The delegates, as has been said, were pledged to secrecy, and this was a wise move, for if the subsequent bitter disagreements on many points among the members had been known to the world, the constitution would probably never have been ratified by the several states. Sessions were held almost every week-day from May to September. Matters were often referred to committees, but all the vital questions were threshed out on the floor by the whole convention. *The procedure.*

It did not take long to discover that among the delegates there were two diametrically opposite opinions as to what the convention ought to do. Some felt that the Articles of Confederation should be used as a basis and that the convention had no authority to do more than supplement or strengthen this agreement. Others were of the opinion that the articles were hopelessly inadequate, that revising them would be a waste of time, and that the convention should simply throw them aside and begin anew. Even before the meetings commenced, in fact, James Madison, with the help of his Virginia colleagues, had prepared a new scheme which disregarded the Articles altogether, and this was at once laid before the convention by Edmund Randolph of Virginia. Known as the Randolph plan, it proposed a real federal union, with a central executive, legislature, and judiciary, with independent taxing powers and with authority to make its mandates fall directly upon the individual citizen, not merely upon the states. The *Fundamental questions: the nature of the union.* *The Randolph plan.*

federal Congress, under this plan, was to be made up of representatives from the several states in proportion to their respective populations. Virginia would thus have fifteen or sixteen representatives, while Georgia, Delaware, or New Jersey would each have only one or two.

*The Paterson plan.* As a counter proposition William Paterson of New Jersey brought forward a wholly different scheme. This plan contemplated the continuance of a Congress on substantially the same lines as that of the confederation — a single chamber with each state having a single vote but with the addition of an executive in the form of a council chosen by the Congress and with provision for a federal judiciary. The Paterson plan also provided for a federal revenue by proposing that Congress be given the power to levy duties and excise taxes.

*Could these two plans be reconciled?* Each of these two plans obtained an almost equal numerical support among the states represented in the convention, the larger states for obvious reasons siding with Virginia, while the smaller states, from equally plain motives of self-interest, ranged up with New Jersey. For days the convention debated the merits and faults of each proposal. One faction pointed out the unfairness of giving to the states which would pay most of the taxes no more representation than those which would contribute little. The other stood firm on the point that to depart from the old doctrine of the equality of all the states, large and small, would be the first step toward the ultimate servitude of the small community. There was no more reason, said a delegate from one of the small states, for giving a large state more votes than a small one than there was for giving a big man more votes than a little man. The appeals, after all, were not to reason but to self-interest. The fundamental trouble was that some states were large and some small; while all were alike sovereign and independent. They had adopted the doctrine of common equality as a makeshift at the outset of the war; now the small states held to it as their inalienable right. For a time it seemed as though the convention would split its keel on this rock. In the end a solution was found through the door of compromise.

This solution is commonly known as the Connecticut compromise, because it was brought forth by the delegates of that middle-sized state, although it is believed to have sprung from the fertile intellect of Benjamin Franklin. In brief, it provided that in the proposed federal Congress the upper House should be based on the equal representation of the states, while the lower House should represent the several states in proportion to their respective populations, with the additional proviso that all bills for raising or appropriating money should originate in the lower House and should not be subject to amendment in the upper chamber. Before the convention finished its work, however, this latter proviso was somewhat modified. With great difficulty the delegates were induced to accept the Connecticut compromise, but it was finally adopted and its acceptance removed the greatest obstacle that the delegates encountered. *The Connecticut compromise.*

This fundamental question out of the way, the convention began to make better progress. But soon another source of friction and disagreement was encountered. The Connecticut compromise had provided that representatives in the lower house of the new Congress should be apportioned among the several states on a basis of population. But in counting the population of a state, were the slaves to be counted or left out? Nothing had been said about that point when the Connecticut compromise was under discussion. The delegates from South Carolina were particularly insistent that the term "population" should be taken to include all inhabitants whether bond or free, black or white. One of the Massachusetts delegates retorted angrily that if such chattels as slaves were counted in the South, other such chattels as horses and mules should be counted in the North. The states opposed to the counting of slaves were in the majority and could have had their way by boldly asserting it; but, after a discussion which made the sparks of animosity fly in showers, they chose to meet the others halfway or rather more than halfway. The outcome was the arrangement known as the three-fifths compromise, by which it was agreed that slaves should be counted in determining the quota of representation from *The "three-fifths" compromise.*

each state, but at three-fifths of their numerical strength only. In other words a hundred slaves were to be counted, for purposes of representation in Congress, as the equivalent of sixty free men. Direct taxes, if levied upon the several states, were to be apportioned on this same basis.

*Illogical nature of this arrangement.*

There was no logic in this compromise except possibly the logic of an awkward situation. A convention of political philosophers would never have devised it or agreed to it. If slaves were deemed to be citizens, they should have been counted, head for head, at full value; if they were deemed to be chattels, they should not have been counted at all. The three-fifths compromise could not be defended except on the hypothesis that slaves were neither one thing nor the other. Illogical as it was, however, this compromise is really a tribute to the sound political sense of the convention. It showed that there were practical politicians at work on the new frame of government, men who were ready to divorce themselves from logic or theory if by so doing they could bring the states into working harmony and thus get a strong union established.

*Other difficulties.*

But there were other questions connected with slavery. Every one agreed that the new federal government should be given some power to regulate commerce. The absence of such authority in central hands had been a glaring weakness under the Articles of Confederation. To what extent, however, and subject to what limitations, should this power be given to the new Congress? This was a perplexing question. If Congress should be given unrestricted power, it might levy duties not only on imports but upon the great exports of tobacco, cotton, rice, and indigo, which the southern states were shipping to Europe. Quite possibly, indeed, the populous northern states, like Pennsylvania, New York, and Massachusetts, might, by their superior representation in the new Congress, try to make the duties on southern exports furnish the bulk of the national revenue. And what about the trade in slaves? Slaves were still being brought from the coasts of Africa in large numbers, and the southern states felt that the new Congress should not have power, under color of regulating trade, to shut down upon these importations of slaves or to tax them too heavily. On the other hand, there were delegates in the convention, even from the South, who openly expressed their longing for the day when this brutal and infernal traffic would come to an end. Must the new constitution, then, to satisfy the southern planters, sanctify and fasten forever upon the land the curse of human servitude?

Another compromise solved these problems. It was agreed that Congress should have full liberty to tax imports but should be forbidden to tax exports; furthermore, that it should not be allowed to prohibit the importation of slaves until the year 1808. Meanwhile, it might levy a tax, not exceeding ten dollars per head, on all slaves brought in. Under this arrangement slaves continued to come for twenty years after the constitution went into force, but when this time-limit expired, Congress promptly forbade further importations. Thereafter the South had to depend upon the natural increase of its slave population. In the meantime, however, slavery gained an almost unshakable hold upon the economic system of these southern communities. What the loosening of this iron grip would ultimately cost the nation the framers of the compromise could not have foreseen; but of all the compromises of the constitution, this was the most heavily paid for in the end. *The commerce-and-slave-trade compromise.*

Various other questions had to be settled before the convention's work was finished, and some of them made heavy demands upon the time and patience of the members. The proper position and powers of the chief executive was one of these. The Articles of Confederation had provided for no separate executive; the Congress possessed both executive and legislative powers and handled its executive functions through its own committees or through officers whom it appointed. This system of carrying on the executive work of government proved, however, to be far from satisfactory. It was inefficient in war and cumbersome in peace. Hence arose the idea of making a place in the new constitution for a powerful and independent executive in the person of a President who would have dignity and authority in keeping with his position as the first citizen of a great nation. Yet the convention felt that there must be care lest the President's powers be made too broad, thus *Other questions.*

giving him at some future time the opportunity to become a virtual dictator with a more agreeable name. Accordingly, the framers of the constitution devised a curious method of choosing the President through the agency of an electoral college, so that he might be independent of Congress. As a weapon of self-defence, moreover, they gave him the power of veto. Likewise they placed in his hands great authority with respect to the making of appointments and the negotiating of treaties with foreign states. But, on the other hand, they hedged the presidential office with stern restrictions. A plan of removal by impeachment was provided to hold him in leash; his appointments were made subject to confirmation by the Senate, and a two-thirds vote of this body was made necessary to the ratification of treaties negotiated by him. The convention, in short, gave with one hand and took away with the other.

*The final touches.* Many other problems had to be worked over patiently. Time and again important matters were settled, only to be reopened and debated again. But in due course the various provisions were ready for a Committee of Detail, which put them into logical form. Then they were gone over again, and, after more alterations, the document was ready in September for a Committee of Revision. Gouverneur Morris, as chairman of this committee, was charged with the function of putting the provisions into terse and forceful English. How admirably he performed this task even a rapid reading of the document will disclose.

On September 17, 1787, the final draft of the constitution was signed by thirty-nine members of the convention. Of the others, some were absent; some refused to sign. *The constitution signed and transmitted to the several states for ratification.* The constitution was then sent to the Congress of the Confederation with the request that copies be transmitted to the legislatures of the several states, to be by them submitted to state conventions elected by the people, for ratification. This done, the convention dissolved. The members started for their own states to explain the new constitution, and there was much explaining to do.

By diligence and patience the constitution had been

framed, but a bigger task was still ahead, that of getting the states to accept it. No one dared to hope that all the states would agree, hence it was provided by the convention that if nine states gave their adhesion, the new central government would be established. There were serious doubts, indeed, whether even nine states would concur. The fact is that the members of the convention were themselves far from being enthusiastic over the product of their summer's labor. Scarcely one of the thirty-nine who signed the constitution regarded the document with whole-hearted approval. Alexander Hamilton, for example, gave his signature gladly, but in doing so took occasion to remind the convention that no man's opinions were more remote from the new constitution than his own. He was ready to accept it because in his opinion no plan of government could be much worse than that provided by the Articles of Confederation. Benjamin Franklin also had misgivings; but after remarking that the experience of fourscore years had taught him to doubt the infallibility of his own judgment, he placed his name at the head of the Pennsylvania delegation. So it was with Madison, the man who had done most to bring things to an auspicious end. The new constitution as finally drafted was a long way from being a true reflection of his clean-cut opinions, but he was ready to shoulder his share of responsibility for it before the people. Some men of inflexible convictions, among them Edmund Randolph of Virginia and Elbridge Gerry of Massachusetts, were so disappointed with the compromise character of the document that they would not sign at all.

*The great question: Would the states accept it?*

As the convention had met behind closed doors no inkling of what the delegates were doing reached the people till everything was done. In lieu of actual information from within the brick walls, however, the newspapers circulated all sorts of gossip as to what was under consideration. Many of these rumors were wild, but even the wildest among them found some believers. Not a few honest men in all sections of the land were afraid that a monarchy was being hatched at Philadelphia. When the constitution was finally made public, it contained, of course, many surprises. Some thought it made the central government too strong; others

*How the new constitution was received by public opinion.*

*The fault-finders.*

that it did not make it strong enough.[1] From all quarters came the serious and well-founded criticism that the constitution contained no bill of rights or group of guarantees for freedom of the press, freedom of speech, religious liberty, and so forth, such as had been incorporated in most of the state constitutions. Thomas Jefferson, for example, regarded this omission as the chief defect in the convention's work. Some grumbled because the constitution gave the new federal government power to issue paper money; others because it took that right away from the states. Many good people stigmatized the document as sacrilegious because it contained no mention of the Deity and did not even require that office-holders should be Christians. In the North there was a feeling that the compromise with slavery went too far; in the South it was regarded as not having gone far enough. The fault-finders were numerous, and among them were many influential men.

*The struggle for ratification in the various states.*

The Congress of the Confederation, after some delay and hesitation, sent copies of the constitution to the legislatures of the several states for ratification. In no case did these legislatures submit the question to a direct popular vote. They followed the policy of asking the people to elect delegates to state conventions which should by majority vote decide the matter. Conventions in Delaware, Pennsylvania, and New Jersey accepted the constitution almost at once; Georgia followed after a few weeks. Then serious obstacles began to appear in some of the larger states: Massachusetts, New York, and Virginia. In these the campaign of opposition became very bitter; an avalanche of criticism was let loose in broadsides, pamphlets, and letters to the newspapers. Personal attacks were launched against the leading men of the convention, and even Washington did not escape the flood of invective. The danger was not merely that fewer than nine states would accept the constitution, but that the refusal of one or two of the largest states might, by reason of their geographical situation and economic importance, practically nullify the whole

---

[1] In Paul Leicester Ford's *Pamphlets on the Constitution of the United States* (Brooklyn, 1888) will be found a collection of criticisms issued by various contemporary opponents of the constitution.

plan. There was New York, for example, where popular feeling seemed to be running most strongly against the constitution. If New York should refuse its adhesion, the assent of all the others would not insure the success of the new federation. Geographically New York lay right athwart the country. Four states were to the north of her and eight to the south. No union could be solid without New York. Yet in the closing days of 1787 it was apparent that if the question of ratifying the constitution were submitted to the people of New York, it would be overwhelmingly rejected. The critical need, therefore, was for a campaign of education which would focus the attention of the people, both in New York and elsewhere, upon the merits of the constitution itself, not upon the foibles and failings of the men who had framed it.

Such a campaign of education was accordingly planned by Alexander Hamilton, who enlisted for the work the coöperation of James Madison and John Jay. During the winter and spring of 1787–1788, these three wrote a series of letters which were printed, sometimes three or four letters a week, in various New York newspapers. The letters were designed to show how necessary some plan of federal union had become to the several states and to demonstrate, point by point, that the new constitution offered the best practicable solution of all the difficult problems involved. Each letter dealt with some phase of the subject in logical order, explaining, defending, and appealing to the patriotism of the people. All the letters bore the common signature "Publius," and the individual authorship of several of them cannot be definitely determined, but it is beyond doubt that the great majority were the work of Hamilton and Madison. *The campaign of education.*

Although these newspaper expositions of the new constitution were written under pressure and as campaign polemics, they set a high standard both in substance and in style. Brushing aside all personalities, all appeals to passion or to sectional prejudice, they went right to the heart of every constitutional question. They were the work of men who were brimful of their subject and who knew, better than any others of their time, just what the provisions of the *Value of the "Publius" letters.*

new constitution expressed or implied. Naturally these arguments exerted a great influence upon the public mind, and particularly upon the minds of those who came to the state conventions without any clear understanding of what powers the new constitution conveyed to the central government and what limitations it imposed. Had it not been for this vigorous publicity campaign, there is every reason to believe that New York would have rejected the constitution. Even as it was, that state was one of the last to ratify, and then this action was taken by the narrow majority of three votes in the state convention.

*The Federalist.*

Even before all the letters had appeared in the newspapers they were collected and printed in book form under the title of *The Federalist*. In that shape they have come down to us, and remain to-day the best contemporary exposition of what the constitution meant to the men who made it.[1] For keenness of analysis, cogency in the statement of arguments, adroitness in reply to critics, and brilliancy of style this volume has stood unrivalled in the field of American political literature for one hundred and thirty years. Seldom is it given to any treatise in political science to hold its place of supremacy so long. True enough, the book is not a trustworthy guide for those who want to know what the various provisions of the American constitution express or imply to-day. In the years since these letters were written eighteen amendments have been added; the courts have interpreted many clauses in a way which the framers of the constitution could never have foreseen, while a legion of political customs and usages, forming an unwritten constitution as it were, have grown up around the original frame of national government. Time in this as in all other things of human handiwork has wrought great changes. But as an elucidation of the basic principles of federal government and of what is compendiously called "the political ideals of the Fathers," there is nothing that approaches in value these campaign letters of Hamilton, Madison, and Jay.

A classic of political science.

While it is impossible to tell with certainty what would

[1] There are many editions of *The Federalist*, but the best for most purposes is Paul Leicester Ford's edition (N. Y., 1898).

have happened had the constitution been submitted for acceptance to the direct vote of the people in the various states, there is every reason to think that it would have been rejected. At the hands of conventions it had a far better chance of ratification because in none of the states save New York were the delegates to these conventions chosen on a basis of manhood suffrage. In all the remaining states there were property or other qualifications for voting, and the propertied classes were, on the whole, favorably disposed towards the constitution. It has been demonstrated, in fact, that most of the men who framed the constitution were themselves the owners of public bonds and other forms of property which were likely to gain in value if a strong federal government could be established. In the various state conventions, moreover, it was the delegates from the towns, the representatives of the mercantile and trading classes, who lined up most strongly in favor of ratification. The constitution drew its chief support from the well-to-do, the merchants and ship-owners, the men of education, — in a word from that part of the population which lived in the better-settled parts near the seacoast. The people of the interior and sparsely settled areas, the struggling farmers and pioneers, were, on the whole, opposed to it. There were exceptions, of course, but this indicates the broad line of division.[1]

*Other influences responsible for the adoption of the constitution by the states.*

*Attitude of the propertied classes.*

The constitution was not carried into operation, therefore, on any tidal wave of popular enthusiasm. Its supporters did not make their chief appeal by extolling the democratic features of the document; on the contrary, they placed their reliance upon arguments which could make little impression except upon the minds of thinking men. They tried to show that its acceptance would establish a safe government, a well-balanced government, a government able to maintain order within and security without, a government which would insure economic prosperity. In our own time we are occasionally told that the na-

*The arguments which prevailed.*

---

[1] For further information on this important point see O. G. Libby, *The Geographical Distribution of the Vote . . . on the Federal Constitution* (Madison, 1894) and C. A. Beard's *Economic Interpretation of the Constitution* (N. Y., 1913).

tional constitution is a reactionary document, framed in the first instance by men who had no faith in popular government, and that even in the days of its origin it did not reflect the political ideals of the people. That is in part true; in part false.

Why the constitution was not more radical.

The constitution was framed and adopted at a time when business conditions were bad and the national outlook unpromising. Men who had just won their independence were feeling the deep responsibility that went with nationhood. Quite naturally the constitution was not so completely imbued with ultra-democratic principles as would have been a fundamental law framed ten years before, by the men who signed the Declaration of Independence, for example. Only six of the fifty-six who signed the Declaration had a hand in making the constitution. Moreover, the framers of the constitution had to keep constantly in mind the fact that their work must go before the representatives of the people, and that whatever theories of government individual members of the convention may have held, these could not safely be given unchastened play. Be it undemocratic or otherwise to the eyes of the twentieth century radical, this constitution was incomparably the most democratic achievement of all the centuries down to its day. No leading nation of Europe in 1787 had a written constitution of any sort; nor, with the single exception of England, did any have even the forms of popular government. The new American constitution provided a scheme of government which was much more democratic than that which England possessed at the time and far more democratic than that which any land had ever possessed at any previous time.

The original constitution of the United States, like any other product of human hands, must be judged in the light of its own day, which was a day with scarcely a glimmer to lighten the darkness of political despotism in nearly all parts of the world. Let it be remembered, again, that this document, as has been well said, was the expression not only of political faith but of political fears. Its framers desired to establish a government which would be a bulwark of popular liberty; but they also wanted one that would defend the nation's borders, keep peace within the land, and

# THE CONSTITUTION AND ITS MAKERS 43

pass its blessings on to posterity. Let the political annals of four generations testify whether or not they acted wisely and well.

They established, in any event, the foundations of a nation which has shown itself able to preserve democracy at home and to fight for it abroad. They deserve the fame and gratitude that history has given them. "Leaders of the people by their counsels, wise and eloquent in their instructions, all these were honored in their generations and were the glory of their times. . . . With their seed shall continually remain a good inheritance, and their children are within the covenant. . . . Their glory shall not be blotted out. . . . Their bodies are buried in peace, but their name liveth forevermore. The people will tell of their wisdom and the congregation will show forth their praise." [1]

But to return to the final ratification. It will be recalled that the constitution was to go into force whenever nine states should have accepted it. By midsummer of 1788 the necessary nine had been secured; the others drifted in one by one. North Carolina did not give assent till the autumn of 1789, however, and Rhode Island delayed ratification until the spring of 1790. *(The constitution finally ratified.)*

The Congress of the Confederation, which had prolonged its feeble existence during all these turmoils, now issued a call to the various states to choose presidential electors, senators, and congressmen; likewise, it designated New York as the temporary seat of the new government, and then itself went out of existence. Ten states responded by choosing electors, and these electors in due course chose Washington as President and John Adams as Vice-President of the union. Likewise, they each chose their quota of senators and representatives in the way prescribed. The new government took office on April 30, 1789. *(The new federal government installed.)*

[1] *Ecclesiasticus* (Apocrypha) 44: 4–13.

# CHAPTER IV

## "THE SUPREME LAW OF THE LAND"

The constitution of the United States, to use its own words, is "the supreme law of the land." It is a short document, as constitutions go, and more concise than the constitution of any other nation or of any among the forty-eight states of the union. Therein it satisfies the first though not the second of the requirements once stipulated by Napoleon Bonaparte, that a good constitution should be "short and obscure." To read it through takes about twenty minutes. In arrangement it consists of a preamble and seven articles of unequal length, to which eighteen amendments have since been added. The three chief articles deal respectively with the legislative, the executive, and the judicial organs of government; the others with miscellaneous matters, such as interstate relations, the admission of new states, the methods of amendment, and the arrangements for its own ratification. Viewing the provisions of the constitution as a whole, certain fundamental considerations stand out prominently, and these will be briefly recapitulated.[1]

[1] The fundamental principles of the American constitution have been expounded at great length by many able writers. Joseph Story's *Commentaries on the Constitution* (5th ed., 2 vols., Boston, 1891) contains what may well be termed the classic exposition. W. W. Willoughby's *Constitutional Law of the United States* (2 vols., N. Y., 1910) is less philosophical and far more closely in touch with the conditions of to-day. Another well-known commentary, J. I. C. Hare's *American Constitutional Law* (2 vols., Boston, 1889), includes an able treatment of some difficult constitutional questions, and mention should also be made of Roger Foster's *Commentaries on the Constitution* of the United States, of which only the first volume was issued (Boston, 1895). John R. Tucker's *Constitution of the United States* (2 vols., Chicago, 1899) gives the Southern point of view on controverted questions. Among the smaller manuals the most useful are W. W. Willoughby's *Constitutional Law* (N. Y., 1912) and Emlin

In the first place the constitution is a grant of powers. It emanated from states which desired union but not unity. To that end they gave over, by mutual consent and irrevocably, certain powers which had hitherto been included in their own attributes of sovereignty. They created a new government, endowed it with definite powers, and made it sovereign within its own sphere. But the new federal government received only such powers as were expressly or by reasonable implication conveyed to it by the specific provisions of the constitution. All other authority was reserved to the states themselves, and any occasion for doubt on that point was speedily set at rest by the tenth amendment.[1] The proper allocation of powers to the Union and the states respectively was a matter of supreme importance, for upon this more than upon all else the success of the new constitution would ultimately depend.

1. The constitution is a grant of powers.

There had been federal governments in other countries before 1787, but their history had been one of failure, partial or complete. Either the federal government had in each case received too little power and hence had perished from general debility, or it had been allowed so much authority that it proved able to crush out the governments of its component parts. The framers of the constitution strove to guard against both these eventualities. They gave large powers to the new federal government, but not too large. They tried to assure it a reasonable revenue, but did not give it unlimited power to tax; they gave it power to borrow; they empowered it to regulate foreign and interstate commerce, to provide an army and navy, to establish and maintain a postal service, and to do various other things which the common welfare of all the states seemed to demand. But on the other hand they reserved to the states the whole

A balanced adjustment of authority.

---

McClain's *Constitutional Law in the United States* (N. Y., 1905). For short discussions on various topics, with well-chosen lists of further references, the reader may be referred to the *Cyclopedia of American Government*, edited by Andrew C. McLaughlin and Albert Bushnell Hart (3 vols., N. Y., 1914).

[1] "The powers not delegated to the United States by the constitution, nor prohibited by it to the states, are reserved to the states, respectively, or to the people."

field of civil and criminal law, the regulation of trade within their own bounds, the "police power," and the whole great list of other functions which the state government exercises to-day.

*The powers in detail.* Here are the chief general powers given by the constitution to the federal government and alongside them are placed some of the most important things left largely or wholly to the jurisdiction of the several states:

| Federal Powers | State Powers |
|---|---|
| 1. Taxation for federal purposes. | 1. Taxation for local purposes. |
| 2. Borrowing on the nation's credit. | 2. Borrowing on state's credit. |
| 3. Regulation of foreign and interstate commerce. | 3. Regulation of trade within the state. |
| 4. Currency and coinage. | 4. Civil and criminal law. |
| 5. Foreign relations and treaties. | 5. The "police power." |
| 6. Army and navy. | 6. Education. |
| 7. Postal service. | 7. Control of local government. |
| 8. Patents and copyrights. | 8. Charities and correction. |
| 9. Regulation of weights and measures. | 9. Suffrage and elections. |
| 10. Admission of new states. | 10. Organization and control of corporations. |

*Does the partitioning of governmental powers mean weak government?* Federalism, it is sometimes said, means weak government.[1] It distributes powers among several governments instead of concentrating them all into one strong hand. From their nature, then, federal states, whether they be monarchies or republics, are inferior in vigor and strength to centralized or unitary states. In the actual workings of federalism this may not be true, because inherent weakness may be more than offset by other factors which make for strength. In the United States it has not been true. The national government here developed through its hold on the loyalty of the people a degree of strength and stability which has served to offset the intrinsic weakness of a federal

[1] A. V. Dicey, *Introduction to the Study of the Law of the Constitution* (8th ed., N. Y., 1915), p. 167.

system. Whether a government will be strong or weak depends more upon the political genius of its people than upon the form of its constitution. It depends also upon the natural resources of the country, the spirit of the laws, and upon the political traditions that are developed. If a federal government proves weak, it cannot be attributed to the system alone.

The form of government established by the constitution through its partitioning of authority is a "federal republic," in other words a republic of republics or a federation of states. The adoption of this form was made necessary by geographical conditions and historical antecedents alike. No unitary republic, with all final powers lodged in the hands of the central authority, would have been practicable under the circumstances as they existed in 1787, and the convention did not consider any such proposal. Federal republics had been established in previous times, but never on so large a scale as this. Here was the world's first great experiment in federal republicanism. *A federal republic.*

A second fundamental characteristic of the American constitution is its recognition of what has commonly been called the principle of "division of powers" or of "checks and balances"; in other words the idea that the three organs of government — legislative, executive, and judicial — should be kept distinct and independent and should each act as a check on the others. The executive should never legislate nor should the legislature ever attempt to administer its own laws. The courts, again, should enforce the laws of the land but should have no hand in making them. *2. The principle of "checks and balances."*

This interesting doctrine has been generally associated with a French writer, Baron Montesquieu, whose two volumes on *The Spirit of Laws* appeared about 1748. But the general idea of differentiating the functions of government is as old as Aristotle. Montesquieu merely gave it a broader and more emphatic expression, and through his writings the leaders of political thought in America were impressed by it. Here is the doctrine in Montesquieu's own words: *Derived from Montesquieu.*

"Political liberty is to be found only in moderate governments; even in these it is not always found. It is there only when there is no abuse of power. But constant experience shows us that every man invested with power is apt to abuse it, and to carry his authority as far as it will go. Is it not strange, though true, to say that virtue itself has need of limits? To prevent this abuse, it is necessary from the very nature of things that power should be a check to power. . . . In every government there are three sorts of power: the legislative, the executive. . . . and the judiciary power. . . . When the legislative and executive powers are united in the same person, or in the same body of magistrates, there can be no liberty. . . . Again, there is no liberty, if the judiciary power be not separated from the legislative and executive." [1]

Montesquieu's doctrine was widely accepted by the leaders of public opinion in the various states during the last two decades of the eighteenth century. John Adams was a firm believer in its soundness and embodied it in the constitution of Massachusetts. The most influential members of the constitutional convention of 1787 accepted it as gospel. "No political truth," wrote Madison, "is of greater intrinsic value. . . . The accumulation of all powers, legislative, executive and judiciary, in the same hands, whether of one, a few, or many, and whether hereditary, self-appointed, or elective, may justly be pronounced the very definition of tyranny." [2] Hence, while no express statement of Montesquieu's principle was incorporated in the national constitution, the separation therein of legislative, executive, and judicial provisions into three separate articles and the establishment of divers checks and balances prove that the doctrine was held clearly in mind.[3]

Why should the writings of a French philosopher have had such an influence upon the structure of American government? One reason is that the doctrine seemed to fit in precisely with the experience of colonial America.

[1] *The Spirit of Laws*, Book XI, chs. 4–6, *passim*.
[2] *The Federalist*, No. 47.
[3] John Adams of Massachusetts, a loyal apostle of Montesquieu, was able to find no fewer than eight separate "checks and balances" in the constitution. See John Adams, *Works* (10 vols., Boston, 1850–1856), Vol. vi, p. 467.

The colonists had repeatedly protested against the interference of their colonial governors in the matters of legislation, and there had been many conflicts over the independence of the colonial judges. On the whole, it looked as though most of the political troubles of the colonial era had arisen from a failure to keep these organs of government from encroaching upon the prerogatives of one another. It was not realized by those who so readily accepted the theory of the separation of powers, however, that Montesquieu's teachings were based largely upon a misconception of existing English government. The Bourbon despotism of his own country seemed to Montesquieu to be the result of concentrating all powers in one centre, namely, in the monarch's hands; his ideal of what a free government ought to be was the government of England under the Hanoverians.

*Reasons for this influence although his teaching was based upon a misconception.*

So far as France was concerned, Montesquieu was right; but as regards England, he was wrong. In France the boast imputed to Louis XIV, "*L'état c'est moi*," expressed no mere fiction of royal power. The king was the state; he made the laws by royal decree, enforced them, and sent men to prison by his personal orders. All governmental power was centralized in him. In England the political situation during the second half of the eighteenth century was very different. There the king had no such unrestrained authority. Yet the principle of checks and balances was not really embodied, as Montesquieu thought, in the English government of his day; the legislature there dominated and controlled the executive. Montesquieu was looking at the ancient theory of English government which gave the crown a position of executive independence; he was unmindful of the actual facts of English government which gave parliament, through a ministry responsible to it, the power to control the actions of the crown.

Despite the rancor which remained in their hearts as the natural result of the Revolution, the political leaders of 1787 admired the spirit and the institutions of English government. It is no wonder that they did. Britain alone of all great countries had at that time even a pretence of free government. Alone among the nations the United Kingdom loomed up as the shadow of a great

*The fathers of the constitution admired but did not fully understand the English system of government.*

E

rock in a weary world of despotisms. Yet even James Madison, with all his political erudition, did not really understand the true spirit of the government under which he was born. Neither he nor Washington, nor Hamilton, nor Franklin, much less the minor lights of the constitutional convention, had any real appreciation of the great hiatus which already existed between the theory and the practice of English government. To-day this gap has become so conspicuous that no elementary student of the subject ever misses it. In legal fiction the crown remains the chief executive, an independent "estate of the realm," as the phrase goes, with all its time-hallowed prerogatives. In actual fact, however, the crown is the mere creature of parliament, doing as it is told and possessing, as was once said in another connection, "neither eyes to see nor tongue to speak" save as parliament may command. In 1787 the supremacy of parliament, although not so clearly marked as to-day, was established beyond any question, but the men who made the constitution of the United States failed to see it. They were misled by the husks of legal fiction which obscured the kernels of actual fact.

*They overlooked the most distinguishing feature of English government — the cabinet.*

Hence it was that they gave little attention to what had already become, without the enactment of a single law, the most distinguishing feature of English government — the responsible cabinet. When they thought of the executive branch of English government, they had their minds on the crown, not on the cabinet. They did not realize that even in their own day the prime minister was the master of the crown and the servant of parliament, and hence that all clean-cut separation of powers between executive and legislative organs of government had vanished. That is why it may properly be said that the system of checks and balances, as woven into the American constitution by its framers, was the outcome of a misconception. Its acceptance sanctified an error.

*Complete separation of powers neither practicable nor desirable.*

In the form which Montesquieu gave it, moreover, the theory is unworkable. The absolute independence of the three great departments of government would bring administration to a standstill. There must be points of contact. Even the framers of the constitution realized this and so made no attempt to secure complete separation of powers. They gave to the Senate, for example, the right to withhold its confirmation of appointments, thereby awarding it a share in the exercise of executive power. On the other hand, they gave the President, through his veto, the power to exercise a check on legislation. Madison, moreover, was at great pains to point out, when the constitution was before the states for acceptance, that Montesquieu himself had not urged complete separation of powers. The French philosopher's dogma, as "illustrated by the example of his eye," aimed merely to secure broad lines of separation and did not seek to preclude slight overlappings of jurisdiction. In this interpretation Madison was right, although it would have been much better, on the whole, if he and his colleagues in the convention had carried their broad interpretation of Montesquieu's doctrine a great deal further.

The notion that there can be no liberty without a separation of governmental powers, without a system of checks and balances, is one that might easily be expected to find favor a century ago; to-day it is far from commanding general acceptance by students of political science. The federal governments of Canada and Australia, for example, with no separation of powers, have demonstrated Montesquieu's dread of centralization to have been in large measure imaginary. It is impossible to say, of course, whether the United States would have fared better or worse under a constitution framed by men who knew not Montesquieu; but there are many thoughtful Americans who nowadays believe that the theory of checks and balances is a delusion and a snare, that it has made for confusion in the actual work of government, that it divides responsibility, encourages friction, and has balked constructive legislation on numberless occasions. On the other hand, the doctrine still retains its stanch friends who point out that some system of restraint must be placed on all governmental authority. In England the main reliance for holding the supreme will of parliament in leash is placed upon public opinion; but in the United States with a wide variation of geographical interests and a polyglot population, it may

*Is the theory of checks and balances sound?*

be that some more rigid check is needed than public opinion could ever be expected to supply.

3. The doctrine of judicial supremacy.

The third fundamental of the American constitution is the doctrine of judicial supremacy.[1] In every sovereign state there must be "a supreme authority whose determinations are final and not subject to any recognized power." In England this supremacy rests with parliament, which can do whatever it will so long as it keeps within the bounds of what is humanly possible. No executive can veto the acts of parliament, no British court declare them unconstitutional. In the French Republic, although there is a written constitution, no court can set aside the mandate of the Senate and the Chamber of Deputies when they act in accord. These two countries, Britain and France, have accepted the doctrine of legislative supremacy. But, in the United States, that is just what the framers of the constitution sought to avoid. Experience with repressive acts of the English parliament in the days before the Revolution had impressed upon them the belief that it is the habit of all legislatures to become tyrannical, and it was not their purpose, as one of them put it, "to create an elective despotism" on this side of the Atlantic.

Did the framers intend to make the Supreme Court the guardian of the constitution?

Yet final authority, as has been said, must in all governments be placed somewhere. So it was placed in the constitution itself, which was declared to be the "supreme law of the land." But that was not enough. A written constitution is not of itself a living, growing organism, able to keep step with the needs of an expanding nation. It must contain within itself some provision for giving it growth and flexibility. The framers of the American constitution avowedly recognized this not merely by making the document a judicious mixture of definiteness in principle with elasticity in details, but of inserting two alternative plans for adding amendments. Did they also have it in mind to give the Supreme Court the function of guarding the constitution, interpreting it, and declaring null any act of Congress that might overstep the allotted bounds of federal power? Did they have clearly in

[1] For a full discussion of this topic, see C. G. Haines, *The American Doctrine of Judicial Supremacy* (N. Y., 1914).

mind the idea of judicial as contrasted with legislative supremacy?

Whether they had such an intent or not is a question too involved for discussion here. Much has been written about it. Two things, however, are certain. One is that the Supreme Court is not endowed with its nullifying powers by any provision of the constitution. Early in the convention's deliberations a proposition was made to establish a council of revision made up of the executive and a convenient number of Supreme Court judges whose duty it should be to examine every act of Congress and whose dissent from any act should nullify it unless the act were subsequently reënacted by a two-thirds vote. But this proposal was rejected, and the veto power was finally intrusted to the executive alone, nothing being settled definitely as to the authority of the judges to declare a law unconstitutional. The other certainty is that the Supreme Court in due course assumed the power to declare laws unconstitutional and unequivocably possesses that power to-day. The doctrine of judicial supremacy is therefore a fundamental fact of American constitutional government. Whether the framers of the constitution intended it to be so is now an academic question, hardly worth further controversy.[1] Many other lands have written constitutions as their supreme law, and they have supreme courts as well, but in none of them has a supreme court ever undertaken to declare unconstitutional any act of the national legislature. *It has, at any rate, become so.*

One other feature distinguishes the constitution of the United States from those of some other countries, from the constitutions of Canada or of Australia, for example. Both of these latter are federations of Anglo-Saxon origin, and their respective constitutions have borrowed much from the United States, but in neither case have they accepted the American theory of "constitutional limitations." The constitutions of Canada and Australia merely establish organs of federal government and allot powers; the constitution of the United States not only does these things, but it also places express limitations upon both the national *4. The theory of constitutional limitations.*

[1] For a summary of the matter see C. A. Beard, *The Supreme Court and the Constitution* (N. Y., 1912).

and state governments. It enumerates various things which no government may do, such as condemning men to death by legislative process or taking private property without just compensation. Hence no government in the United States, whether national or state, is absolutely sovereign. They are sovereign only within the limits of the constitution. The only absolutely sovereign authority in America is that authority which can change the federal constitution, namely, two-thirds of the members of both houses of Congress and a majority of the members in each of three-fourths of the state legislatures acting in accord, or, alternatively, a majority of the members of a national convention together with a majority of the members in each of three-fourths of the state legislatures, all acting in accord. Whether all the limitations which appear in the constitution of the United States have really served a useful purpose is a matter to be discussed in another chapter; they form, at any rate, a distinctive feature of the document.

*Constitution contained few wholly new principles.*

These are the fundamental doctrines of the national constitution. No one of them was wholly new even in 1787. The idea of a written constitution as a grant of powers is as old as the Lycian Confederacy; the theory of separation of powers harks back to Polybius and Aristotle. The doctrine of judicial supremacy and the idea of constitutional limitations were both evolved out of hazy notions concerning the paramountcy of the common law in colonial times, and for the former there were well-defined precedents before the Revolution. When, after the constitution had been some time in operation, the Supreme Court announced its right to declare an act of Congress unconstitutional, it impressed the people as doing nothing revolutionary. At common law any act done by any official beyond the limits of his legal jurisdiction was void. The doctrine of judicial supremacy was merely the same general notion greatly enlarged and somewhat modified.

*And few practical innovations.*

And what has been said of fundamental doctrines is also true of the actual provisions of the constitution from preamble to conclusion. Few of them represent real innovations. Many go back to the great landmarks of civil liberty like Magna Carta and the Grand Remonstrance. Nearly all have their roots deep down in the soil of English history. What did not come from England came chiefly from the rich granary of colonial experience. Let it not be forgotten that Englishmen had been adapting their ancient political institutions to the environment of the New World for over a hundred and fifty years — a longer period than that which has to-day elapsed since the American constitution went into force. They had tried many things, had succeeded in some and failed in others. They had a large fund of homeland data to draw upon. To foreign lands, accordingly, the framers of the constitution went for very little.[1] The experiences of ancient confederacies, mediæval republics, and eighteenth century absolutisms were instructive mainly in showing them what to avoid. They took comfort from one other dictum of Montesquieu, that the best government is "that which best agrees with the humor and disposition of the people in whose favor it is established."[2] Their minds were therefore set upon the task of framing a constitution which would fit the "humor and disposition" of the three million souls who lived along the Atlantic seaboard. Scholars have wasted much energy in trying to find out-of-the-way origins for some of the things which went into the constitution. For the electoral college which was established to choose the chief executive of the United States there is no need to seek precedents in the college of cardinals or the princely electors of the Holy Roman Empire. Even this strange institution was not improbably suggested by a somewhat analogous arrangement which already existed in Maryland. The constitution, in a word, contains very little that is

[1] "With the exception of the method of electing the president there is not a clause of the constitution which cannot be traced back to English statutes of liberty, colonial charters, state constitutions, the articles of confederation, votes of congress, or the unwritten practice of some of these forms of government." — A. B. Hart, *National Ideals Historically Traced* (N. Y., 1907), p. 139. For a further discussion of this point the following books may be indicated: J. H. Robinson, *The Original and Derived Features of the Constitution* (Philadelphia, 1890); C. E. Stevens, *Sources of the Constitution of the United States* (2d ed., N. Y., 1894), and Sydney G. Fisher, *The Evolution of the Constitution of the United States* (N. Y., 1897).

[2] *The Spirit of Laws*, Book I, ch. 3.

not indigenous. It is Anglo-American from start to finish. Its genesis is to be found at Runnymede and Westminster, not at Philadelphia; it is the handiwork not alone of Madison and Wilson and Morris but of Simon de Montfort, Edward Coke, John Hampden, and Oliver Cromwell. What its framers did not get from England they took from the stock of past and present institutions in America. Discreet selection rather than random borrowing marked their work.

The constitution, indeed, contains very few marks of creative genius; there is practically no provision of any importance for which some well-known Anglo-Saxon precedent cannot readily be found. The most solid and excellent work done by the convention was its enumeration of the eighteen powers of Congress [1] and its definition of the judicial power of the United States.[2] In both these cases the experience of the country during the critical years between 1781 and 1787 served the framers as virtually their sole guide.

[1] Article i, Section 8.      [2] Article iii.

# CHAPTER V

## HOW THE CONSTITUTION HAS DEVELOPED

PROFESSOR DICEY, in his interesting discussion of parliamentary sovereignty, divides all constitutions into two general classes, flexible and rigid. The English constitution, he says, is flexible because its provisions may be changed in the same way as any ordinary law, by the regular lawmaking authority of the realm, which is parliament. The constitution of the United States, on the other hand, he calls rigid, because it cannot be so altered by the regular law-making authorities, that is, by the President and Congress. Flexibility, he suggests, makes for constitutional progress and easy change; rigidity for conservatism. In illustration of this he asserts that the constitution of the United States did not undergo a tithe of the changes which marked the constitutional development of England during the nineteenth century.[1] *Flexible and rigid constitutions.*

This difference between flexible and rigid constitutions, however, is easy to exaggerate, and Professor Dicey, in contrasting English with American constitutional development, has laid undue emphasis upon it. If the American constitution could only be expanded or developed by actually amending it in the way prescribed, there would be good reason for calling it rigid, because the method of amendment is tedious and difficult. But there are other ways, quite as effective and much simpler. The constitution of the United States has been enabled to keep pace with the economic and social needs of the country by various other agencies of development, and these processes of change move so insidiously that they do not seem to be fully appreciated by foreign students of American government. *The distinction has been overemphasized.*

[1] *Law of the Constitution*, p. 120.

*English and American definitions of "constitutional development."*

The haziness on this point is in part due to the fact that, in contrasting English with American constitutional evolution, due care has not always been given to terminology. When we wish to compare the constitutions of different countries, we should first reduce them to a common denominator. It is misleading to contrast the *constitution* of England, meaning thereby the whole body of fundamental laws, court decisions, and usages which determine the way in which Englishmen are governed, with the *constitution* of the United States, meaning by that term only the written document and taking no cognizance of the whole body of interpreting laws, decisions, usages, and devices which supplement and determine the real application of those written provisions. Americans are governed by laws, judicial decisions, and usages quite as much as by the strict wording of their national constitution.

*The English constitution is not really more flexible than the American.*

If we look at matters in this light, meaning by the American constitution that whole body of organic jurisprudence which fundamentally determines the forms and facts of actual government, it is not true that the constitution of the United States has shown itself to be far less flexible than the constitution of England. Let the following example illustrate this point. Among the great constitutional changes in England during the past hundred years not the least important are those embodied in the Reform Acts of 1832 and 1867 which greatly widened the suffrage. These reforms stirred public discussion to its depths. The whole world realized at both these dates that England was undergoing a great constitutional transition. But sub-

*Suffrage widening as an example.*

stantially the same widening of the suffrage, and indeed an even greater widening, took place in the United States during the first half of the nineteenth century without any actual amendment of the constitution, but merely through the enactment of new suffrage laws by the various states. When the national constitution went into force, manhood suffrage existed almost nowhere. To-day it is universal throughout the Union, and in a dozen or more states the suffrage has been extended to include women as well. The national constitution did not lay down any definite rule as to who should vote at national elections. It left the matter to be determined, under certain limitations, by the several states themselves. Then, one by one, all the states accepted the principle of manhood suffrage, and one by one they are now giving women the right to vote at national elections. In the course of a hundred years property qualifications for voting have been everywhere abolished in this country. The wording of the constitution remains absolutely unchanged on this point, yet the actual situation with reference to suffrage (apart from negro suffrage) is vastly different from what it was at the end of the eighteenth century.

Take another example, the power of the Supreme Court to declare a law unconstitutional. The constitution, as has been already pointed out, conveys no such right in express terms. The court assumed it, whether with or without good reason is not the question here. The fact that this change did not come by formal constitutional amendment is no good reason why it should be placed outside the field of constitutional development. Some of the most notable mutations in the spirit and facts of American government have taken place without the necessity of altering a single word in the supreme law of the land. To regard a written constitution as rigid, merely because it is not easy to amend in the prescribed way, is to overlook other great agencies of elasticity which not only exist but are unceasingly at work.

*Another example—Supreme Court's power.*

Whether a written constitution may properly be called "rigid" depends, therefore, not only upon the degree of ease or difficulty with which the document itself may be amended, but upon the breadth of its various provisions, upon the powers and policy of the authorities who interpret these provisions and upon the extent to which development may take place by usage. Under certain conditions a written constitution may be more flexible and more easily brought into tune with new and popular demands than one which has not been embodied in writing.

*The true test of flexibility.*

The constitution of the United States is precise in its enunciation of principles, but not nearly so definite in its prescription of details. It leaves many things to be worked out by law either in Congress or in the various state legislatures. There was no compelling desire to have all things

*How the American constitution has developed: 1. development by law.*

exactly uniform throughout the country except in matters which absolutely required uniformity. The makers of the constitution did not endeavor to settle every detail of national government. Knowing that they could not provide for all contingencies, they did not try to do so, but trusted to future Congresses, or to the various state legislatures, to provide whatever detailed arrangements might prove necessary.

<sub>Other examples.</sub> In this way great scope was left for the development of the constitution by merely changing the national or state laws. And in the last century and a quarter there has been a tremendous development through this channel. The whole structure of the subordinate federal courts is provided for by federal statutes, since the constitution merely handed over to Congress the duty of making such provisions in whatever way it deemed best. The succession to the presidency, in the event of the Vice-President not being available, is similarly arranged by law. There is scarcely a word in the constitution relating either to the President's Cabinet or to the organization of the various executive departments. All that is provided for by the federal laws. The present method of governing territories and insular possessions again rests wholly upon law and not upon constitutional provision. So, likewise, the methods by which members of Congress are nominated and elected, and even the determination of who shall vote at congressional elections, is left to be arranged by the laws of the several states. Of the actual present-day workings of the federal government one cannot, indeed, get an adequate knowledge by merely studying the words of the constitution itself. By far the greater portion of what the student of actual government desires to know is not there but is set forth in the statute-books of the nation and the states.

2. development by judicial interpretation. In the second place, the constitution has been developed by judicial and administrative decisions. Montesquieu urged that the judiciary should never be allowed to make or alter the constitution or the laws, and this doctrine is agreed to in all countries to-day. The courts should merely interpret the constitution and the laws. *Jus dicere, non dare*, the saying is. Ostensibly all they ever

do is to interpret and apply; but the plain fact remains that to interpret a phrase often means to give it a new application, and the Supreme Court of the United States has read into the American constitution many things which are not there visible to the naked eye. For one hundred and thirty years question after question has come before it as to the meaning and scope of various provisions, phrases, and words in the organic law of the nation. "Congress," the constitution declares, "shall have power . . . to regulate commerce. . . ." But what is included within the term "commerce"? In matters of trade and industry the United States has been moving forward with phenomenal rapidity, each year bringing new problems concerning the relation of government to business. It has been the work of the Supreme Court, through its power of judicial interpretation, to "twist and torture" (as Lord Bryce puts it) the term "commerce" so that it will cover them all. What, again, does the constitution mean by the words "to regulate"? By its regulating power may it tax, may it even prohibit? The Supreme Court has answered that it may do either or both. It has held at various times that the commerce power of Congress extends not only to the transportation of freight and passengers, but to the transmission of telegrams, telephone messages, light and power, the sending of oil through pipe lines, to pilotage, maritime contracts, and many other things.[1]

Here we have, therefore, a new element of flexibility. *Its scope.* The student who wants to know what the actual powers of Congress are to-day will get a scant idea of their scope and ramifications by merely surveying the eighteen formal powers granted in the words of the constitution itself. Hundreds of Supreme Court decisions have widened these original powers beyond recognition, yet never in a single instance has the court asserted its power to make any change in the phraseology. The stretching of a phrase in one decision gives a foundation for some further elongation in the next; the lines of development are pricked out by one decision after another until the last has carried matters a long way from the point at which the interpreting

[1] See below, pp. 249–250.

process began. The framers of the constitution realized, of course, that differences of opinion would arise as to what various provisions expressed or implied, and they took it for granted that the Supreme Court would resolve those differences. But they could not have foreseen the stupendous amount of interpreting that would have to be done, or the subtle way in which this process would in the end spell actual change.

*The process of interpretation.*   Provisions of the constitution are subjected to judicial interpretation only when actual disputes concerning them have arisen. The procedure is usually as follows: Some power is claimed and exercised by a national or state legislature or official; it is then challenged by any citizen as not warranted by the constitution and the issue goes to the courts. Not always directly to the Supreme Court of the United States, however, although if the issue be important, it eventually comes to that tribunal ultimately for final decision. In determining what any phrase in the constitution means, the Supreme Court has the last word. This, it need hardly be reiterated, is a tremendous power, and one which has never yet been assumed by the paramount judicial authority in any other land. Its exercise has greatly modified and expanded the provisions of the constitution; it is probably true that a greater development has taken place through this than through any other channel. The study of American constitutional law to-day is chiefly the study of judicial decisions.[1]

*Its effect in strengthening the national government.*   How has this method of development affected the relative powers of the nation and the states as originally adjusted by the constitution? On the whole the course of judicial interpretation has greatly widened the actual powers of the national government, carrying them far beyond what the framers of the constitution could ever have foreseen or intended. The Supreme Court at an early

[1] The most important of these decisions have been brought together in various compilations, of which the best is James Bradley Thayer's *Cases in Constitutional Law* (2 vols., Cambridge, 1895). A smaller collection, Lawrence B. Evans, *Leading Cases on American Constitutional Law* (Chicago, 1916), will be found more convenient for student use. Emlin McClain, *Selection of Cases on Constitutional Law* (2d ed., Boston, 1900), is also well worth notice.

date accepted the doctrine of "implied powers"; in other words the idea that whenever the constitution gives to Congress a general power in express terms, it conveys by implication all the collateral authority that may be necessary or proper for carrying such general power into effective operation. The constitution, for instance, gives Congress no express power to charter banks, but it does give a general power to borrow money. Hence the Supreme Court long ago decided that if Congress regards the establishment of banking institutions as a necessary or proper aid to the exercise of its borrowing power, it may establish banks.[1] Within the general power to tax, to borrow, to regulate commerce, to establish post-offices and post-roads, one action after another on the part of Congress has been upheld. The distance between some action of Congress and the literal words of the constitution which authorize such action often seems very great, but a chain of decisions bridges the gap between. Every general power of Congress has been as a sun, developing its group of planets or subsidiary powers, while around these in turn have grown up a girdle of satellites.

But it is not the courts alone that interpret the constitution, although in the main this function is assumed by them. Administrative officers from the President down are often confronted with the necessity of acting promptly when their constitutional powers are not clear. Their actions may in most cases be challenged and subjected to judicial review, but usually they are accepted without any such protest. In that event the action stands and forms a precedent for the future. It does not form a binding precedent, of course, for no administrative ruling, however long acquiesced in, is certain to be upheld by the courts. Nevertheless, when any legislative or administrative construction of a constitutional provision has been allowed to pass for a long time unchallenged, and particularly when important public or private rights have been based upon it, such construction is altogether likely to be accepted. In recent years there have been many administrative rulings which virtually operate as agencies of constitutional development. The opinions of the Attorney-General, given for the guid-

*The construing of constitutional provisions by administrative rulings.*

[1] See below, p. 237.

ance of the executive departments, afford the most conspicuous illustration.

*3. development by usage.*

In the third place the constitution has been developed, expanded, and modified by usage or custom. Alongside the written document there has grown up a body of practices based neither on laws nor judicial decisions, but merely the result of long-continued habit, and these form what is sometimes called the "unwritten constitution" of the United States.[1] Custom everywhere plays a large part in actual government. England is the classic example of a land ruled largely by political customs or usages, but even written constitutions have not precluded the development of usages elsewhere. While traditional ways of doing things have no force when they come into actual conflict with the letter of the constitution, usages do grow luxuriantly within the broad limits permitted thereby, and it is necessary to reckon with them in any survey of actual government.

*Some examples: (a) the actual method of electing the President.*

What are some of the customs that have thus developed in the practice of the national government? One concerns the actual method of electing the President. It was assumed by the framers of the constitution that the electors in the several states would meet, each at his own state capital, and would survey the whole field of possibilities before casting their votes. By custom they do nothing of the sort. They have become, as every one knows, mere instrumentalities with no deliberative function. They form to-day a wholly superfluous cog in the machinery of election. Yet there is nothing to prevent their doing just what the constitution contemplated that they would do. The custom has become stronger than the constitution itself. To-day the President of the United States is as directly chosen by the voters as though there were no intervening electors at all. In other words, there has developed precisely the system of election which the designers of the constitution sought to avoid. They did not desire any direct, popular election of the nation's chief executive officers and spent much thought in devising an elaborate scheme for preventing it.

[1] C. G. Tiedeman, *The Unwritten Constitution of the United States* (N. Y., 1890).

## HOW THE CONSTITUTION HAS DEVELOPED 65

Again, the constitution empowers the President to make appointments subject to "the advice and consent of the Senate." But by usage the Senate's advice is never asked and by usage also its consent is in some cases never refused. The Senate never declines its consent, for example, to those whom the President may select for Cabinet offices. The Cabinet itself, indeed, represents a development based partly on law and partly upon custom. The various executive departments are organized by law, but usage alone has determined what heads of departments shall be called to Cabinet meetings. Mention might also be made of the principle known for so many years as "senatorial courtesy," by virtue of which presidential appointments were under certain circumstances not confirmed by the Senate unless they were first approved by the senators from the state directly concerned. This somewhat pernicious practice had no warrant in either the constitution or the laws, but merely grew up and became strong enough, at one period, to be rightly regarded as an important feature of actual government. In the matter of removals, too, the rules have been established by usage and not by constitutional provision. As to how removals should be made, other than by impeachment for high crimes and misdemeanors, the constitution is silent, and the question early arose as to whether the "advice and consent of the Senate" were needed for removals in the same manner as for appointments. The President, however, assumed the responsibility of removing officials without seeking the Senate's concurrence, and usage, now supported by judicial decisions, has established his right in the matter. *(b) the confirmation of presidential appointments.*

The most important development which has come about in the whole field of American government as the result of both extra-legal and extra-judicial forces, however, has been that complicated political fabric which we call the party system. The framers of the constitution regarded the rivalry of political parties — the violence of faction, they termed it — as a thoroughly vicious feature, inimical to the best interests of free government. It was their hope and expectation that there would be no political parties in America, hence the constitution contains no men- *(c) the machinery and work of political parties.*

F

tion of them. Its provisions, indeed, were framed on the assumption that there would be no party organizations. Yet political parties sprang into being almost at the outset of the Union and they soon became dominating factors in the work of the new federal government. The whole mechanism of the political party, its caucuses, primaries, and conventions, its platforms and pledges, its campaigns and committees, its manipulations both in Congress and outside — all this has been developed for the most part in the realm of unwritten law. Yet who will say that party organizations do not profoundly affect the political life of the American people? Custom has here revolutionized in its spirit, if not in its form, the whole governmental structure and made it, whether for good or ill, far different from what its architects designed it to be.

(d) money bills.

Occasionally it happens that the usage proves even stronger than the literal wording of a constitutional provision. The constitution, for instance, stipulates that all bills "for raising revenue" shall originate in the House of Representatives. Nevertheless, as a matter of actual practice, some bills for raising revenue do originate in the Senate. On the other hand, the constitution makes no stipulation as to where bills for spending money shall originate. By usage, however, all such bills originate in the House. It will be easily seen, therefore, that the words of the constitution furnish no guidance whatever on matters of financial procedure.

(e) other examples.

Various other examples of institutions and practices which owe their existence to usage and not to enactment might easily be given. The Speaker of the House has developed most of his powers by custom. The caucus system in Congress is the child of custom alone; no provision for it exists in the constitution or in the laws. So is the committee system, including the policy of appointing a committee of conference whenever the two chambers fail to agree. The principle that no President should hold office for more than two terms has become a strong tradition, although this was far from being the intention of those who framed the constitution.[1]

[1] *The Federalist*, No. 68.

# HOW THE CONSTITUTION HAS DEVELOPED 67

Even usages, however, may change. For a full century no President ever read his messages to Congress. The custom was to send them in writing by messenger. But President Wilson changed this custom, setting aside the precedents of a hundred years, and it is quite possible that the new practice may be continued by his successors. Usage has profoundly influenced the actual workings of national government in America, building up an elaborate unwritten constitution and thus giving to the written document a much greater resiliency.

Finally, the constitution has been developed by amending it. Its framers foresaw that the need for amendments would arise, but it was not their opinion that the need would be frequent nor was it their desire that the process of amendment should be easy. Hence they provided a rather cumbrous amending machinery which ordinarily involves action not only by Congress but by three-fourths of the states. There are two alternative methods of amending the constitution of the United States and they cannot be more clearly or concisely described than by using the exact phraseology of the document itself. "The Congress, whenever two-thirds of both Houses shall deem it necessary, shall propose amendments to this constitution, or, on the application of the legislatures of two-thirds of the several states, shall call a convention for proposing amendments, which, in either case, shall be valid to all intents and purposes as parts of this constitution, when ratified by the legislatures of three-fourths of the several states, or by conventions in three-fourths thereof, as the one or the other mode of ratification may be proposed by the Congress."[1]

<small>4. development of the constitution by amendment.</small>

Only eighteen amendments have been made to the national constitution in one hundred and thirty-one years. The number is really much smaller, for the first ten amendments, all made at the same time, might easily have been combined into a single one. Taken as a whole the eighteen fall into four groups. First there are these initial ten amendments which are commonly called the Bill of Rights. They should have been put in the original document, and the campaign for the ratification of the constitution would have

<small>The first ten amendments.</small>

[1] Article v.

been less arduous if that had been done. Much of the opposition to the acceptance of the constitution was based upon its failure to provide any of the safeguards for individual liberty which had been incorporated into the constitutions of the various states. Immediately after the constitution had gone into force, therefore, a series of amendments covering these matters was submitted to the states and ratified. These ten amendments, indeed, ought not to be regarded as amendments at all, but as forming, to all intents and purposes, an integral part of the original constitution.

<small>Later amendments.</small>

The next two amendments, the eleventh and twelfth, were designed to remedy what appeared to be ambiguities and defects in the original provisions — perfecting amendments, they might be called. The former was a direct result of a Supreme Court decision which held that a citizen could sue a state in the federal courts. This interpretation of the judicial power conferred by the constitution aroused the more ardent champions of state rights, who bestirred themselves to have the judicial sovereignty of the states made clear.[1] The other amendment, the twelfth, was proposed and adopted because the presidential election of 1800 demonstrated the need of changing that section of the original constitution which dealt with the choice of a President and Vice-President. In the third group come the post-bellum amendments, thirteenth, fourteenth, and fifteenth, embodying the principles which the victorious northern states insisted upon after the Civil War, and forming, as it were, the terms of peace. Lastly, there are the sixteenth, seventeenth and eighteenth amendments dealing respectively with income taxes, the method of electing senators, and national prohibition. All of these amendments have been adopted in our own day and all of them may be regarded as the product of the changed political and social ideas which marked the incoming of the twentieth century. A proposed nineteenth amendment, on woman suffrage, is now before the States.

After all, the constitution has not been greatly changed by actual amendment. This is partly because the process of amendment, with forty-eight states now concerned, is

[1] See below, p. 347.

much more difficult than its framers expected or intended, but it is also because there are easier ways of gaining the same end. By means of their senatorial primaries, for example, many of the states, long before the adoption of the seventeenth amendment, had virtually acquired the system of choosing senators by popular vote.[1] The election of the President by what is virtually a direct popular vote has been secured by the pliancy of the state legislatures, no formal amendment being necessary. If the various state legislatures, however, had persisted in naming the presidential electors themselves and had not turned this function over to the people, there is little question that a constitutional amendment would have been used to accomplish the change. The amendment of the constitution is the last resort of those who desire new political institutions. It is a method of obtaining what cannot be had by statute, by usage, or by judicial interpretation. The relative infrequency with which amendments have actually been made is a tribute to the foresight of those who couched the provisions of the constitution in broad language and gave it thereby an inherent quality of suppleness.[2]

Great changes may take place in the spirit of a government without much alteration in the phraseology of its organic law. That is what has happened in the United States. The federal government has become far stronger than a literal reading of the constitution would indicate. It has steadily gained power, chiefly through channels of judicial interpretation, and the end is not yet. And this is despite the provision that all powers not given to the federal government shall revert to the states.

*Results of constitutional development: (a) increased strength of national government.*

As for the distribution of powers between the three organs of government,—executive, legislative, and judicial,—the balance as originally adjusted in 1787 has remained without rude disturbance. The executive, in relation to Congress, may appear to have grown stronger during the last half-century, and its authority in war-time is assuredly

*(b) division of powers not disturbed.*

[1] Below, p. 151.
[2] While only eighteen amendments have been adopted, a great many more have been proposed. See H. V. Ames, "Proposed Amendments to the Constitution of the United States," in American Historical Association's *Annual Report* (1896).

impressive, but Congress is still all that it was designed to be. The judiciary is the organ that has developed the largest measure of unexpected strength. It is well, however, that this has been the case; for, to be successful, a federalism must have a tribunal strong enough to act as an impartial arbiter between contending states, to protect the constitutional rights of minorities, and to safeguard the liberty of the individual.

(c) government has become more democratic.

It is not in the general organization but in the practical workings of American government, in the things which the laws and usages determine, that most of the development has taken place. The people of the United States live under a far more democratic government to-day than in the closing years of the eighteenth century. This is not because they have had a revolution, bloodless or otherwise. It is merely because a steady popularization in the spirit, usages, and methods of government has been entirely possible within the original framework. If the national constitution, as some now profess to believe, is a mere travesty upon the principles of popular government, enshrining the ideas of eighteenth-century reactionaries who had no confidence in democracy, it has at any rate afforded scope for the development of democratic institutions on a scale such as the constitutions and laws of no other country have ever permitted. The constitution of the United States, whatever one may think of its underlying philosophy, has served the cause of human freedom and world democracy as no other document has ever done.

The form of a government, after all, reaches only a little way. "Constitute government how you please," Edmund Burke once wrote, "the greater part of it must depend upon the exercise of powers which are left at large to the prudence and uprightness of ministers of state. . . . Without them your commonwealth is no better than a scheme on paper, and not a living, active, effective organization."

# CHAPTER VI

### THE CITIZEN AND HIS RIGHTS

THE framers of the constitution, notwithstanding their aversion to the extremes of democracy, had implicit faith in the principle of government "by the consent of the governed." They began with the humanistic postulate that man is a superior creature, wholly competent to determine his own political destinies. Accordingly they accepted the people as the source of all political power and agreed without reservation upon the principle of ultimate popular sovereignty. What they limited was not the sovereignty of the people, but the way in which this sovereignty might be exercised. Sovereignty in the United States rests, therefore, in the hands of the citizens, acting through their representatives in the manner prescribed by the constitution. There is nothing in the form or mechanism of American government which the citizens of the United States cannot change, provided they go about it in the proper way. It is important, therefore, that we should have some definition of the citizen, his status, his rights, and his duties. *The sovereign citizen.*

The constitution of the United States at the time of its adoption made use of the term "citizen," but did not define the term. It was taken for granted, no doubt, that the rule of English law, as laid down in Calvin's Case, would be followed, namely, that allegiance would be the test of citizenship, that all persons owing allegiance to the United States or to a state of the Union would be accounted citizens. The wording of the constitution seems to recognize this double citizenship, state and national, for it speaks of "citizens of different states" and also of "citizens of the United States." But no hint is given as to *Who are citizens?*

71

what difference, if any, was assumed to exist between the two.

**The old controversy over dual citizenship.** Until the adoption of the Fourteenth Amendment there was a great deal of controversy as to the interrelation of these two lines of allegiance. Those who upheld the doctrine of states' rights inclined to the view that citizenship of the United States was merely the consequence of citizenship in some state of the Union, and that not every citizen of a state became *ipso facto* a citizen of the United States. **The Dred Scott decision.** In the Dred Scott case (1856), the Supreme Court took the same attitude. "It does not by any means follow," declared the court in this decision, that "because he [a negro] has all the rights and privileges of a citizen of a state, he must be a citizen of the United States. He may have all the rights and privileges of the citizen of a state and yet not be entitled to the rights and privileges of a citizen in any other state. For, previous to the adoption of the constitution of the United States, every state had the undoubted right to confer on whomsoever it pleased the character of citizen, and to endow him with all its rights. But this character, of course, was confined to the boundaries of the state, and gave him no rights or privileges in other states beyond those secured to him by the laws of nations and the comity of states. Nor have the several states surrendered the power of conferring these rights and privileges by adopting the constitution of the United States. Each state may still confer them upon an alien, or any one it thinks proper, or upon any class or description of persons; yet he would not be a citizen in the sense in which that word is used in the constitution of the United States, nor entitled to sue as such in one of its courts, nor to the privileges and immunities of a citizen in the other states."[1]

**Reversed by the Fourteenth Amendment.** But the Fourteenth Amendment, adopted in 1868, reversed this doctrine, asserting that "all persons born or naturalized in the United States, and subject to the jurisdiction thereof, are citizens of the United States and of the states wherein they reside." This amendment declared citizenship to be primarily of the United States and only consequentially of the several states. Citizenship of the

[1] *Dred Scott* v. *Sandford*, 19 Howard, 393.

United States was made fundamental. Since 1868 any citizen of the United States by birth or naturalization becomes a citizen of a state by merely taking up his residence there. No state can either bestow American citizenship or withhold it.

So far as the rules of international law are concerned, only one citizenship is recognized, namely, citizenship of the United States. In relations with foreign powers all citizens of the United States, wherever resident, are alike; they are equally entitled to the protection of the national government; they carry the same sort of passport; they have the same privileges and immunities abroad. But constitutional law, the supreme law of the United States, still recognizes the dual nature of American citizenship, the Fourteenth Amendment being explicit on that point when it uses the words "citizens of the United States and of the states wherein they reside," although no one can now possess one form of citizenship without the other. Apart from the question of determining the courts in which suits shall be brought, however, the duality is not of any practical importance because citizens of the United States have the same privileges and immunities in all the states.[1] *The duality, however, still exists, although it is of no general importance.*

Who are citizens? The Fourteenth Amendment authoritatively defined the term for the first time in American constitutional jurisprudence as "all persons born or naturalized in the United States and subject to the jurisdiction thereof." Citizenship may thus be acquired either by birth or naturalization. But as a matter of fact not all persons who are actually born in American territory are citizens of the United States. The words "subject to the jurisdiction thereof" introduce a qualification. Children born to foreign ambassadors at Washington are not citizens of the United States, for example, because even though born on American soil they are not subject to the jurisdiction of the United States. On the other hand, the children of American ambassadors, when born abroad, or children born of American parents on American vessels at sea are deemed to have been born in the United States and to be "natural- *Citizenship by birth.*

---

[1] Arnold J. Lien, *Privileges and Immunities of Citizens of the United States* (N. Y., 1913).

born citizens," eligible as such for election to the presidency. But apart from various exceptions of this sort, which are not of great practical importance, all persons born in the United States, of whatever parentage, are citizens. The old common law doctrine of the *jus soli*, embodying the principle that allegiance and citizenship are in the first instance governed not by parentage but by place of birth, is the pivot of all American rules regarding citizenship. In addition to this, however, the federal laws provide that "all children born out of the limits and jurisdiction of the United States, whose fathers were or may be at the time of their birth citizens thereof, are declared to be citizens of the United States; but the rights of citizens shall not descend to children whose fathers never resided in the United States." [1] In other words the principle of the *jus sanguinis* or doctrine of citizenship by reason of parentage is also recognized.[2]

*Citizenship by naturalization.*

Citizenship may also be acquired by naturalization. The constitution confers on Congress the right "to establish an uniform rule of naturalization," thereby giving it complete power over the admission of aliens to citizenship. Congress accordingly determines the conditions and procedure in naturalization.

*1. Naturalization by statute or by treaty.*

Naturalization may be either collective or individual. In the former case whole bodies of persons may be admitted to citizenship at one stroke, as when new territory is annexed to the United States and the inhabitants of such territory taken within the fold of American citizenship by treaty or by act of Congress. This was done in the case of Texas. When Texas joined the United States in 1845 after a successful revolt from Mexico, all citizens of Texas were made citizens of the United States by resolution of Congress. So the act of Congress which provided a civil government for Hawaii (April 20, 1900) conferred American citizenship on all those who had been citizens of the Hawaiian Republic.

[1] *Revised Statutes*, Section 1993.
[2] Two monographs which deal fully with this general subject are F. Van Dyne, *Citizenship of the United States* (Rochester, 1904), and J. S. Wise, *A Treatise on American Citizenship* (N. Y., 1906). An informing "Report on Citizenship of the United States" was issued as an official publication in 1907 (59th Congress, 2nd Session, House Document, No. 326).

On several occasions, when the United States has acquired new territories by treaty, the inhabitants of these territories have been made American citizens *en bloc* by the terms of the treaty.[1]

But the mere acquisition of new territory by the United States does not admit to American citizenship the inhabitants of such territory. There must be a specific provision to that effect either in a treaty or in an act or joint resolution of Congress. The treaty with Spain in 1898 by which the United States acquired Porto Rico and the Philippines did not contain any such provision, nor were the inhabitants of either at once admitted to the full status of American citizenship by any act of Congress. Congress in 1917 granted to the Porto Ricans full status as citizens of the United States and to the Filipinos it has given some of the privileges and immunities of citizens; but the Filipinos are not yet American citizens in the strictly legal sense of that term. In the phraseology of international law they are called "nationals" of the United States, which means that they are entitled to the protection of the American government, to have American passports when they go abroad, and in general to enjoy all the rights of an American citizen when outside American territory. They have, moreover, the promise of eventually independent citizenship.

Mere conquest does not entail collective naturalization.

Collective naturalization by treaty or by action of Congress is not common. When one speaks of naturalization, it is ordinarily of the other form, namely, the naturalization of individuals. This is a judicial process the nature of which is prescribed, even to its smallest details, by the federal laws. There are two chief steps in the procedure, both of which must be taken before a duly authorized federal or state court. The first step is a formal "declaration of intention" to become a citizen. This formal declaration may be made by any alien who is "a white person, or of African nativity or of African descent,"[2] before any federal court or any state court of record having jurisdiction over the place in which he lives. Such declaration may not be

2. Naturalization by judicial process.

[1] For example the Louisiana treaty of 1803; the Florida treaty of 1819; the Alaska treaty of 1867, and others.
[2] It will be noted that this wording excludes most Asiatics.

*(a)* the declaration of intention ("first papers").

filed, however, until the alien has reached the age of eighteen years. The declaration must contain information as to the applicant's name, age, parentage, occupation, country of origin, and time and place of arrival in the United States; and it must further announce his intention to become a citizen, and thereby to divest himself of all allegiance to any foreign sovereign.[1] A copy of this document, under the seal of the court, is given to the alien, and must be presented by him when he applies for final naturalization.

*(b)* the letters of citizenship ("final papers").

After not less than five years' continuous residence in the United States and not less than two years after an alien has filed his declaration of intention, he may file a petition for letters of full citizenship in any one of the various courts designated by law as having authority over naturalization matters, provided that he has lived within the jurisdiction of this court at least one year immediately preceding the filing of his petition.[2] The petition must be signed by the applicant himself, and must give full answers to a set of prescribed questions. If the alien has arrived in the United States since June 29, 1906, his petition must be accompanied by a document from the United States immigration authorities certifying the time and place of his arrival. In addition, he must, when he files his application, bring forward the sworn statements of two witnesses (both of whom must be citizens of the United States) in personal testimony to his five years' continuous residence and his moral character, and in substantiation of the other claims made in his petition. After this paper has been left with the clerk of the court it must lie on file for at least ninety days, during which notice of its filing is posted. In this interval, also, an investigation of the petitioner's claims is undertaken by one of the federal agents employed for the purpose. All these formalities having been attended to, the court sets a date for a hearing upon the petition. This hearing must be public, and cannot take place within thirty days preceding any regular federal or state election. Both

[1] Citizenship may be acquired, however, without formal declaration of intention by aliens who have served a certain term in the United States army or navy and have been honorably discharged therefrom.

[2] These requirements are waived in the cases of persons who, in time of war, are members of the armed forces of the United States.

witnesses must attend the hearing with the applicant, and must answer such questions as may be put to them by the presiding judge, who may also demand from the applicant assurance that he is not affiliated with any organization teaching disbelief in organized government, and that he is attached to the principles embodied in the constitution of the United States. If the court is satisfied upon these various points, the clerk will issue letters of citizenship, or final papers, as they are more commonly called, and the alien is thereafter a full-fledged citizen.

These strict rules concerning naturalization procedure are the outcome of an attempt to put an end to various abuses that existed under the provisions of previous naturalization laws. Prior to 1906, when the process of naturalization was simpler and easier, fraudulent admission to citizenship was not uncommon. Sometimes an alien got himself enrolled as a citizen upon the voters' list by means of forged papers; and, since there were so many courts with authority to grant these papers, the detection of forgeries was not easy. More often, crowds of aliens were admitted to citizenship during the days preceding an election, when no careful investigation of their statements was possible. Paid witnesses were sometimes provided by the party managers to take oath as to matters which they knew nothing about. In fact, the naturalization of foreigners became one of the regular undertakings of the ward organization: the applicant's petition was made out for him, his witnesses were supplied, the foreigner being nothing more than a participant in formalities which he did not even understand. The handling of fifty or sixty naturalizations per hour was not a rare achievement in New York courts before the stricter rules went into force. Under such pressure during the days preceding the registration of voters, all careful scrutiny of petitions was out of the question; and the voters' lists of the larger cities were regularly padded with the names of persons who had not fulfilled the stated qualifications at all. Since 1906 these abuses have been almost wholly eliminated.

But however their citizenship may have been acquired, whether by birth or naturalization, all citizens of the United

*Reason for the strictness of the present naturalization laws.*

States are on a plane of legal equality. They have the same rights under the constitution save in one respect, namely, that only citizens by birth are eligible to the office of President or Vice-President. One other difference, the outgrowth of international comity, should also be mentioned because it is in some cases of great importance. Several European states, Italy and Germany for example, do not recognize the right of persons born in those countries to become naturalized citizens of the United States and then, on returning to the land of their birth or parentage, to set up this American citizenship as a means of evading compulsory military service or other such obligations. Hence it has been generally conceded by the United States that if a naturalized American citizen chooses to return to his native country, he will not be protected there against the exaction of any obligations which accrued by its laws before he left his native land. A naturalized citizen has the same right of protection as a native-born citizen so long as he remains in the United States or if he goes to any country other than his own native land; but if he returns to the land of his original citizenship, he does so at his own risk.

Citizens of the United States, whether natural-born or naturalized, are not only entitled to protection in foreign countries but they are safeguarded against adverse discrimination in any state of the Union. The Fourteenth Amendment provides that "no state shall make or enforce any law which shall abridge the privileges or immunities of citizens of the United States." What are the privileges and immunities of citizenship? Political privileges, for example, are not necessarily an accompaniment of citizenship. American citizenship does not necessarily imply the right to vote or to hold office. Women are citizens as well as men, yet in the majority of the states they are without political privileges. On the other hand, the right to vote, even at presidential and congressional elections, has been given in various states to persons who are not citizens. The relation between citizenship and the right to vote is at best an incidental and not a necessary relation. The Supreme Court has made it clear on more than one occasion "that the constitution of the United States does not confer the right of suffrage upon any one, and that the United States have no voters of their own creation."[1] The attempt was made, by the adoption of the Fifteenth Amendment, to enforce the granting of voting rights to negroes in the southern states. This amendment does not specifically mention negroes; it merely forbids the denial of voting rights by any state on the ground of "race, color, or previous condition of servitude"; but the purpose of this provision is unambiguous. {The Fifteenth Amendmen attempt to secure political privileges for the negroes.}

This purpose, however, has not been fulfilled. The southern states have been able, in a roundabout way, to shut out negroes from voting. This is usually done by requiring that no one may vote unless he can read and write. Inasmuch as the percentage of illiterates among negroes is very large, the requirement that voters shall be able to read or write is one which, when strictly administered, shuts out a large proportion of them. But there are also many illiterate white citizens who would be excluded by the test; and for their benefit Alabama, Louisiana, Mississippi, North and South Carolina, and Virginia have provided means whereby the requirement can be easily circumvented by the white element of the population. Various devices are employed to this end. In one case the provision is that the voter must either read the constitution or "give a reasonable interpretation thereof," the question whether the interpretation is reasonable or not resting with the white officials in charge of the registration.[2] In another state the so-termed "grandfather clause" relieves from the necessity of passing the educational test all those who enjoyed voting rights before 1867 and all descendants of such voters, which is a way of giving complete exemption to all native-born white citizens.[3] Still another of the southern states exempts all owners of property who have paid the taxes assessed for the year preceding enrolment. As the percentage of property-owning negroes is small in the southern cities, and the proportion of those who promptly pay their taxes even {How this constitutional guarantee is circumvented: 1. the literary test. 2. the "grandfather clause." 3. the tax requirement.}

---

[1] *Minor* v. *Happersett*, 21 Wallace, 162.
[2] *Constitution of Mississippi*, 1890. Article xii, Section 244.
[3] *Constitution of Louisiana*, 1898. Article cxcvii, Sections 3–5.

smaller, it follows that not many illiterates get their names upon the rolls by the use of this exemption.[1]

Finally, there is a way of permitting the negroes to vote but depriving them of all real share in the selection of representatives. Practically all the southern states are overwhelmingly Democratic. The candidates who receive the nomination of that political party are certain to win at the polls, hence the real fight is for the nomination. The plan pursued in some of these states, therefore, is to exclude negroes from voting at the primaries where the real contest takes place. Each state has full power to determine who shall be enrolled as members of any political party and hence entitled to a share in the selection of the party candidates. The Fifteenth Amendment does not forbid the exclusion of any one from membership in a political party by reason of race or color.

*4. exclusion from the primaries.*

All of these provisions keep within the letter of the Fifteenth Amendment, even if they disregard its spirit. They illustrate how easy it is, after all, to find ways of evading a constitutional provision when Congress does not provide adequate machinery for enforcing it, and, indeed, when public opinion throughout the country does not feel sufficiently interested to demand its enforcement. These various devices have been established for the sole purpose of disfranchising the negroes. That they have done this effectively is proved by the estimate, based upon careful study, that in some of the southern states not more than one adult male negro out of every hundred is allowed to vote at presidential elections.[2]

*The letter and the spirit of the law.*

The question of granting complete voting rights to women has been much discussed for many years in the United States. The first grant of full suffrage to women was made by the territory of Wyoming in 1869. This privilege was continued when the territory became a state in 1890,

*The Woman Suffrage Movement. Its progress and the reasons therefor.*

---

[1] *Constitution of South Carolina*, 1895. Article ii, Section 4. For a further discussion of these matters, see J. B. Phillips, *Educational Qualifications of Voters* (University of Colorado Studies, III, No. 2); and, for a defence of the policy pursued by the southern states, see F. G. Gaffey's article on "Suffrage Limitations at the South," in *Political Science Quarterly*, XX, 53–67 (March, 1905).

[2] J. C. Rose, "Negro Suffrage," in *American Political Science Review*, I. 20 (November, 1906).

and since that date about a dozen other states have given full voting rights at all elections,[1] while many of the remaining states have granted them the right to vote at some elections but not at others. Considerations both of sentiment and of expediency have led to this extension of suffrage. The doctrine of natural rights has been revived to do service. More influential, however, have been the distinctly practical considerations; for example, the fact that women are in many cases taxpayers and hence should have a direct share in their government, and that many are wage-earners and hence deserve a share in determining the relation of the laws to industry. The progress of the movement for woman suffrage is also in some measure the outcome of American social usages which have placed the two sexes on a plane of equality in nearly all non-political fields of activity.

Various arguments are advanced both for and against the policy of giving full voting rights to women. Women are citizens; many of them own property; and all are so affected by the workings of government as to be directly interested in its efficiency. In some fields of law and regulation, such as those relating to the care of the dependent and delinquent classes, to hours and conditions of female and child labor, women have a particularly vital interest. It is claimed that the extension of the suffrage to women would in some degree offset the political influence of the foreign-born element in large communities since the figures show that far more male than female immigrants come to this country. It is said that women, if given the ballot, would constitute a powerful element in opposition to the vicious influences in American political and social life, the saloon, the gambling den, the brothel, and so on. And finally, it is urged that where women have been given the suffrage the result has been made manifest in the humanizing of the laws and in the improved tone of political life. *Arguments in favor.*

In opposition to the policy it is argued that women would not use the ballot wisely, being actuated by their sympathies *Arguments against.*

---

[1] They are as follows: Colorado (1893); Utah (1896); Idaho (1896); Washington (1910); California (1911); Arizona (1912); Kansas (1912); Oregon (1912); Montana (1914); Nevada (1914); New York (1917); Michigan, South Dakota, and Oklahoma, 1918.

G

and emotions rather than by their judgment; that they would not develop an active interest in politics or come to the polls in reasonably large numbers; that the extension of the suffrage to women would tend to weaken the family as a social and economic unit; that it would greatly increase the expense of elections without making government more truly representative; and that it would merely widen the area of political activity at the expense of normal domestic life.

*What experience proves.* The results of woman suffrage in the states which have had a sufficient experience with the institution seem to show that neither the merits nor defects of the policy have been as marked as its advocates or opponents respectively would have us believe. Women have used the suffrage much as men have used it, showing no more interest and no less, using the ballot with great intelligence at some times and with little at others, even as men have done for many generations, influenced by their prejudices, whipped into line by party bosses, all as men are, and apparently to the same degree. The granting of voting rights to women in a dozen states of the Union has not demoralized domestic life in any of them, nor, on the other hand, has it had noticeably effective results in the way of securing these states a priority over the others in the humanitarianism of their laws. The chief merit of woman suffrage in these communities has been that of rendering content a large group of citizens without in any perceptible measure impairing the economic, social, or political order.

*Other things which are not "rights" of a citizen.* The privileges and immunities of a citizen of the United States, again, do not include the right to serve on a jury in any state court. A state may restrict that privilege or duty to its own citizens, or in other words to citizens of the United States who reside in the state concerned. So with many other privileges which do not appertain to a citizen as such. The right to practice law or medicine in one state, or to drive a motor car there, gives no privilege of doing the same in any other state. These are on the same plane as the right to vote, save that the discretion of the state is even wider. A state may allow its own citizens and no others to be lawyers, physicians, druggists, school teachers, chauffeurs, or what not. Where a state grants to outsiders the same privileges as to its own citizens in any of these things it does so as a matter of comity or interstate courtesy, not because it is compelled so to do by any constitutional requirement.

The right to vote, to hold office, to serve on a jury, or to practice a profession — these rights do not appertain to citizens as such. They are privileges granted or withheld by the several states as expediency may dictate. There are, however, other privileges which do appertain to American citizenship, the "privileges and immunities of citizens," as the constitution terms them. These words are comprehensive, and the Supreme Court has wisely refrained from any attempt to make a complete list of the American citizen's privileges and immunities.[1] But in general they include the right to pass freely from state to state, to reside in any one of the states, and to have all such privileges as are accorded to residents there; to own property, whether real or personal, in any state; to sue in the courts of the state in which a citizen resides; to appeal, when necessary, to the federal courts, and to have when abroad the protection of the federal government for his life, liberty, and property. Nor may a citizen of the United States be deprived by legislation of his life, liberty, or property without "due process of law," that is to say, except by the proper exercise of a state's police power; in other words, its power to protect the safety, health, and morals of its own people.[2] These are the real "rights" of the citizen, his constitutional privileges, which no law of any state may abridge.

[1] The nearest approach to any full enumeration, perhaps, is that made in the *Slaughter House Cases* (16 Wallace, 36), where the Supreme Court included among the privileges and immunities of citizens the right "to demand the care and protection of the federal government over his life, liberty and property when on the high seas, or within the jurisdiction of a foreign government; to peaceably assemble and petition for the redress of grievances, the privilege of habeas corpus; to use the navigable waters of the United States however they may penetrate the territory of the several states; all rights secured to citizens by treaties with foreign states . . . the right on his own volition to become a citizen of any state of the United States by a *bona fide* residence therein, with the same rights as other citizens of that state."

[2] For an explanation of "due process of law" and its history see below, pp. 291–294.

## 84   THE GOVERNMENT OF THE UNITED STATES

**Is a corporation a citizen?**

For most judicial purposes a corporation is a citizen. It is deemed to be a citizen of the state in which it has been organized. A corporation chartered in New Jersey, for example, is by legal assumption a citizen of that state and as such entitled to the equal protection of the laws in all other states.[1] In determining whether a suit to which a corporation is a party shall be brought in the federal courts (in accordance with the constitutional provision which gives these courts jurisdiction over controversies "between citizens of different states") the corporation is deemed to be a citizen of the state in which it was chartered. But while it is regarded by the courts as having in many respects the same rights as a natural person, a corporation is not a citizen in the same sense as an individual and is not entitled to all the "privileges and immunities" which the constitution guarantees to the individual citizen. It is quite permissible, accordingly, to make reasonable discriminations by the laws of any state, between corporations chartered there and those chartered elsewhere, and to give to the former privileges which are denied to the latter. That policy, however, is not usual.

**The inalienable rights secured by constitutional limitations.**

The rights of the citizen, both in the states and in the United States, are formulated in a series of limitations which the constitution contains, some of them in the original document and some in the articles of amendment, particularly in the first ten amendments which, taken together, are commonly called the Bill of Rights. These rights, as there stated, include the right to be immune from punishment by any bill of attainder or ex post facto law, to have the privilege of the writ of habeas corpus except when the public safety may require its suspension, to enjoy freedom of worship, freedom of speech, freedom of the press, freedom to assemble peaceably, and freedom to petition the government for the redress of grievances. They include likewise the right to keep and bear arms when so authorized

---

[1] The legal doctrine may be briefly stated as follows: The citizenship of a corporation is determined by the citizenship of the persons composing it; but when the corporation receives its charter in a state, the presumption is that its members are citizens of that state, and this presumption may not be rebutted by any averment or evidence to the contrary. See *Mississippi R. R. Co.* v. *Wheeler*, 1 Black, 286.

by the militia laws of any state, to be immune from the billeting of soldiers except in time of war and then only in a manner prescribed by law, to be secure in person and in home against unreasonable searches and seizures and from the issue of search-warrants without probable cause supported by oath, to be given in the federal courts all manner of judicial protection including securities against trial for any serious crime except upon action of a grand jury, and against being twice placed in jeopardy for the same offence, to be assured a speedy and public trial by jury, to be informed of charges, confronted with witnesses, to have the assistance of counsel, to have jury trial also in important civil cases, to be free from the requirement of excessive bail and not to be subjected to any cruel or unusual punishment. Finally they comprise the right to be free from bondage or involuntary servitude save as a punishment for crime; the right to be protected in life, liberty, or property unless deprived thereof by due process of law, and to receive in all parts of the Union the equal protection of the laws.

This long enumeration of the citizen's rights is not to be construed, the constitution expressly provides, to deny or disparage others retained by the people. It does not, accordingly, profess to be a complete catalogue of them all, but only of the fundamental ones. Taken together they form, nevertheless, a large portion of the general category known to students of American government as "constitutional limitations." The exact scope of these limitations, however, will be the theme of a later chapter.[1] *The foregoing list is not exhaustive.*

In general, we hear far more about "natural rights" and the "rights of the citizen" than we do about natural and civic duties. Yet every right, of whatever sort, carries a duty and a responsibility along with it. What, then, are the duties of the citizen? They are not definitely set forth in the constitution, it is true, but they are implied by the very nature of free government. The citizens of a democracy who act upon the assumption that popular government prefigures rights alone will in time have no rights worthy of the name. Popular government implies not only government for the people but government by the people. The *Correlation of rights and duties.*

[1] See ch. xx.

latter makes large demands in the way of patriotism, self-sacrifice, public spirit, intelligence, and activity. No one, therefore, should fix his eyes upon his civic rights to the exclusion or to the derogation of that equally important factor in free government, civic duties.

*Proper performance of civic duties is essential to good government.*

The constitution of the United States guarantees to every citizen that he shall have the privilege of living under a "republican form of government." But the literal terms of this guarantee do not mean much. A government may be republican in form and yet be a very bad government, autocratic, inefficient, and corrupt. All the governments of Central and South America are republican in form, yet most of them have never been popular governments and some are nothing but guerilla dictatorships. A republican form of government will provide and preserve the blessings of liberty to such extent as its citizens may entitle themselves by their intelligence, patriotism, initiative, and forbearance. "Every nation," somebody once wrote, "has as good or as bad government as it deserves." That is sound, democratic doctrine. The excellences of a constitution or of laws will avail little if the actual machinery of government be not kept to the proper pitch of efficiency and responsiveness. Political philosophers talk of a "government of laws, not of men," but the world has never seen such a government. All laws outside of Holy Writ depend for their actual application, interpretation, and enforcement upon human agencies.

*But in a true democracy the citizen will perform his civic duties if given a fair chance.*

It is the crowning glory of a democratic form of government, however, that the people can be counted upon to do their duty. Where they fail, it will usually be found that their democracy has been spurious. Democracy has often been badly alloyed with political autocracy by reason of party manipulations, cumbrous nominating machinery, the blanket ballot, lobbying in legislatures, and by the various other appurtenances of ramshackle government. If the issues can be fairly set before the citizens, however, they can invariably be depended upon to do their share. Genuine democracy spells patriotism. Were it not so, democracy would have a poor chance of survival, since autocracy is in many ways a more simple and less expensive form of rule.

The duties of the citizen in a free land are too numerous and too varied to be set down on the pages of any man's book. Their name is legion. The duty to know his country's history and to be proud of it; to understand his own government and to honor it; to know the laws and to obey them; to be respectful of all duly constituted authority; to be loyal in action, word, and thought; to look upon the privilege of the suffrage as a sacred thing and to use it as becometh a sovereign prerogative; to bear his portion of the common burdens cheerfully; to serve in public office at personal sacrifice and to regard it as a public trust; to fight and die if need be in the nation's cause — these are the first obligations which a free government imposes upon its citizens. The vision of duties as well as of rights must be always before the citizen's eyes, for where there is no vision the people perish.

*Some outstanding duties of the citizen in a free land.*

# CHAPTER VII

## THE PRESIDENT

*The need of a centralized executive.*

IN the Articles of Confederation there was no provision for a chief executive. The Congress of the Confederation chose its own presiding officer, but he had no executive powers, and such executive work as could not be performed by the Congress itself was deputed either to specially appointed officials or to committees. This arrangement proved far from satisfactory as any one who reads Washington's letters will learn, and the framers of the constitution agreed that in the new government a strong and separate executive was necessary. Their experience during the years prior to 1787 had clearly taught this lesson, for the need of a supreme guiding hand had been sorely felt on many occasions during the critical days of the Revolutionary War. But how the executive should be chosen, whether he should be independent of Congress or not, and what powers he should have — these matters were not so easily decided. No part of the convention's work gave it more trouble, or caused so many changes of front, or seemed less calculated to inspire a feeling of satisfaction when the task was done.

*A single executive decided upon.*

As to the proper organization, powers, and functions of the executive there were, at the outset, nearly as many different opinions as there were delegates. The examples of arbitrary power afforded by the reign of George III led some to favor the idea of a plural executive or group of persons no one of whom should be superior to the others, but all of whom should act by joint decision. This would provide security against executive despotism. It was realized, however, that whatever might thereby be gained in security would be more than offset by the ever present danger of friction and conflict of opinion in national emergencies. So the convention finally committed itself to the single executive plan. This was an eminently wise decision, for history had not disclosed plural executives to be satisfactory either in peace or war. The Directory which handled the affairs of the new French republic during the years 1795–1800 was soon to give a fresh demonstration of that fact.

Having decided to place the supreme executive authority in the hands of a single individual to be called the President, the next question concerned the method of selecting this official. Many of the delegates favored a proposal to let Congress choose the President, and that plan was provisionally adopted. But later on, when the convention became convinced that this arrangement would virtually destroy the whole system of checks and balances, the question was reopened and finally settled in an entirely different way, namely, by the expedient of indirect election. There were a few who favored direct popular election, but the majority were unalterably opposed to that plan, regarding it as the open door to the choice of demagogues and perhaps, eventually, to the usurpation of monarchical power. The fear that somehow or other a monarchy might grow out of the new national government haunted the delegates at every turn, and they were desirous of guarding against such a possibility in every practicable way. On the other hand, they were equally disinclined to set up a mere paper executive with the functions of a figurehead, the mere creature of Congress and incapable of effective leadership. What they did, accordingly, was to give the President a position of circumscribed independence with powers which they deemed to be adequate in normal times and which might be considerably expanded if emergencies should arise.[1]

*His position in relation to Congress.*

What was the mechanism finally adopted by the convention for securing the choice of President? It was relatively simple and allowed a large degree of latitude to the states. Briefly, the constitution provided that each state should "appoint" in "such manner as the legislature thereof may direct" a number of "electors" equal to the

*The original method of choosing the President.*

[1] The development of the presidential office is fully discussed in Edward Stanwood's *History of the Presidency* (2 vols., Boston, 1916).

state's combined quota of senators and representatives in Congress. A state having, for example, two senators and five representatives was thus to choose seven electors. In due course these electors were to meet, each group in its own state, and were to give their votes in writing for two persons, of whom both should not be inhabitants of its own state. These ballots were to be sealed and transmitted to the president of the Senate, who was directed to count them in the presence of both Houses and to announce the result. The person receiving the most votes was to be President and the one obtaining the next highest number was to be declared Vice-President.

*Motives which dictated the selection of this mechanism.* The ends which the makers of this plan had in mind were made quite clear during the debates in the constitutional convention. The delegates believed that the selection of the nation's chief executive officers should be made solemnly and with deliberation, by electors specially chosen for this task alone. It was their hope that the electors so gathered together would be men of high repute in their respective communities, and that the function of choosing the President would be completely left to them by the people. That, indeed, is what happened at the first two elections. Then a different course began to shape itself. At the third election (1796) it was well understood, even before the electors met, that most of the electors would vote for either John Adams or Thomas Jefferson, although in no case were any pledges exacted. In 1800 things were carried a step further. Two well-defined political parties had now arisen, and at the election of that year both put forth their regular candidates. Electors were chosen upon the understanding that they would vote for one or the other of these candidates. The function of deliberation so far as the electors were concerned now became a mere fiction; henceforth the electors were to serve as mere automatons, selected because they would do what they were told to do. The heart of the original plan was thus cut out within ten years, and never since has there been any serious attempt to restore it. The mechanism of indirect election has been retained because no practical purpose would be served by abolishing it. The saving clause in the original provision, namely, "in such manner as the legislature thereof shall direct," has proved quite broad enough to permit the complete substitution of direct for indirect election.

The constitution in its original form provided that the electors should vote for "two persons" without designating which was the elector's choice for President and which for Vice-President. But this indefiniteness led to serious trouble at the election of 1800 when two aspirants, Thomas Jefferson and Aaron Burr, each received an equal number of votes. Both candidates had been put forward by the same political party with the intention that Jefferson should be chosen President and Burr Vice-President; and the electors, voting strictly on party lines, gave one as many votes as the other. Now the constitution made provision that in case of a tie the House of Representatives should determine the choice, and the House did so, choosing Jefferson President after an exciting contest. The episode proved, however, that under the party system a tie vote might often occur and that a change in the method of voting would be advantageous. In 1804, therefore, the Twelfth Amendment was added to the constitution providing, among other things, that thereafter the electors in the several states should "name in their ballots the person voted for as President, and in distinct ballots the person voted for as Vice-President." *A defect in the original plan.*

For more than seventy years thereafter presidential elections were held without any trouble of a serious nature. In 1824, it is true, no candidate for President received a clear majority of the electoral votes, and the House of Representatives once again had to make a choice. There was some talk of changing the mechanism of election once more, but nothing was actually done. Through the political tumults of the Civil War period the system worked without mishap. It was not until the election of 1876 that a perplexing difficulty arose. From several states, on that occasion, two different sets of electoral votes were received. Who should determine which of these sets should be counted and which rejected? The constitution had not anticipated any such eventuality; there was nothing in the laws, either of the United States or of the states themselves, to provide a satisfactory answer. If the president of the Senate, whose *The Hayes-Tilden controversy.*

duty it was to open and count the votes, should accept one set of returns from the disputed states, the election of Rutherford B. Hayes, the Republican candidate, would be assured; if he should accept the other, the election would go to Samuel J. Tilden, his Democratic opponent. As a way out of the difficulty it was agreed to create a special electoral commission of fifteen persons, five senators, five representatives, and five justices of the Supreme Court, with authority to decide which sets of votes should be counted. The decisions of this body determined the election of President Hayes.[1]

While the matter was eventually settled in this way without disturbance, the situation was fraught with danger for a time and Congress sought to make sure that a controversy of the same sort should not occur again. How to do this, whether by an entire reconstruction of the plan of election (which would require an amendment to the constitution) or by merely making clear the procedure in cases of doubt (which could be done by law), was much discussed for some years. In 1887 Congress solved the problem by a statute which deals with the subject of disputed votes. In general each state must now determine, in accordance with its own laws, any disputed questions concerning the choice of presidential electors from that state. If in New York, for example, two groups of electors claim to have been chosen at the polls, the laws and courts of New York must settle the dispute before the votes of either contesting group can be counted.

*Its sequel — the act of 1887.*

From neither the constitution nor the laws, however, can one get an adequate idea of the way in which the Presi-

---

[1] Of the 369 electors, 184 were pledged to Tilden (Democrat), 164 to Hayes (Republican), and 21 votes were in dispute, namely, those of South Carolina, Florida, Louisiana, and Oregon. To the electoral commission the Senate appointed three Republicans and two Democrats, while the House of Representatives appointed three Democrats and two Republicans. Of the five Supreme Court justices, three were Republicans before their appointment to the bench and two were Democrats. Thus the electoral commission, as finally constructed, contained eight Republicans and seven Democrats. All, however, took an oath to decide the issue on its merits and impartially. On every disputed question, however, the commission divided on straight party lines and gave the entire twenty-one disputed votes to Mr. Hayes, this being necessary to secure his election.

dent of the United States is actually chosen.[1] The constitution provided three steps — the choice of electors, the voting by electors, and the counting of the votes. By usage two other steps have developed, so that there are now five steps in all. The first three are of great importance, while the last two, the voting by electors and the counting of the votes, have become mere formalities.

*The present method of election.*

First of all there is the nomination of candidates, a matter on which there is not a word in the constitution, for it was not intended that there should be any formal nominations. The initial step is taken with the calling of the national party conventions. Each of the great political parties maintains a general executive body known as its national committee, made up of one delegate from each state. Each national committee decides when and where the convention of its own party shall be held. Usually the calls are issued in January of a presidential year, and the conventions meet in June.

*First step: nomination of candidates.*

*Stages in nomination procedure:*
*(a) the calls for the party conventions.*

Then in the following months the different political parties in each state select their own delegates to these conventions.[2] Every state is entitled to twice as many delegates to each convention as it has senators and representatives combined. Massachusetts, for example, has two senators and sixteen representatives. It sends, therefore, thirty-six delegates to each of the national conventions. Not so many, as a matter of fact, go to any except the Republican and Democratic conventions. National conventions of other parties, such as Prohibition and Socialist parties, rarely or never draw their full quota from all the states. It is also usual in the case of the major parties to select an equal number of alternates, to serve in case regular delegates are absent, and these alternates, or most of them, go to the place where the convention is being held.

*(b) selection of delegates to the party conventions.*

All delegates to national conventions are now chosen at the party primaries, that is, by the members of each party in the various states at ballotings held for the purpose or by

[1] A full account of both the law and the practice may be found in J. H. Dougherty's *Electoral System of the United States* (N. Y., 1906).
[2] The history and methods of presidential nominations are fully dealt with in F. W. Dallinger's *Nominations for Elective Office in the United States* (N. Y., 1897) and in E. C. Meyer's *Nominating Systems* (Madison, 1902).

conventions made up of party delegates. Until recent years the delegates have been chosen to use their own discretion at the national convention, but now the laws of some states permit the voters of each party to instruct or pledge their delegates, that is, to indicate on the ballot what presidential candidate the delegates are to support at the convention.

(c) the conventions.

Then comes the meeting of the convention, an unwieldy and often boisterous body of a thousand members or more. The Republican convention meets usually in one city, the Democratic convention in another, and the two do not meet at the same time. The procedure in each, however, is much the same. In a great hall the delegates are seated by states. After the various formalities of choosing a chairman and examining the credentials of delegates are gone through, the convention proceeds to the adoption of the party platform. This platform has been framed in advance by a committee. Then nominations are called for. The roll of the states is called in alphabetical order, Alabama first and Wyoming last. The chairman of any state delegation, or any one deputed by him, may make a nomination. The nominations are usually supported by speeches.

(d) balloting on nominations.

After the nominations have been made the balloting begins. At Democratic conventions the "unit rule" is frequently applied, that is, the vote of the entire delegation from each state is given intact, whenever the state convention so directs and the state laws so permit, the majority in each delegation deciding how it shall be cast. At Republican conventions, on the other hand, the votes of a delegation may always be split if the delegates wish, although that does not usually happen. At any rate, the votes are given, counted, and announced. At Republican national conventions a candidate receives the nomination if he secures a clear majority of all the delegates; at Democratic national conventions he must obtain a two-thirds vote. In either case, when several candidates have been placed in nomination it is often necessary to take ballot after ballot before a choice is decided upon. The weaker candidates drop out; votes are shifted around on successive ballots, and the convention keeps at work until a decision comes. Mr. Garfield, in 1880, was nominated on the thirty-sixth ballot. The selection of the party nominee for the vice-presidency is made in the same way, but usually with less difficulty.

When the party conventions have finished their work, the next step is the nomination of electors in the several states. In each state the political parties put forth their slates of electors, nominated in whatever way the state laws prescribe. In some the electors are nominated at primaries, in others by state party conventions. These electors are usually prominent party men, but must not be federal office-holders. Their names go on the ballot in parallel columns, and on the Tuesday after the first Monday in November the voters in each state decide which group of electors shall be chosen. When the voter marks his ballot for a certain group of electors, however, he is in reality indicating his preference for one or other of the candidates already named by the national conventions. The ballots do not bear the names of these nominated candidates, or, if they do, it is only to guide the voters in voting for the desired group of electors. To all intents and purposes, nevertheless, the balloting is just as direct as though there were no intervening electors at all. The real election takes place on this election day; what occurs later, unless some unusual mishap occurs, is nothing but formality. *Second step: the nomination of electors.* *Third step: the election of electors.*

Yet the constitution requires two further steps in the election of a President and Vice-President. In January following the election the electors chosen in each state come to the state capital and there go through the procedure of balloting for the candidates whom their party nominated at the national convention six months before. No constitutional provision or law prevents them from marking their ballots as they please, voting for some one other than the prescribed candidates, but they never do so unless, perhaps, a candidate chosen by a national party convention has died in the meantime. Then they vote as the national committee instructs them to vote. *Fourth step: election of the President by the electors.*

The votes are attested, sealed up, and sent to Washington. In February the president of the Senate supervises the counting of the votes in the presence of both Houses of Con-

**Final step: transmission and counting of the votes.**

gress. As a rule this is only an uninteresting ceremony, nothing more. But it may happen that the result is a tie, or that no candidate has received a clear majority of the total electoral vote. In either case the House of Representatives proceeds to choose a President from among the three candidates who have stood highest. In making this choice, however, the representatives do not vote as individuals; each state has one vote and the representatives from a state merely decide by majority action among themselves just how the vote of their state shall be cast. In case the electoral college fails to elect a Vice-President by a clear majority, the Senate makes the choice from the two highest candidates, but the senators vote as individuals and not by states. On only two occasions, the last of them more than ninety years ago, has Congress been called upon to make the selection.[1] The result having been announced, the inauguration of the President and Vice-President takes place upon the following fourth of March.

**Lord Bryce on the presidency.**

In Lord Bryce's admirable analysis of the spirit and workings of American government a chapter is devoted to the question, "Why great men are not chosen Presidents." "Europeans often ask," wrote Bryce in 1884, "and Americans do not always explain, how it happens that this great office, the greatest in the world, unless we except the Papacy, to which anyone can rise by his own merits, is not more frequently filled by great and striking men." "Since the heroes of the Revolution died out with Jefferson and Adams and Madison," he continues, "no person except General Grant has reached the chair whose name would have been remembered had he not been President, and no President except Abraham Lincoln has displayed rare or striking qualities in the chair."[2]

**The nation has not always utilized its greatest men.**

These statements are scarcely as defensible to-day as they were thirty odd years ago. Many Americans regard Grover Cleveland as a "great" President, even when measured with John Adams or James Madison; and there are few who would deny to either Andrew Jackson or Theodore

---

[1] The election of Thomas Jefferson in 1800 and of John Quincy Adams in 1824.

[2] *The American Commonwealth*, I, ch. vii.

Roosevelt the possession of "striking qualities." Surveying the history of the presidency as a whole, however, one may properly admit that the query propounded by Lord Bryce is a fair one and deserves discussion. The nation has failed to utilize in the presidential office a long line of notable statesmen: Hamilton, Marshall, Gallatin, Webster, Clay, Calhoun, Seward, Sumner, Hay, and others. On the other hand, it has bestowed its highest honor on men like Polk, Fillmore, Pierce, and Arthur, of whom no one now knows much except that they are on the roll of the Presidents. Certain it is, at any rate, that things have not turned out exactly as the Fathers of the Republic intended, for Hamilton in 1788 voiced the prediction that in view of the plan of indirect election provided by the constitution "the office of President will seldom fall to the lot of any one who is not in an eminent degree endowed with the requisite qualifications. . . . It will not be too strong to say that there will be a constant probability of seeing the station filled by characters preëminent for ability and virtue."

In the United States several factors have contributed from time to time in placing at the head of the nation men who did not possess conspicuous qualifications for so great a responsibility. In the first place, the greatest asset of one who aspires to political office in any country having a free government is the general quality of being acceptable to a wide variety of political interests. A candidate is acceptable, if his temperament, his associations, and his reputation seem to fit the political needs of the moment. These needs are sometimes easy to meet; at other times very difficult. At the approach of one election campaign there may be many aspirants with the desired qualities; at other times a party may be hard pressed to find any one who comes at all near the assumed requirements. It often happens, therefore, that one who is by common agreement the strongest possible candidate in one year may be wholly out of the running a year or two later. The political stage shifts its background quickly. *Factors which determine the choice of a President: 1. acceptability to a wide variety of interests.*

Long experience in political life is one of the things which ought to make one an acceptable candidate for high office; but in practice it usually does not. The man who spends *2. experience, or the lack of it.*

a long term in the public service has either proved himself a trimmer or else by standing up courageously for his own opinions has made himself many enemies. If he has served several terms in Congress, he has necessarily supported some measures and opposed others. He has probably offended some elements of his own party. He is indeed fortunate if he has not antagonized some economic interests and made himself unpopular in various sections of the country. In other words he has "made a record," and a public record, no matter how good it may be, usually presents opportunities for partisan or sectional attack. The Blaine-Cleveland campaign of 1884 afforded a good illustration of this factor. Mr. Blaine had given the country twenty years of aggressive service in Congress. Mr. Cleveland had all the advantage of being only three years in the public eye, and of never having held a national office at all. Mr. Blaine was beaten by the enemies he had made in his congressional career. A considerable section of his own party, although fully recognizing his personal ability and his qualifications for the presidential post by reason of long familiarity with national problems, had been antagonized by his record in Congress. Of the five Presidents since the first election of Cleveland, only Harrison and McKinley served in Congress prior to assuming the presidential office. All the others had been in public life as governors of states or of insular possessions; but they had not identified themselves too closely with matters of national legislation.

3. the influence of the "pivotal" states.
It is strategically desirable, again, that presidential candidates shall be taken from what are called the pivotal states. This results from the fact that the outcome of the election is not determined by the plurality of the total votes cast by the people but by a majority of the electors chosen. The successful candidate must carry enough states to control this majority, and he may do this (and sometimes has done it) without getting a popular majority. At the election of 1860 Lincoln's electors received a million fewer votes than those of his opponents, yet he had a comfortable majority in the electoral college. Harrison in 1888 and Wilson in 1912 received a minority of the popular ballots but were elected nevertheless. A majority of many thou-

sands in any state is no better for practical purposes than a majority of one. When Cleveland carried New York by less than twelve hundred, he captured that state's entire slate of presidential electors. A change of six hundred ballots would have given the electoral vote of the state, and with it the election, to his opponent.

An aspirant from a small state is, therefore, at a disadvantage as compared with one from a large state, for a presidential candidate should at least carry his own state and it ought to be a state worth carrying. The man who can deliver the twenty-four electoral votes of Ohio is, accordingly, a better candidate, if other things are equal, than the one who could bring with him merely the three votes of Nevada. It is, moreover, not merely a question of carrying one state, sometimes, but a whole group of neighboring states, of swinging New England, or the Middle West, into line. Another consideration also comes in. Many states are sure states, that is, they can be carried, under normal conditions, by the regular candidate of one or other political party no matter who he is or where he comes from. Nearly all the southern states are in this class. They are solidly Democratic. Why then nominate a Southerner as the Democratic candidate? It is the big, doubtful states which count, that is, the states like New York and Ohio, which are not so strongly welded to the fortunes of either party. Every President since the Civil War has come from Ohio or New York, with the exception of Woodrow Wilson, whose state is New York's next-door neighbor.[1]

Many other factors influence the choice of candidates. Religious affiliation, business association, party loyalty, the general impression which a candidate will make upon the public imagination must all be taken into account. Yet none of these things is necessarily related to the possession of "great and striking qualities" in a man. The ablest statesman in the land may be inferior, in point of political availability, to some favorite son of a pivotal state. Great men do not always make strong candidates, and it is the business of the national conventions to select candidates, not Presidents.

4. personal factors.

[1] Harrison, though a resident of Indiana, was born in Ohio.

5. the time of the election.

The policy of fixing rigidly the date at which a presidential election shall take place has also had its effect. In England a general election must ordinarily occur at least once in every five years. But within this limit an administration can "go to the country" whenever it pleases. It can avoid a time when public opinion seems to be running adversely and can choose a moment when some striking administrative success or some popular stroke may operate heavily in its favor. In America the party leaders cannot do this. They must take the times as they are. If the presidential election comes along during a year of business depression or of slender harvests, the party in power is likely to be at a disadvantage. Candidates are chosen to suit the times; there are fair-weather candidates and there are those to whom the parties are more apt to turn when the skies are darkening.

Ups and downs of the presidency.

Yet the presidency, when all is said, has maintained a reasonably high level of ability and statesmanship, save for a lapse at one period. It has been "one thing at one time, another at another, varying with the man who occupied the office and with the circumstances that surrounded him." [1] During the first thirty-five years of its existence the standard was high. No wonder men felt that the arrangements devised by the constitution had proved a great success. Washington, Adams, Jefferson, and Madison represented the best the country could give. All the Presidents prior to Andrew Jackson, indeed, were just about what the framers of the constitution expected the incumbents of the office to be. Jackson, first elected in 1828, was not a man of great intellectual qualities; but he was surely an aggressive and virile figure, the personification of a new era in the nation's politics. His successor, Van Buren, has been accurately characterized as a "first-rate second-class man," which is rather more than can be said of any among the seven presidents who intervened between him and Lincoln.[2] During this quarter of a century, the mediocrities had their day, varied on two occasions by the election of

[1] Woodrow Wilson, *Constitutional Government in the United States* (N. Y., 1911), p. 57.
[2] T. F. Moran, *American Presidents* (N. Y., 1917).

soldiers who had made reputations in the War of 1812 or in the Mexican war. The outstanding figures of American statesmanship during this period, Webster and Clay among them, were either passed over by conventions or defeated at the polls. In the late fifties, accordingly, it might well have been said that the presidency was entirely failing to justify the high hopes placed upon it by the creators of the constitution.

Then came the election of Lincoln and the Civil War. In Lincoln's day the prestige and powers of the presidency rose enormously. And after a lurid interval marked by unseemly quarrels between Congress and Andrew Johnson (who became President on Lincoln's death) General Grant was chosen as the nation's chief executive on his military reputation alone. It is yet too early to determine how posterity will regard the line of Presidents since Grant finished his second term. As for prior political experience, Hayes, Cleveland, McKinley, Roosevelt, and Wilson were governors of states before becoming candidates for the presidency, while Taft had served as governor-general of the Philippines. During the last fifty years, in fact, the governorship of any one of the great doubtful states has become a far more reliable stepping-stone for presidential aspirants than long or conspicuous service in Congress. This is natural enough. The man who can secure a large plurality as a candidate for governor in his own state is reasonably sure to carry it with him at the national election. He has shown his vote-getting power. Moreover, the experience which a governor gains in office is exactly in line with what he most needs as President, and the governor's post always gives its occupant the chance to initiate striking reforms, to declare policies, to show just what he stands for. One may, from the nature of things, be a long time in the Senate or House without obtaining any such opportunity. There a member is bound by the trammels of party loyalty, and the stand he takes is often determined for him by the party caucus or by the force of circumstances beyond his own control.

The history of the presidency, therefore, falls into four periods: the first from Washington to John Quincy Adams, inclusive (1789–1829), when the government was "getting a footing both at home and abroad, struggling for its place among the nations and its full credit among its own people; when English precedents and traditions were strongest; and when the men chosen for the office were men bred to leadership in a way that attracted to them the attention and confidence of the whole country."[1] The second period, from Jackson to Buchanan (1829–1861), was a day of cruder and more intense politics, with the influence of the frontier making itself dominant while sectionalism worked havoc with the solidarity of political parties. The third era, from Lincoln to Arthur (1861–1885), was dominated by the war and its legacies, including the question of greenbacks, to the exclusion of most other things. Finally, in the epoch between the first election of Cleveland in 1884 and the opening of the European War in 1914 questions of domestic policy were once more uppermost in the minds of the people, and the presidency neither rose to the heights of the first period nor descended to the depths of the second.

*Quo vadis?* As for the future, there is nothing to indicate the probability of any marked change from the course which has so long been run. The presidential primary system of selecting delegates to the national conventions and of pledging these delegates in advance has already been adopted in many states and is not unlikely to gain acceptance in all the others. What effect its use would have upon the selection of candidates, if adopted by them all, is hard to say. Delegates cannot well be sent to national conventions with definite instructions covering all eventualities. Situations will at times arise in which a delegation must be free to act. The candidate to whom they were pledged may withdraw or his chances of nomination may altogether disappear. Then the delegation must have discretion. The pledging process can hardly ever operate conclusively unless the nation-wide fight narrows down to two or three candidates, and this, if the future is anything like the past, it is not apt to do.

Will the use of the presidential primary secure the nomi-

[1] Woodrow Wilson, *Ibid.*, p. 58.

nation of better candidates? Probably not. State conventions, as nominating bodies, have been in many parts of the Union supplanted by state primaries. The results have not been up to expectations. Campaigns for the nomination have become far more expensive to candidates and their political friends; the voters are called out to the polls on an additional occasion; the deliberations and compromises which marked a convention are no longer possible; and on the whole there has been no appreciable improvement in the types of men nominated. If any improvement in the great and striking qualities of American presidents is to be sought, therefore, it will probably have to be by some more comprehensive plan than the selection and pledging of delegates at presidential primaries.

*Will the presidential primaries secure better candidates?*

The remuneration of the President is fixed by Congress, but it may not be either increased or diminished during the term for which he was elected. At present it is $75,000 per annum. In addition, various appropriations for secretaries, clerks, travelling expenses, the care and maintenance of the White House, and so on are annually made, amounting to more than a quarter of a million dollars.

*Salary and allowances.*

"In case of the removal of the President from office, or of his death, resignation, or inability to discharge the powers and duties of the said office, the same shall devolve upon the Vice-President."[1] On five occasions since 1789 the death of a President has devolved his duties upon the Vice-President in accordance with this provision of the constitution. No President has resigned and in no case has the devolution come because of inability to discharge the presidential functions, although President Garfield during his last illness was for more than two months in 1881 physically unable to perform any important official act. In case the Vice-President is for any reason not available to succeed the President, the constitution gives Congress the right to determine the order of succession, and Congress has so provided by law, naming the various cabinet officers according to the seniority of their posts: the Secretary of State, the Secretary of the Treasury, and so on. But no one of these officials may in any event succeed to the presidency if he

*Succession to the presidency.*

[1] Article ii, Section 1.

be constitutionally ineligible. Where a vacancy occurs in the office of Vice-President, it is not filled till the next election.

*The vice-presidency.*

A few words, but only a few, should be added with reference to the vice-presidency. The framers of the constitution intended the office to be a dignified and important one, its incumbent to be a man second only to the President in the favor of the electors. During the first few decades that idea persisted; but with the practice of nominating the candidates at national conventions it was gradually lost to view. During the last fifty or sixty years the vice-presidential nomination has been used, for the most part, as a means of strengthening the party ticket. It has gone to some one who can placate a discontented faction of the party, or bring some doubtful state into line, or secure large contributions to the party's campaign funds. The personal merit and capacity of the candidate usually count for very little.

*Constitutional qualifications of the President and the Vice-President*

No one is eligible to the presidency or the vice-presidency, either by election or by succession, unless he be a natural-born citizen, thirty-five years of age or more, and unless he shall have been a resident of the United States for at least fourteen years. A special exemption was made in the constitution for those who were citizens at the time of its adoption, this being done as a matter of courtesy to Alexander Hamilton, James Wilson, and others who, although not born in the territory which formed the Union, had taken a considerable share in establishing the new government.

# CHAPTER VIII

### PRESIDENTIAL POWERS AND FUNCTIONS

FREE government has developed two different types of executive power, which are commonly known as parliamentary and presidential, or, as they are sometimes called, responsible and independent, respectively. A parliamentary or responsible executive is one which derives its power from the legislature and is responsible to that body for all its official acts. Under this arrangement the legislature is the supreme organ of government, for it can change the executive at any time. England is the classic example of a country with a parliamentary executive, the prime minister being directly responsible to the House of Commons. A presidential or independent executive, on the other hand, derives its powers not from the legislature, but from the people directly, and forms a coördinate branch of the government. Such an executive is not responsible to the legislature, which cannot alter its tenure or prerogatives. The United States affords the best example of this type. The powers of the President are on the same solid ground as are those of Congress. They are more varied, more comprehensive, and more momentous than those possessed by the national executive of any other land.[1]

*Parliamentary and presidential executives.*

The powers and functions of the President may be conveniently grouped under the five main heads of strictly

[1] For the views of recent Presidents concerning what the functions of the presidential office are, or ought to be, the reader may be referred to W. H. Taft's *Our Chief Magistrate and his Powers* (N. Y., 1916); Grover Cleveland's *Presidential Problems* (N. Y., 1904); Theodore Roosevelt's *Autobiography* (N. Y., 1913), especially ch. x.; Benjamin Harrison's *This Country of Ours* (N. Y., 1898), especially chs. iv-xix; and Woodrow Wilson's *Constitutional Government in the United States* (N. Y., 1911), ch. iii.

executive, diplomatic, legislative, military, and political. The first four are devolved upon him by the constitution and the laws; the last is an outgrowth of the party system.

The President is the nation's chief executive. The constitution enjoins him to "take care that all the laws be faithfully executed." While the government of the United States is designed to be "a government of laws, not of men," laws are not self-executing. They must have officials to apply them and courts to enforce them. As chief executive, accordingly, the President is authorized to appoint both the administrative officials of the federal government and the judges of the federal courts. This places in his hands one of the most important executive powers that he exercises. It gives him more political influence than he derives from any other function intrusted to him. The constitution divides all appointive offices into two classes, namely, those higher posts which must be filled by the President with the advice and consent of the Senate and those "inferior" offices which should be filled, if Congress should so provide, by the President alone, or by the heads of departments or by the courts. In the category of higher offices, appointed by the President with the concurrence of the Senate, are the members of the Cabinet, all ambassadors, ministers, and consuls, all judges and court officials, members of the various federal commissions such as the Interstate Commerce Commission, the Federal Trade Commission, and the Tariff Board, together with postmasters in the larger communities and officials who have to do with the collection of revenues. In all such cases the President sends his nomination to the Senate, and this body may confirm or reject it. If the Senate be not in session when the nomination is made, the nominee takes office at once and holds what is termed a "recess appointment" until the Senate has had the opportunity to take action.

The Senate has an undoubted right to refuse assent to any nomination which the President may send. But in practice it allows the President to name the members of his own Cabinet, confirming these nominations as a matter of course. It has taken the proper ground that if the President is to be held responsible for the acts of those whom

*Classification of the President's powers.*
*1. Strictly executive powers.*
*(a) appointments.*
*Limitations upon the appointing power: senatorial confirmation.*

he selects to be members of his Cabinet, he should be given a free hand in choosing them. In all other cases, however, the Senate's power is one to be reckoned with. It has refused its assent to appointments in a great many cases. As a rule it does not withhold its consent except for some good reason, but much depends upon whether the President and a majority of the senators are of the same political faith and are working in harmony. To confirm a nomination sent to it by the President a bare majority of the senators present is required. It does not take a two-thirds vote as in the case of confirming treaties.

While the words "advice and consent" might seem to indicate that the Senate was to have advisory as well as confirming functions, it was not the intention of those who provided the plan of senatorial confirmation that the constitution should give the senators any actual initiative in the making of appointments. Nor has the Senate openly laid claim to such right. In due course there developed, however, the unwritten rule known as the "courtesy of the Senate." Stated briefly, this was the practice of refusing to confirm the nomination of any local officer, such as a postmaster or collector of internal revenue, unless the nominee proved satisfactory to the senator or senators from the state concerned, provided of course that these senators were of the same political party as the President himself. Or, to put it more concretely, a Republican President should not nominate any one as postmaster at Philadelphia without first consulting the Republican senators from that state. If he did so, the other senators, out of courtesy to their Pennsylvania colleagues, were under obligation to refuse confirmation. Senatorial courtesy has had its ups and downs; it has been strong enough at times to tie the President's hands considerably; on the other hand, some Presidents have been able to disregard it with impunity. From the nature of things, however, a President usually finds that he can avoid endless trouble and can get much-needed support for more important things by consulting the two senators from the state concerned, if they be of his own political party.[1]

The rule of senatorial courtesy.

[1] See also below, p. 164.

In the case of the "inferior" offices, such as postmasters in small communities, or clerkships, or the host of subordinate positions in the various departments, the whole list running up to several hundred thousand minor offices, the power of appointment is vested by law, for the most part, in the President alone. Some of these are still treated as "patronage" and are filled at the suggestion of senators or representatives from the districts concerned; but by far the greater portion of them are now dealt with in accordance with the civil service regulations.[1]

The civil service system.

The beginnings of the civil service system go back to 1883 when the United States Civil Service Commission was established and given authority to hold examinations whenever there were positions in the classified service to be filled. Although at first rather limited, the scope of the classified service has been gradually extended until to-day it includes nearly all the subordinate administrative positions. They number nearly a quarter of a million, including almost all the clerks and other civilian departmental employees in Washington, the postmasters in all but the largest cities, the letter carriers, mail clerks on trains, employees in customhouses, in the revenue service and in practically all the other governmental activities except, of course, the army, the navy, and the courts. The Civil Service Commission itself is made up of three members appointed by the President with the confirmation of the Senate. This body has general supervision of the competitive examinations, including the selection of the examiners. As to the practical workings of the civil service system, whether in national, state, or local government, more will be said later. The merit system has, at any rate, greatly improved the efficiency and the whole temper of the public service.

(b) removals.

The constitution says nothing about the power of removal, but at the first session of Congress in 1789 the question was debated and settled by a tacit agreement that the President should have power to remove without securing the consent of the Senate. On one or two subsequent occa-

[1] Many further details concerning the methods of appointment are given in the essay on "The Appointing Power of the President" by Lucy M. Salmon, in the American Historical Association's *Papers* (1886).

sions Congress undertook to restrict the President's freedom in making removals, but without much success.[1]

The President, accordingly, can now remove all appointive civil officials at his discretion. But upon this power there are two limitations: first, it does not include judges, who can be removed by impeachment only; and second, those who secure appointment under the civil service system may not be removed "except for such causes as will promote the efficiency of the service." This latter limitation is not necessarily a serious obstacle to a President who desires to make removals on political grounds, but in practice its spirit has been tolerably well respected. *Limitations upon the power of removal.*

Taken in all its bearings, the appointing power of the President is of great extent. No head of any other nation has powers approaching it. Many have equal or greater appointing powers in theory, it is true; but the personal desires of the American President have more actual weight in a larger number of cases than do those of prime ministers, chancellors, or monarchs. Of all the presidential powers, moreover, it is the most disagreeable in its exercise, the one that makes most demand upon the President's time, and the one that may be most easily used for wrongful purposes. The framers of the constitution had no suspicion that this would be the case, nor did it become so for more than forty years after the federal government was established. But when Andrew Jackson became President in 1829, he at once promulgated the famous doctrine that "to the victors belong the spoils" and followed it up by wholesale removals from office. Thus was inaugurated the spoils system and the vice of political patronage. From Jackson to Cleveland *Importance of the appointing power.*

---

[1] Notably in 1867 when Congress passed the "Tenure of Office Act" with the plain purpose of preventing President Andrew Johnson from removing various officers. It provided that any person holding a civil office to which he had been appointed with the confirmation of the Senate should hold such office until a successor was in like manner appointed; that during a recess of the Senate the President might suspend but not remove, the Senate having authority to concur or not to concur when it resumed its session. The Act was vetoed by the President and passed over his veto. President Johnson disregarded it as unconstitutional, and this action was one of the grounds upon which he was impeached. The Act was partly repealed in 1869, and practically altogether repealed in 1887. It is now generally conceded to have been an unconstitutional enactment.

every President was forced to give a large part of his attention to the pressure for partisan removals and appointments.[1] Not until Cleveland enunciated the far more wholesome doctrine that "public office is a public trust," and laid thereon the foundations of the civil service system, did the burden of importunities appreciably diminish. Even yet the President finds the demands of patronage to be considerable, for the more lucrative offices are still within his discretion to bestow. For these he is pressed from all sides by office-seekers and their friends; he is held responsible for appointments which of necessity he must make without accurate personal knowledge, and there is the ever present temptation to use the appointing power in such a way as to insure his own renomination or to promote the interests of his own party. On the whole, however, this temptation has been well resisted. A strong-willed President, if he chose to use without scruple his powers of appointment and removal, could in four years build up a personal and political machine of almost irresistible strength; for with the enormous growth in the functions of national government the appointing power has extended over a far wider range than could ever have been foreseen when the foundations of the Republic were laid.

(c) the power of pardon. Another power, sometimes spoken of as quasi-judicial, but really executive both in its origin and in its nature, is the power to "grant reprieves and pardons." The President may pardon any offence against the federal laws, but he has, of course, no authority to grant pardons for offences against the laws of any state. The pardon may be either partial or complete. One limitation is imposed upon the President by the constitution, however, in that he can grant no pardon to any one convicted by the process of impeachment. This embodies a lesson which the framers of the constitution drew from the Stuart period of English history when the monarch, on more than one occasion, relieved his advisers in this way from penalties imposed by parliament.

Another group of executive powers are those which

[1] For a full account of this development, see Carl Russell Fish, *The Civil Service and the Patronage* (N. Y., 1905).

relate to diplomacy, treaties, and the general handling of foreign affairs. American ambassadors and ministers to foreign countries are appointed by the President (with the consent of the Senate), and their instructions in all important matters are given by him through the Secretary of State. Ambassadors who come to Washington from foreign lands are accredited to the President. What the general course of foreign relations will be rests to a large extent in the President's hands.[1] In all important negotiations he assumes personal supervision of the communications sent to foreign governments, even to the extent of frequently preparing them himself. The initiative in foreign affairs, which the President possesses without any restriction, is a very great power and at times amounts to the absolute control of such matters.

*2. Powers relating to diplomacy.*

But there are limitations upon the President's powers in relation to foreign policy. He can authorize the making of a treaty with any foreign state, but no treaty can go into effect until it has been ratified by a two-thirds vote of the Senate. He can break off diplomatic intercourse with any other nation, and may take various other steps which are tantamount to a declaration of war; but a formal declaration of war can be made only by Congress. In practice the President does not usually venture to direct the foreign relations of the United States without relying on the advice of others. He depends for guidance to some extent upon his Cabinet, to some extent upon the leaders of his own party in both Houses of Congress, and he is always subject to the pressure of public opinion. In speaking of this matter one must always afford considerable scope for the interplay of men and circumstances. Some Presidents have made the handling of foreign affairs their special hobby, leaving but little to the discretion of the State Department and rarely deigning to consult the congressional leaders; others have shown far less inclination to deal personally with diplomatic negotiations. When matters of great importance are in controversy, however, the nation expects the President to take the reins of foreign policy into his own

*Limitations upon these powers.*

[1] Edward S. Corwin, *The President's Control of Foreign Relations* (Princeton, 1917).

hands. But under no circumstances may the President finally commit the nation to an alliance or to any other obligation based upon a treaty. This power he must share with the Senate.[1] The framers of the constitution realized the dangers which might arise from clandestine alliances and secret diplomacy. They were determined that there should be no place for these things in the New World. On the whole they took a wise precaution. At times the Senate, by withholding its assent, has prevented the conclusion of arbitration treaties and other agreements which would probably have benefited the nation, but on the other hand its insistence upon a full and frank discussion of every proposed international compact has saved the United States from being drawn into that maelstrom of duplicity and intrigue which has so long and so steadily cursed the diplomacy of Europe.

**3. Powers in relation to legislation.**
One might judge from the reverence with which the statesmen of 1787 regarded Montesquieu's doctrine of checks and balances that the President would have been given no share in national legislation. But he was, in fact, endowed with some powers in relation to the making of the national laws, and by usage these powers have been greatly expanded. By the terms of the constitution he was intrusted with certain advisory or initiatory functions, on the one hand, and with the power of restricting legislation or the veto power, on the other.

**Restrictions upon the power to call, adjourn, or dissolve Congress.**
Unlike the chief executive in most European states, the President does not call the national legislature together except in special session. The time for the beginning of regular sessions of Congress is fixed by law. Nor does he adjourn Congress unless the two Houses fail to agree between themselves as to the time of adjournment. The power of dissolution, so important in England, does not exist in the United States. Congress finishes out its two-year term, no more, no less. It cannot be dissolved by executive action.

**The President's messages.**
The constitution, again, requires the President to "give to the Congress from time to time information on the state of the Union, and recommend to their consideration

[1] See below, pp. 164–167.

such measures as he shall judge necessary and expedient." This is the basis of the President's right to send messages to Congress, a right which has been freely used from the outset. Washington and Adams delivered their recommendations by addressing Congress in person; but Jefferson began the practice of sending written messages to be read in both Houses by the clerks, and this plan was consistently followed until 1913, when President Wilson reverted to the earlier method. But whether read or sent in writing, the messages may come at any time and may deal with any subject. Usually there is a long message prepared for the beginning of each congressional session; then there are special messages dealing with particular subjects and sent as often as the President may see fit.

But while the President may recommend many things, some of them with great earnestness, it does not follow that Congress must act upon these recommendations. A President's annual message is not, like the speech from the throne in England, an outline of what will almost surely come to pass before the session ends. What the speech from the throne recommends is almost certain to be followed by parliament because the men who really frame these recommendations, namely, the prime minister and his colleagues, have a majority in parliament ready to do their bidding. The President, on the contrary, may have no such congressional majority in sympathy with him. The other political party may control a majority in either or both Houses of Congress. That has frequently been the case. Or even if his own party does control both Houses, the President has no assurance that the senators and representatives will do what he advises. The result is that projects of legislation, however urgently recommended to Congress by the President, often fail to receive acceptance. *How far do they produce results?*

On the other hand, presidential recommendations always carry weight, and there are many occasions upon which they move Congress to action. When the President's own political party is in control of Congress; when he has taken counsel with the party leaders and obtained their support — in such cases he can make recommendations with reasonable ground for expecting that they will be followed. He *Their influence on legislation.*

may even go so far as to have bills prepared and presented by some senator or representative, he may send for influential members of Congress and solicit their assistance, and in many other ways he may exert great influence from behind the scenes in getting these bills enacted. In no field of actual government does more depend upon the President's political and personal relation to Congress than in this. Here, more than anywhere else, the function is the measure of the man. Andrew Johnson, opposed and disliked by a majority in both Houses, found his advice rebuffed and all manner of unfriendly legislation sent to him for his signature. Woodrow Wilson, on the other hand, has given in our own day an extraordinary example of the way in which a President, when favorably placed in relation to Congress and when possessed of the requisite personal qualities, can make himself a parliamentary leader. The constitution, as Mr. Wilson once declared in the days before he became the nation's chief executive, does not forbid a President to back up his messages, as General Washington did, with such personal force and influence as he may possess. The constitution, indeed, failed to provide for Congress any definite leadership. Yet leadership of some sort there must be if work of legislation is to be carried through effectively. Hence the President is warranted in assuming the rôle of a prime minister so far as the constitution will permit him to do so. The people look to the President rather than to Congress for the redemption of pledges made in the platform of a victorious party. He must, therefore, be active in promoting legislation or he will be forced to bear the onus, under the party system, of failing to fulfil his preëlection promises. This is an outgrowth of the President's status as a party leader, a matter to be discussed presently.

Another phase of the President's legislative powers: the system of "executive orders."

Within the last few decades there has grown up in the United States, moreover, the practice of determining many matters by means of "executive orders," issued by the President and having virtually the force of law. These orders may almost be regarded as constituting what is known in France as ordinances, although the theory on which the ordinance power rests in the French Republic is commonly thought to be foreign to the entire spirit of American institutions. In France it is customary to have parliament enact the laws in general terms, leaving the executive branch of the government to make all the necessary detailed provisions by ordinance. In the United States the laws are avowedly framed to cover all contingencies and to leave no considerable discretionary margin to the executive, yet executive orders are frequently issued prescribing various regulations concerning the postal and immigration service, the collection of internal revenue, the civil service system, the patent, pension, and land offices, and many other branches of public administration. In purport these "orders" do not make, amend, or repeal or even supplement any law; they merely explain and apply the provisions of laws made by Congress. In effect, however, they do far more than that: they actually modify the strict application of legal provisions with a great deal of freedom. For that reason they may be looked upon as embodying a form of executive legislation, strange as that term may sound to American ears, for while these orders are to some extent the result of discretionary authority conferred by general laws, they are in even larger measure issued without any such warrant; in other words, they are the manifestations of inherent executive power. This development, as will appear more clearly in connection with the work of the executive departments, is a tacit admission that under the complex economic and social conditions of to-day a government cannot well remain strictly a "government of laws" in the narrow sense. The inflexibility of law must in some way be made capable of relaxation.

More important, however, than the function of recommending legislation to Congress or of prescribing rules by executive order, is that of vetoing any measure which does not meet the President's approval. The scope and nature of this power cannot be more succinctly expressed than by quoting the exact words of the constitution on the point:  *The veto power.*

"Every bill which shall have passed the House of Representatives and the Senate shall, before it becomes a law, be presented to the President of the United States; if he approve he shall sign it, but if not he shall return it, with his objections, to that House in which it shall have originated, who shall enter the objections at large on their journal, and proceed to reconsider it. If after such reconsideration, two-thirds of that House shall agree to pass the bill, it shall be sent, together with the objections, to the other House, by which it shall likewise be reconsidered, and if approved by two-thirds of that House, it shall become a law. But in all such cases the votes of both Houses shall be determined by yeas and nays, and the names of the persons voting for and against the bill shall be entered on the journal of each House respectively. If any bill shall not be returned by the President within ten days (Sundays excepted) after it shall have been presented to him, the same shall be a law, in like manner as if he had signed it, unless the Congress by their adjournment prevent its return, in which case it shall not be a law." [1]

*The qualified veto is a compromise.*
On the question of the President's relation to lawmaking the framers of the constitution tried to steer carefully between two extremes. They were not prepared to give the President an absolute veto such as had been possessed by the governor in every one of the thirteen colonies or by the king in relation to colonial laws. They were mindful of the indictment of George III in the Declaration of Independence for having "refused his assent to laws the most wholesome and necessary for the public good." It was not their desire to give any like weapon of despotism to the chief magistrate of the Republic, although Alexander Hamilton argued that it would never be abused in the future as it had been in the past. On the other hand, they were unwilling that laws should be made in entire disregard of the President's rights or wishes. Experience with parliament in colonial days had shown that a legislature could be quite as tyrannical as a monarch, that it could usurp the prerogatives of the other departments of government, and that legislatures could not be kept within their own sphere of action by any "mere parchment delineation of boundaries." [2] The executive must, therefore, have some sort of bludgeon to wield in its own defence. The qualified

[1] Article i, Section 7.  [2] *The Federalist*, No. 73.

veto was devised as a thrust-and-parry arrangement, establishing what Hamilton was ready to defend as "a salutary check upon the legislative body" and at the same time a "shield to the executive." Apparently the veto was regarded as a legislative rather than as an executive function, for provision was made for it in that part of the constitution which relates to the organization and powers of Congress.[1]

Was it intended that the veto should be used freely or only on rare occasions? Washington, Adams, Jefferson, and Madison, the Presidents of the constitutional group, used it with great restraint. During the first forty years of the Republic, only nine bills were vetoed, an average of less than one for each administration. Andrew Jackson, however, set a new record in this as in several other things by vetoing nearly as many as all his predecessors put together. This was because Jackson interpreted the veto power in a way quite different from that of his six predecessors. Their attitude had been one of non-interference with the lawmaking authority of Congress except where intervention by means of the veto power was necessary to protect the executive department from legislative encroachment. But Jackson took a more aggressive stand, using the veto to stay the hand of Congress whenever its action seemed to run counter to his own political or personal aims. This interpretation was bitterly criticised in its day as revolutionary and a usurpation, but with the lapse of time it has gained general acceptance. From Jackson's time until after the Civil War, however, vetoes did not increase, and during his entire term of office Lincoln negatived only two general measures. President Johnson during his quarrel with Congress swung his battle-axe right and left, but not to much avail because Congress regularly passed its measures over his veto. Since 1867 the only President to use the veto power unsparingly was Grover Cleveland, who applied it to a large number of private

[1] "It has been suggested by some that the veto power is executive. I do not quite see how. . . . The character of the veto power is purely legislative."— W. H. TAFT, *Our Chief Magistrate and His Powers* (N. Y., 1916), p. 14.

pension bills, but all of the Presidents since his time have employed it more freely than it was used in the first quarter of the nineteenth century. They have not confined themselves, moreover, to measures which by any stretch of the imagination could be regarded as encroachments upon their own constitutional prerogatives, but have assumed the duty of vetoing any measure that seemed to be unwise or inexpedient. What was intended, therefore, to be a presidential weapon of self-defence has developed into an implement which can be and is regularly used for guiding and directing the law-making authority of the nation. As now interpreted the veto power makes the executive a far more active factor in legislation than he was originally intended to be.[1]

*How the veto power is exercised.* In vetoing a measure the President not only returns it without his signature, but he must also send to Congress his reasons for this action, although such reasons need not be lengthy or definite. Any general statement will serve. He may allege the bill to be unconstitutional, although it has sometimes been remonstrated that this is a matter which he should leave to be settled by the courts. He may allege it to be unwise, untimely, extravagant, or may register any other objection to it. As a rule, a presidential veto is decisive, for a two-thirds vote to overcome it cannot usually be had. There are exceptions, however, as for example in Andrew Johnson's time, when both Houses of Congress by large majorities were opposed to the President.

*The "pocket veto."* A word should be added in explanation of what is called the "pocket veto." If the President neither signs nor vetoes a bill, it becomes a law upon the expiration of ten days, unless Congress should adjourn in the meantime, in which case the bill expires without becoming a law. Now there is usually a great congestion of bills passing through their final stages in Congress near the close of a session and many of these come to the President during the last week before adjournment. Those which the President favors he may pick out and sign; those which he opposes he need merely

[1] E. C. Mason, *The Veto Power* (Boston, 1890), gives a full account of the use and abuse of the veto power during the first century of its history.

ignore, and they will meet their fate by the "pocket veto." This puts much less personal responsibility on the President than the process of vetoing bills in the ordinary way, and yet is just as effective. On the other hand, if a President neither favors nor opposes a measure which comes to him in good season before the adjournment of Congress, he may allow it to become a law without his signature, merely by inaction during the ten prescribed days. Some Presidents have taken this course as a means of indicating their indecisive attitude on certain measures, a notable example being the Income Tax Law of 1894, which became a law without the signature of President Cleveland and was later held by the Supreme Court to be unconstitutional in that it levied a direct tax without apportionment among the states, as the constitution required.

It is asked whether the veto power has, on the whole, served a good purpose. Lord Bryce believes that it has, and most students of the subject are inclined to agree. Apart from private pension bills and other measures of personal, political, or sectional favoritism, the vetoes have not averaged one per year. Ninety-nine per cent of all the measures passed by Congress regularly go upon the statute-book. The veto power, save in very exceptional instances, has not been abused. For the most part it has been exercised prudently and with good reason. Its ruthless use by Jackson and Tyler led to an agitation for its abolition or amendment, and Henry Clay in 1842 proposed that a mere majority instead of a two-thirds vote should be prescribed as sufficient to pass any measure over the veto, but the plan never made much headway, and the agitation soon subsided. There is at present no serious or widespread feeling that the veto power ought to be taken away or made less effective, and on the whole the system is now regarded as one of the excellences of the American political system, yet no European country or colony has seen fit to copy it. Other federations, particularly Canada and Australia, have borrowed considerably from the political institutions and experience of the United States, but the qualified veto is not among the things to which they have accorded the flattery of imitation.

*Merits and defects of the veto system.*

# 120  THE GOVERNMENT OF THE UNITED STATES

*Veto power does not extend to items in a measure.*

One improvement in the existing veto system has been strongly urged, namely, that the President be allowed to strike out single items in an appropriation bill, a power which he does not now possess. At present he must either veto the bill as a whole or not veto it at all. In consequence the President must often give his consent to items which he does not approve; otherwise the entire bill would fail. This is particularly true of appropriation bills which often include hundreds of items, all of which, save a very few, may be entirely proper ones. These few may be pernicious and wasteful, yet the President must take the chaff with the wheat. Many wasteful expenditures have gone past the most vigilant Presidents in this way. A constitutional amendment giving the President power to veto some items while accepting others might serve in some ways a good purpose; on the other hand it would enormously increase the influence of the President in legislation, giving him a new form of patronage almost equal to that which he now has through the exercise of his appointing power. All congressmen, both senators and representatives, are greatly interested in securing appropriations for use in their own states or districts. The partial veto, in the hands of a partisan or vindictive President, could easily be used to penalize those who oppose him and to advance the interests of those who support his policies. The remedy might readily prove worse than the existing evils. With a proper budget system in operation, however, the danger of discrimination would not be so great.[1]

*Nor to constitutional amendments nor to concurrent resolutions.*

Proposals to amend the constitution, when passed by a two-thirds vote of Congress, do not require the President's signature and hence cannot be vetoed by him. The same is true of the "concurrent resolutions" which both Houses of Congress adopt from time to time and which are merely expressions of congressional opinions, not having the force of law. "Joint resolutions," however, do have the force of law, and being submitted for the President's signature,

---

[1] The constitution of the Confederate States, adopted in 1861, conferred upon the President of the Southern Confederacy the right to veto individual items.

may be vetoed. The difference between a bill and a joint resolution is only of technical importance.

Surveying as a whole the President's powers in relation to law-making, it will be seen that whatever the purpose of the constitution may originally have been, the actual influence now exerted by the executive in matters of federal legislation is in reality very extensive. It is both positive and preventive. The President, in a positive sense, recommends legislation to Congress by message, follows up his recommendations by the use of political and personal pressure, and may use his patronage, if need be, to make his wishes prevail. In a preventive sense, on the other hand, his influence is exerted by the exercise of his veto power. Save in rare cases no law goes on the statute-book against his pronounced objection. Putting the two forms of influence together, one can readily grasp the far-reaching nature of his legislative influence. *Conclusions on the President's powers in relation to law-making.*

By express provision of the constitution the President is commander-in-chief of the army and navy of the United States, and this includes the militia forces when called into the federal service. He appoints all the regular and reserve officers of the army and navy, but officers of the militia, when not in the service of the United States, are appointed as the laws of their several states may direct. Congress votes the appropriations for the military and naval forces, but the expenditure of these funds is in the hands of the War and Navy departments, both of which are directly under the President's control. Congress also makes the general laws under which the military and naval forces are organized and maintained, but a large discretion in the making of detailed regulations is left with the President and his advisers, particularly in time of war. The President directs the location and movement of the nation's armed forces and by the exercise of this authority may bring about a state of war, leaving Congress no option but to recognize an accomplished fact by the issue of a formal declaration. Under his war powers the President may provide by proclamation for the government of conquered territory until Congress provides a permanent form of administration. No man has ever accurately defined the *4. Military powers.*

powers of the President as "commander-in-chief," and no court has ever placed any fixed limit upon them. They expand with the needs of the situation in war time and potentially are as great as any ever exercised by Oliver Cromwell or Napoleon Bonaparte. Lincoln, in his day, demonstrated that the war powers were enormous, and President Wilson, in our own time, is showing that these powers have in no wise diminished. It is one of the cardinal virtues of the American constitution, despite its reputed inflexibility, that in neither of two great military emergencies has it prevented the "incisive application of a single will."

The maintenance of domestic peace.

In the matter of guaranteeing to each of the states a republican form of government, protecting them from invasion, and putting down internal disorders, the constitution intrusts powers to the federal government which the President usually exercises on its behalf. In the event of an invasion or of any attempt to supplant the republican form of government the intervention may take place without any request from the state concerned. But in the case of domestic violence the federal government may not step in unless its assistance is requested by the authorities of the state in which the disorder has arisen. This request is made by the state legislature if in session; if the legislature be not in session, it is made by the governor. When, however, the disorders within any state obstruct any function of the federal government, such as the collection of import duties or the carrying of the mails, the President may intervene without waiting for any invitation from the state authorities. President Cleveland, in 1894, sent federal troops into Illinois, despite the opposition of the authorities in that state, to secure the free passage of the mails and of interstate commerce during a railway strike. The Supreme Court upheld the exercise of this authority.[1]

---

[1] "The entire strength of the nation may be used to enforce in any part of the land the full and free exercise of all national powers and the security of all rights intrusted by the constitution to its care. The strong arm of the national government may be put forth to brush away all obstructions to the freedom of interstate commerce or the transportation of the mails. If the emergency arises, the army of the nation, and all its militia, are at the services of the nation to compel obedience to its laws." *In re Debs*, 158 U. S. 564.

# PRESIDENTIAL POWERS AND FUNCTIONS 123

All the foregoing powers are vested in the President by the constitution and the laws of the United States as interpreted by the courts. There is a fifth class of powers, or to speak more accurately a form of official influence, which the President does not obtain from this source, but which he possesses by virtue of his position as leader-in-chief of his own political party. The President is a partisan, elected as such. The National Committee of his party is so organized as to be in sympathy with him. His party leaders in Congress must work in reasonable harmony with their chief, otherwise the party is likely to go down to defeat at the next election as the penalty of its own disunion. The President, therefore, while not himself possessed of a seat in Congress, is far more influential there than any member of it, and usually more influential than any score of members. The country has often had party bosses in its cities and occasionally in its several states, but never yet a national party boss. That position, or something very akin to it, is at times assumed by the President himself. As the constitution makes no provision for either parties or bosses, this attribute of the national executive is wholly extra-constitutional and the outcome of usage.

<small>5. Political powers.</small>

Yet the President's functions as the dominating figure in the councils of his own political party cannot be ignored. His wishes are consulted in the framing of the party platform because it is highly desirable that the platform and the candidate should be articulated. If he is interested in any important legislative or administrative project, the party platform usually embodies his programme on that point. Just as the constitution enjoins upon the President the faithful execution of the laws, so the unwritten rules of party loyalty enjoin upon him the earnest endeavor to carry into legal effect, either by his own authority or by pressing action upon Congress, whatever promises have been incorporated in the platform of his party. The platform is a series of pledges, or is intended to be. Members of the party in both Houses of Congress, as well as the President, are bound by it. The President can demand their support in many things, therefore, not merely as the first citizen of the nation but as the commander-in-chief

<small>The President's relation to his party.</small>

of his party cohorts. His appeal, when put in this form, is usually influential, for legislators on the whole desire to be accounted "regular," and there are ways of penalizing them by withholding patronage if they are not. It happens at times that even in his capacity as party leader the President fails to move his co-partisans in Congress, or, on the other hand, that he may feel constrained to veto laws which they have passed; but that is not the usual course of events. Between his authority as chief executive and his influence as a party leader it is a weak or untactful President who cannot obtain from Congress, provided his party controls a majority in both Houses, the chief measures which he determines to secure. Party regularity in Congress is far from being as strict as it is in the British House of Commons, and the President's wishes are by no means so implicitly respected in the one as are the dictates of the prime minister in the other, yet the difference is not nearly so great as the disparity in the framework and theory of the two governments would imply. The unwritten constitution of the United States is in this matter to be reckoned with, and by foreign students of American government it is too often overlooked. "The personal force of the President," as the contemporary incumbent of the office has expressed it, "is perfectly constitutional to any extent to which he chooses to exercise it; and it is by the clear logic of our constitutional practice that he has become alike the leader of his party and the leader of the nation." [1]

The President and the courts.

The President of the United States, during his term of office, is immune from control by the courts. There is only one tribunal before which he can be called to answer for any offence or dereliction of duty, and that is the Senate of the United States sitting as a court of impeachment. There are two good reasons for this immunity. One is that the President, as commander-in-chief of the armed forces of the nation, controls the ultimate power which enforces any judicial decision. Against him the courts would be powerless unless he chose to accept their decisions, and the Supreme Court long ago wisely decided that it would not

[1] Woodrow Wilson, *Constitutional Government in the United States* (N. Y., 1911), pp. 71–72.

attempt what Chief Justice Marshall termed "an absurd and excessive extravagance" of jurisdiction. The other reason for the President's immunity from ordinary judicial process is to be found in his unlimited power to grant pardons save upon conviction by impeachment. There is no disability or restraint that the courts might impose upon him but could be at once removed by one stroke of his own pardoning power. The one great safeguard which the constitution provides against the abuse of presidential powers or presidential malfeasance of any sort is the privilege of impeachment.

## CHAPTER IX

### THE CABINET AND NATIONAL ADMINISTRATION

The genesis of the Cabinet.

THE practice of surrounding the chief executive with a circle of advisers, chosen by himself, is one of the oldest in the history of government. It appeared in England under the Anglo-Saxon kings and became fully recognized as an integral feature in the government of the realm under the Normans. During the long period between the first of the Plantagenets and the last of the Stuarts the institution known as the Privy Council, composed of the royal ministers or advisers, assumed administrative functions of comprehensive importance in England, and it was from this body that an inner circle, henceforth known as the Cabinet, developed under the Hanoverians to the position which it occupies at the present day. Originally made up of advisers selected by the crown and not accountable to parliament, the English Cabinet has become, during the past two centuries, the creature of the majority party in the House of Commons, and responsible to the crown in legal fiction only. It is to-day the real executive organ of the United Kingdom, the great standing committee of parliament.

Its lack of legal basis both in England and in the United States.

In one sense the English and American Cabinets are alike. Neither has any constitutional foundation. In England the basis upon which the Cabinet stands is usage alone; in the United States the constitution contains no provision for a Cabinet and makes only incidental references to "heads of departments," from whom the President may ask opinions and who may be authorized by law to appoint their own subordinates. Here, too, the Cabinet as a body rests upon usage. But aside from this similarity in the mutual lack of any legal basis the Cabinets of the two countries are unlike in every important respect. Without the

Cabinet the whole scheme of English government would fail to function; if the Cabinet were to be abolished, the entire frame of English administration would have to be remodeled, for it has become the pivot around which all else now revolves. But in the United States the Cabinet, as such, plays no such all-essential part. The wheels of federal government would run just about as smoothly if the heads of departments formed no organized group and if no Cabinet meetings were held from one end of the year to the other.[1]

The builders of the American federal system were indistinctly aware of the important rôle which the Cabinet had assumed in the practical working of English government during the eighteenth century, and they were also well acquainted with the work of the executive councils which had existed in some of the colonies before the Revolution. That they did not make specific provision for any such body in the constitution of 1787 is presumptive evidence that they at least did not regard it as a necessity, and perhaps did not desire any body of the sort. They realized, however, that the President could not alone perform all the administrative functions that the Union would require, and indeed the experience of the nation under the Articles of Confederation had shown that executive officers, each in charge of a department, were essential to the proper despatch of business. So the framers of the constitution merely assumed that the President would have subordinates in charge of the various departments, but specified neither what these departments should be, nor what authority they should exercise. They did not even indicate in the constitution whether these departments should be established by the President or by Congress. "The President . . . may require the opinion in writing of the principal officer in each of the executive departments. . . ." That is all the constitution has to say about the President's relation

*The framers of the constitution did not regard a Cabinet as essential.*

*But made provision in the constitution for heads of departments.*

[1] John A. Fairlie's *National Administration of the United States of America* (2d ed., N. Y., 1914) is the best book on the subject of cabinet organization and functions. On the development of the Cabinet, its personnel at various periods, and its relations with the President, see H. B. Learned, *The President's Cabinet* (New Haven, 1912), and M. L. Hinsdale, *History of the President's Cabinet* (N. Y., 1911).

**Departments which have been established by Congress.**

to his chief executive advisers. As a matter of fact, however, the various departments one after another have been created by Congress. Three of them, indeed, were established at its first session in 1789. These were the Department of State, the Department of the Treasury, and the War Department. The offices of the Attorney-General and Postmaster-General, which were established in the same year, did not at first rank as regular departments. They became departments, however, in the course of time, and Congress has also added others: the Navy in 1798, the Interior in 1849, Agriculture in 1889, Commerce in 1903, and Labor in 1913. There are now, accordingly, ten administrative departments whose heads are by custom entitled to membership in the Cabinet.

**Status of these department heads.**

The head of each department (Secretary of State, Attorney-General, Postmaster-General, as the case may be) is appointed by the President with the consent of the Senate. But this consent, as has already been stated, is now never withheld. The President announces his selections immediately after his inauguration, and the heads of departments, as a rule, hold their posts till the end of the President's term, although they may be removed by him at any time. Removals in the ordinary sense have not been common, but resignations because of failure to work in entire harmony with the President have been numerous. Only in rare cases can it ever become necessary for the President to dismiss any member of his Cabinet. A hint that a resignation would be acceptable is ordinarily quite enough. Occasionally the head of a department may serve through the term of more than one President, particularly if the succeeding President be of the same political party. No head of a department may sit in either the Senate or the House of Representatives; in this respect there is a marked contrast with the English system, which requires that every member of the Cabinet shall have a seat in parliament. Nor has any member of the American Cabinet the right to be heard in either House of Congress, although he may and frequently does confer with congressional committees.

**How selected.**

In selecting the ten heads of departments who form his Cabinet the President is not limited by the constitution or laws as to the range of his choice. He may select whom he pleases. But there are practical considerations which to some extent direct his actions. As a rule all are chosen from his own political party. Washington endeavored to select his Cabinet from among the men of different political inclinations, but the result proved embarrassing and the precedent has not been followed save in very exceptional cases. The selections are made, moreover, with an eye to giving general representation to all sections of the country. A President does not take all his Cabinet secretaries from the North or the South, or from the East or the West. Regard is also paid to the desirability of representing different factions in the party, if such there be, and some of those who have been the President's right-hand men during the campaign for his nomination and election are sure to expect, and usually receive, recognition. Frequently, in past years, the President's strongest competitor for the party nomination has been taken inside the breastworks after the battle and made Secretary of State. Now and then the selection is made solely because the appointee is peculiarly well fitted by administrative experience to be placed at the head of some department; but in the main the choice is determined by personal or political reasons.

In discussing the powers and functions of the Cabinet it is advisable to make a distinction between those functions which are performed by the Cabinet as a whole, and those which are exercised by the members of the Cabinet individually, as heads of their own departments. *Powers and functions of the heads of departments:*

It has already been stated that the Cabinet, as a body, has no constitutional or statutory powers. There is nothing which can be done with its consent which could not be done without its approval if the President should so decide. It is merely a group of high officials whom the President may or may not call together for consultation as he chooses. Yet its members meet in council once or twice each week and seem to find plenty to do at these meetings. What is there to do? Briefly the Cabinet discusses whatever the President may see fit to lay before it and gives its advice to him when he asks for it. Sometimes the President has already made up his mind and *1. as a body.*

merely brings a matter before the Cabinet for suggestions as to details. Lincoln, for instance, did not consult his Cabinet on the Emancipation Proclamation until he had himself fully decided that it ought to be issued. In general, however, the President submits a great many matters to his Cabinet for discussion before a decision is reached. He is not bound to follow the Cabinet's advice, and in practice questions are rarely put to a vote, but from the nature of things the discussion which takes place at Cabinet meetings is likely to influence the President's attitude. This is because it is a discussion participated in by ten men, all of whom the President has himself chosen as sound and sensible advisers.[1] Yet every President realizes, or ought to realize, that the Cabinet has no collective responsibility and that the onus of every executive action must rest upon the shoulders of the President alone.

Meetings of the Cabinet are secret, and no formal record of the discussions is ever kept or given to the public. Whether the President asks, receives, accepts, or disregards advice from his Cabinet is never known, save in rare instances, and then long after the event has passed. Outwardly the Cabinet, as in England, must display the appearance of solidarity. If there are important differences of opinion, they must be composed within the Cabinet itself by the President's friendly intermediation. No head of a department can openly criticise either the President or his own colleagues and remain a member of the Cabinet. In estimating the influence of the Cabinet a great deal depends, of course, upon the temperament of the President himself, whether pliant or strong-willed, and much will also hinge upon the personality of the men who make up the Cabinet. The best service performed by the frequent Cabinet meetings, however, is that of avoiding conflicts or misunder-

[1] There has been a world of difference among Presidents in this respect. Four or five members of his Cabinet virtually controlled President Buchanan during the latter part of his term, and Franklin Pierce was commonly spoken of during his administration as a President who always sought Cabinet advice and followed it. Jackson and Grant, on the other hand, carried their military traditions into the White House and dealt with members of the Cabinet as subordinates whose duty it was to carry out the orders of the commander-in-chief, rather than as advisers whose function it was to help reach a decision.

standing among the several departments, thus enabling the administration to put unity into its programme.

More vital than the functions of the Cabinet as a whole are those of its members as individuals, as heads of departments. Every head of a department is responsible to the President and is under his direction at all times, but in practice each is allowed a considerable range of independence. This must necessarily be the case, for if everything could be supervised directly by the President himself, there would be no need for departments at all. Even in a single department, indeed, there is always more to do than the official at its head can personally attend to, hence each department is divided into two or more bureaus under bureau chiefs or commissioners. This internal organization of the departments is in almost all cases prescribed by law; it is not left, as in most other countries, to be arranged by executive orders. The scope of work to be handled by these bureaus and divisions is very extensive. No head of a department, much less a President, can ever hope to keep the run of it. With the expanding functions of federal government, moreover, it is growing by leaps and bounds. The administrative machinery at Washington is now a dozen times more complex than it was a generation ago. Not only has the work of the various departments been divided, redivided, and subdivided among subordinate bureaus, but many new administrative boards and commissions, some of them exercising functions of the highest importance, such as the Interstate Commerce Commission, the Federal Trade Commission, the Civil Service Commission, and the Tariff Board, have been established altogether outside the purview of the ten regular departments. Of these, however, more will be said presently.

2. as individuals.

The disintegration of departmental machinery.

Each department and each board or commission has its own special functions to perform, these functions being roughly indicated by their respective titles. The exact scope of their work is largely defined by law. Within the bounds thus set the head of the department has the right to make regulations affecting the conduct of business within his own jurisdiction. Each has also been given by law, in many cases, the right to issue departmental orders, some of

General work of the departments.

which may be of great importance. The amount of work to be done by the different departments varies greatly — in ordinary times the Treasury Department has probably the largest amount of business to handle, while the Department of Labor has the smallest, although its functions are by no means inconsiderable.

*The State Department: its functions:*

*1. diplomatic.*

Let us examine, one by one, the organization and chief functions of these various executive agencies.[1] The State Department is the oldest, and the Secretary of State is for that reason the senior member of the cabinet. But he is not a prime minister in any sense of the term. His department deals chiefly with foreign and diplomatic affairs. He is the channel of intercourse between the government of the United States and all foreign governments; likewise the medium of communication between the national and state governments in this country. The State Department does the actual work of negotiating treaties, sending and receiving diplomatic correspondence, giving instructions to American ambassadors abroad, issuing passports, communicating with the governors of the various states, and so on. The Secretary of State, therefore, is the American minister of both interstate and foreign affairs. This field, however, is one in which the President himself is likely to take a direct interest, and the foreign work of the State Department is usually performed under the President's close supervision.

*The diplomatic service.*

A word as to the diplomatic service. The United States sends to and receives from all the sovereign states of the world certain diplomatic officials known as ambassadors or ministers, according to their rank. Those who are sent from this country are appointed by the President with the consent of the Senate; their function is to look after American interests in the countries to which they go; they report regularly to the Secretary of State and get their instructions from his office. At the more important foreign capitals the American diplomatic representatives have the rank of ambassadors; at the less important capitals the rank of

---

[1] The best discussion of the organization and work of the various executive departments is that contained in John A. Fairlie's *National Administration of the United States* (2d ed., N. Y., 1914).

ministers. In duties and authority, however, there is no important difference between the two. The United States also sends and receives other officials known as consuls, and the consular service is also in charge of the State Department, but consuls or consuls-general are not primarily diplomatic officials. They are concerned chiefly with the task of furthering the commercial interests of their own countries.

The Secretary of State has functions also in relation to home affairs. He promulgates the laws when they are passed by Congress; he is the custodian of the national archives or original documents; he countersigns the President's proclamations and he is the keeper of the great seal. To assist him in the performance of all his functions the Secretary of State has three assistant secretaries, also appointed by the President. The State Department is divided into eight bureaus, each of which takes its own share of the general work. Some notable figures have served the nation as secretaries of state, among them John Quincy Adams, William H. Seward, James G. Blaine, and John Hay. In the early days of the Union the post was utilized on several occasions as a stepping stone to the presidency, but since the Civil War no one has moved from one office to the other.[1]

2. internal.

The Department of the Treasury is next in order of seniority. While the name might give the impression that this department corresponds to the Exchequer or Ministry of Finance in other committees, its powers of financial leadership are somewhat less extensive. In most other governments the chief financial minister possesses a well-defined initiative in matters relating to fiscal legislation; he introduces all such measures and defends them on the floor of parliament. In the United States the Secretary of the Treasury has no such formal authority. Financial measures are brought before Congress by its own committees. The Secretary may advise or recommend; but his counsel may be and too often

The Treasury Department.

Unlike the English Exchequer or French Ministry of Finance.

---

[1] For a further discussion of the history and work of this department see Gaillard Hunt, *The Department of State of the United States, Its History and Functions* (New Haven, 1914), and W. H. Michael, *History of the Department of State of the United States* (Washington, 1901).

is disregarded in matters affecting both revenue and expenditures. As Congress has no regular budget system the Secretary of the Treasury lacks the outstanding function of a European finance minister, namely, the preparation and presentation of the budget. And it is right here that the doctrine of separation of powers has worked its greatest havoc in wastefulness and extravagance. The services of the one official who ought to know most about the financial resources and needs of the government have been utilized to a surprisingly small extent in this country. Congress has guarded with extreme jealousy its control of the purse, even to the extent of frequently resenting advice from the administrative officials who are best equipped to tender it.

*One result of this difference.*

If it be asked, Who, then, is responsible for the financial policy of the United States? the answer is, that real responsibility belongs to nobody. It is the waif of dark-lantern politics. For a few years in the early days of the Union, when Alexander Hamilton was Secretary of the Treasury, the United States had a definite financial policy and a statesman who was responsible for it; but that day has long gone by. The initiative, influence, and responsibility which Hamilton took into his own aggressive hands is now dissipated among various committees of both congressional chambers to an extent which only those well-versed in legislative procedure can possibly appreciate.[1]

*Work of the Treasury Department.*

The actual work of the Treasury Department, nevertheless, is extensive and important. It may be grouped into four divisions. First, there is the collection of revenue, especially the supervision of work performed by customs officers and collectors of internal revenue. This includes the duty of issuing all regulations relating to this revenue service and the deciding of appeals which come to the department from the rulings of subordinate officers. Second, there is the custody of the public funds and the paying of all bills for expenditures which have been properly authorized. Sub-treasuries have been established in various large cities of the country to serve as depositories of public funds, and these are under the department's immediate direction.

[1] See below, pp. 302–307.

Government money may also be deposited in national and state banks at the discretion of the Secretary of the Treasury under restrictions provided by law. Third comes the entire supervision of the currency, including control of the mints which coin the money. These functions are directly intrusted to the Comptroller of the Currency, the Director of the Mint, and other officials of the department. With this goes also the supervision of the Federal Reserve Bank system and the inspection of the national banks. The issue of bonds, likewise, when authorized by Congress, is in the department's charge. The accounts of every other executive department, moreover, are audited under the supervision of the Secretary of the Treasury. Finally, there are some miscellaneous powers relating to the lifesaving service, the secret service, the quarantine and public health services, and the system of war risk insurance. This bare enumeration of important functions will at least suffice to show what a large and varied amount of work the Treasury Department has to do. The headship of this department has been held at various times by men of great financial ability, beginning with Alexander Hamilton and including among his successors Albert Gallatin, Salmon P. Chase, and John Sherman.

The War Department in the United States is chiefly concerned, of course, with the maintenance and administration of the army. It has to do not only with the enlistment and equipment of men for all branches of the service, but with contracts for supplies, with fortifications, and the transportation of troops. Even in time of peace these functions are of no inconsiderable importance, but in time of war, as recent years have shown, they become tasks of stupendous magnitude, involving millions of men and billions of dollars. Even before the United States entered the Great War the internal organization of this department, with its eleven different bureaus, was complicated enough; to-day it is so elaborate that even the most elementary description would fill many pages. In addition to these military functions, moreover, the Secretary of War has two important fields of civil authority. One is the supervision of certain public works undertaken by the

The War Department.

national government, such as the dredging of harbors or the improvement of waterways. All the navigable waters of the United States are under the final jurisdiction of the War Department. No obstructions to navigation (in the way of bridges or piers, for example) may be erected anywhere without this department's consent. The other function is that of supervising the administration of the insular possessions. The Philippines, Porto Rico, and the Panama Canal Zone are under the care of the War Department, the two former having been left there since they were occupied by the armed forces of the United States during the Spanish War. Unlike the chief European countries, the United States has no department of colonies. The War Department looks after the possessions just mentioned, but Alaska and Hawaii, being ranked as territories, are under the supervision of the Interior Department.

*Its head is usually a civilian.* The head of the War Department has usually been a civilian, but men of large military experience, Grant and Sherman, for example, have held the post at times. This is quite in contrast with the practice in the countries of continental Europe, where high officers of the army are practically always selected for the post. Both methods have their respective advantages. An army officer is likely to have a better appreciation of the technical phases of the work, while a civilian may be much better qualified to handle such matters as contracts, transportation, the construction of public works, and the administration of the insular possessions. The danger, of course, is always that of friction between a civilian secretary and the military heads of the various technical bureaus in his department. This danger has from time to time been encountered both in the United States and in England where a similar system is in operation. In spite of this, however, the subordination of the military to the civil branch of the government is something that should at all times be clearly provided for in a democracy, even at the risk of some slight lapse in military efficiency. The ablest and most successful Secretary of War among the many who held that office during the nineteenth century was a civilian, Edwin M. Stanton.

The Department of the Interior has various functions

which, in the main, are not at all analogous to those possessed by similar departments in other countries. It does not, as in France, for example, exercise a general supervision over the government of cities and towns. It has nothing whatever to do with local government, police administration, and the other functions which Europeans associate with the "interior" work of national government. Its functions, in fact, are of such a miscellaneous character that it has been jocularly termed the "Department of Things in General." They can be enumerated, but not easily classified. The department has the control of all the public lands, including national parks, and the handling of Indian affairs. It has direct supervision over the territorial affairs of Alaska and Hawaii. It has charge of patents, pensions, the geological survey, and various other things which have no relation to one another. Finally, it distributes the government appropriations to various educational institutions and supervises certain hospitals in the District of Columbia. *Department of the Interior.*

The Postmaster-General is what his title implies. His department has the largest number of employees and hence the greatest range of political patronage. He awards contracts for the transportation of the mails and for all other forms of service in his department. He assumes the oversight of the entire postal business of the United States, which is the largest single business enterprise of any sort in the world if one includes the parcels post system, the handling of money orders, and the postal savings banks. An important authority possessed by the Postmaster-General is that of denying the use of the mails to any concern which may come under the ban for using the service wrongfully. He may also debar any obnoxious publication from passage through the mails. This latter power has been extensively used during recent years. *The Postmaster General.*

The Attorney-General is the head of the Department of Justice and the chief legal adviser of the national government. He is its representative in all legal proceedings to which the United States is a party. He conducts proceedings against corporations or individuals who violate the federal laws and supervises the work of the federal district attorneys throughout the country. He investigates and *The Department of Justice.*

138 THE GOVERNMENT OF THE UNITED STATES

reports to the President upon all applications for reprieves or pardons. His department has general oversight of the federal penitentiaries and other institutions of correction. The post is always held by a lawyer of high standing.

The Navy Department.
The functions of the Navy Department are for the most part implied by its designation. The construction, arming, and distribution of the naval vessels, both regular and auxiliary, the establishment and maintenance of navy yards, the enlistment of men, the making of contracts for supplies, and the general administration of the country's armed forces afloat — all these branches of work are included. The Secretary of the Navy, like the Secretary of War, is practically always chosen from civil life, and the technical work of the department is performed by various subordinate bureaus, each of which is headed by a naval officer of high rank. Although the chief insular possessions of the United States are administered under the supervision of the War Department, the Secretary of the Navy has charge of the smaller islands, Tutuila (in the Samoan group), Guam in the Pacific, and the recently acquired Danish West Indies.

The Department of Agriculture.
The Secretary of Agriculture has acquired many branches of jurisdiction, all of which have to do with agriculture either directly or indirectly. They include the maintenance of agricultural experiment stations, the distribution of seed, the establishment of cattle quarantines, the inspection of meats and other food products, the making of scientific studies relating to agriculture and the issue of bulletins, the control of the weather bureau and the forest service, the management of the crusade against noxious insects, and many other things of an allied nature. The work of this department is supplemented by the states, most of which maintain their own departments of agriculture.

The Department of Commerce.
Two departments of relatively recent establishment are those of Commerce and of Labor. They were originally united but were divided in 1913. The Department of Commerce has to do with the development of foreign and domestic trade, the control of corporations, the licensing and inspection of steamboats, the regulation of fisheries, the lighthouse service, the taking of the census, and some

minor matters. The Department of Labor has direction of the immigration service, the administration of the naturalization laws, and the adjustment of relations between labor and capital. It includes a children's bureau to which is intrusted the execution of the federal laws relating to the employment of child labor in industry. In a word it seeks to do for the interests of labor what other departments have done for agriculture and commerce respectively. *The Department of Labor.*

The heads of the ten departments, namely, the Secretary of State, Secretary of the Treasury, Secretary of War, Secretary of the Interior, Postmaster-General, Attorney-General, Secretary of the Navy, Secretary of Agriculture, Secretary of Commerce, and Secretary of Labor, make up the Cabinet. Subject to the general direction of the President and within the range of the laws, each has control of things in his own division of work. The degree of independence possessed by each is nowhere exactly defined. One thing is certain, however, and that is the absence of any jurisdiction on the part of the Cabinet over its individual members. The Cabinet as a whole cannot give any orders to its own members. That can be done only by the President. Members of the Cabinet do, however, consult the President on all important problems within their departments, and he may, of course, not only lay these before the whole Cabinet for discussion but may be governed thereby.

In addition to these ten regular departments, there are some other branches of national administration whose heads are not members of the Cabinet. These federal agencies, which are not called departments but bureaus, commissions, or boards, have been established from time to time under the authority of acts passed by Congress, but the chiefs of the bureaus and the members of the commissions are appointed by the President with the consent of the Senate. For the policy of placing these bureaus and boards outside the purview of any of the regular departments there have been various reasons, historical, political, and personal. In the main, however, these administrative agencies deal either with functions which are rather too important to be committed to subordinate officials in one of the regular departments and yet are not important *The detached bureaus and boards.*

enough to warrant the creation of a new department, or they are functions which from their intrinsic nature can most appropriately be handled by a board of several officials responsible directly to the President.

*The Interstate Commerce Commission.* The most widely known among these bodies is the Interstate Commerce Commission, established in 1887 to supervise the execution of the national laws relating to foreign and interstate trade, with power to investigate complaints. The original powers of the commission have since, by successive acts of Congress, been greatly extended. It is now composed of nine members, each appointed for a seven-year term by the President with the consent of the Senate. The work of the commission is quasi-judicial in its nature, for it adjudicates controversies between interstate transportation companies and shippers relating to rates and conditions of service. From its rulings there is, however, an appeal on points of law to the Supreme Court of the United States. The commission has become the right hand of Congress in the exercise of its commerce power.[1]

*The Federal Trade Commission.* Another board which exercises authority in the domain of commerce and industry is the Federal Trade Commission established in 1914. It is composed of five members, each appointed by the President with the concurrence of the Senate for a seven-year term. This commission took over the work formerly handled by the Bureau of Corporations in the Department of Commerce, but it has acquired from Congress other authority in addition. It is empowered in a broad way to investigate and to prevent all unfair competition in commerce and industry, save among transportation companies and banks, both of which are under the supervision of other federal authorities.[2]

*The Tariff Commission.* Still more recently, in 1916, Congress authorized the establishment of a Tariff Commission with a membership of six, each appointed by the President with senatorial confirmation, for the unusually long term of twelve years.[3]

---

[1] So long as the railroads remain under government operation, however, its influence is much diminished.

[2] See also below, p. 259.

[3] The initial appointments were in all cases except one made for shorter terms in order that the various members might end their terms periodically and not all together.

It is intended that this board shall make a thorough study of all questions relating to the importation of merchandise and shall thus provide data upon which the tariff, in future years, can be framed with reference to the real economic needs of the country rather than in obedience to sectional or class or political pressure. The commission has, of course, no powers except those of an advisory nature. Congress retains full authority over the traffic schedules.

Another important federal board is the Civil Service Commission which helps to recruit the public service. The Spoils System flourished in all its vigor from the first inauguration of President Jackson in 1829 until the assassination of President Garfield in 1881, a period of more than half a century. During all of these years it was a persistent troubler in Israel, giving successive Presidents no end of embarrassment and taking from them the time and strength which should have been given to things far more important. Public opinion, however, gradually solidified against the system, and the tragic end of President Garfield at the hands of a disappointed office-seeker gave a new impetus to the movement for civil service reform. In 1883 Congress passed the act which laid the basis of the present civil service system and authorized the establishment of a commission to carry out its provisions. This commission is a body of three members, each appointed by the President with the Senate's approval, but not more than two of the members may belong to the same political party. It prepares the rules governing civil service competition, supervises the work of examining candidates, and certifies the successful candidates for appointment. With more and more offices placed within the classified service, the functions of the commission have steadily become greater in scope. *The Civil Service Commission.*

A few other executive agencies remain to be mentioned. The Bureau of Efficiency, established in 1917, has for its chief function to suggest improvements in the system and business methods of the various government offices in Washington. The Library of Congress, the largest repository of books in the country and one of the largest in the world, is not included in any of the regular departments, its librarian *Other executive agencies.*

being responsible directly to the President. The government printing office is also a detached unit of administration, although there is no sensible reason why it should be.

*The decentralization of administrative agencies.*

It will be seen from the foregoing enumeration that the agencies of national administration are diverse in their methods of organization and even more varied in the scope of their work. They are not more numerous, however, than in the national government of any other great nation. Their relation to one another is neither intimate nor at all times accurately defined, but the saving grace of the whole system is the fact that it revolves on a definite centre, the executive supremacy of the President. There is no diffusion of administrative responsibility in the national government, such as so commonly exists in the government of American states and cities. The President is the apex of the executive pyramid. All administrative responsibility converges in his hands. So long as that remains true, so long as he appoints all heads of departments, chiefs of bureaus, and members of commissions, and so long as he may remove them at will, the elaboration of administrative machinery need bring no friction or working at cross purposes. If, however, Congress should ever succeed in limiting the right of the President to remove members of his Cabinet and other executive officers, as it tried to do by the Tenure of Office Act in 1867, the system of centralized administrative responsibility would quickly break down. So long as the separation of powers remains a corner stone of American government the supremacy of the chief executive in all strictly administrative matters must be closely guarded or chaos in the business affairs of the nation will inevitably ensue.

*Relation of national administration to Congress.*

While, however, the executive branch of the government is not directly responsible to Congress in the sense that the English Cabinet is responsible to parliament, this does not mean that Congress can in no way influence the course of national administration. On the contrary it is Congress that authorizes the establishment of each department, bureau, or commission; it is Congress that gives each its functions; it is Congress that grants the money which enables every administrative agency to carry on its work.

# THE CABINET AND NATIONAL ADMINISTRATION 143

Congress can reorganize any department or even abolish it altogether, subject of course to the obvious condition that to do so it would probably have to override a presidential veto. Most important of all among congressional powers over the administration, however, is the authority to give or withhold appropriations. This, in the last analysis, is the weapon with which it can bring any administrative officer, and sometimes even the President, to terms. From the various departments, moreover, Congress can and does require reports and information; it can investigate any department at will, and in the last resort it has the power of impeachment. Let it not be thought, accordingly, that because administration shares place with legislation as a coördinate and not as a subordinate function of government it is altogether immune from legislative contact or influence.

It has often been urged that a greater degree of harmony and coöperation between the executive and legislative branches of the national government would be secured if members of the Cabinet were allowed to sit and speak (although not to vote) in both Houses of Congress. Congress has an undoubted right to give them this privilege under the provision of the constitution which authorizes both Houses to make their own rules of procedure. For a hundred years, moreover, delegates from the territories have been allowed to sit in the House of Representatives and to speak there, although having no right to vote. The constitution excludes any person "holding any office under the United States" from being "a member of either House during his continuance in office," but the head of a department, by taking a part in the deliberations of either House, would not become a member of it any more than the chaplain or the clerk. He would have no official term, no privilege of immunity from arrest, no vote, none of the constitutional attributes of a member. *Should members of the Cabinet sit in Congress?*

Admitting, however, that Congress has the power to admit the members of the Cabinet to its sessions, would it be expedient to do so? That question has been many times discussed, and there are undoubtedly two sides to it. On the one hand, it has been urged that Congress could, *Merits and defects of the proposal.*

in this way, obtain more useful and more exact information than it now obtains through roundabout channels; that the change would inspire the President to choose, as members of the Cabinet, men of greater public experience, and that it would also compel these men to become proficient in the affairs of their several departments, for no incapable head of a department could hope to influence the deliberations of Congress day by day. On the other hand, it is replied that to place on the floor of each chamber ten cabinet secretaries of national prestige and long public experience would give the executive branch of the government a greatly increased influence over the making of laws and appropriations. Members of the Cabinet, it is also said, have already too much to do in their several departments without daily attendance at congressional debates. Frequently they have complained of the time required of them in appearing before congressional committees. There are those who suspect, moreover, that the admission of administrative officers to the floor of Congress would be the thin end of a wedge which would ultimately be driven deep into the principle of checks and balances, thus breaking down a political tradition which still has its vigorous supporters. It is not unlikely, however, that the experiment will some day be tried.

English and American Cabinets contrasted:

A favorite theme of writers in the field of comparative government has been the series of contrasts between the cabinet system of England and that of the United States. The differences, of course, are wide and fundamental. It is hardly worth while to discuss them at length, for they are relatively easy to comprehend. Here are the chief discrepancies set down under three main heads:

1. qualifications of members.

The members of the English Cabinet must be members of one or other branch of parliament; in the United States the members of the Cabinet cannot be members of either House of Congress.

2. powers of initiative in legislation.

In England the Cabinet is the "great standing committee of parliament," arranging all important business in advance, championing these measures on their way through both chambers, and assuming the function of legislative leadership. In the United States the Cabinet may, in an informal way, help the President with proposed projects of legisla-

# THE CABINET AND NATIONAL ADMINISTRATION 145

tion, but it can assume no formal responsibility and it can take no open share in facilitating the progress of legislation. The most important practical power of the English Cabinet, that of guiding the business of national legislation, does not belong to the Cabinet in America.

Finally, the English Cabinet is responsible to the House of Commons, while the Cabinet of the United States is not responsible to Congress. An adverse vote in the House of Commons is sufficient to overthrow the Cabinet in England; a hundred adverse votes in the Senate or the House of Representatives do not necessarily cause the members of the American Cabinet to resign. Their responsibility is to the President alone. This is, after all, the most outstanding of all differences between the two Cabinets. In England the executive power is dependent upon the will of parliament; in America it is independent of Congress, supreme within its own sphere and accountable to the people alone.

3. responsibility.

To attempt any demonstration that either system is superior to the other would be profitless. It would be like engaging in a controversy upon the relative prowess of an elephant and a whale. Each is fitted to its own element and would make a ludicrous showing were it to change habitats. Both the English and American Cabinet systems have served satisfactorily, each in its own political environment, and the adaptation of the agent to its environment is as essential in the body politic as in other organisms. If the American system shows its weakness in the defective coöperation which it provides between the two great arms of government, it has an offsetting merit in the protection which it affords against any undue gravitation of power into a few hands.

## CHAPTER X

### THE SENATE: ITS ORGANIZATION

*Why the double-chamber system was first adopted.*

DURING the Revolutionary War and under the Articles of Confederation, the common affairs of the thirteen states were managed by a Congress which consisted of a single chamber. It was decided by the constitutional convention of 1787 at an early stage in its deliberations, however, that the new government should provide a Congress of two chambers. This decision was reached with practical unanimity, as it seemed unwise to give to a single chamber, particularly to one chosen by popular vote, the great legislative authority which it was proposed to vest in the new government. Such a single chamber might enact laws hastily, might be moved by gusts of prejudice, and might become in the end a legislative octopus. Most of the colonies, moreover, had maintained two legislative chambers, likewise all of the new state constitutions except those of Pennsylvania, Georgia, and Vermont made provisions for the double-chamber system. The bicameral system seemed to be indicated by the lessons of experience and by considerations of prudence, in view of the "propensity of all single and numerous assemblies to yield to the impulse of sudden and violent passions, and to be seduced by factious leaders into intemperate and pernicious resolutions." But there was another consideration, namely, the desirability of embodying, somewhere in the new government, the principle that all the states were equal. Without provision for two houses, the terms of the first great compromise would not have been possible.[1] The adoption of the double-chamber system was settled before the dispute over the basis of representa-

---

[1] See above, p. 33.

# THE SENATE: ITS ORGANIZATION

tion became acute, but the compromise sealed the matter beyond the possibility of reopening it.

The basis of representation in Congress, therefore, is this: two interests are to be represented, namely, the states and the people of the states. The states as such are equally represented, by each having two senators in the upper branch of Congress, the Senate. The people of the several states, on the other hand, are represented by a varying number of representatives in the lower branch of Congress, the House of Representatives. In both cases the unit of representation is the state. Congress, accordingly, is a bicameral convention of state envoys; its members are officers of the states from which they come and not officers of the national government. *The Constitutional basis of representation in Congress.*

In the constitution, as originally adopted, it was provided that the Senate of the United States should be made up of two senators from each state, chosen by the legislature thereof for six years. In making this provision that senators should be chosen by the various state legislatures two purposes were in view. First, it was the intention that the Senate should be a conservative body, made up of men who had gained political experience and distinction in their own states, — men who might not possess the attributes of popularity but who would command respect by their personal attainments. The fear of demagogism, of legislation dictated by selfishness or ignorance, cropped out persistently in the deliberations of 1787. "A good government," wrote one of those who had much to do with the framing of the constitution, "implies two things: first, fidelity to the object of government, which is the happiness of the people; secondly, a knowledge of the means by which that object can be best attained. Some governments are deficient in both these qualities; most governments are deficient in the first. I scruple not to assert, that in American governments too little attention has been paid to the last."[1] Honesty and good intent, in other words, would not of themselves suffice as the basis of an enduring government. Precaution must be taken to make place in the national legislature for a small body of men who would *Reasons for the original method of choosing senators: 1. the desire for a mature and conservative element in Congress.*

[1] Alexander Hamilton in *The Federalist*, No. 62.

be chosen because of their knowledge, judgment, and maturity.[1] Such men would, it was felt, be more readily chosen by the state legislatures, they having, as it was asserted, "more sense of character" than the people at large.

2. to guarantee the permanence of the state legislatures.

But there was a second reason for intrusting the selection of senators to the legislatures of the several states, namely, to insure the permanence of these legislatures themselves. The popular fear that the creation of a vigorous national government would be the first step towards the ultimate destruction of the new state administrations was one which had to be reckoned with. Hence an important wheel in the national machine was geared directly to the mechanism of state government so that the state legislatures could never be eliminated without bringing down one branch of Congress as well. The Senate was to be a constitutional link binding together the two spheres of government, state and national. It was a hostage given to the states to insure the permanence of their legislatures.

The Senate was intended to be the balance wheel of the new government. It was to serve as a Privy Council and House of Lords combined, a check on certain powers of the executive (in the matter of treaties and appointments), and a brake upon the radicalism of the lower chamber. Senators were given the longest terms provided for any non-judicial officers, — six years, — in order to reduce the evils of what Hamilton termed "the mischievous effects of a mutable or unstable government," to trace which, he declared, "would fill a volume."[2] If Hamilton had been given his way, they would have been chosen for life. While his colleagues were not ready to go so far, they concurred in the opinion that one of the two legislative chambers should be so constituted as to protect the rights of property against the possible, and even probable, inroads of an aggressive and capricious majority among the people.[3] It was Washington, according to a somewhat dubious tradi-

[1] George H. Haynes, *The Election of Senators* (N. Y., 1906).

[2] *The Federalist*, No. 62.

[3] So far as the records of the convention of 1787 disclose, James Wilson of Pennsylvania was the only delegate who urged the direct popular election of senators.

tion, who remarked that the Senate was to be a saucer into which the hot tea which came steaming from the House might be poured to cool.

The Senate, as originally designed and established, is a purely American product. Some antiquarians have unearthed a precedent for it in the ancient confederation of Hellenic states "where each city, however different in wealth, strength, and other circumstances, had the same number of deputies and an equal voice in everything that related to the concerns of Greece." Others have found its prototype in both the United Netherlands and the Swiss Confederation. There is no need, however, to have gone seeking so far afield. The framers of the constitution were quite familiar with upper chambers in colonial times, some of which, like the council in Massachusetts, were made up of members chosen to represent districts, and all of which were intended to serve as checks upon the popular assemblies. Starting with this upper chamber of colonial days the organization of the new Senate was merely adapted to the political exigencies of the time. *The Senate an indigenous institution.*

For more than a century senators were elected by the state legislatures as the constitution originally provided. Each legislature, in the first instance, was left to determine the procedure by which the choice should be made, whether by its two branches acting separately or in joint session. But in various states controversies arose between the two legislative chambers, and these controversies sometimes prevented any choice being made at all. In 1866, therefore, Congress passed a law making the procedure uniform in all the states. In brief, the provision was that the two branches of a state legislature should first ballot separately, and if they could each elect the same candidate by a clear majority, well and good. But if the two chambers could not agree on the choice of a senator in that way, they were then to meet in joint session and keep balloting day after day until some one obtained a majority. If a vacancy in the senatorial representation from any state occurred at a time when the state legislature was not in session, the governor of the state was empowered by the constitution to name some qualified person to serve until the legislature *Older plan of choosing senators described.*

could meet and make a choice, or should adjourn without making a choice.

**Objections to this plan.**

But as time went on there came a growing demand that senators should be chosen by direct popular election, and not by the state legislatures. Various factors contributed to this demand. Far from always choosing men of ripe political judgment and stanch integrity, some of the state legislatures allowed their choice of senators to be dictated by ulterior motives. The choice was never determined, in fact, by the legislature but by a party caucus of the majority members. Partisan service, without any other qualification, on many occasions placed senators in their seats. The dictation of political bosses counted for more with members of state legislatures than the promptings of their own judgment or the trend of public opinion. The influence of great corporations was able, time and again, to determine the election. Even outright bribery was not unknown. Not that all senators, of course, or even most of them, were chosen in obedience to reprehensible motives; the great majority of United States senators obtained their seats by methods which were perfectly proper and beyond criticism, being chosen because the several legislatures regarded them, sometimes in the narrow perspective of their political bias, as worthy representatives of their various states. But departures from the paths of legislative rectitude were all too frequent, and they stamped upon the public mind the impression that indirect election inevitably meant intrigue, that it gave an unfair advantage to the candidate with large funds at his disposal, and that it made of the Senate a reactionary body. There were frequent deadlocks, too, ballot after ballot being taken daily for weeks and even for months without any one obtaining a clear majority. In this way a state was often deprived of its full representation in the Senate over considerable periods of time.

**The movement for the direct popular election of senators.**

At any rate, the antipathy to the old plan grew apace, and projects for changing the constitution so as to permit direct election came to the front in the closing decades of the nineteenth century. Several times the House of Representatives passed by the requisite two-thirds vote a proposition to submit such an amendment to the states for their approval, but the instinct of self-preservation led the Senate to refuse concurrence. Meanwhile, some of the states evolved a plan by which they virtually secured the popular choice of their senators without waiting for a change in the constitutional machinery. The general features of this plan were as follows: whenever the term of a senator was about to expire a direct primary was held in which each political party chose its candidate for senator. Candidates for election to the state legislature were then asked by the voters to pledge their support to the people's choice at the primary. The legislators were, of course, under no legal obligaticn to keep such preëlection pledges, but in the main they did so, and the choice of the majority party at the primary was regularly chosen for the Senate by the majority members of the same political party in the legislature. The whole proceeding was directly contrary to the spirit of the constitution but quite within the letter of its requirements.

In 1913 the Seventeenth Amendment to the national constitution was finally adopted. It provided that hereafter senators should be chosen directly by the voters of the several states, not by the legislatures. No longer was there any hesitation about snapping the ancient link between the state and national governments; the danger that federal usurpation would extinguish the state legislatures had long since passed away, if, indeed, it had ever had any real existence. To-day, therefore, the post of United States senator is elective, but the term and the qualifications of senators remain as before. A senator must be not less than thirty years of age, a citizen of at least nine years' standing, and at the time of his election an inhabitant of the state which he is to represent. *Culmination of this movement in the Seventeenth Amendment.*

But while the term of senators, as has been said, is six years, one-third of the Senate's membership is renewed every two years. No state elects both its senators in the same year, unless some unexpected vacancy should occur in one of the senatorships. The choice is made by the voters at the regular state election, and the qualifications for voting are the same as those required at the election of representatives. When a vacancy occurs through the death, disqualification, or resignation of a senator from any state, the governor issues a writ for a special election, unless a regular polling day is near at hand; and the state legislature may empower the governor to appoint some qualified person as senator temporarily, to sit until this election is held.

Equality of representation in the Senate must remain.

The Seventeenth Amendment made no change, moreover, in the equal representation of the states, although, with the present great disparity of population among the various commonwealths, this feature has become a great anomaly. Nevada, with about 100,000 population, has two senators, while New York, with over 10,000,000, has the same number. Proportionally, New York would have two hundred senators. But, anomalous or not, this equality of representation was an essential feature of a bargain made by the larger with the smaller states, and in the constitution a pledge was given that no state without its consent should ever be deprived of its equal suffrage in the Senate. That pledge will of course be respected. No matter how widely the states may vary in area, population, or resources, the principle of equality must remain so far as the upper branch of Congress is concerned. This is one respect in which the constitution is practically unamendable. Strictly speaking, of course, the sovereignty of a nation cannot be restricted in this way; an unamendable constitution, or part of a constitution, is incompatible with the principle of ultimate popular sovereignty. But the pledge was made in good faith and it will be kept.

Organization of the Senate.

The Senate of the United States holds its regular sessions each year in its own chamber at the national capital. It may also be called by the President in special session, even when the House of Representatives is not sitting. This is because the Senate, as will be pointed out in the next chapter, has some special functions which are not shared by the other branch of Congress, the trial of impeachments and the approval of treaties, for example. By the terms of the constitution the Vice-President of the United States is the Senate's presiding officer, and he possesses the customary powers and duties of that post. But he has no vote except in the case of a tie. This restriction was thought prudent in order that the state from which the Vice-President happens to come would not regularly have three votes on all questions. In the earlier days of the Union, when the Senate was a small body of less than thirty members, tie-votes were not uncommon; but nowadays, with the membership increased to ninety-six, the Vice-President rarely gets the opportunity to give a casting vote. In the absence of the Vice-President the Senate elects a president pro tempore. It also chooses its other officers, sergeant-at-arms, chaplain, and clerks.

The Senate makes its own rules of procedure. On the whole its rules are simple, far more so than those of the House. They require that every bill or joint resolution shall receive three readings before being passed, but the first two readings are merely nominal and are given before the bill is referred to the appropriate committee. The real contest, if any, comes upon the occasion of the third reading, when amendments may be offered and voted upon. No general priority is given in the Senate, as in the House, to any class of measures, except that appropriation bills have a certain precedence. Debate in the Senate is not limited by the rules save in one particular, namely, that a senator may not speak more than twice upon the same question during the same day without permission of the Senate. This great freedom of debate has had an important influence upon the work of the chamber, as will be indicated presently. While most of the daily meetings are public the Senate meets occasionally in "executive session" behind closed doors. This is usually the case when the confirmation of treaties is under discussion. *Its procedure.*

Like all great legislative bodies, the Senate of the United States does a large part of its work through standing committees, of which it has more than sixty. Some of them are important and have substantially the same designation and jurisdiction as the chief committees in the other chamber; but most of them have only perfunctory work to do and scarcely ever meet at all. The most important committees of the Senate are those on finance, appropriations, foreign relations, the judiciary, and interstate commerce. The first two have the consideration of all measures affecting revenue and expenditures respectively; the next two owe much of *Its committees.*

their importance to the fact that all the President's nominations to the diplomatic service and to the courts are referred to them. Likewise, the committee on foreign relations considers all treaties before they are discussed by the Senate as a whole. The committee on interstate commerce has the preliminary consideration of all measures in the important field of administration which its title indicates. Senate committees contain from five to fifteen members, and every senator is likely to be assigned to one or more of them. The Senate also meets in committee of the whole for the detailed consideration of measures.

*How committees are chosen.* The selection of the various committees is made, at the beginning of each Congress, by special committees chosen for that purpose by the caucus of each party. These special "committees on committees" make up a slate or list of committee assignments, and this is ordinarily accepted by the Senate without change. The real selections are, therefore, made by the committee and not by the Senate itself. Invariably, of course, the majority party in the Senate is given a safe numerical margin on every committee of importance. Each committee has its chairman, who is named on the slate in the same way, but in the naming of these chairmen it is usual to respect the principle of seniority in service. Senators of the majority party who have had long service, especially on particular committees, are usually given the important chairmanships. Every committee has its "ranking member," the one who stands next in order of seniority and who is in line for promotion to the chairmanship when a vacancy occurs, provided his own party retains a majority in the Senate.

*Freedom of debate in the Senate: its merits and defects.* Mention has been made of the fact that in the Senate freedom of debate is unrestricted to an extent unknown in any other legislative body throughout the world. There is no closure system such as exists in England, and until recently no other means of shutting off discussion. This plan has, of course, some great advantages in that it encourages spirited and continued discussion; it gives a minority a fair chance to fight matters to a finish and to let the country know the facts. But like all such unwonted freedom, this latitude in debate may be abused, and it sometimes has been abused. It affords obstructionist senators the opportunity to talk measures to death. It gives a factious minority the opportunity to use dilatory tactics and to wear out the patience of the majority by conducting a "filibuster," as it is called. When the Senate's session is drawing to its close, this freedom of debate sometimes permits a relatively small minority to defeat any measure by resort to filibustering tactics, and many measures have perished in this way. Indeed it can fairly be said that legislation in the closing days of the Senate's session virtually requires unanimous consent. Everyone remembers, for example, the way in which "twelve wilful men" in a total membership of ninety-six endeavored to prevent the arming of American merchant vessels for self-protection in the spring of 1917. This action caused the Senate to alter its rules somewhat and the previous question may now be moved as a means of closing an unduly prolonged debate.

Notwithstanding the incentive afforded for long and carefully prepared speeches, the Senate's debates do not nowadays, in general, reach the high standards of seven or eight decades ago, the days of Webster, Clay, Calhoun, Hayne, and Sumner. Speeches of sterling quality in substance and of rhetorical excellence are still delivered on occasions when some matter of special importance or solemnity gives the opportunity; but a senator no longer hopes to convert his colleagues by eloquence. Speeches in the Senate, in fact, are addressed to the country at large rather than to immediate hearers. By the way, it is not the practice of the Senate, as it is of the House, to give members "leave to print" speeches which they have not delivered or "leave to extend" a few remarks into many pages of the printed record. *Quality of the Senate's debates.*

Yet the standards of debate maintained by the United States Senate to-day are not below those of the British House of Commons, and they are certainly above those of legislative bodies in other lands. Legislative eloquence has suffered an eclipse in our time, not merely in this country but everywhere. Party lines have tightened, so that only the authorized spokesmen of the party are now listened to *Comparison with other countries.*

with great interest; the others merely repeat, expound, and amplify. The senator who is merely a loyal supporter of his party programme cannot thrill the country with something new and startling, the outcome of his own initiative and reflection. If he did, he would no longer be accounted a loyal party man, and under the party system which now rules the Senate there is no influential place for any one else.

*Influence of the party spirit.*

The party whip cracks frequently in the Senate as in other legislative chambers. Its custodian is the caucus. Each party, majority and minority, has its own caucus, made up solely of its own members, and at these meetings the action of each group is decided upon. The majority senators, whether Republicans or Democrats, agree as to

*The caucus system in the Senate.*

the measures which they will support; the minority members, on the other hand, map out their counter-operations, deciding whether to oppose, or to offer amendments, or to filibuster, or to let measures go through. Only the majority party, however, uses the caucus regularly. Every senator who attends his party caucus is bound to abide by any decision which the caucus may make, bound by a merely moral obligation, to be sure, but that is enough for all practical purposes. Thus it comes to pass that when a majority caucus has pledged its members to support any measure, the ultimate issue is virtually sealed. The majority, being pledged by caucus resolution to stand together, can insure its enactment. In the Senate, as in the House, vigorous

*Merits and defects of the caucus.*

protests against the caucus system have been voiced from time to time, and there is throughout the country a good deal of prejudice against caucus legislation; but the system provides the only way in which responsibility for legislation, under a system of divided powers and partisan government, can be adequately centralized. When a majority caucus pledges its members, this means that the party is ready to take the entire responsibility for some action. The proposal then becomes what in England would be termed a "government measure." Reformers are continually urging that the Senate should replace "irresponsible party action in a secret conclave" by some form of "public, personal, and individual responsibility"; but the whole history of representative law-making proves that no well-ordered legislative programme is ever carried through by placing undue emphasis upon the duty of every legislator to run off on his own tangent. The legislative caucus, or something akin to it, is a fixture in all countries having systems of free government. It is not, as some imagine, a vicious instrumentality which the politicians of America have devised for their own benefit.

The Senate has the usual rights of a legislative body, and its members enjoy the customary immunities. They are privileged from arrest on civil process during their attendance, or in going to, or in returning from, the sessions. For what a senator may say in the course of a debate, moreover, the constitution provides that he "shall not be questioned in any other place"; in other words, he is not subject to the ordinary law of libel as administered by the courts. But the Senate itself can punish a member for disorderly conduct and by a two-thirds vote may even expel him. It may compel the attendance of absent senators, may conduct investigations, may summon witnesses, and, in the event of their refusal to appear or to answer questions, may punish them for contempt. It has the right to determine the qualifications of its own members. It may do more than merely examine into these formal qualifications, for it may investigate the question whether any senator has been properly chosen, whether bribery or other reprehensible means have been employed to influence his election. It has the power to declare an election void if reasons for so doing should appear. A senator is not, however, a "civil officer of the United States," as defined by the constitution, and hence may not be impeached before the Senate itself.[1]

*Privileges and immunities of senators.*

In political influence and prestige the Senate remained, during the early years of the Union, quite inferior to the House. The latter took the initiative in legislation of all kinds, the Senate devoting more time to revising the measures which came up to it from the lower chamber than in originating bills of its own. It was a small body, sitting behind closed doors, and regarded by the public as a private conference of provincial notables in which there was no

*The place of the Senate in American political history.*

[1] See below, p. 170.

(a) from 1789 to 1830.

(b) from 1830 to 1870.

opportunity for the exercise of brilliant political talents.[1] In the original Senate Chamber (now occupied by the Supreme Court) there were no seats installed for the public. Madison, on one occasion, remarked that being desirous of increasing his reputation as a statesman, he could not afford to accept a seat in the Senate. The centre of political gravity during this period, which extended from 1789 to about 1830, was lodged in the House.

But with the Jacksonian revolution this situation underwent a change. The abolition of the congressional nominating caucus, which the House through sheer weight of numbers always controlled, reduced the influence of that body.[2] The Senate began to come into its own. Men of great power and prestige came into its membership during the three decades which intervened between the inauguration of Jackson and the Civil War. The outstanding political questions of this epoch were connected mainly with the subject of state rights, and in these the Senate, as the chamber representing the interests of the several states, became the great forum of discussion. Controversies and compromises relating to the admission of new states centred about the ultimate control of the Senate by the pro-slavery or anti-slavery sections of the Union. The permanence of its organization, the longer terms for which its members were chosen, its smaller and more wieldy size, the reputation for skill and eloquence in debate which it developed — these things helped to make the Senate the real battle-ground upon which the great national issues of the ante-bellum era were fought out. Both at home and abroad the Senate gained a name for talent, dignity, and aggressiveness. So quickly and so completely was the balance of power shifted from the lower to the upper chamber that a distinguished French student of American democracy, writing in the middle thirties, was impressed by the wide discrepancy between the two.[3] The great debates which preceded the War

[1] Henry Jones Ford, *The Rise and Growth of American Politics* (N. Y., 1911), pp. 260–261.

[2] Cf. below, p. 332.

[3] "On entering the House of Representatives at Washington, one is struck by the vulgar demeanor of that great assembly. Often there is not a distinguished man in the whole number. Its members are almost

of 1812 took place in the House; but the oratorical battles which foreshadowed the Civil War were fought in the Senate. Its zenith of prestige was reached at the close of the Civil War when it sought, under Andrew Johnson, to usurp a share of the President's executive authority and ended by almost removing him from office by conviction on impeachment. No upper chamber in any other country matched the Senate of the United States in influence and power at that point.

Then came the inevitable reaction. By its undue emphasis upon "senatorial courtesy" and by its disposition to hamper the hands of the executive in foreign affairs the Senate overreached itself. Grant and Garfield each took a hand in clipping its wings, the former by rebuffing its claim to any control over removals from office; the latter by defying its rule of courtesy. Questions of economic policy, moreover, now came to the front, and in its handling of these the sectional spirit of the upper chamber became all too plain. The growth of huge corporations and of great fortunes brought new elements into its membership, senators who owed their selection either to personal wealth or to the fact that they were well backed from opulent sources. The ranks of those who owed their seats to intellectual eminence or skill in debate or long political experience grew thinner as the years went by. The Senate began to stamp itself upon the public imagination as the stronghold of vested economic interests and the foe of popular rights.

(c) since 1870.

Other things, moreover, contributed to the decline of the Senate's prestige during the closing quarter of the nineteenth century, particularly the frequent scandals connected with the choice of senators by the legislatures in various states and the reputed alliance between certain

all obscure individuals. . . . At a few yards distance is the door of the Senate, which contains within small space a large proportion of the celebrated men of America. Scarcely an individual is to be seen in it who has not had an active and illustrious career; the Senate is composed of eloquent advocates, distinguished generals, wise magistrates, and statesmen of note, whose arguments would do honor to the most remarkable parliamentary debates of Europe." — ALEXIS DE TOCQUEVILLE, *Democracy in America* (2 vols., London, 1835–1840), I, ch. xiii.

160    THE GOVERNMENT OF THE UNITED STATES

senators and great railroads or industrial corporations. The great and dominating figures of the golden age disappeared, one by one, and the new senators who came to take their seats did not share to a like degree the public confidence. During the past twenty-five years the senatorial firmament has contained very few stars of the first magnitude. Yet the Senate has relaxed its grip very slowly, and even yet it retains a large portion of its earlier strength and prowess.

*Will the new plan of election improve the Senate?*  By some this deterioration in personnel and in influence has been attributed to the old method of choosing senators, and the prediction has been made that, under the new scheme of popular election provided by the Seventeenth Amendment, the Senate will soon regain its unquestioned hegemony. It is yet too early to pass judgment upon the soundness of this expectation, but the lapse of a few years has given no tangible indication that it will ever be fulfilled. Popular election, when used in connection with the direct primary, has not shown itself in any field of American political life to be a certain method of securing for the public service men of high intelligence, sound judgment, or rugged integrity. The new plan is not likely to do worse than the old, perhaps, but the hope for a marked improvement leans upon a slender reed.

*The many-sided Senate.*  "It is very difficult to form a just estimate of the Senate of the United States. No body has been more discussed; no body has been more misunderstood and traduced. There was a time when we were lavish in spending our praises upon it. We joined with our foreign critics and appreciators in speaking of the Senate as one of the most admirable, as it is certainly one of the most original, of our political institutions. In our own day we have been equally lavish of hostile criticism. We have suspected it of every malign purpose, fixed every unhandsome motive upon it, and at times almost cast it out of our confidence altogether. The fact is that it is possible in your thought to make almost anything you please out of the Senate. It is a body variously compounded, made many-sided by containing many elements, and a critic may concentrate his attention upon one element at a time if he chooses, make the most of what is good and put the rest out of sight, or make more than the most of what is bad and ignore everything that does not chime with his thesis of evil. The Senate has, in fact, many contrasted characteristics, shows many faces, lends itself easily to no confident generalization." [1]

[1] Woodrow Wilson, *Constitutional Government in the United States* (N. Y., 1911), p. 112.

# CHAPTER XI

## THE SENATE: ITS FUNCTIONS

<small>The Senate an executive as well as a legislative body.</small>

THE United States Senate was designed to be more than a branch of Congress and the right arm of the legislative power. It was intended to serve, in some degree, as an executive council as well. If the framers of the constitution made no regular provision for any body like the English Privy Council, it was possibly because they felt that they had assigned to the Senate the most important things upon which it was desirable that the President should have advice and assistance. Washington, when he became President, fully expected that the Senate would act as an advisory council, deliberating with him on treaties and appointments. The Senate at this time consisted of twenty-eight members only, so that it was not too large a body for informal and confidential discussion. At any rate, it was Washington's practice, in the earlier years of his administration, to attend in person whenever executive sessions of the Senate were held for the consideration of treaties. But the senators did not relish this practice; they felt that it was a restraint upon free discussion, and soon adopted the plan of postponing all matters laid before them by the President until they could be taken up in his absence. In time there developed, accordingly, the practice of merely sending appointments and treaties in formal written communications, leaving the Senate to make up its mind without presidential assistance.

<small>Is this consistent with the principle of separation of power?</small>

When Alexander Hamilton wrote of the executive power as being divided between the President and the Senate, he had in mind, doubtless, the great executive functions which the constitution gave to the latter, namely, those of confirming appointments and of approving treaties.

# THE SENATE: ITS FUNCTIONS

The idea of vesting executive functions to any extent in the upper chamber of Congress came, no doubt, from colonial experience, for in several of the colonies the same body which advised the governor formed a branch of the legislature. On the whole this scheme had served with a reasonable degree of satisfaction because the governor's council in colonial days had given stability, character, and continuity to the whole administration. It was no great innovation, at any rate, to bestow upon the Senate some special functions of an executive nature.

The constitution provides that appointments made by the President shall be subject to the "advice and consent" of the Senate. The appointing power is one of the greatest of all executive functions, too portentous, it was felt, to be given without restraint to the President alone, lest he permanently intrench himself in office by filling the great offices of state with his own minions. Although the President is commonly spoken of as *appointing* a justice of the Supreme Court or an ambassador, his action in reality is merely that of *nominating*. When he desires to fill any office, the President sends a nomination to the Senate, and this nomination, after being announced, is referred to the appropriate committee. If it be the nomination of a federal judge, it goes to the judiciary committee; if that of an ambassador, to the committee on foreign relations. These committees may, and often do, assign such presidential nominations to special sub-committees for investigation as to the qualifications of the person nominated. If there are objections to the nominee, the committee or sub-committee hears such objections, and in due course a report, favorable or unfavorable, is made to the whole Senate. Then comes the vote to consent or to refuse consent. The Senate is not bound, of course, to follow the recommendations of its committees on such matters; but it does so except in unusual cases. If consent is refused, the same nomination may be submitted a second time, but this is not commonly done.

Rejections have not been uncommon, and they have at times developed considerable bitterness, but the vast majority of presidential nominations are confirmed with

*Special functions of the Senate: (1) the confirmation of appointments.*

little or no hesitation. Much depends, of course, upon whether the Senate contains a majority representing the same political party as the President, and the general temper of the Senate with reference to appointments has changed from time to time. It is now pretty well conceded, however, that the responsibility for selecting appointees rests, and was intended to rest, chiefly upon the President's shoulders and that the Senate should not impair this clear responsibility by insisting upon a share of the initiative. Hence the senators do not ordinarily reject nominations without good reason. A bare majority is needed to confirm nominations sent to the Senate by the President.

Recess appointments.

What happens if a post becomes vacant and the President desires to fill it when the Senate is not in session? In that case the President may make what is known as a "recess appointment." The recess appointee assumes office at once and holds it until the Senate has an opportunity to confirm him as the regular incumbent. If, however, the Senate declines to confirm him, he ceases to hold the office whenever the Senate's session comes to an end. Then, of course, the President can bestow upon the same individual another recess appointment if he chooses to do so. It has occasionally happened that by a succession of these recess appointments an office has been kept occupied, despite the non-concurrence of the Senate, for several years.

(2) the approval of treaties.

The second executive power shared by the Senate is that of approving treaties.[1] In dealing with this matter the framers of the constitution faced a dilemma. If they gave the President sole power to make treaties, they would endow him with the absolute control of foreign affairs including the power to make alliances, and they were not prepared to face public opinion with a proposal so startling. On the other hand, they realized that in the making of treaties, as John Jay phrased it, "perfect secrecy and immediate despatch are sometimes requisite." [2] And these requisites, it was easy to see, could scarcely be had if the President

---

[1] S. B. Crandall, *Treaties, Their Making and Enforcement* (2d ed., Washington, 1916), and C. H. Butler, *The Treaty Making Power of the United States* (N. Y., 1902).
[2] *The Federalist*, No. 64.

were forced to submit his negotiations, step by step, to any considerable body of men. In the end it was decided to take chances with the less dangerous of the two alternatives and to stipulate that the President should make treaties "with the advice and consent of the Senate, provided two-thirds of the senators concur."

In treaty negotiations, as in the selection of persons for appointment to office, the Senate's advice is not asked in any formal way, although on some occasions the President has sounded the Senate before actively beginning treaty negotiations. In any event a President rarely goes ahead and definitely concludes the terms of an important treaty without making sure of his ground. He is likely to keep in touch with the leaders of the Senate, especially with the chairman of its committee on foreign relations, and through them to ascertain in advance what the action of the Senate is likely to be on any treaty that may be framed. No President likes to carry treaty negotiations to a conclusion, only to have the Senate reject his work. When it is borne in mind, moreover, that two-thirds of the senators must give assent, the difficulty of securing this approval in all cases is by no means negligible. Hence the President is constrained to unfold his plans in part at least to influential senators, bearing in mind always that the Senate is very jealous of its share in the treaty-making prerogative and that a relatively small group of senators can completely spoil the fruit of his negotiations. While it is true that a President does not ask the Senate's advice, it is equally true that he cannot profitably ignore that body until the time comes to send the treaty to it for ratification. Many instances of this consultation and of its successful outcome might be given, and many illustrations, likewise, of the failure of a treaty to be ratified by reason of a President's disinclination to act in harmony with the ascertained convictions of Senate leaders. President Grant's treaty for the annexation of San Domingo in 1870 was rejected by the Senate because Charles Sumner, the chairman of the committee on foreign relations, fought it to defeat.

*How the President and the senators share this power.*

The negotiations which precede the making of a treaty with any foreign country are conducted on behalf of the

United States by the Department of State. This may be done either at Washington or at a foreign capital, the American ambassador or minister acting as intermediary in the latter case. After the general provisions have been informally agreed upon, the formal document is prepared and signed by diplomatic representatives of the countries concerned. At this stage the treaty goes to the Senate for approval. If approval is given, the treaty is formally ratified and goes into force, but if the Senate's approval is refused, the whole proceeding comes to naught. Every form of international agreement to which the United States is a party must be submitted to the Senate in this way.

A treaty, when duly approved and ratified, becomes, like the constitution, the supreme law of the land, "and the judges of every state are bound thereby, anything in the constitution or laws of any state to the contrary notwithstanding." No state may make a treaty nor may it enforce any law which contravenes the terms of a treaty made by the national government. The national government, moreover, may conclude treaties covering matters on which Congress would have no right to pass laws. The right of foreign citizens to acquire and hold property in the United States, for example, is a proper subject of a treaty provision, although the regulation of land-holding in any state does not come within the legislative jurisdiction of Congress. If a treaty and a state law or state constitution are in conflict, the treaty prevails. If, however, a treaty conflicts with a national law, whichever is later in time will control, and the same is true as between two conflicting treaties.

May the Senate amend a treaty laid before it by the President? It may, and sometimes has done so. In that event, however, the negotiations with the other country must be reopened in order that its consent to the amendments may be obtained. But it sometimes happens that the nature of the Senate's amendments precludes any such agreement altogether. Thus the general arbitration treaty of 1897 was thwarted by hostile amendments. Not only may the Senate amend a treaty, but it may by resolution, either of itself or jointly with the House of Representatives, request the President to open negotiations on any matter with a foreign power. The President is of course under no legal obligation to comply.

Strictly speaking, the House of Representatives has nothing to do with treaties, but occasions may arise in which action on its part is virtually necessary to give a treaty effect. No money can be appropriated for any purpose, no laws passed, no changes made in the tariff, for example, without affirmative action on the part of the House. Treaties sometimes include stipulations that money will be paid, or that reciprocity in tariff matters will be granted by the United States. The treaty with Russia whereby the United States purchased Alaska in 1867 is an example; likewise the treaty with Spain in 1898, which provided for the payment of twenty million dollars in connection with the transfer of the Philippine Islands. What if the House of Representatives had stood on its prerogative and refused to join in appropriating the money stipulated in the terms of these treaties? That is a very old constitutional question, for it was raised and discussed in connection with the Louisiana Purchase of 1803, and it has been debated several times since, but it is still an unanswered question because the House has, thus far, never failed to do its part. The House has on more than one occasion asserted its right to refuse, but it has made no actual refusal. The best legal opinion inclines to the view that while the refusal of the House to do its part in carrying out the provisions of a treaty after such agreement had been approved by the Senate and finally ratified would place the nation in an awkward predicament, it would none the less be within the constitutional privilege of the House to take that stand. *Relation of the House to treaties.*

It is often said that treaty-making arrangements such as exist in the United States would be intolerable in any European land. In England treaties are made by the Secretary of State for Foreign Affairs without the necessity of submitting them to any body outside the Cabinet. In the various countries of Continental Europe certain treaties must be submitted to the legislative chambers, but not the ones which require secrecy. Alliances and obligations of that nature have been made and assumed by the chief executive alone. Hence it is that in things of the *The treaty-making power and secret diplomacy.*

most transcendent importance, in things which are most likely either to bring on wars or to prevent them, the direct representatives of the people in European countries have had no immediate influence at all. Bismarck, the Iron Chancellor of the German Empire, once spoke of public opinion as "the great enemy of efficient diplomacy." If that be true, American diplomacy can never be very efficient, for public opinion must always be a controlling factor in it. From a European point of view the necessity of secrecy in the making of treaties has been taken for granted, and secret diplomacy has been the tap-root of that continent's overwhelming catastrophes. The men of 1787 were prudent in their day and prophets in their generation when they raised in the New World an insuperable barrier against anything of the sort. At times, no doubt, the requirement that treaties must go before the Senate has been a stumbling-block. It has occasionally prevented the President from making a good bargain. It has sometimes compelled him to enter a diplomatic tussle with one hand tied behind his back. When John Hay was Secretary of State, he fumed against it as the weakest feature of America's whole governmental scheme. But it has been on the whole a salutary provision. It has held rash Presidents in bounds. It has kept the nation on its course for one hundred and thirty years without a single entangling alliance. Of no other great country can that be said.

(3) the power to try impeachments.

The Senate, as the constitution declares, has "the sole power to try all impeachments." Several important questions arise with respect to the scope and incidents of this impeachment power. How did this process of impeachment originate? Why did the framers of the constitution establish it in the United States? Who may be impeached, for what offences, and what are the penalties in the event of conviction? Does the procedure in impeachments differ from that of an ordinary trial by jury? And to what extent has the impeaching power been used in the national government of this country?[1]

[1] One of the best general surveys of this whole subject is that contained in Roger Foster's *Commentaries on the Constitution of the United States* (Boston, 1895), pp. 505–632.

## THE SENATE: ITS FUNCTIONS

The impeachment is of English origin. It dates back into mediæval times, and for many centuries before the development of Cabinet responsibility it afforded the only means whereby any minister of the crown could be brought to account by the House of Commons. The Commons preferred the charges; the House of Lords heard the evidence and gave its decision. Many high executive officials who used their power oppressively were brought up with a sharp turn in this way. An impeachment, however, should be clearly distinguished from the enactment of a "bill of attainder," which was a way of condemning men to death by ordinary legislative process, without formulating any definite charges or giving them any form of trial. Bills of attainder are prohibited by the constitution of the United States, and they have long since become obsolete in England. The impeachment procedure, on the other hand, commended itself to the pioneers of the American political system as a necessary safeguard against the exercise of arbitrary power. They found difficulty, however, in determining just how the English impeachment system could best be adapted to the needs of a purely representative government. "A well-constituted court for the trial of impeachments," declared Hamilton, "is an object not more to be desired than difficult to be obtained in a government wholly elective. The subjects of its jurisdiction are those offences which proceed from the misconduct of public men, or, in other words, from the abuse or violation of some public trust. They are of a nature which may with peculiar propriety be denominated *political*, as they relate chiefly to injuries done to the society itself. The prosecution of them, for this reason, will seldom fail to agitate the passions of the whole community, and to divide it into parties more or less friendly or inimical to the accused. . . . In such cases there will always be the greatest danger that the decision will be regulated more by the comparative strength of parties, than by the real demonstrations of innocence or guilt." [1]

For this reason it was suggested that the impeachment power should be given to the Supreme Court, or to the

[1] *The Federalist*, No. 65.

Supreme Court and the Senate sitting together. But there were great practical objections to both these alternatives. Would it be wise, for example, to leave the duty of passing judgment upon the President to judges whom he had himself appointed? So the convention decided to follow the traditional English practice of allowing the lower house to prefer the charges and the upper house to determine them. Its members were well aware that this was by no means an ideal arrangement. But if mankind, as one of the delegates sagaciously expressed it, "were to agree upon no institution of government until every part of it had been adjusted to the most exact standard of perfection, society would soon become a general scene of anarchy, and the world a desert."

Who may be impeached? Who may be impeached? Only the "President, Vice-President, and all civil officers of the United States." The list of civil officers includes ambassadors, members of the cabinet, judges of all federal courts, even postmasters; but it does not include members of either branch of Congress, nor, of course, officials of the several states. Members of the Senate and the House may be expelled by a two-thirds vote of their respective chambers, but not impeached. They are not civil officers of the United States.[1] This was decided by the Senate in the famous Blount case (1797). Senators and representatives are responsible to the states and to the people of the states. State officers may only be impeached in their own states under such regulations as are provided in the state constitutions.

A civil officer of the United States is liable to be impeached for any offence committed while holding office even though he should resign his post before the impeachment proceedings begin. That was one of the points made clear in the Belknap case (1876). Military and naval officers are not liable to impeachment, but are subject to trial by court-martial.

The constitution also sets forth the offences for which

---

[1] Notice, in corroboration of this, the wording of another clause in the constitution (Article I, section vi), which provides that "no senator or representative shall, during the time for which he was elected, be appointed to *any civil office.*"

a civil officer of the United States may be impeached; **For what offences?** but it does not do this with unmistakable clearness. The grounds for impeachment, as therein stated, are "treason, bribery or other high crimes and misdemeanors." The first two words of this phrase are definite enough, but the remaining part of it is ambiguous and has given rise to some differences of opinion. In general, however, it is now understood that civil officials are not to be impeached except for offences of grave misconduct or malfeasance in office. Inefficiency or partisan favoritism or the abuse of an official's discretionary authority are not accounted grounds for impeachment although they may afford reason for an officer's removal by the President, except in the case of the judges.

When an officer is convicted by the Senate in an impeachment trial, he cannot be punished to any further extent than removal from office and disqualification from ever holding a federal position again. He cannot be put to death, imprisoned, or fined. But conviction upon impeachment does not prevent additional proceedings against an official in the ordinary courts of the land if he has committed an indictable offence, and such penalties may be imposed by these courts. A two-thirds vote of the Senate is necessary for a conviction, and no pardon from any human source is possible in the case of one convicted on impeachment. **The penalties.**

The procedure in impeachments may be briefly outlined.[1] First, the accusation is made by some member of the House of Representatives from the floor of that body. A committee of the House is then appointed to investigate the charges. If it finds that an impeachment should be proceeded with, the committee so reports to the House and the latter may vote to accept this recommendation. In this case the articles of impeachment are sent to the Senate. The Senate has no discretion as to whether it will accept these articles or not. It merely sets a date for the trial and furnishes the accused official with a copy of the charges preferred against him. In hearing an impeachment the Senate sits as a court, the senators being "placed on oath **The procedure.**

---

[1] Alex. Simpson, Jr., *A Treatise on Federal Impeachments* (Philadelphia, 1916).

or affirmation," as the constitution requires, before the proceedings begin. The Vice-President of the United States presides on this as on other occasions in the Senate, except when the articles of impeachment are directed against the President, in which case the Chief Justice of the Supreme Court presides. This provision is made for an obvious reason. The Vice-President would not be an appropriate presiding officer when the outcome of the trial might determine his own promotion to the presidency. In impeachments the usual rules of evidence are observed: the accused official is allowed to be heard in his own defence, he may summon witnesses and have his own counsel. The proceedings are public until the senators begin to vote upon a verdict. Scrupulous provision is therefore made for fairness and impartiality.

*Famous impeachments.* In all there have been nine federal impeachments, only two of which have come within the last forty years. Only three have resulted in convictions. The most notable cases were those of William Blount, senator from Tennessee, in 1797, Andrew Johnson, President of the United States, in 1868, and William W. Belknap, Secretary of *Blount.* War, in 1876, all of whom were acquitted. Senator Blount was charged with having a part in a conspiracy to stir up troubles in the Floridas and Louisiana, which at that time belonged to Spain. The Senate, after receiving the charges, expelled him from its membership, but refused to convict him on impeachment, holding that he was not a "civil officer *Belknap.* of the United States." Secretary Belknap was charged with the acceptance of bribes from an officer whom he had appointed to an Indian post-tradership. Belknap resigned before the impeachment proceedings began, and President Grant accepted his resignation. The point was raised that, being no longer the occupant of a civil office, the accused was now a private citizen and not subject to impeachment, but the Senate overruled this claim and proceeded with the impeachment. In the end Belknap was acquitted. The charges *Johnson.* against President Andrew Johnson in 1868 were eleven in all, most of them having to do with reputed violations of the Tenure of Office Act which Congress had passed over the President's veto in 1867. The trial was conducted during the month of March, 1868. At its conclusion the Senate voted thirty-five to nineteen for conviction, but this was one vote short of the required two-thirds. It was a close call. In the autumn after Johnson's acquittal the next presidential election took place, and the accession of Grant put an end to the highly strained relations which had existed between the executive and legislative branches of national government. The most recent instance of a federal impeachment occurred in 1912 when a judge of the short-lived federal Commerce Court was impeached. The charges related to the acceptance of bribes from litigants in his Court, railroad officials, and attorneys practising before him. In this case the accused was convicted and removed from office.[1]

An impeachment procedure is at best a cumbrous and costly proceeding. It is not a method to be used if there is any simpler way of securing an officer's dismissal. But in the case of judges, or of other civil officers whom the President may decline to dismiss, an impeachment is the only other way of securing involuntary removal. Of the nine impeachments, six have concerned members of the federal judiciary, and three of these ended in convictions.

The three special functions of the Senate, — confirmation of appointments, approval of treaties, and the trial of impeachments — have combined to give it dignity and prestige as well as power. The Senate, however, in addition to these special prerogatives, is a regular branch of Congress, sharing with the House of Representatives the function of making the federal laws. With one important exception its legislative authority is coördinate with that of the House. This exception relates to measures for raising the revenues, all of which, by the terms of the constitution, must "originate in the House of Representatives; but the Senate may propose or concur with amendments as on other bills." This devolution of the initiative upon the popular branch of Congress was one of the concessions made to larger states by the First Compromise. It was

*The authority of the Senate in legislation.*

*Money bills.*

---

[1] For data concerning these various impeachment trials see the *Cyclopedia of American Government* (edited by A. C. McLaughlin and Albert Bushnell Hart, 3 vols., N. Y., 1914), *passim*.

in imitation of the English parliamentary rule which, however, goes a good deal further, in that it gives the House of Commons the sole right to originate all money bills, whether relating to revenue or to expenditure.[1] In the United States the limitation upon the Senate's authority, as expressed in the constitution, has not proved to be of great importance, for the Senate can virtually initiate new revenue proposals under the guise of amendments. On the other hand, while the constitution of the United States is silent as to which chamber shall originate bills for spending money, thus creating the presumption that they may originate in either, the practice has been to leave this function wholly in the hands of the House. Usage has made this an unwritten law of the constitution.

*Legislative powers of the Senate and the House are substantially co-ordinate.*

In all other matters the powers of the two chambers, both by the constitution and by usage, are equal in scope. No bill can become a law without the Senate's approval. At various times and on various matters one chamber or the other may have the greater amount of legislative influence because of its better organization or stronger hold upon public opinion. The Senate, being the smaller and more wieldy body, usually has this advantage. If the two chambers fail to agree on any measure, one or the other must give way, or a compromise must be arranged by both receding in part. This is effected by means of a conference committee, representing both chambers, and made up of three members from each. In these compromises the Senate has the reputation of usually getting the better of the bargain. It is, for the most part, represented on conference committees by stronger personalities, and as a rule it gives its conferees a firmer degree of support. Senators, too, are more experienced legislators, on the average, than are the members of the House. Many of them have served terms in the lower chamber before being chosen to the Senate and have thereby acquired proficiency in all the subtleties of legislative practice. The older senators, who guide the upper chamber in its work, regard themselves as experts in the science of lawmaking, whereas the members of the House are to be reckoned rather as mere

*Disagreements between the two chambers — how settled.*

[1] See below, p. 306 *n.*

amateurs, serving a two-year term only. They are legislative birds of passage, as it were, who abide their destined hour and go their way. Even upon the President, as Woodrow Wilson remarks, the older members of the Senate look with "unmistakable condescension." If the Senate has at any time been an *imperium in imperio*, it is not that the constitution, laws, or usages of the land have made it so, but because it is a more compact body than the House, better organized, more tractable to leadership, and less subject to fluctuations of opinion.

# CHAPTER XII

## THE HOUSE OF REPRESENTATIVES: ITS COMPOSITION

*The "popular branch" of government.*

THE House of Representatives was intended to be a reformed and popularized House of Commons. It was designed to be a very different chamber from the Senate, in that it should represent not the states but the people of the states. In the original frame of government it was the only authority so constituted as to obtain its mandate directly from the people. The other agencies of the new government, the President and the Senate, were to be chosen by indirect election. Hence the House of Representatives was from the first designated as the "popular branch." It was assumed as a matter of course that any such body, directly elected, would be radical, impulsive, vacillating. The provisions relating to the organization and powers of the House were avowed concessions to the principles of democracy, made rather reluctantly by some members of the convention, but regarded by all as a practical necessity. To establish a government with no branch of it directly responsible to the people was out of the question. In all the colonies popular assemblies had grown up and all the states in 1787 had provided for at least one such body in their new legislatures. In view of the bitter protests which had been raised against taxation without representation in revolutionary days, moreover, the claim of the people to direct representation in that branch of Congress which was to have the initiative in taxation was one which could not well be denied.

*The basis of representation in the House.*

The constitution, accordingly, provided that "the House of Representatives shall be composed of members chosen every second year by the people of the several states." In accordance with the compromises which had been agreed upon, it was further stipulated, first, that the several states should be represented according to their respective populations, and, second, that in estimating this population all other than free white persons were to be counted on a three-fifths basis; in other words that negro slaves were to be counted at only sixty per cent of their numerical strength. The first House of Representatives was to have sixty-five members, distributed among the states in a way which was assumed to be roughly proportional, but a census was to be taken forthwith and a redistribution on a more accurate basis was to be arranged on these figures. Further provision was made that a similar redistricting should take place after every decennial census, but that the House should never contain more than one member for every thirty thousand population. No state, nevertheless, was ever to be left without at least one representative. Within these limits the size of the House is fixed by action of Congress.

As to who should have the right to vote at congressional elections, the framers of the constitution did not venture to decide. There were at the time the widest differences among the thirteen states in the matter of suffrage requirements, and it was not deemed advisable to impose upon any of them a general provision which might be out of accord with their own practice. Hence the convention gracefully evaded the difficult question by leaving it to be settled by the state constitutions. This, to be sure, was not the logical thing to do when so much care was being bestowed upon the proper adjustment of minor questions, for the suffrage is one of the fundamentals of free government. Yet it was the best of the practical alternatives. To have reduced the diverse requirements of the several states to one uniform rule would have satisfied nobody. To have left the matter open for Congress to settle would have vested in that body the power to create an oligarchy by law. Nor could the determination of the suffrage at congressional elections be left, without restriction, to the legislatures of the various states, for that would have made the federal House of Representatives too dependent upon the state legislatures when it was designed to be responsible to the

*Who vote at congressional elections?*

people alone. Hence the provision which was finally accepted seemed to the builders of the constitution "to be the best that lay within their option." Each state, accordingly, determines by its own constitution who may vote at elections held to choose "the most numerous branch" of its own state legislature. These same voters, whoever they may be, must receive the right to vote at congressional elections. On this local discretion, however, one important restriction is now imposed, namely, that there must be no exclusion of citizens from voting rights because of "race, color, or previous condition of servitude." This limitation is imposed by the Fifteenth Amendment. If any state withholds voting rights from any adult male citizen of the United States "except for participation in rebellion, or other crime," a reduction may be made in the congressional representation from such state. This provision, it may be added, has not been enforced.

*Citizenship and the right to vote are two different things.*

There is a clear distinction, as has been already pointed out, between *citizenship* and the *right to vote*.[1] In the popular mind the two things are often confused, but they rest upon entirely different legal foundations. Citizenship does not necessarily carry with it the right to vote, nor, on the other hand, is it always necessary for one to be a citizen in order to be a voter. Thousands of American citizens, women, residents of the District of Columbia, untaxed Indians, to give a few examples, have no right to vote, while there are thousands of voters who are not American citizens. There is no requirement that only citizens shall vote at national elections, and in several states of the Union a declaration of intention to become a citizen, which is something far short of actual citizenship, is all that is required. In a dozen or more states of the Union, moreover, women are permitted to vote for the election of congressmen; while in the remaining states they have not been given that privilege.

*One is a federal, the other a state matter.*

All this ought to impress upon the reader's mind the fact that citizenship is a matter of *federal* jurisdiction, while the suffrage, as the constitution now stands, is wholly a matter of *state* control. The national government determines

[1] See above, p. 78.

who may become citizens and under what conditions. Each state, on the other hand, determines by its constitution and laws who shall have the right to vote at all elections, whether national, state, or municipal, subject to the restrictions contained in the Fourteenth and Fifteenth Amendments. The constitution of the United States as has been already shown, does not treat the right to vote as an inalienable right like the right to freedom of speech or to trial by jury. It deals with it rather as a privilege which may, under certain broad restrictions, be given or denied, narrowed or widened, by the several states at their own discretion and upon considerations of expediency.

The result is that the suffrage requirements at congressional elections are not alike in any two states of the Union, or, if they are, the identity is by mere accident. Some states, as has been said, demand full citizenship; others only a declaration of intention to become a citizen. Some require a longer period of residence than others, the time ranging from three months to a year; a few exclude all persons who are unable to read and write. Some require that a voter shall be a taxpayer or at least shall have been assessed as a taxpayer. Most of the states exclude paupers, criminals, and idiots, with varying degrees of strictness, from their electoral lists. The most important difference of all is to be found, however, in the fact that some states have opened the suffrage to women while as yet the majority of the states have not done so. About the only requirement that seems to be uniform in every one of the states is the rule that a voter, whether male or female, must be at least twenty-one years of age.[1] *The actual suffrage requirements.*

No definition of American suffrage requirements can, therefore, be given in general terms. Manhood suffrage is not the rule, although it comes nearer to being the rule than the exception. Between the suffrage as it existed in 1787 and the suffrage as it exists to-day, however, there is a world of difference. The process of widening has gone a long way, not steadily, but by fits and starts. When the national constitution went into operation, property or *The gradual extension of the suffrage.*

---

[1] The detailed provisions relating to the suffrage in all the states may be found in the *Cyclopedia of American Government*, iii, pp. 449–456.

taxpaying qualifications for voting existed in most of the original states. The negroes, or, at any rate, the great majority of them, being in bondage, were not allowed to vote although they were counted on a sixty per cent basis in determining each state's quota of representatives in Congress. Women were nowhere entitled to a share in the elections. The potential voters formed but a small percentage of the adult population.[1] During the past one hundred and thirty years all this has changed. Beginning with the era of Jacksonian democracy the property qualification went overboard. The constitutional amendments of the reconstruction period forbade all suffrage discriminations against the negro and provided, moreover, that he should be counted at full value in determining the apportionment of representatives.[2] And finally, a generation or more later, came the extension of voting privileges to women, a movement which has been gaining impetus in recent years.

*How voters are registered.* Not only are the suffrage requirements different in the several states, but the machinery for registering or enrolling voters varies from place to place. The most common plan is to require every voter to present himself before a registrar or some similar official and there to take oath that he is qualified by citizenship, age, residence, and whatever else the laws of the state may demand. This registration takes place at designated places and on assigned dates some time in advance of each election, and from the registration books the voters' lists are compiled. Usually the same lists are used at all elections, whether presidential, congressional, state, or municipal, but this is not always the case. Occasionally it happens that a state allows women to vote at some elections but not at others; as, for example, in Illinois where they now have the suffrage at presidential but not at congressional elections. Ordinarily no one may vote whose name is not on the list as a qualified voter.

The constitution does not require that members of the federal House of Representatives shall be elected by con-

---

[1] A. E. McKinley, *Suffrage Franchise in the Thirteen English Colonies* (Philadelphia, 1905).
[2] See above, p. 79.

gressional districts or by secret ballot or in all states on the same day. But the federal statutes have now established these requirements. The district system is now universally used except in cases where a state legislature has neglected to make provision for a division or redivision into districts, in which case all the congressmen from such state are elected at large. This function of districting is devolved by Congress upon the legislatures of the several states, but there is no way of compelling a legislature to assume this duty. When a legislature proceeds, however, to the work of dividing the state into congressional districts, the only limitations imposed upon its discretion are that these districts must be approximately equal in population and must not be made up of scattered units of territory. All the territory within the limits of any congressional district must be contiguous.  *Congressional districts.*

The arranging of congressional districts, each of which elects one representative, is carried out as follows: After the national population has been ascertained by a decennial census, Congress by law fixes the number of members to be elected to the House of Representatives and then figures out the "ratio of representation" for the whole country; that is, the uniform quota of population which is entitled to elect one representative. This is done by dividing the total population by the number of members in the House. After the census of 1910 the size of the House was fixed at 435 and the ratio of representation was found to be somewhat above 200,000, since the total population of the country was 92,000,000 or thereabouts. The limit fixed by the constitution upon the size of the House is absurdly high, namely, that it shall not exceed one member for every thirty thousand population. Were this limit reached to-day, the national House of Representatives would have more than three thousand members. The country's population has grown, therefore, beyond the wildest anticipation of its Fathers. The exact size of the House is fixed every ten years far below the constitutional limit and at such a figure as Congress may determine. Under this arrangement the House has been steadily growing larger. In 1789 it started with only 65 members; in 1820 it had 213; in 1880  *How created.*  *The ratio of representation.*

the number had risen to 292; in 1900 it was 386, and it now stands at 435. It is, therefore, more than four times as large as the Senate. It is becoming so unwieldy, in fact, that the periodical increasing of its membership must before long come to an end.

*Apportioning representatives among the states.* Having found the ratio of representation to be 200,000 or thereabouts, it becomes a simple matter to determine how many representatives each state shall have. If Rhode Island has about six hundred thousand population, it gets three; while New York with ten millions of people would get fifty. But no state, however small its population, may ever be left without at least one representative. The constitution makes that rule. Four states, namely, Arizona, Delaware, Nevada, and Wyoming, would be without a single representative were it not for this provision, because the population in each is below the ratio. In the larger states considerable changes take place every ten years. Some gain rapidly; others stand still or even lose. Hence some receive additional representatives after every census, while others have their quotas reduced. This means that every ten years the congressional districts within each state must be mapped out anew, or, as it is commonly termed, a "redistricting" must take place.

*Principles on which districts are based* This work of redistricting a state, when it gains or loses representatives, is nominally performed by the state legislatures, but in reality the task is deputed in the first instance to a legislative committee appointed for this purpose. The recommendations of this committee then go before the legislature and are there acted upon. So far as practicable, an effort is made to respect local boundaries by placing a whole city or town in one congressional district, but at times it becomes necessary to place one part of a municipality in one congressional district, while the remaining part goes into another. In large cities it is thought desirable, also, to respect the ward boundaries, and in great rural areas the aim is to put whole counties into the same district wherever it is practicable to do so. To accomplish all these things and yet have districts approximately equal in population is sometimes quite a problem. The task of redistricting is one requiring careful study and absolute fairness.

Too often, unhappily, the work of redistricting a state is performed with neither care nor impartiality. State legislatures are partisan bodies, and so are their committees. Because of their partisanship the attempt is often made to so lay out the districts that the interests of the dominant political party may be served. This practice of "gerrymandering" is more than a century old; it took its name from Governor Elbridge Gerry of Massachusetts, who apparently sanctioned one of the first flagrant cases of partisan district-making in that state.[1] By adding one county and taking off another, by shaping the district in some unnatural way, so that in configuration its nearest resemblance may be to a lizard or a starfish, it is quite possible to make the area yield a comfortable majority for the candidate of the right political party. The hostile votes, on the other hand, can be "hived" or massed into a few districts which are likely to go to the opposition party in any event. The gerrymander has been a pernicious factor in American politics, but of late years popular sentiment has been developing against it. This resentment now reacts at times against the party which performs the work of redistricting in a way that is flagrantly unjust to its minority opponents.

*The practice of "gerrymandering."*

The congressional districts having been fixed, they remain unaltered for ten years, or until after the next decennial census. Each district elects one member of Congress every second year. Candidates are nominated as the laws of each state may provide. Some states still retain the district convention of party delegates as the nomination body, but the majority of the states have now provided for the

*Nominations and elections.*

---

[1] Mr. John Fiske has given the following account of the incident:
"In 1812, when Elbridge Gerry was governor of Massachusetts, the Republican legislature redistricted the districts in such wise that the shapes of the towns forming a single district in Essex county gave to the district a somewhat dragon-like contour. This was indicated upon a map of Massachusetts which Benjamin Russell, an ardent Federalist and editor of the 'Centinel,' hung up over his desk in his office. The celebrated painter, Gilbert Stuart, coming into the office one day and observing the uncouth figure, added with his pencil a head, wings, and claws, and exclaimed, 'That will do for a salamander!' 'Better say a Gerrymander!' growled the editor; and the outlandish name, thus duly coined, soon came into general currency."

nomination of candidates at a direct popular primary.[1] The change, it was thought, would bring forth candidates of a better type, but it has apparently wrought no great alteration in this respect. The elections are held throughout the country on the same day, namely, on the Tuesday following the first Monday of November in every alternate year.[2] The voting must be by secret ballot, but this does not preclude the use of voting machines. Usually candidates for other offices, state or national, are chosen at the same election and on the same ballot, the so-called Australian type of ballot being the one most commonly used.

*Contested elections and recounts.* When any dispute arises in connection with the result of the voting or the validity of the election, the House of Representatives is the deciding authority, having the sole power to declare which of the claimants is to be seated. The procedure in such cases is for the defeated candidate to serve notice upon the one who has been reported as elected, setting forth the grounds of his protest. To this the latter makes formal reply, and the papers are then transmitted to the Clerk of the House. The matter is then referred to one of the committees on elections, of which the House maintains three, and this committee hears the evidence in the case. When this is concluded, the committee reports to the House, where its recommendation is almost invariably accepted. Contested elections are not common in the United States. The general tendency is to accept the results of the balloting as announced when the polls are closed. When the successful candidate's lead is very small, however, a recount of the votes is sometimes asked for and granted under such conditions as the state election laws provide.

*Qualifications of representatives.* The technical qualifications of a representative, as set forth in the constitution, are merely that he shall be a citizen of at least seven years' standing, at least twenty-five years of age, an inhabitant of the state from which he is elected, and not the holder of any federal office.[3] Nothing

[1] For an explanation, see below, pp. 418–419.

[2] A few states, Maine, for example, hold their elections earlier in the year.

[3] Even army and navy officers are regarded as coming within the scope of this prohibition.

# HOUSE OF REPRESENTATIVES: ITS COMPOSITION 185

is said about his being an inhabitant of the congressional district which elects him. Indeed, it is quite possible for a congressional district to elect a non-resident, and that has occasionally happened. But there is a strong prejudice against the outsider who ventures to seek the votes of any community in opposition to local candidates, and he is not likely to make much headway against it. Residence within the district is, therefore, an unwritten requirement. This is a matter in which American political usage differs greatly from that of England. In that country, the election of a non-resident to the House of Commons is not at all uncommon; on the contrary many of the political leaders represent districts (or constituencies) in which they do not reside and which they may rarely visit except on the eve of an election. The merit of the English practice is that it encourages a member of parliament to make his work appeal to more than a single district, to develop himself into a national figure. A strong man in English politics need never be without a seat in parliament; but the ablest statesman in the United States has practically no chance of a seat in Congress if his own home district should contain a majority of voters who belong to the opposite political party. *The unwritten law as to district residence. English and American usage on this point.*

The reasons for the American prejudice on this point are purely practical, and they have been summarized by Lord Bryce in a way which can hardly be improved upon. Local pride and jealousy, he points out, are factors. Members of the House of Representatives are reasonably well paid and every district has its own crop of payroll-patriots. They are ready to join in the hue and cry against the "carpet-bagger" who comes in from outside. Every district, moreover, wants a share in the annual appropriations for post-offices or for the improvement of rivers, harbors, or roads, and the general feeling is that a local man can best discern the local needs. Hence, although the constitution intends the House of Representatives to represent the people of states and not the people of districts, the unwritten rule as to district residence has narrowed the horizon of the members to the bounds of their own communities. *Why the American voter insists upon resident candidacies.*

All this suggests a query as to the proper function of a

popular representative, whether in Congress or in a state legislature or in any other elective body. Is it his duty to act in accordance with the dictates of his own judgment and in obedience to his own conception of the general welfare, regardless of whether this may reflect the opinion of his own particular district? Or, is the sole function of a representative to represent, in other words to discover, what his district desires and to be governed accordingly? These are fundamental questions of duty which every representative must face. A legislator may, for instance, be personally opposed to the use of the initiative and referendum as a method of making laws, and may sincerely believe this movement to be at variance with the best interests of the whole country. Yet if a majority of the voters in his own district be known to him to favor the initiative and referendum, how shall he vote upon the project in Congress or in the legislature? Shall he stultify his own judgment and convictions, or shall he disregard the logic of his own status as a popular representative? Is it conscience or constituents that should determine his vote?

*The logical function of a representative.*

*A concrete example.*

Congressmen are often confronted by this dilemma. Students of political philosophy, too, have long wrestled with the fundamental question but have reached no agreement upon it.[1] It may not be inappropriate to quote in this connection, however, the famous dictum of Edmund Burke in his address to the electors of Bristol when he defended certain unpopular votes which, as their representative, he had given in the House of Commons. "I maintained your interests against your opinions," he declared. "A representative worthy of you ought to be a person of stability. I am to look indeed to your opinions; but to such opinions as you and I must have five years hence. I am not to look to the flash of the day." The idea that a representative should reflect the sentiment and desires of his district rather than his own judgment or inclinations is, nevertheless, firmly bedded in the average American voter's mind.

*The dictum of Burke.*

[1] For a further discussion see J. W. Jenks, *Principles of Politics* (N. Y., 1909), pp. 76–80.

The House of Representatives holds one session each year, so that there are two regular sessions between elections. These two sessions, however, are not of equal length or importance. One is a short session, beginning in December and concluding not later than the following fourth of March; the other is a longer session, beginning in December of the year following and extending through July or August. The House assembles for its short session soon after the congressional elections take place in the even-numbered years; but the newly elected congressmen do not take their seats at this session because their terms of office do not officially begin until the following March. Hence it is normally thirteen months after his election before a new congressman actively begins his legislative duties. It is unfortunate enough that a new President, elected in November, should not take office till the following March, but that congressmen should not begin their actual service until still another nine months have passed seems to involve an inexcusable departure from the realities of representative government. It means that for thirteen months the business of legislation and the spending of public money may remain under the control of men who have been defeated at the polls. Large appropriations are sometimes carried through by the votes of congressmen who have been defeated for reëlection. Moreover, the present arrangement means that although a representative serves for two years only, the interval between the beginning of his campaign for a nomination and the close of his actual service in one Congress is almost four years, during all of which interval he must give a large part of his time to the public. To earn two years' salary requires nearly four years of effort. *Sessions of the House.*

*The long interval between a congressman's election and the beginning of his active duties.*

The two-year term for which representatives are elected is too short for the best results. Members of the popular chamber in every other country serve a longer period. The system of biennial elections was adopted in America at a time of strong partiality for short terms, and if some of the delegates in the constitutional convention of 1787 could have had their way, the congressional term would have been one year only. It is quite true that congressmen are frequently reëlected, and that some of them manage *Should congressmen be chosen for longer terms?*

to retain their seats for ten or twenty years; but that is exceptional. A great many are retired to private life after one or two terms, before they have had a real opportunity to demonstrate their capacity as legislators or even to acquire much familiarity with national problems. The frequency with which the elections come, moreover, is distracting in its effects. A congressman who manages to retain his seat has a double contest on his hands every second year, a fight with his political friends for the nomination and another with his political enemies for election. The political exigencies of his own district, therefore, are always before his eyes, and the opportunity to see national affairs in a broad light is correspondingly restricted.

<small>Effect of short terms upon congressional leadership.</small> The few members who manage to secure reëlection to Congress term after term become, therefore, its recognized leaders although they may not be fitted for that rôle by natural capacity. Seniority of service determines the chairmanships of important committees and gives to the few congressmen who have been repeatedly reëlected an influence which their own merits would never earn. No other practice, as Lord Bryce has pointed out, could more effectually discourage noble ambition or check the growth of a class of accomplished statesmen. There are few walks of life in which experience counts for more than in politics. No one comes to Congress with an intuitive knowledge of what to do. The new member is handicapped by the complexity of the rules and by a natural disinclination to push himself too far forward until he has acquired a sure footing. Far from making the House a democratic body, responsible to the fluctuating pulse of public opinion, the short term has in reality tended to centre its great powers in the hands of a few old-timers, while the great body of newer members have to be content with a minor share in the determination of legislative policy. The situation in this respect is not now so bad, however, as it was before the congressional revolution of 1910.[1]

The debates in the House of Representatives are not of a high order. Nor are they as good as they used to be. This is in part due, no doubt, to the great size

[1] See below, pp. 197–198.

of the chamber in which the sessions are held. Only a leather-lunged orator can make himself heard in every part of it. "It does not always happen that a powerful mind and a powerful voice are combined in the same individual, and often the member with the real message cannot be heard, while the member with nothing to say has no difficulty in filling the chamber with sound. . . . This condition tends to develop a manner of speaking that is gladiatorial and declamatory . . . and except on occasions much too rare the House does not strike the spectator in the gallery as an impressive body."[1] Prior to 1909 the situation was much worse, but since that time the auditorium has been reduced in size. The acoustic facilities of the House remain, however, the worst of any great legislative chamber in the world.

*The standards of debate in the House.*

*Chamber not well adapted to forensic argument.*

To some extent, again, the paucity of good speeches is due to strict limitation upon the time that any speaker may keep the floor, and something may be credited to the custom of allowing a member to have his speech printed in full without delivering it at all. Why should a representative make long speeches, or why should others listen to them, when it is so easy to place an argument in printed form, at the public expense, into the hands of every one? Members, therefore, ask for "leave to print" or to "extend in print" a few remarks made on the floor, and this request, while it must be unanimous under the rules, is usually granted. Copies of such speeches, printed without ever having been delivered, are then struck off by the thousand and sent through the mails, free of postage, to the voters of the districts from which the congressmen come. The "franking" privilege, or right to make free use of the mails for all official business, has been grossly abused in this way. Magazine articles and even whole books have sometimes been reprinted and distributed broadcast by congressmen at the public expense.

*It is easier to print speeches than to deliver them.*

These things contribute to the absence of much genuine oratorical effort in the House, but they do not account for it entirely. The stupendous mass of routine business which comes before the House day after day is the great deterrent

[1] S. W. McCall, *The Business of Congress* (N. Y., 1911), pp. 108–109.

*The pressure of routine business leaves little time for speechmaking.*

to prolonged deliberation. The merely mechanical work of putting the grist of bills through their various stages takes a great deal of time. The last Congress, at its two sessions, received more than twenty-six thousand bills, not to speak of joint resolutions, concurrent resolutions, and reports by the hundreds. Of this total the great majority never received any serious consideration, even by a sub-committee, but of those which did receive consideration about seven hundred public bills and seven thousand private bills were finally passed. If there were an earnest consideration of every measure, the House would never get its work done by sitting twenty-four hours throughout every day in the year. Routine business, therefore, must have the right of way. Discussion has been transferred to the committee rooms, and it is only on matters of unusual importance that a real debate takes place on the floor of the House itself. Herein the popular branch of Congress differs greatly from the House of Commons, where the art of public discussion has not yet become wholly obsolete.

## CHAPTER XIII

THE HOUSE OF REPRESENTATIVES: ORGANIZATION AND PROCEDURE

WHEN a new House assembles, its first duty is that of organizing. The roll is called to determine the presence of a constitutional quorum. During this proceeding the clerk of the last House presides. Then the election of a Speaker is in order. The House also chooses its other officers, including the chaplain, sergeant-at-arms, clerk, and doorkeepers. The rules, usually those of the presiding Congress, are then provisionally adopted to stand until altered; the oath is administered to the members, and the House is then ready to proceed with the business of legislation. At this point the lower chamber joins with the Senate in sending a committee to notify the President that both bodies are ready to receive any communication he may desire to make. *How the House organizes.*

The House of Representatives has full power over its own rules of procedure. The first House, in 1789, adopted a set of rules based largely upon those which had been used in the Congress of the Confederation. These, again, had been modelled on the rules of the colonial assemblies which harked back to the procedure of the English House of Commons. Each succeeding House since 1789 has re-adopted these original rules with various changes from time to time. On a few occasions there has been a considerable revision, but many of the provisions which were adopted in 1789 remain substantially unaltered at the present time. The rules of Congress, therefore, are not the work of any one man. They are an evolution, the growth of many centuries of legislative experience. Some of them, as, for example, the provision that a bill shall be given three read- *The House rules.*

ings, go back a long way in English parliamentary history. In 1837 the House adopted a provision, which is still in force, that it should be guided by Jefferson's famous parliamentary manual in all matters not covered by its own rules and not inconsistent therewith, but this compendium is not now referred to very frequently.[1] The House rules and the precedents cover practically everything that can possibly arise.[2]

*The Speaker.*

*Origin of his office.*

The Speaker is the presiding officer. The men who framed the constitution decided without much argument that the House should have such an official, chosen by itself, thus perpetuating in the New World a post that had acquired a tradition of democracy in the Old. In English parliamentary annals the Speaker had more than once stood forth as the tribune of the people, defying the arbitrary authority of the crown. On one occasion well known to students of English constitutional history, for example, Charles I strode into the House of Commons with a body of soldiers to seize five of its members and demanded that the Speaker point them out to him. But the Speaker with unconquerable self-assertion merely replied that he had "neither eyes to see nor tongue to speak save only as this House shall command."[3] The speakership was in due course transplanted to the colonial assemblies in America, and here also its tradition continued good. So there was written into the constitution of the United States a provision that "the House of Representatives shall choose their own Speaker."

*Attributes of the Speaker's office in England.*

But the office of Speaker in America presently came to differ from that which had so long existed in the land of its origin. In the House of Commons the Speaker is and always has been a mere presiding officer, with no powers except those which one ordinarily associates with the chair-

---

[1] S. W. McCall, *The Business of Congress* (N. Y., 1911), p. 33.

[2] These precedents have been brought together in Asher C. Hinds, *Precedents of the House of Representatives of the United States* (8 vols., Washington, 1907–1908), published also as House Document, No. 355, 59th Congress, 2d Session.

[3] Josiah Royce, in his *Philosophy of Loyalty* (N. Y., 1909), cites this incident as a conspicuous historical example of loyalty to a cause (pp. 102–107).

manship of any gathering. He has a few honorary functions and privileges, but they are of no political account. Usually he is a man of political distinction and long parliamentary service, but not one who has been overmuch in the public eye as a party leader. Above all things, he is expected to be fair, tactful, and firm in the discharge of his duties, and absolutely neutral, never giving members of his own party an obvious preference nor allowing himself to be drawn into the thick of partisan controversy. The English Speaker is commonly reëlected by his constituency to successive parliaments without opposition and often serves for a long term of years despite changes in the political complexion of the House. He appoints no committees, and his position is certainly not one of either open or covert leadership. His position, in fact, comes as close to absolute non-partisanship as is possible in any legislative body.[1]

In the colonial assemblies of pre-Revolutionary America the office of Speaker soon began to show the effects of a new environment, particularly as political controversies grew acute. Men like Otis and Randolph, who served as speakers in Massachusetts and Virginia, could not constrain themselves to any attitude of scrupulous neutrality. In the days of passive resistance they perforce assumed the function of active leadership. Whether the makers of the constitution, when they gave the House of Representatives the right to choose its own Speaker, had in mind the English or the colonial model is not easy to say, for they were quite familiar with both. They were also familiar with the position held by the presiding officer of the Congress under the Articles of Confederation. In the absence of an independent executive this personage had been the highest officer of the confederated government. At any rate the constitution places no restrictions upon the office, and in the course of time the Speaker of the House began to gather power into his own hands. Ultimately he became the most powerful figure in national administration, next to the President himself.[2]

*Development of the Speaker's office in America.*

---

[1] Michael McDonagh, *The Speaker of the House* (London, 1914).
[2] M. R. Follett, *The Speaker of the House of Representatives* (N. Y., 1909).

**Groundwork of the Speaker's powers.**

Why and how did this development take place? Well, to begin with, it arose out of the fact that the constitution provided the House with no official leadership. Apparently the statesmen of 1787 took it for granted that both Houses of Congress would be able to do their work smoothly without any official leadership, a strange assumption as it appears at this day. The House was a small body to start with; at first it had only sixty-five members, or about two-thirds of the Senate's present membership. But it grew rapidly with the increase of national population. In twenty years it had doubled in size, and before the Civil War it had doubled again. Even then it had only about two hundred and forty members, to which it has since added nearly two hundred more. With this growth, and with the increase of business to be done at every session, the need of a steering hand became steadily more urgent. This function could not, as in England, devolve upon members of the Cabinet because they did not possess seats in the House. What more natural, therefore, than its gravitation into the hands of the Speaker as the only conspicuous officer provided by the constitution to be chosen by the House itself? That, at any rate, is what happened. The Speaker became the recognized leader of the majority party, chosen virtually by the caucus of that party, and one who could be depended upon to use his office for its benefit.

**How the Speaker is chosen.**

A word as to this caucus method of selecting the Speaker. In name the choice is always made by the House itself at the beginning of each Congress, that is, every second year. In practice, however, it is always agreed upon, before the House meets, by a caucus composed of members of the majority party. To be chosen speaker is a high honor, one which goes only to a man of considerable experience in Congress and of undoubted prominence in his party. If a change takes place in the relative strength of the parties as the result of an election, the next Speaker is altogether likely to be the man who served as leader of his party when it was in the minority. The caucus makes the choice and the House merely ratifies it.

The powers of the Speaker have been developed from three sources: first, his formal authority as a presiding officer;

second, his function of appointing committees;[1] and third, his position as a party leader.  Only the first of these is implied in the constitution; the others have come to him either by the rules of the House itself or by usage.

*Sources of his authority.*

Except when the House is sitting in Committee of the Whole, the Speaker is in the chair.  He has the customary prerogatives of a presiding officer; he recognizes members wishing to speak or make motions, decides all points of order subject to overruling decisions which may be made by a majority of the House, puts questions to a vote, announces the result, and so on.  The power to recognize one member rather than another is one which can be used to some extent for partisan advantage, although the Speaker is accustomed to observe certain long-standing usages of the House in relation to this matter.  Members who desire to be heard rise in their places and address the presiding officer as "Mr. Speaker."  The Speaker, turning to the member whom he decides to recognize, asks, "For what purpose does the gentleman rise?"  After being thus recognized, a member may be interrupted by any other representative and asked to "yield the floor" in order that some explanation or brief interpolation may be made.  This the member having the floor may do or not as he chooses, but the usual practice is to yield when requested.

*The Speaker's powers: 1. As a presiding officer.*

*(a) the right to recognize members.*

The Speaker may himself take the floor, and occasionally does so.  In such case he calls some member to take the chair temporarily.  Likewise he has a vote on all questions and not merely in the event of a tie, as is the case with the Vice-President of the United States who presides in the Senate.  By becoming Speaker he loses none of his rights or privileges as a member.  Having once voted on a question, he may not, however, vote again to break a tie.  In the case of a tie, if the Speaker has voted, the motion is deemed to be defeated.

The Speaker's right to determine, in the first instance, all points of order, procedure, or privilege gives him the opportunity to help his own party or to embarrass its opponents.  His discretion in this field is by no means unrestrained,

*(b) the right to rule on points of order.*

---

[1] This branch of his authority has now been largely taken away.  See below, p. 197.

however. The rules of the House on many matters are plain, and the Speaker has no authority to set them aside. The rulings made by previous speakers, especially when these have been long acquiesced in, are also regarded as binding; although on occasions a Speaker has had the hardihood to set one of these rulings aside and to establish a new precedent.

*Limitations on this right.*

The most notable example of this precedent-breaking, and the one most commonly cited, is a ruling once made by Speaker Thomas B. Reed with reference to what constitutes a quorum of the House. The constitution prescribes that "a majority shall constitute a quorum to do business," but does this mean that a majority of the House must be recorded as voting on a measure or merely that a majority of the members must be present, whether voting or not? For more than a hundred years the former interpretation was accepted and a quorum was not deemed to be present unless the roll-call showed a majority of the entire membership to be recorded either for or against a measure. This repeatedly led to the blocking of business by members of the minority party who, although in their seats, would concertedly refrain from voting and thus prevent the official record from showing the presence of a quorum. In 1890, Speaker Reed directed that the names of all those present but not voting should be added to the record and that if the total should prove to be a majority of the entire membership, the House should be deemed to have a quorum. Although this new ruling was bitterly attacked as unconstitutional the Supreme Court later upheld it and it is the rule to-day.

*The Speaker is not rigidly bound by precedents.*

This instance has been mentioned because it involved an exceptional exercise of the Speaker's authority to rule on a point of order in defiance of the established precedents. Controversies concerning procedure come up frequently, but the Speaker has an ample store of precedents to which he can refer for guidance. Where there is no precedent, he usually follows the general rules of parliamentary practice. Yet despite restrictions the Speaker retains a considerable amount of discretion which he may use to the advantage of his own political friends in the House. On occasions

*His authority on points of order is always subject to the control of the House itself.*

this power has been used ruthlessly, to the point of causing an open revolt on the part of the minority; but surveying congressional history as a whole it cannot be said that the Speakers have abused it badly. There is no Speaker's ruling, moreover, which cannot be set aside by a majority of the House. When, therefore, a Speaker is permitted to be an avowed partisan, the dominant party must share the responsibility.

For a long period the power upon which the Speaker chiefly relied as a means of guiding legislation was the right to appoint all committees. This authority was cut to pieces during the congressional revolution of 1910–1911, but for many decades prior to that time it was a source of great prestige and influence. It enabled the Speaker to organize all the important committees of the House in such way that he and his party were maintained in absolute control of legislation at every stage. True, the Speaker deferred in most cases to the advice of the party leaders and to the decisions of party caucuses, but his own hand was always firmly on the tiller. He became in newspaper parlance the "Czar of the House." Loud murmurs were heard from time to time against this virtual dictatorship, as wielded by a succession of strong willed Speakers such as James G. Blaine, Samuel J. Randall, John G. Carlisle, Thomas B. Reed, and Joseph G. Cannon; but it was not until 1910–1911 that strong-headedness in the Speaker's chair induced a successful revolt against the old arrangement.

*2. The right to appoint committees.*

To understand this important change in the Speaker's authority, however, it is necessary to know something about the influential part which had been assumed during the years preceding 1910 by one small committee of five members, the Committee on Rules. Originally the only function of this committee, with the Speaker himself as chairman, was to prepare and to recommend a set of rules for the House at the beginning of each Congress. These rules, which were usually not much more than a repetition of the ones used by the preceding Congress, served for the guidance of business throughout the sessions. Thus the Committee on Rules was in its origin a special or select committee; but in 1880 it became a regular or standing

*Special influence of the Speaker as chairman of the Committee on Rules.*

committee with the function of considering and reporting upon any proposed changes in the rules which might be made during the sessions. Finally, in 1891, it was given the right to report a new rule at any time or for any purpose, thus enabling it to intervene and cut a knot whenever business in the House should become tangled. Out of this authorization the Committee on Rules, with the Speaker as its chairman and dominating spirit, steadily developed a preponderating influence, amounting at times to a practical control over legislation. With the Committee on Rules ready to do his bidding and a majority of the House on his side, the Speaker could secure at any time the adoption of a special rule to advance measures which he favored or, on the other hand, to retard measures which he opposed. The "grand remonstrance" of 1910 took from the Speaker the power to appoint this Committee on Rules, increased its membership from five to ten, and made the Speaker ineligible to a place on it. In the following year the House went a step further and made provision that all other committees should likewise be chosen by itself.

The "revolution of 1910–1911."

3. The Speaker as a party leader.

The House of Representatives is an organ, not of popular government merely, but of party government. The Speaker is the choice of the majority party; he is the party's mentor. It is upon him that the party depends to get its programme through. "The power to govern, the power to act or to force action when the House desires, and thus to set aside obstructions and suppress those who would prevent the action of the House, — this power must be lodged centrally somewhere. In England it is in the Cabinet, that is the central guiding committee who manage the business of government." [1] In the House of Representatives it is the Speaker and his fellow party leaders who perform this function. The real question, therefore, is not whether a certain measure can worm its way through the House if it gets a chance. It is rather the question whether the Speaker and the other leaders of the majority party ought to give it a chance. As the recognized head of his party in the House the Speaker must be to some extent a legislative censor, but

[1] J. A. Woodburn, *The American Republic* (2d ed., N. Y., 1916), p. 269.

let it not be forgotten that two things have combined to make him so: first, the omission in the constitution of any provision for official legislative leadership, and, second, the development of party responsibility for legislation. Two things, indeed, there must be in every well-ordered government, leadership and responsibility. The constitution did not provide a means of supplying them, hence usage has stepped in to fill the void.

So much for the Speaker. It is next appropriate to say something about the committees of the House, their organization and the work which they do, for most of the real legislative work is done by them.[1] There are now fifty-eight regular or standing committees of the House, but at least half of them have practically nothing to do. These inactive committees are maintained year after year because the chairmanship of a committee, however unimportant, carries with it certain perquisites, including an office and stenographic service.[2] Out of the entire fifty-eight committees not more than a dozen are of consistent importance, while perhaps a half dozen more have substantial work to do on infrequent occasions. The most important committees are those on Appropriations, Ways and Means, Rules, Interstate and Foreign Commerce, Judiciary, Post Offices and Post Roads, Military Affairs, Naval Affairs, and Agriculture. The temporary prominence of some particular issue may give some other committee a fleeting importance, but when the agitation has subsided, the committee again lapses into innocuous desuetude. In addition to its standing or regular committees, the House may also establish special or select committees to deal with any particular matter which may arise from time to time outside the ordinary run of business. When standing and special committees are appointed, the member whose name appears first on the list is chairman and presides at all committee meetings. The rank of the other members of each committee is also determined by the order in which their names appear on the committee rolls.

*The committees of the House.*

[1] L. G. McConachie, *Congressional Committees* (N. Y., 1898).
[2] For example the Committee on the Disposition of Useless Papers, the Committee on Mileage, etc.

**Committee of the Whole.** Mention should also be made of one other congressional institution, the Committee of the Whole. This is merely the entire membership of the House sitting as a great committee. There are several important differences, however, between the House in Committee of the Whole and in regular session. In Committee of the Whole the Speaker does not preside, but calls upon some member to act as chairman; the strict rules of procedure do not apply; one hundred members make a quorum; there are no roll-calls on any measure under consideration — in a word the arrangement enables the House to deliberate informally. Large use is made of this facility, and the House probably sits a larger number of hours in Committee of the Whole than in regular session.

**How places on committees are assigned.** Places upon important standing committees are much sought after. What factors determine who shall get the most coveted assignments? Length of service counts for a great deal, more than any other single factor. Places on important committees naturally go to congressmen of experience, not to new members. The chairmanships go to the leaders of the majority party; indeed it is sometimes said that the chairmen of the chief committees form the closest American analogy to the "members of the government" in the House of Commons. The chairman of each committee is selected as a rule from among those who have in previous years served as members of that committee. The senior or "ranking" member is next in line for promotion, provided, of course, that his party continues in control of the House. So, also, members of minor committees, after doing good service in one Congress, if reëlected, are deemed entitled to promotion in the next. A member's own personal preferences are also ascertained and, so far as practicable, respected.

**The mechanism by which assignments are made.** Subject to these general principles, then, this is what now happens: first of all, the members of the House, each in their own party caucus, select the Committee on Ways and Means. The majority party selects fourteen members of this committee, while the minority chooses seven. This Committee on Ways and Means then presents for adoption by the House a slate of all the other committees. On every

Committee the dominant party is invariably given a majority. When the slate is presented, the House usually accepts it without any material change, and the committees so constituted remain intact until the end of that Congress, in other words during two sessions.

So far as the actual composition of committees is concerned, too much weight must not be attached to the changes of 1910–1911. It is true that these changes impaired the Speaker's authority considerably, but in the main the members of the House get just about the same committee assignments to-day that they would have obtained before the change was made. Length of service, personal ability, amenability to party discipline, willingness to work harmoniously with others — these things rather than the vagaries of either Speakers or caucuses have always determined and are always likely to determine whether a congressman will be placed high up or low down on the list, no matter what the rules may provide. In that respect Congress is no different from any other body of sensible men. *Service and merit the chief factors.*

The functions and powers of the committees may best be made clear, perhaps, by a brief explanation of the way in which bills are dealt with, step by step. In the first place any member of the House may present a bill or draft of a proposed law. It may be one that he himself has prepared and favors, or it may be one that any outside individual or organization has asked him to introduce. The procedure is simplicity itself; the congressman merely writes his name on the bill and places it in a box at the clerk's desk. Thousands of bills are put in during the opening days of each session. This freedom with which bills may be introduced has both good and bad features. It gives reality to the citizen's constitutional right of petition and perhaps encourages the putting forth of new legislative ideas. On the other hand, it permits Congress to be deluged with all manner of eccentric proposals which have no chance whatever of being adopted. *Work of the committees: 1. How bills are introduced.*

Presently all these bills are sorted out and are referred, under the rules of the House, to appropriate committees. If there is any doubt as to what committee should have a particular bill, the Speaker decides. If a measure is of *2. Reference of bills to committees.*

great importance, the committee to which it is referred may assign it for preliminary consideration to a sub-committee. The work of these sub-committees has become increasingly important in recent years and in many cases the real work of getting measures in shape for presentation to Congress is performed by them. Committee proceedings are usually public, but executive sessions may be held when desired. In any case the committee or sub-committee will hear all who want to be heard either for or against the bill. This is done as a matter of courtesy, not of constitutional or legal right; but the opportunity to be heard is practically never denied to any one. If many persons desire to appear before the committee, the hearings may last, day after day, for weeks. Committees usually sit in the forenoon, and no committee, except the Committee on Rules, may hold meetings while the House is in session unless it secures special permission from the House itself. During these hearings a record of the proceedings is kept by the clerk of each committee. When a hearing is finished, the committee decides, either at once or on a later day, what report, if any, it will make to the House on the measure.

Several courses are open to any committee with reference to a bill which it has had under consideration. It may favorably report a bill just as it stands. In that case the measure will have, under ordinary conditions, a good chance of passing, especially if the favorable recommendation of the committee is made unanimously. Or, again, the committee may approve the bill in some points but not in others. In that case it may redraft the measure and report it favorably in a new form. Here too the chances of passage are good. When a favorable report is made upon any measure, either in its original or revised form, the report goes to the Clerk of the House, who enters it upon the journal, and in due course it is set upon one of the calendars for a first reading. Certain committees have the privilege of reporting at any time directly from the floor of the House, although this is now not usually done.

But in the great majority of cases the committee will not be favorably impressed with the measure at all, in which

# ORGANIZATION AND PROCEDURE

case it usually makes no report whatever. Over twenty thousand bills are introduced at each session of Congress, but the great majority of these have not the slightest chance of ever "coming out of committee." The simplest way to kill any proposal is, therefore, to have a committee refrain from reporting it, because no bill can be acted upon by the House until a committee sends it up. Since 1910 it has been possible, in certain cases, for the House to call up a bill from the hands of a committee and proceed to action upon it; but this is very rarely done. While favorable action by a committee does not, therefore, mean that a bill is assured of passage, adverse action, which is no action at all, is automatic execution. Most bills are guillotined by committees, as indeed they ought to be. The committees of Congress are, therefore, the great sifters of legislative proposals. Without them the introduction of bills would have to be rigidly limited or the whole mechanism of law-making would soon become hopelessly clogged.

When a measure is reported to the House by a committee, it is placed on one of the calendars so that it will be given its various readings and voted upon. There are three calendars. One of them, known as the Union Calendar,[1] contains all favorably reported measures relating to revenue, appropriations, and public property. A second, called the House Calendar, includes all public bills not included in the foregoing category. The third, known as the Calendar of the Committee of the Whole, or the Private Calendar, makes a place for all measures of a private character. Matters on each calendar are not necessarily, or even usually, taken up in order; they may be called up out of turn.

*Procedure in the House:*
*1. The calendars.*

At every daily session there is a "morning hour," so-called (it may be an hour or a whole day), for the consideration of general bills called up from one of the calendars by committees which have favorably reported upon them. Then, if time permits, the House goes into Committee of the Whole to discuss revenue or appropriation bills, or, failing these, some other public bills on the House Calendar. The regu-

*2. Calling up bills.*

---

[1] Its full title is "Calendar of the Whole House on the State of the Union."

lar order of business is frequently interrupted, however, by reports from privileged committees, by the established practice of setting aside certain days each month for the consideration of particular matters, or by the discussion of business brought in under a suspension of the rules which the House can authorize at any time by a two-thirds vote. It is desirable, moreover, that important measures, usually those which provide money for urgent purposes, may on necessary occasions gain the right of way, and this is secured by the action of the Committee on Rules, which may report a special rule putting such bills ahead of other business.

3. The three readings.

Every bill, of whatever sort, must have three readings in the House. The first reading is by title only; the second is a reading of the whole measure, and at this stage amendments may be offered; the third reading is also by title unless some member requests that it be again read in full, which hardly ever happens. If the measure passes to its third reading, it is engrossed and must go through a further formal stage of being finally passed by the House before it is sent to the Senate for concurrence. Four methods of voting are used. The common plan is by *viva voce* vote. Any member may doubt the result and call for a rising vote. If a certain number of members so demand, the vote is again taken by tellers who are appointed by the Speaker. The members pass between the tellers and are counted. Finally, the constitution provides that if one-fifth of the members ask for it, the ayes and nays shall be recorded. A roll-call must always take place when the passing of any measure over the President's veto is being decided.

The debate on a bill almost invariably takes place upon the question of ordering it to a third reading, although it sometimes continues upon the question of final passage. Reconsideration may also be asked for after the House has voted at either of these stages. When the measure succeeds in running this entire gantlet of readings and votes, it does not become a law, of course, but merely goes to the Senate, where substantially a similar course of procedure is encountered.

4. The debate.

When a bill is reached on one of the House calendars or is called up out of turn, the usual practice is for the chairman or some other member of the committee which has reported it favorably to open the debate. If the favorable report has not been made unanimously, some minority member of the committee then follows with a speech in opposition. When members of the committee have had their say, other congressmen are recognized in their turn, and thus the debate runs on. No member may address the House for more than one hour without unanimous consent, and when the House is in Committee of the Whole, speeches are limited to five minutes only. If there is any likelihood of a long debate, it is customary for the House, by unanimous consent at the beginning of the discussion, to fix a time at which a vote will be taken. The previous question may also be moved at any time as a means of bringing a debate to a close. The best discussions do not take place when the House is in regular session, but in Committee of the Whole, under the five minute rule. This is because short, snappy speeches, with members answering quickly the arguments of each other, hold the attention of the House, while long and carefully prepared addresses do not.

When the House has finished with a measure, it goes, as has been said, to the upper chamber. What may the Senate do with it? It may do any one of three things: It may pass the measure without change. It may defeat it or let it die in committee. Or it may pass the measure after making some amendments. In this last case the bill must come back to the House for a vote on the amendments; if the House accepts them, well and good, but if it declines to accept the Senate's amendments, the usual plan is to ask for a Committee of Conference. This is usually made up of three members from each chamber, and its function is to reach some agreement by way of compromise. Conference committees meet behind closed doors, and the matters dealt with are only those upon which the two Houses have failed to agree. The committee is not supposed to touch provisions which have been accepted by both. As a rule the conferees from each chamber make mutual concessions and in that way secure a meeting of minds. If the committee can reach an agreement, the two Houses usually accept their recommendation; if they cannot agree, the measure fails. Noth-

*Bills sent to the Senate for concurrence.*

*Conference committees.*

ing can become a law unless both Houses have concurred on every point.

<small>The final steps in congressional legislation.</small>
When a bill has passed its various stages in both chambers, it is "enrolled" or written on parchment. It is then signed by the Speaker of the House and the presiding officer of the Senate, after which it is laid before the President for his approval or veto. If signed by the President, it goes to the archives of the State Department and in due course is published in the statute book.

The powers of the House and the Senate in law-making are exactly the same, save for the exceptions already noted, namely, that the House has by constitutional provision the sole right to originate bills for raising revenue, and by usage it has acquired the exclusive power to initiate appropriations. But the Senate may amend bills of either sort, even to the extent of making practically new measures out of them.

<small>The House of Representatives compared with the House of Commons.</small>
Comparing the House of Representatives with the House of Commons, some striking similarities and contrasts come into view. Both do most of their work through committees, and the general procedure followed in the passing of measures is in both substantially alike. But in Congress no broad distinction is made between public and private bills. All are dealt with in the same way. In parliament there is a special procedure for private bills, that is, for those which concern only an individual or an organization or a locality, and which accordingly are not deemed to be of general importance. Relatively little time is devoted in the House of Commons to this category of measures, and hence more time is left for the consideration of general laws. This permits and encourages more discussion and debate in the English chamber. The great powers of Congress, again, are almost equally shared by the two chambers, while in parliament the lower chamber has long been dominant, and since 1911 it has become potentially supreme. The presence of executive officers in parliament and their absence in Congress is another striking difference and one which has far-reaching results upon the course of business. Finally, and perhaps most important of all, the members of the House of Commons and of the House of Representatives are alike ranged into two well-defined and relatively

permanent party divisions, one supporting and the other opposing the administration. It is this phenomenon more than any other that betrays the kinship of the two great English-speaking organs of popular government. It is this unified party system which differentiates them both from the parliaments of Continental Europe. The House of Representatives was created in conscious imitation of the House of Commons. In its traits and temperament, if not in its external features, it bears unmistakably the marks of its parentage.

# CHAPTER XIV

## THE GENERAL POWERS OF CONGRESS

*The law of legislative powers in the United States.*

THE Senate and the House of Representatives together constitute the Congress of the United States, which is the law-making department of the national government, the organ through which the people frame and declare the policies of the nation. But this power of the people to declare through their representatives in Congress the laws by which they wish to be governed is not an unlimited power. Unlimited power cannot be exercised by any arm of the national government, executive, legislative, or judicial, or even by all three acting together. Limitations there are to a greater extent than in any other country, and the greatest of these limitations upon the powers of Congress arises from the theory of the constitution itself.

*The powers of Congress are delegated powers.*

The constitution of the United States, as has been already shown, is a grant or delegation of powers. In that respect it differs from the constitutions of the several states, for in the latter all powers accrue as an incident of their original sovereignty. By the national constitution Congress gets only what is therein given; by the state constitutions every state legislature gets whatever is not expressly taken away. In the case of Congress the appropriate question is: Has the power been granted? In the case of a state legislature it is: Has the power been handed over to the national government, or limited, or withdrawn? This difference is of vital importance, so much so that even a repeated mention of its existence may be pardoned. Without having it constantly in mind there can be no proper understanding of the way in which Congress acts or of the limitations that surround its sphere of action. The government of the United States has no powers *ex proprio vigore*, none save such as are expressly or by reasonable implication conveyed to it by the terms of the constitution. The constitution is the source, and the sole source, of all its authority.

Never has this principle been more clearly or cogently stated than in the writings of Thomas Jefferson. "To take a single step beyond the boundaries thus specifically drawn around the powers of Congress," wrote the great Virginian, "is to take possession of a boundless field of power no longer susceptible of any definition. The government created by the constitution was not made the exclusive, or final, judge of the extent of the powers delegated; since that would have made its discretion and not the constitution the measure of its powers." This doctrine has been upheld by the Supreme Court for over one hundred years, and it is not now open to controversy. *Jefferson's statement of the matter.*

It is true that the doctrine of "inherent powers" has at various times been set forth as justifying the exercise by Congress of powers which the constitution does not either expressly or by implication convey; but that doctrine is not constitutionally sound. The Supreme Court, to be sure, has not been unequivocal in repudiating this theory that the national government possesses certain powers which are deducible from the simple fact of national sovereignty, and at times has used language which at least suggests that the theory has some color of validity. But the court has never yet justified any act of Congress on the ground of inherent powers. It has always found some warrant, either express or implied, in the constitution itself.[1] *The contrary doctrine of "inherent" powers.*

Until the several states accepted the Articles of Confederation each was sovereign and unrestricted in its freedom of action. Each was free to do as it pleased, to wage war or make peace independently if it so chose, to coin money, issue bills of credit, conclude treaties, establish a tariff, maintain its own postal service, even to set up a monarchy if it so desired.[2] But upon ratifying the Articles of Confed- *First step in the delegation of powers: the Articles of Confederation.*

---

[1] W. W. Willoughby, *Constitutional Law of the United States* (2 vols., N. Y., 1910), pp. 67–69.

[2] This, at any rate, is the author's conviction. For a statement of the evidence which leads to such conclusion, see Roger Foster, *Commentaries on the Constitution of the United States* (Boston, 1895), pp. 63–70. For a

P

eration during the years 1777 to 1781 each of the thirteen states gave up, in the general interest, a certain amount of this freedom. They all agreed, for example, that none would make treaties separately; they agreed to contribute men and money to the common cause when called upon by the Congress of the Confederation, to maintain a common postal service, and to do various other things together. But they still remained sovereign states, for these concessions, even when taken all together, were not a serious impairment of their sovereignty.[1]

*Second and final step in the delegation of powers: the Constitution.*

By accepting the constitution of 1787, however, the several states took a far more important step. They surrendered powers of greater variety and extent. The nature of the change was clearly expressed by Chief Justice Marshall in one of his great decisions: "It has been said that they (the states) were sovereigns, were completely independent, and were connected with each other only by a league. This is true. But when these allied sovereigns converted their league into a government, when they converted their congress of ambassadors, deputed to deliberate on their common concerns, and to recommend measures of general utility, into a legislature, empowered to enact laws on the most interesting subjects, the whole character in which the states appear underwent a change, the extent of which must be determined by a fair consideration of the instrument by which the change was effected."[2] They gave up, in fact, some of the most important prerogatives of sovereignty, and although we still speak of them as sovereign states, they are not in a strictly juristic sense entitled to be so termed. They are sovereign within their own residual sphere of action, and there alone.

*The delegation of powers was made in perpetuity.*

There is no denying that the states gave up large powers when they accepted the federal constitution. Did they, however, surrender these powers to the national government

contrary view, see Albert Bushnell Hart, *National Ideals Historically Traced* (N. Y., 1907), p. 136.

[1] "Each state retains its sovereignty, freedom, and independence, and every power, jurisdiction, and right which is not by this Confederation delegated to the United States in Congress assembled."—*Articles of Confederation*, Article ii.

[2] *Gibbons* vs. *Ogden*, 9 Wheaton, 1.

forever, or did each state impliedly reserve the right to resume them at some future time if circumstances should so dictate? That is a question which bulked large in American political controversy during the decades preceding the Civil War. Could a state, in other words, nullify a power given by the constitution to Congress by insisting upon its own interpretation as to what such power was meant to include? Could a state secede from the Union and thus resume its full sovereignty? These two questions, involving respectively the right of nullification and the right of secession, were eventually answered, not by political philosophers or jurists but by the logic of events.

South Carolina in 1832 asserted its famous policy of nullification based upon the contention that whenever Congress ventured to transcend the limits of power granted to it by the constitution, any state was at liberty to declare such action unauthorized and null. This doctrine found its protagonist in John C. Calhoun.[1] In his interpretation the constitution gave the various states a "negative power, the power of preventing or arresting the action of the government, be it called by what term it may — veto, interposition, nullification, check, or balance of power." Acting upon this conception of ultimate state sovereignty, South Carolina in 1832 attempted by ordinance to nullify certain acts of Congress. The federal authorities under President Jackson's sponsorship promptly took up this gage of battle, and in the end South Carolina receded from her position of defiance.

Nullification and its failure.

The question as to whether a state had the right not merely to refuse obedience to acts of Congress but to withdraw from the Union altogether and thus to repudiate the compact of 1787 came to the front in a much more serious form twenty or more years later. Threats of secession had been made by various states from time to time during the first half of the nineteenth century, but it was not until December 20, 1860, that any state took the actual step of seceding. On that date South Carolina once again took the initia-

Secession — a far more difficult problem.

[1] For a full statement of the doctrine, see his *State Papers on Nullification* (1834); also David F. Houston's *Critical Study of Nullification in South Carolina* (N. Y., 1896).

212    THE GOVERNMENT OF THE UNITED STATES

tive with the issue of a declaration that "the union now subsisting between South Carolina and other states under the name of the United States of America is hereby dissolved." Within a few months ten other southern states took similar action.

*Claims of the secessionists.*

The right to secede from the Union and thus to reacquire all the powers which had been surrendered to Congress in 1787 was based upon several contentions which need not be enumerated here. They may be epitomized in the claim that the constitution was nothing more than a treaty or compact among the states, and that the violation of its terms or spirit by some of the states freed the others from the obligation of being further bound by it.[1]

*The Civil War settled the question.*

During the years preceding the Civil War this question was discussed from many angles, but to no solution. Nor was it one that could be settled by any reference to clear understandings at the time the constitution was adopted. The constitution itself is silent on this point. Nothing was said about it in the convention of 1787 and practically nothing during the discussions while the campaign for ratification was under way. The matter was not then of immediate interest. So men argued bitterly about it, went to war over it, and finally settled it at Appomattox.

*Perpetual nature of the Union established.*

Since 1865, therefore, this stormy petrel of American politics has been at rest. No state has the right to take back any of the powers or functions which it agreed to give to the national government by the compact of 1787. These powers form the permanent endowment of Congress. They can be withdrawn in one way only, that is by the concurrence of three-fourths of the states as provided in the constitution.

*Summary of the constitutional bases of congressional powers.*

Three points, accordingly, are now well established in American constitutional jurisprudence. First, that the constitution is a grant or delegation of powers and that Congress has no lawmaking authority save as is therein conveyed; second, that within its own legislative sphere, as delimited by the constitution, the authority of Congress

---

[1] Jefferson Davis, President of the Confederacy, in his message to the Congress of the Confederate States (April 29, 1861) gave a full statement of the secessionist doctrine. This is elaborated in his *Rise and Fall of the Confederate Government* (N. Y., 1881), i, pp. 1–258.

is supreme; and, third, that no state has the right to nullify this supremacy by a refusal of obedience or to withdraw from the jurisdiction of the federal government.

Turning now to the actual powers of Congress, these may be classified in various ways. One method of classification is in accordance with the form in which they are granted, whether in express terms or by implication. Another is according to the degree of obligation imposed by various powers, in other words whether they are permissive or mandatory. Finally, and most significant, is the classification of the powers of Congress according to their scope, nature, and importance. {The classification of the powers of Congress.}

Does Congress possess only those powers which are granted by the constitution in express terms? Or does Congress also possess powers which, though not expressly granted, may be reasonably implied? This was a point of clash between the Federalists and the Anti-Federalists during the early years of the Union. Hamilton and the Federalists argued that there should be no strict construction of the constitution's terse phraseology, and that where an express power had been granted, this should be construed to carry with it any authority desired by Congress to make such power effective. "Is the end included within the expressed powers?" asked Hamilton. "If it is so included," he answered, "the means requisite and fairly applicable are constitutional." The Federalists thus related their contention chiefly to that clause of the constitution which confers on Congress the right "to make all laws which shall be necessary and proper for carrying into execution" the powers expressly granted. The Anti-Federalists took the opposite ground, maintaining that the long enumeration of express powers granted to Congress in the constitution was meant to be complete and that nothing should be added by implication. Between these divergent views the Supreme Court, in one of its notable decisions a century ago, took a stand which involved a near approach to the Federalist claim. "The sound construction of the constitution," said Chief Justice Marshall in this decision, "must allow to the national legislature that discretion with respect to the means by which the powers it confers are to be carried {Express and implied powers.}

into execution, which will enable that body to perform the high duties assigned to it in a manner most beneficial to the people. Let the end be legitimate, let it be within the scope of the constitution, and all means which are appropriate, which are plainly adapted to that end, and which are not prohibited but are consistent with the letter and spirit of the constitution are constitutional." [1] The doctrine of implied powers was thus given legal recognition, and it is now a well-established principle of American constitutional interpretation.

Scope of the "implied" powers.

Some of the most important functions which the federal government performs to-day have their basis in "implied" powers. The right of Congress to provide for the establishment and supervision of national banks, for example, is not an express power. It is implied, or at any rate has been held by the Supreme Court to be implied, in the express power "to borrow money on the credit of the United States." The right of Congress to authorize the enforcement of wheatless and meatless days in war-time or to compel the shutting down of stores and industries in order to conserve the fuel supply is nowhere expressly granted in the constitution. It is implied, however, in the express power "to raise and support armies." Nor, again, does the constitution expressly give Congress the right to own and operate railroads, yet this authority may be and doubtless is implied in the power "to establish post-offices and post-roads" or in the power to regulate commerce among the several states. The power to establish carries with it the power to maintain; and the power to regulate carries with it the authority to choose any agencies of regulation which are in fact adapted to the end in view.

Mandatory and permissive powers.

The powers of Congress, as expressly or by implication granted in the constitution, are for the most part permissive in character. That is to say, Congress may exercise them or may not as it sees fit. It may make use of them much, little, or not at all. The clause which provides that Congress "shall have power . . . to borrow money" does not, obviously, mean that Congress shall borrow money whether the country is in need of it or not. But on the other hand,

[1] *McCulloch* vs. *Maryland*, 4 Wheaton, 316.

## THE GENERAL POWERS OF CONGRESS

there are some powers which notwithstanding their permissive phraseology are mandatory in effect. Wherever, for example, some action on the part of Congress is necessary to make any provision of the constitution effective, it can hardly be maintained that the function of Congress is a discretionary one. To give an illustration: the constitution provides that the Supreme Court shall have appellate jurisdiction "under such regulations as Congress shall make." But if Congress should not make any regulations, the court would have no appellate jurisdiction at all and the entire judicial system would be dislocated. Again, the constitution provides for a re-apportionment of representatives after each decennial census, this census or enumeration to be taken in such manner as Congress shall by law direct. But if Congress should fail to provide the machinery and the money for taking the census, the re-apportionment prescribed by the constitution could not be made. Congress is, therefore, under constitutional obligation to make use of its powers in such cases. If it should decline to do so, however, there is no way of applying compulsion. The Supreme Court will not order Congress to pass a law. No judicial body in any country has power to compel the enactment of a law, no matter how remiss the legislature may be. The mandatory functions of Congress are unenforceable obligations, it is true, but obligations nevertheless.

Broadly speaking, all legislative powers are divided by the constitution into four groups. First, there are certain powers which are forbidden to be exercised either by Congress or by the state authorities. Second, there are various powers which are vested in Congress alone, to the exclusion of all state authority. Third, there are certain concurrent powers, which Congress and the state authorities may share, although the latter in case of conflict must give way to the former. And, finally, there are all the remaining powers of government forming the residuum which reverts to the states. *The four groups of powers provided for in the constitution.*

The powers prohibited either to Congress, or to the states, or to both, are of a considerable range. Some are powers which no free government ought ever to exercise; for example, the power to pass bills of attainder, or to enact *ex post facto* laws, or to deprive any one of his life, liberty, or property without due process of law. The exercise of these powers is forbidden to both the national and the state governments.

*1. Powers prohibited to both the nation and the states.*

But in addition there are other powers, not by their nature despotic or arbitrary, which had to be vested in some central authority and hence were prohibited to the states so that they might always be exercised by Congress alone. The states, accordingly, were forbidden to make treaties, or to coin money, or to lay taxes on either exports or imports.

*Powers prohibited to the states only.*

The constitution contains eighteen clauses expressly granting powers to the national government, hence the customary reference to "the eighteen powers of Congress." There are really more than eighteen separate powers, however, as some of the clauses convey more than one. The section which contains the enumeration of these powers is the longest single section in the constitution and also the most important.[1] It furnishes the national government with its motive power, and indeed without this particular section Congress would be a wholly impotent body. The powers granted to Congress by these eighteen clauses are those which the makers of the constitution agreed upon as either being necessary for the maintenance of a vigorous central government or of such a general character that they could not be left to the precarious tutelage of the several state legislatures.

*2. Powers expressly given to Congress.*

Taken as a whole they may be grouped under eight heads: (1) *Financial*, the power to levy taxes and to borrow money. (2) *Commercial*, the power to regulate foreign and interstate commerce. (3) *Military*, the power to declare war, to raise and support armies, to provide for the organization, arming, and calling forth of the militia, and the power to maintain a navy. (4) *Monetary*, the power to coin money, to regulate the value thereof, and to protect the currency against counterfeiting. (5) *Postal*, the power to establish post-offices and post-roads. (6) *Judicial*, the power to constitute tribunals inferior to the Supreme Court. (7) *Miscellaneous*, including powers in relation to naturaliza-

*How these powers may be classified.*

[1] Article 1, Section 8.

tion, bankruptcy, patents, copyrights, and to the government of the national capital. (8) *Supplementary,* the power to make all laws which may be found "necessary and proper for carrying into execution the foregoing powers." Not all of these powers are of equal scope and importance. The first three categories — financial, commercial, and military — are probably of greater moment than all the others put together. They form the mainstay of congressional powers.

The fact that a power is given to Congress by the constitution does not imply, however, that Congress alone may exercise it, and that it may not also be shared by the states as well. Some congressional powers are by their nature practically indivisible, as for example, the power to declare war; but there are others which can readily be shared, for instance, the power to punish counterfeiting. These latter powers are usually spoken of as concurrent powers, or powers which the states may use so long as their action does not conflict with laws made by Congress. To take an illustration: Congress is given by the constitution the power to establish "uniform laws on the subject of bankruptcies throughout the United States." If, however, Congress does not enact such uniform laws, any state may make its own rules on the subject and apply them within its own borders. But when Congress does provide uniform laws, all conflicting rules in any state become unconstitutional.

3. Concurrent powers.

Naturally enough, no enumeration of powers retained by the states is made in the constitution. The states merely retained the whole residuum. Subtracting from the totality of all governmental powers those which are expressly forbidden to them and also those which are granted to Congress the states have what remains. All powers not mentioned or implied in the constitution are state powers. If this was not sufficiently clear at the outset, the Tenth Amendment soon made it so.[1] The residuum which remains with the states is very large, including as it does nearly the whole field of civil and criminal law, the chartering of corporations, the supervision of local government, the maintenance of order, the control of education, and the general adminis-

4. Powers retained by the states or "residual" powers.

[1] See above, p. 45, footnote.

tration of nearly all the things which touch the daily life of the people.

**Constituent powers and lawmaking powers.**

This distribution of powers and the limitations on the national government, as a thoughtful writer has pointed out, will enable any one to understand why the British parliament is termed a constituent body while Congress is only a lawmaking body.[1] Legally speaking, parliament is the British empire. Its powers embrace the sum total of all governmental authority. There is no political power above it, competent to restrain or overrule its acts; there is no sphere or field of government in which it may not operate, no act of government which it may not perform. Congressmen *represent* the people; but parliament *is* the people. Congress is merely an agent, while parliament is a principal. Whatever the nation can do in its sovereign capacity, parliament can do. It is not restrained by a constitution, because its acts make up the constitution, and hence nothing that it does can be unconstitutional. Congress, on the other hand, is the American nation for one purpose alone, namely, for exercising certain powers delegated to it by the states.

**Are the powers of Congress adequate?**

Does the constitution give Congress powers enough? Construed strictly, it does not. But the literal powers conveyed by the constitution, as has been already shown, have been greatly broadened by the process of judicial interpretation so that they are now reasonably adequate for all that a central government needs to do. The convention of 1787 was undertaking a great experiment in the division of governmental powers. It is small wonder that its members should have gone cautiously. Since their day a dozen other nations have established federal constitutions, including Australia, Canada, Switzerland, and South Africa. In every case these constitutions give more powers to the federal government than does the supreme law of the United States. The old fear of federal despotism has passed away.

---

[1] J. A. Woodburn, *The American Republic* (2d ed., N. Y., 1916), p. 89.

# CHAPTER XV

## THE TAXING POWER

OF all the prerogatives that can be lodged in any government, the taxing power is the most important. When Chief Justice Marshall spoke of the power to tax as the "power to destroy," he meant that this great economic weapon, if unrestrained, might be used by a government to destroy any form of business or to wipe out any form of property.[1] It is a power, nevertheless, which in some form or other every government must possess. No government can exist without income, and taxation is the natural source of governmental income. The Articles of Confederation gave no power to tax, and that is the chief reason why the Confederation tottered. It was chiefly to create a taxing power that the framers of the new constitution were brought together. The Union was born of the desire for a central authority with an assured income. It is appropriate, therefore, that the authority "to lay and collect taxes, duties, imports and excises" should stand first among the eighteen enumerated powers of Congress.

*Importance of the power to tax.*

A tax may be defined as a burden or charge imposed by a legislative authority upon persons or property to raise money for public purposes. Taxation, accordingly, is simply the confiscation of private property for public use under conditions determined by law. The only difference between modern taxes and the predatory exactions of tyran-

*Definition of a tax.*

---

[1] "That the power to tax involves the power to destroy; that the power to destroy may defeat and render useless the power to create; that there is a plain repugnance in conferring on one government a power to control the constitutional measures of another, which other, with respect to those very measures, is declared to be supreme over that which exerts the control, are propositions not to be denied." — *McCulloch* vs. *Maryland* (1819), 4 Wheaton, 316.

nical times is that the former are levied upon the people by action of their own representatives and in accordance with certain principles which aim to insure a fair adjustment of the burden.

*Essentials of a good tax.*

Nearly one hundred and fifty years ago the greatest of political economists, Adam Smith, laid down four rules or canons which ought to be observed in the levying of taxes, and these rules, despite great changes in both economic and political conditions, are recognized as sound at the present day. Adam Smith's canons of taxation may be briefly summarized as follows: that the citizens of a state should be taxed according to their ability to pay; that taxes should be certain, not arbitrary; that they ought to be "levied at the time and in the manner which is most likely to be most convenient for the contributor to pay"; and, finally, that taxes should be so contrived as to take out of the pockets of the people as little as is possible above what is actually needed by the public treasury.[1]

*Classification of taxes:*
*1. According to purpose: fiscal and regulative.*

Taxes are of various sorts and may be classified in several ways. According to their purpose, taxes may be divided into two kinds, fiscal and regulative. The former are levied with the sole purpose of securing revenue; the latter are imposed, either in whole or in part, from motives of social or economic improvement and without prime regard for their value as revenue producers. The general property tax is the best example of taxation for purely fiscal purposes, while taxes levied upon alcoholic liquors may be looked upon as being to a large extent regulative in character, designed to discourage consumption. Taxation may, of course, be both fiscal and regulative. A protective tariff on imports is a good illustration. High duties yield a large annual revenue and in addition afford a measure of protection to home industries against foreign competition.

*2. According to incidence: direct and indirect.*

Another classification of taxes is based upon their assumed incidence or final resting place.[2] Direct taxes, such as taxes on land and poll taxes, are supposed to rest finally upon those who pay them in the first instance; while indirect

---

[1] *The Wealth of Nations*, Book v, ch. ii, pt. ii.
[2] For a discussion of this subject see E. R. A. Seligman, *The Shifting and Incidence of Taxation* (3d ed., N. Y., 1910).

taxes, such as customs duties and excises upon spirituous liquors, are laid with the expectation that they will be shifted to the shoulders of the ultimate consumer. These suppositions, however, are not always in accordance with the facts. Even direct taxes are occasionally shifted, while indirect taxes under some circumstances remain where they are placed. For this reason the classification of all taxes into two categories, direct and indirect, according to incidence, is not a satisfactory one from the standpoint of the economist. In political science and in actual legislation, nevertheless, this distinction between direct and indirect taxes has been of great importance, particularly in the United States.

The chief taxes levied in the United States today, whether fiscal or regulative, direct or indirect, are taxes on property, real and personal, taxes on incomes, duties on imports, excises on liquors, tobacco, railroad and theatre tickets, telegrams, and so forth, taxes on the excess profits of industry and commerce, inheritance taxes, and poll taxes on persons. The national government is permitted by the constitution to levy taxes in all these seven forms, but it has not for more than fifty years made use of the first or the last, both of which, if imposed, must be apportioned among the states according to their respective populations. 3. According to subject.

But although the taxing power of Congress is extensive in scope, it is by no means unlimited. Restrictions of various sorts are provided in the constitution. The first of these limitations relates to the purposes for which taxes may be imposed. Congress may only levy taxes in order "to pay the debts and provide for the common defense and general welfare of the United States." That, to be sure, is not a stringent limitation, for nearly every tax that Congress desires to levy may be brought within the broad confines of "general welfare." This general welfare clause, it should be mentioned, is not a grant of legislative authority to Congress, as might appear from a rapid reading of its context, but a limitation upon the taxing power.[1]

---

[1] "Some, who have not denied the necessity of the power of taxation, have grounded a very fierce attack against the constitution, on the language in which it is defined. It has been urged and echoed, that power 'to lay and collect taxes, duties, imposts and excises, to pay the debts, and provide for the common defense and general welfare of the United

In various forms the question as to what is a "general welfare" purpose has been presented to the courts for interpretation. May taxes be imposed in order to pay bounties to growers of sugar beets or some other commodity which Congress desires to encourage? In such matters the courts have held that incidental private benefits do not preclude the main purpose from being a public one. Rarely, therefore, have tax laws been declared invalid on this account.

2. Taxes must be uniform

In the second place, the constitution requires that all duties, imposts, and excises imposed by the authority of Congress shall be uniform throughout the United States. This does not mean, however, that all the states must contribute equally or in proportion to their population. Congress, in the exercise of its discretion, may adjust the burden of national taxation so that more will fall upon one area or section of the population than upon another. A tax on tobacco is not void for want of uniformity because tobacco happens to be grown in some states of the Union and not in others. Uniformity, within the meaning of the constitution, is secured if the levy bears with equal burden wherever the subject of the impost is found. For example, a tax upon alien immigrants has been held to be uniform even though nine-tenths of it was shown to fall upon the port of New York. On the other hand, a tax would not be uniform if it should make discriminations between the same things in different parts of the country; for example, if it should be levied upon inheritances at one rate in some states and at a different rate in others. When customs duties are collected, to give another illustration, the rates upon any class of commodities must be the same at all ports of entry. No preference may be given by any regulation of commerce or revenue to the ports of one state over those of another.

3. No tax may be laid on exports.

A third limitation upon the taxing powers of Congress relates to exports and to internal tariffs. "No tax or duty," declares the constitution, "shall be laid upon articles ex-

States,' amounts to an unlimited commission to exercise every power which may be alleged to be necessary for the common defense or general welfare. No stronger proof could be given of the distress under which these writers labor for objections, than their stooping to such a misconstruction." — *The Federalist*, No. 41.

## THE TAXING POWER 223

ported from any state." Congress may not, therefore, tax the exports which go from the United States to foreign territories. It may tax imports only. The restriction upon the states is even more rigid, since a state cannot, without the consent of Congress, impose taxes upon either imports or exports under any circumstances whatever. In this connection the insular possessions, such as Porto Rico and the Philippines, have been held to be neither states nor foreign territory, hence trade between the United States and these areas may be made subject to taxation. In one of the famous Insular Cases the Supreme Court held that Porto Rico, upon its cession to the United States, ceased to be foreign territory, but did not thereby become incorporated into the Union.[1]

The prohibition of any tax upon exports was one of the compromises of the constitution. It was a concession to the southern states, which were at that time large exporters of rice, tobacco, and similar staples. The current economic notion of the day was that export duties always fell upon the exporter, while duties on imports fell upon the consumer. Hence the southern delegates were firmly opposed to giving Congress any right to impose export duties which would fall wholly upon the planters, and in the end they had their way. In some respects, however, the restriction has proved unfortunate. It has at times deprived Congress of a means whereby the depletion of natural resources might have been prevented. Exports of timber amounting to many millions per year have gone forth untaxed. It should be noted, however, that the prohibition of taxes on exports does not restrain Congress from regulating export trade in any reasonable way otherwise than by taxing it. Nor does it exempt goods from the payment of ordinary internal taxes merely because they are being manufactured for export. As regards duties on imports, Congress has full power. It may levy import duties of any sort and at such rates as it may determine, provided of course that the rates are uniform at all ports where the goods come in.

*Reason for this rule.*

*Its unfortunate influence.*

A fourth constitutional limitation on the taxing power of Congress relates to the imposition of capitation and other

[1] 183 U. S. 151.

direct taxes. Congress has power to lay and collect direct taxes, as often and in such amounts as it may see fit. But the amount which it requires to be raised by direct taxation must be "apportioned among the several states according to their respective numbers, counting the whole number of persons in each state, excluding Indians not taxed."[1] In other words, direct taxes must be distributed throughout the Union according to population, not according to wealth, income, or any other common denominator. This provision of the original constitution, somewhat modified by the Fourteenth Amendment, was part of the Great Compromise.

<small>4. Direct taxes must be apportioned.</small>

But what are direct taxes within the scope of this restriction? At the time the constitution was adopted it seems to have been taken for granted that the only direct taxes were poll taxes and taxes on land. Taxes of every other sort were regarded as indirect taxes. Ten years later the Supreme Court affirmed this assumption in an opinion which declared that a tax on carriages was not a direct tax; that capitation taxes and taxes on land were the only forms of direct taxation; and that all other taxes were included within the comprehensive phrase "imposts, duties and excises," or indirect taxes.[2] Three of the four justices who heard the arguments in the controversy had been members of the constitutional convention. "As all direct taxes must be apportioned," said one of the justices in this case, "it is evident that the constitution contemplated none as direct but such as could be apportioned." Congress also levied at various times a tax upon bank circulation, a tax upon the receipts of insurance companies, and a tax upon the inheritance of real estate; but it did not regard these as direct taxes and hence made no provision for apportioning them. All these taxes were contested as unconstitutional, but the Supreme Court held that none was a direct tax and hence that none needed to be apportioned.[3]

<small>What are "direct taxes" in this sense?</small>

<small>Some examples of early taxes not held to be "direct" taxes.</small>

Finally, in 1862 and 1864, under the stress of heavy demands for war revenue, Congress proceeded to lay taxes

---

[1] Amendment XIV, Section 2.
[2] *Hylton* vs. *United States*, 3 Dallas, 171.
[3] *Veazie Bank* vs. *Fenno*, 8 Wallace, 533; *Pacific R. R. Co.* vs. *Soule*, 7 Wallace, 433; and *Scholey* vs. *Rew*, 23 Wallace, 331.

on incomes, without provision for apportionment. Then, for the first time, arose the question whether an income tax was a direct tax. After reviewing its attitude in previous cases relating to the taxing power of Congress, the Supreme Court unanimously decided that an income tax was not a direct tax, declaring categorically that the only direct taxes, within the meaning of the constitution, are poll taxes and taxes on real estate.[1] This decision was not given for many years after the passage of these income tax laws. Meanwhile, the need for great increases in the federal revenue had passed and the laws were repealed.

*The income tax controversy: its various stages.*
*1. The income tax law of the Civil War period.*

This long line of decisions might well have been thought to settle the matter forever, but in the next generation the question as to the status of income taxes was once more revived, and this time it was answered in a different way. Congress in 1894 passed a new income tax law imposing a levy of two per cent on all incomes above four thousand dollars from whatever source derived. This law was promptly attacked as unconstitutional, and the Supreme Court, after prolonged delays and two hearings, finally decided in 1895 that a tax on the income from property is virtually a tax on the property itself, and accordingly that a tax on such income must be held to be a direct tax.[2] A tax on land, the court pointed out, was admittedly a direct tax, and a tax upon the income of land is not distinguishable on any broad principle from a tax on the land itself. The law of 1894, having levied a direct tax without provision for apportioning it among the states according to population as the constitution requires, was therefore declared to be unconstitutional. Thus, by a close decision, in which four out of the nine justices dissented, the court reversed the ruling which it had made on the nature of income taxes fourteen years before. From 1895 to 1911, accordingly, Congress was not able to enact a valid income tax law without providing for an apportionment among the states. To have apportioned an income tax according to population would have been highly inequitable, since population and total income do not bear any fixed ratio to one

*2. The income tax law of 1894.*

---

[1] *Springer* vs. *United States*, 102 U. S. 586.
[2] *Pollock* vs. *Farmers' Loan and Trust Co.*, 157 U. S. 429; 158 U. S. 601.

another. Massachusetts, for example, has a smaller population than Texas, but a far larger number of taxable incomes.

*3. The Sixteenth Amendment, 1913.* This legal obstacle was finally removed, however, in 1913, when a sufficient number of the states gave their assent to the Sixteenth Amendment, the adoption of which was in effect a reversal of the Supreme Court's decision on the law of 1894. This amendment provides that "Congress shall have power to lay and collect taxes on incomes, from whatever source derived, without apportionment among the states and without regard to any census or enumeration." Shortly after the adoption of the Sixteenth Amendment a new federal tax upon incomes was imposed, and this tax, which is now collected directly by the federal authorities, brings in a considerable share of the nation's income.[1] The power of Congress to levy upon incomes, without apportionment, is now beyond question; but this does not mean that no income tax law can henceforth be held to be unconstitutional. The constitution provides, for example, that the salaries of judges "shall not be diminished during their continuance in office." Notwithstanding the provision that Congress may tax incomes "from whatever source derived," it is quite possible that a tax upon the salaries of judges would be held to be an impairment of their protection against any diminution of remuneration, and hence to be unconstitutional.

*4. The income tax law of 1913.*

*Constitutionality of the tax on corporations.* In 1909, before the adoption of the Sixteenth Amendment, a tax was imposed by Congress upon the net income of corporations. This levy was upheld as being an excise, not an income tax; in other words as a tax upon the privilege of doing business under the corporate, as distinguished from the individual, form of organization. Being an excise, it could be levied without apportionment.

All of the foregoing limitations are expressly laid down in the constitution. In addition, there is an implied limitation arising out of the very nature of the federal union, and one that is necessary to the continued free working of the state governments. If the states are to be secured in the full enjoyment of their reserved powers, Congress must not be permitted to hamper their agencies of administra-

[1] E. R. A. Seligman, *The Income Tax* (2d ed., N. Y., 1914).

tion by imposing taxes upon them. For let it once be admitted that Congress may tax the mechanism through which the state performs its functions and the supremacy of Congress over the states would soon become established. One hundred years ago it was decided by the Supreme Court that no state could tax the instrumentalities of the federal government, such as post-offices, customhouses, or the notes of national banks. This decision was based upon the argument that the various states, if given authority to tax the mechanism of federal administration, would possess the power to stop its wheels entirely. This argument, however, if valid in one direction is equally valid in the other, as is now well recognized. Congress may not tax the property of a state or the salaries of its officers.[1] It may be that the Sixteenth Amendment has now altered this situation as respects incomes derived from state employment.

*May Congress tax the instrumentalities of a state?*

These, then, are the limitations imposed by the constitution upon the taxing power of Congress. Now as to the way in which the taxing power is actually exercised. It was assumed by the framers of the constitution that Congress would frequently levy direct taxes and apportion them among the states, but direct taxes have proved far less important sources of federal revenue than was anticipated in 1787. On five occasions only has Congress levied direct taxes: once in 1798, three times during the War of 1812, and once during the Civil War. In each case Congress set the total amount to be raised and then allotted to each state its due proportion according to its population. In each case also, Congress specified the subjects upon which the tax was to be levied and indicated the machinery for collecting it. Lands and slaves were the subjects taxed by the earlier laws, while the act of 1861 laid a direct tax upon land alone. The seceding states refused to pay this levy. No direct tax has been apportioned among the states since that date.[2]

*How Congress has exercised its taxing powers.*

*1. Direct taxes.*

---

[1] *Tax Collector vs. Day*, 11 Wallace, 113.
[2] Data concerning the taxing policy of the federal government during various periods may be conveniently found in D. R. Dewey's *Financial History of the United States* (5th ed., N. Y., 1915).

2. Indirect taxes.

At all times since its establishment the national government has depended for the bulk of its revenue upon indirect taxes, and particularly upon three forms of indirect taxation, namely, customs duties, excises upon liquors and tobacco, and, more recently, taxes levied upon the net earnings of individuals and corporations. Until the time of the Civil War the proceeds from import duties upon merchandise formed the most important source of national income. The entire national revenue in 1860 was about sixty millions, of which nearly ninety per cent came from duties upon imports. In 1916, the year before the United States entered the war, the national revenue from taxation had increased to more than seven hundred millions, of which the import duties contributed considerably less than one-half. Excises, or internal revenue taxes upon spirituous liquors, tobacco, and a few other articles had grown to be the most lucrative source of national income and yielded in 1916 much more than duties on imports. Some years previously Congress imposed a tax upon the net income of corporations, and in 1913, after the adoption of the Sixteenth Amendment, the policy of taxing the net incomes of individuals and partnerships was revived. These four forms of taxation, customs duties, excises, taxes on corporations, and taxes on individual incomes formed the mainstay of federal revenues in the years just prior to 1917.

The war taxes.

In April, 1917, when the United States declared war upon the German government, the certainty of huge military expenditures necessitated an increased revenue. It was not deemed to be just or expedient that all the funds needed for carrying on the war should be raised by borrowing, but rather that the present generation of taxpayers should be made to bear its proper share of the burden. Hence Congress, by a series of war revenue measures, not only extended and increased some of the existing taxes but resorted to new forms of federal taxation as well. The excises on liquors and tobacco were made higher, while many new excises were imposed, for example, upon telegrams, railroad tickets, automobile sales, certain legal papers, and so forth. The rates of taxation, both upon the net income of corporations and the net income of individuals, were much increased. A tax upon excess profits, that is, upon all business profits above a certain point, was levied for the first time in American history. By these various tax measures the nation's normal income was many times multiplied.

This great widening in the area of federal taxation means that both the nation and the states are now to some extent taxing the same things. From the citizen's point of view this is double taxation. Contrary to the popular impression, however, there is nothing in the constitution of the United States which forbids double taxation. The taxing powers of the states clearly overlap those of Congress, for the states are at liberty to tax practically anything except imports, exports, the instrumentalities of interstate commerce, and the agencies of the federal government. Many states now have inheritance taxes and taxes upon corporations, while some have income taxes. In all such cases the inheritance or corporation or income is subjected to two different levies, one by the nation and the other by the state. Such double taxation, while not constitutionally forbidden, is unsound policy. It means that revenues are being drawn from the same source by two different authorities, neither of which pays much attention to what the other is taking. Each imposes what it regards as a necessary and reasonable burden, yet the two levies put together may prove to be more than can be borne without forcing great economic readjustments. A system of taxation, to be highly efficient and at the same time equitable, should be coördinated in all its bearings. In each designated field either the nation or the states, wherever practicable, should be given the right of way. Competition for revenues between two different authorities, each of which has the right to gather all it can from the same sources, can hardly ever be made the basis of sound public financing. *The widening field of federal taxation.*

Not all this extension of federal taxation has been due to the need for more revenue. The corporation and income taxes were levied before the huge expenditures on military account began. These taxes, along with the inheritance tax, have had in view, to some extent at least, the readjustment of the entire national tax-burden, so that a larger por- *Federal taxation as a weapon to compel economic readjustments.*

tion of it may be borne by the well-to-do than was the case in the earlier days when customs duties furnished the bulk of the revenue. During the whole of the nineteenth century the larger part of the national revenue was not raised in conformity with the principle that those who are best able to pay should contribute accordingly. The high customs duties were spread upon the whole population in the form of higher prices. The rich, being larger purchasers, doubtless assumed some share; but relatively the load was much lighter upon them than on the poor. The excises on liquors and tobacco, moreover, fell chiefly upon the masses of the people and not upon the well-to-do. The income tax, on the other hand, with a rate which becomes higher as the size of the income increases, is a charge which adjusts itself to the financial resources of each individual citizen. The inheritance tax also represents an endeavor to make wealth rather than population the measure of the public demand from different sections of the country. Taxation, in a word, is becoming in the twentieth century not only a means of raising money for public use, but of compelling such economic reconstruction as Congress thinks desirable for American society as a whole. Many people believe that "swollen fortunes" are an evil in a democracy. The inheritance tax is one agency for reducing them; the income tax with a progressive surtax affixed is another. Incidentally these taxes bring in a large revenue, and thus relieve the national government from depending so heavily upon duties and excises.

*The future of national taxation.* The future of national taxation ought to have a word because certain features of congressional policy in the domain of public finance are now becoming clear. It is unlikely that tariff duties will for some years after the war contribute as large a proportion of the total revenue as in the years preceding it. The adoption of the Eighteenth Amendment, which prohibits the manufacture and sale of intoxicating liquors, deprives the national treasury of large sums which have hitherto been obtained from liquor excises. On the other hand, there will be a continuing need for a far greater revenue than in pre-war days, to pay interest upon the billions of war bonds, to provide pensions, to carry through domestic enterprises which have been suspended during the war years, and to take care of many things which the nation's participation in the great conflict will inevitably throw upon the public treasury. Where is all this revenue to be had? If the signs of the present day are not misleading, we may reasonably look for the continuance of taxes on incomes, inheritances, and excess profits. Possibly there may be a resort to direct taxes on property, apportioned among the states, although this will never be the case until the other producers of national revenue have been used to their full carrying capacity. In any case the history of American federal taxation during the first quarter of the twentieth century is certain to be altogether unlike that which marked the closing quarter of the nineteenth.

The work of collecting the national revenue is in the hands of the Secretary of the Treasury, but is performed by two agencies in that department, namely, by the customs and the internal revenue services. For the collection of duties upon imports the country is divided into about fifty customs districts, each with a main port of entry in charge of a collector or deputy collector of customs. For the collection of internal revenue taxes the country is divided into a larger number of similar areas, about sixty-five in all, each also in charge of a collector. The work of these collectors of internal revenue includes not only the levy of the regular excises on spirits, tobacco, and so forth, but the collection of the corporation and income taxes as well. The assessments upon which corporation and individual income taxes are levied depend, in the first instance, upon sworn declarations which must be filed by every corporation, partnership, or individual liable to taxation. Incomes of business corporations and of individuals below a designated sum are exempt. All collections are turned into the general treasury of the United States. *How the federal taxes are collected.*

This general treasury consists of the main vaults at Washington and nine sub-treasuries located in as many large cities throughout the country.[1] These sub-treasuries are the government's chief agencies, not only for receiving the *The general treasury and the sub-treasuries.*

[1] At present these are: Baltimore, Boston, Chicago, Cincinnati, New Orleans, New York, Philadelphia, St. Louis, and San Francisco.

**United States depositaries.**

**Audit.**

revenue but for paying it out on warrants. The law also permits the Secretary of the Treasury to designate various national banks as depositaries and to keep funds in these institutions. In such cases, however, approved securities must be placed with the Secretary, to be held by him as a guarantee for the safety of the government deposits. The accounts of every officer who has to do with the collection of the revenue are regularly audited by officials of the national auditing service who are agents of the Treasury Department, but who occupy positions of independence so far as the conduct of their investigation is concerned. This auditing work, it need scarcely be added, is of huge dimensions.

## CHAPTER XVI

### THE BORROWING POWER, THE NATIONAL DEBT, AND THE NATIONAL BANKING SYSTEM

NOT all national expenditures can be defrayed out of income. Extraordinary undertakings which involve great outlays, such as the financing of a war or the construction of an inter-oceanic canal or the creation of a great fleet of merchant vessels, cannot be carried through from the funds which the ordinary revenues provide. All governments, accordingly, must have command of resources which will enable them to handle such out-of-the-ordinary projects when the need arises. The constitution provides for such eventualities by giving to Congress the unlimited right "to borrow money on the credit of the United States." *Purpose of the borrowing power.*

This is one of the few powers upon which the constitution places no limits whatsoever. Congress can borrow as much as it pleases and in whatever manner it may deem expedient. There was a good reason for dealing liberally with the federal government in this field because in 1787 the national credit was at its lowest point. The Congress of the Confederation had encountered the greatest difficulty in borrowing upon any terms. Moreover, it was all too plain in 1787 that the new central government would start off with a heavy burden of debt on its shoulders. Bonds had been issued during the Revolutionary War both on the authority of the Confederation and by the several states themselves. The former would certainly be a charge upon the new federal administration, and the latter would in all likelihood be taken over as a part of the national debt. That, indeed, is what soon came to pass. *Absence of limitations upon it.*

*Beginnings of the national debt.*

The funding of these obligations, which amounted in all to over $125,000,000, was the work of Alexander Hamilton,

## 234  THE GOVERNMENT OF THE UNITED STATES

*The legacy of the Revolutionary War.*

*Alexander Hamilton's work in funding it.*

who served as Secretary of the Treasury during the years 1789–1795. To Hamilton also is due the beginnings of a system of federal revenues which not only provided for the ordinary expenses of government, but made possible the gradual extinction of the nation's indebtedness. During the War of 1812 some new bonds were issued, but twenty years after the close of this war the entire national debt had virtually been paid off. Not only that, but there was a surplus in the federal treasury which Congress distributed among the states although there was no legal obligation to do this. For twenty-five years, 1836–1861, the United States was the only great country in the world without a national debt of any appreciable dimensions. Then came the Civil War, and during the years 1861–1865 the debt rose by leaps and bounds to an unprecedented height.

*The Civil War debt.*

*The national debt since the Civil War.*

At the close of this war the interest-bearing indebtedness of the nation stood at about three billions of dollars, but this does not tell the whole story, for much borrowing had in reality taken place through the issue of paper currency.

This fiscal heritage of the conflict was steadily reduced, however, and during the twenty years which followed Lee's surrender the national debt was brought down to about six hundred millions.[1] Then the pendulum began to swing once more in the other direction. In the second Cleveland administration bonds were issued to replenish the gold reserve in the treasury, and later, during the war with Spain, there were additional borrowings. The building of the Panama Canal, during the ensuing era, added several hundred millions to the total, so that the national debt, on the eve of America's participation in the European War, was about a billion dollars in round figures. Viewed in the light of to-day this single billion of only a year or two ago seems insignificant. The war borrowings for the two years 1917–1918 alone amounted to over fifteen billions, or more than five times the highest figure ever reached at any previous time.

*The "Liberty" issues.*

During the first quarter of the nineteenth century the Supreme Court was called upon to interpret the scope of the

---

[1] For the exact figures and further details, see Henry C. Adams, *Public Debts* (N. Y., 1898).

powers conferred by the borrowing clause; in other words to settle the question whether Congress might, under cover of its power to borrow money, establish a national bank. The constitution contains no mention of banks or banking. A proposal to give the national government such power in express terms was rejected by the constitutional convention. Accordingly, the power to charter and regulate banks might at first glance be looked upon as falling within the residuum of jurisdiction reserved to the states.[1] But Alexander Hamilton, as Secretary of the Treasury, outlined a plan for the establishment of a great national bank, somewhat after the model of the Bank of England, and in 1791 Congress chartered the first Bank of the United States, the ostensible purpose of this action being to provide a financial institution which would assist the national government in the exercise of its borrowing power, in the collection of its revenues, and in the custody of its funds.[2] Washington was in serious doubt as to whether he should sign the bill which chartered this bank, but Hamilton in an able state paper persuaded him to give his signature despite the strenuous opposition of Jefferson, who was also a member of the Cabinet as Secretary of State.[3]

*Scope of the borrowing power. May Congress charter banks?*

*The first Bank of the United States, 1791–1811.*

The first Bank of the United States continued in existence until 1811 when its twenty-year charter expired. It had a capital of ten millions and established eight branches in different parts of the country. It served as a depositary for public funds and also loaned the government consider-

*Its history and end.*

---

[1] James Madison, as is well known, took this ground, declaring that the establishment of a national bank would be unconstitutional, and asserting that the claim of Congress to charter a bank was "condemned by the silence of the constitution; was condemned by the rule of interpretation arising out of the constitution; was condemned by its tendency to destroy the main characteristics of the constitution; was condemned by the expositions of the friends of the constitution whilst depending before the people, etc."

[2] In 1781, several years before the adoption of the constitution, the Bank of North America had been chartered by the Congress of the Confederation. This institution, however, encountered popular opposition and soon surrendered its charter from the Congress, obtaining instead a charter from the state of Pennsylvania. See Lawrence Lewis, *History of the Bank of North America* (Philadelphia, 1882).

[3] This document is reprinted in H. C. Lodge's edition of Hamilton's *Works* (Federal edition, 12 vols., N. Y., 1904).

able sums from time to time. The bank was well managed and proved profitable, but its charter was not renewed in 1811, chiefly because it had aroused the opposition of many small state banks whose jealousy of the national institution was now strongly reflected in Congress.[1]

*The second Bank of the United States.*

Five years later, however, the financial embarrassments caused by the War of 1812–1815 determined Congress to establish the second Bank of the United States, and its charter was signed in 1816 by President Madison, whose misgivings on the question of constitutionality had now become somewhat mollified. The capital of this bank was fixed at thirty-five millions; it was empowered to issue paper money; it served as a depositary for public funds; it assisted the treasury department in the collection of the public revenues and at times made temporary loans to the national government. Its charter was to run for twenty years.

*The question of its constitutional status.*

Prior to 1816 the authority of Congress to charter a bank had not come squarely to issue before the Supreme Court, but the second Bank of the United States had no more than begun its operations when the question of constitutionality was brought forward in a way which enabled the point to be settled for all time.

*The decision in McCulloch vs. Maryland.*

In 1818 the legislature of Maryland imposed a stamp tax on the bank's paper money, and the cashier of the Baltimore branch, McCulloch, refused to pay this tax. The matter in due course went before the Supreme Court of the United States. This tribunal, in 1819, set a new landmark in American constitutional development by its opinion in the famous case of *McCulloch* vs. *Maryland*.[2] The decision in this case, written by Chief Justice Marshall, has become a classic of American jurisprudence. It is the most cogent elucidation ever made of the doctrine of "implied powers." In words which for clearness and force cannot be improved upon, Marshall laid down the principle that though the national government "is limited as to its ob-

*Chief Justice Marshall on the implied power to charter banks.*

---

[1] The Bank of the United States had also allowed more than two-thirds of its capital stock to pass into the hands of foreigners, and this fact was urged as an additional reason for not renewing its charter. For the history of this bank see J. T. Holdsworth, *The First Bank of the United States* (Philadelphia, 1910).

[2] 4 Wheaton, 316.

jects," it is none the less "supreme with respect to those objects," and hence that where an express object is authorized by the constitution, "any means adapted to the end, any means that tend directly to the execution of the constitutional powers of government, are in themselves constitutional." In express terms the constitution had given the national government the power "to lay and collect taxes" and "to borrow money on the credit of the United States." It had also expressly granted to Congress the right "to make all laws which shall be necessary and proper for carrying into execution the foregoing powers." Putting these provisions together, the Supreme Court held that Congress must be allowed discretion in choosing the sort of laws "necessary and proper" for carrying out its undoubted right to collect revenue or to borrow.

Congress being thus authorized to provide its own financial mechanism, it followed that any administrative agencies created for this purpose must not be subjected to factious interference by the states. "If," declared the Court, "the states may tax one instrument employed by the [national] government in the execution of its powers, they may tax any and every other instrument. They may tax the mail; they may tax the mint; they may tax patent rights; they may tax the custom-house; they may tax judicial process; they may tax all the means employed by the government to an excess which would defeat all the ends of government." For this convincing reason the law of Maryland which taxed the circulation of the United States Bank was declared unconstitutional. *No state may tax the circulation or deposits of banks chartered by Congress.*

The decision in this case was of the highest national importance, for it set the authority of the federal government upon a firm and sure foundation. Its reasoning is a tribute to Marshall's intellectual power, to his political sagacity, and to his mastery of the English tongue.[1] Al- *Importance of the decision.*

[1] "Marshall was probably the greatest judge that ever lived, when one considers the wonderful cogency and beauty of his judicial style, his statesman's foresight, the accuracy of his legal learning, the power of his reasoning, his soundness of judgment, his wonderful personal influence over his colleagues, and the fateful influence of his work upon the structure of our great government." — W. H. TAFT, *Our Chief Magistrate and His Powers* (N. Y., 1916), p. 46.

though not relished at the time by the extreme champions of state rights, it is to-day universally conceded to have marked a triumph of union over sectionalism and to have saved the nation from what would surely have been the first of a series of inroads upon its constitutional prerogatives.[1]

*Jackson's war on the Bank.*

The second United States Bank came to an end in 1837, but not because of any doubts as to its constitutional status, nor yet because it lacked prosperity. It was drawn into the political arena, where Andrew Jackson and his political supporters waged war upon it. The allegation was that managers of the bank's branches in different parts of the country were showing political favoritism in making loans, and that the bank itself was endeavoring to crush local banking institutions, thus aiming to become a great financial monopoly. This line of attack proved effective in a day of strong anti-capitalistic feeling. Jackson vetoed a bill passed by Congress for renewing the bank's charter and withdrew all government deposits from it.

*Its exodus.*

Forced to the wall, the institution was in 1836 converted into a state bank, but in this field it was unsuccessful and finally went out of existence altogether.[2]

*Banks and banking from the Jacksonian era to the Civil War.*

Although movements for the establishment of a new bank with a federal charter were set afoot from time to time during the next twenty-six years, none of them resulted in success. The banking of the country was carried on during this period by institutions chartered in the several states. But in 1863, under the financial stress of the Civil War, when the Secretary of the Treasury was hard pressed in his effort to sell bonds on reasonable terms, Congress was induced to pass the first of the laws which laid the foundations of the American national banking system as it exists at the present day.

*The National Banking Acts of 1863–1865.*

Briefly, the National Banking Act of 1863, as considerably amended by other statutes passed in the two following years, imposed a heavy tax upon the circulating notes of all state banks, with intent to drive this paper currency out

---

[1] See J. P. Cotton, Jr., editor, *The Constitutional Decisions of John Marshall* (2 vols., N. Y., 1905), i, 302–345.

[2] The full history of its vicissitudes may be found in R. C. H. Catterall's *Second Bank of the United States* (Chicago, 1903).

of existence. It then provided that any bank incorporated under the new law might issue untaxed circulating notes, provided it bought United States bonds to a designated amount and deposited these bonds in Washington as security for its note issues. Fundamentally, then, this legislation was merely a scheme to create an artificial market for government bonds at a time of great national need, although a secondary purpose was to substitute uniform bank notes with a federal guarantee for the multifarious and voluminous issues of state banks, thus placing a limit upon inflation. But the legislation worked out surprisingly well, and since the war its main provisions have been retained although many amendments to it have been made. Nearly eight thousand national banks are now included within the system. At any rate the federal government's present-day control and supervision of the national banking system is a corollary from the express power of Congress "to borrow money on the credit of the United States."

The supervision of the national banking system is in charge of the Comptroller of the Currency, an official in the Treasury Department who is responsible not only for the general examination of their accounts but for the approval of applications to establish new banks. He has charge of the corps of national bank examiners who go about inspecting the banks, one by one, and he has power to intervene whenever a bank seems to be insolvent. *Supervision of national banks.*

For many years prior to 1913 it was generally recognized by financial authorities that the national banking system of the United States might be considerably improved. The rigid provisions relating to the reserves were regarded as particularly embarrassing in times of commercial depression. All national banks must keep on hand a reserve amounting to a designated percentage of their deposits, but the smaller banks have been permitted to keep a portion of this reserve in the banks of certain large cities, and these latter banks, again, have been allowed to keep a part of their reserves in the banking institutions of New York City. This policy of fixing the amount of reserves in terms of definite percentages and of tying them up among a hierarchy of banks served for many years to deny the American banking *Defects of the national banking system.*

system that considerable measure of flexibility which is to be found in the financial arrangements of other countries. The reserve requirements proved to be higher than necessary in times when deposits were coming in freely, and not high enough when heavy withdrawals were being made. When a financial crisis occurred, as in 1893, the smaller banks did not find it easy to call in their reserves promptly.

**The federal reserve banking system.** To give the national banking system greater elasticity, therefore, the Federal Reserve Act was passed by Congress in 1913. By the provisions of this statute the entire territory of the United States is divided into twelve federal reserve districts, with a federal reserve bank in each. The capital stock of each reserve bank is contributed by banks within the district, the national government also subscribing if necessary to make up the amount. Each reserve bank is controlled by a board of directors chosen in part by the banks who own stock and in part by the national government through a body known as the Federal Reserve Board. This board is composed of the Secretary of the Treasury, the Comptroller of the Currency, and five other members appointed by the President. These twelve federal reserve banks are now the reserve depositaries for such smaller banks as have subscribed to their capital stock, and they also lend funds to the smaller banks upon approved security when funds are needed. The Federal Reserve Board has authority to change the percentage of reserves required, and each of the twelve federal reserve banks has the right to issue paper money. In time these notes will replace the notes which have been issued by the national banks. The new system thus secures leeway in the amount of reserves required; it discourages the piling-up of funds in any one large financial centre; it enables small banks to get their reserves quickly when needed and also to borrow or rediscount easily; and finally, it provides in the Federal Reserve Board a central authority which is able to furnish the entire banking interests of the nation with guidance in an emergency. It gives the United States, in a word, the larger part of the advantages which other great countries derive from their centralized banking systems, yet it does not create a single gigantic institution like the Bank of England or the Bank of France.

These agencies, then, the national banks and the federal reserve banks, provide the government with an adequate means of regulating the flow of currency, collecting the revenues, and borrowing money. Now as to the methods by which the national government exercises its power to borrow. The most common plan has been to secure loans by the issue of bonds. These bonds are promises to pay on the expiration of a designated period, say twenty, thirty, or forty years, with interest, at a stated rate during the lifetime of the bond. For the most part the national government has borrowed from banks or groups of banks, giving them the bonds which they either resell to private investors or deposit at Washington as security for their own circulating notes. But at times the bonds have been offered for public sale, and subscriptions have been taken not only by banks but by post-offices and other government establishments. To facilitate a direct and general sale to the public, some of the bonds sold during the Spanish War were issued in denominations as low as twenty dollars, and the "Liberty bonds" issued during the European war were put on sale in denominations as low as fifty dollars. Even so, however, a very large proportion of these bonds were sold to the public through the banks.

<small>The methods of national borrowing.</small>

Bonds are of two types, registered and coupon. The former are registered in the name of the owner upon the books of the Treasury Department. The interest is paid by cheque from Washington to the holder whose name is so registered. Registered bonds can be transferred only by written indorsement. Coupon bonds, on the other hand, are made payable to bearer, and the owner secures his interest by presenting the coupons which are attached to the bond and which are also payable to the bearer. Coupon bonds are transferable by mere delivery. The Treasury Department keeps no record of those who hold them. For permanent investment the registered bond is preferred; the holder does not suffer loss if his bond is stolen or destroyed; and the interest payments come to him regularly without any action on his part. Coupon

<small>Types of bond issues.</small>

R

bonds are preferred by those who hold bonds for speculation or who desire to have securities which may be quickly turned into money when needed. As the greater part of the bonded debt of the United States prior to 1917 was held by banks and other institutions of investment, the registered bonds formed until recently the major part of the total issues. But the huge borrowings of the last two years, being floated largely by the issue of coupon bonds, have changed this situation.

*Treasury notes.* From time to time the United States has also borrowed money by the issue of treasury notes. These are promissory notes issued in denominations of from five to one thousand dollars and maturing within a short time, usually from one to three years, or even on demand. In some cases they have been issued bearing interest, in other cases without interest. During the Civil War these treasury notes, of all varieties, were issued to a total of nearly two billion dollars. At the close of the war most of them were converted into bonds. Those which remain in existence bear no interest and have become part of the national currency. During the last few years large issues of interest-bearing treasury notes have also been put on the market, but merely as a preliminary to the selling of bonds, the notes being issued to provide money until the bonds could be sold and paid for.

*Borrowing by the issue of currency* Certain issues of currency, for example the silver dollar, the silver certificate, and the fractional coins, have sometimes been referred to as examples of a method of borrowing money, inasmuch as they yield more to the national government than it costs to issue them. Ordinarily the silver dollar does not cost a dollar to coin, nor does the nickel represent five cents' worth of that metal. The difference between what they cost and what the government gets for them, however, is a profit rather than a loan. They do not, at any rate, form part of the interest-bearing debt and do not increase the burden placed upon the taxpayer.

Bonds issued on the credit of the United States are not taxable by the states or the municipalities without the consent of Congress. This is a logical corollary from the general rule laid down in *McCulloch* vs. *Maryland.* Both the bonds themselves and the income derived from them may, however, be made subject to federal taxation. This, nevertheless, has not been the policy of Congress until within very recent years and then only with reference to bonds which have a relatively high rate of interest. The first war bonds of 1917 were made exempt from all taxation whatsoever; the later issues gave to each holder a limited exemption. *U. S. bonds are not subject to state taxation without the consent of Congress.*

In no case has there ever been a repudiation of the national debt of the United States or any part of it. Repudiation of the debts owed by some of the individual states, however, has occurred on several occasions.[1] Where such action takes place, the holder of a repudiated bond has no effective legal redress. He cannot sue the state except in its own courts, and even there he has no status as a plaintiff unless the state gives it to him, which it is not likely to do. He cannot enter suit in the federal courts, because the Eleventh Amendment prohibits federal courts from hearing any citizen's suit against a state. *Repudiation of public debts.*

After the Civil War there was a fear in financial circles that some portions of the national debt might be repudiated. To allay these misgivings the Fourteenth Amendment provided in 1868 that "the validity of the public debt of the United States, authorized by law, including debts incurred for payment of pensions and bounties for services in suppressing insurrection or rebellion, shall not be questioned." It was furthermore stipulated that neither the United States nor any state of the Union should assume or pay any debt or obligation incurred in aid of insurrection or rebellion against the United States, or any claim for the loss or emancipation of any slave. Debts incurred by the Confederacy or by any state of the Confederacy in connection with the Civil War were thus nullified by constitutional provision. *The Fourteenth Amendment as a security against repudiation.*

The burden of a national debt may at times be lessened by the process known as refunding. The government, when bonds are issued, may reserve the right to pay them *The practice of refunding.*

---

[1] Eleven states, mostly in the South, have repudiated some of their State issues at various times. W. A. Scott, *The Repudiation of State Debts* (N.Y., 1893).

off at any time after a designated date. If at that date the general rate of interest has fallen, it may secure the money to make the repayment by the issue of new bonds at such lower rates. Or at the expiry of the term designated in the bonds it may offer the holders their choice either of cash payment or of new bonds bearing a lower rate of interest. If the government, for example, borrows a billion dollars at five per cent in war time on bonds which are to run for twenty years, this does not mean that it must either repay the loan at the expiry of that period or keep on paying interest at five per cent. It can, and probably will, "refund" the loan at its expiration by the issue of new bonds bearing only four or perhaps even three per cent interest. This is entirely fair to the original bondholders, who get their option of either taking cash payment as promised or new bonds at current rates. It is thus possible to lessen the real burden of a national debt without actually paying it off.

*Absence of a national debt limit.* Many of the states have placed in their constitutions various provisions which limit the total amounts which the state authorities may borrow on the public credit. They have even more rigidly limited the amounts which may be borrowed by counties, cities, and towns. But there is no limit on the amount which the nation may borrow, because none was placed in the national constitution. States and municipalities are often prohibited from borrowing for certain purposes, and they are sometimes required, when they do borrow, to establish a sinking-fund which, by reason of the annual contributions made to it from revenue, will be sufficient to extinguish the debt at its maturity. No such limitations are placed upon the borrowing powers of Congress. It may borrow for any purpose, at any time, from any source, and without making provision for repayment at all. This is a sweeping power, but necessarily so in view of the emergencies which may arise.

*Is a public debt a public evil?* Until within the last generation or two all public debts were popularly looked upon as public evils. To get the nation out of debt altogether was deemed to be an end worth making sacrifices for, and the national surplus was used to lessen the load even when public improvements were greatly needed. To-day, however, the old notion has passed away. The whole national bank circulation of the United States, for example, rests upon evidences of public indebtedness.

Economists agree that the creation of debt for certain purposes and within reasonable limits is entirely justified. The doctrine propounded by the first Secretary of the Treasury, Alexander Hamilton, that a public debt, if not excessive, is a source of public strength in that the holders of government bonds become influential factors for political stability would hardly receive general acceptance at the present day; yet the opposite contention that all public debts are public afflictions is still further from popularity among authorities on public finance. Enterprises which result in permanent or semi-permanent value to the people, such as the building of the Panama Canal, or the purchase of forest reserves, or the extension of national territory ought not, in all fairness, to be paid for entirely by the taxpayers of a single year; that is, they ought not to be wholly paid for out of current revenues. Borrowing money in such a way that the cost will be gradually liquidated in the course of a term of years is the fairer plan, provided, of course, that this policy is not so distorted as to pile up huge increments for future generations to bear. A nation may be both prosperous and thrifty while yet having a national debt of large dimensions. So, too, the huge national expenditures which result from participation in armed conflict cannot be placed entirely upon the taxpayers of the day, for the dead-weight thus imposed upon the nation's whole economic system would handicap production and thus serve to impair its military resources. Business conditions take time to adjust themselves to a new and unexpected situation, hence too severe a dislocation should not be brought about if it can be avoided by a reasonable exercise of the borrowing power. Practically the entire debt of the United States has been incurred for one or other of two purposes, public improvements or war.

# CHAPTER XVII

## THE POWER TO REGULATE COMMERCE

Commerce and national prosperity.
"THE prosperity of commerce," wrote Alexander Hamilton in 1788, "is now perceived and acknowledged by all enlightened statesmen to be the most useful as well as the most productive source of national wealth, and has accordingly become a primary object of their political cares."[1] It was in recognition of this truth that the framers of the national constitution gave to the federal government what have proved to be powers of paramount importance in the matter of encouraging, maintaining, and regulating the commerce of the several states both with foreign countries and among themselves.[2]

Commercial chaos before the formation of the Union.
The chaotic condition of American commerce, indeed, did about as much as anything else to bring the states together in constitutional union. After the close of the Revolutionary War some discriminatory rules against American commerce were made by Great Britain, and the Congress of the Confederation had no way of making reprisal. The various states themselves were adopting commercial tariffs against each other. Connecticut, for example, threw her ports wide open to British shipping

---

[1] *The Federalist*, No. 12.
[2] The clauses in the national constitution directly relating to the regulation of commerce are as follows:

The Congress shall have power . . . to regulate commerce with foreign nations, and among the several states, and with the Indian tribes. (Article i, section 8.)

No tax or duty shall be laid on articles exported from any state. (Article i, section 9.)

No preference shall be given by any regulation of commerce or revenue to the ports of one state over those of another; nor shall vessels bound to, or from, one state be obliged to enter, clear, or pay duties in another. (Article i, section 9.)

while all goods imported into Connecticut from Massachusetts were subjected to duties.[1] Such commercial discriminations, as the world has too often found out, lead eventually to retaliation and often to open hostilities. The mischief was great and the dangers for the future were alarming. Never could the several states hope to live in peace and amity among themselves if each preserved the right to secure its own commercial advantage by setting at naught the welfare of all the rest. The forward-looking men of the thirteen states realized, therefore, that the commerce of all must be placed under uniform direction or the "most productive source of national wealth" would not be available in proper measure. The regulation of commerce must be made uniform, and uniformity could only be had by giving the regulatory power to some central body.

The constitution, therefore, gives to Congress complete power to regulate commerce with foreign nations and among the several states, but subject to the limitation that such regulation shall not give to one state any preference over another, and that no export duties may be levied. These provisions are deceptively simple on their face; in reality they have become, in their application to present-day commerce and commercial methods, more difficult to define with exactness than almost any other powers granted in the constitution. They were framed in days when life was simpler, when the agencies of commerce were pack-wagons and sailing vessels, when there were no steamships, railroads, telegraphs, or telephones, and almost no manufacturing for sale outside the immediate locality. The task of fitting these phrases of the eighteenth century to the intricate commercial and industrial conditions of the twentieth has devolved upon the Supreme Court. It has been performed, however, with a degree of persistence and of ultimate success which provides us with a striking illustration of constitutional expansion. As the Supreme Court frankly avowed in one important decision, the commerce power has been extended "from the horse with its rider to the stagecoach, from the sailing vessel to the steamboat, from the

*What the constitution gives to Congress in the way of powers over commerce.*

*The expansion of these powers.*

[1] For many other examples of interstate commercial rivalry, see A. C. McLaughlin, *The Confederation and the Constitution* (N. Y., 1905).

coach and the steamboat to the railroad, and from the railroad to the telegraph, according as new agencies are successively brought into use to meet the demands of increasing population and wealth." [1]

*The first landmark in this expansion: Gibbons vs. Ogden (1824).*

No one in the constitutional convention could have had even a remote idea of the vast potentialities which lay concealed in these three words "to regulate commerce" nor did the full import of the authority begin to be realized until at least a generation after the Union was established. The decision in the famous case of *Gibbons* vs. *Ogden* (1824) first brought home to the states the extent of the jurisdiction which they had handed over to Congress, and from that time forward the commerce clause has been steadily including one thing after another within its broad bounds. The elasticity of the written word finds ampler illustration here than in any other field of American constitutional development. Words and phrases, when used in a constitution, have dynamic properties. Their meanings keep step with social and economic changes; they expand to cover the necessities of each new age; they signify one thing in this generation and another in the next. Those who deplore the cold rigidity of written constitutions and laws make the error of postulating the static character of legal phraseology.

*Exact definition of the commerce power is impossible.*

In endeavoring to explain what the phrase "to regulate commerce" means to-day one is confronted with an initial difficulty. The phrase has never been authoritatively defined, and cannot be. The Supreme Court has never ventured to say that here the power begins and there it ends. An authority so vast and so steadily expanding does not, indeed, yield to exact definition. Yet from the multitude of its decisions the general lines of jurisdiction may be staked out, always with the reservation, however, that what is the law of the land to-day may not be so to-morrow.

*What is commerce?*

What, then, is the commerce which Congress under certain limitations may regulate? We have the word of Chief Justice Marshall that "commerce is intercourse," but that does not carry us far when it is further explained

[1] *Pensacola Tel. Co.* vs. *W. U. Tel. Co.*, 96 U. S. 1.

that not all intercourse is commerce.[1] Does commerce include not only trade in merchandise but the transportation of passengers and the sending of messages by telegraph or by telephone? The answer is that the term "commerce," whatever it may have meant to those who gave Congress the power to regulate it, includes all these things to-day. It embraces navigation in all its phases, and every form of transportation by land. It includes the transmission of intangible things, such as messages sent by wire or by wireless. It has broadened its scope to cover transportation through the air as well.

Mention has been made of the first great milestone in the evolution of the power to regulate commerce, the decision in the case of *Gibbons* vs. *Ogden*.[2] In this instance the Supreme Court held that commerce among the states is not the mere buying and selling, or trading in goods, but includes all the instrumentalities of trade such as vessels carrying goods or passengers from the ports of one state to those of another. Hence it was declared that no state might prevent the use of its own waters by vessels plying between the ports of two different states, that is, by vessels engaged in interstate commerce. This was but the first of a long line of decisions, which, especially during the last forty years, have steadily widened the federal law of commerce. By one decision the term "commerce" has been held to include passenger traffic; by another to include telegrams; by another telephone messages; while by still another the transportation of oil in pipe lines has been held to come within the scope of the term. On the other hand, it has been declared by the Supreme Court that such things as traffic in bills of exchange or the selling of fire and life insurance policies are not commerce. Nor does it in any event include the manufacture of goods even when they are intended to become articles of interstate commerce. Commerce does not begin until the product has started on its way. Commerce may begin after manufacture has been completed but is not a part of it.[3] In a word the term "commerce" to-day "embraces navigation, intercourse,

*Stages in the broadening of the term.*

*Passenger and freight traffic, telegrams, telephone service, pipe lines, etc.*

---

[1] *Brown* vs. *Maryland*, 12 Wheat. 419 (1827).    [2] Above, p. 248.
[3] *U. S.* vs. *Knight*, 156 U. S. (1895).

*Does not include bills of exchange, insurance, or manufacture.*

communication, traffic, the transmission of persons, and the transmission of messages,"[1] but does not include banking transactions, insurance, or manufacture. All commerce, as thus defined, when carried on either with foreign countries or among the several states, is from start to destination wholly under the regulatory power of Congress.

*The relation of manufacturing to federal control.*

When it is said, however, that manufacturing has not been held to be included in the term "commerce," this does not mean that the processes and incidents of industry cannot be to some extent controlled by the federal government. All large industries of to-day depend on a large area for their raw materials and desire a wide market for the distribution of their products. Their import of materials and their export of products, if not their actual work of manufacture, fall within the scope of commerce. They buy raw materials in one state, make them up in another, and sell the finished products in several more. Even the processes of manufacture must depend to some extent upon the regulations under which this interstate buying and selling goes on.

*Congress cannot by the exercise of its commerce power, control the incidents of manufacture.*

But the extent to which Congress may make such regulations is not well defined. During the years immediately preceding 1918 it was assumed in many quarters, for example, that Congress might prohibit the sale in foreign or interstate commerce of goods made by child-labor, thus placing a damper upon that sort of employment. But the Supreme Court decided in 1918 that the act of Congress which imposed such prohibition was unconstitutional, being a federal interference in a matter which belonged to the states alone. For the time being, therefore, it is settled that Congress cannot, under color of regulating interstate commerce, dictate the conditions under which manufacturing shall be carried on.

*The child-labor decision (1918).*

*But Congress may exercise some control through taxation.*

On the other hand, the Supreme Court is clearly on record as upholding the right of Congress to tax the manufacture of a product, even to an extent which actually operates to prohibit manufacture.[2] Manufacturing is not commerce or subject to regulation as such; but by virtue of its taxing power the national government has a method of controlling to some extent the processes and

---

[1] *Champion* vs. *Ames*, 118 U. S. 321 (1903).
[2] The Oleomargarine Case (*McCray* vs. *U. S.*, 195 U. S. 27), 1904.

incidents of manufacture whether for sale within the bounds of a single state or outside.

So much for a short survey of what commerce is. When does commerce concern a single state alone, and under what circumstances, on the other hand, does it come within the scope of "commerce with foreign nations or among the several states"? The division of power between the federal and state governments on this point is now well settled, although it is not a logical division. All commerce which begins and ends wholly within the bounds of a single state is intrastate commerce. The state alone can deal with it. But if at any point between its beginning and its end it passes outside the boundaries of the state, no matter for how short a distance, the whole transaction goes out of the state's jurisdiction and into the domain of Congress. Goods shipped from Boston to New York are under federal regulation from one place to the other, not merely while crossing the intervening states. In other words, the only way to keep from coming under the federal commerce power is to live, move, and have one's being wholly within a single state. Under present-day conditions of general economic intercourse that is a practical impossibility. The federal government has thus become the great regulator of American commercial and industrial life. That is why economic problems have thrust themselves so far to the front in discussions of national policy.

Having pointed out in general terms the extent of the commerce power possessed by Congress, it remains to indicate more specifically the limitations placed by the constitution upon the exercise of this authority. In the first place when Congress undertakes to regulate foreign commerce, it must do so uniformly. It cannot discriminate in favor of one section of the country, or in favor of one part of the population as against any other. If it imposes duties upon imports coming into the United States from foreign lands, those duties must be levied at the same rate in all ports to which the goods may come. The same rules must determine the method of valuing the goods, collecting the duties, giving refunds, and so on. Congress must regulate with an even hand. There must be no sectional

*Limitations on the power of Congress to regulate foreign commerce.*

partiality or discrimination. If Congress should try to collect a higher duty on sugar coming from Cuba to New York than on sugar coming from Cuba to New Orleans, its action would be clearly unconstitutional. So long as it observes the rule of uniformity, however, Congress may levy duties either as a means of regulating commerce or of securing revenue, without any limitation as to their nature or amount.

*The tariff as an instrument of commercial regulation.*

Strictly speaking, a tariff imposed for revenue only is imposed by virtue of the taxing power, while a tariff avowedly framed for protection comes more properly within the scope of the commerce power. But this distinction is of no practical importance, for Congress has never imposed any duties which could not easily be justified as coming well within both of these powers. A word on the tariff policy of Congress may not inappropriately be added here, for tariff questions have bulked large in the history of American politics, more consistently so, perhaps, than any other single issue or group of issues.[1] To begin with, the prevailing opinion in the thirteen states at the close of the Revolutionary War leaned rather strongly to the doctrine of free trade. That was natural, because the taxing of trade by parliament had been one of the causes of the war. But when the constitution had been adopted and a new national government established, one of the first acts of Congress was to enact a tariff in which the desirability of protecting the industries of the country was frankly asserted. The duties imposed by this first tariff of 1789 were relatively low, but they mark the beginning of the protectionist movement.

*Beginnings of American tariff history.*

*Hamilton's Report on Manufactures (1791).*

This movement soon gained force, moreover, by reason of the cogent arguments put forth in its behalf by Alexander Hamilton in his famous Report on Manufactures (1791), a document which still ranks as a classic of protectionist literature. Nevertheless, the duties on imports continued to be fixed at low figures, and there was little in the way of tariff controversy until the war with England began in 1812. Duties were then doubled, and when the war was over, they were not materially reduced. During the next

[1] For a full narrative see F. W. Taussig, *Tariff History of the United States* (6th ed., N. Y., 1914).

two decades, indeed, they kept going up; the principle of tariff-for-revenue being relegated to the background, while protectionist sentiment gained headway. The northern states favored protection, and they were for the time in the ascendant. By 1832 the tariff had become a powerful weapon of industrial protection. Then came a reaction, slow at first and temporarily interrupted on one occasion, but gaining in impetus as the years went by. The tariff was revised downward from time to time until it was substantially upon a revenue basis once more.  *The tariffs of the period preceding the Civil War.*

The Civil War inaugurated a third period in tariff history. So much money was needed to finance the struggle that duties again shot up to high levels. And when the war ended, the need of revenue to liquidate the debt was urged as a reason for keeping the duties where they were. The Republicans were in the saddle, and they were committed to the policy of protection. So firmly did the gospel of protection seem to be anchored in the public mind that General Hancock, the Democratic candidate for the presidency in 1880, suggested that the tariff was nothing more than a "local issue."[1] But it soon became a national issue of great prominence, and with various ups and downs it has not ceased to be such. On a dozen or more occasions since 1880 Congress has revamped the tariff, revising it up or revising it down, narrowing or widening the free list; but it has never departed altogether from the principle of protection. Congress continues to regulate foreign commerce by taxing it for the benefit of American industry. The constitutionality of its power to do so is not doubtful in the slightest degree. The right to regulate commerce includes the right to tax imports or even to prohibit imports altogether.  *The Civil War tariffs.*  *Tariff developments since 1880.*

In the enactment of tariff legislation, however, the national legislature has not always shown itself at its best. The machinery of Congress is not well adapted to secure the best results in tariff-making. Since 1861 all tariff measures  *The procedure of Congress is not well adapted to tariff-making.*

[1] Hancock's words were "the tariff is a local affair," but his dictum has passed into popular currency as "a local issue." What he meant was that the country as a whole favored protection but that every local area wanted a different sort of tariff.

have been framed by the Ways and Means Committee of the House of Representatives. After this committee has prepared the bill and its accompanying schedules, the measure is taken up by the entire House. Here it may be amended at will in the interest of any proposition that can secure a majority. Then the bill as amended goes to the Senate, where the process of overhauling is continued, and in the end it invariably goes back to the House again. To reconcile whatever differences may exist between the action of the two chambers a Committee of Conference is appointed, and this committee makes the final readjustments. In the end the tariff is altogether likely to be a medley of compromises and trades, bearing little resemblance to the measure as originally drawn and with no one directly responsible for its final form. On rare occasions, however, this has not been the case. When one political party controls a working majority in both House and Senate, a tariff bill can be drawn and pushed through without substantial change if the leaders are agreed upon what they want and if they have the support of the President. That is what happened in 1913. But the ordinary vicissitudes of American politics are such that legislative and executive solidarity of this nature is quite the exception.

The Tariff Commission. To better this situation resort has been had to the expedient of a tariff commission. The first step in this direction was taken as early as 1865, but the work of the commission appointed in that year amounted to little and it soon went out of existence. Then in the early eighties another attempt was made. A commission of nine members was appointed; it studied tariff questions carefully and made recommendations to Congress, but the latter gave little heed to its advice. No further steps towards a more efficient tariff policy were taken until 1909, when Congress provided for the creation of a Tariff Board made up of three members appointed by the President. The duties of this board were to investigate and to report upon the condition of various American industries, their relation to the tariff, their production-costs, the rate of wages paid in such industries, and the rates paid in corresponding manufactures in other countries. But before this board could accomplish more than a small part of the work planned for it, Congress refused to continue the appropriations for its support and it went out of existence in 1912. The sentiment in favor of some such body would not down, however, and in 1916 Congress was persuaded by President Wilson to provide once more for a tariff commission. This board now consists of five members appointed by the President, one of the number being designated as chairman. Its duties are to study the tariff needs of the country from every point of view and to report annually with recommendations. It has, of course, no power to make any changes in the tariff, its functions being of an informational and advisory nature only. Even so, its work may be of the highest value in adjusting future tariffs to the actual needs of the country, whether for revenue or protection, rather than leaving the matter a prey to partisan and sectional intriguery.

By virtue of its power to regulate foreign commerce Congress has also passed numerous laws relating to the immigration of aliens. These laws prescribe the conditions under which immigrants may enter the United States and exclude some classes of aliens altogether. For example, the federal laws exclude all persons, except those engaged in the various professions, who come to the United States to perform labor under contracts made before their arrival. They also prohibit, with certain exceptions, the immigration of Chinese.[1] More recently a literacy test has been provided by law for all otherwise admissible immigrants. Among those inadmissible under all circumstances, however, are insane persons, those likely to become public burdens, or afflicted with serious ailments, polygamists, anarchists, and persons who have been convicted of serious crimes. Admissible aliens are required to pay, upon entering the United States, a small head tax. *The control of Congress over immigration.*

The administration of these rules is in the hands of the commissioner-general of immigration, an officer appointed by the President. At each port of entry for immigrants there is a board of inquiry, under his jurisdiction, and this board determines whether an immigrant is entitled to enter. If it decides that he is not entitled to be admitted, he is *How the immigration laws are administered.*

[1] The exceptions include students, merchants, and professional men.

ordered to be deported and the steamship company bringing him in must take him away. Appeals from the decisions of these boards may be carried to the commissioner, however, and as a last resort to the Secretary of Labor. There is no appeal to the courts from the Secretary's decision.

<small>Methods of regulating interstate commerce.</small>

It is by means of the tariff and the immigration laws that Congress chiefly exercises its power to regulate commerce with foreign nations. Commerce among the several states, on the other hand, is an entirely different matter to which these laws have obviously no direct relation. Interstate commerce has been the subject of many regulating laws relating not only to the rates charged and the service rendered by transportation companies but to combinations in restraint of trade between the states, to unfair competition, the inspection of food and drugs, and to a multitude of other matters. These laws, however, are not self-enforcing, hence a considerable amount of administrative machinery has been created to see that their various provisions are duly applied. The scope of the laws, in fact, may best be understood from a general survey of the work which these federal regulating bodies perform.

<small>The Interstate Commerce Commission: Its composition.</small>

First in point of importance among these administrative regulating bodies is the Interstate Commerce Commission. It was established in 1887 and at the outset consisted of five members named by the President. The number of members has subsequently been increased to nine and the powers of the commission have also been greatly widened during the last thirty years by various acts of Congress.[1]

<small>Its functions.</small>

The functions of the Interstate Commerce Commission include the general carrying out of the federal laws relating to steamship and railroad companies, express and sleeping car companies, telegraph and telephone companies, and oil pipe companies, all when engaged in interstate commerce. It may investigate, either upon complaint made to it or on its own initiative, any allegations of overcharge, or faulty

---

[1] The Acts of March 2, 1889, and of February 11, 1893; the Hepburn Act of June 29, 1906; the Act of June 18, 1910, and so on. Members of the commission are paid salaries of $10,000 per year and are appointed for seven-year terms.

service or discrimination in rates. By the Act of 1906 the commission is authorized to fix, when petitioned to do so and after proper hearings, the maximum rates to be charged and also to make reasonable rules as to service. The Act of 1910 further enlarged these powers by empowering the commission to prescribe maximum charges even when no complaint against existing rates had been filed with it.

As the regulations now stand, all railway rates in interstate commerce must be reasonable in the judgment of the commission; there must be no favoritism as between different shippers or patrons, no rebates, and no discrimination against any person or locality. With certain specified exceptions no free passes may be given; and no railroad is allowed to transport any merchandise which it is itself engaged in producing. There are many other regulations applying to all companies engaged in interstate commerce. Schedules of rates must be public, kept open to inspection, and must not be changed without due notice to the commission, which may withhold its approval of the changes. All the companies must keep their accounts in the way which the commission prescribes and must make periodical reports to it. It will be seen, therefore, that the commission has functions of a wide variety and great importance.[1] It is the country's most powerful administrative tribunal. In addition to all these things, moreover, it was given, a few years ago, the enormous task of securing a physical valuation of all the railroads in order that a more intelligent determination of rates might be made possible. *The regulation of rates.*

From the rulings of the Interstate Commerce Commission an appeal may be taken on matters of constitutional privilege to the federal courts. There is no escape from the necessity of granting this right of appeal. The constitution does not permit Congress to endow the commission with final powers. No law of the land may deprive a citizen or a corporation of judicial protection against a deprivation of their property. Hence the regular federal courts have many appeals from decisions of the commission brought before them, so *Appeals from the Commission's rulings.*

[1] During the period in which the railroads are under federal operation (see below, p. 259) these functions are naturally diminished.

s

many, indeed, that these appeals form a serious tax upon their time. In order to lighten this load, Congress in 1910 established a new Commerce Court, to be composed of judges selected from the federal circuit courts. This new tribunal was to hear, in the first instance, all appeals from the orders of the Interstate Commerce Commission. The Commerce Court, however, soon came into disfavor by its frequent reversals of these rulings, and in 1913 it was abolished.

*The division of authority over commerce between federal and state governments.*

It should again be pointed out, even at the risk of overemphasis, that the Interstate Commerce Commission has no authority over intercourse which keeps strictly within the bounds of a single state. So far as such commerce is concerned, each state provides its own regulations and its own regulating body, commonly known as a railroad commission or public service board. This division of authority over transportation, telegraph and telephone companies has been a great source of friction and of working at cross purposes. Every large railroad does both sorts of business, carrying some goods and passengers from one point to another within the same state under state regulation, and carrying other goods and passengers between points in different states under federal regulation. The states, moreover, regulate the organization, the capitalization, and the borrowing powers of these companies (because each obtains its charter from the state and not from the federal authorities), while the nation, through the Interstate Commerce Commission, is usually the deciding factor in determining the revenues and the conditions of service. The spirit and methods of regulation have not always been the same from both quarters, hence the double and divided supervision has in many cases unreasonably hampered the railroads in their efforts to give good service at fair cost. Regulation can never be altogether satisfactory until it is wholly placed in the same hands, that is to say until some one authority is vested with power to control the organization, borrowing powers, income, rates, service, hours of labor, and every other incident of transportation. All such problems are interlocking and no one can be solved without regard to the others. The solution of the matter is not a simple one, however, for there are serious objections to vesting all of this power in the hands of the federal government.

On December 27, 1917, the President of the United States, by virtue of war powers conferred upon him by Congress, took over the operation of all the important railroads of the country, placing them for the time being under a Director-General named by himself. In the spring of 1918 Congress by law provided that the owners of the railroads should be compensated during the period of federal operation by being guaranteed a net income equal to the average net earnings of the three preceding years. This statute likewise provided for the physical upkeep of the roads and for their re-delivery to the owners in as good condition as when taken over, this return to private operation to take place not more than twenty-one months after the close of the war. The President was given authority to fix rates and terms of service subject to the approval of the Interstate Commerce Commission, but all such determinations of the President were authorized to take effect at the date of their issue and to remain in effect until overruled. *Federal operation of the railroads in war time.*

Another important agency of Congress in carrying out its laws relating to interstate commerce is the Federal Trade Commission, established in 1914.[1] Its organization has been already described.[2] The commission's functions are twofold. In the first place it is charged with the duty of preventing unfair competition in foreign or interstate trade by manufacturers or manufacturing corporations or any other concerns except banks and common carriers. The latter are under separate federal supervision, one under the Comptroller of the Currency and the other under the Interstate Commerce Commission. The Federal Trade Commission may, after due investigation and hearings, issue orders designed to prevent unfair competition, but appeals from such orders may be taken to the Circuit Court of Appeals and from its decision, again, to the Supreme Court. The other function of the commission is to investigate, when *The Federal Trade Commission.*

---
[1] This commission took over the powers of the federal Bureau of Corporations which had been created in 1903.
[2] See above, p. 140.

asked to do so, the facts in any judicial proceeding which may be begun by the federal government to dissolve an illegal combination.

*The attempts to suppress combinations in restraint of trade.*

Combinations organized for the purpose of stifling competition or otherwise restraining interstate trade have long been under the ban. It is a principle of the common law that all combinations designed to restrain trade *unreasonably* are illegal. This was the legal situation in the United States until 1890. In that year, however, Congress went a step further and passed a law, commonly known as the Sherman Anti-Trust Act, the first provision of which was as follows: "Every contract, or combination in the form of trust or otherwise, or conspiracy in restraint of trade or commerce among the several states or with foreign nations, is hereby declared to be illegal." This provision, it will be noted, makes no distinction between combinations which are unreasonable and those which are not. Going further than the common law its wording seemed to forbid all combinations in restraint of trade, whatever their nature.

*The Sherman Anti-Trust Law of 1890.*

For a dozen years or more this provision slumbered on the statute books;[1] but in 1904 it was brought to activity by the decision of the Supreme Court in the Northern Securities Case.[2] This decision arose out of an action entered by the federal authorities to dissolve what amounted to a virtual merger of two great railroads, the Northern Pacific and the Great Northern, through the agency of a holding corporation known as the Northern Securities Company, which had acquired a majority of the common stock of each railroad. The Supreme Court held that the combination was in restraint of trade and ordered it to be dissolved.

*The Northern Securities Case (1904)*

Then came some other decisions, notably in the Standard Oil Company's Case (1911) and the American Tobacco Company's Case (1911), which held that these concerns were also combinations in restraint of trade and ordered their dissolution. But in rendering its decision in these cases the Supreme Court gave for the first time a definitive

*Other decisions under the Sherman Act.*

---

[1] In 1895 the Supreme Court decided (*U. S.* vs. *Knight Co.*, 156 U. S. 1) that the Sherman Act did not forbid the merging of manufacturing companies.

[2] *Northern Securities Co.* vs. *U. S.*, 193 U. S. 197 (1904).

interpretation of the Sherman Act. The court explained that the mere existence of a combination in relation to trade did not, according to the provisions of the Sherman Act, render it illegal, but that every such combination must be adjudged in accordance with its purpose and in the light of reason. Hence the court, although it held these particular concerns to be illegal, set forth the principle that it would not order the dissolution of combinations merely because they happened to restrain trade but only when it appeared that they were able and ready to restrain trade *unreasonably*. This dictum passed into popular discussion as "the rule of reason." The gist of the rule is that while the exact wording of the Sherman Act differs from the old rule of the common law with reference to combinations in restraint of trade, it was not the intent of Congress to change that rule in substance but merely to provide for its more efficient application.

The "rule of reason."

In its practical applications the Sherman Act has clearly demonstrated the inferiority of purely legislative as compared with the administrative regulation of trade. Its enforcement no doubt put an end to some huge commercial abuses but, on the other hand, it has in many cases proved an obstacle to the proper consolidation of business in the interest of economy. Competition is often a prolific source of wastefulness so that in the end the public gains nothing from it. When the national government in 1917 took over the operation of the railroads it at once proceeded to do on an unparalleled scale what it had always prevented the railroads themselves from doing. It put everything under central control, eliminated duplications in service, cut away every vestige of competition and operated every mile of trackage as part of one giant transportation monopoly. Enormous savings were made in this way, thus demonstrating that more can be had in the matter of results through the elimination of competition than through the compulsory fomenting of it. Administrative supervision such as is exercised over railroads by the Interstate Commerce Commission, over the banks by the Comptroller of the Currency, and over industrial concerns by the Federal Trade Commission is much more flexible and in the long run more salutary from the

Merits and defects of the Anti-Trust Law.

public point of view than the sweeping prohibitions of the law can ever hope to be.

**The extent to which the states may restrain commerce.** These, in brief, are the powers and instrumentalities of the national government with respect to commerce. Lest a misleading impression has been given let it be repeated, however, that federal jurisdiction in many of these matters is not exclusive; the several states have some powers even with respect to foreign and interstate commerce. The constitution expressly permits a state to lay duties on imports or exports whenever such "may be absolutely necessary for executing its inspection laws," but it may not use this power as a means of obtaining revenue. Moreover, the Supreme Court has consistently upheld the doctrine that reasonable **Police power in its relation to interstate trade.** state laws for the protection of the public safety, health, and morals, even when they operate to restrain interstate commerce, are valid. Thus a state may establish its own quarantine, may prohibit the operation of freight trains on Sundays, may regulate the maximum speed of trains, and so on, even though such regulations interfere with carriers engaged in interstate commerce. The state regulations must be reasonably designed to protect its own citizens and no more; they cannot interfere with interstate commerce on any other ground.

There is, accordingly, a margin for conflict between two spheres of authority, the commerce power of Congress and the police power of the states. This was well illustrated in **The Original Package Decision (1890).** the so-termed Original Package Case. Various states have laws forbidding the manufacture or sale of intoxicating liquors within their own borders, Maine, Kansas, and Virginia, for example. Do these prohibitory laws operate to prevent the importation of liquor from other states and its sale within the prohibition area? Many years ago the Supreme Court in a well-known decision which passed into popular parlance as the Original Package ruling held that the prohibitory laws of states cannot ordinarily interfere with the importation and sale of any merchandise so long as the commodity remained in the unbroken package in which it was delivered for transportation into the state from a point outside.[1] The court did not lay this down as an

[1] *Leisy* vs. *Hardin* (135 U. S. 100), 1890.

absolute rule but as a general principle to be followed whenever special circumstances did not seem to require a departure from it. This decision established the doctrine that in the absence of permission from Congress the states cannot ordinarily prohibit unbroken importations from abroad or from another state.

Congress, however, soon cleared up this difficulty so far as the importation and sale of liquors is concerned. Immediately after this decision it passed the Wilson Act of 1890, which provided that all intoxicating liquors brought into any state should be subject to the state laws as regards their sale even in original packages, and in 1913 it went still further by forbidding altogether the importation of liquors into states which have laws against importation. In 1919 the Eighteenth Amendment was adopted, making provision for national prohibition. The "original package" doctrine still holds in a general way as regards tobacco and other articles of general trade. *The Wilson Act.*

The regulating power of Congress over foreign and interstate commerce, therefore, while paramount whenever exercised, is not exclusive. When a state, for example, makes laws for the sanitary protection of its harbors, these laws apply to foreign merchant vessels in port, and if they are not in conflict with laws made by Congress they are held to represent a reasonable exercise of the state's police power.[1] What the constitution requires is that the states shall not set out to determine the course of commerce and that they shall not, under color of their police power, undertake to raise revenues from any form of commerce which is not wholly carried on within their own boundaries. Within this latter sphere the states may tax, license, regulate, or even prohibit as they see fit, provided they do not deprive any one of his property without due process of law or deny to any one the equal protection of the laws.

[1] "The fact that state regulations adopted in the exercise of the general police power may incidentally affect foreign commerce does not render such state regulations necessarily invalid. If they are not unreasonable, nor calculated to effect a discrimination, and do not in substance amount to general regulations of such commerce as is placed within the control of Congress, they will be upheld." Emlin McClain, *Constitutional Law in the United States* (2d ed., N. Y., 1913), p. 153.

**Federal taxation of corporations.**

Since 1909 all corporations doing business in the United States, even when such business is wholly within a single state, have been subject to a federal corporation tax.[1] The levy of this tax has been upheld, not as a regulation of commerce, but as an excise laid upon the privilege of doing business under a corporate form of organization. As a means of assessing the tax, every corporation is required to make to the national government an annual report disclosing its earnings and expenses, so that the weapon of publicity as a means of corporate regulation is now in the government's hands.

**Proposed federal incorporation.**

But although business corporations pay federal taxes and make an annual report to the national authorities, nearly all of them are operating under powers conferred by the states. In other words, nearly all have state charters. Congress undoubtedly has authority to charter corporations provided they are to engage in foreign or interstate commerce and at times has exercised this authority, but not to any large extent. It has frequently been proposed, however, that the national government should require all concerns engaged in such commerce to take out national charters, so that the charters of all corporations might be made uniform and federal control rendered more effective. Another suggestion is that while leaving the states to provide corporations of all kinds with their charters, the national government might prescribe a federal license for all those desiring to carry on foreign or interstate commerce, thus providing itself with a strict and effective regulatory power through the possibility of revoking a license at any time. Thus far, however, nothing tangible has been brought to pass along either of these lines.

[1] Provided their net earnings are more than a designated amount.

## CHAPTER XVIII

### THE WAR POWERS

"SECURITY against foreign danger is one of the primitive objects of civil society. It is an avowed and essential object of the American Union. The power requisite for attaining it must be effectually confided to the federal councils." That, in the words of Madison, is the reason why war powers of practically unlimited extent are conferred upon the national government by the constitution. Seven specific grants of war power to Congress appear in that document, namely, to declare war, to raise and support armies, to provide and maintain a navy, to make rules for the government of the land and naval forces, to provide for calling forth the militia to execute the laws of the nation, to provide for organizing, arming, and disciplining the militia, and to exercise exclusive legislation over places acquired for forts, magazines, arsenals, dockyards, and other needful buildings. Among the eighteen clauses of the constitution which enumerate the powers of Congress, therefore, more than one-third deal with the various branches of military and naval authority.[1]

*Scope of the war powers.*

[1] The exact wording of these various clauses is as follows: "To declare war, grant letters of marque and reprisal, and make rules concerning captures on land and water."
"To raise and support armies, but no appropriation of money to that use shall be for a longer term than two years."
"To provide and maintain a navy."
"To make rules for the government and regulation of the land and naval forces."
"To provide for calling forth the militia to execute the laws of the Union, suppress insurrections, and repel invasions."
"To provide for organizing, arming, and disciplining the militia, and for governing such part of them as may be employed in the service of the United States, reserving to the States respectively the appointment of the officers, and the authority of training the militia according to the discipline prescribed by Congress."

## 266 THE GOVERNMENT OF THE UNITED STATES

1. The power to declare war.

Congress alone can declare war, but a formal declaration is not an essential preliminary to the outbreak of hostilities. Such declarations are customary among nations, but no rule of international law requires their issue. Declarations of war are not issued primarily for the benefit of the adversary but for the information of neutrals so that they may observe the strict rules of neutrality and keep out of the way. Not infrequently a declaration of war is issued after the hostilities have actually begun, as, for example, in the Spanish-American War of 1898. When Congress does act, however, a declaration of war is usually embodied in a resolution passed in both Houses and signed by the President. This resolution recites the reasons for the resort to arms and ends by declaring that a state of war exists.

2. The power "to raise and support armies."

The power "to raise and support armies" is vested in Congress without any limitation save that no appropriation of money for this purpose shall be made for a longer term than two years. In other words no Congress may commit succeeding Congresses to a programme of military expenditures. In all other respects, whether as to the size of the army, the method of recruiting it, or the measures necessary for supporting it, Congress has unlimited discretion. This wide latitude was wisely given because no one could foresee the dangers with which the Union might some day be confronted, but it was assumed that no standing army of any considerable size would ordinarily be required.

The regular army.

During Washington's two terms as President the army of the United States (as distinct from the militia of the states), never exceeded five thousand of all ranks. But even this was regarded by the anti-Federalists as too large, and in 1798 the legislature of Virginia, under the inspiration of Jefferson and Madison, voted that "our security from invasion and the strength of our militia render a standing army unnecessary." The danger of a war with Napoleonic France, however, soon led to a temporary increase in the size of the regular forces. During the War of 1812 Congress authorized the raising of about thirty-five thousand men by enlistment in the army, but men did not enlist readily and the war was fought chiefly by the militia called into the national service. After peace had been made in 1815 the regular army again dropped in numbers and was not again substantially increased until a few years prior to the War with Mexico. Even in the Civil War the strength of the regular army was not raised to any formidable proportions. By far the greater portion of the fighting forces were obtained by calling out the militia of the several states and by encouraging volunteer organizations. After the war the maximum size of the regular army was fixed at twenty-five thousand, a figure which was raised to sixty-one thousand for the Spanish War in 1898. Thereafter it continued to range between sixty and one hundred thousand until after the outbreak of hostilities in Europe when comprehensive measures for its further increase were taken. The regular army has always been recruited by voluntary enlistment. It has never contained any units raised by conscription. It is, as its name implies, a permanent establishment, composed of trained officers and men who give their entire time to the service.[1]

*The volunteer forces.*

Although the regular army, upon the participation of the United States in the European War, was recruited by enlistment to the highest figure in its history, and although the organized militia of the various states was called into the federal service, the bulk of the expeditionary forces were raised by the application of the so-termed Selective Service Law, passed by Congress in 1917.[2] This act, with its amendments, provided at first for the selective conscription of male citizens between the ages of twenty-one and thirty-one and later for an extension to include all between the ages of eighteen and forty-five. A registration of all such persons was ordered and the first increment of the new army was drawn from the lists by lot after a due apportionment of the required number had been made among the states. For subsequent increments, however, all registrants were divided according to their circumstances into various classes, the first class including physically fit persons without dependents,

*The national army.*

---

[1] By the provisions of the National Defence Act of 1916 the authorized strength of the Regular Army of the United States was fixed at about 133,000 of all ranks.

[2] Approved by the President, May 18, 1917; amended August 30, 1918.

not engaged in necessary war work or in essential employments. Selections were then made wholly from the first class. The entire work of selecting men for the army was performed under the supervision of the provost-marshal-general, an official of the War Department, assisted by civilian boards in all parts of the country.

*Scope of the power "to support armies."* The power "to raise and support armies" gives to Congress in war time an authority over every branch of national life which is well-nigh unlimited. The events of recent years have shown this impressively. When an army is in training or in the field every branch of commerce or industry, even the home life and habits of the people, may be placed under any necessary restraint to facilitate its "support." It was by virtue of this authority that Congress empowered the President to establish systems of food and fuel administration with power to regulate supply and to control consumption. It is by virtue of this authority "to support armies" that the compulsory shutting down of industries for short periods was decreed. The taking-over of the railroads likewise came within the scope of this power. That action may also be within the power which Congress possesses to regulate commerce; but there was no need to have recourse to that interpretation. The war authority is broad enough to cover it. The huge shipbuilding program upon which the nation embarked in 1917 is also within the same category. In time of peace the commerce clause might be invoked to validate the construction, ownership, and operation of merchant vessels by the national government, although it is not certain that it could be invoked successfully. But so long as the nation is at war there appears to be very little, if anything, in the way of construction, conservation, or regulation that Congress cannot command. The last ounce of national energy may be necessary to support military operations; if so, Congress may call for it. This is as it ought to be. The framers of the constitution acted with great foresight when they set no shackles upon the national government in time of war.

*Control of the food and fuel supply.*

*Operation of the railroads.*

*The shipbuilding program.*

Power "to provide and maintain a navy" is also given to Congress, in this case without any restriction as to the period for which appropriations may be made. The naval authority includes the right of Congress to make rules for the general administration of the sea forces, including the organization of the navy department and its various technical bureaus. It also authorizes the voting of money for the construction of vessels, the determination of the type of ships to be built, the provision of navy-yards and repair depots, and the entire general direction of the nation's naval policy. While the immediate direction of the navy is in the hands of the President as its commander-in-chief, acting through the Secretary of the Navy, the organization and general policy are both within the jurisdiction of Congress.

3. The power "to provide and maintain a navy."

Five years after the establishment of the national government Congress provided for the construction of six frigates, which became the nucleus of the United States navy. A few years later a separate Department of the Navy was created, naval affairs having been theretofore under the control of the War Department. Some impetus to naval construction was given by the War of 1812, but from the close of this war until 1861 the armed sea forces of the government received astonishingly little attention. A large naval establishment was built up during the Civil War, but it was allowed to disintegrate when the struggle was over. The navy of to-day began its real development about 1885, when a complete reorganization of the department took place; but it received new impetus during and immediately after the War with Spain in 1898. At the outbreak of the European War the navy of the United States ranked third among the fleets of the world.

History of the navy.

The authority to "make rules for the government and regulation of the land and naval forces" is also devolved upon Congress by the constitution. The general rules for the government of the land forces are contained in the Articles of War. On the outbreak of the Revolutionary War in 1775 the Continental Congress adopted with some changes the code of military rules which governed the English army at that time. These were continued in force, with some further modifications, by resolution of the first Congress of the United States in 1789, and by successive

4. The power to make rules for the land and sea forces.

The Articles of War.

enactments thereafter until 1806, when they were revised and somewhat altered. Although further amendments were made, particularly during the Civil War, the Articles remained without great changes until 1912 when another general revision took place with numerous alterations.[1] The navy is also governed by a general code of regulations which Congress has enacted.

**Military law: what it implies.** These codes of rules, enacted by Congress for the government of the land and naval forces, make up that branch of jurisprudence which is commonly known as military law. It should be clearly distinguished from martial law. Military law applies only to persons who are in the military or naval service. Martial law is a term used to designate the government of any territory when the ordinary civil administration is superseded by the military authorities.

**Distinguished from martial law.** When martial law is proclaimed the ordinary laws and courts are no longer paramount: the military authorities prescribe the rules and administer them for the time being. Martial law applies to the inhabitants of the area in which it is proclaimed. It may, but does not necessarily, include within its scope the members of the armed forces.

**Military law and military tribunals.** Military law establishes many rules of conduct to which civilians are not subject but which are regarded as essential for the proper maintenance of discipline. The enforcement of these rules of military law is not intrusted to the ordinary courts but to special tribunals known as courts martial composed of officers named for the purpose.

**Courts martial.** There are three types of courts martial, — summary, special, and general. A summary court martial is held by a single officer and deals with minor offences. A special court martial consists of from three to five officers and has a broader jurisdiction. A general court martial is made up of from five to thirteen officers and may try any crime or offence made punishable by the Articles of War. Every special or general court martial is assisted by a legal adviser known as a judge-advocate, who prosecutes the case in the name of the United States, examines the witnesses, keeps a record of the proceedings, and is the legal adviser of the court. A prisoner on trial by such courts martial is also

[1] The latest edition is the Code of 1916.

permitted to have his own counsel. Punishment in varying degrees up to and including the death penalty may be awarded; but the sentence of a court martial must always be submitted for approval or disapproval to the commanding officer by whose order the court was convened. In certain cases the approval of the President is required before the sentence of a court martial can be carried into effect.[1]

Martial law may be proclaimed in any area at any time by Congress, or by the President if such action is urgently required before action by Congress can be had. It is not proclaimed except in case of invasion, insurrection, civil or foreign war, and then only in districts where the ordinary law proves itself unable to secure the public safety. There are no prescribed rules of martial law. The orders of the officer commanding the military forces, when duly promulgated, are to be obeyed and their disobedience may be summarily punished by the military authorities. In other words martial law is not a statutory code but is made up of the day-to-day regulations which are rendered necessary by the exigencies of military occupation. Special military tribunals, which should be distinguished from courts martial, are established to administer martial law if necessary; but occasionally the existing courts are retained. Martial law was administered on an extensive scale over large sections of territory during the Civil War. *What martial law means.*

While the establishment of martial law in any area deprives the inhabitants of their ordinary civil law and civil courts it does not of itself withdraw from them the constitutional rights of citizens. Military as well as civil officials are bound by the constitution and the substitution of martial for ordinary law does not change the relation between the individual and the nation. The privilege of the writ of habeas corpus is not suspended by the mere proclamation of martial law. This suspension must be specifically made and in a strictly legal sense it can only be made by Congress although the suspension was ordered during the *Limitations on martial law.*

---

[1] The details are too numerous to be given here. They may be found in the *Manual for Courts-Martial* (Washington, 1917, War Dept. Doc. No. 560), par. 378. See also G. Glenn, *The Army and the Law* (N.Y., 1918).

Civil War by the President. The privilege of this writ enables any one held in custody to obtain a speedy hearing before a regular court; its suspension means that a prisoner may be held indefinitely without a hearing. The constitution requires, accordingly, that this privilege be not suspended except when in case of rebellion or invasion the public safety demands it.

*Military government.* When territory is conquered and held by an invading force it is usually given, for the time being, a military government. This, again, should be distinguished from the administration of martial law, for while the establishment of military government involves the superseding of the old sovereignty it does not usually abrogate the existing legal system. A military government, for example, was established by the United States in Porto Rico after its conquest from Spain in 1898, and remained in charge of the island until Congress made provision for a civil administration, but martial law was not proclaimed, nor was the old Spanish jurisprudence at once abrogated.

Military law, martial law, and military government, accordingly, are three quite different things although they are often confused. The first, which applies during peace as well as during war, includes within its jurisdiction only members of the land and naval forces. It is the system of law which the courts martial enforce. The second replaces the ordinary civil law whenever, either in peace or war, the ordinary administration proves inadequate to maintain the public safety. It applies to all the inhabitants of the area in which it is proclaimed. The third, military government, is a form of rule temporarily set up in conquered or occupied territory.

*5. The power to call forth the militia.* When the military provisions of the federal constitution were being agreed upon, it was taken for granted that a well-regulated militia rather than a standing army ought to be the backbone of national defence. The militia of the colonies had done good service during the French Wars and a large part of the Continental Army during the Revolution had been created by the mustering-in of militia organizations. The dread of a standing army, which had been so long a bugbear of public opinion in England, was quite as strong in America, hence the prominence given to the militia in

1787 "as the only substitute that can be devised for a standing army and the best possible security against it."[1]

As defined by the national laws the militia includes all citizens between the ages of eighteen and forty-five and this entire force is legally subject to the call of the President to enforce the laws, to suppress insurrection, or to repel invasion; but in actuality only a small portion of this body is regularly organized into the militia or National Guard of the several states. *Who constitute the militia?*

The constitutional status of the militia is somewhat complicated, and widespread misunderstanding exists concerning it. The militia, as such, cannot be used outside the United States. The constitution allows the federal authorities to call out the militia for three purposes only, "to execute the laws of the Union, to suppress insurrections and to repel invasions," none of which operations contemplate service on foreign soil. Whenever it has been desired, therefore, to use the organized militia of the states in service outside the national boundaries the practice has been to organize a federal volunteer army and to permit the transfer of the militia to this branch of the forces. That is what was done in 1898. The National Defence Act of 1916 (Section 111) provides, however, that the President may "draft into the military service of the United States" any or all members of the National Guard whenever Congress authorizes the use of armed forces in excess of the regular army. This "federalizing" of the militia units takes them wholly out of state jurisdiction and places them on exactly the same footing as the other national forces. *Legal status of the militia.* *Mustering the militia into the federal service.*

During periods when the militia are not in the service of the nation the constitution provides for a division of jurisdiction. Congress has power to provide for the "organizing, arming, and disciplining" of the militia, but "the appointment of officers and the authority of training the militia according to the discipline prescribed by Congress" are matters which are expressly reserved to the states. The reasons for this separation of functions are to be found in the public sentiment of the post-Revolutionary era. The *6. The power to control the organization, arming, and disciplining of the militia at all times.*

[1] *The Federalist*, No. 29.

274    THE GOVERNMENT OF THE UNITED STATES

states were jealous of their military privileges and would not have tolerated a complete extinction of their rights in this field. On the other hand it was obvious that if each state was left entirely to itself in the matter of organizing, arming and drilling its militia the country would never be able, in time of emergency, to call forth a homogeneous army. Accordingly the national government was given such authority, and only such authority, as would suffice to secure the necessary uniformity in the militia systems of the several states, while the states themselves were allowed to retain the reins of direct control, including the appointment of all militia officers. This latter right was the one upon which the states laid the greatest emphasis.

The exercise of this control.

As early as 1792 Congress passed the first act for "organizing, arming, and disciplining" the militia, and this statute continued in effect without very material changes until 1903, although the various wars of the nineteenth century showed that most of its provisions were absurdly inadequate. In this year a general measure for the improvement of the militia was passed by Congress. Provision was made for supplying all militia units with the same uniforms and equipment, also for their instruction by officers of the regular army and for a periodic inspection in the interests of efficiency. An important stipulation of this act was that militia units might be mustered into the federal service in time of war by a procedure therein set forth. A few years later (1908) Congress provided for the distribution to the states of an annual grant to assist them in the maintenance of their militia, and in 1916 various other changes were made, chiefly in the direction of accentuating the federal government's control.[1]

While the division of military authority, as provided for

[1] These provisions were embodied in the National Defence Act (approved, June 3, 1916). The numbers of the National Guard were fixed in each state at 200 rank and file for each of its senators and representatives in Congress, with a provision that in each succeeding year this number is to be increased by 50 per cent until a total peace strength of 800 for each senator and representative is reached. Various provisions relating to the disciplining of the state militia, the qualifications and pay of officers and men, and as to closer federal supervision were also included. This legislation may be found in John H. Wigmore's *Source Book of Military Law and War-Time Legislation* (St. Paul, 1919), pp. 384–444.

in the constitution, was a necessary concession to the states and could not have been avoided, its practical workings have been at all times far from satisfactory. The federal government makes the rules of organization and discipline, but so long as these rules are carried out by officers whom the states appoint the hands of the War Department are benumbed. In many of the states the appointment of militia officers has been largely a matter of personal and political favoritism, with little regard for the military capacity or experience of the persons appointed. The annual training of the militia, extending over a few days only, has too often been the occasion of large expenditures without any substantial results. The militia of the United States will not be an effective force until its entire control, whether in peace or war, passes into the hands of the federal government.[1]

*Weakness of the militia provisions.*

When the militia of the states was called out by the national government in August, 1917, the requirements of defence at home were met by the organization of a federal force known as the United States Guard and of local forces, commonly known as home guards or state guards. The United States Guard was under federal jurisdiction, but the state or home guards were wholly under state control. The rules concerning organization, equipment, and discipline, the appointment of officers, and the methods of training for state guards were established by the legislature of each state. The cost of maintaining such organizations was also borne entirely by the states.

*Home guards and similar organizations.*

In various parts of the country the national government has acquired land for the construction of navy-yards, forts, arsenals, and other military or naval works. Over such property, the constitution provides, Congress may exercise "exclusive legislation"; in other words, Congress alone may make laws relating to such areas. The military and naval works of the United States are not subject to taxation by the states in which they happen to be located, nor

*7. Powers over forts, arsenals, etc.*

[1] In 1918 all outward marks of distinction between members of the Regular Army, the federalized Militia of the States and the National Army were abolished for the duration of the War. This action, however, did not abolish distinctions made between these various organizations in the constitution or the laws.

may the states apply to them any restrictions inconsistent with a proper fulfilment of the purposes for which such works are constructed. They are to all intents and purposes federal areas, outside the legislative jurisdiction of the states. No property may be acquired by the national government in any state for military or naval purposes, however, without the consent of the state legislature.

Conclusion. On the whole the war powers of Congress have proved ample. If demonstration of this fact were needed it has been forthcoming within the last couple of years. The relative slowness with which the United States has been able to put forth its whole military strength cannot be laid at the door of inadequate constitutional powers. The inaction of Congress in making preparations and the apathy of public opinion have been the real causes. When Congress decided to act the power was there.

[1] Under authority vested in the President by Congress many important boards and commissions were created during the years 1917–1918. Among these may be mentioned the War Industries Board, the Emergency Fleet Corporation, the Shipping Board, the War Labor Board, the War Labor Policies Board, the War Trade Board, the Council of National Defence, the federal Board for Vocational Education, the Bureau of War Risk Insurance, the Committee on Public Information, the Censorship Board and the War Finance Corporation. Some of these were created for the duration of the war only, but others will probably remain in existence for many years to come. On the organization and work of these various boards see the *American Year Book* for 1918, especially pp. 38–81.

# CHAPTER XIX

## MISCELLANEOUS POWERS OF CONGRESS

OF the great powers granted to Congress by the eighteen endowment clauses of the national constitution the four most important have been discussed in the immediately preceding chapters. The others must have less extended consideration, not because they are of little importance (for some of them are of large consequence), but because the limits of space preclude any attempt to trace the ramifications of them all. Nor is a knowledge of these powers in detail necessary to a reasonably clear grasp of the main principles. A statement of these remaining powers, with a few comments upon the scope of each, must therefore suffice.

Congress has power to establish uniform rules upon two subjects, naturalization and bankruptcy. The procedure in naturalization has been already explained. Over the rules as to citizenship Congress has complete and exclusive jurisdiction, having fully covered the matter by law. As regards bankruptcy laws, or laws which provide for the distribution of a debtor's assets among his creditors after he becomes insolvent, Congress has not assumed jurisdiction to the exclusion of the states, but where any state law conflicts with a provision of the National Bankruptcy Act, the former becomes inoperative. The present national law provides for both voluntary and involuntary petitions in bankruptcy. In the former cases the insolvent himself files a petition in a federal district court and officials are appointed by the court or elected by his creditors to take over his assets; in the case of involuntary petitions the application is made by one or more of the insolvent's creditors. After the assets have been liquidated the insolvent

*Naturalization and bankruptcy.*

may under certain conditions obtain from the court a discharge from bankruptcy which relieves him of further legal liability with respect to all debts unpaid at the time of filing the petition. For the security of interstate trade on credit it is obviously desirable that the rules relating to bankruptcy should be uniform throughout the country.

Coinage and currency.

Congress, again, is given power by the constitution to coin money and to fix the standard of weights and measures. The power to coin money belongs to the federal government alone; it is prohibited to the states. Immediately after the formation of the Union a mint was established at Philadelphia (1792) and other establishments for minting coin have since been provided for in other cities.[1] Provision was also made for adopting the decimal system, with eagles, dollars, dimes, and cents as the chief units. The ratio of silver to gold was fixed at fifteen to one, that is to say the weight of the silver dollar was made fifteen times that of the gold dollar.[2] But changes in the supply of the two metals and in their market value made it necessary to change the ratio to sixteen to one in 1834. This ratio continued until 1873 when the coinage laws were entirely revised and the minting of silver dollars discontinued. Gold alone now became the standard of values. The country passed from a bimetallic to a gold basis. But vigorous opposition at once developed, with the result that in 1875 Congress restored the silver dollar to the list of legal tender coins, and in 1878 the minting of silver dollars in limited quantities was resumed. This policy continued until 1890, when an increase in the coinage of silver was provided for, but the continued decline in the market price of that metal led to the complete discontinuance of further silver purchases for coinage.

The conflict over bimetallism.

This action of Congress divided the two great political parties on the issue of free silver. The Democrats, under the leadership of Mr. Bryan, fought the election campaign of 1896 on a platform which demanded the free and unlimited

[1] There are four mints at present, namely at Philadelphia, Denver, San Francisco, and New Orleans. Assay offices have been established at nine other places.

[2] Gold dollars were actually coined during the period 1849–1889 only.

MISCELLANEOUS POWERS OF CONGRESS 279

coinage of silver dollars at a ratio of sixteen to one. The Republicans, on the other hand, supported the monometallic or single gold standard. The Republican victory at this election did not end the free silver agitation, but it virtually insured the continuance of the gold basis, and the matter was definitely settled by the Gold Standard Act of 1900. Into the economic merits of this famous controversy it is not necessary to proceed; but the question bulked large in political discussion during the decade 1890–1900.[1] Silver dollars continue in circulation, but they are not a basis of the currency. The gold dollar, which is no longer coined at all, is the legal standard of values in the United States.

Congress is not given any express authority to issue paper money, the constitution being dumb on this point, although it definitely forbids any of the states to "emit bills of credit." It has been held, however, that Congress may not only issue paper money as an incident of its borrowing power, but may make such notes legal tender in payment of debts. Treasury notes were issued during the War of 1812 and during the Mexican War, but not until 1862 did Congress designate anything except gold and silver coin as a legal tender. In that year, due to the urgent needs of the government in Civil War times, a larger issue of notes than ever before was made, and in order to float them more readily these so-called "greenbacks" were declared to be a legal tender for all payments except customs duties and interest on government bonds. Other issues followed and these also were made legal tender. It was a moot question whether Congress had any right to make this paper money a legal tender, but the Supreme Court finally decided in 1871 that this authority was within the jurisdiction of Congress as an incident to its power to borrow money.[2]

The legal tender issue.

When the Civil War was over there was a clamor from various quarters that these paper notes be withdrawn and

---

[1] J. L. Laughlin, *History of Bimetallism in the United States* (4th ed., N. Y., 1900), and F. W. Taussig, *The Silver Situation in the United States* (3d ed., N. Y., 1898).
[2] *The Legal Tender Cases*, 110 U. S. 421.

*The greenback controversy, 1866–1880.*

that specie payments be resumed. Various difficulties stood in the way of this policy, however, and the controversy over the greenbacks continued for a decade. One faction, both in and out of Congress, sought to continue the greenbacks in circulation and even to increase them; the other sought to have them removed from circulation so as to make room for metallic currency and national bank notes. The organization of the Greenback Party which figured prominently in the elections of 1876 and 1878 was an outcome of this political conflict. Congress, however, agreed that in the matter of returning to a specie-payment basis "the way to resume is to resume" and a considerable portion of the notes were retired by virtue of an act passed in 1875. The remainder are still in circulation.

*Present factors in the currency.*

The present currency of the United States falls into at least six classes: (1) gold coin, minted at various times in denominations from one to twenty dollars; (2) silver dollars, fractional silver (half-dollars, quarters, and dimes), and fractional small coins (nickels and cents); (3) gold and silver certificates issued against deposits of gold and silver bullion held in the federal treasury; (4) United States notes or "greenbacks," and treasury notes, both of which are redeemable in coin; (5) national bank notes, which are protected by deposits of government bonds, and (6) federal reserve bank notes issued against the security of commercial paper deposited by subscribing banks for re-discount. This is a greater variety of currency than one can find in the peace-basis circulation of any other great country. Yet it is not to be assumed that there would be any great advantage in reducing it all to the same type.

The entire currency, metallic and paper, is issued under the authority of Congress; no state can either coin money or "emit bills of credit." A state may authorize a bank to issue paper money, but as such notes are subject to a heavy federal tax they are non-existent.

*Weights and measures.*

In the matter of weights and measures Congress has full determining power. Many laws were put upon the statute book relating to this subject during the course of the nineteenth century, but no comprehensive attempt was made to deal with the standardization of weights and measures in a scientific way until 1901, when the national Bureau of Standards was established to undertake the work of securing accuracy and uniformity. This bureau now supplies the various states with exact standards. The inspection of weights and measures, on a basis of their conformity to these standards, is in the hands of state and municipal authorities. The old English standards (pound, yard, gallon, etc., and their derivatives), somewhat modified, are generally used; but the metric system was also made legal by Congress more than fifty years ago and the standards of the international metric system are supplied to all the states.

Congress has power to provide for the punishment of counterfeiting either the money or the securities of the United States or those of foreign countries, but this does not preclude the punishment of such offences by state laws as well. As a rule, however, these offences are left to be dealt with by the federal courts. The wilful uttering of counterfeit money or notes, apart from the actual counterfeiting, is commonly made an offence by state law and punished by the state courts.  *The punishment of counterfeiting.*

Then there is the postal power, or as the constitution puts it, the power "to establish post-offices and post-roads." "No other constitutional grant," as one distinguished writer has remarked, "seems to be clothed in words which so poorly express its object or so feebly indicate the particular measures which may be adopted to carry out its design."[1] The reason, perhaps, is that the framers of the constitution merely sought to perpetuate in central hands a power which was already there and which in its actual workings was well comprehended by everybody. The postal system of the country is older than the federal government itself, extending back into colonial times. In the interval between the outbreak of the Revolution and the adoption of the constitution it was first in charge of the Continental Congress and later by the Articles of Confederation was given to the Congress established by that agreement.  *The postal power.*

By virtue of its postal power the federal government

[1] J. N. Pomeroy, *An Introduction to the Constitutional Law of the United States* (10th ed., Boston, 1888), Section 411.

*What it includes.*

*"Fraud orders."*

*How far does the postal power extend?*

not only maintains the country's elaborate network of post-offices and delivery routes but conducts the money-order service and the postal savings bank system.[1] It likewise exercises a considerable degree of control over certain lines of business by virtue of its power to refuse the use of the mails to any concern which has been found to use the service fraudulently. This is done by the issue of "fraud orders." The right to deny the use of the mails represents a large power, capable of wide extension and indeed with possibilities of serious abuse. Many years ago the Supreme Court sustained the right of postal authorities to exclude from the mails any matter that they deem objectionable,[2] and also declared that no state might establish a postal system in competition with the federal government. Congress may likewise delegate to the Postmaster-General the right to determine what matter shall be so excluded, and this delegated authority is not subject to review by the courts. Decisions of the Postmaster-General, in the case of fraud orders, are final and conclusive.[3] The denial of the right to use the mails is not a deprivation of property, for no one can acquire a property right in postal facilities paramount to the proper handling of the service.[4]

The power to establish and maintain "post-roads" is an authority which has thus far been used but slightly, yet it might well be utilized to amplify the functions of the federal government in an enormous degree. The original intention may have been to vest in Congress the right to build and maintain roadways if that should be necessary to secure the carrying of mail from one town to another. But mails are not now for the most part carried by road; they are handled by the railways. To interpret the term "post-roads" as including railways involves no greater stretching of a constitutional phrase than that which the

---

[1] There are four classes of post-offices, ranged according to their gross annual receipts. All postmasters are appointed by the President, but appointments to practically all post-offices are now made under civil service rules.

[2] *Ex parte Jackson*, 91 U. S. 727.

[3] *Public Clearing House* vs. *Coyne*, 194 U. S. 497.

[4] For a survey of the postal authority in its legal phases, see Lindsay Rogers, *The Postal Power of Congress* (Baltimore, 1916), especially ch. vii.

Supreme Court has so freely permitted by including telegrams and telephone messages within the word "commerce." Although the nation has taken over the operation of the railroads as a war measure, Congress has not committed itself to a programme of government ownership; but if it should ever do so this post-road provision would in all likelihood be construed as sufficient to warrant such action. *(Does the phrase "post-roads" include railroads?)*

In his message vetoing the Cumberland Road bill in 1822 President Monroe asserted that Congress had no power under the constitution to embark upon a policy of highway construction by virtue of its postal authority, but that the postal service must use the existing roads provided by the states. That doctrine, however, has long since become unorthodox. The power of Congress to construct not only roads but railways across either territories or states has been upheld by the Supreme Court to be implied not only in the "post-roads" clause of the constitution but also in the authority to regulate commerce.[1] *(The Supreme Court's answer.)*

Again, Congress is given power to "promote the progress of science and the useful arts, by securing for limited times to authors and inventors the exclusive right to their respective writings and discoveries," in other words to grant patents and copyrights. A patent is a certificate given to an inventor, securing for him during a designated term of years the exclusive right to make such profits as there may be in his invention. The issue of patents is in the jurisdiction of the Patent Office, a bureau in the Department of the Interior. The rules relating to them are elaborate and complicated.[2] A patent is valid for seventeen years during which time the holder is protected by the courts *(Power to grant patents.)*

---

[1] *California* vs. *Central Pacific R. R. Co.*, 127 U. S. 1.

[2] Here are a few general provisions: The applicant for a patent must make a sworn statement that he believes himself to be the original inventor of the article or process which he seeks to patent; he must submit descriptions and drawings, also a model if required; and must pay a fee of fifteen dollars. Not everything new can be patented; it must be both "new and useful." It must be something "not patented or described in any printed publication in this or any foreign country prior to the invention and not in public use or on sale in the United States for more than two years prior to the application." When applications come in they are referred to examiners in the Patent Office, and if a patent is issued, another fee of twenty dollars is exacted.

against infringement. Trade-marks have no necessary relation to inventions or discoveries and do not come within the power to issue patents or copyrights. But trade-marks used in interstate commerce may be registered at the Patent Office. When intended for use in trade within a single state they can be protected only by state registration. It should be mentioned, moreover, that the granting of a patent does not give an inventor the right to manufacture or to sell his invention except under such conditions as the police power of the states may impose. Even patented articles, if dangerous to the safety, health, or morals of the community, may be excluded by the laws of any state. The imposition by the states of a license fee for the sale of any article, moreover, would apply as well to patented merchandise as to any other. The right to manufacture or sell is not derived from the patent and is neither increased nor diminished thereby.

**Power to issue copyrights.**
A copyright secures exclusive rights to publish and sell any book, manuscript, musical composition, drawing, photograph, or similar matter having inherent value. A mere label or advertisement, not having value as a composition, may not be made the basis of a copyright. The present term of a copyright is twenty-eight years with the opportunity for a further renewal during an equal term. To obtain copyright in the United States a book must be actually printed in this country; but this does not apply to books in languages other than English.[1] Many attempts have been made to secure some form of international copyright agreement so that an author may have protection in all countries, and some progress in this direction has been made by means of treaties.

**Power to establish subordinate courts.**
Congress is given power to create tribunals inferior to the Supreme Court, in other words to provide a system of subordinate federal tribunals. The Supreme Court is the only federal tribunal for which the constitution expressly provides; the other courts were left to be organized at the discretion of Congress but subject to the general provisions

---

[1] Application for copyright is made to the Librarian of Congress. The fee is only one dollar, but two copies of the copyrighted publication must be given to the Library.

relating to the security of judges in tenure and remuneration. In virtue of this power Congress has established the system of district and circuit courts which are described in a later chapter, and has allotted to them their respective spheres of jurisdiction.

"To define and punish piracies and felonies committed on the high seas, and offences against the law of nations" is another power granted to Congress. The high seas are the waters outside the three-mile limit, or, to speak more accurately, beyond a distance of one marine league. International law recognizes that the territorial jurisdiction extends to this distance from the shore, but beyond this limit the salt waters of the earth are the "high seas" over which all are free to travel in time of peace without restriction. Over American vessels on the high seas the federal government has sole jurisdiction. Piracy is now a thing of the past; it was the offence of committing depredations at sea without color of authority derived from any government. Regarded as the enemy of mankind a pirate might lawfully be captured by any one on the high seas and punished in any country. Offences against the "law of nations" or against the rules of international law are for the most part breaches of neutrality. Congress has defined the duties of American citizens when other countries are at war and forbids the commission of unneutral acts on American territory, as, for example, organizing armed expeditions or fitting out armed vessels in aid of a belligerent power. Such "offences against the law of nations" are punished by the federal courts.

As for the national government's authority to issue letters of marque and reprisal, in other words to grant authorizations to privateers or predatory private vessels — that authority, although granted by the constitution, is of no consequence to-day. For while the United States has not, like all the chief European states, relinquished formally the right to use privateers in time of war, the practice of privateering will, in all probability, never again be revived. The rules of international law are not always exact and definite; but most of them are sufficiently so to permit their being properly applied. International law, unlike

*Powers in relation to the high seas.*

the law of a single country, has no single tribunal with authority to enforce it. The federal courts of the United States apply the rules of international law only where the controversy arises within American jurisdiction.

**Exclusive jurisdiction over the national capital.**

The question of a national capital gave the makers of the constitution some trouble. The prize was coveted by various cities, both north and south. To avoid an embarrassing difficulty, therefore, the whole matter of selecting a capital was left to be decided by Congress after the constitution should go into operation. It was felt that an entirely new city should be founded to serve as the seat of national government, and with that idea in mind provision was made for creating a small district completely under national control. In establishing the District of Columbia, Congress later availed itself of this power "to exercise exclusive legislation in all cases whatsoever, over such district (not exceeding ten miles square) as may, by cession of particular states and the acceptance of Congress, become the seat of government of the United States." The jurisdiction of Congress over this area is complete. As will be seen later, the District of Columbia has no system of local self-government, and Washington is the only large municipality in the country of which that can be said.[1]

**The "implied powers."**

Finally, there is the national government's right to make all laws which shall be necessary and proper for carrying any of its general powers into execution. This is sometimes referred to as the "implied powers clause" of the constitution, or as vesting in the national government a "coefficient power." Laws are the agencies through which all the powers granted by the constitution either to Congress or to the President are carried into effect. The exercise of every constitutional power requires a law. The law adds nothing to the scope of powers already possessed; it merely makes the powers effective. Where a power is granted, the right to carry it into effect is implied. To desire the end is to tolerate the means. The Supreme Court, as already indicated, has interpreted this clause liberally, giving to the central government a large range of choice as to the means which it will employ in carrying its powers into effect. The

[1] Below, pp. 384–388.

"implied powers clause," moreover, extends not only to the enumerated powers of Congress but to whatever authority is granted by the constitution to any officer or department of the national government.

These, then, are the powers of Congress as enumerated in the constitution. The simple words in which they are clothed give rather scant guidance to any proper conception of what these powers express and imply at the present day. The lapse of time has shown that, if anything, the constitution gave to Congress too few powers rather than too many. It might well have included the authority to make uniform rules concerning the chartering of corporations, concerning marriage and divorce, and concerning the rights of aliens in the several states. These matters, being left to each state for its own determination, have been dealt with by some in ways which not only operate unfairly toward others but which are contrary to the best interests of American society as a whole.

*The powers of Congress in general.*

## CHAPTER XX

### CONSTITUTIONAL LIMITATIONS ON THE POWERS OF CONGRESS

Constitutional limitations; their nature and importance.

IN the preceding chapters the various powers of Congress, express and implied, have been outlined. The constitution, however, does more than grant certain powers. It imposes limitations upon Congress in the exercise of its legislative authority, and these limitations are matters of supreme importance in American constitutional law. Some of them relate only to the way in which a power may be exercised, as for example the provision that all taxes shall be uniform, and these limitations have been already indicated in connection with each of the congressional powers concerned. But others are in the nature of general prohibitions which forbid the exercise of certain powers under any circumstances. These restrictions and prohibitions are either expressly set forth in the constitution or may be reasonably implied from its provisions.

The chief limitations upon legislative power:

1. As to bills of attainder.

Congress is forbidden to pass any bill of attainder. A bill of attainder may be defined as a legislative act which inflicts a penalty without a judicial trial.[1] Legislation of this sort was frequent during the Tudor and Stuart periods of English history. By bills of attainder men in high office were "attainted" of treason and sent to the scaffold without even the forms of judicial process; their descendants even unto the third and fourth generation being deprived of civil rights. By a modified form of attainder known as bills of pains and penalties men were fined, or thrown into prison, or had their property confiscated. The enactment of attainders in any form is prohibited by the constitution because its makers did not believe that any legislature ought

[1] W. W. Willoughby, *Constitutional Law of the United States* (2 vols., N. Y., 1910), ii, 801.

to assume the function of condemning men without the safeguards of judicial process. After the Civil War some of the border states tried to exclude from officeholding all who refused to take an oath that they had not voluntarily borne arms against the Union; but the Supreme Court held this to be unconstitutional in that it imposed a penalty without judicial condemnation.[1] There are only two ways in which a penalty can ordinarily be imposed upon any one in the United States; one is by the verdict of some regular court of competent jurisdiction (including courts-martial); the other is by a legislative body serving as a tribunal of impeachment.[2]

The same provision of the constitution that prohibits attainders forbids also the passing of *ex post facto* laws. Not all laws which are retroactive in effect, or which date back and cover events antecedent to their passage are in this class, however. The limitation applies to criminal laws only, and even here it does not include any legislation but that which operates to the disadvantage of the accused. In this matter one can tread upon firm ground, for the Supreme Court many years ago gave a full and exact definition of the *ex post facto* clause. It includes "every law that makes an action done before the passing of the law, and which was innocent when done, criminal; and punishes such action; every law that aggravates a crime, or makes it greater than it was, when committed; every law that changes the punishment, and inflicts a greater punishment than the law annexed to a crime when committed, and every law that alters the legal rules of evidence and requires less, or different testimony, than the law required at the time of the commission of the offence, in order to convict the offender."[3] In a word it includes any law which operates to the detriment of an accused person, provided such law was passed after the alleged crime was committed.

2. As to *ex post facto* laws.

Taking a lesson from the annals of parliament the makers of the constitution limited the power of Congress with respect both to the definition and the punishment of treason. Treason is the oldest of crimes. In the history of Eng-

3. As to the definition and punishment of treason.

[1] *Cummings* vs. *Missouri*, 44 Wallace, 277.
[2] Cf. below, p. 292.   [3] *Calder* vs. *Bull*, 3 Dall. 386.

u

land it goes back to the time of the Saxon kings. Originally it was the offence of killing the sovereign, but as time went on various other offences were included, such as the killing of the king's relatives and the levying of war against the established government. During several centuries the category of treasons steadily widened, all manner of "new-fangled treasons" being added to the list from reign to reign until the unrestricted power to make and alter the law of treason became a great weapon of abuse and oppression. To make sure that there should be no such extension in the United States the constitution restricts the designation of treason to a certain definite offence, namely, that of levying war against the United States, adhering to their enemies, giving them aid and comfort. It further provides that "no person shall be convicted of treason, unless on the testimony of two witnesses to the same overt act, or on confession in open court," and, moreover, that no penalty for treason shall extend beyond the life of the person convicted. No punishment may be extended to descendants, or, as the words of the constitution express it, the penalties shall not "work corruption of blood or forfeiture, except during the life of the person attainted."

To constitute the crime of treason there must be an overt act of levying war or assisting the enemy. Ordinary resistance to public authority in the form of riots does not come within this definition, but any rising of armed men with intent to overthrow the government or to deprive it of its functions is an overt levying of war and hence constitutes treason. Mere conspiracy to create an insurrection, and even the enlistment of men, do not amount to overt acts of treason; there must be an actual assembling of men for a treasonable purpose.[1] In general the Supreme Court has declined to extend the definition of treason to doubtful cases and has required that the offence shall come well within the words of the constitution. Treason may be committed not only by a citizen but by an alien, provided he is, at the time of the offence, within the jurisdiction of the United States. The punishment of treason against the United States, as fixed by statute, is death. Crimes against

[1] *Ex parte Bollman*, 4 Cranch, 75.

the security of the nation not amounting to treason, such as inciting to rebellion, sedition and seditious conspiracy, are also made punishable by statute, but not with the same degree of severity.  *The penalty.*

Treason against the United States should be distinguished from treason against a state of the Union. The federal constitution makes no mention of the latter, hence each state may make its own definitions and provide its own degree of punishment. All of the states, either in their own constitutions or by statute, have exercised this right, but in the main they have followed the federal practice.  *Treason against a state.*

Among the provisions of the Great Charter which the barons of England wrung from King John in 1215 there was a stipulation that no freeman should be in any manner penalized save by "the lawful judgment of his peers or by the law of the land." This fundamental right of all freemen, after an existence of more than five hundred years in England, made its way into the constitution of the United States as a part of the Fifth Amendment, which provides that "no person shall be . . . deprived of life, liberty or property without due process of law." [1] The meaning and scope of these four words "due process of law," however, have given the courts and the commentators a plenitude of trouble, and even to-day their exact application is not absolutely clear. Few legal phrases in the whole history of jurisprudence, indeed, have proved so elusive of exact comprehension. The highest American tribunal has refrained from committing itself to any hard and fast definition of the term, preferring rather that "its full meaning should be gradually ascertained by the process of inclusion and exclusion in the course of decisions in cases as they arise." [2]  *4. As to the deprivation of life, liberty, or property without due process of law.*

But all students of constitutional law know in a general way what the phrase means. Due process of law is an approximate equivalent of the *per legem terrae* of the Great Charter. It means that there must be in all actions to deprive a man of his "life, liberty or property" an observance  *The meaning of "due process."*

---

[1] The phrase "due process of law" first appeared in a statute passed by parliament in the fourteenth century (28 Edw. III, 3). We have the word of the great English jurist, Sir Edward Coke, in his *Institutes*, that it was there used as the equivalent of the older phrase "law of the land."

[2] *Twining* vs. *New Jersey*, 211 U. S. 78.

of those general rules which are essential to the safeguarding of the individual's rights, those judicial forms and usages which by general consent have become inseparable accompaniments of fair procedure. Daniel Webster in a famous argument before the Supreme Court gave a definition of due process which has been much quoted and which will probably serve the layman as well as any other. It is the process of law, he asserted, "which hears before it condemns, which proceeds upon enquiry, and renders judgment only after trial. The meaning is that every citizen shall hold his life, liberty, property and immunities under the protection of the general rules which govern society."[1]

*Webster's definition.*

Where the difficulty comes, however, is in the application of these "general rules which govern society" to particular cases. In the main the courts have held that due process of law always involves a hearing of the issue by competent authorities before it is decided; but they have not been ready to go much further than this so far as procedure is concerned. It is now settled that due process of law does not necessitate a trial by a jury or even by a court of law at all, but that issues involving a deprivation of property may in certain instances be determined by administrative officers, for example, that a man's property may be taken and sold upon the order of city officials for failure to pay taxes, provided the owner has been given fair notice. Due process does not require that an accused be given the right to appeal from a lower to a higher court or that the incidental forms of judicial procedure at any trial shall be rigidly adhered to.[2]

*The application of due process: (a) to judicial procedure.*

The chief application of this phrase has not been to judicial procedure but to what is compendiously called the "right to freedom of contract." This right to make contracts and to have them enforced is a corollary from the general rights of liberty and property which the Fifth Amendment guarantees against deprivation. The Supreme Court has stood guard against frequent attempts to deprive individuals and corporations of their freedom of contract

*(b) to freedom of contract.*

---

[1] *The Dartmouth College Case*, 4 Wheaton 518.
[2] L. P. McGehee, *Due Process of Law under the Federal Constitution* (Northport, L. I., N. Y., 1906), and the cases there cited.

by the mere enactment of laws, whenever such laws are not demanded by the needs of public safety, health, or morality. Federal laws providing for the regulation of rates in interstate commerce concerning workmen's compensation, the limitation of hours of labor and a great many other matters in the field of industry have come before the court for review upon the allegation that these laws involved a deprivation of liberty or property without due process. Some have been upheld, others declared unconstitutional; but in this way the Supreme Court has assumed a considerable censorship over the economic legislation of Congress.

The due process requirement, as it appears in the Fifth Amendment, does not apply as a limitation upon the legislatures of the several states, but only upon Congress. The Fourteenth Amendment, however, imposes the restriction upon the state legislatures in exactly the same terms, so that "due process of law" is a general requirement which binds all American legislative authorities. The state legislatures, far more frequently than Congress, have sought to interfere both with freedom of contract and with property rights, hence the larger number of appeals to the Supreme Court against alleged deprivations have been made on the basis of state laws.

It is to-day well recognized that "due process of law" is not a stereotyped thing. A true philosophy of liberty must permit a progressive growth and wise adaptation to new circumstances. It follows, therefore, that any legal proceeding enforced by public authority, whether sanctioned by age or custom, or newly-devised in the discretion of the legislative power, in furtherance of the general public good, which regards and preserves the principles of liberty and justice, must be held to be due process of law.[1] To declare once and for all that certain formalities of procedure must in every case be observed where personal liberty or property are concerned would be to mummify legal progress. The general requirement as to due process affords an adequate protection to the individual or corporation against gross legislative unfairness; it was not

[1] *Hurtado* vs. *California*, 110 U. S. 516.

intended to be a barrier to the reasonable regulation of property in the interests of social and industrial justice. Linked with due process in the Fifth Amendment is a provision that "private property shall not be taken for public use without just compensation." Before explaining this provision a word must be said about the right of eminent domain upon which the foregoing provision operates as a limitation. It is a necessary attribute of every government that it shall have the right to acquire for public purposes the ownership or control of private property even without the consent of the owner. Such property is essential to the carrying on of governmental functions; it is needed for forts, navy-yards, post-offices, custom-houses, prisons, highways, and so on. The *domain* or property-taking right of the government must therefore be *eminent* or paramount, that is, superior to the property-holding right of any individual. This is a well-recognized doctrine of both jurisprudence and political science, so well recognized, in fact, that it is now never disputed. In the absence of constitutional limitations, therefore, the nation and the several states might each take, at their own will and pleasure, any private property for any purpose and under such terms of payment as their legislatures might provide or even without any payment at all. In England, parliament has that unfettered authority, although it does not practise the tyranny of taking property without paying for it. But in America the constitution contains express limitations upon the power of eminent domain. The nation is restricted by the terms of the Fifth Amendment and the states are limited, for the most part in the same words, by the terms of their own respective constitutions.

The limitations in both cases are twofold : the taking of property must be for a public purpose, and just compensation to the owner must be given. But what is a public purpose? The courts have been liberal in their interpretation of this term. They have upheld the taking of land for post-offices and other buildings, for parks, and for all other purposes related to the functions of government. Not only may the government itself exercise this right of taking private property for public purposes, moreover, but it may confer the same right by franchise-grant upon railroads and other corporations engaged in public or quasi-public enterprises. It is with reference to these public service corporations, indeed, that the chief difficulty is found in determining the constitutional limitations upon the right of eminent domain. It may be generally stated, however, that such power as the government itself possesses in the matter of condemning private property it may delegate to any public utility corporation. On the other hand, whatever limitations apply to the original authority of the government in this field also apply when the power is delegated to a subordinate corporation.

The private owner, when his property is taken for public use either by the government itself or by some corporation authorized by it, must always receive "just compensation." What is just compensation and how is it determined? As a rule the officers of the government or corporation make a valuation and offer the owner the sum so determined. Then, by the usual process of refusal, counter-proposals, and compromises, an adjustment may be made. If the private owner cannot get what he believes to be just compensation in this way, however, he has an appeal to the courts, where a jury will decide what he may receive and must accept. Where private property is taken by the authority of any state in the Union the laws of that state prescribe the method by which compensation will be determined.

(b) as to just compensation.

Many express limitations with respect to the methods of judicial procedure are incorporated in the national constitution, especially in the first ten amendments, and these restrict the powers of Congress to determine the process which may be used in the federal courts. These limitations relate to jury trial, to certain rules of evidence, to the nature of punishments, and to second jeopardy for the same offence. They will be more appropriately explained in a later chapter dealing with the judicial power of the United States.[1]

6. As to judicial forms and procedure.

As there are implied powers in the Constitution, so there are some implied limitations, in other words, some restric-

[1] See ch. xxiv below.

296   THE GOVERNMENT OF THE UNITED STATES

*Implied limitations on the powers of Congress.*

tions which are not set forth specifically but which follow logically from the general nature, form, and purposes of the federal government. The constitution, for example, does not expressly forbid Congress to delegate any of its legislative powers to the President or the heads of departments or to the various administrative boards. Yet it is

*The rule as to delegation of legislative power.*

"one of the settled maxims in constitutional law," according to America's foremost authority on this subject, "that the power conferred upon the legislature to make laws cannot be delegated by that department to any other body or authority. Where the sovereign power of the state has located that authority, there it must remain, and by that constitutional agency alone the laws must be made until the constitution itself is changed. The power to whose judgment, wisdom and patriotism this high prerogative [of legislation] has been intrusted cannot relieve itself of the responsibility by choosing other agencies upon which the power shall be devolved, nor can it substitute the judgment, wisdom, and patriotism of any other body for those to which alone the people have seen fit to confide this sovereign trust."[1]

*Forbids resort to a nation-wide referendum.*

Because of this well-recognized limitation a nation-wide referendum as a means of accepting or rejecting a law would not be constitutional. Congress might, if it so chose, submit a question to the people as a means of securing an advisory test of public sentiment; but the formal enactment of all federal statutes, and the undivided responsibility therefor, must remain where the constitution placed it. Congress cannot delegate its legislative power and responsibility even to the whole people. To establish the principle of direct legislation by the people, so far as national law-making is concerned, would require the amendment of the federal constitution.

*Administrative discretion may be delegated.*

But while Congress may not delegate its law-making power it may depute to some other body or authority the function of determining when and how the provisions of the law are to be carried out. This latter is held to be a ministerial, not a legislative function. It is permissible for Congress,

[1] T. M. Cooley, *Constitutional Limitations* (7th ed., Boston, 1903), p. 163.

where it has passed a law, to provide, for example, that it shall go into effect whenever the President shall adjudge certain conditions to exist and shall so announce by proclamation.[1] While Congress, therefore, cannot delegate its power to make a law, it can authorize the exercise of administrative discretion with respect to matters which are closely related to law-making. Just when this discretion becomes so broad as virtually to constitute legislative power is a question which cannot be answered by rule. The tendency of the Supreme Court in later years has been to give administrative discretion a large amount of play.

This is of great practical importance because of the steadily increasing control of business by the law. Laws are not by nature resilient, and regulation by laws alone, unmodified by the exercise of official discretion, is reasonably sure to work injustice. The best system of regulation is one which can bear heavily when the need arises but relax its weight when the need disappears. Hence it has been the policy of Congress to delegate to various federal boards, such as the Interstate Commerce Commission, the Federal Reserve Board, the Federal Trade Commission, and even various administrative officials such as the Postmaster-General or the Commissioner of Immigration, discretionary powers of a comprehensive and varied character. This action has been furiously attacked in the courts as constituting a delegation of legislative authority. In practically every instance, however, the action of Congress has been upheld.

*Importance of this administrative discretion.*

One result of this frequent delegation of ministerial discretion has been to take the country, in actual practice, a long step away from old legal traditions. As official discretion widens, a government becomes more and more a government of men. Hence we have had in the United States during the past quarter of a century a steady growth of "administrative law," a rather incongruous term in a country which still professes allegiance to the doctrine of separation of powers. So rapidly has this system of administrative discretion been extended that to-day a considerable part of the federal government's regulating authority is actually carried into

*It has introduced a new feature into American government.*

[1] *Field* vs. *Clark*, 143 U. S. 649.

*The conflict of theory and practice in delegation.*

operation by the promulgation of administrative rules and ordinances, thus approximating the practice of European countries. Administrative supervision is far more just and more effective than legislative dictation couched in unbending terms, and before the pressure of this practical advantage the ancient theories of government by law alone are being relentlessly pushed off the stage. Let it be made clear, however, that in no case may any administrative board or officer change any express provision of a law, even though such provision may seem no longer calculated to fit the needs of the situation. Administrative officers, no matter how wide their discretion, can insert nothing, change nothing, repeal nothing. Their discretion extends only to such latitude, within the written provisions of the law, as Congress may designate.

*Importance of the whole subject.*

The foregoing are not the only limitations placed by the constitution upon the powers of Congress. Some others, which relate more particularly to the inherent rights of the citizen, have been already discussed under that heading; others, again, which appertain to the forms of judicial procedure will be explained more fully in connection with the jurisdiction and work of the federal courts. Constitutional limitations, a subject which concerns the student of European governments very little or not at all, can never be lightly brushed aside by any one who desires to understand the spirit and the scheme of government in the United States. Nor is Congress alone in its subjection to organic limitations. The state legislatures also have their constitutional shackles, as will in due course appear. American constitutional law, indeed, is fundamentally the law of constitutional limitations.

# CHAPTER XXI

## THE WORKINGS OF CONGRESSIONAL GOVERNMENT WITH SPECIAL REFERENCE TO CONGRESSIONAL FINANCE

THE Congress of the United States, as the foregoing chapters have tried to show, is a legislative organ of intricate mechanism, with its complicated rules and methods of procedure, its multitude of committees, its varied powers, and its equally significant limitations. How well or how poorly does it do the work which a legislature ought to do? Does it function smoothly as a legislature should? The acid test of a constitution is the success with which the various organs established by it perform their functions and hold their proper relations to one another. *The merits and shortcomings of Congress as a legislative body.*

First among the merits of congressional government, as it has existed in the United States for over one hundred and thirty years, is the fidelity with which law-making has reflected the public opinion of the country. That is not to imply that Congress has at all times been immediately responsive to popular sentiment; but on the whole it has not often failed to act when the country spoke its mind. A characteristic of American public opinion is that it does not readily grow solid the country over. Sentiment on great political issues of American history, states' rights, slavery, secession, the tariff, the currency, the regulation of business, has shown great sectional divergences and on many occasions Congress failed to act decisively because no audible mandate came to it from the country as a whole. *Its responsiveness to public opinion.*

Herein one finds a fundamental difference between the American and the English conceptions of what a law-making body ought to do. Englishmen speak of the "governing classes" who have virtually dominated parlia- *Its function is to follow, not to lead.*

ment for many generations and whose function it is to assume the rôle of leadership, guiding public opinion along definite lines. There are no governing classes in America and save for a few years after the establishment of the Union there never have been. It has been the function of Congress to keep its finger on the public pulse and to be guided in its actions accordingly. Its duty has been to transform national desires into statutory enactments rather than to formulate policies for the nation to follow. So far as the national sentiment is crystallized into definite proposals, this has been the work not of Congress but of the men who make the party platforms.

*Lack of inherent leadership makes this necessary.*

It is well, on the whole, that Congress has not essayed the function of leadership, for its organization is not well adapted to that task. Someone has remarked that even if every Athenian citizen had been a Socrates, the Athenian assembly would still have been a mob. So if every member of Congress were a Washington or a Webster, its methods of doing business would in themselves preclude the planning and consummation of a well-defined legislative policy. The House of Commons has been able to guide political opinion in Great Britain because it is itself endowed with an administrative leadership. The doctrine of separation of powers has denied that advantage to Congress. Congress is not, therefore, to blame for the lack of continuity in American legislative policy or for the paucity of well-grounded legal traditions. A new and rapidly growing country changes its mind frequently; it is proverbially fickle in its desires, and Congress has mirrored these transformations in public opinion with a reasonable degree of accuracy.

*The liberty of the individual Congressman compared with that of a member of parliament.*

The eulogists of the British system of representative government have laid emphasis upon the way in which public proposals can be formulated by a few ministerial leaders and carried through parliament without the likelihood of their being mutilated beyond recognition. A government measure, when once laid before the House of Commons, is reasonably sure of adoption without material change. From the standpoint of clarity and expedition in law-making, and the concentration of responsibility for it, this is a great merit, but it is achieved by sacrificing the personal discretion of the individual member. In the House of Commons it has reduced the greater number of the members, the "back-benchers" as they are called, to a position of virtual impotence in the making of the laws. They have no personal discretion as to whether they will or will not support the decisions of their leaders. A member of the majority party can vote against the policy of the cabinet only at the risk of being branded as a political renegade. If a member of the minority should support any proposal of the majority, that would be an equally grave breach of party allegiance. Such things happen on occasions, it is true, but they are in the highest degree exceptional and contrary to the spirit of party government as it exists in Great Britain. So long as the English legislator stands by his leaders he takes no risks, for such action is always in itself a sufficient justification to his constituents. In Congress, on the other hand, the discretion of the individual member is more extensive and his responsibility more general. The obligation to support the measures of his party does not transcend the obligation to do what his conscience directs or what his constituents desire. The ultimate character of legislation is not, as a rule, determined in advance by a few leaders; and it is never safely settled until the members of both Houses have registered their individual opinions upon it. So far as caucus action is taken upon measures before Congress this liberty of the individual member is impaired, but relatively few measures are made the subject of caucus decision. One of the striking characteristics of congressional government, therefore, is the emphasis which it places upon the discretion and the responsibility of the individual member. This is a feature which secures to every congressional district its due share in the law-making process.

The theory of English parliamentary government is that a minority party has no right to influence the legislative policy of the majority. But the business of Congress is not conducted on that principle. A minority there has powerful weapons by virtue of the rules and the usages. The presence of a majority of the members being necessary to do

*Congressional deference to the rights of the minority*

business in Congress, it is often within the power of the minority, when the ranks of the two parties are not widely apart, to prevent the progress of business. If Congress is to get through its huge program at any session, moreover, the advancing of measures must be had in a great many cases by unanimous consent, and a minority, however small, may establish a legislative blockade by refusing this. But most important of all is the fact that a party majority in Congress is not always to be counted upon. Sectional interests often outweigh party allegiance. Relatively few measures pass both Houses of Congress by a straight party vote. Hence the individual member of Congress has a much greater personal share in moulding the policy of the country than has the member of parliament unless the latter happens to be also a member of the ministry.

*Where Congress fails.*

On the other hand Congress has the defects of its qualities. The absence of official leadership is the source of friction, log-rolling, working at cross purposes, and hopeless diffusion of responsibility. As an appropriating body Congress appears at its worst and in handling that branch of public business can scarcely bear favorable comparison with the national legislature of any other country. Its methods are clumsy, provocative of delay, and an incentive to extravagance. In no other field of Congressional activity is the need for reform more urgent than in this.

*Its inefficiency in public finance.*

*Stages in the making of appropriations.*

It is a fundamental principle of popular government that public expenditures shall not be authorized save by the representatives of the people. Accordingly it is provided in the constitution of the United States that "no money shall be drawn from the Treasury but in consequence of appropriations made by law." The first essential step in all national expenditure is, therefore, that Congress shall make an appropriation in the form of a law. Before an appropriation bill is submitted to Congress, however, there are some preliminary steps which should be indicated.

*1. The estimates: how prepared.*

Most of the functions of national government (such as the maintenance of the army, the navy, public works, the administration of justice, and so on) are in the jurisdiction of some executive department. Each of these departments, therefore, submits an estimate of the amount of money that it needs for the ensuing fiscal year. These estimates are made out in detail. The sheets are then put together and given as a whole to the Secretary of the Treasury who transmits them to the Speaker of the House. In printed form they make up a volume of many hundred pages. Along with these departmental estimates the Secretary forwards his forecast of probable revenues for the year.

In preparing their estimates the various departments act independently. Each formulates its own requirements without any reference to the needs of the others, and without knowing how much there will be to spend. The Secretary of the Treasury has no power to prune these estimates; he is merely a channel for transmitting them to Congress. As a natural consequence the estimates, when totalled together, are always far in excess of the probable revenues. Since March 4, 1909, the law requires the Secretary, whenever he finds the estimated expenditures in excess of the probable revenues, to "transmit a detailed estimate of all said estimates to the President, to the end that he may, in giving Congress information of the state of the Union, and in recommending to their consideration such measures as he may judge necessary, advise Congress how in his judgment the estimated appropriations could, with the least injury to the public service, be reduced so as to bring the appropriations within the estimated revenues, or, if such reduction be not in his judgment practicable without undue injury to the public service, that he may recommend to Congress such loans or new taxes as may be necessary to cover the deficiency." [1]

*Lack of joint action in preparing them.*

*2. Sent to the Secretary of the Treasury.*

*The change of 1909.*

Since the adoption of this provision it has been the practice of the President to name a committee of the Cabinet to go over the estimates before they are sent to the Secretary of the Treasury. But the task is so large that no group of busy men can attend to it properly in their spare time. Despite the act of 1909 the estimates continue to be framed and sent to Congress without any mutual coöperation among the executive departments.

*Has not accomplished much.*

Now comes the next step. The Speaker of the House

[1] Henry Jones Ford, *The Cost of Our National Government* (N.Y., 1910), p. 128.

3. Reference of estimates to committees.

receives the estimates from the Secretary of the Treasury. His function, thereupon, is to refer them to the several committees of the House for consideration. Eight or nine different committees each get a portion. The largest share goes to the Committee on Appropriations; but the Committee on Military Affairs, the Committee on Foreign Affairs, the Naval Committee, the Post-Office Committee, and various others each get the estimates relating to their several branches of administration. These committees then proceed to hear what the various heads of departments or chiefs of bureaus have to say in explanation of their estimates. No official of an executive department may sit or speak in Congress, but he may appear before one of its committees, and in the long run that is about as effective a way of making his opinions known.

Each of these eight or nine committees does its work independently. No one knows what the others are doing; each is solely concerned with its own estimates. To make matters worse, supplementary estimates keep coming in after the committees have their work under way. These supplementary estimates are to provide for things which have been overlooked by executive departments in making out their original estimates, or for new and unforeseen demands which have arisen.

4. Supplementary estimates straggle in.

5. Bills are also filed by individual Congressmen.

Various bills involving expenditures, again, are filed by Congressmen after the session begins. Such measures include bills for the erection of post-offices and other public buildings, for dredging rivers and harbors, for the construction of roads, and for various other matters in which the representatives are directly interested. These bills also go to the proper committees for consideration.

6. The appropriation measures framed by the committees.

After each committee has deliberated upon all these proposals to spend money it reports one or more appropriation measures in which the expenditures, as the committee has finally decided upon them, are provided for. These measures are either in the form of the regular appropriation bills,[1] based upon the estimates sent in by the

---

[1] Ordinarily there are fourteen regular appropriation bills, as follows: (1) Legislative, executive, and judicial expenditure, (2) District of Columbia Appropriation bill, (3) Fortification bill, (4) Pension bill, (5) Army

# THE WORKINGS OF CONGRESSIONAL GOVERNMENT 305

executive departments, or they take the form of "omnibus" bills, made up by lumping together such separately-introduced proposals for expenditure as the committee may favor. It is with respect to these omnibus bills that the greatest opportunities for log-rolling are presented. Nearly every congressman has some project for spending public money in his own district, and if it is not recommended in the estimates of some executive department, he endeavors to get it wedged into one of the omnibus enactments. Every year many millions of dollars are appropriated in this way for post-office buildings which the Postmaster-General's department has not asked for and which it would advise against if its advice were asked.

These bills are then reported to the House, where they are put through their several stages. To give them detailed consideration is quite out of the question in a body which numbers four hundred members. Consequently they go through, for the most part, just as they come from the committees. A little may be added here and taken off there, but great increases or reductions are rarely made. In appropriation bills totalling nearly a billion dollars reported by committees in 1916 the House made changes amounting to less than five millions in all. The spending-power of the House is thus diffused among various committees which do not work together on any single plan. 7. Put through their various stages in the House.

Having passed the House the bills go to the Senate. Here the system of consideration by committees is much simpler. All appropriation bills go to one Committee on Appropriations, with the exception of the Rivers and Harbors bill, which is referred to the Committee on Commerce. Before these two committees the senators may urge amendments, and many of them do so, usually in the way of proposed increases or new items. When the bills are reported to the whole Senate, accordingly, the aggregate amounts are almost always increased. With these amendments and others that may be added in the Senate itself 8. Sent up to the Senate.

bill, (6) Military Academy bill, (7) Naval bill, (8) Post-Office bill, (9) Indian Affairs bill, (10) Rivers and Harbors bill, (11) Agricultural bill, (12) Diplomatic and Consular bill, (13) Sundry Civil bill, and finally (14) the Deficiency Appropriation bill.

x

## 306   THE GOVERNMENT OF THE UNITED STATES

**9. The Senate's part in appropriations.**

**10. The final compromising and the executive approval.**

**Influence of the President in appropriations.**

after the committees have reported, the bills are finally sent to Committees of Conference made up of selected senators and representatives. It is the function of these conference committees to adjust the items so that both chambers may agree and get them finally passed. Compromises here and there are made; the conferees report these to their respective chambers, which then pass the bills and send them to the President to be signed.

When an appropriation bill has been passed by Congress the President has practically no alternative but to accept it. He can veto the whole bill if he chooses to do so; but he cannot veto any items in a bill, leaving the rest to stand. To veto a whole appropriation bill because certain items in it are objectionable, thereby depriving some department of the national government of funds for carrying on its work, is a rather drastic step. Consequently the President, as a rule, registers his objections to the offensive items but signs the bills all the same. The result is that the veto power, so far as the spending of public money goes, is reduced almost to a nullity. Such a situation is both embarrassing to the President and costly to the taxpayers. Public opinion holds the President responsible for extravagances which he is in reality quite powerless to prevent.

**How appropriations are made in other countries.**

In this complicated procedure two things stand out prominently, first, the marked difference between the way appropriations are made in the United States as compared with other countries, and second, the considerable share which the Senate has assumed in the authorizing of expenditures. In England, in France, and indeed in every country having constitutional government except the United States and the Latin-American republics, there is a centralization of responsibility for all proposals to spend public money. In England, no proposal to spend money can be considered by the House of Commons unless it comes from the crown, that is, unless it comes to the House with the indorsement of the cabinet.[1] No proposal of expenditure

---

[1] Here is the rule (adopted more than two hundred years ago): "This House will receive no petition for any sum relating to the public service, or proceed upon any motion for a grant or charge upon the public revenue — unless recommended by the Crown."

can reach the Chamber of Deputies in France unless it is sent by the executive branch of the government. In the United States, on the other hand, any head of a department, any senator, any representative, any citizen through the agency of his congressman in fact, may obtain a hearing upon proposals to spend the nation's money.

Lord Bryce quotes an unnamed American publicist as the source of the following shrewd observation on this point: "So long as the debit side of the national account is managed by one set of men, and the credit side by another set, both sets working separately and in secret without public responsibility, and without intervention on the part of the executive official who is nominally responsible; so long as these sets, being composed largely of new men every two years, give no attention to business except when Congress is in session, and thus spend in preparing plans the whole time which ought to be spent in public discussion of plans already matured, so that an immense budget is rushed through without discussion in a week or ten days — just so long the finances will go from bad to worse, no matter by what name you call the party in power. No other nation on earth attempts such a thing, or could attempt it without soon coming to grief, our salvation thus far consisting in an enormous income." [1]

*Lord Bryce's comment.*

The second feature which stands out prominently in the mechanism of national expenditure is the relatively large power of the Senate. It was taken for granted by those who framed the constitution that the House of Representatives would "hold the purse," as Madison phrased it. But the actual words of the constitution do not so specify, for they give the Senate equal powers with the House in all financial matters except the originating of bills for raising money. There is nothing in the constitution which requires that bills for spending money shall originate in the House, although by custom they always do originate there. It was expected that the House would become practically supreme in all financial matters because the framers of the constitution had before their eyes the example of England, the one country having real parliamentary government in

*The influence of the upper chamber upon financial policy.*

[1] *American Commonwealth*, i, pp. 182–183.

1787. There, without any formal provision of law, the House of Commons had acquired a complete mastery over both revenue and expenditure.

*The House was intended to be the dominant factor in that field.*

In one of the Federalist letters Madison brought his historical knowledge to bear on this point. "Notwithstanding the equal authority which will subsist between the two Houses on all legislative subjects, except the originating of money bills, it cannot be doubted," he declared, "that the House . . . will have no small advantage. . . . The House of Representatives can not only refuse, but they alone can propose, the supplies requisite for the support of government. They, in a word, *hold the purse* — that powerful instrument by which we behold, in the history of the British Constitution, an infant and humble representation of the people gradually enlarging the sphere of its activity and importance, and finally reducing, as far as it seems to have wished, all the overgrown prerogatives of the other branches of the government. This power over the purse may, in fact, be regarded as the most complete and effectual weapon with which any constitution can arm the immediate representatives of the people, for obtaining a redress of every grievance, and for carrying into effect every just and salutary measure." [1]

*But it has not succeeded in becoming such by any means.*

No expectation of the Fathers has been denied realization to a greater extent than this. The House of Representatives, unlike the House of Commons, has obtained no financial mastery. Where the Senate and the House have come into conflict upon questions either of revenue or expenditure the Senate in nearly every case has had its way. Instead of becoming the dominant chamber the House has hard work to maintain its place as a coördinate arm of the national legislature. It has never gained that power of the purse which was originally regarded as its peculiar prerogative. Instead of being strong and masterful in its relations with the Senate, as was anticipated, the House has been forced on numberless occasions to take refuge in compromise. The fact is worth remarking that in the United States, almost alone among the world's great nations, the lower chamber of the national legislature has failed to gain control of the national pocket-book.

[1] *The Federalist*, No. 58.

CONGRESSIONAL GOVERNMENT 309

...ed that the United States is also the ...hout a budget system. Whether that ...lepends upon what one means by a ...defined as "a statement of probable ...ires and of financial proposals for the ...presented to or passed by a legislative ...then Congress does have each year a series of such statements emanating from various sources, and these taken together make up a national budget. But if a budget be defined as "a collection of documents assembled by an officer who is at the head of or is responsible for the administration and submitted to the legislative branch of the government." [2] then the United States does not have a national budget system. Some of the documents are prepared by the executive departments under the President's direction; others are prepared by the committees of the House. Neither the executive nor the legislative branch of the government is wholly responsible for the programme of expenditures. There is no correlation, moreover, between those committees which prepare bills for raising revenue and those which prepare the appropriation and the "omnibus" bills. If the expenditures keep within the income it is by happy accident rather than by careful design.

How might this serious defect be remedied? One change would certainly be of advantage, namely, the adoption in both the House and the Senate of a standing rule providing that no proposal of expenditure should be in order unless recommended by the executive branch of the government. It may be urged that such a provision would be unworkable because the executive and legislative branches are not always, as in England, harmonious as to public policy. In reply it need only be pointed out that political inharmony between the mayor and the council is often found in American municipal government, yet the provision that no appropriation can be considered by the city council unless it is recommended by the mayor has been inserted with good

*The lack of a national budget.*

*Suggested changes in rules relating to appropriations.*

---

[1] Boston Budget Commission's *Report* (1915), p. 4.
[2] *Report of the President's Commission on Economy and Efficiency. The Need for a National Budget* (Washington, 1912. 62d Congress, 2d Session, House Document 854), p. 8.

results in many city charters. Congress could man[age] expenditures under the operation of a similar rule if [com]pelled to do so. It would still have the right to strike out [or] to reduce any item, but not to insert or increase. It may be of interest to note that the framers of the short-lived constitution for the Confederate States of America in 1861 adopted a provision of this nature.[1]

*A budget system recommended.*

Some years ago, on the recommendation of President Taft, Congress authorized the appointment of a special commission to examine the existing methods of national finance and to recommend improvements. This commission, after a thorough investigation, recommended the establishment of a budget system under which all estimates for the year would be transmitted to Congress by the President in a single list and incorporated into one great appropriation measure. Congress, however, did not take kindly to this proposal and the system remains as before.

*Congress works too hurriedly*

Not merely in the matter of appropriations but in the enactment of all its measures the great handicap upon Congress is the perennial need for haste. The first and in some cases the only object of its multifarious rules is to hurry business along. Everything else is subordinated to the problem of getting things out of the way. So much is each year laid out for it to do that only by skimming the surface can Congress hope to do its work at all. Legislation is never an easy business in a democracy where many discordant voices are shrieking their desires and counsels at the same time.

*And has too much to do.*

If a country makes up its mind to have a government of laws it must expect a plenitude of laws, for it takes a whole volume of laws to do what one administrative official, with sufficient discretionary authority, could perform without overworking himself. The American doctrine of government by laws alone has brought in its train the greatest outpouring of statutes that the world has ever seen. Law has become the popular panacea for all political, social, and industrial evils. Congress is not the inspirer

---

[1] Art. I, Sec. 9. "Congress is forbidden to appropriate money from the treasury except by a vote of two-thirds of both Houses, unless it be asked by the head of a department and submitted by the President, or be asked for the payment of its own expenses, or of claims against the Confederacy declared by a judicial tribune to be just."

but merely the reflection of this national eccentricity. The enacting, revising, amending, repealing of laws has become a great national industry. Statutes fly from forty-nine legislative capitals in the United States like sparks from so many forges.

Laws beget laws. Give a statute time and it will have its own progeny. The increase is like that of micro-organisms, by geometrical progression. The fathers of the Republic foresaw the dangers of over-legislation and desired to guard against it. "It will be of little avail to the people," wrote one of them in the *Federalist*, "that the laws are made by men of their own choice, if the laws be so voluminous that they cannot be read, or so incoherent that they cannot be understood; if they be repealed or revised before they are promulgated, or undergo such incessant changes that no man who knows what the law is to-day can guess what it will be to-morrow."

*The plethora of laws.*

But such safeguards as the constitution provides against law-making *en gros* have not proved effective. The chief shortcoming of Congress, and of the state legislatures as well, is the sacrifice of quality to quantity in the process of law-making.

# CHAPTER XXII

## POLITICAL PARTIES IN NATIONAL GOVERNMENT: THEIR HISTORY AND FUNCTIONS

Opposition of the founders to the party system.

THE history of political parties in the United States began with the constitutional convention of 1787, yet the men who made the constitution were not believers in party government. On the contrary they were at great pains to provide a scheme of government which would be free from party animosity or the "violence of faction" as James Madison expressed it.[1] This attitude of Madison and his colleagues was quite in tune with the eighteenth century Whig idea of government which regarded parties as barnacles upon the ship of state or cancers in the body politic. Before 1787 no English political writer of any consequence except Edmund Burke had dared to defend the party system, and his arguments were regarded as disingenuous attempts to gloss over the iniquities of cabals and cliques. The fathers of the American republic chose rather the political gospel of Bolingbroke and Chatham, which frowned sternly upon the "pestilential influence of party animosities."

[1] "Among the numerous advantages promised by a well constructed union, none deserves to be more accurately developed than its tendency to break and control the violence of faction. . . . By a faction I understand a number of citizens, whether amounting to a majority or a minority of the whole, who are united and actuated by some common impulse of passion or of interest, adverse to the rights of other citizens, or to the permanent and aggregate interests of the community. . . . The latent causes of faction are sown in the nature of man; and we see them everywhere brought into different degrees of activity, according to the different circumstances of civil society. A zeal for different opinions concerning religion, concerning government, and many other points . . .; an attachment to different leaders . . . have in turn, divided mankind into parties, inflamed them with mutual animosity, and rendered them much more disposed to vex and oppress each other than to co-operate for their common good." *The Federalist*, No. 10.

The eighteenth century knew little of the practice of free government. The statesmen of the period could not foresee that political parties would come into being in a democracy no matter what constitutional barriers might be set up against their existence. Give any people the right to govern themselves, the right to think their own thoughts and to speak their minds aloud, and political parties are inevitable. The political experience of the nineteenth century was to prove that parties will come and flourish under all forms of popular government, that they are an essential of sound democracy and not an excrescence upon it. But Madison and his colleagues, guided by the relatively brief history of political parties in England prior to 1787, were earnestly concerned to keep the party system from getting any foothold in the New World. How futile were their endeavors the whole history of American politics can now attest. The stone which the builders rejected has become the chief corner-stone.

<small>Yet parties are inevitable in all free governments.</small>

The abhorrence of party divisions continued, for a time at least, after the new government had been established. Washington's farewell address was as much an admonition against party divisions within the Union as against permanent alliances outside. "In the most solemn manner," the first of the presidents warned the nation "against the baneful effects of the spirit of party generally," and pilloried it as the worst enemy of popular government.[1]

<small>Washington's antipathy to the "spirit of party."</small>

[1] "I have already intimated to you the danger of parties in the state, with particular reference to the founding of them on geographical discriminations. Let me now take a more comprehensive view, and warn you in the most solemn manner against the baneful effects of the spirit of party, generally. . . . It serves always to distract the public councils, and enfeebles the public administration. It agitates the community with ill-founded jealousies and false alarms, kindles the animosity of one part against another, foments occasional riot and insurrection. . . . There is an opinion that parties in free countries are useful checks upon the administration of the government, and serve to keep alive the spirit of liberty This within certain limits is probably true — and in governments of a monarchical cast, patriotism may look with indulgence, if not with favour, upon the spirit of party. But in those of the popular character, in governments purely elective, it is a spirit not to be encouraged. . . . A fire not to be quenched; it demands a uniform vigilance to prevent its bursting into a flame, lest, instead of warming, it should consume." "Farewell Address" (*Writings of Washington*, edited by L. B. Evans, N. Y., 1908), p. 539.

Yet although there existed in high places this animosity to political parties in the closing decade of the eighteenth century it was then, nevertheless, that American political parties came into being. The members of the constitutional convention were themselves aligned into two political parties. They did not realize it, of course, and would have resented the imputation; but to any one who follows their daily deliberations the fact is readily discernible. From the very outset of their deliberations the delegates divided themselves broadly into two groups on questions of general policy. There were those who believed in a real union, who wanted to subordinate the states to the nation, to bestow large powers upon the central government. These were the Federalists. On the other hand there were delegates, and they formed a minority, who desired that no power should go to the central government if it could be safely left to the several states. They believed that the central government should care for the common defence and such other things as could not be handled by the states acting separately. These were the Anti-Federalists. American political parties began with federalism and anti-federalism, with Edmund Randolph and William Paterson leading the delegates into two groups on the first great question that came before the convention. They crystallized into permament form when Alexander Hamilton lined up one half the country against Thomas Jefferson and the other half, during Washington's first administration.

It may be contended, of course, that political divisions in the New World antedated even the framing of the constitution.[1] In a sense that is true. There were Whigs and Tories in colonial days: there were Whigs and Tories during the Revolution. But between these analogues of the great English parties and the new divisions based upon federalism and its antithesis, there is no close connection. Nor, indeed, is there any close continuity between these new divisions and the American political parties of to-day. The

---

[1] "You say our divisions began with federalism and anti-federalism! Alas! they began with human nature; they have existed in America from its first plantation. In every colony, divisions always prevailed." John Adams, *Works* (10 vols., Boston, 1850–1856), x, pp. 22–23.

Republican party, when first organized, drew from both Federalists and Anti-Federalists and it, in turn, became the progenitor of both our present great parties. In the history of American political parties this exchange of names is a confusing factor.[1]

During the early years of the Union the Federalists, under the leadership of Alexander Hamilton, gained the upper hand. The reaction against the weaknesses of the old confederation ran strongly in the minds of the people and they were willing to have the central government gain in strength. The excesses of the French Revolution (1789–1802) likewise disposed many sober-minded Americans to place more emphasis on order and authority than upon the natural liberty of states or individuals. Washington was not a party man. He was elected without opposition and showed his sincerity as a non-partisan by choosing his Cabinet from both political groups. Hamilton and Jefferson, therefore, were members of his first official family. But while Washington was neither by temperament nor by training a party President, he gravitated steadily towards the Federalist point of view. During the eight years of his administration the first United States Bank was established; the first tariff on imports was framed; the national credit was put upon a firm basis and a system of taxation created. Provision, likewise, was made for taking over and paying off the debts incurred by the various states in the Revolution. In all these things the handiwork of Hamilton, the Federalist leader, was made manifest.

*The Federalists in the saddle, 1789–1800.*

This rapid centralization of functions, however, aroused strong opposition, particularly among that part of the population which had no important financial or commercial connections. To the farmers in most of the states the national policy looked like a surrender to the moneyed and shipping interests. Jefferson, whose antagonism to the Federalist attitude was not concealed even while he was a member of the Cabinet, came to be recognized as the champion of

---

[1] For the history of American parties, see Henry J. Ford, *Rise and Growth of American Politics* (N. Y., 1898), and J. A. Woodburn, *Political Parties and Party Problems* (N. Y., 1903), also the references given below, p. 330, *note*.

the opposition, and his followers adopted for themselves the name of Republicans or Democratic-Republicans. Their strength among the people soon increased, and at the election of 1796 they almost defeated John Adams, the Federalist candidate for the presidency.

*Their disunion under Adams.*  The administration of John Adams gave the opposition a chance to make headway owing to the divided leadership of the Federalists. Hamilton, the most brilliant spirit in the ranks of the latter party, did not manage to work in harmony with Adams. The two were not alike in temperament or ways, and their relations ended in an open breach. By their support of the Alien and Sedition Acts (1798), moreover, the Federalists made a serious error, giving Jefferson and his friends a fine opportunity to make political capital. The country rang with the clamor of the Republicans that these measures were designed to buttress the falling fortunes of the Federalist party by repressing freedom of speech and stifling criticism. Every prosecution under these laws provided occasion for a demonstration against the Federalists. The result was that at the election of 1800 Jefferson was triumphantly returned and the Democratic-Republicans assumed control of the national government. Before the close of his administration, however, Adams succeeded in clinching for many years the hold of the Federalists upon one department of the government. This he did when he appointed John Marshall to be Chief Justice of the Supreme Court.

*The Jeffersonian victory of 1800.*  The election of 1800 disclosed for the first time a definite political alignment not only among the leaders but among the people. The agricultural population of the country, the small farmers of the North and the planters of the South, supported Jefferson. The industrial and the trading interests, the seaboard towns and the Puritan strongholds of New England, were behind Adams. The change from Adams to Jefferson was, therefore, a turnover of great political significance. The Federalists had been conservative, aristocratic, even reactionary. They had clung with great tenacity to theories of government which placed more emphasis upon order than upon liberty. They strove to make the central government a real power in the land, construing in a broad way the powers granted to Congress by the constitution. Jefferson and his Democratic-Republican followers, on the other hand, professed those theories of government which laid stress upon the natural liberty of the citizen. They asserted that the provisions of the constitution which gave powers to the federal government should be strictly construed. They were partisans of state rights and gave their allegiance to what they liked to call "democratic principles." Yet they did not, after their accession to power, throw overboard what the Federalists had acquired for the new government. They continued the protective tariff, established another United States Bank, and in the purchase of the Louisiana Territory gave the broadest possible interpretation to the powers of the national government. The Alien and Sedition laws were allowed to lapse; but the Embargo Act which shut off American commerce with Europe (1807), and the methods used in its enforcement constituted quite as great an interference with individual liberty. *Supremacy of the Republicans, 1800–1824.*

Jefferson remained strong, however, in the confidence of the people, as his reëlection proved in 1804, and he was able to pass on the presidency to his disciple, Madison, at the close of his second term in 1809. During the two administrations of Madison the Federalist party still further disintegrated, and at the election of 1820 placed no candidate before the people. The Republicans with the election of James Monroe in 1820 were in complete control, their candidate having carried every state in the Union.[1] The Federalist party went out of existence. *Disintegration of the Federalists.*

But no one party can long remain in sole control of any free government. A majority party, no matter how strong, has within itself the germs of decay. The more pronounced its ascendency, in fact, the more quickly is it apt to relax its vigilance and to afford opportunities for disintegrating forces to do their work. Signs of disunion promptly showed *The party chaos of 1824.*

---

[1] One elector from New Hampshire gave his vote for John Quincy Adams for President, and thus deprived Monroe of the honor of a unanimous election. It has been frequently said that this recalcitrant elector did so in order to prevent any one else from sharing with Washington the honor of a unanimous choice; but this statement is not true. The elector had other reasons for his action. See Edward Stanwood, *A History of the Presidency* (2d ed., 2 vols., Boston, 1916), i, p. 118.

themselves among the Republicans. Before long the party divided itself into various factions which eventually coalesced into two prominent groups, one of them led by John Quincy Adams, Daniel Webster, and Henry Clay, the other by Andrew Jackson and John C. Calhoun. But before this consolidation was accomplished the country was compelled to pass through ten years of personal and factional politics. During these years it seemed impossible to restore the popular alignment into two great divisions, and at the election of 1824 there were four candidates for the presidency, Jackson, John Quincy Adams, Crawford, and Clay. No one of these obtained a majority of the electoral vote, and the choice of Adams was made by Congress. Thus ended the rule of the Virginia dynasty.

Evolution of the new parties.

The new administration began its work in a whirl of charges and recriminations. Rumors of corrupt and underhand dealings were in the air. Congress was hostile to Adams and his administrative plans frequently missed fire. The factional bickerings seemed interminable. By 1828, however, the various groups had consolidated. The more nationalistic factions, now known as the National Republicans, in that year supported Adams for reëlection; while the more radical elements of the old Republican party, taking the name Democrats, supported and secured the election of Andrew Jackson.

The election of Jackson and the era of Democratic supremacy, 1828–1844.

"The election of General Jackson to the presidency," says Professor Channing, "was the most important event in the history of the United States between the election of Jefferson in 1800 and that of Lincoln sixty years later. Madison, Monroe, and John Quincy Adams belonged to the Jeffersonian school of statesmen who, while holding liberal views, yet represented in their education and habits of thought the older and more courtly type of which Washington was the most conspicuous example. Jackson, on the other hand, was an indigenous product of the American soil. Vigorous and absolutely without fear, he was a born leader of men. The Jeffersonian theory aimed rather at the establishment of state democracies, while Jackson's mission was the founding of a national democracy." [1]

[1] *The United States*, 1765–1865 (New York, 1896), p. 208.

The election of Jackson, at any rate, is a great landmark in the history of American political parties. His views and policies were forceful; they made him warm friends and bitter enemies; and they accentuated the division of the people into two great parties, Whigs and Democrats.[1] Jackson's extension of the spoils system promoted the efficiency of party organization by giving his party followers something tangible to fight for. But even more important was his successful fight to break up the congressional caucus as a machine for nominating presidential candidates, thus paving the way for the rise of the national party conventions.

The Democrats continued to hold power until the inauguration of 1841, having reëlected Jackson in 1832 and secured the choice of Van Buren in 1836. Then commenced an era of party alternation in office. The issue of slavery began more and more to dominate the political arena, and in the end it managed to split both the Whig and Democratic parties asunder. During the middle fifties the new Republican party arose out of the ruins of the old Whig alignment and secured the election of Lincoln over a divided opposition in 1860. This election ushered in a period of Republican supremacy which lasted for twenty-four years, from 1861 to 1885. *The alternations and reorganizations of the period 1844–1860.*

The Civil War, while it lasted, drew into the Republican ranks all those who believed in "the unconditional maintenance of the Union, the supremacy of the constitution, and the complete suppression of the existing rebellion with the cause thereof by all apt and efficient means." It was by appealing to the voters on this programme that the Republicans reëlected Lincoln in 1864. When the war ended it left the Republican party strongly intrenched. Then intervened the difficult tasks of reconstruction which kept sectional bitterness alive, and it was not until the end of Grant's second term (1877) that the two great parties began to align themselves upon present rather than upon past issues. *The effect of the Civil War on party strength.*

One of the legacies of the war was a high tariff, and the continuance of a protective policy during the later sixties

---

[1] The Whig party was organized in 1834 by a combination of the National Republicans with one faction of former Democrats.

and seventies drew to the Republicans the support of the large business interests of the country. The questions of finance and currency which came to the front during this period had a similar influence, the Republicans handling these matters in a way to draw the support of those who had most to gain from conservative financial legislation. The Democrats, on the other hand, made their appeal to the friends of tariff reduction, to the agricultural voters of the South, to those who had radical views on matters of finance and currency. Grant, Hayes, and Garfield successively carried the Republican standard to victory during these years when questions relating to the tariff and the currency were the great issues. It was not until the election of 1884 that the Republican hold upon the presidency was relaxed, and the triumph of Grover Cleveland in that year was due as much to the lack of *élan* among his opponents as to the strength of his own party.

At each of the next four elections the tariff continued to be a prime issue, although the Democratic adoption of a free-silver programme in 1896 thrust the question of bimetallism for the moment into the foreground. Until 1912, in fact, the cleavage between the parties remained tolerably clear, and it related more directly to the tariff than to any other issue. In that year came a schism in the Republican ranks, a revolt against the alleged reactionary methods and tendencies of its leaders, with the resulting formation of the short-lived Progressive party. This division in the Republican ranks made certain the success of the Democrats in the election of that year. By 1916 this breach had been to a large extent healed, but the issues between the Democrats and the reunited Republicans were no longer so clearly marked out as in the years before the Progressive insurrection. The tariff dropped out of public discussion and there were no currency questions in controversy. The relation of the United States to the great war which for two years had been raging in Europe was the chief problem in the minds of the people. It was upon the presumed attitude of the candidates with reference to this question and not upon issues of old-style domestic policy that the election turned. The margin of Democratic victory was so narrow that a change of fewer than two thousand votes in what turned out to be a pivotal state would have altered the outcome.

This rather curious and complicated history of political parties in the United States may be marked off, by way of summary, into three periods. The first extends from 1787 to 1820, an era in which the Federalists and the Democratic-Republicans, the exponents of national centralization and of state rights respectively, aligned the people into two well-marked political groups. Until 1800 the Federalists maintained their hold; then with the election of Jefferson their opponents began their march to a position of supremacy which in time caused the Federalists to disappear as a party altogether.

<sub>Summary of party history: First period: 1787–1820.</sub>

The second period extends from about 1820 to 1860. It was marked by a succession of party crumblings and new integrations. First came the break-up of the old Democratic-Republican organization into groups of which some eventually united to form the Democratic party under the leadership of Andrew Jackson, while the others consolidated into the Whig party under the leadership of Adams, Webster, and Clay. Then, in due course, ensued the disruption of the Whigs in the campaign of 1856 and the rise of the new Republican party, followed in turn by the disruption of the Democrats in 1860.

<sub>Second period: 1820–1860.</sub>

The third period covers the years since the Civil War. During that time the alignment of Republicans and Democrats, save for temporary defections, has been reasonably well preserved. These two great parties, since 1860, have had a longer and more intelligible history than any of their predecessors. It is during this period, moreover, that in addition to the regular political parties, various other organizations based upon social or economic principles have come into the field and have managed to continue their existence over considerable periods of time.

<sub>Third period: 1860–</sub>

Two of these minor parties deserve mention in even the briefest outline of party history. One of them is the Prohibition party, which held its first national convention in 1872. Its fundamental principle, as its name implies, is opposition to the manufacture and sale of intoxicating

<sub>The Prohibition party.</sub>

Y

liquors, but in recent years the party platform has expressed itself on various other issues as well. The Prohibition party regularly nominates its candidates for President and Vice-President. Although at times a considerable popular vote has been polled for these candidates (more than a quarter of a million on one occasion), the party has never yet secured a single vote in the electoral college.

*The Socialist party.* The Socialist party in the United States virtually began its career as a national party in 1900, although for some years previous to that date a Socialist-Labor and a Social-Democratic party had been in existence. The Socialist party of to-day is the result of the union of these two earlier organizations, although a Socialist-Labor party still continues *Its platform.* in the field. Its platform calls for both economic and political reforms. Among the economic demands are the public ownership of railroads, telegraphs and telephones, the extension of state ownership to mines, forests, and other natural resources, the socialization of industry, the provision of work for the unemployed, and the establishment of pensions for the aged. Among the political reforms which the party desires are equal suffrage, the initiative and referendum, the abolition of the United States Senate, the popular election of all judges for short terms, and the abolition of the Supreme Court's power to declare laws unconstitutional. At the presidential election of 1912 the Socialist candidate polled a popular vote of more than eight hundred thousand, but in 1916 the total dropped to six hundred thousand. The party organization includes all members who pay small monthly fees, such funds as are needed for election campaigns and for propaganda being obtained in this way.

*Definition of a political party.* It is sometimes said that the genius of a nation for self-government can be best judged by a study of its political parties. The strength of parties is an index of popular interest in public affairs; their weakness and disintegration is a sign of a political indifference among the people. What, after all, is a political party? Edmund Burke defined a political party as "a body of men united for the purpose of promoting by their joint endeavors the national interest upon some particular principle on which they are all agreed." That is, at any rate, a good definition of what a political party ought to be.

Political parties, in short, are groups made up of voters who profess to think alike on public questions. Their aim is to promote the success of those policies and methods in which they believe. They are a perfectly natural outcome of the fact that all people do not think alike nor yet do they all think differently. Left to themselves they will gravitate into political groups just as people range themselves as the result of passive inheritance or active choice into various sects or denominations in matters of religious belief. Parties are, in fact, the denominations or sects of statecraft. Most people inherit their political as well as their religious beliefs, although in the one field as in the other there may be defections due to the influence of environment or propaganda.

*Parties are natural and essential in popular government.*

If all people thought alike on political questions we could have no political parties; if every man thought differently from his fellows we could have no parties, for every voter would then be a political party unto himself. The political party is therefore a logical phenomenon in all forms of government, except in a despotism on the one hand or an anarchy on the other. Their existence is the outcome of a trait which is characteristic of free men everywhere. John Adams was right, in a sense, when he declared that parties began with human nature. The desire, if not the opportunity, for group-expression is primeval. No country has ever been able to maintain, over considerable periods of time, any form of responsible government without the aid of political parties. And it is safe to prophesy that no country ever will.

Yet essential as political parties are to the proper workings of government in all democratic countries, they have been compelled to grow up without much nursing from constitutions or laws. The latter have either ignored the existence of political parties altogether or have sought to hold them in check by regulatory provisions. Parties, whether in England, France, or America, are extra-constitutional institutions, not formally recognized as having any influence upon the actions of the government. Neither

*But they have not been so recognized.*

parliament nor Congress has ever admitted that any political organization is entitled to delineate its policies or determine the obligations of its members. Yet every careful observer is well aware of the dominating influence exerted by party platforms, party discipline, and party allegiance in both these great legislative bodies.

<small>The functions of political parties:
1. To select public issues and present them to the electorate.</small>

What are the functions of a political party? In general a party has three functions. In the first place it singles out and frames political issues for presentation to the public. Such issues come to the front gradually and do not, as a rule, assume at the outset a very definite form. By means of the party platforms various major and minor issues are succinctly stated and the attitude of the party upon each of them is made a matter of record. "We believe in the adoption of a non-contributory old-age pension system," may be a plank in the platform of one party. "We view with alarm the proposal to spend large sums of public money in old-age pensions except upon a contributory basis," the platform of the other party may make reply. Party assertions of this type put questions of public policy squarely before the voter. Indeed, it may well be said that in order to get any important principle of public policy transformed into legislation the first step is to have it enunciated in one or both of the party platforms.

<small>Importance of this function.</small>

An election under the party system is therefore not merely a means of choosing candidates but a referendum to the people of the various matters contained in the platforms upon which the respective candidates stand. The specific political views of men range over a wide area; but in a democracy they must be willing to make sacrifices of individual opinion to reach common ground. A democracy of irreconcilables, of men who would not sacrifice to reach common ground, could not long endure. It is the function of party organizations to find that common ground which will attract the greatest number of individual preferences among the voters. Or to express it in another way: the function of preparing a political creed upon which large numbers of men can substantially agree, a creed made up by selecting those aspirations which are uppermost in the minds of the people and embodying them in a programme—that is the first function of a political party. It is a duty that needs to be performed in every well-governed country, yet it is difficult to see how, in the absence of political parties, it would be performed at all. The political party, by its performance of this function, enables men to act in masses.

It is quite true, of course, that political parties do not always perform with frankness and simplicity this work of delineating the issues. Sometimes their platforms present questions to the people in a bewildering or evasive form. Sometimes, again, they dress up the party's principles in resounding platitudes which may mean anything or nothing at all. At times the platforms evade important issues or straddle them, as in 1892, when neither of the great parties ventured to take an unambiguous stand on the free silver question. But on the whole the main issues at each election are made fairly clear, and certainly they are much less obscure than if there were no party platforms at all. *Although it is not always well performed.*

In the second place, it is the function of political parties to provide a system of collective and continuing responsibility. Responsibility, to be real, must be both collective and continuing. The mere fact that individual officers of government are responsible to the people does not guarantee a responsible government. They must be collectively responsible, and to this end there must be some group or organization which stands sponsor, shouldering the responsibility for what they do. As a penalty for inefficiency and a deterrent to any repetition of it, the mere turning of an officer out of his post when his term has expired avails but little. The penalty, to be effective, must also fall on his bondsmen, that is, upon the political party which by nominating him vouched for his fitness. *2. To establish a collective and continuing political responsibility.*

The party thus serves as a guarantor, pledging its own interests and reputation, at times staking even its existence upon the ability and integrity of the men whom it places in nomination for public office. If its candidates are elected and make good, the party gets the credit; if they are elected and fail, the party cannot evade the responsibility. The Democratic party was still carrying the responsibility for having placed James Buchanan in the presidential office, the Republican party was still reaping the credit of having made Abraham Lincoln his successor, long after both these men were in their graves. It is a rare Republican platform in our own day, indeed, which does not seek in some ingenuous way to remind the electorate of the great service which that party rendered the nation at the memorable convention of 1860. Democratic platforms, for their part, as seldom fail to pay homage to the principles and policies of Thomas Jefferson. In a word the party system makes for organic as well as personal responsibility, establishing an accountability which is real, continuing, and effective, serving as the guarantors of all who enter public office as party nominees. Without parties the responsibility would go no farther than the office-holder himself, and it would end with the expiry of his term.

3. To serve as agencies of civic education.

Finally, the political parties assist the practical workings of popular government. A democracy is ever subject to the danger of popular indifference, yet eternal vigilance is indispensable to its success. The education of the voter on political questions, the awakening of his interest, the promotion of political discussion, are essentials in any democracy which seeks to be worthy of its name. The kinship of democracy is with knowledge, straight-thinking, and intelligence, not with ignorance of public affairs, apathy, or the blind following of individual prejudice or caprice. If every voter were left to inform himself on political questions and to vote without either guidance or leadership, no democratic scheme of government would survive. A government will not long remain popular in the true sense if public issues do not at all seasons occupy a place in the minds of its people.

The political parties perform great services in the field of political education. They stimulate discussion, fill the newspapers with their controversies, attract the attention of the people by their rallies, parades, and demonstrations, deluge the voter with their circulars and harry him to the polls on election day. "If all men took a keen interest in public affairs, studied them laboriously, and met constantly in a popular assembly where they were debated and decided, there would be no need of other agencies to draw attention to political questions. But in a modern industrial democracy, where the bulk of the voters are more absorbed in earning their bread than in affairs of state, these conditions are not fulfilled, and in case no one made it his business to expound public questions or advocate a definite solution of them they would commonly go by default."[1]

These three functions, the formulating of issues, the maintenance of a collective and continuing responsibility, and the political education of the electorate, would not be performed if the party organizations did not take them in hand, yet their value, indeed their indispensableness, is beyond question. Political parties, as Lord Bryce has well said, are "to the organs of government almost what the motor nerves are to the muscles, sinews, and bones of the human body. They transmit the motive power, they determine the directions in which the organs act." They link private opinion to public policy and thus make concrete for millions of men and women what would otherwise be mere abstractions. *Summary of functions.*

Political parties, therefore, have important and useful work to perform. To do it effectively they require machinery. Candidates must be brought forward, hence the need for caucuses or conventions or primaries. Candidates, moreover, cannot be elected without effort, and a good campaign requires funds, workers, and discipline. Hence the need for party committees and officials, for party contributions, and for the whole complicated mechanism of party organization. American party machinery is not a chance development. Neither is it the product of human perverseness. It is not even the outcome of political indifference on the part of a people so engrossed in their private vocations as to surrender the conduct of public business into professional hands. It is merely the result of a desire to do in an efficient way the things that have to be done in every popular government and cannot be so well done by any other machinery. *Need of machinery to carry out these functions.*

When reformers, therefore, plead for the abolition of parties or for the breakdown of party organizations through the development of individual political independence they display unfamiliarity with the fundamentals of democratic *Independence of party is not necessarily a virtue.*

[1] A. L. Lowell, *Public Opinion and Popular Government* (N. Y., 1913), p. 61.

government. President Lowell quotes "a prominent reformer" who urged that it was the duty of every good citizen to go to the polls and to vote for the man he thought most fit for an office, whether other people proposed to vote for him or not.[1] And he adds, quite rightly, that a more certain way of insuring the victory of undesirable candidates could hardly be devised. One might as well say that every good soldier should fight as his own conscience directs, and not as the interest of the whole army seems to demand. An army acting on that principle would be sure to lose, but no surer than a body of voters following the same principles of discipline. In matters affecting individual conduct only, each member of the community may let his own political individuality have free rein; but the election of competent officials, the putting of good laws on the statute book, and the inauguration of reforms in government are matters that require unity of effort. It is the function of the party to provide the means for this concerted action, hence the stanchest party man may be in reality the most effective reformer.

*It is one way of insuring bad government.*

It will now become more readily apparent, perhaps, why third parties come into existence only when the regular party system is not working smoothly. The most satisfactory working of representative government is secured under a two-party system, one party unitedly supporting the administration, the other presenting a vigorous opposition. When its support is divided, an administration cannot be sure of its ground; it must compromise; its policy will not be firm and decisive. If, on the other hand, the opposition is divided, the administration will not be subjected to that unrelenting pressure which is necessary to keep it on its mettle, endeavoring to do its best. Where there are three, four, or five parties there is no distinctness of issue and the elections decide nothing permanently. In France and in Italy, where there are several political parties, the effect has been to hinder the continuity of public policy, to weaken the administration, and to becloud the issues which go before the people. The steady maintenance of the two-party system in both Great Britain and the United States

*Advantages of the two-party system.*

[1] *Public Opinion and Popular Government* (N. Y., 1913), p. 67.

is not indicative of a public opinion which lacks independence but is a tribute to the practical political capacity of the Anglo-Saxon race.

Where two political parties are well organized and where their leaders are alert there is no room for a third party. Things which the voters desire will be taken in hand by one or other of the two regular parties and incorporated into its own programme long before they can be used as the endowment of a new party. If the two regular parties do not use unceasing vigilance in this direction, and if they are not always on the lookout for new and popular issues, they fail to fulfil one of their chief functions. There should be no issues left for a third party to pick up but those which are either unpopular or impractical. All political issues, by the way, may be grouped into three classes; those which are popular but impractical; those which are practical but not popular; and those which are both popular and practical. The regular parties capture all of the last; no party wants the second; the third parties usually take possession of the first.

*No room for third parties in a smooth-working democracy.*

*Two parties can cover the issues.*

# CHAPTER XXIII

## POLITICAL PARTIES IN NATIONAL GOVERNMENT: THEIR ORGANIZATION AND METHODS

A POLITICAL party depends for its success upon individual discipline and united effort, both of which are the outcome of careful organization. American party organizations have developed from rudimentary beginnings, but they are now the most elaborate and efficient institutions of their type in any country.[1]

*Early organization: the caucus.*

During colonial days there existed in Boston and in other New England towns various clubs or cliques which were at first social in character, but which became hotbeds of political discussion during the stormy days of stamp taxes and tea parties. The Caucus Club in Boston was a conspicuous example.[2] At its more or less secret meetings the wheels were set in motion for influencing the deliberations of the colonial assembly and the town meeting. After the Revolution some similar clubs or "Democratic Societies" were formed in the cities and towns of the various states, but public opinion did not take kindly to these self-created organizations and they eventually went out of existence.

---

[1] There are several excellent monographs on the organization and methods of American political parties, but special mention should be made of Jesse Macy, *Party Organization and Machinery* (N. Y., 1904); M. Ostrogorski, *Democracy and the Organization of Political Parties* (2 vols., N. Y., 1902); and P. Orman Ray, *Political Parties and Practical Politics* (2d ed., N. Y., 1917).

[2] The origin of the term "caucus" is not known. Some believe it to have been derived from the Algonquin Indian *kaw-kaw-was*, meaning to talk or confer. Others have derived it from " caulkers " because secret political meetings, which are said to have originated in Boston, were held by the ship caulkers to make protests against the actions of English soldiers. For further details, see M. Ostrogorski, *Democracy and the Party System* (N. Y., 1910), pp. 3–4.

Party machinery did not, therefore, obtain its earliest development through organizations of the people themselves. It came through another channel, namely, the organization of caucuses in the national and state legislatures, in other words through the development of party nominations for office.

In local elections, during the earlier part of the nineteenth century, nominations were made at town or county meetings where the number of the voters was sufficiently small to permit their coming together. Not only the town and county officers but the representatives in the state legislature and in Congress were nominated in this way.[1] Quite often the candidates were virtually picked out beforehand by small groups of men who represented different shades of political opinion, and the general town or county meetings merely indorsed these selections. There were no regular town or county committees in charge of the local party interests, and no party funds.

*Party organization in the early part of the nineteenth century.*

*1. Local party organizations.*

In the case of state elections, for such offices as those of governor or lieutenant-governor, however, the plan pursued in local elections could not so easily be followed. The function of making the preliminary selection of party candidates for state offices was therefore taken in hand by the members of the state legislature. This was natural enough, because the legislators formed the only available body of delegates representing the entire state. Hence arose the legislative caucuses, in which the members belonging to the same party in both Houses came together, decided upon their respective nominations, and announced them to the voters. The legislative caucus spread to all the states. It was not the creation of any individual or party, but arose from the simple fact that it was at the time the only practicable way of making selections on behalf of the voters throughout the whole state. It was not easy in those days

*2. State party organizations.*

*The legislative caucus.*

---

[1] "To nominate candidates for elective offices which went beyond the limits of the county, delegates from several localities often assembled. But these meetings were composed in an anything but regular way; too often the representation of the different localities was neither complete nor direct. The decisions taken in them, however, were not binding; neither voters nor candidates considered themselves bound by the nominations made." M. Ostrogorski, *Ibid.*, p. 5.

to gather a special convention of party delegates together; travelling was difficult and costly; the local party organizations were not strong, and there were no party funds. The spoils system, moreover, had not yet been devised to furnish a corps of aspiring office-holders, party enthusiasts, and professional workers wherewith to fill a convention hall.

*3. National party organization.*

In Congress also the legislative caucus as a means of expressing the consensus of each party in nominations for office was soon adopted. In 1800 both the Federalist and the Democratic-Republican members of the Senate and the House of Representatives held secret conclaves and nominated their respective candidates for the Presidency and the Vice-Presidency, recommending these candidates to the presidential electors in the several states. At the election of 1808 they did the same thing; but on this occasion their caucuses were not secret. There were plenty of protests against this arrogation of nominating authority, but the presidential electors accepted the advice given them by their respective congressional caucuses, for there seemed to be no practical alternative. The congressional caucus included senators and representatives from all over the country. Surely these congressmen were able to express the sentiment of their states quite as well as any other body of men could do it. No other gathering so representative of the whole party could have been brought together in those days.

*The congressional caucus.*

*Opposition to the congressional caucus.*

Yet the congressional caucus was not favorably regarded by public opinion at any time, and popular antagonism grew stronger as time went on. This antagonism reflected itself in Congress to such an extent that in 1820 President James Monroe was renominated without the indorsement of a congressional caucus at all, and in 1824 the last attempt to nominate candidates by caucus action proved a hopeless fiasco. The ostensible objection to the congressional caucus was its defiance of the spirit of the constitution. Congress, the people felt, was virtually usurping the function of choosing the President. There was also the practical objection that the congressional caucus represented only a portion of those who made up the party. Districts represented in Congress by members of one party had no representation in the caucus of the other party. Yet such

*The practical objection to it.*

districts might contain large numbers of voters professing allegiance to this other party. At any rate the legislative caucus, both in national and in state campaigns, completely disappeared after 1824.[1] *Its decline.*

The rise of the nominating convention overlapped the decline of the legislative caucus in the states. To meet the practical objection referred to in the preceding paragraph it became the custom, when the legislative caucus met for the purpose of nominating candidates for state offices, to call in some outside delegates chosen for the purpose, particularly from those towns or counties which would not otherwise have representation there. These mixed bodies, made up of legislators and delegates, soon gave way, however, to regular party conventions made up wholly of delegates chosen for this purpose alone. The first regular convention of this type to nominate state officers was held in Pennsylvania in 1817. Gradually the plan spread to the other states as well. *Rise of nominating conventions:* *(a) in the states.*

In the field of national government the transition from legislative caucus to national convention was through a somewhat different channel. The congressional caucus practically disappeared, as has been said, after 1824. What took its place? In the campaign of 1828 the candidacy of Andrew Jackson was announced by the legislature of his own state, Tennessee, and was indorsed by a number of informal public gatherings elsewhere. His opponent, John Quincy Adams, was not formally nominated by any caucus or convention. Having served one term as president, he was by general acquiescence deemed to be a logical candidate of his party for another term. *(b) in the nation.*

Four years later, however, a different course was taken. As the campaign of 1832 was about to open, assemblies made up of delegates from the several states were called together, and these bodies placed the various candidates in nomination. As yet they could scarcely be called conventions, for they did not contain delegates from all the states and the basis on which they were chosen was not definitely settled. But in due course national conventions, *The system of national conventions makes headway.*

[1] C. S. Thompson, *The Rise and Fall of the Congressional Caucus* (New Haven, 1902).

made up of party delegates from all the states and chosen on a recognized basis of apportionment, became the recognized agencies of nomination. As time went on these conventions developed a systematized organization; they were brought to some extent under the supervision of the law, and they became an integral part of American electoral machinery.

*Organization of the national party.*

To nominate their respective candidates for the Presidency and the Vice-Presidency, each political party holds a national convention once in every four years. Republicans, Democrats, Prohibitionists, and Socialists each have their own gathering of this sort. The time and place of meeting are decided in each case by the party's national committee, a body which will be described presently. The national convention is made up of delegates from every state, each state having twice as many delegates as it has presidential electors, in other words, twice as many delegates as it has United States senators and representatives combined. Massachusetts, for example, has two senators and sixteen representatives in Congress. It is entitled, therefore, to eighteen presidential electors and it sends to each national convention, Republican or Democratic, thirty-six delegates. An allotment of delegates is also made to the District of Columbia, Hawaii, Porto Rico, the Philippines, and Alaska, so that the total membership of a national convention is about one thousand. In addition it is the practice to provide each delegate with an alternate, that is, with somebody to take the delegate's place if the latter should be absent from any of the convention's sessions.

*Conventions.*

*How delegates are chosen.*

Prior to 1912 the delegates to both the Republican and the Democratic national conventions were practically everywhere chosen by state or local conventions; but in recent years this plan has given way to the method of selection by party primaries in about half the states.

*Work of the national party conventions:*
*Adopting the party platform.*

The nomination of candidates is not the only function which party conventions, whether in the nation or in the states, are expected to perform. They also prepare and issue the party platforms, the actual work being done by a committee and submitted to the convention, which almost invariably accepts it without much amendment. Until 1912 the conventions also chose the national committees, but in that year the Democratic convention provided that the national committee of that party should be chosen, one member from each state, by the voters at the primary. The Republican convention continues to name members of its national committee wherever the state laws do not provide for their election by popular vote.

The national committee has its chairman, who may or may not be one of its members. He is the party's chief of staff and head strategist. Ostensibly he is chosen by the national committee, but in reality he is the personal choice of the party's candidate for the presidency. No man can have too much skill, ingenuity, resourcefulness, or patience for this position. "He must be a master of details, and at the same time capable of taking a correct view of the general situation and endowed with an unlimited capacity for hard work. He must possess the confidence of party leaders and have an almost intuitive grasp of the popular feeling. He must keep in touch with every fibre of the organization, holding frequent conferences with state chairmen in the most important and doubtful states. He must be conciliatory, secretive yet approachable, keen in his choice of helpers, able to command the services of the most effective workers in the party, and capable of making them work in unison without overlapping."[1] The ideal national chairman is a rare individual, for nature does not often combine all these qualities in the same personality.

*The national party committee.*

*Its chairman.*

The national chairman is often a factor of great importance in determining the party's success or failure at a presidential election. He must plan the campaign, select the vulnerable spots in the embattlements of his adversaries, and bolster up the weak places in his own. It is for him to determine what states need particular attention and what states need little or none. He virtually decides how and where the campaign funds of his party shall be spent, allotting them as his judgment dictates to this or that purpose, or to this or that section of the country. President Harrison probably owed his election in 1888 to the skill and energy of Senator Quay of Pennsylvania, then chairman of the

*His functions.*

[1] P. O. Ray, *Political Parties and Practical Politics* (2d ed., N. Y., 1917), pp. 235–236.

National Democratic Committee, and although President McKinley would probably have been the victor at the election of 1896 in any event, his large majority was mainly due to the work of the Republican national chairman, Senator Mark Hanna of Ohio.

*The secretary of the national party committee.*

Next in point of importance to the national chairmen are the secretaries of the national committees. Each is in charge of his party's national headquarters, supervising the enormous amount of correspondence which pivots on that point, and handling a legion of details relating to the itineraries of campaign speakers, the publication of campaign literature and the coördination of every campaign activity. These secretaries are paid and permanent officials.

*Auxiliary committees.*

Each national committee maintains a number of sub-committees or auxiliary committees, made up to some extent from its own members but to a much larger proportion by the selection of prominent party workers outside. Among these auxiliaries are finance committees of each party, publicity committees, speakers' bureaus, organization committees, and so on. Each of these groups is responsible for some special branch of campaign activities, but all are under the general direction of the national committee and under the immediate supervision of the national chairman.

*The congressional campaign committees.*

The work of the national committee of each party is primarily concerned with presidential elections. The special function of assisting the party's candidates for Congress is devolved upon separate committees, known as the congressional campaign committees. Each party maintains a committee of this type. The chief work of these committees comes midway between presidential elections when congressmen are being chosen in the "off-years." In organization they are like the national committees, being composed of one member from each state and territory.[1] They likewise have their respective chairmen and secretaries. But their members are chosen differently. Both political parties select their congressional campaign committees by means of legislative caucuses. The Republicans make their selections at a joint caucus of the Republican senators and representatives in Washington; the Democrats convene

[1] The Democratic committee has nine additional members.

their senators and their representatives in separate caucuses. The committees are made up mainly from among the congressmen themselves.[1]

The work of these party committees, each in its own field, covers a wide range. Details of the nominating convention have to be arranged. Then there is the general planning of the election campaign and the selection of subcommittees to take charge of different branches of the work. There is the preparation of campaign literature and its effective distribution. Speakers have to be secured; meetings provided for and announced; local committees must be set to work; causes of friction or dissatisfaction here and there have to be eliminated; campaign funds must be raised and apportioned, canvassing and newspaper propaganda organized, and arrangements made for getting out the vote on election day.

*Work of the party committees.*

It is not to be assumed, of course, that the national committee looks after all these matters in a presidential campaign. Each member of the committee is to some extent in charge of the arrangements for his own state, coöperating with the state committee. But the detailed work is in large measure delegated to state committees, auxiliary committees, or local party organizations. The general responsibility, however, cannot be delegated, so that, to borrow a military metaphor, the national committee serves as the general staff of the party forces. The state and local organizations form a hierarchy of divisional, brigade, and regimental staffs who direct the operations of their respective units. The theory of party organization is that it is controlled from below, by the men and women in the party ranks. In actual fact, however, the control and direction, as in military organization, comes always from above. It is only in the event of a mutiny that the ordinary soldier in the party's ranks gets any measure of control.

*The devolution of party functions.*

Political campaigns are not waged with uniform aggressiveness all over the country. In some sections, where the party is strong and united, the national committee finds

[1] For a further description see Jesse Macy, *Party Organization and Machinery* (N. Y., 1912), ch. vii.

338   THE GOVERNMENT OF THE UNITED STATES

*The theory and the practice of party organization.* little to do. In other sections, where the party's chances of success seem to be hopeless, it will also put forth little of its energy. The Democratic national committee does not bother itself much about a presidential campaign in Texas. Nor does the Republican national committee give its chief thought to Pennsylvania. The result is that efforts are largely concentrated from both sides upon the doubtful states, the states which may be swung from one party column to the other by dint of good strategy, careful organization, and the free expenditure of party funds.

*The need of tense effort in a presidential campaign.* In a national campaign all the machinery of the party, and every wheel in it, must be run at full speed. From the smallest village or township committee through the district and state organizations the party's entire strength must be put forth in perfect articulation. For it must always be remembered that the outcome in the nation may hinge upon victory or defeat in a single state. New York turned the scale in 1884; California did likewise in 1916. A relatively slight lapse from sound political strategy was responsible for the defeat of Mr. Blaine in the one case and of Mr. Hughes in the other. On either occasion the shifting of about a thousand votes would have changed the line of presidents. Mishaps of this sort have taught party leaders the value of capable guidance, good discipline, and thorough organization.

*Party finance.* The activities of a political party in a national campaign require large expenditures. In the campaign of 1916 the Democrats spent nearly two million dollars while the Republicans disbursed almost twice that amount. Nor do these figures tell the whole story of actual expenditures, for while each national committee has its own fund, so has every state committee. Likewise the various city, county, district, and town committees have special campaign funds of their own. Being raised and spent independently, these latter are not included in the national totals.

*The quest for contributions.* To secure these funds every committee, national, state, and local, has its treasurer and usually its subcommittee on finance. The first step is usually to send out circulars asking for contributions. These circulars go to all party leaders, to all candidates and office-holders belonging to the party, to all who have contributed in previous campaigns, and to all others from whom subscriptions may for any reason be expected. Much money comes in by way of response to this preliminary call. Then a second and more urgent appeal is commonly sent to those who have not responded. But no party war chest can be filled by impersonal solicitation. Personal canvassing must also be undertaken, especially to get large contributions. This work is done by the national chairman and the treasurer, hence it is desirable to have as treasurer some one who has a large personal acquaintance with men of means. The national and state committees also have auxiliary committees on finance, the members of which assist the treasurer in this work.

Subscriptions to party funds on the eve of a national election come from many sources. Some of them are made by persons who, acting for themselves or for corporations, have more than merely altruistic ends to serve. Men who aspire to office or to future political favors of any sort usually find places for their names upon the subscription rolls. Large sums often come from those who anticipate that the success of one or the other party would affect their own business profits. In the election campaign of 1896 millions were given to the Republican fund by manufacturers who sincerely believed that the Democratic programme of free coinage of silver and tariff reduction threatened the business interests of the country with ruin. There was a time when corporations and public officials were literally black-jacked into making contributions. Regular assessments were levied upon federal office-holders in proportion to their salaries. These are now things of the past. They are forbidden by the laws and by the civil service regulations. Corporations are now pretty well protected against blackmailing politicians, for by law they have been forbidden to contribute anything to national campaign funds. *Where the money comes from.*

Another factor which has proved of great service in lessening the evils connected with the raising of campaign funds is the practice of requiring the publication of the subscription lists. An act of Congress, passed in 1910, requires the national party committees to file before the day *The control of campaign finance by publicity.*

of the election detailed statements of all their receipts and expenses, showing who have contributed to the funds and where the money is being spent. The law no longer looks upon the national party funds as private patrimony to be used as its custodians see fit, but as semi-public money to be collected and disbursed under strict governmental supervision. One salutary result of this has been to make the party leaders more dependent upon small contributors and hence more directly accountable to the rank and file of the voters. In recent presidential campaigns every effort has been made by both parties to gather large numbers of small subscriptions, and to an astonishing degree these endeavors have proved successful.

*Ramifications of party influence.* The party system, not only during an election campaign but in the intervals between elections, permeates every phase of American political life. The framers of the constitution, were they to emerge from their graves, would doubtless view this situation with amazement, yet it is difficult to see how any other outcome of their work could have been looked for. In a federalism where national and state governments have independent spheres of jurisdiction, *Why strong parties are needed in America.* with a government based upon the principle of division of powers between executive and legislative organs, the party system furnishes the one great coördinating force. The expression and the execution of the people's will must somehow be conjoined in every system of popular government. If an articulation is not provided for by the constitution or the laws, it will develop outside, usually in the form of a party system. And the greater the official barriers in the way of coördination the more elaborate and the more centralized will be the party organization needed to overcome these obstacles.[1]

*Relation of partyism to the American system of government.* This is one reason why the American party system has developed so much more machinery than have the party systems of England or France. The correlation between central and local administration, and between the legislative and executive organs in these countries is provided for within the frame of government itself. In the United

---

[1] For an elaboration of this point, see F. J. Goodnow, *Politics and Administration* (N. Y., 1900), especially ch. ii.

States no single organ of government, President or Congress, has power to shape the entire national policy. Yet public policy ought to be carried into operation by the organs of government acting in unison, and to secure this accord is the aim of each political party. Whatever the theory of the constitution may be, the party organizations have become in fact the great policy-determining factors in American government. By far the larger part of what Congress does is at the behest of party leaders. By far the larger part of what it puts upon the statute-books is by way of redeeming promises made in the platform of the majority party. "Congress as at present constituted," a recent writer complains, "is ninety-nine per cent politics," and he proceeds to urge that "the first concern of every economic and moral interest should be to reverse this relation."[1]

*Partyism controls Congress.*

Such comments display a poor mastery of the science of government. The destruction or even the serious weakening of partyism, whether in Congress or out of it, would in all probability impair, not improve, the practical workings of American national government so long as the present constitution of the United States is retained. A federalism, and particularly a federalism which possesses a central government based upon the principle of division of powers, demands the centripetal influence of partyism. Most of the assaults which have been made upon the party system are the result of a failure to comprehend the true aims and functions of political parties. It is quite true that in their organization and work political parties have developed many excrescences and have often been guilty of public abuses. But to get rid of parties altogether on that account would be a ruthless sort of political surgery. The true task of the reformer, and the one to which too much attention cannot be given, is that of making the party system conform to its professed and proper functions.

*The elimination or weakening of the party system would not improve legislation.*

[1] Lynn Haines, *Your Congress* (Washington, 1915), p. 40.

# CHAPTER XXIV

## THE JUDICIAL POWER OF THE UNITED STATES

*The need of a strong judiciary.*

A FEDERAL system of government, if it is to be successful, must have a provision for a strong judiciary. Federalism by its very nature implies a division of authority between the central and the state governments with the certainty that disputes concerning the exact range of their respective powers will arise. There must, therefore, be a judiciary strong enough to settle such controversies with fairness to both authorities. The makers of the constitution realized that a decentralized judicial organization would be "a hydra in government from which nothing but contradiction and confusion could proceed," hence by deliberate choice they set up a tribunal which in the extent of its powers had no counterpart in any other land. The wisdom of this action has been fully demonstrated by the manner in which the guiding hand of a strong judiciary has become the most notable feature of American constitutional evolution. It may fairly be said, in fact, that the development of a Supreme Court into a final arbiter of constitutional disputes is America's most conspicuous contribution to the science of government.

*What the constitution provides.*

Lord Bryce tells of an educated Englishman who heard that the Supreme Court of the United States had authority to annul as unconstitutional the laws of Congress and spent two days reading up and down the constitution in a hunt for that particular provision.[1] It is no wonder that his quest proved vain, for the constitution has nothing to say on that point and very little about the powers of the judiciary in any connection. It provides for a Supreme Court, but leaves the organization of that tribunal to Congress. It likewise protects the judges in all the federal courts against

[1] *American Commonwealth*, i, 246.

improper removal and secures them from either legislative or executive interference. But it is far less explicit with reference to the rights, powers, and organization of the judiciary than with regard to the composition, authority, and procedure of Congress. This was not, however, because the makers of the constitution failed to recognize the importance of the federal courts. They did recognize it. But they were of widely different minds as to how such courts ought to be constituted, and they ended by merely laying down a few general principles upon which they were agreed, leaving to Congress the task of determining the details later on. And Congress, by the Judiciary Act of 1789, performed this task at its first session.[1]

What need is there for federal courts? Why was not the nation's entire judicial business left to be handled by the state courts? That had been done during the period before the constitution was framed. The answer is that this selfsame experience had shown the weakness of such a plan. The lack of a federal judiciary had been strongly felt during these years, and it was realized that the new national government, with its greater powers, would have to lean more heavily than ever upon the sympathy and support of the tribunals. Questions would arise among the states themselves, moreover, and there should be some judicial authority, standing outside them all, to settle these controversies. There would be controversies bearing on the relations of the United States with foreign powers, on matters covered by treaties, for instance, which could not safely be left for decision by each state through its own tribunals. But most important of all, disputes would arise as to the meaning of various clauses in the constitution and concerning the interpretation of laws passed by Congress. By whom should such contestations be decided? To leave them to the various state courts would be to invite chaos. Each court might render a different decision, so that the constitution and the federal laws would mean one thing here and another thing there. To make the Union real there must be a coördinating judicial organization, in other words one or more tribunals wholly

*Why federal courts were deemed necessary.*

---

[1] This law remained in force, with amendments, for well over a hundred years. It was not superseded until 1911.

independent of the states. "If there are such things as political axioms," wrote Alexander Hamilton, "the propriety of the judicial power of a government being coextensive with its legislative, must rank among the number. The mere necessity of uniformity in the interpretation of the national laws decides the question. . . . Any other plan would be contrary to reason, to precedent, and to decorum."[1]

*Two complete sets of courts have arisen.* These reasons, however, did not necessitate the creation of a whole hierarchy of federal courts. One Supreme Court would have sufficed to maintain the federal supremacy and to insure the uniform interpretation of the laws, leaving to the state courts the function of hearing all cases in the first instance. Nor does the constitution expressly require that there shall be any federal courts other than the Supreme Court.[2] Might it not have been possible, then, for Congress to have refrained from establishing subordinate federal courts and to have empowered the state courts to take cognizance of cases falling within the judicial power of the national government? The framers of the constitution appear to have thought so. As Hamilton distinctly pointed out, the power "to constitute tribunals inferior to the Supreme Court," as enumerated among the powers of Congress, was "intended to enable the national government to constitute or *authorize*[3] in each state or district of the United States a tribunal competent to the determination of matters of national jurisdiction within its limits."[4] But Congress decided that it would be better for the new national government to have a complete series of its own courts from the lowest to the highest, and on the whole this decision has turned out to have been wise. The Supreme Court, moreover, decided some years after the Judiciary Act was passed that Congress has no power to confer jurisdiction on any courts not created by itself.[5]

Before the structure and powers of the various federal

[1] *The Federalist*, No. 80.
[2] "The judicial power of the United States shall be vested in one Supreme Court and in such inferior courts as Congress may from time to time ordain and establish." Article iii, Section 1.
[3] The italics are Hamilton's, not mine.
[4] *The Federalist*, No. 81. [5] *Houston* vs. *Moore*, 5 Wheaton, 1.

courts are explained, it may be well to notice the division of jurisdiction between the federal courts, taken as a whole, and the state courts.¹ The federal courts have jurisdiction over certain classes of controversies named in the constitution; the state courts have jurisdiction over all others. These matters of federal cognizance cannot be more concisely or more clearly summarized than by quoting the exact words of the constitution itself: {The sphere of the federal courts.}

"The judicial power shall extend to all cases in law and equity arising under this constitution, the laws of the United States, and treaties made, or which shall be made, under their authority; to all cases affecting ambassadors, other public ministers, and consuls; to all cases of admiralty and maritime jurisdiction; to controversies to which the United States shall be a party; to controversies between two or more States, between a State and citizens of another State; between citizens of the same State claiming lands under grants of different States, and between a State, or the citizens thereof and foreign States, citizens, or subjects." ²

As a model of concise legal phraseology this paragraph of the constitution is probably unsurpassed in the whole range of jurisprudence. If any one has doubts on this score let him try to recast its phrases in his own words. But the very compactness of the wording makes some explanation necessary in order that the full force and effect of these provisions may be properly understood.

First and most extensive of the controversies enumerated as within the judicial power of the federal government are those arising under the constitution and under the laws or treaties of the United States. Where a controversy involves the interpretation of any clause in the national constitution or in a federal law or in a treaty to which the United States is a party, such issue is for the federal courts to settle. {1. Cases arising under the federal constitution, laws, and treaties.}

---

[1] B. R. Curtis, *The Jurisdiction, Practice and Peculiar Jurisprudence of the Courts of the United States* (2d ed., Boston, 1896); Joseph Story, *Commentaries on the Constitution of the United States* (5th ed., 2 vols., Boston, 1905), §§ 1573–1795; W. W. Willoughby, *Constitutional Law of the United States* (2 vols., N. Y., 1910), ii, 970–998; and R. M. Hughes, *Handbook of Jurisdiction and Procedure in United States Courts* (2d ed., St. Paul, 1913).

[2] Article iii, Section 2.

Any one who claims a right under the constitution, laws, or treaties of the United States may claim it in the federal courts.[1] To take an example: If a person or corporation is being prosecuted in any state court on grounds which seem to infringe any rights guaranteed in the federal constitution (for instance, the right not to be deprived of life, liberty, or property without due process of law), relief may be sought in the federal courts. Or if any law made by Congress is being applied, all controversies relating to it must come to the federal courts. Or, again, if a foreign citizen claims that rights given to him by treaty are being denied by any state of the Union, he comes to the federal courts for the enforcement of his claims. Whenever, in fact, one of the parties to a suit asserts that he has a substantial right which arises from the constitution, laws, or treaties of the United States, this gives the federal courts jurisdiction.

2. Cases affecting ambassadors, other public ministers, and consuls.

Again the federal courts have jurisdiction over all cases affecting foreign diplomats. A diplomatic agent of a foreign state is by international law immune from prosecution in the courts of the country to which he is accredited. The provision of the American constitution which extends federal jurisdiction to diplomats merely operates, therefore, to keep the state courts from a possible infringement of such rights at international law. If an ambassador or other public minister of a foreign state commits an offence his recall may be requested, or he may even be expelled; but so long as he remains an accredited diplomat his freedom from legal process is guaranteed. This rule as to diplomatic immunity has been recognized from ancient times.

3. Admiralty cases.

By "admiralty and maritime" jurisdiction is meant authority over cases which relate to American vessels travelling on the high seas or in the navigable waters of the

[1] "The jurisdiction of the courts of the United States is properly commensurate with every right and duty created, declared, or necessarily implied by and under the constitution and laws of the United States" (*Irvine* vs. *Marshall*, 20 Howard, 558). But the right must be a substantial and not merely an incidental one in order to warrant its assertion in the federal courts. "It must appear on the record . . . that the suit is one which does really and substantially involve a dispute or controversy as to a right which depends on the construction of the constitution or some law or treaty of the United States, before jurisdiction can be maintained." *Cableman* vs. *Peoria, etc. R. R. Co.*, 179 U. S. 335.

United States. Such, for example, are controversies regarding seamen's wages, damages due to collisions, and offences committed on shipboard. In England for many generations prior to 1787 admiralty courts had exercised jurisdiction over cases connected with sea-borne commerce. Admiralty law is a distinct branch of jurisprudence, differing both in substance and in procedure from the common law and equity of the regular courts. Both for that reason and because foreign commerce was placed within the regulating power of the federal government, it was deemed wise to vest admiralty jurisdiction exclusively in the federal courts.

Likewise the federal courts have jurisdiction whenever the United States is one of the parties to a suit, or whenever the contestation is between two states of the Union, or between a state and a citizen of another state. On this last point the wording of the constitution at the time of its adoption gave ground for difference of opinion. Did the words "between a state and citizens of another state" intend that suits might be brought in the federal courts whenever an outsider wished to proceed against a state?

4. Cases in which the United States or a state of the Union is a party.

An issue on this matter was soon raised, and in a noteworthy decision the Supreme Court ruled that such suits might be maintained.[1] This ruling was a surprise, because it had been openly asserted, when the constitution was before the states for acceptance, that no state would be amenable to the suit of an individual without its own consent. But the Supreme Court in making its adjudication merely followed the literal wording of the constitution which plainly allowed such construction if it did not actually require it. The decision was regarded by the states as an impairment of their legal sovereignty, since the principle that a sovereign state is not liable to suit without its own consent had been a maxim of public law from time immemorial. Blackstone had spoken of it as "a necessary and fundamental principle." Popular resentment against this new subordination of the states to outside jurisdiction was aroused, and five years later (1798) the Eleventh Amendment was added to the constitution, making the situation clear for the future.

The suability of a state.

[1] *Chisholm* vs. *Georgia*, 2 Dallas, 419.

*The Eleventh Amendment.*

By the terms of this amendment the federal courts are expressly forbidden to take cognizance of any suit brought against a state "by a citizen of another state, or by citizens or subjects of any foreign state." Any one who desires to sue a state must bring his suit in the state's own courts and these courts will not entertain such suits unless they have been authorized to do so by the state laws, in other words unless the state has consented. But the states do, as a general rule, permit themselves to be sued in their own courts under prescribed conditions. A state may be sued in the federal courts only by the United States or by another state of the Union.

*May state officials be sued in the federal courts?*

While the doctrine that no state may be sued in the federal courts by either its own citizens, by citizens of another state, or by foreign citizens is now well established, the question whether the officials of a state are equally immune is by no means so unclouded. In general the Supreme Court in such cases has endeavored to determine whether the suit is really against the state through one of its officers, or whether it is against a state officer as an individual. In the former case it will not assume jurisdiction; in the latter it has maintained its right to entertain suits against those who "while claiming to act as officers of the state, violate and invade the personal and property rights of the plaintiffs under color of authority."[1]

*5. Controversies between citizens of different states.*

Finally, the jurisdiction of the federal courts extends to all controversies between foreign and American citizens, and between citizens of different states. It is cases of this sort that bring the largest grist to the federal mills. A corporation or company is presumed for purposes of jurisdiction to be a citizen of the state in which it was chartered or incorporated, although it may be doing the larger part of its business in other states.[2] When a corporation brings a suit, or when a suit is brought against it, the chances are, therefore, that the other party to the suit will not be of its own citizenship, in which case the issue will come to the federal courts. The same is true of foreign companies doing business in the United States. They sue and are sued in the federal tribunals. National banks are for purposes of

---

[1] *Hagood* vs. *Southern*, 117 U. S. 52.   [2] See above, p. 84.

# THE JUDICIAL POWER OF THE UNITED STATES 349

jurisdiction designated by law as citizens of the states in which they are located. All other corporations chartered by Congress, unless their charters provide to the contrary, may invoke the jurisdiction of the federal courts.

The authority of the federal courts covers a wide area and the amount of judicial business which comes before them is very large. Summarizing it all, one can say that many suits arise in the federal courts because of their subject-matter, that is because they concern matters dealt with by the constitution, laws, or treaties of the United States; that others arise there because of the sovereign character of the parties concerned, as for example suits to which the United States is a party or in which two states are contestants; while yet others go to the federal courts because the suitors are not of the same citizenship. *Summary.*

So much for the jurisdiction of the federal courts. What is the law which they administer? Speaking broadly, it is made up of two branches, the common law and statutes. The common law is the oldest branch of American law. Its development began in mediæval England when there were few written rules and when the royal courts decided cases, so far as they could, in accordance with the unwritten usages or customs of the people. Gradually the decisions of the courts in such matters grew more and more uniform, until this judge-made law or body of usages became "common" to the whole realm of England, although it had never been enacted as the law of the land by any parliament or other law-making body. It is not to be assumed, however, that the common law stood unstirred and changeless on its mediæval pedestal. Developing in accordance with the needs of civilization, it slowly broadened down from precedent to precedent. It adapted itself through the centuries to the genius of the Anglo-Saxon race. In the course of time, moreover, this whole system of common law was reduced to written form by great text-writers or commentators, Glanvil, Bracton, Coke, Littleton, and Blackstone.[1] *The law and equity of the United States. The two branches of law: (a) The common law. Its history in England.*

During the colonial period the common law followed the

[1] The best general account of this development is that given in Blackstone's *Commentaries on the Laws of England*, § 3.

English flag across the Atlantic. Its principles and procedure were applied by the judges in the American colonies. The Declaration of Rights adopted by the first Continental Congress in 1774 spoke of it as a heritage. "The respective colonies," it asserted, "are entitled to the common law of England." When the thirteen colonies shook off British political control, therefore, they did not root out the common law. It remained, and still persists, as the foundation of the legal system in the nation and in all the states but one.[1] Only in Louisiana did the common law fail to get an initial foothold. There, through the colonization of the country by the French, the jurisprudence of France became the basis. Even in Louisiana, however, the system of trial by jury and other common law institutions have had a profound effect upon the judicial system.

*Its development in America.*

*(b) Statutory law.*

But although the common law of England remains the basis of the American legal system, it has ever kept growing and changing, widening and narrowing, in the New World as in the Old. This steady transformation of the American legal system has been accomplished in part by judicial decisions but in larger measure by the enactment of statutes which have modified or even supplanted the rules of common law on many matters. A statute or act of a legislature may merely reënact with slight changes what has been the common law, or it may set the rules of the common law on any point entirely aside. Where the common law and a statute are inconsistent the latter always prevails.

*Its extent.*

Statutory law, as has been indicated, is law made by an established law-making body. It may be framed by a constitutional convention, in which case we call it a constitution. A constitution is of the nature of statutory law, supreme statutory law. By far the greater part of statutory law is made, however, by the regular legislative bodies, by Congress, or by the state legislatures. The output of these bodies is called laws, acts, or statutes. These enactments supplement or alter the common law as the case may be. The total production of statutory law by Congress and by forty-eight state legislatures is of great proportions,

[1] The standard American treatise on common law principles is O. W. Holmes, *The Common Law* (Boston, 1881).

hence this branch of the law now forms by far the larger part of American jurisprudence; but the underlying principles are still provided by the common law.

The constitution speaks of the federal courts as being entitled to jurisdiction "in law and equity." What is equity? To explain the substance, procedure, and limitations of equity jurisprudence would take far more space than could be accorded to that subject in any general treatise on American government. The layman thinks of "equity" as something inseparably associated with abstract justice and conscience, but equity as administered by the courts is merely a formal set of rules which must be applied with an unfaltering hand, even as laws are applied. {Equity. What it is.}

The origins of equity are interesting. In mediæval England there grew up, side by side with the common law, a system of rules administered by a special royal court, the Court of Chancery, which aimed to give redress to individuals in cases where the common law afforded such redress inadequately or not at all. This Court of Chancery was the "keeper of the king's conscience" and its intervention at the outset was confined to the granting of relief from the legal consequences of accident or mistake. Every such case was adjudged on its own merits. Gradually, however, definite principles or rules were evolved to cover all cases of the same sort. In the course of time these rules were reduced to written form; and taken together they became known as equity. {Its origin.} {Its development.}

Equity came to the American colonies with the common law. It was retained after the Revolution and has been developed. To-day both law and equity are administered by the same federal courts. The differences between the two are both numerous and technical, but in general equity applies only to certain classes of civil actions and never to criminal cases; its procedure is simpler; a jury is not ordinarily used to determine the facts at issue, and its remedies are more direct. A suit at law, for example, is a request for an award of damages, a petition in equity usually asks for a decree or for an injunction, that is, for an order specifically compelling a person to do or not to do a thing. It is characteristic of equity that it deals directly with persons or acts {Its nature.}

*in personam*, while the law in civil actions deals chiefly with material things at issue, or acts *in rem*. Over some matters equity has exclusive jurisdiction; over others its jurisdiction is concurrent with that of the law. Within the first category redress must be sought at equity; in the latter there is, under certain limitations, the option of equity procedure.

International law as administered by the courts. The federal courts, within the fields of jurisdiction allotted to them by the constitution, administer both common and statutory law, and equity as well. The common law applied by the federal courts is the common law of the states.[1] The statutes which they administer are for the most part acts of Congress but very frequently (as in the case of controversies between two states or between citizens of different states) the work of the federal courts is concerned with the interpretation and application of either the common law or the statutes of the states. In such cases, if the state courts have already given an interpretation of the state law concerned, the federal courts will ordinarily accept such interpretation. So far as they are applicable, the federal courts also apply the recognized rules of international law when cases involving that branch of jurisprudence arise. "The law of nations," said Marshall in one of his decisions, "is part of the law of the land."[2]

Congress controls the procedure of the federal courts. The procedure of the federal courts, including their rules of evidence, the regulations concerning appeals, and all other matters relating to their actual work are for the most part left by the constitution to the discretion of Congress. These matters are covered to some extent by the Judiciary Act of 1789 and by the various amendments to that statute, all of which were revised and codified by a general law in 1911. On many points of detail Congress has empowered the courts to make their own rules of procedure.[3]

The constitution, however, contains many limitations

---

[1] "There is no body of federal common law separate and distinct from the common law existing in the several states, in the sense that there is a body of statute law enacted by Congress separate and distinct from the body of statute law enacted by the several states." *Western Union Tel. Co.* vs. *Call Publishing Co.*, 181 U. S., 92.

[2] *The Nereide*, 9 Cranch, 388.

[3] A revision of equity procedure was made a few years ago; a revision of the procedure in cases at law is also needed.

upon this power of Congress to regulate the procedure in the federal courts, limitations designed to insure fair trials and to preclude injustice to any of the parties. These limitations, which are to a large extent set forth in the Bill of Rights, relate to such matters as grand jury hearings, jury trials, promptness and publicity in judicial proceedings, double jeopardy, self-incrimination, the issue of warrants, and the nature of punishments.[1] They apply to the federal courts only.

*But subject to various limitations.*

No one may be held to trial in a federal court for any "capital or otherwise infamous crime unless on a presentment or indictment of a grand jury."[2] A grand jury is a body of men, not exceeding twenty-three in number, selected by lot or by some other established procedure, and sworn to discharge impartially the duty of investigating all alleged offences which may be brought to their attention by the prosecuting officers of the government. It conducts an inquest or investigation, not a trial. If it finds that there is a *prima facie* case against any person, it returns an indictment against him and he is held for trial. If, on the other hand, it finds no reasonable ground for holding a person to trial, it returns a "no bill" and he is discharged.[3]

*Nature of these limitations: (a) the need of grand jury action. What the grand jury is and does.*

In all criminal cases (except impeachments) and in all civil suits at common law, where the amount involved is more than twenty dollars, the constitution requires that the trial shall be by jury.[4] This jury, in criminal cases, must be selected from the state and district in which the crime is alleged to have been committed. If the offence is committed

*(b) the requirement of jury trial.*

[1] Amendments I–X. See T. M. Cooley, *Constitutional Limitations* (7th ed., Boston, 1903), *passim*, and F. Lieber, *Civil Liberty and Self-Government* (3d ed., Philadelphia, 1911).

[2] Amendment vi. An "otherwise infamous crime" has been construed to be one to which a penalty of imprisonment for more than one year is attached. The constitution makes an exception to the grand jury requirement in the case of the military and naval forces. The distinction between presentment and indictment is now of no practical importance.

[3] G. J. Edwards, *The Grand Jury* (Philadelphia, 1906).

[4] Article iii, Section 2; also Amendment viii. It is not necessary that all such trials in the lowest court shall be by jury; it is sufficient if the accused has the right of appeal from such tribunal to a higher court which provides a jury. The constitutional right to a jury trial is one which may be waived in any case by the consent of both parties.

2 A

outside the limits of any state, the trial may be held and the jury selected wherever Congress shall by law direct. No fact, moreover, when tried and determined by a jury, may be reëxamined in any court otherwise than according to the rules of common law, that is to say a higher court sitting without a jury cannot set aside conclusions of fact reached by a jury in a lower court. In such cases it can only hear appeals on points of law.

*What a trial jury is and does.* A trial jury, or petit jury as it is sometimes called, is a body of twelve qualified persons, selected either by lot or in accordance with other legally established methods, and sworn to try impartially a particular case, rendering a true verdict thereon in accordance with the evidence. It is usually required that persons called for jury service shall be qualified voters but there is no necessary connection between the right to vote and the obligation of jury service. Certain classes of persons are exempted by law from the obligation, including physicians, attorneys, public officers, teachers, and so on. Persons selected for service at each term of the court are called veniremen or talesmen, and from among them the twelve jurors are selected after due inquiry has been made concerning their impartiality and competence. Each party to the trial, plaintiff and defendant, has the right to challenge any venireman for stated cause. The right to challenge peremptorily, that is, without assigning any cause, is also granted under certain limitations. The selection of the jury is complete when twelve persons, against whom no valid objection or peremptory challenge is interposed, have been duly sworn.

*Functions of the jury.* The jury hears such evidence as the presiding judge permits to be presented. The admissibility of evidence is a matter of law for the judge, and not for the jury, to decide. The value of evidence, when once admitted, however, is a matter of fact for the jury to determine. Most suits at law resolve themselves into questions concerning the relative credibility of evidence submitted by the opposing sides. When the evidence has been presented and the arguments of counsel heard, the judge instructs or charges the jury on their legal duties and on matters of law only, with no comments upon the weight of the evidence. Jury verdicts must be unanimous. If a jury fails to reach unanimity a disagreement is reported and no verdict or judgment can be rendered except after another trial. A presiding judge may set aside a unanimous verdict if he finds that the jury has disregarded his rulings on points of law, or if he is satisfied that the verdict is clearly unsupported by the evidence, or if there has been any serious irregularity in the methods by which the jurors have reached their verdict. In such cases the presiding judge cannot himself render a different verdict, but merely orders a new trial.[1]

*No reopening of facts except by another jury.*

Certain essentials of all trials in the federal courts are made mandatory by the constitution. It is required that trials shall be "speedy and public," that a person charged with crime shall "be informed of the nature and cause of the accusation"; that he shall "be confronted with the witnesses against him" and shall "have compulsory process for obtaining witnesses in his favor," but no person in any criminal case may be compelled to be a witness against himself. Finally, an accused person is entitled to have the assistance of counsel in his defence.[2] "Excessive bail shall not be required, nor cruel and unusual punishments inflicted."[3] No warrants may be issued, except upon probable cause supported by oath and definitely describing the place to be searched or the persons to be arrested.[4] All these requirements are imposed by the supreme law of the land and Congress has no power to set any of them aside. Let it be repeated, however, that they apply to the federal administration of justice only and have no relation to the procedure of the state courts. But most of the state constitutions impose similar limitations upon their own courts.

*(c) other securities for fair trials.*

The constitutional protection of all accused persons against second jeopardy requires a word of explanation. "Nor shall any person," the provision recites, "be subject for the same offence to be twice put in jeopardy of life or limb."[5] The application of this rule is that where a person accused of crime has been tried and acquitted, he may not

*(d) the rule against second jeopardy.*

---

[1] For a discussion of jury procedure, see S. E. Baldwin, *American Judiciary* (N. Y., 1914), Ch. xii.
[2] Amendment vi.   [3] Amendment viii.
[4] Amendment iv.   [5] Amendment v.

be again tried for the same offence. It matters not if new evidence has been discovered; the verdict of acquittal is conclusive and cannot be reopened. When an accused person is acquitted, the government has no right of appeal to any higher court against such verdict. But if an accused is convicted an appeal may be taken in most cases on his behalf. Instances arise occasionally in which the same act may be made the basis of two distinct accusations, as for example the wilful passing of counterfeit money, which is both a statutory offence under the laws of the United States and a fraud under the laws of a state. In such cases the acquittal on one charge is not a bar to trial on the other. In general, however, an acquittal in connection with any act relieves an accused from all further criminal liability in connection with that act.

Conclusion. The insertion of these various limitations in the Bill of Rights shows the jealousy with which Americans in the closing years of the eighteenth century regarded the fundamental rights of the citizen. These were the fruit of struggle and sacrifice during many centuries. It was not thought safe to take any chance of their being swept away by some arrogant Congress in days to come.

# CHAPTER XXV

### THE SUPREME COURT AND THE SUBORDINATE COURTS

THE regular tribunals of the United States consist of a Supreme Court, nine circuit courts of appeals (one for each of nine circuits into which the country is divided), and eighty district courts. In addition there are two special courts, namely, the Court of Claims and the Court of Customs Appeals. The courts of the District of Columbia, the courts of Hawaii, of Alaska, and of the insular possessions are also federal courts inasmuch as these territories are completely under the control of the national government. Names of the federal courts.

The Supreme Court of the United States is composed of a chief justice and eight associate justices, each appointed by the President with the consent of the Senate to hold office during good behavior.[1] No justice may be removed except by impeachment. The Supreme Court meets at Washington and its sessions usually last from October until May. It has its own court officials and makes its own rules of procedure. With the exception of two classes of controversies, namely, those involving ambassadors or other public ministers, and those to which a state is a party, all matters heard before the Supreme Court come to it from lower federal courts or from state courts. In the two instances mentioned the Supreme Court has original jurisdiction. The exercise of original jurisdiction is, however, very uncommon. The Supreme Court: how constituted.<br>Its original and appellate jurisdiction.

The Supreme Court, when in session, meets in the Capitol at noon on each week-day except Saturdays. Its sessions are mainly devoted to hearing the oral arguments of attorneys, How its business is done.

---

[1] For its history and organization, see H. L. Carson, *History of the Supreme Court of the United States* (2 vols., Philadelphia, 1902), and W. W. Willoughby, *The Supreme Court of the United States* (Baltimore, 1890).

who subsequently file printed briefs for the justices to study. On Saturday of each week the justices confer upon the cases which have been argued; the various points presented to them in the oral arguments and in the printed briefs are discussed, and a decision is reached by majority vote. The chief justice then designates one of his associates to write the court's opinion in full.[1] When this has been prepared there is a further discussion, with such changes in the wording as may be decided upon, and the document is then handed down to be printed as the decision of the court. Any justice who dissents from the decision of the court may write a dissenting opinion and have it printed also; or several justices may join in submitting a dissenting opinion. If a justice should agree with the decision of the majority, although not agreeing with the reasons for it, he may write a "concurring opinion."

*How cases may come before it:*

*1. By original suit.*

*2. By removal.*

*3. By appeal.*

Cases may be brought before the Supreme Court in any one of three ways, by original suit there, by the removal of a case from a state court, or by appeal. The original jurisdiction of the highest tribunal is limited, as has been said, to two classes of controversies which arise but rarely. Jurisdiction by removal is much more common. Whenever a suit is brought in a state court and one of the parties believes that because of its subject-matter, or the diverse citizenship of the suitors, or for any other legal reason it ought to be tried in a federal court he is privileged to ask its removal thereto. When so removed it may go directly to the Supreme Court, but more often it will be transferred to one of the lower federal courts.

Most cases come before the Supreme Court by appeal either from a state court or from a subordinate federal tribunal. The usual process of appeal is by writ of error. A writ of error is a formal order by which a superior tribunal instructs a subordinate court to transmit to it the record of any case which has been decided in the court below. The suitor who secures such a writ is then called "the plaintiff in error" and his opponent becomes "the defendant in error" no matter what their respective positions may have been originally.

[1] In some cases the chief justice may himself write the opinions.

The popular notion that any one not satisfied with the decision of the highest tribunal of his own state may carry his case before the Supreme Court of the nation is far from being in accord with the facts. No case may be appealed from state to federal jurisdiction except where the interpretation of the constitution, statutes, or treaties of the United States becomes involved, and more particularly where some right, privilege, or immunity guaranteed by the federal constitution is in jeopardy. Most controversies which begin in the state courts end there. If, however, a case is carried through the state courts and an appeal is permitted, this appeal goes directly to the Supreme Court of the United States. No subordinate federal court has any authority to hear and determine an appeal from the state courts. {Not all cases may be appealed.}

The amount of business which comes before the Supreme Court is very large. It is not uncommon to find a thousand cases upon the docket when its session begins in the autumn. To keep pace with this work the court's adjudications must maintain an average of about thirty cases a week, which means a great deal of drudgery in the studying of briefs and the writing of decisions. In printed form these decisions make up three large volumes each year.[1] {The pressure of Supreme Court business.}

The Supreme Court began its work in 1790 with John Jay as its first chief justice. He had with him five associate justices, more than were really needed to handle the small amount of business which came before the court. At its first meeting no cases appeared; the court appointed a clerk and then adjourned for lack of anything else to do. During the first ten years of its history the court decided only six cases involving questions of constitutional law, and when John Marshall became chief justice in 1801 there were altogether only ten cases awaiting him on the docket. Thus far the court had not exercised any great influence on the nation's political development. Its most important de- {Landmarks in the Supreme Court's history.} {Its chief justices.}

---

[1] The official reports of the Supreme Court were published in each year prior to 1875 under the name of the reporter; since that date they have appeared as successive volumes of *United States Reports*. The names of these court reporters are as follows: Dallas (1790–1800); Cranch (1801–1815); Wheaton (1816–1827); Peters (1828–1843); Howard (1843–1860); Black (1861–1862); Wallace (1863–1874).

cision upon a constitutional question had been set aside by the action of the states in adopting the Eleventh Amendment.[1] The prestige of the court was small, and a position upon its bench during these early years was regarded as less alluring than the post of a governor or senator. Chief Justice Jay, for example, resigned from the Supreme Court in 1795 to serve as governor of New York.

*John Marshall.* During the next few years the position of chief justice was bandied about somewhat; but in 1801 John Marshall was given the reins and he held them firmly for more than three decades.[2] Born in Virginia, he saw service as a captain in the Revolutionary army when only twenty-one years of age. While still a young man he studied law and entered politics, like so many other young Southerners of his day. Although not one of those who framed the federal constitution, Marshall was a member of the Virginia convention which ratified it in 1788, and was on intimate terms with the founders of the Virginia dynasty. He declined the post of Attorney-General in Washington's cabinet, but in 1798 was elected to Congress and in 1800 became Secretary of State under President Adams. He held this post when he became chief justice. Marshall was a Federalist in the original and genuine sense, a believer in the need of strengthening the Union, and he lost no opportunity of making his influence

*His constitutional views and influence.* effective in that direction. When he became chief justice the powers of the national government under the constitution were not sharply defined; scarcely a clause of the constitution had been subjected to judicial interpretation. To the work of making it "efficient," however, Marshall and his associates promptly set their hands. A succession of great decisions during the next thirty years not only cleared the constitutional horizon but strengthened the arm of the national government and incidentally raised the court to a position of great authority.

Marshall was not only a great jurist but a man of firm

[1] *Chisholm* vs. *Georgia* (1793). See above, p. 347.

[2] On Jay's resignation John Rutledge was named chief justice and assumed the office, but was not confirmed. Then the post was offered to William Cushing, who was already an associate justice, but he declined it. Oliver Ellsworth was then (1796) appointed and confirmed. He resigned in 1799.

and clear convictions. He had the advantage of writing upon a clean slate. There was as yet no long train of decisions to hamper the court's freedom, and of course no doctrine of *stare decisis* when there were no decisions to follow. Yet the period through which he guided the Supreme Court was a critical one in many ways. The chief problems which came up for adjudication were drawn reeking from the shambles of partisan warfare, and the court on more than one occasion had to take grounds which aroused strong resentment. State officials everywhere looked with suspicion upon what seemed to be a judicial encroachment upon state powers. During his thirty-four years of service Marshall wrote the decisions of the court upon no fewer than thirty-six important questions of constitutional law.[1] In these he not only laid the foundations but raised the whole framework of federal jurisprudence.

Two principles of constitutional construction Marshall enunciated and maintained. In the first place he insisted that every power claimed by Congress must be articulated to some provision of the constitution, the onus of finding an express or implied grant of power being imposed upon the federal authorities. But, in the second place (and here is where the doctrine of broad construction obtained full play), Marshall held that once any grant of power was found it should be interpreted liberally, giving to Congress all reasonable discretion as to how the authority should be exercised. Both these principles are in full force and effect to-day.

"No other man," says Lord Bryce, "did half so much either to develop the constitution by expounding it, or to secure for the judiciary its rightful place in the government as the living voice of the constitution. No one vindicated more strenuously the duty of the court to establish the authority of the fundamental law of the land, no one abstained more scrupulously from trespassing on the field of executive administration or political controversy. The admiration and respect which he and his colleagues won for

---

[1] These include such landmarks as *Marbury* vs. *Madison*, *McCulloch* vs. *Maryland*, *Gibbons* vs. *Ogden*, and the *Dartmouth College Case*. See J. P. Cotton Jr., *The Constitutional Decisions of John Marshall* (2 vols., N. Y., 1905).

the court remain its bulwark: the traditions which were formed under him and them have continued in general to guide the action and elevate the sentiments of their successors."[1]

It was under Marshall's leadership that the court first undertook to assert its place as the guardian of the constitution, with authority to invalidate any law, whether state or federal, that contravened the provisions of this instrument. By so doing the court assumed a power which was not expressly committed to it by the constitution, a power which even at the present day some students of political science believe to have been a usurpation. Whether the court's action was originally the exercise of a right or a usurpation is not an appropriate question to argue here;[2] but in the light of present-day constitutional jurisprudence three propositions are beyond the pale of controversy.

*The court's power to declare laws unconstitutional.*

In the first place the Supreme Court has long since made good its claim. No lawyer would to-day deny its absolute and entire right to nullify any law that conflicts with the federal constitution no matter by whomsoever enacted. That is now as well settled as any point of law can be. Congress, the state legislatures, and the country have tacitly accepted this doctrine for more than one hundred years.

*1. This power is now beyond dispute.*

Second, the action of the court in thus asserting the doctrine of judicial supremacy has proved beneficial in its results. Had the court assumed a different attitude the American constitutional system would have become a hydra-headed monstrosity; it would never have gained that strength and regularity of operation which it has to-day. For the preservation of individual liberty there must be an

*2. Its exercise has proved beneficial.*

---

[1] *The American Commonwealth*, i, 268. The best short biography of Marshall is James Bradley Thayer's *John Marshall* (Riverside Biographical Series, Boston, 1901).

[2] For a full discussion of it see C. A. Beard, *The Supreme Court and the Constitution* (N. Y., 1912); C. G. Haines, *The American Doctrine of Judicial Supremacy* (N. Y., 1914); E. S. Corwin, *The Doctrine of Judicial Review* (Princeton, 1914); A. C. McLaughlin, *The Courts, the Constitution and Parties* (Chicago, 1912); Brinton Coxe, *Judicial Power and Unconstitutional Legislation* (Philadelphia, 1893), and J. B. Thayer, *The Origin and Scope of the American Doctrine of Constitutional Law* (Boston, 1893).

arbiter between the governing powers and the governed. The integral maintenance of a proper balance of authority between the nation and the states also demands it; and so does the preservation of the adjustment between the executive and legislative organs of government. "The constitutional powers of the courts constitute the ultimate safeguard alike of individual privilege and of governmental prerogative. It is in this sense that our judiciary is the balance-wheel of our whole system."[1]

Third, the power now exercised by the Supreme Court of the United States is one which is not actively asserted by any other tribunal in the world. No court in any other land has ventured to nullify a law enacted by the highest legislative authority. No court has any such authority in other democracies such as Great Britain, France, or Switzerland Even in the South American republics, in Argentina and Chile, for example, where there are supreme courts modelled on the American pattern, no national law has ever been declared unconstitutional by them.

3. It is a unique power.

While the power exercised by the Supreme Court of the United States is unique in the history of government, it has great merits. No part of the American scheme of government, indeed, has worked out to better purpose. It means that Americans refer to an impartial tribunal, made up of eminent jurists, men habituated to reflection and straight-thinking, the great questions of governmental jurisdiction which are so liable to excite the political passions of the people. If the rulings of this body are not always agreeable to the popular sentiments of the day it is because neither judicial nor public opinion is infallible. The doctrine set forth by Jefferson in the Virginia and Kentucky resolutions that "as in all other cases of compact among parties having no common judge, each party (presumably each state) has an equal right to judge for itself" would have utterly disintegrated the nation. That absurd theory has long since been ridiculed out of existence. If these constitutional questions, moreover, had been left for settlement to the Senate, as some proposed in the constitutional convention, they would never have had a

[1] Woodrow Wilson, *Constitutional Government in the United States* (N. Y., 1911), p. 142.

chance of being determined on their merits. The political majority would always have settled them to its own advantage. The Supreme Court, when all is said, represents as near an approach to a strictly non-partisan body as the makers of any government have ever been able to devise.

*What it needs for continued success.*

But the smooth working of this judicial supremacy predicates among the people what Professor Dicey calls "the spirit of legalism." A better phrase would be "popular respect for judicial decisions." Such an attitude exists in the United States, and its importance can hardly be overestimated. The country accepts the rulings of the Supreme Court, whatever they may be, without outbursts of resentment or accusations of unfairness. This is not because Americans have an exaggerated respect for the wisdom or impartiality of their highest tribunal, but because they have a traditional admiration for the constitution itself and for the scheme of free government which that document establishes. "Not having a king to venerate," a facetious European once remarked, "the American people lavish their reverence upon a constitution."

But if that be true, it is small wonder. The reign of the constitution has been long in the land. No monarch was ever so full of years or saw so much accomplished in his day. It commands the veneration of the people because they have found it to be no mere welter of words set down on paper but a vital factor in the life and development of the nation. The Supreme Court has had no small part in making it so. It was the judges who drew water from the rock by commanding arid phraseology to yield forth national strength and power. No people have an intuitive readiness to accept judicial decisions which are not to their liking. They must be schooled to it by habit. It is a genuine compliment to the American judiciary to say that a spirit of legalism prevails among the people.

*Its abstention from political opinions.*

Another reason why the Supreme Court has gained in such large measure the confidence of the people is to be found in its consistent refusal to decide political questions. On various matters which have come before it the court has ruled that questions of public policy must be left within the discretion of Congress and the decisions of this body accepted as final.

# THE SUPREME COURT AND SUBORDINATE COURTS 365

In one notable instance the Supreme Court held that it was for Congress and the President, and not for the judiciary, to decide which of two rival governments within the same state ought to have recognition.[1] In another case it declined to render any opinion as to the length of time during which the military occupation of Cuba might continue, holding that matter to be entirely "the function of the political branch of the government."[2]

The foundations of the Supreme Court's prestige and powers were firmly laid in Marshall's time. Marshall died in 1835. His successor, Roger B. Taney of Maryland, was a man of different stripe, a disciple of Andrew Jackson, and a stanch exponent of the doctrine of states' rights. Under Taney's guidance there was a reaction against the centralizing of powers in the federal government, although the work of the court under Marshall was now too firmly fixed to be seriously dislodged. Taney's most notable decision was that delivered in the Dred Scott Case (1857). In this case the court applied rules of strict construction to the powers of Congress even within the territories of the United States, holding that Congress had no right to prohibit any citizen from owning slaves in such areas. "No word can be found in the constitution," said Taney, "which gives Congress a greater power over slave property, or which entitles property of that kind to less protection than property of any other description." In some of his decisions during the early years of the Civil War, moreover, Taney placed obstacles in the way of a full exercise of the national government's powers, notably in his decision that the President could not of his own authority suspend the privilege of the writ of habeas corpus.[3]

*Marshall's successor: Roger B. Taney.*

Taney in 1864 gave way to Salmon P. Chase of New Hampshire, after a service of twenty-eight years. Chase had served during the first three years of the Civil War as a member of Lincoln's cabinet. During his term of nine years as chief justice the problems of concluding the war and of reconstruction sent many vital questions before the

*Salmon P. Chase.*

---

[1] *Luther* vs. *Borden*, 7 Howard, 1.
[2] *Neely* vs. *Henkel*, 180 U. S. 109.
[3] *Ex parte Merryman*, Taney's Reports, 246 (1861).

Supreme Court for adjudication. But in the main the court upheld the hands of the national government, especially in practically sustaining the constitutionality of the reconstruction acts.[1] Since this troublous era the course of the great tribunal has been relatively serene. Its traditions are well settled and it has been able to continue without mishap the work of steadily weaving together the golden strands of liberty and law.

**Summary of the Supreme Court's history.**

In summary fashion, then, the history of the Supreme Court may be divided into three periods. The first, which extended from its establishment in 1789–1790 to the death of Marshall in 1835, may be called the period of nationalism, the era in which the constitutional provisions relating to the powers of the national government were construed to that government's upbuilding. The second period, extending from 1835 to the Civil War, may be called the era of states' rights, an epoch in which the court for the most part interpreted strictly the constitutional powers of the national government. Finally, in the third period, extending from the Civil War to the present time, there has been a return on the whole to the policy of broad interpretation, particularly with reference to the regulating powers of Congress in relation to industry and commerce.

But whatever its tendencies at any time, the powers of constitutional construction possessed by the court are great. "The provisions of the constitution," as Justice Holmes once remarked, "are not mathematical formulas having their essence in their form; they are organic living institutions, transplanted from English soil. This significance is vital, not formal; it is to be gathered not merely by taking the words and a dictionary, but by considering their origin and the line of their growth."[2]

**Some eminent associate justices.**

Not a few great jurists have adorned the supreme bench of the United States during its thirteen decades of history. Marshall was the primate of them all, and his generation knew not his equal anywhere. In the court's earlier years it numbered among its chief and associate justices several of the "Fathers" themselves, John Rutledge, James Wilson,

---

[1] *Texas* vs. *White*, 7 Wallace, 700 (1868).
[2] *Gompers* vs. *United States*, 233 U. S. 604.

Oliver Ellsworth, John Blair, and William Paterson.  Later, during the first half of the nineteenth century, Joseph Story served his long term of thirty-four years (1811–1845). Story may rightly be regarded as the classic expounder of the constitution; and his commentaries have not ceased to hold the admiration of legal scholars at the present day.[1]  Next to Marshall, moreover, Story had the largest influence in shaping that notable series of Supreme Court decisions which reared the structure of American constitutional law.  When Marshall and Story were together they formed a great team.  Two others whose names stand out conspicuously on the roll of justices are Stephen J. Field and Horace Gray.  The former served a term of thirty-four years, from 1863 to 1897; the latter was in office from 1881 to 1902.  Both were men of rare legal erudition and uncommon personality.  It is a great art to write decisions which combine law, logic, and literature.

*Joseph Story.*

*Field and Gray.*

The Supreme Court in session is an impressive body.  Each day at noon the justices, wearing their gowns of black silk, walk in formal procession from their consultation rooms to their chamber, which is the old hall used by the Senate in years when that body was small.  The atmosphere of this chamber is one of great dignity.  Only a few spectators are ever present and silence is rigidly insisted upon.  There is no jury in appellate cases, of course, and no examining of witnesses.  The court merely listens to the arguments of counsel, the rule being that no oral argument may be longer than one hour and a half except with the court's special permission.  In addition each justice reads the printed briefs submitted by both sides and also the official record of the case in the courts below.

*Impressive character of the court.*

No decision or opinion on any constitutional question is ever given by the Supreme Court until some case actually involving the determination of the point comes before it. Even then the court will not rule on the constitutional aspect of the case if the decision can be made upon any other ground. Washington, in 1793, submitted to the Supreme Court certain general questions concerning rights of the federal government, but the justices declined to express any opinions

*No "advisory" opinions ever given.*

[1] See above, p. 44, *note.*

save in actual controversies duly brought before them. In some of the states, however, provision is made for such advisory judicial opinions to be rendered by the highest state tribunal to the governor or legislature.¹ The federal rule, on the whole, has much to be said in its favor because the frequent submission of hypothetical questions to the court would place an additional burden upon an already overloaded tribunal. Advisory judicial opinions, moreover, are rendered without hearing the arguments on either side, and they have no binding force even upon the judges who render them. It would be an advantage, of course, if Congress could always know in advance whether a proposed measure would be constitutional, but this gain would hardly offset the disadvantages of the advisory system. Reasonably good advice upon points of constitutional law, moreover, can always be had by Congress by asking the opinion of the Attorney-General.

*The doctrine of stare decisis.*

When the Supreme Court has once established a principle of law in any case actually before it, such ruling becomes a precedent and will generally be adhered to in future cases of the same nature. This is known as the doctrine of *stare decisis*. The court has not often altered any constitutional stand taken by it, although there have been a few notable cases of such reversal. For instance it decided in 1880 that an income tax might be levied by Congress without apportionment among the states, but fourteen years later it ruled that such taxes must be apportioned.² On one occasion the court decided that Congress might not by law make paper money a legal tender in payment of debts incurred before the passage of such legislation.³ A year later it reversed this decision and held that Congress did have power to take such action.⁴ More commonly, however, the court finds it possible to reconstruct or modify a prior decision by some means other than a frank reversal. No two cases are exactly alike, and a later case can usually be distinguished in some particular from an earlier, thus affording an opportunity for the modification of a rule.

*It is not always followed.*

¹ See below, p. 413.  ² See above, p. 225.
³ *Hepburn* vs. *Griswold*, 8 Wallace, 603.
⁴ *Knox* vs. *Lee*, 12 Wallace, 457.

The liberty to reverse its decisions on questions of constitutional law, whenever the urgent occasion to do so requires, is one of the things which enable the Supreme Court to endow the constitution with dynamic quality. In cases strictly affecting private intercourse it is essential that the rules of law be not subject to frequent and capricious change. That is why the doctrine of *stare decisis* was evolved by lawyers and courts. But where issues of public policy are concerned the rigid application of that doctrine would tend to slow up the machinery of political and social progress. In the administration of the law as in other fields of human activity the reverence for precedents, which too often are merely the embalmed prejudices of a past generation, may easily be carried to an absurdity.

*Inadvisability of following it too strictly.*

Changes in the organization and procedure of the Supreme Court have been suggested from time to time. One suggestion is that the number of judges be increased and the court divided into sections after the European fashion. Different sections or groups of justices, say three or five in each group, would then deal with civil controversies, criminal appeals, admiralty and maritime affairs, and so on. This would no doubt expedite business, but it would destroy that uniformity in the application of the laws which was one of the prime reasons for the Supreme Court's original establishment. The entire court would still have to pass on all the important questions of constitutional interpretation, and for that reason would probably develop into a cumbrous tribunal of appeal from the decisions of its own sections. The burden upon the court, as at present constituted, might easily be reduced by placing more obstacles in the way of frivolous appeals.

*Some proposed changes in the organization and procedure of the Supreme Court.*

By the Judiciary Act of 1789 which organized the Supreme Court a system of subordinate federal courts was also created, consisting of Circuit and District Courts. This Act was at various times amended, and the original scheme underwent many important changes during the next century until the judicial legislation became extremely complicated. In 1911, accordingly, the whole legislation was revamped by Congress in the so-called Judicial Code which went into operation on January 1, 1912. This code is now the ground-

*The subordinate federal courts.*

2 B

work of the entire system of federal courts subordinate to the Supreme Court.

**The Circuit Court of Appeals.** Next below the Supreme Court comes the Circuit Court of Appeals. The territory of the United States is divided into nine circuits, each circuit containing three or more states. There is a Circuit Court of Appeals for each of these nine circuits, such courts having from two to four judges according to the amount of business to be done. In addition, one justice of the Supreme Court is assigned to each circuit, but in practice, these justices do not go the circuits at all, their whole time being taken up at Washington. The Circuit Court of Appeals in each circuit holds sessions at various cities, hearing appeals from the District Courts below. In many cases, where the issue of the constitutionality of a law is not raised, the Circuit Court of Appeals has final authority. But when this issue is raised, as it is in a multitude of cases, an appeal may be carried to the Supreme Court.

**The District Courts.** Then come the federal District Courts. The entire territory of the United States is divided into eighty districts, each state constituting at least one district and the more populous states having two districts or even more within their boundaries. New York State is divided into four districts. Each District Court has its own judge as a rule; but in a few cases one judge serves two districts and a few districts have more than one judge. Every District Court holds several sessions every year, sometimes sitting in more than one city within the district. It is a court of first instance, and the only federal court in which a jury is used. Every district has its United States district attorney and United States marshal, appointed by the President with the concurrence of the Senate. The function of the district attorney is to act as the representative of the nation in prosecutions before the court. The marshal executes the court's orders and judgments, attends to the service of its writs, and is its general executive officer. Both are under the direction of the federal Department of Justice. Each District Court also has a federal commissioner who conducts the preliminary hearing in criminal cases and decides whether an accused shall be held for the grand jury. Most cases under federal jurisdiction are entered in the District Courts and the great majority of them are finally disposed of there, only a small percentage going thence to the Circuit Court of Appeals and a still smaller proportion to the Supreme Court.

A word should also be said about the two special courts. The Court of Claims, established in 1855, consists of a chief justice and four associate judges appointed by the President. Its business is to hear and determine the merits of all claims against the federal government, such as claims for salaries due or for supplies delivered. With certain restrictions there is a right of appeal to the Supreme Court. The other special court, the Court of Customs Appeals, is a recent creation, dating only from 1909. It has the same number of judges as the Court of Claims and they are similarly appointed. Its function is to serve as a final court of appeal in all controversies regarding the administration of the tariff laws, as for example, controversies over the appraised valuation of goods, the proper rate of duty and so forth. *[margin: The Court of Claims. The Court of Customs Appeals.]*

The courts of the District of Columbia, of Hawaii, Alaska, Porto Rico, and the Philippines are also federal courts. Their judges and other officers are appointed by the President with the consent of the Senate and their jurisdiction is assigned to them by Congress. Their organization will be described in the next chapter.[1] *[margin: Other federal courts in the territories.]*

In all the federal courts the judges are appointed for life or during good behavior. They are removable only by impeachment before the Senate of the United States.[2] Their salaries may not be diminished during their tenure of office. The rule covering these matters cannot be paraphrased into any clearer or more concise language than that of the constitution itself: "The judges both of the supreme and inferior courts shall hold their offices during good behavior, and shall, at stated times, receive for their services a compensation which shall not be diminished during their continuance in office." *[margin: Protections for the independence of the federal courts.]*

[1] For a word on the short-lived Commerce Court, see above, p. 258.
[2] On this and related subjects see the discussion in W. S. Carpenter, *Judicial Tenure in the United States* (New Haven, 1918).

# CHAPTER XXVI

## THE GOVERNMENT OF TERRITORIES

<small>The United States as a colonizing power.</small>

IT is not customary to think of the United States as a colonizing country, yet the whole history of the nation from 1787 to the present has been one of steady territorial expansion. The area of the original thirteen states forms less than one-tenth of the territory which is under the flag of the United States to-day. No other nation has relatively increased its territory to so great an extent and colonized its acquisitions so largely with its own people.

<small>The two periods of expansion:</small>

The history of American expansion may be divided into two periods. First there is the era extending from the close of the Revolutionary War (1783) to the year 1867. It was during this interval that the United States acquired by successive treaties with Great Britain, France, and Spain all the land included in the Northwest Territory as it was then called,[1] in the Louisiana Purchase, and in Florida. During this interval also, the nation secured by conquest from Mexico and by the admission of territories which had declared their independence of Mexico, the enormous areas of Texas, the Southwest, and the Southern Pacific slope.[2] All this territory was contiguous; it included

<small>1. within the present boundaries.</small>

---

[1] The Northwest Territory was acquired by the Treaty of 1783 and before the adoption of the constitution was governed by the provisions of the famous Northwest Ordinance which was framed in 1787 by the Congress of the Confederation. In 1789, on the establishment of the new national government, the provisions of this ordinance were re-enacted into law by Congress. See William MacDonald, *Select Documents Illustrative of the History of the United States, 1776–1861* (N. Y., 1907), pp. 21–29; also B. A. Hinsdale, *The Old Northwest, the Beginnings of Our Colonial System* (2d ed., Boston, 1899).

[2] A general account of these various additions to the national territory may be found in Edward Bicknell, *The Territorial Acquisitions of the United States 1787–1904* (3d ed., Boston, 1904).

nothing remote from lands already possessed, and its acquisition did not impair the compactness of American territory. All of it, moreover, is territory which was intended to be and indeed has now been parcelled into states of the Union with full rights of statehood. The expansions of this period merely represented the logical rounding-out of national boundaries.

The second period, extending from 1867 to the present time, has been marked by territorial acquisitions much less extensive and of a different sort. By the purchase of Alaska from Russia in 1867 the United States acquired its first non-contiguous possession. This precedent was not followed by any further ventures into distant territories, however, until 1898, when by conquest from Spain the Philippines, Porto Rico, and Guam were acquired; and in the same year Hawaii was annexed at the request of its own government. In 1900 a treaty with Great Britain and Germany gave to the United States certain islands in the Samoan Archipelago, and in 1904 the Panama Canal Zone came virtually into American hands by a treaty made with the new Republic of Panama. Finally, in 1917, the Danish West Indies were acquired by purchase.

2. outside territories and insular possessions.

All these acquisitions differed from those of the preceding period in that they are separated from the main territory of the United States and cannot well be assured of any certain admission to statehood at a future date. They are colonies in the ordinary sense of the word, although for sentimental reasons they are designated in official phraseology as insular possessions. In all prior expansion there was some assurance of ultimate incorporation on a basis of equality with the states already in the Union, but since 1898 the United States has faced the practical certainty that for many years to come its jurisdiction will include two classes of territory; one constituting the United States proper with its people enjoying full constitutional rights and privileges, the other made up of insular possessions which cannot well be dealt with on that basis but can only be brought by gradual stages to the attainment of full self-government. "In a word, whatever may be the theory, as a practical condition the United States, through these

Differences between the two forms of expansion.

acquisitions, is now confronted with the problem of governing and administering dependent or colonial possessions in precisely the same way as is England or are other European nations that have deliberately embarked on a colonial policy." [1]

*The constitutional basis of expansion.*

The makers of the constitution foresaw that the Union would eventually comprise more than the thirteen original states. Hence they made provision that new states might be admitted by Congress and that any territory belonging to the United States, if not admitted to statehood, should be governed in such way as Congress might decide. The constitution did not, however, in express terms bestow on Congress the right to acquire new territory, and in connection with the Louisiana Purchase of 1803 it was urged that Congress had no such right. The Supreme Court in 1810, however, settled this question by asserting the doctrine that the United States as a nation has the right to acquire territory either by conquest or by treaty to the same extent that any other nation has that right.[2]

*Constitutional questions connected with outlying possessions.*

But assuming the right of the United States to acquire territory many other questions arose to be settled. Is the control of Congress over such territory complete and unrestricted, or is Congress bound there by all the limitations of the national constitution? Have the inhabitants of insular territories the constitutional rights of American citizens, the right to freedom of speech, to assemble peaceably, to be immune from unreasonable searches and seizures, the right to keep and bear arms, and the right to trial by jury? Is a Filipino or a Porto Rican entitled to these rights by the mere fact that the American flag flies over his islands? And what about the operation of such laws as Congress may make? Do they apply, *ex proprio motu*, to these territories or do they apply only when their extension thereto is expressly provided for? Does a tariff law, for example, apply only to merchandise which comes into the United States proper, or to all that may come into any

---

[1] W. F. Willoughby, *Territories and Dependencies of the United States* (N. Y., 1905), p. 8.

[2] *Sere* vs. *Pitot*, 6 Cranch, 332. See also J. K. Hosmer, *The History of the Louisiana Purchase* (N. Y., 1902).

territory under the sovereignty of the United States? All these questions have come before the Supreme Court at one time or another and all have been answered by that tribunal, so that the constitutional status of territories and insular possessions is now determined with reasonable clearness.

Summarizing the main features in this chain of judicial decisions one may lay down the following general rules: The power of Congress over the territories of the United States is practically complete. The inhabitants of the insular possessions are not citizens of the United States unless and until Congress expressly extends citizenship to them. The provisions relating to the rights of citizens, for example the right of trial by jury, do not extend to the inhabitants of these territories unless and until Congress so provides. Congress, however, has to some extent made provision in this direction. As respects tariff laws, the Supreme Court has held that duties may be exacted on commerce between the United States and its insular possessions.[1] *The rules as enunciated by the Supreme Court.*

The problem of citizenship with reference to inhabitants of the Philippines is even yet, however, a little perplexing. They are, of course, no longer subjects of Spain, nor are they citizens of the United States. What is their status? International law has coined a new term for them. Filipinos are now by general usage called "nationals" of the United States. This means that they are entitled to the protection of the United States government and to its assistance in all international matters. So far as international law is concerned they are, accordingly, American citizens to all intents and purposes. But by constitutional law, the law of the United States itself, they are not citizens, and are not entitled to the privileges and immunities of citizens save in so far as Congress may grant such rights to them. *Status of Filipinos and Porto Ricans.*

Owing to a diversity in local conditions among the various possessions of the United States, no attempt has

---

[1] These various points were settled by the decisions rendered in a series of controversies commonly known as *The Insular Cases.* See especially *De Lima* vs. *Bidwell,* 182 U. S. 1, and *Downes* vs. *Bidwell,* 182 U. S. 244.

376  THE GOVERNMENT OF THE UNITED STATES

**Present government of American dependencies: Hawaii**

ever been made to establish a uniform scheme of government for all of them. Hawaii is at present the only insular possession which has full status as a "territory," that is to say the territorial status enjoyed by the various western areas of the United States before they were admitted to statehood. Prior to 1893 the Hawaiian Islands had a monarchical form of government with a native dynasty.

**How acquired.**

But in that year a revolution abolished the monarchy and set up a provisional government which, in turn, gave way to a republic in 1895. Three years later the government of the Hawaiian republic applied for and obtained annexation to the United States; and in 1900 Congress established a territorial government in the islands.

**Its administration to-day.**

Under this arrangement the federal government at Washington directly controls such matters as fall within its province on the American continent, for example, the postal service, the collection of customs, taxes, and excises, the coinage, and the national banks. On the other hand, local functions in Hawaii are controlled by its own territorial government under the federal government's general supervision. The territorial governor of Hawaii is appointed by the President of the United States. He is assisted in executive work by various administrative officials, a secretary, treasurer, attorney-general, and so on. Then there is a territorial legislature of two Houses. Of these the Senate is composed of fifteen members elected from the four counties and serving for a four-year term, while the House of Representatives consists of thirty members chosen from the six representative districts into which the islands are divided. All persons who were citizens of Hawaii at the time of its annexation (1898) became forthwith citizens of the United States. At present the voters who elect the Senate and the House comprise all male citizens who are able to speak, read, and write either the English or the native language.

**Laws and appropriations.**

Subject to the general control of Congress the Hawaiian legislature, consisting of these two Houses, makes the laws, determines the taxes, and provides for the annual expenditures. The governor possesses the usual right of veto, which may be overridden by a two-thirds vote of both

Houses. There is, moreover, an important provision "that in case the legislature fails to pass appropriation bills providing for payment of the necessary current expenses of carrying on the government and meeting its obligations as the same are provided for by the then-existing laws, the governor shall, upon the adjournment of the legislature, call it in an extra session for the consideration of appropriation bills and until it shall have acted the treasurer may with the advice of the governor make such payments for which purpose the sums appropriated in the last appropriation bills shall be deemed to have been reappropriated." In other words the territorial legislature cannot use its control of expenditures in such way as to coërce the executive into submission by stopping the wheels of government. Hawaii also has its own territorial courts, besides a federal district court. The territory sends one delegate to the House of Representatives at Washington, but he has no vote.

From the date of its purchase from Russia (1867) until 1884, Alaska was not given any system of territorial government. It was kept during these seventeen years directly under the control of the national authorities at Washington. In 1884, however, Congress passed an act establishing a civil government for Alaska and in its general outlines this has remained unchanged to the present day. The administration of Alaska is in charge of a governor appointed by the President. A legislature was established in 1912. The executive departments at Washington still control various Alaskan matters, for example, the system of education is under the Secretary of the Interior. From 1884 to 1900 the general laws of the state of Oregon were applied to Alaska so far as practicable; but in the latter year Congress provided Alaska with a special code of laws and a code of civil procedure. Arrangements have been made whereby settlements may become incorporated as towns, and may establish a system of elective town government. *Alaska.*

During the war with Spain the American army occupied Porto Rico and in the two years following the withdrawal of the Spanish forces the island continued under military government. People do not always realize how easy it is *Porto Rico.*

for an army to provide, out of its own resources, all the administrative machinery that is necessary for temporarily governing a conquered territory. The commander-in-chief with his staff transform themselves into a governor and council; the engineer corps provides a department of public works; the paymaster's department takes charge of the finances; the medical and sanitary corps become a department of public health; the judge-advocate sets up a judicial system; the military police take over the work of policing, and so on. To say that Porto Rico was for two years under military rule does not mean, therefore, that the affairs of the island were crudely or arbitrarily handled. Quite the contrary. The system of military rule did not give way to an organized civil government because it was found to be inefficient but because of the general aversion of the American people to continued military government in any portion of their territory.[1]

The present frame of government in Porto Rico has its basis in the Foraker Act of 1900, considerably modified by the organic statute of 1917, commonly known as the Jones Act.[2] At the head of the island administration is a governor, appointed by the President with the consent of the Senate. He holds office during the President's pleasure. The governor is assisted by six heads of executive departments of whom two (the attorney-general and the commissioner of education) are appointed by the President, while the remaining four (treasurer, commissioner of the interior, commissioner of health and commissioner of agriculture and labor) are appointed by the governor. These six heads of departments form an executive council, assisting the governor in an advisory capacity.

The Porto Rican legislature consists of two chambers, the Senate and the House of Representatives. The Senate contains nineteen members, of whom two are elected from each of seven senatorial districts and five are elected by the voters of the island at large. The House of Representatives is composed of thirty-nine members, one from each of

[1] L. S. Rowe, *The United States and Porto Rico* (N. Y., 1904).
[2] Approved, March 2, 1917. 39 U. S. Statutes at Large, Pt. I, pp. 951 ff.

thirty-five districts and four elected at large. Porto Rico has practically manhood suffrage.

The legislature may levy taxes (except taxes on exports) and may authorize borrowing on the credit of the island. It also determines the expenditures, but since 1909 it has been provided that if the two chambers cannot agree on appropriation measures for the support of the island government, the governor may himself promulgate a budget the total of which shall not exceed the entire appropriations of the year preceding. This amendment to the Foraker Act was made by Congress because a serious deadlock between the two chambers on one occasion prevented any appropriations being made at all. Measures of every sort, to be effective, must be accepted by both chambers of the island legislature. The governor has the customary right of veto subject to being overridden by a two-thirds vote of both chambers if the President approves. Every measure, after it has been enacted, must be reported to Washington, where Congress has power to annul it. As a matter of fact, however, Congress does not interfere, and Porto Rico virtually enjoys a full measure of colonial autonomy similar to that possessed by the self-governing colonies of Great Britain.

Porto Rico has its own system of courts, the judges of the higher tribunals being appointed by the President and those of the lower courts by the governor of the island with the consent of the executive council. There is also one federal District Court for the island. All the judges hold office for life. *Its courts.*

One delegate from Porto Rico, elected by popular vote, has the right to sit in the House of Representatives at Washington, but has no vote in that body. Free trade exists between the island and the United States, but the regular United States tariff laws are applied in Porto Rico as against the rest of the world. All customs duties and internal taxes go into the treasury of the island. *The Porto Rican delegate in Congress.*

By the treaty with Spain in 1898 the Philippine Islands were ceded to the United States. Military rule continued, however, until September 1, 1900. During this interval a commission was sent to the island to study conditions and *The Philippines.*

to report upon a system of civil government for the islands, and its recommendations became the basis of later action by Congress. Meanwhile, President McKinley also appointed a civil commission to serve temporarily as a legislative body for the island while executive powers remained vested in the military governor.

*The preliminaries of civil government.*

Up to 1902 Congress took no action in the matter of a permanent scheme of government for the Philippines. The President controlled the administration of the islands by virtue of his powers as commander-in-chief of the army. But in order to remove any possible doubts as to the legality of this situation, Congress in March, 1901, gave the President in express terms "all the military, civil and judicial powers necessary to govern the Philippines . . . until otherwise provided."[1] The combination of military, executive, and civil legislative commission continued, however, until September 1, 1901, when a civil governor was appointed with William H. Taft as first occupant of that post. Meanwhile various administrative departments were organized and a beginning was made toward the reconstruction of local government.

*The present frame of administration.*

In July, 1902, came the next step, when Congress passed the Philippine Civil Government Act which remained in force for a period of fourteen years.[2] The chief provisions of this law were as follows: The executive power was vested in a governor-general, appointed by the President with the consent of the Senate, and in the heads of the administrative departments, who were similarly appointed. These administrative officials were also members of the Philippine Commission, which included along with them four other persons named by the President. This commission remained the sole legislative body of the islands until 1907; from that time until 1916 it served as the upper chamber of the legislature.[3]

[1] This act was popularly known as the Spooner Amendment.
[2] 57th Congress, 1st Session, Chap. 1369; 32 Statutes at Large, Pt. I, p. 691.
[3] The Commission was abolished by the new organic act for the government of the Philippines which was approved by the President on August 29, 1916. A summary of the provisions of this act may be found in the *American Year Book* for 1916, pp. 239–240.

## THE GOVERNMENT OF TERRITORIES 381

The Act of 1902 did not provide for the immediate establishment of an elective assembly or House of Representatives. It merely stipulated that such a body should be called within a certain time after the islands had been pacified and a census taken. These conditions were eventually fulfilled, and the first Philippine Assembly met at Manila in the autumn of 1907. *The Philippine Assembly.*

In 1916 a further step was taken by making both branches of the legislature elective. The Philippine Commission was replaced by an elective Senate of twenty-four members, of whom twenty-two are chosen by the voters in eleven senatorial districts, while the remaining two are named by the governor-general to represent the non-Christian provinces. The Assembly has ninety members, of whom eighty-one are elected by districts and nine appointed. *The Act of 1916.*

The Philippine legislature is now made up of two chambers, therefore, the Senate and the Assembly. Its powers include the levy of taxes, the making of laws, the borrowing of money, and the voting of annual appropriations. The governor-general is given the right to veto measures passed by the legislature and no legislation may be passed over his veto without the assent of the President of the United States. All appointments to headships of departments, made by the governor-general, must be submitted for confirmation to the Philippine Senate. The governor-general holds office during the pleasure of the President. Philippine senators sit for six years and members of the lower house for three. Two delegates from the Philippines, chosen every two years by the Philippine legislature, are entitled to sit but not to vote in the House of Representatives at Washington. *The powers of the legislature.* *Delegates in Congress.*

The United States is under virtual pledge to accord full independence to the Philippines when the appropriate time arrives. It is not unlikely that this will be done within a few years if the international situation permits.

The judicial organization of the Philippines is much like that of Porto Rico. There are local courts, district courts (or courts of the first instance), and a supreme court for the islands. Under certain conditions appeals may be taken from the decisions of this last-named court to the Supreme *Judicial organization.*

Court of the United States. Judges of the subordinate courts are appointed by the governor-general with the consent of the Senate; those of the supreme court by the President. Congress has extended to the Philippines all the constitutional rights which belong to the citizens of the United States, excepting only the right of trial by jury and the right to keep and bear arms. The old legal system of the Spanish period remains substantially unchanged; but Spanish judicial procedure in both civil and criminal trials has been abolished. Common-law procedure, with the exception of the jury system, has supplanted it.

*The provincial governments.*

A system of local government has also been established in the islands. There are thirty-one "regular" provinces, each with a provincial governor and certain administrative officials assisting him. The provincial governor is elected every two years by a convention made up of the councillors of the municipalities within the province; the administrative officials are selected under civil service regulations and appointed by the governor-general. There is no elective council in any of these provinces. The functions of the provincial governments are to look after the collection of taxes, to care for main roads, and to supervise the work of the municipal authorities. The taxes, after they are collected, go in part to the island treasury, in part to the municipalities, and in part to the province; but the province is the chief unit for collecting them. Seven other non-Christian provinces are entirely under the control of the executive department and have no local government of their own.

*Municipal government.*

*Manila.*

Of municipalities there are several hundreds, large and small. Manila, the capital, is governed by a board of six commissioners of whom three are appointed by the governor-general with the assent of the Philippine Senate, one is a member *ex officio* (the city engineer), and two are elected by the people of the city. In the event of a deadlock in the board, the governor-general is empowered to appoint a seventh member. This board has the usual powers of an American city government. It appoints the city officials, enacts the local ordinances, and controls the various administrative departments such as public works, police, health, and schools; it also determines the general course of municipal enterprises.

Apart from Manila all the municipalities are grouped into four classes according to their size. Each has an elective municipal government which includes a municipal council of from eight to eighteen members. These local governments, however, are under strict provincial control. *The smaller municipalities.*

The fiscal relations between the United States and the Philippines are different from those which exist between the United States and Porto Rico. Trade between the Philippines and the United States, both ways, is subject to a special tariff. There is also a great variety of internal taxes. Much revenue is needed, especially to cover the cost of the elaborate public school system which has been developed under American rule.[1] *Fiscal relations.*

In Samoa all governmental authority is vested in the hands of a commandant designated by the Secretary of the Navy. The commandant appoints a governor for each of the three districts into which the American islands are divided. Local government is left to the natives. The same system of administration by naval commandant exists in the island of Guam. In the case of the Panama Canal Zone, that strip of territory across the isthmus about ten miles in width, of which the United States acquired in 1904 from the Republic of Panama "the perpetual use, occupation and control," the administration is in the hands of the War Department and is exercised through a governor appointed by it. The newly-acquired Danish West Indies or Virgin Islands are for the time being in charge of the Navy Department. Cuba is not in any sense a possession of the United States, although it is virtually under American protection in international affairs. *Samoa and Guam. The Panama Canal Zone. The Virgin Islands.*

Unlike other countries which possess important overseas dependencies, the United States maintains no Department

[1] For further information concerning the government of the Philippines, see W. F. Willoughby, *Territories and Dependencies of the United States* (N. Y., 1905); F. Chamberlin, *The Philippine Problem* (Boston, 1913); W. H. Taft, *Special Report to the President on the Philippines* (Washington, 1908); J. M. Dickinson, *Special Report to the President on the Philippines* (Washington, 1910); and Dean C. Worcester, *The Philippines, Past and Present* (2 vols., N. Y., 1914).

384    THE GOVERNMENT OF THE UNITED STATES

The decentralized supervision of external possessions. of Colonies. The general supervision of the affairs of Porto Rico, the Philippines, and the Panama Canal Zone is intrusted to the War Department. In the case of the Philippines this supervision is directly exercised by the Bureau of Insular Affairs, one of the War Department's bureaus. The minor island dependencies, as has been said, are under the jurisdiction of the Navy Department, for no other reason than that the navy took over possession of them in the first instance and Congress has not since intervened. Hawaii and Alaska are to some extent under the supervision of the Interior Department.

The District of Columbia. The District of Columbia occupies a somewhat anomalous position in the governmental system of the United States.[1] It is neither a state nor a territory but by virtue of its being the national capital it is directly under the control of the federal government. From the beginning of the Revolutionary War to the formation of the constitution, Philadelphia served as the continental headquarters save for a short period in 1783 when the Congress of the Confederation was driven from its meeting place by a band of Revolutionary soldiers clamoring for their pay. Sessions for a few weeks Early vicissitudes of the federal capital. were then held at Princeton. This incident carried its lesson, however, to the members of the constitutional convention in 1787. While they were not ready to designate any city as the permanent seat of the new national government, lest by so doing they should create sectional jealousy and perhaps lead to the rejection of the whole constitution, they did make provision for the eventual selection of a capital which would be exempt from the jurisdiction of any state.

What the constitution provides. At Madison's suggestion, accordingly, the constitution was worded to provide that Congress should have power "to exercise exclusive legislation in all cases whatsoever over such district (not exceeding ten miles square) as may, by cession of particular states and the acceptance of Congress, become the seat of government of the United States." [2] The selection of the exact place was left for the future, but with

---

[1] The best full account of its government is that given in W. F. Dodd, *The Government of the District of Columbia* (Washington, 1909).

[2] Article i, Section 8.

the stipulation, as indicated above, that the territory acquired for the new capital should be wholly under the control of Congress.

When the first Congress of the United States met in 1788–1789 after the adoption of the constitution, there was a long and bitter struggle on this question, particularly between representatives of the northern and the southern states. Each wanted the capital located in its own region. In the end it was agreed to accept a location on the Potomac, which was in reality a victory for the South.[1] *Choice of the Potomac location.*

So Maryland and Virginia each jointly ceded some territory to the federal government, too much of it in fact, and in 1846 Virginia was allowed to take back part of what she had given, so that the area of the district is now sixty-nine square miles instead of the hundred originally ceded. During the course of the years 1790–1791 legislation was enacted locating the new federal district, and accepting the cession of territory from Maryland and Virginia. Meanwhile Congress held its annual sessions first in New York (1789–1790) and then in Philadelphia (1791–1800). *The site acquired from Virginia and Maryland.*

The statute establishing the new home of the nation's government on the Potomac also provided for the establishment of a commission to lay out the streets, the sites for public buildings, and so on. The commission acted wisely in the work, for at Washington's suggestion it brought from France Major Pierre-Charles L'Enfant, an engineer who had served in the Revolutionary War, and intrusted the city-planning task to him. L'Enfant did his part well, although he planned upon a rather too elaborate scale. It is due largely to his skill and foresight that the national capital is to-day the best-planned large urban area in the world. The planning and construction of the public buildings took nearly ten years, and it was not till 1800 that the President and Congress moved to their new quarters in the District of Columbia. *The planning of the district.* *Work of L'Enfant.*

[1] The selection was the result of a deal between the sectional leaders by which southern congressmen supported a measure for the assumption of state debts by the national government, a project in which the business interests of the northern states were much interested. For the whole story, see Gaillard Hunt's article on "Locating the Capital" in the American Historical Association's *Annual Report* (1895), pp. 287–295.

**Early government of the district.**

In the following year (1801) an act was passed by which Congress assumed complete control over the district and divided it into two counties, one on the south and the other on the north shore of the Potomac. In due course two cities were chartered in the northern area under the names of Washington and Georgetown, each with its own local government, and in this shape matters drifted along until 1871. The divided municipal authority naturally gave rise to friction and the interests of the national government finally impelled Congress to consolidate the whole area into one municipality, known as the District of Columbia. But the scheme of municipal government provided for the district soon proved extravagant and unsatisfactory. In 1874, accordingly, Congress again intervened by putting all the affairs of the district in the hands of three commissioners appointed by the President, thus abolishing local self-government altogether. This plan was made permanent in 1878 and with minor changes it remains.

**Present administration.**

The executive administration of the District of Columbia is vested in an appointive commission of three. Two of these commissioners are appointed by the President, with the consent of the Senate, from among the residents of the district. They hold office for a four-year term and one must be chosen from each of the two leading political parties.

**The commissioners.**

The third commissioner is detailed by the President from the engineer corps of the United States army. He must be an officer with the rank of captain or higher rank, but is not detailed for any definite term. Subordinate officers of the engineer corps are assigned to assist him.

**Their powers.**

These three commissioners of the District of Columbia, as a body, have large powers. They make all municipal appointments, supervise the local public services such as streets, water supply, policing, fire protection, schools, and charities; and have power to make the ordinances or regulations relating to the protection of life, health, and property. Each member of the commission takes immediate charge of certain departments, for example, the engineer member has charge of streets, water supply, sewerage, parks, and lighting. In a word they exercise the functions which in many cities of the United States are given to the mayor, the heads of municipal departments, and the city council.

The laws applying to the District of Columbia are practically all made by Congress, although usually on the commission's recommendation. So also are the appropriations for carrying on the government of the district. The commissioners each year make their estimate of what is required and submit it to a congressional committee. After this committee has considered the estimates, and changed them as it sees fit, an appropriation act embodying them is passed by Congress. Half the annual cost of governing the district, as thus appropriated, is paid from the national treasury; the other half is levied upon the district by taxation. A very great amount of property in the district belongs to the national government and is exempt from taxation. That is why the national treasury bears part of the cost. *The laws and the appropriations, how made.*

The District of Columbia has its own system of courts, comprising a police court, a court of appeals, and a supreme court. All the judges are appointed by the President. The Supreme Court of the United States holds its sessions there also; but it has no direct concern with local jurisdiction. *The local courts.*

The inhabitants of the District of Columbia are entirely disfranchised. They have no vote for President, since the district is not entitled to any presidential electors. They have no senators, no representatives in Congress, no mayor, aldermen, or councillors. The only way in which any inhabitant of the District of Columbia ever manages to cast a ballot is by being a "legal resident" of some other place. That is the way many of them arrange it. When men are appointed to federal positions which involve their living in Washington they often retain their legal residences in the states from which they come, and go back to these states to cast their votes on election day. But there are many thousands who are born in Washington and live there who have no such opportunity. They pay taxes regularly but they have no representation either in the national government or in the management of their own local affairs. The government of the District of Columbia affords the most *Absence of local autonomy.* *The anomaly of the situation* glaring example of taxation without representation that exists in any democracy. No sophistry can explain that simple fact away.

<small>Efficiency of the district's government.</small>

But as a practical matter the people of the district are far better off than they would be if Congress allowed them to elect all their local officers and to pay all their own expenses. The District of Columbia is one of the most efficiently and most economically governed urban areas in the world. Its administration has been free for more than forty years from scandal and corruption. Local self-government would more than double the rate of taxation and the people of the district would probably get less for their taxes than they do under the present system.

<small>Washington as a capital city.</small>

The selection of Washington as the site of a political metropolis was a serious mistake. The Potomac location has no marked natural advantages, and as a place in which thousands of public officials must work throughout the summer months it has obvious drawbacks. The difficulty of defending it from attack was amply proved during the War of 1812, and in the Civil War the necessity of guarding the capital interfered greatly with the strategy of the federal armies. Nevertheless it has become one of the world's best cities.

# CHAPTER XXVII

### THE PLACE OF THE STATES IN THE NATION

THERE are two sorts of republics, national and federal. A national republic is one in which the smaller communities are merely administrative subdivisions of the whole, and possess only such powers as are delegated to them. France, for example, is a national republic. A federal republic, on the other hand, is an aggregation of states, commonwealths, or other divisions, each of which possesses its own inherent powers. The United States is a republic made up of smaller republics, a federal republic, an indissoluble league of republican states. And a republic, as Madison defined it, "is a government which derives all its powers directly or indirectly from the great body of the people." The states of the Union are not, like the *departments* of the French republic, mere administrative divisions created for the more efficient carrying on of government. The American state has its own assured powers; within its own sphere it is supreme; and within broad limits it determines its own frame of government. Its powers are inherent, not delegated. It possesses these powers *ab initio* and does not receive them by grant from the federal constitution or from any other overhead source. There were states before there was a national constitution and they possessed the attributes of sovereignty. Despite the assertion in the preamble of the federal constitution that "We, the people of the United States" ordained and established that document, the fact is that the people as such had nothing directly to do either with its making or adoption. The states through their delegates framed the constitution and through their conventions ratified it.[1]

*A federal republic defined.*

*Place of the states in a federal republic.*

[1] See footnote on next page.

But although the government of the United States is federal in form, it is national as respects the mode in which it exercises its powers. The national government in the United States acts directly upon the individual citizen. The coöperation of the state governments is not absolutely needed for the operation of federal powers to the extent that it was before 1787. The nation claims its own citizens, and over them it exercises direct authority in its own right. This dual nature of the American republic has been the mainspring of much diacritical controversy, but the framers of the constitution knew exactly what they were doing when they established it and explained it fully at the time. Madison, in *The Federalist*, gave it a lucid exposition and one that for conciseness has not since been excelled. "The proposed constitution," he wrote, "is in strictness neither a national nor a federal constitution, but a composition of both. In its foundation it is federal, not national; in the operation of its powers it is national, not federal; in the extent of them, again, it is federal, not national; and finally, in the authoritative mode of introducing amendments it is neither wholly federal nor wholly national." [1]

In the American scheme of government the states are the original source of governmental powers. All powers now possessed by the national government have been delegated by the states at some time or other.[2] By their adoption of the national constitution, the states parted with certain great powers, delegating them to a new national government

[1] *The Federalist*, No. 39.
[2] This doctrine of original state sovereignty and of state-delegated federal powers was not in favor among Northern constitutional jurists before the Civil War. Daniel Webster, for example, was at great pains to explain that although the constitution had been ratified state by state, yet the process of adopting it was, after all, not the act of each state individually "but of the whole people united into a political unity by that subjective feeling of nationality which is the ultimate foundation of every sovereign state," or in other words, that the whole people merely used their existing state machinery to act *en masse*. This sounds a good deal like juridical sophistry; and indeed it sets forth a proposition which no mortal man can either prove or disprove. What the "subjective" attitude of the whole people really was in 1787–1788 no one can say. So far as the written records of the time can be appealed to, they show a variety of attitudes both as to what sort of action the constitution contemplated and as to whether that action ought to be taken at all. See W. W. Willoughby, *The American Constitutional System* (N. Y., 1904), pp. 18–19.

in order "to form a more perfect union, to establish justice, insure domestic tranquillity, provide for the common defence, promote the general welfare and secure the blessings of liberty." The states on establishing the national government parted with various powers forever, for example, the power to make treaties, to wage war, or to coin money. They parted forever with all the exclusive powers which the constitution gives to Congress and became forever subject to the limitations which the constitution places upon themselves, subject of course to the right of amendment which the constitution itself provides may be exercised in ways prescribed. *The delegation of powers to the nation*

The states have also delegated certain powers downward, that is to counties, cities, towns, and other subordinate corporations. But here there is a great difference. What the states have given to these communities may at any moment be taken back again. The grant of power upwards is an irrevocable grant; the grant of power downwards can be revoked. There is a fundamental difference, accordingly, between the federal constitution and a city charter although both are examples of a delegation of power. The city, the county, and the town are the mere creatures of the state, established by it as a matter of administrative convenience. They may be divided, amalgamated, or even extinguished at any time. They have no vested authority. The nation, although it was at its formation the handiwork of the states, was endowed with attributes of sovereignty which have proved sufficient to guarantee its indissolubility. *The delegation of powers to subordinate communities.* *Difference between the two.*

State government in the United States accordingly represents the exercise of powers which have not been irrevocably delegated. It covers a field originally unlimited but now confined within strict bounds by the supreme law of the land. It was assumed that the policy of assuring to the states the "residuum" of governmental powers would eventually make the authority of the states outweigh that of the national government, but in the course of events such has not proved to be the case. The elasticity of federal powers, as interpreted by the Supreme Court, has enabled the national government to assume functions which would have fallen within the residual field if a policy of strict construction had been consistently *The "residuum" of powers.*

## 392    THE GOVERNMENT OF THE UNITED STATES

<small>Failure of this residual idea.</small>

followed. Nevertheless the state is still the pivot around which the whole American political system revolves. Were it not for the states and their reserved powers the American scheme of government could not well continue; were it not for the work of the state governments a President could not be elected, nor could congressmen be chosen, for the states determine the voting qualifications, the states mark out the congressional districts, and the states provide all the machinery of elections. Neither would there be any county or city or town governments, for all of these derive their existence and their authority from state constitutions and state laws.

<small>Are the states "sovereign"?</small>

Much ink and paper have been wasted in discussing whether the several states of the Union are now "sovereign." Here, as in so many other political disputations, a great deal depends upon definitions. If by sovereign one means "possessed of absolutely unlimited political power" then no state of the Union is sovereign. None of them is without constitutional shackles; all are restricted in what they may do. The true situation was tersely set forth by Chief Justice Marshall a hundred years ago and it has not since been materially changed. "In America the powers of sovereignty are divided between the government of the Union and those of the states. They are each sovereign with respect to the rights committed to it, and neither is sovereign with respect to the rights committed to the other."[1] This doctrine, however, did not find unanimous concurrence throughout the country during the period preceding the Civil War. "Sovereignty," declared John C. Calhoun, "is an entire thing; to divide it is to destroy it. . . . We might just as well speak of half a square or of half a triangle as of half a sovereignty."[2] To-day, however, Marshall's doctrine is accepted by the weight of authority.

Much of the confusion has resulted from a failure to

---

[1] *McCulloch* vs. *Maryland*, 4 Wheaton, 316. Alexander Hamilton, in 1788, had expressed the same doctrine in somewhat different words. "The laws of the United States," he declared, "are supreme as to all their constitutional objects; the laws of the states are supreme in the same way. These supreme laws may act on different objects without clashing."

[2] *Disquisition on Government* (1851).

distinguish sovereignty, as such, from the exercise of those governmental powers which one commonly associates with sovereignty. Sovereignty is by nature indivisible; for there obviously cannot be two wills, each supreme, in the same body politic. On the other hand the sovereign will may find expression through various channels, legislative and executive, and in federal states it may find expression through both central and local authorities. In the United States this is the case. There is a division of governmental powers between the nation and the several states, but no partition of sovereignty, no division of the supreme will. The authority which gave these powers and which can take them away is the ultimate sovereign in the United States and it remains, in fact, undivided. That ultimate sovereignty is the authority which can make or unmake the federal constitution.

*Reason for misunderstandings on this question.*

Where does it rest? To say that ultimate sovereignty rests with "the people" is not to express it correctly. A majority of the people of the United States cannot by direct action change the federal constitution; a minority might in some circumstances accomplish it. Action by a two-thirds vote on the part of Congress, ratified by the legislatures of three-fourths of the states in ways prescribed, or action by a convention called together at the request of two-thirds of the state legislatures with subsequent ratification by three-fourths of them — that is the manner in which ultimate sovereignty can be exercised. Upon such action as may be taken in such ways are no limitations whatsoever, and of no other governmental action taken in the United States can the same be said. The constitution-making authority has the last word in all things.[1] But this sovereign in the United States, as Lord Bryce puts it,

*The real American sovereign.*

[1] "The task of running the sovereign to cover, especially in the composite states of to-day, is not always easy, and when discovered it is not always recognized. It is extremely difficult to place one's finger on the exact spot where it reposes. The constitutional lawyer and the layman do not always travel the same path in the search for it, and they do not always find it in the same place. But it is always present somewhere in the state; and if in the search we push our inquiry until we find that authority which has the power to say the last word in all matters of authority, we shall find ourselves in the presence of the sovereign." J. W. Garner, *Introduction to Political Science* (N. Y., 1910), p. 263.

is "a sovereign who sleeps," a sovereign who is only at intervals roused forth to action, and whose supreme authority has been exerted only twice during the last half century.

<small>The states are equal.</small> It is a principle of the American constitutional system that all the states are equal. No one of them possesses any governmental powers not enjoyed by all the rest. Congress may exact, however, and sometimes has exacted, certain conditions as the price of a new state's admission to the Union. It can do this because full discretion as to whether a state shall be admitted or not rests in its own hands. In 1894, for example, Utah was required as a condition of its admission to abolish plural or polygamous marriages forever. But once a state is actually admitted to the Union there is no longer any legally binding force in these promises or conditions. Upon being granted by Congress the privileges of statehood, a state "becomes entitled to and possesses all the rights of dominion and sovereignty which belong to the original states" and stands upon an equal footing with them in all respects whatsoever.[1] No continuing limitations other than those provided for all the states by the terms of the federal constitution can be imposed.

<small>Creation of new states.</small> The constitution places no restrictions upon the creation of new states except that "no state shall be formed or erected within the jurisdiction of any other state, nor any state be formed by the junction of two or more states, or parts of states, without the consent of the legislatures of the states concerned."[2] The process of admission to statehood is relatively simple, the usual first step being the presentation of a petition to Congress from the people of a territory asking that they be organized as a state of the Union. If Congress regards this petition favorably it passes an Enabling Act, authorizing the people to draw up a state constitution and prescribing the way in which they shall proceed to do this. The constitution having been framed and accepted by the people it is submitted to Congress and then, by a resolution of that body, the territory is declared to be a state.

All the states, old or new, are entitled to certain guarantees at the hands of the national government. The first of

[1] *Boln* vs. *Nebraska*, 176 U. S. 23.   [2] Article iv, Section 3.

these, as set forth in the constitution of the United States, is the guarantee of "a republican form of government."[1] Just what is meant by that phrase the constitution does not explain; but it is reasonable to assume that what its makers had in mind was the general type of government existing in the original states at the time the national constitution was adopted. "No particular form of government," declared the Supreme Court on one occasion, "is designated as republican. . . . All the states had governments when the constitution was adopted. . . . These governments the constitution did not change. . . . Thus we have unmistakable evidence of what was republican in form, within the meaning of the term as employed by the constitution."[2] So long, therefore, as a state continues to maintain any reasonable approximation to "a government which derives all its powers, directly or indirectly, from the great body of the people," it is deemed to have a government republican in form. The denial of suffrage to women does not, accordingly, make a government unrepublican. Neither does the partial substitution of direct for representative methods of legislation by means of the initiative and referendum. The Supreme Court has wisely refrained from any attempt to restrain the development of state government within rigid bounds by construing the term "republican" too narrowly.

*Federal guarantees to the states:*
*1. a republican form of government.*

The constitution also guarantees to the states that the whole nation shall "protect each of them against invasion; and on the application of the legislature, or of the executive (when the legislature cannot be convened), against domestic violence."[3] This guarantee is couched in terms sufficiently definite to prevent any serious misconception of its scope. In case of invasion the federal government's intervention does not have to be invited; but in the event of riots or other internal disorder an express request must be made by the state authorities in the manner prescribed. The national

*2. protection against invasion and aid against internal disorder.*

---

[1] Article iv, Section 4. Some thought the insertion of this guarantee to be a needless precaution. "But who can say," wrote Madison, "what experiments may be produced by the caprice of various states, by the ambition of enterprising leaders or by the intrigues and influence of foreign powers?"

[2] *Minor* vs. *Happersett*, 21 Wallace, 162.     [3] Article iv, Section 4.

government may, however, intervene to quell disorder, even without a state's invitation or consent, if local violence is impeding the proper exercise of any federal function such as the transmission of the mails or the collection of the national revenues.[1]

*The powers of the states are not enumerated in any constitution.* The powers of the several states are of course not enumerated in the federal constitution. To look for them there would be to misconceive the fundamental nature of that document. When one man gives to another a deed of certain lands he does not include a list of all the property he still has left. Neither did the states, in surrendering certain powers, make any catalogue of those retained. All unmentioned governmental powers remain where they were originally — with the states. This point will bear repetition, for despite its simplicity and importance, there is no feature of the American constitutional system so persistently misunderstood by the average citizen.

The federal constitution curtailed the governmental authority of the states in three ways, by transferring certain powers to the national government, by prohibiting the states from doing various things, and by placing some interstate obligations upon them. The powers transferred to the nation have already been discussed. The prohibitions laid upon the states are to some extent similar to those placed upon Congress; but with some important additions. The obligations have to do, as will be seen presently, with matters of interstate comity.

*Prohibitions upon the states:*
*1. in general.* The prohibitions laid upon the nation and the states alike are those relating to bills of attainder, *ex post facto* laws, and titles of nobility, all of which are forbidden. In addition the constitution forbids the states to enter into any treaty or alliance, to coin money or to issue paper money, to make anything but gold and silver a legal tender in payment of debts, to lay any duty on imports or exports, to keep troops or ships of war in time of peace, or to engage in war unless in imminent danger of invasion. These various restrictions were placed upon the states in order that various powers of the national government (such as the conduct of foreign affairs and the control of commerce) might not be interfered

[1] See above, p. 122.

with. They are intended to render certain federal powers exclusive in their nature.

A restriction upon the states which has given rise to some famous controversies is that which forbids the passage of any "law impairing the obligations of contract." One of the earliest, and certainly the most notable, of these was the Dartmouth College Case which came before the Supreme Court in 1819.[1] The point at issue was as to whether the charter of Dartmouth College was a "contract" and hence protected against any hostile interference on the part of a state legislature. The Supreme Court held that it was a contract and that the state legislature had no power either to revoke it or to impair its value. This does not imply, however, that when a private corporation is given a charter it can never be taken away or changed. The state legislatures, in granting charters, can make them revocable at will and many of them now do this. But even when such reservation is not made, a charter is no more sacred than any other form of property and it can be taken away whenever the public interest so requires, provided just compensation be given. Not only that, but if the impairment of a corporate charter be demanded by the interest of public safety, health, or morals, the police power of the state is a sufficient warrant for abrogating or changing it without any compensation.

The rule in the Dartmouth College Case applies to the charters of private corporations only. The charters of public corporations, such as cities, counties, or boroughs, are not contracts and are in no case protected by this constitutional provision against revocation or change at will. The municipality is merely the agent of the state established for the more convenient administration of its local functions and so far as the federal constitution is concerned the legislature has unlimited power to repeal or amend its charter. But in many of the state constitutions, as will be seen later on, a certain degree of protection or "home rule" is guaranteed to cities and various limitations are placed upon the legislature's authority with reference to them.

A contract is an agreement enforceable at law. When the

[1] *Dartmouth College* vs. *Woodward*, 4 Wheaton, 518.

398    THE GOVERNMENT OF THE UNITED STATES

parties to a contract acquire rights of property therein, the state is not permitted, by the passage of any adverse law, to impair such rights without compensation unless the interests of the public safety, health, or morals so require.[1] In determining what relations come within the category of contracts and are hence entitled to this protection, the courts, however, have held to rules of strict construction. A license to carry on any given form of business, for example, is not a contract within the meaning of the impairment prohibition. It does not give its holder a vested right.

3. limitations of the Fourteenth Amendment.

The Fourteenth Amendment, in addition to imposing upon the states the same limitation which applies to Congress with reference to the deprivation of property without due process of law, adds the provision that no state shall make or enforce any law abridging the privileges and immunities of citizens of the United States, "nor deny to any person within its jurisdiction the equal protection of the laws." [2]

Purpose of this provision.

This broad limitation upon the states has had, during the half century which has elapsed since its insertion in the constitution, an interesting history. Its general intent was simple and plain enough. The negro had been set free during the Civil War and the main purpose of the Fourteenth Amendment was to provide him with an effective guarantee against hostile discrimination in the future laws of the southern states. So clearly was this purpose apparent that not long after the adoption of the amendment the Supreme Court expressed its doubt "whether any action by the state not directed by way of discrimination against the negroes as a class or on account of their race" would ever be held to be an infringement of its provisions.[3]

Its scope widened.

Yet, strangely enough, the negro has managed to obtain during the past forty years scarcely a whiff of this solicitude. The Supreme Court presently resolved its own doubts by ruling that "every one everywhere," including corporations, was included among those entitled to the equal protection

[1] There is no provision in the federal constitution prohibiting Congress from passing any law which impairs the obligation of a contract. The prohibition applies only to the states.

[2] H. E. Flack, *The Adoption of the Fourteenth Amendment* (Baltimore, 1908).

[3] *Slaughter House Cases*, 16 Wallace, 36.

of the laws.[1] And at once the court's docket began to fill up with the appeals of corporations against alleged discriminations on the part of various states, while the negro, for whose particular benefit the amendment was provided, soon dropped out of the reckonings altogether. The litigation based upon this interpretation of the Fourteenth Amendment has been inordinately large. The Supreme Court, during the forty-four years from 1868 to 1912, rendered more than six hundred decisions in elucidation of its provisions. Less than a score of them had to do with alleged discrimination against negroes.[2] More than half the six hundred were controversies in which corporations invoked the provisions of the amendment against the exercise of state authority.

*The flood of litigation in consequence.*

As the Fourteenth Amendment parallels to a certain extent the wording of the Fifth, its guarantees against deprivations without due process of law and in relation to the taking of private property for public use have already been discussed.[3] But the requirement as to "the equal protection of the laws" is an additional one and demands a word of explanation.[4] The words do not require that all individuals and corporations shall be treated absolutely alike by the laws of a state. They merely insist that where any distinction is made by law between different classes of individuals and corporations it shall be based upon some reasonable ground and shall not be of the nature of an unfair discrimination. It is proper, for example, to restrict certain professions to residents of the state as against non-residents, or to persons of the male sex. It is allowable to make rules relating to one class of industries but not to others, provided the classification is a reasonable one. Such distinctions are not regarded as denying the equal protection of the laws. But where the laws of a state are clearly intended to impose a disability upon

*"The equal protection of the laws."*

---

[1] *Santa Clara Co.* vs. *Southern Pacific Co.*, 118 U. S. 394.

[2] C. W. Collins, *The Fourteenth Amendment and the States* (Boston, 1912).

[3] Above, pp. 293-295.

[4] See also Henry Brannan, *A Treatise on . . . the Fourteenth Amendment* (Cincinnati, 1901), and F. J. Swayze, "The Judicial Construction of the Fourteenth Amendment," in 26 *Harvard Law Review*, No. 1 (1912).

certain persons or corporations while giving immunity therefrom to others whose position is substantially similar, then the protection of the Fourteenth Amendment may be invoked. Even "though a law be fair on its face and impartial in appearance, yet, if it is applied and administered by public authority with an evil eye and unequal hand so as practically to make unjust and illegal discriminations between persons in similar circumstances, material to their rights, the denial of equal justice is still within the prohibition of the constitution." [1]

Constitutional obligations on the states:

1. "Full faith and credit."

The obligations placed upon the states by the federal constitution relate to interstate comity and to extradition. In general the several states are independent of one another. Each has its own laws, courts, and officials whose authority does not extend beyond the state limits. Yet matters often arise which involve a reference to the laws or judicial decisions of another state and the constitution lays down the principle of interstate comity which shall apply in such cases. "Full faith and credit," it stipulates, "shall be given in each state to the public acts, records, and judicial proceedings of every other state." [2] When, therefore, a civil issue has been tried by the courts of one state the judgment will be recognized and if necessary enforced by the courts of every other state without a retrial of the issue. The provision does not apply to criminal judgments; no state may be required to enforce the criminal laws of any other state.

What interstate comity requires.

The obligation of interstate comity requires that when any legal proceeding is carried out within the jurisdiction of one state in proper accord with the laws and usages of that state, it will be recognized as a valid act by all the other states. A marriage, if legally contracted in one state, is held to be valid in all the others, however different their rules may happen to be. So with deeds, wills, or contracts. The laws of Massachusetts require that a valid will shall

[1] *Yick Wo* vs. *Hopkins*, 118 U. S. 356. The law in question was one which required that all persons desiring to establish laundries in frame buildings in San Francisco should first obtain licenses from city officials. It was evidently designed to provide the local politicians with a new source of revenue.

[2] Article iv, Section 1.

have three witnesses, each of whom shall sign in the presence of the testator and in the presence of each other. Yet if some other state requires only two witnesses, a will so witnessed in such jurisdiction is held valid in Massachusetts as affecting property there. So in the matter of contracts. The *lex loci contractus* or law of the state in which the contract is made governs the making of it. If valid there the courts of any other state will lend their aid toward having it carried out.

In the matter of divorces the "full faith and credit" clause has had the greatest strain put upon it. Divorces are granted in different states under widely varying conditions. One state (South Carolina) allows no decree of divorce to be given by any of its courts for any reason whatsoever; a few others maintain rules so strict that divorce decrees are infrequent; others, again, let people obtain them more easily, while one or two states, finally, have divorce regulations of the most lenient sort both as to the grounds necessary to be alleged and as to the evidence required to secure a decree. Yet despite this diversity of practice throughout the country a decree of divorce, if granted by any court having rightful jurisdiction in one state, is valid in every other state. The Supreme Court has laid down some rules as to the essentials of rightful jurisdiction, however. It has ruled, for example, that no court in any state may render a decree of divorce which will be binding in other states unless the plaintiff in the case is a *bona fide* resident of that state. Certain formalities in the way of notice to the defendant must also be complied with. Nevertheless the obligatory recognition of divorce decrees, so easily obtained in some states, has been grossly unfair to others in which better standards are maintained. It is unfortunate that the whole matter of determining the legal grounds for divorce and of regulating the procedure in such controversies was not at the outset given to Congress so that it might be dealt with uniformly throughout the country. This would have saved the nation from what has proved to be, in numberless cases, a mockery of justice and a challenge to social morality.

<small>The recognition of divorce decrees.</small>

The extradition of criminals is another obligation placed

**2. The extradition of criminals.** by the constitution upon the several states. "A person charged in any state," the provision reads, "with treason, felony, or other crime who shall flee from justice and be found in another state, shall on demand of the executive authority of the state from which he fled, be delivered up, to be removed to the state having jurisdiction of the crime."[1]

**Extradition among nations.** Among the nations of the world the extradition or delivering up of criminals is provided for by treaty and is governed by some general limitations contained in these treaties. Between different nations there is no extradition of offenders unless the offence be one enumerated in the treaty. An accused person, moreover, if he be extradited for one crime may not, on being brought from his foreign place of refuge, be placed on trial for some different crime. It is usual to provide in extradition treaties, again, that a nation shall not be bound to hand over its own citizens to any other country nor to give up persons charged with political offences. Subject to these limitations a criminal who makes his escape from the United States to another country can now be extradited or brought back. The procedure is by a request sent through the Department of State at Washington accompanied by various documents showing the nature of the charge against the individual whose delivery is desired. These go to the other country through the regular diplomatic channels.

**How interstate extradition differs.** As between the various states of the Union the general idea is the same although the detailed arrangements and conditions are quite different.[2] Extradition between the states is not subject to the limitations which are imposed upon international extradition. There is no enumeration of the offences for which the return of an offender may be requested. The words of the constitution are "treason, felony or other crime." Nor is there any rule against extraditing an offender on one charge and trying him upon another. States freely give up their own citizens, moreover, to be tried in other states of the Union when properly asked to do so.

---

[1] Article iv, Section 2.
[2] John Bassett Moore, *A Treatise on Extradition and Interstate Rendition* (Boston, 1891).

No one may be brought back to a state for trial, however, unless he is actually a fugitive from justice as the words of the constitution expressly require. A state cannot demand the return of any one, for example, who was not within its jurisdiction at the time the offence is alleged to have been committed.

The procedure in securing the return of a fugitive is simple enough. Legal proceedings are initiated in the state where the offence was committed, and an indictment obtained. The arrest of the offender, wherever he happens to be, is arranged for. Then a requisition, signed by the governor of the demanding state, is taken by a police officer to the governor of the state in which the offender has taken refuge. If this requisition is found to be in proper form it is honored by the latter and the prisoner is handed over to the officer to take him back. *The procedure in interstate extradition.*

Occasionally a prisoner, through his counsel, resists extradition, in which case the governor will hold a hearing to determine whether the requisition shall be acceded to. At times the surrender of a prisoner is refused, although there is usually no disinclination to honor requisitions when they come in proper form. But if a governor should for any reason decline to hand over an offender, there is no legal way of compelling him to do so. True, the words of the constitution are "shall be delivered up"; but the Supreme Court has simply declared that it will not undertake to force any governor to act against his will in this matter. The power is mandatory in form, but discretionary if a governor chooses to make it so. Happily there has been no considerable abuse of this discretion. *Mandatory in form but discretionary in fact.*

While these two obligations of interstate comity and interstate extradition are imposed upon the states by the federal constitution in express terms, there are others which, while not so expressed, may rightly be regarded as of equal force. To further the interests of the whole Union the states must provide the machinery for the election of senators and representatives; they must place no obstacles in the way of national officers in the proper performance of their duties; they must give loyal adherence to the spirit of the constitution and by the enlightened character of their laws endeavor to promote the national prosperity. *The general obligations of states.*

## CHAPTER XXVIII

### THE STATE CONSTITUTIONS

The original state constitutions.

THE basis of state government is the state constitution. Each of the thirteen original states adopted a constitution before 1787 and thus was able to come into the Union fully organized. These constitutions had been adopted by the states in various ways, but in no case save that of Massachusetts was one of the original state constitutions adopted by popular vote. In the other twelve states the ratifying action was taken by the legislature or by a convention called for the purpose. Virginia was the first to provide itself with a constitution (1776) and Massachusetts the last (1780).

Their relation to the colonial charters.

These state constitutions were the descendants of the old colonial charters. The earliest American settlements were founded by trading companies which were chartered by the crown and thus it was that Massachusetts and Virginia began their political history as chartered colonies. The charter of Massachusetts Bay, granted in 1628, provided for a frame of government constituted of a governor, various assistants, together with a "Great and General Court" or assembly of freemen. In 1691 this charter was revoked and a new one issued with various changes. This continued to be the basis of Massachusetts government until it was replaced, after the Revolution, by the state constitution of 1780. This latter document took over bodily a large part of the charter, retaining not only much of the old nomenclature but many of the general provisions as well.[1] In Connecticut and Rhode Island, the other two colonies which had succeeded in retaining their

[1] The constitutional title of the Massachusetts legislature, for example, is still " The General Court."

charters down to the eve of the Revolution, these charters were transformed into state constitutions without any substantial change. The remaining ten colonies had no charters to perpetuate. Some had never received charters; in others the charter had been revoked. These colonies had to devise new constitutions, but in so doing they followed the traditional lines.

The adoption of the thirteen original constitutions established as a fundamental principle the distinction between law-making power and constituent power, between ordinary and organic legislation, between statutes and constitutions.[1] Legislatures were set up to make the laws; but their powers in legislation were circumscribed by the terms of constitutions which no legislature could change. The state constitution became, prior to 1787, the supreme law of the state. To-day this distinction between the legislative power on the one hand and the constituent power on the other has become a commonplace of political science. In the closing decades of the eighteenth century it was quite novel, although it cannot be said to have been wholly unknown. *The distinction between "constituent" and "law-making" power.*

If this distinction between the organic and the ordinary laws of the state, the constitution and the statutes, did not exist at the close of the eighteenth century either in England or in the great countries of continental Europe, where did those who framed the constitutions of the thirteen original American states derive it? It was one of the lessons which they drew from their own colonial history. Before the Revolution, as has been said, certain of the colonies had their charters from the crown. These charters contained *Whence derived?*

[1] On the various matters discussed in this chapter the following books will be found useful: J. A. Jameson, *A Treatise on Constitutional Conventions; Their History, Powers and Modes of Proceeding* (4th ed., N. Y., 1887); W. F. Dodd, *The Revision and Amendment of State Constitutions* (Baltimore, 1910); J. Q. Dealey, *Growth of American State Constitutions* (Boston, 1915); Roger Sherman Hoar, *Constitutional Conventions* (Boston, 1917); C. Borgeaud, *The Adoption and Amendment of Constitutions in Europe and America* (N. Y., 1895); and C. S. Lobingier, *The People's Law* (N. Y., 1909). The constitutions of all the states are printed in F. N. Thorpe's *Federal and State Constitutions* (7 vols., Washington, 1909) and an *Index Digest of State Constitutions* was prepared for the New York Constitutional Convention (Albany, 1915).

various provisions relating to the government of the colony within the bounds of which the colonial assemblies had to do their work. The assemblies could make laws and regulations, but were restrained within the limits laid down by charters which only the home government could change. The charter was, in a way, the constitution of each colony that had a charter; and the people valued it accordingly. Naturally enough, when the colonies became states, they sought to establish some analogous form of security against the abuse of public authority.

*Freedom of the states to make and change their constitutions.*

The power to make and to alter their own constitutions is a power which belongs wholly to the states. The national constitution merely assumes the existence of this power and places various limitations upon it. Subject to these limitations the states are free to change their constitutions at will and in any manner they choose. Each state decides for itself the procedure by which a new constitution shall be adopted or an old one amended. Of the thirteen original constitutions all but one have been supplanted by new ones. Massachusetts alone retains its first constitution of 1780.

*Common features in the earlier state constitutions.*

When the earliest state constitutions were adopted no two of them were in all respects alike, although there was a general similarity among them all. In each a scheme of state government was provided, consisting of a governor (with sometimes a lieutenant-governor), a legislature usually of two chambers, and a system of state courts. In a few there was a specific provision that the three departments of government, executive, legislative, and judicial, should be kept distinct and that no one of these should ever assume the functions which properly belonged to the others.[1] The Massachusetts constitution of 1780, for example, set forth this doctrine of divided powers in unambiguous terms. This doctrine of separation of powers did not find its way into most of the original constitutions, but the states which did not accept it at the outset became converts later on.

*1. The frame of government.*

*2. Separation of powers.*

*3. Bill of rights.*

A few of the earliest state constitutions also included a bill of rights, in other words a declaration of what the framers

[1] See above, pp. 47*ff*.

of these documents believed to be the inalienable rights of men in general and of citizens in particular. Such rights, for example, were the right to freedom of speech, to freedom of worship, to trial by jury, and to the privilege of the writ of habeas corpus; the right to a speedy and public trial, and so on. These were not new rights, of course. They had existed for centuries in England and had for the most part been fully recognized in the American colonies. But here was an opportunity to place them beyond the power of future governors or legislatures to destroy. So they were enumerated in some of the original state constitutions and gradually found their way into all of them.

In all American constitutions, whether national or state, the bill of rights is historically the most ancient and most interesting feature. It is there that the intimate connection between American constitutional rights of to-day and the hard-won privileges of Englishmen in past centuries can be most clearly traced. The political dogmas, such as the right of the people to change their government, echo the theories of John Locke and the Puritan Revolution. These bills of rights embody in each state constitution the essentials of civil liberty as the American people understand them. *Historical significance of the bill of rights.*

Since 1780, when the last of the thirteen original states framed its original constitution, thirty-five other states have been admitted. In every case the framing of a satisfactory state constitution has been a prerequisite of admission to statehood. No state has ever been admitted to the Union without a constitution. Congress decides whether this constitution is satisfactory; it may refuse admission upon this or any other ground, but having once admitted a state Congress has no further control over any action which the state may take in revising or amending its constitution. Arizona, for example, was at first refused admission to the Union because its new constitution provided for the recall of judges by popular vote. This provision was omitted; Arizona was then allowed to come in, but no sooner was the new state government established than the objectionable provision was restored to the constitution.[1] *Later state constitutions.*

[1] See also above, p. 394.

## 408  THE GOVERNMENT OF THE UNITED STATES

*Their characteristics.*

In addition to provisions respecting the frame of government and a declaration of rights, American state constitutions contain many paragraphs relating to a wide range of miscellaneous matters such as the militia, taxation, expenditure and debt, impeachment, local government, education, and the methods whereby amendments may be made. Whenever, during the last half-century a new state constitution has been framed by any state, or an old one revised, many new provisions dealing with matters of administrative detail have been put in. State constitutions, therefore, have steadily grown to be longer documents; every one of them is now far more exhaustive than the constitution of the United States. Some of them have become veritable codes of law.

*The tendency to put too many things in state constitutions.*

The tendency is to put more things in the constitution and to leave fewer things for the legislature to deal with. The first of all the state constitutions, that of Virginia, for example, contained less than fifteen hundred words; the present constitution of that state runs to more than thirty thousand. Oklahoma, to take another example, is not a state which has particularly complicated problems of government, yet its constitution contains more than fifty thousand words, which is the record for prolixity.

*Baneful effects of this policy.*

This practice of crowding a multitude of detailed matters into the state constitutions has been unfortunate in its results. It has multiplied the opportunities for litigation and has tended to give a legalistic and technical tone to discussions of social policy. Details, when placed in the constitution, shackle the hands of both legislators and courts. The more voluminous a constitution the more quickly it loses touch with the social and economic needs of a rapidly growing community. The federal constitution has been a marvel of flexibility because its provisions are broad and general. Its framers were wise enough to leave it silent on all matters which could be trusted to work themselves out aright in the process of time. The makers of state constitutions, during the past fifty years, have not been so sagacious. They have too often fastened upon future generations the prejudices and whims of the moment.

There are two methods by which a state constitution may be prepared. The work of drafting it may be assumed by the legislature. That plan was followed by some of the thirteen original states. To-day, however, the other method, namely, that of having the constitution framed by a convention chosen for that purpose is almost invariably followed. This body, the constitutional convention, is a distinctively American institution. Its members, usually called delegates, are elected by the people. The most common plan is to provide that some shall be chosen at large by the voters of the entire state, while others, the greater number, shall be elected by districts. Nominations are made in such manner as the state laws provide, but the usual plan nowadays is by a primary election. The ballots in some cases bear no party designations, and that is the proper procedure to follow, for the questions with which a constitutional convention has to deal are not, in the main, party questions. Members of a constitutional convention are usually paid for their services.

*Methods of framing state constitutions.*

*The constitutional convention.*

In due course the delegates assemble in convention at the state capitol, elect their own presiding officer, appoint their committees, and proceed to the only business of the convention, which is that of preparing the draft of a new constitution or suggesting amendments to the existing one. A few state constitutions provide that a convention must be called at stated intervals, as for example every twenty years; but most of them make no such stipulation and a convention is only called when either the legislature, or the people, or both of them, decide to call one. These conventions are usually large bodies, containing from eighty to four hundred delegates.

The superficial resemblances between a constitutional convention and a legislature are so numerous that the fundamental differences between the two are apt to be overlooked. A legislature is avowedly a partisan body; its members are divided into two well-defined party groups, each committed to the carrying-out of a party programme. In a constitutional convention, on the other hand, party lines are not so sharply drawn. Compromises are more frequent, for the constitutional convention is above all things a deliberative body. Of itself it can take no final action. All that it prepares must go to the people for rati-

*Conventions and legislatures compared.*

fication.[1] Compared with a legislature the number of matters with which a constitutional convention has to deal are relatively few and they touch the fundamentals of government. Hence a full and free discussion on every subject is not only more practicable but more urgently desirable in the latter. The rules of a legislature are designed to expedite business; those of a constitutional convention aim rather to afford an opportunity for careful consideration without an undue prolongation of sessions.

*Procedure of constitutional conventions.*

When a constitutional convention assembles it is practically supreme with reference both to its procedure and to the scope of its work. As a rule, however, any delegate is allowed to present written proposals as to what the new constitution should contain or what amendments should be made to one already in existence. These proposals are referred to committees of the convention for consideration and report.[2] Then they come back to the whole body to be debated and voted upon.

*Committees.*

*Committee of the whole.*

As a rule, also, the debate upon matters which are reported by committees takes place in committee of the whole. This parliamentary device, which, as has already been indicated, is used by Congress, permits informal discussion under a general relaxation of the regular rules. In committee of the whole there are no roll-calls, a member may speak as often or as long as he pleases, and when decisions are reached they are only provisional. They must be ratified by the convention in regular session before becoming effective. The obvious defect of the plan, of course, is its tendency to waste time. When any large body gives its members the privilege of unlimited debate, or anything approaching it, the days are likely to slip by without due progress being made.

[1] In only one state of the Union during recent years has the work of a constitutional convention been put into effect without popular ratification.

[2] The committees are usually appointed by the presiding officer of the convention. The Michigan convention of 1907 had 28 standing committees; the Ohio convention of 1912 had 25; the New York convention of 1915 had 30, and the Massachusetts convention of 1917–1918 had 24. In size these committees ranged from 5 to 21 members. The function of the committees is to hold public hearings upon the various proposals and on the conclusion of these hearings to make recommendations to the convention.

The committee of the whole reports its decisions to the convention, which may accept or reject them. Such as are adopted go usually to a committee on form and phraseology for touching-up. Then, when finally accepted by the convention, they are ready for submission to the people. Whether its resolutions shall be submitted as a whole, or one by one, is a matter for the convention itself to decide. The convention may submit an entirely new constitution, or a revision of the old one, or merely a few amendments. So, also, the convention decides when and how its work shall be submitted, whether at a regular or a special election. If it so choose it may remain in session to receive the returns and to announce the verdict of the people on its work. No time limit is ordinarily set upon the duration of a convention's sessions. It can continue in existence till its work is done. The Massachusetts convention of 1917–1918, for example, sat from June until November and then adjourned until the following summer. Ordinarily, however, a constitutional convention will not long remain in session after the appropriations for the payment of its members have become exhausted. Aside from preparing and submitting a constitution or individual amendments a convention has no functions. When this work is done it dissolves.[1]

*Submission to the people.*

A constitutional convention, as has been said, can decide nothing finally. What it does is merely to prepare; the people have the final voice in ratifying or rejecting. This was not so in the early days. Twenty-five states framed their constitutions before 1801; but only three of these constitutions were submitted to the voters. As time went on, however, the practice of popular submission developed steadily. In one or two states of the Union, the people have not yet acquired this determining power, but in the great majority of them nothing nowadays goes into the constitution without the assent of a majority of those who vote upon the question at an election. This requirement that

*Conventions have no final powers.*

---

[1] For a description of the way in which the work of a constitutional convention is performed, see Bulletin No. 1 of the Massachusetts Constitutional Convention entitled "The Procedure of Constitutional Conventions" (Boston, 1917).

the people shall pass upon all constitutional changes is America's most striking illustration of the doctrine of popular sovereignty.

**How constitutions may be amended.**

When it is desired merely to amend a state constitution in certain definite particulars it is not necessary or even usual to call a convention of delegates. Most state constitutions provide simpler methods of amendment. One of these ways permits the legislature (although sometimes requiring more than a majority vote, and sometimes requiring that the resolution be passed more than once) to submit proposals of amendment. In such cases, after it has duly passed the legislature, the proposed amendment goes on the ballot, and if accepted by the voters becomes an effective part of the constitution.

**1. By legislative proposal and popular ratification.**

**2. By the Initiative and Referendum.**

The other way is by the use of the initiative petition. This institution, which in its application to constitutional amendments originated in Oregon in 1902, will be more fully discussed in a later chapter; it will suffice here to say that the voters of their own accord may in some states present proposals of constitutional amendment by petition. If this petition bears the requisite number of valid signatures, the proposal goes by referendum to the people, without any affirmative action of the legislature being necessary, and if adopted at the polls becomes a part of the constitution. Either method allows the submission of several amendments on the same ballot, and almost every year, in many states, one or more amendments are submitted.[1]

**Supremacy of the state constitution in its own sphere.**

Within its sphere the state constitution is supreme. It binds the executive, legislative, and judicial branches of state government. The state legislature, in the exercise of its law-making authority, must respect all the limitations placed upon it by the state constitution. In case of controversy the highest court of the state will decide whether the legislative measure in question is or is not constitutional. As a matter of judicial practice the courts always assume that the legislature has a power until the contrary is shown.

**Method of interpreting it.**

This rule, it will be noticed, is just the reverse of that applied in interpreting the powers of the national government. Congress is not deemed to possess any power unless an actual

[1] See also below, pp. 505 *ff*.

grant of that power can be demonstrated. If there be any reasonable doubt as to whether a measure passed by a state legislature is unconstitutional, the measure will be upheld.

Strictly speaking, then, the only way in which a state legislature can determine whether any law is constitutional or not is to pass it and see. There is, however, a plan by which some states have managed to obtain authoritative opinions in advance, and thus to guard against the passing of laws which would be thrown overboard by the courts. This is known as the plan of obtaining advisory judicial opinions. Where it is in operation the governor or either house of the legislature may call upon the highest court of the state for an opinion upon any constitutional question which arises in connection with a pending legislative enactment. But these opinions, when given by the judges, are not binding upon them in case the same point should later arise in a suit at law. They are merely advisory, and being arrived at without hearing the arguments on both sides can never be regarded as final. On the other hand they are usually safe enough to follow.[1] *Determining in advance the probable constitutionality of laws. Advisory judicial opinions.*

Year by year it becomes increasingly difficult to keep all the laws of a state within the bounds of constitutionality. This is because state constitutions are steadily narrowing the legislature's freedom. Things which a half-century ago were left to the legislators are nowadays being dealt with by constitutional provision. This, no doubt, is a sign of declining public confidence in the wisdom and integrity of legislatures. The constitutional convention is becoming not only the ultimate but the proximate law-making body of the state, dealing with all fundamental questions and with a great many which are not fundamental. Conventions, however, meet infrequently, and in the interim the legislature must provide whatever laws are needed. The demand for social and industrial reform presses the legislature on one side; the limitations of the state constitution restrain it on the other. Between the two the plight of legislators is often embarrassing. To escape it they sometimes enact laws which they believe to be unconstitutional, leaving the courts to take the odium of destroying their work. *The increase of unconstitutional state laws.*

[1] See also above, pp. 367–368.

One reason for it.

During the first half of the nineteenth century state laws were not often declared to be in contravention of state constitutions. The general quality of legislation was good, and in all doubtful cases the courts were disposed to give the legislature the benefit of the doubt. But now that constitutions have become so prolix and intricate, now that laws are passed in such large numbers that circumspection by the legislatures is no longer possible, the courts have quite properly become less lenient. Public opinion, or at least the loose-thinking portion of it, is disposed to brand the courts as despotic and to assail them as obstacles in the way of social progress because they fail to perform the impossible task of reconciling exact constitutional requirements with slipshod legislation. The real fault is with the making of the constitution, or the laws, or both.

# CHAPTER XXIX

## THE STATE LEGISLATURE

THE legislature is the paramount branch of American state government. It makes the state laws, controls the appropriations, and determines in considerable measure the functions which the executive authorities perform. Constitutional limitations in steadily increasing number have everywhere circumscribed its authority; the use of the initiative and referendum in many of the states has further impaired its supremacy; while the development of independent administrative officials and boards has taken from it many of its regulatory functions. Yet the legislature maintains, on the whole, its position as the dominating branch of state government. *Important rôle of state legislatures in American government.*

The organization of the legislature differs from state to state, but in essentials it is everywhere the same. In every state it is made up of two elective chambers with substantially concurrent law-making powers. The upper chamber, called the Senate, is the smaller of the two. Its members are elected from senatorial districts and their term of office is either two or four years, except in New Jersey, where it is three years. Massachusetts abolished annual elections in 1918. The lower chamber, which is variously known as the House of Representatives, or Assembly, or House of Delegates, is a much larger body; its members are chosen from smaller districts and the term of office is shorter, as a rule, being in most states only one or two years.[1] *General organization of the legislature.*

[1] The smallest state Senate is that of Delaware, with 17 members; the largest is that of Minnesota, with 67. The smallest lower chambers are those of Arizona and Delaware, with 35 members each; the largest is that of New Hampshire, with 404. In New York the Senate has 51 members and the Assembly 150; in Massachusetts, the figures are 40 and 240; in Illinois, 51 and 153; in Pennsylvania, 50 and 201. A table showing the

Except in New England the unit of representation is almost always the county, or group of counties, or portion of a county. In New England it is the town or group of towns. These units are rearranged from time to time, usually after each decennial census, with a view to making each of them approximately equal in population. This redistricting gives an opportunity for gerrymandering which the majority party in the legislature almost invariably seizes to its own advantage.[1]

**Why the bicameral system has been adopted.** Why have all the states adopted this double-chamber or bicameral system? To some extent the reason may be found in certain reputed merits of the plan, but the influence of the national system has also been important. Only a few of the thirteen colonies had even the semblance of a bicameral system, and in their original constitutions after the Revolution some of the states made no provision for an upper chamber. But when a two-house Congress was provided in the frame of national government, the example was naturally a stimulus to the states. Those states which began with one chamber replaced it in due course with two, while new states, as they were formed after 1787, established bicameral legislatures one after another. There also developed in the public mind, moreover, a belief in the usefulness of a divided legislature as a security against hasty, indiscreet, secret, unnecessary, or partisan action, as a protection for the rights of minorities, and as a part of the system of checks and balances.

**Is it necessary to-day?** These are the grounds upon which the continuance of the bicameral system is commonly justified to-day, but they are not so convincing as they were a century ago. The danger of hasty or secret action, under modern rules of legislative procedure, with the printing of proposed measures, with committee hearings open to all, with three readings of every

membership, term, frequency of sessions, and limit of sessions in all the states and territories is printed in *Bulletin* No. 9 of the Massachusetts Constitutional Convention (1917), pp. 7–8.

[1] Occasionally, as in New Jersey, each county is equally represented in the upper chamber, no matter what its population may be. In Connecticut the lower chamber represents the towns irrespective of their population. Not a few states have so arranged the basis of representation that the rural districts get more than their due share of legislators.

measure in the legislature, with ample opportunity for reconsideration, and with a governor's veto power in the background — with all these safeguards the opportunities for slipping measures upon the statute book without publicity are very few. Nor does the theory that one chamber will exercise a wholesome check upon the other always work out satisfactorily when put to the test of actual practice. Both chambers are made up of party men. If the same political party controls a majority in both, the check imposed by one House upon the other is rarely of much practical value; if different political parties control the two chambers, the checking or negativing of each other's acts often becomes so persistent that deadlocks ensue and all progress with important measures of legislation is impeded. There was a time when the state Senate, chosen by a different electoral process or with a property qualification for membership, might be said to represent an aristocracy of wealth or intellect, while the lower chamber reflected the interests of the masses. To-day there is no basis for any such distinction. Both Houses are everywhere chosen by the same voters, in substantially the same way, and with relatively unimportant differences as to the qualifications of their members. The only distinction between state senators and representatives nowadays is that the former are usually chosen by larger districts, for a longer term; they enjoy a somewhat greater prestige and in the natural course of events are men of greater political experience.

The arguments for the bicameral system in state government are not, therefore, of preponderating weight. On the other hand, the division of legislative authority has some serious defects. It increases the cost and the complexity of the legislative machinery; it facilitates and even actively encourages the making of laws by a process of compromise, bargaining, and log-rolling; it compels all legislative proposals to follow a circuitous route on their way to final enactment; it provides countless opportunities for obstruction and delay; and it makes easy the shifting of responsibility for unpopular legislation. Finally, it has proved a barrier to the planning of the laws. There may be some degree of leadership and planning in each House, but rarely

2 E

is there any coördination of the work in both chambers unless some dominating governor oversteps the strict limits of his own functions to provide it. The bicameral system is continued, in spite of its defects, because the country has become thoroughly habituated to it and because most people are inclined to accept, without analysis of their merits, the formulas of government which have come down from past generations. The same system in municipal government was retained for many decades after its shortcomings had been demonstrated beyond all controversy. Whether the states could get along as well, or better, with single-chambered legislatures is a question which cannot be answered by a discussion of probabilities, but only by actual test. Some day a state with radical inclinations will take the step, just as a few courageous cities took the lead in breaking away from the bicameral obsession in municipal government.[1]

*Methods of nominating state legislatures.*

Candidates for election to the legislature are nominated in the various states either by a caucus, a convention, or a primary. The caucus method can exist only where the district is so small that the voters of a party can be brought together in a single meeting. But even in small districts this plan of nomination has largely gone out of use. The convention, or body of delegates chosen by caucuses in various parts of the district, still retains its hold in some states, chiefly in the South. The primary has become the most common agency of nomination.[2] Candidates are usually required to secure the signatures of a small number of voters in order to have their names placed upon the primary ballot, and at this primary the voters of each political party determine which of the various aspirants shall stand at the election as the authorized party candidate. In some cases there is, at the primary, a separate ballot for each party; in others, all the names are in different columns on the same ballot.

*The caucus, convention, and primary.*

The direct primary, as a method of nominating officials

[1] In two states, Oregon and Kansas, the adoption of the single-chambered plan has been seriously considered. In the former the question was submitted to the voters in the form of a proposed amendment to the state constitution (1912), but was rejected by them.

[2] C. E. Merriam, *Primary Elections* (Chicago, 1912).

and representatives, was welcomed as a device which would help to raise the standard of candidacy at elections. The old convention, it was said, encouraged manipulation and trickery. It allowed political bosses to put forward candidates who would never be selected by the rank and file of the voters on their own initiative. The way to remedy that situation, reformers urged, was to place directly in the hands of the people the nomination as well as the election of their representatives. This would give a fair chance to men of ability and independence, to men who were not professional politicians, to men who could appeal for nomination upon their own merits and not merely upon grounds of party regularity. *Purpose of the primary.*

The new method of nomination has now had a fair trial. Has it proved superior to the convention as a means of securing capable legislators in the several states? On the whole, perhaps it has, although there is no certainty in that direction. At its best the convention was capable of making excellent selections, the fruit of careful deliberation. The primary has not often shown itself able to reach as high a standard. On the other hand the convention at its worst could strike occasionally a plane of arrogance, trickery, and corruption to which a primary rarely if ever descends. In a word, the primary seems to afford protection against the worst fault of the convention, which was the frequent selection of incapable and corrupt candidates at the behest of a few political leaders. But it has not, in twenty years or more of experience, demonstrated that it can achieve positive results of a measurably satisfactory character. It has not rid the states of boss domination; it has increased the expense which every candidate must incur, and it gives a marked advantage to the man whose name is well known to the voters, whether he be a professional politician or not. To say that the primary secures on the average somewhat better results than the old convention may be stating the truth, but it is not high praise. *Has it achieved its purpose?*

State elections are by secret ballot, although voting machines are sometimes used. The polling is in some cases held upon the same date as the congressional and presidential elections; in others on a different date. Each *The election of state legislators.*

state, under the constitutional limitations already set forth, determines who may vote for members of its own legislature. A plurality of votes is ordinarily sufficient to elect. Only one state, Illinois, provides for minority representation.[1] Many of the states have laws for the prevention of corrupt practices at elections, and in some cases these laws impose strict limitations upon the amounts which candidates may spend. Contributions to campaign funds must also, as a rule, be made public.

*Pay and privileges of state legislators.*

Members of state legislatures are usually paid an annual salary, which varies from five hundred to fifteen hundred dollars. In some of the states no annual salary is fixed, but a per diem rate of from five to ten dollars is paid while the session lasts. Usually, too, they are given an allowance for expenses in travelling to and from the state capital. Their privileges of free speech and their immunity from arrest on civil process are substantially the same as those given to members of Congress.

*Frequency and length of legislative sessions.*

In most states the legislature holds its regular sessions every two years. In only a few are annual sessions regularly convened.[2] These sessions, whether biennial or annual, ordinarily continue for two months or more with brief adjournments from time to time. In many states the constitution provides that the legislative session may not continue during more than a prescribed number of days.[3] In others the same end is virtually achieved by a provision that the legislators shall be paid so much per day for so many days and no longer. Special sessions may be convened by the governor when necessary.

[1] Illinois is divided into 51 districts, each of which elects three representatives. Every voter is allowed three votes, all of which he may give to one candidate, or one to each, or two to one and one to another, as he chooses. This permits the minority to elect one of the three representatives in the district.

[2] These are Georgia, Massachusetts, New Jersey, New York, Rhode Island, and South Carolina.

[3] The limit ranges from forty days in Oregon and Wyoming to ninety days in Maryland and Minnesota, and five months in Connecticut. In California the legislature holds a thirty-days session during which bills are introduced. Then comes a recess of equal length during which the legislators discuss these measures with the organizations and voters of their respective districts. Following this interval the legislature resumes, with no limit upon the duration of its session.

# THE STATE LEGISLATURE 421

The powers of state legislatures are broader and more important than the casual student of American government is apt to realize.[1] They comprise every field of governmental activity not restricted by the federal constitution and by the constitution of the state itself. Those limitations upon the states which are provided by the federal constitution have already been mentioned. Those which the state constitutions impose relate not only to the rights of the citizen, but to many other matters on which the limitations differ from state to state. A few examples will illustrate the general character of these prohibitions.

*Powers of state legislatures.*

*Limitations thereon:*
*1. in the federal constitution.*

Legislatures are sometimes forbidden by the terms of their own state constitutions to grant special charters to municipalities or to private corporations, or to authorize public borrowing beyond a fixed point, or to impose property qualifications for voting, or to grant public money to sectarian institutions of education, or to give perpetual franchises to public service corporations, or to lend the state's credit to private enterprises, or to change county seats without the consent of the voters concerned, or to reduce the salaries of judges, or to make discriminations in the tax laws, and so forth. In addition to these actual prohibitions the state constitutions often prescribe in detail the way in which many things shall be done and even fix the salaries to be paid to state officials. The tendency is to increase the number and extent of these restrictive provisions, so that the state constitutions have become much more than codes of fundamental law.

*2. in the state constitution.*

Yet despite its narrowing sphere of action the work of the state legislature comes much nearer than that of Congress to the daily routine of the citizen. The state laws, for example, provide for the proper registration of a child's birth; they determine the qualifications of the physician who attends him during infancy; they establish the schools in which he gets his education. When the child becomes a man, the state laws regulate the profession or the trade he enters; the state laws enable him to marry, to accumulate

*The broad field which remains within these limits.*

---

[1] For a full survey of these powers, see P. S. Reinsch, *American Legislatures and Legislative Methods* (N. Y., 1907), especially chs. iv–x; and A. N. Holcombe, *State Government in the United States* (N. Y., 1916), ch. v.

property, to vote, to hold office; the state laws provide for the issuance of a burial permit when he dies and regulate the transmission of his property to his heirs. From his birth to his death the state laws, through the agency of subordinate municipal authorities, provide the citizen with police protection, with redress for wrongs done to him, with highways and sanitation, with libraries and recreation facilities. The state laws determine most of the taxes which he pays; they impose penalties upon him when he does wrong. The state laws reach out into the shops and factories, regulating the hours and conditions of labor. They provide for the care of the poor, the insane, and the delinquents of all ages. Where federal statutes touch the citizen once, the state laws influence his actions a hundred times. The average citizen does not realize all this because he has become so completely habituated to it.

*Legislative procedure.*

In the exercise of its lawmaking function throughout this broad expanse of jurisdiction each state legislature determines its own forms and rules of procedure. Practically all of them, however, have followed the general example of Congress, so that legislative procedure in all the states is not far from uniform. This applies to the presiding officer of each House, the system of committees, the methods by which the two chambers take action upon pending measures, and the general rules of debate.

*Modelled on that of Congress.*

*The presiding officers of state legislatures.*

As for the presiding officers, the influence of the federal analogy is everywhere apparent. When a state has a lieutenant-governor, he usually (but not always) presides over the state Senate just as the Vice-President of the United States is the presiding officer in the upper house of Congress. Otherwise the state Senate chooses its own chairman, usually calling him the president of the Senate. The lower chamber of the state legislature chooses its own Speaker. In practice, the choice is first determined by a caucus of the members of that political party which controls a majority in the House and is then formally ratified by the chamber as a whole. This Speaker has the usual functions of a presiding officer, including in most legislatures the duty of appointing all members of committees from his own chamber. Each House of a state legislature also chooses

THE STATE LEGISLATURE 423

its other officers, chaplain, clerk, sergeant-at-arms, and messengers.

Much of the preliminary work of state legislation is performed by committees, and every legislature maintains a considerable number of these subordinate bodies. There may be separate committees for each chamber, appointed in each case by the presiding officer, or there may be joint committees made up of members from both chambers. In size the committees vary, running from as few as five to as many as twenty-one members or more. The committees are also of varying degrees of importance. Some of them, such as the committees on finance, or ways and means, on rules, on the judiciary, on labor and industries, on cities, on education, on public institutions, and on public utilities may have a great deal to do. Others, such as those on printing, on fisheries and game, on pensions, and on federal relations may have very little. In addition to these regular or standing committees there are special committees which are appointed whenever the occasion arises. *Legislative committees.*

Every measure introduced into either House of the legislature is forthwith referred to the appropriate committee. There, in regular order, hearings are held, and at those hearings both the supporters and opponents of the measure are entitled to appear. In some states, Massachusetts included, the rules require that a hearing shall be advertised upon every measure, and that before a certain date every matter referred to a committee shall be reported back, favorably or otherwise, to the legislature. In some other states such hearings are not held except upon important matters, or when asked for, and committees are not under any obligation to report upon every proposal that is turned over to them. Hence in some state legislatures, as also in Congress, matters may die in committee; that is, may be left on the committee's files without any action until the legislative session ends. *Their functions.*

The committee system in its actual operation among the several states has displayed great merits and equally grave defects. Legislation without the aid of committees is practically impossible so long as legislatures retain their present size, for only by some such division of labor can the huge grist of bills be given any consideration at all. Where the committees are intelligently constituted the committee system means that all measures are intrusted for preliminary consideration to those legislators who know most about them. Legislators who sit on the municipal committee of a state legislature, for example, inevitably learn a good deal about city problems and become after a while the legislature's experts in that field. In principle, therefore, the committee system is sound. The trouble is that too often the committees are not properly constituted, but are made up by a process of political trading. Their members frequently have neither interest in the measures before the committees nor desire to learn much about them.

Another feature which is destructive of efficient committee work is the too frequent tendency of the legislature to disregard the reports of its committees and by its own votes to reject, without adequate reason, the decisions which committees have arrived at after prolonged discussion. It is true that in most legislatures the recommendation of a committee, particularly if it is made unanimously, carries considerable weight; but nowhere is there any certainty that such recommendation will be accepted. Traditions and practice in this matter differ greatly among the states, but in general it can be said that the unconcern with which legislatures set aside the work of their own committees is a serious weakness in the American system of lawmaking.

The details of legislative procedure are too complicated to be set forth in brief form without the risk of serious inaccuracy.[1] Yet this is a branch of the subject which cannot be entirely omitted from any discussion of American government, however general. The spirit and form of the laws are determined in some measure at least by the system of legislative procedure. The quality of the statute book depends thereon. Simplicity of procedure is essential to the making of good laws. On the other hand a certain amount of intricacy and formality is necessary to insure that laws shall not be made or unmade hastily, or in obedience to the dictates of prejudice and excitement. American

---

[1] A full description may be found in H. W. Dodds, *Procedure in State Legislatures* (Philadelphia, 1918).

legislative procedure has been severely criticised because of its complexity, and it is indeed over-complex; but lawmaking is a serious business and must be carried on under adequate safeguards. It is wiser to tolerate a system which slows down the process of legislation than to incur the danger of letting unjust or untimely measures pass too easily. Even with the restraint of cumbrous procedure the output of legislation is prodigious. What would it be if the barriers were cut away?

Let a single state serve to illustrate the successive steps which must be taken in the process of legislation from the introduction of a measure to its final enactment. Massachusetts furnishes an appropriate example for this purpose, because its rules of legislative procedure have long since become firmly established and because impartial students of the subject have commended the Massachusetts system of lawmaking as worthy to serve as a model elsewhere. "The General Court of Massachusetts," Professor Reinsch declares, "is in all respects nearest the people and the most responsive to public opinion of any American legislature." [1] *How a state legislature enacts a law.*

As between Massachusetts and the other states there is no great difference in the printed rules of legislative procedure; it is in the interpretation and application of the rules that the difference arises. In Massachusetts the rules are followed with scrupulous fidelity; in many of the others they are honored by frequent suspension or evasion. Even when the state constitution requires that bills shall be read verbatim before final passage, or passed through their successive stages on different days, these requirements are often evaded by a merely fictitious compliance which is set down upon the official records as a compliance in fact. In these states no one can get an exact idea of the actual procedure by merely reading the rules. *Variety and uniformity in such matters.*

In Massachusetts the first step in the making of a law is the presenting of a petition accompanied by a bill.[2] Any citizen may present a petition; that is his constitutional *1. The introduction of a bill.*

[1] P. S. Reinsch, *American Legislatures and Legislative Methods* (N. Y., 1907), p. 174.
[2] In nearly all the other states no petition is necessary, the bill itself being sufficient.

privilege. One signature is enough. Getting the bill properly drafted is not so simple, however, hence a great many measures are presented in ungainly form, with provisions crudely expressed, ambiguous in wording, and otherwise defective. The trouble is that we assume the competence of any citizen to frame a law, an assumption which may have had some warrant in early days when conditions of life were simple, but which in its application to the intricate mechanism of modern society is a gross absurdity.

*Provision for bill-drafting by experts.*

The proper drafting of a law requires skill and experience. In recognition of that fact some legislatures have made provision for the maintenance of legislative reference bureaus, with expert officials whose function it is to draft measures whenever requested, and to procure for legislators any additional data or information that may be desired. It is only by some such provision that legislatures can be spared the hopeless task of straightening out all the inconsistencies and ambiguities of bills which have been prepared by amateurs.

*Restrictions on the introduction of bills.*

The Massachusetts rules require that some member of either the Senate or House of Representatives shall indorse each petition for legislation before it is formally presented. This does not mean that the member approves the petition; it is merely a way of making sure that petitions are presented in good faith. Bills may be introduced in either House, at the discretion of the petitioner, but must be filed before a certain date, otherwise they can be introduced only under suspension of the rules, and this requires a four-fifths vote in each chamber. As a practical matter all such requests for the suspension of rules go first to the Committee on Rules, and on its recommendations, in most cases, the request is granted or denied.

*2. The first reading and the reference to a committee.*

When bills are introduced, they are read by title only. Thereupon the presiding officer refers each bill to an appropriate committee. Ordinarily there is no doubt as to what committee should have a particular measure. Bills relating to taxation go to the committee on taxation; those relating to city affairs to the committee on cities. Those affecting the courts go to the committee on the judiciary; those relating to labor to the committee on labor and industry. But occasionally a measure comes forward dealing with some matter which seems to be on the border line between the jurisdiction of two different committees. Take the subject of workmen's compensation, for instance. Should a bill relating to that matter go to the committee on labor and industry, or to the committee on insurance, or to the committee on social welfare? In such cases the assignment made by the presiding officer may be discussed by the legislators and possibly overruled. Or a compromise may be made by referring the bill to two committees sitting jointly.

What happens after a bill reaches the committee? The first step is to place it on the committee's calendar and to assign a date for a public hearing upon it. When that date arrives, the hearing is held. Advocates and opponents of the measure appear and argue for or against it. Sometimes the hearing may take an hour or less; sometimes it may continue all day or for several days. When both sides have had their say, the hearing is closed; the committee goes into executive session and decides whether it will report favorably or unfavorably. Or the committee may postpone this decision until some convenient time several days or even weeks after the hearing is over. In Massachusetts each legislative committee *must* report before a given date upon every matter referred to it. In Congress, it will be recalled, there is no such requirement.

3. The committee hearing and report.

When a committee sends back a bill with its report, favorable or unfavorable, it is listed upon the calendar of the House or the Senate as the case may be, and in due course comes before the whole chamber for action. There the committee's report may be accepted or rejected; in the former case the measure is advanced to its next stage. The chief debate takes place at this point, namely, the second reading. If not defeated at that point, it is placed on the calendar for a third reading, being referred meanwhile to a committee on Bills in the Third Reading for careful inspection and for any verbal changes that may be needed. When reached again on the calendar, a further discussion may take place, although that is not customary. Having passed its third reading, it is ordered to be engrossed and then forwarded to the other chamber. There it must go

4. The committee's report presented.

5. Second reading.

6. Other steps in legislation.

through a similar course of three readings. If the other chamber makes no amendments, the measure is finally enacted and goes to the governor for his signature. But any amendment, however unimportant, brings the bill back to the original chamber for concurrence, and in case the two Houses fail to agree, a committee of conference, representing both chambers, is named to effect a compromise if possible. If the committee fails to reach a satisfactory compromise, the bill is dead, but relatively few measures perish in this way.

*Lawmaking a tedious process.*

It will be seen, therefore, that the making of a state law is a long process.[1] It is even longer than the foregoing outline would indicate, because reconsideration may be moved at almost any stage. Important bills often take several weeks and even months in going through their various stages. Emergency measures can be rushed through in a few days, but only under suspension of the rules, and this requires unanimous consent.

*Urgent measures.*

*The intricate procedure does not guarantee the quality of legislation.*

Notwithstanding all this formality in the way of committee hearings, reports, three readings in each chamber, and frequent motions to reconsider, the fact remains that many measures go through the legislature without being even read by any considerable portion of the members. The elaborate mechanism of legislation is depended upon to accomplish what can never be secured without patient study and care on the part of the legislators themselves. The result is seen in the all-too-common enactment of laws which contain "jokers"; or provisions which on careful scrutiny are not what they appear to be at the first glance. Provisions inconsistent with each other, and even ludicrous absurdities, are sometimes found in bills after they have passed through all their stages. Measures are occasionally passed without enacting clauses or without some other indispensable feature. These mishaps are not peculiar to any one state. They are common in them all.[2] The reason is plain enough.

[1] The reader who is interested in the scope and methods of lawmaking in the United States may be referred to Chester Lloyd Jones, *Statute Law Making* (Boston, 1912).

[2] A few examples:

"If any stallion escape from his owner by accident, he shall be liable for all damages, but shall not be liable to be fined as above provided."

"No one shall carry any dangerous weapon upon the public highways

# THE STATE LEGISLATURE

It is everybody's business to see that defects are weeded out of a bill during the time it is under consideration. This means that it is nobody's business. Prolonged and varied formalities are substituted for individual scrutiny. There is too much of the one, too little of the other.

American state legislation has not set a high standard either in form or in substance. The popular tendency to look upon law as the remedy for all political, social, and economic evils is one fundamental reason for this. Legislation in America has been called upon to perform functions which in all other countries are turned over to administrative officials with discretionary power. The laws which are annually enacted by the legislature of Massachusetts fill two large volumes; the forty-eight states of the Union produce nearly thirty thousand pages of statutes every session. A large part of this annual production is rushed through by the use of rapid-fire methods in the closing days of legislative sessions. Small wonder it is that under such conditions a sizable portion of it should prove to be of inferior quality.

*Reasons for the inferior quality of state laws.*

There are other reasons, too, why so many state laws prove unsatisfactory. The haphazard way in which bills are drafted, without attention to clearness or brevity, is responsible for a share of the trouble. The absence of recognized legislative leadership, due to the separation of executive and legislative organs, is another feature which has encouraged careless lawmaking. The attempt to make formalities of procedure take the place of personal alertness on the part of legislators has proved a failure. Overproduction of laws, however, is the fundamental difficulty. The legislative promoter or lobbyist who earns his living by buttonholing legislators in favor of one measure and against another, being paid in either case by interested

except for the purpose of killing a noxious animal, or a police officer in the discharge of his duty."

"All carpets and equipment used in offices and sleeping rooms of hotels and lodging houses, including walls and ceiling, must be well plastered and kept in a clean and sanitary condition at all times."

"Any seven persons, residents of the state, may organize a co-operative association with capital stock . . . provided however, that not more than one-tenth of said capital stock shall be held by any one stockholder."

outside parties, has been a contributory factor to this orgy of lawmaking. The British parliament passes fewer laws for fifty million people each year than the Massachusetts legislature enacts for four million. That is because in Great Britain matters of detail are left to the discretion of administrative authorities and are not allowed to cumber the law books.

Conclusion.

Every statute that passes a legislature affords a basis for future amendments, elaborations, or repeals. "Once begin the dance of legislation and you must struggle through its mazes as best you can to its breathless end — if any end there be."[1] The social and economic system of the United States has become extraordinarily complex during the last half century. The task of adjusting legislation to it has become correspondingly difficult, requiring far greater caution, sagacity, and courage on the part of those who make the laws of the land, and also requiring more efficient machinery for lawmaking. Legislators have not, however, improved in quality during this period, nor has the machinery of legislation been greatly bettered. The trouble, therefore, is not merely on the surface but in the foundations of American state government. Its elimination calls for a considerable reconstruction, and not merely for a few minor changes.

[1] Woodrow Wilson, *Congressional Government* (N. Y., 1884), p. 297.

# CHAPTER XXX

### THE GOVERNOR

EVERY state of the Union recognizes in its scheme of government the principle of checks and balances. Each state accordingly has established an executive department, independent of the legislature and possessing executive powers only. This executive department consists of a governor and various state officials. As to these state officials there is considerable variation, but most of the states have a lieutenant-governor, a secretary of state, a treasurer, an attorney-general, an auditor, and a superintendent of education. Many have other executive officials, such as a superintendent of public works, a commissioner of agriculture, a superintendent of insurance, and a tax commissioner. Nearly all of the states have various administrative boards, such as boards of health, public service commissions, boards of charity, and the like, whose functions will be described in the next chapter. The governor is the dominating figure of this whole executive group. *Organization of the state executive departments.*

The office of state governor is the oldest executive post in America.[1] More than three hundred years ago, before the first colonial assembly was called into existence, the position of governor made its first appearance in Virginia, and it has continued as an American political institution ever since.[2] Each of the thirteen colonies had a governor in the days before the Revolution; in two of them the office was elective, in the others it was appointive, the power of appointment resting either with the crown, as in Massa- *The office of governor, its history.*

---

[1] E. B. Greene, *The Provincial Governor* (N. Y., 1898).
[2] The title of the office came directly from the official terminology of the trading companies.

chusetts, or with the colonial proprietor, as in Pennsylvania. When the colonies became states and adopted their own constitutions, they provided in every case for continuing the office of governor, but placed it upon a responsible basis. In a few of the states the function of electing the governor was given to the people, but in most of them it was left to the legislature. Gradually, however, the latter plan was abandoned, and to-day in each of the forty-eight states the governor is chosen by popular vote.[1]

**Term and method of election.** The term of the governor is either two or four years. It is four years in Pennsylvania, Virginia, Missouri, and several other states. Two years is the more common term. Governors in nearly all the states are eligible for reëlection, and in those states where the term is short, re-elections are common. There are various formal requirements as to citizenship, length of residence in the state, and age, but no property qualification is now necessary, except in a few states. Everywhere candidates are nominated either by a party convention or at a primary; the election is in all cases by secret ballot, and a plurality of votes is ordinarily sufficient to determine a choice. In a few states, however, a majority is required; otherwise the choice is made by the legislature. The elections everywhere are party contests; but in states where one political party is largely in the majority the real struggle for the governorship takes place in the primary. Salaries of governors range from $2500 in Vermont to $12,000 in Illinois.

**Removal of governors by impeachment.** All state constitutions make some provision for filling the governor's post in case it should become vacant during the term for which he was elected. Such vacancy may be by reason of the governor's death or through his conviction and removal on impeachment. The constitutions of nearly all the states make provision that the governor and other civil officers shall be liable to impeachment for crime or misconduct in office. The lower house of the legislature, following the federal analogy, has the power to begin the impeachment proceedings; the upper house as a rule hears and determines the issue. Occasionally, as in New York, the jus-

---

[1] He is chosen by direct popular vote in all the states but one. The exception is Mississippi, where the choice is made indirectly by the people.

tices of the highest state court sit with the upper chamber during the trial. A verdict of conviction, which usually requires a two-thirds vote, ousts the governor from office and may disqualify him from holding in the future any civil office in the state's service. As a matter of history very few governors have been brought to book in this way and convictions resulted in only about half these cases.

In a few states the governor may be removed from office by recall. This involves, as will be explained a little later, the presenting of a petition bearing a designated number of signatures with the request that the matter of removing the governor from office before the expiring of his full term be placed before the voters on the ballot at an election. Reasons, as a rule, must be given in the petition for a governor's recall, but they need not amount to allegations of misconduct such as would be required for an impeachment. Thus far no governor has been removed by means of the recall procedure. *Removal by recall.*

When a governor is convicted on impeachment, or dies in office, he is succeeded, according to the provisions made in more than two-thirds of the states, by the lieutenant-governor. This official is ordinarily chosen for the same term as the governor and by the same process of popular election. His main function, apart from that of being heir-apparent, is to preside at sessions of the upper branch of the state legislature and in a few states at meetings of the governor's council. Failing the lieutenant-governor (or in states where there is no such officer), the succession usually passes to some designated state official or to the Speaker of the lower chamber, as the constitution may provide. If a governor is removed by means of the recall, however, this order of succession does not go into effect. His successor is elected by the people. *How a vacancy in the governorship is filled.*

The powers of the governor are for the most part executive powers.[1] The theory of American state government is that the governor has no legislative functions, and from a reading

---

[1] J. H. Finley and J. F. Sanderson, *The American Executive and Executive Methods* (N. Y., 1908); A. N. Holcombe, *State Government in the United States* (N. Y., 1916), ch. x; and J. M. Mathews, *Principles of American State Administration* (N. Y., 1917), ch. iii.

## 434   THE GOVERNMENT OF THE UNITED STATES

*The governor's powers:*
*1. legislative.*

of the various state constitutions one might readily conclude that this would be true in practice as well. These constitutions give the governor no formal voice in the making of laws. Some of them explicitly forbid all executive participation in lawmaking. Nevertheless, the governor's

*How the governor secures his legislative influence.*

influence upon the course of legislation is almost everywhere considerable and far more extensive than any reasonable interpretation of his strictly constitutional powers would imply.[1] This is because of the close relation which exists in the states, as in the nation, between lawmaking and the party system. Members of state legislatures are almost invariably elected on a party basis, pledged to carry out a programme of legislation set forth in the platform of their party. As a rule, though of course not always, the governor

*His influence as a party leader.*

is a leader of the party which controls a majority in the legislature. When, therefore, the governor urgently insists that some particular measure be passed or another one rejected, he does not speak primarily as the executive head of the state government but as the leader of his party in the state. His recommendations may be communicated to the legislature formally by means of official messages, or informally by conferences with prominent members of his own party in the legislative chambers. The latter is often the more effective way.

*The spell of his influence with individual legislators.*

Members of the legislature, moreover, are to some extent under the spell of a governor's influence. They are interested in the appointments to paid positions which the governor has power to make; they are interested in the passage of bills which will come before him for assent or veto; they are interested in appropriations which he may or may not recommend. By the strategical use of his authority and discretion in these matters a governor can, if he so desires, bring many members of the legislature into sympathy with his own legislative recommendations. The governor, moreover, has ready access to the ear of public opinion. He can often present his recommendations in such way that they

---

[1] J. W. Garner, "Executive Participation in Legislation," in *Proceedings of the American Political Science Association*, x, pp. 176–190 (1914). See also the discussion of the same subject in the *Proceedings of the Academy of Political Science*, v, pp. 127–140 (1914).

stir up a popular demand which in its turn reacts upon the legislature. The pressure of public opinion acts upon the executive and legislative branches of state government alike; but the former usually secures the first opportunity to sense it and to act accordingly. The strict constructionists continue to urge the doctrine that the American state governor has no share in the making of laws, but even the casual observer of practical politics knows that this doctrine does not accord with the facts. The governor's legislative authority is not founded upon either law or logic; it is not to be discovered by a reading of constitutions or statutes, but rather by keeping an eye on those legislators who visit the governor's ante-chamber and then become his spokesmen in the committee rooms or on the floor.[1]

Nor is the governor's influence over the course of state legislation confined to positive channels only. Like the President in relation to Congress he also possesses, by express constitutional provision, that effective weapon of legislative obstruction known as the veto power or the power of withholding his assent to bills passed by the legislature and thereby preventing their enactment into law. This veto power now exists in every state of the Union except North Carolina. It was not given to the governor in any of the original thirteen state constitutions except those of Massachusetts and New Hampshire, as it seemed to savor of executive despotism.[2] But having been adopted in the

The governor's veto power: its origin and development.

[1] Some years ago, in answer to inquiries, fourteen governors expressed their opinions with reference to the scope and importance of executive influence upon state legislation. Their replies made it quite clear that, whatever the constitutional limitations upon executive influence might be, the state governor is everywhere an important factor in lawmaking. See John H. Finley and John F. Sanderson, *The American Executive and Executive Methods* (N. Y., 1908), pp. 181–183.

[2] The framers of the thirteen original state constitutions were much more afraid of executive than of legislative tyranny. This was, of course, a legacy from colonial days when the governor had to carry out the instructions which came to him from England and hence obtained on many occasions a reputation for high-handedness which was not of his own making. These original constitutions reduced the governor's office to a post of relatively small importance, making the legislatures the predominant arm of the government in all the states. As Madison expressed it during the debates in the federal convention of 1787, "The executives of the states

federal constitution of 1787 the veto ultimately made its way into the organic laws of all the forty-eight states but one.

*How the veto power is exercised.*
In principle and in practice the governor's veto power and the veto power of the President are much alike. With a few minor exceptions every bill or resolution which passes both Houses of the state legislature must be presented to the governor for his signature. Like the President he has three options; he may sign it, or within the prescribed period send it back without his signature, or do neither. In the first case it becomes a law. In the second case it does not become a law unless both houses of the legislature, by a prescribed majority (usually two-thirds or three-fifths), pass the measure over his veto. In the third case, at the expiration of the prescribed time, from three to ten days, it becomes a law without the governor's signature, provided the legislature does not in the meantime end its session, in which case it does not become a law but receives what is commonly termed in state as in federal politics the "pocket veto."

*The power to veto parts of measure.*
In many of the states the governor cannot veto particular clauses or sections of a measure, but must sign or reject it as a whole. In the case of appropriation bills this is a serious drawback to the effective exercise of the veto power, for a governor is often faced with the alternative of letting an objectionable item of expenditure pass or of tying up the entire list of appropriations. In some states the veto of individual items is permitted, and this, it has been found, not only enhances the authority of the governor in the determination of the state's financial policy but places upon him a corresponding responsibility for the economy of his administration.

*The "pocket veto."*
The governor's power over lawmaking, through the use of the veto, is greatly increased by the common practice (in which most state legislatures indulge) of letting bills drag along until near the end of the session. Then they are hurried through their final stages and sent to the governor in large numbers during the last week of the legislative term. In such cases the governor has very little chance to examine

are in general little more than ciphers; the legislatures omnipotent." It is hardly necessary to remark that this situation has been greatly changed during the intervening hundred and thirty years.

## THE GOVERNOR

the various measures carefully, yet any of them that he does not actually sign are bound to be slaughtered by the "pocket veto." To ameliorate this situation many states have provided that measures shall become effective unless vetoed by the governor within a specified period after the legislature closes its session.[1]

Executive vetoes have been much more frequent in state than in federal lawmaking. They are much more common in some states than in others, but in all the states together the total number of vetoes nowadays exceeds a thousand a year. This is due in part, no doubt, to the large number of measures which come to the governor's desk and are there found to be badly drawn, or unintentionally in conflict with laws already passed, or of doubtful constitutionality, or defective in some other way. These shortcomings give a governor his opportunity. Yet the entire number of measures vetoed in whole or in part is but a small fraction of the total number which comes to the executive officers for approval, probably not more than five to ten per cent on the average for the whole country. On the other hand the repressive influence of the governor is not to be accurately measured by merely counting his actual vetoes. A word in advance from the governor's office to the effect that any particular measure, if passed, will not receive the executive signature is often quite sufficient to prevent its further progress in the legislature. A governor's vetoes are in most cases final, for it is only in exceptional cases that a two-thirds vote of both chambers can be mustered to override them.

*Workings of the veto system.*

This means that governors have obtained, through the free use of the veto, a degree of influence over the course of legislation which they were not originally intended to have. The veto power was given to the executive, in the first instance, as a weapon of defence, as a shield against possible assaults made by the legislature upon executive independence. It was not assumed that a governor would veto measures passed by the legislature whenever, in his opinion, they might seem to be of doubtful constitutionality. The determination of a measure's constitutionality is a judicial

*How its use has increased executive influence.*

---

[1] See J. A. Fairlie, "The Veto Power of the State Governor," in *American Political Science Review*, xi, p. 473 (August, 1917).

function. Nor was it expected that the possession of the veto power would make of the governor a third chamber of the legislature, ready to share with the two regular houses the function of determining whether any proposal of legislation is the embodiment of good public policy. Yet governors have assumed both of these rôles. They have arrogated to themselves the duty not only of protecting their executive prerogatives but of safeguarding the state constitution from violation and of sharing in the determination of expediency as respects all matters of legislative policy.

*The governor's executive powers:*

The most important gubernatorial powers are, however, executive, not legislative. In the realm of executive authority the law and the facts coincide. This executive authority includes the power of appointment and removal as regards many positions in the state service, the power to pardon offenders convicted by the state courts, various military powers, the general supervision of state administration, and certain powers of a miscellaneous nature.[1]

*1. The appointing power.*

The appointing power of the governor is great, and is steadily increasing. Time was when most of the higher state officials were chosen by the legislature, but now very few are selected in that way. The practice of choosing officials of state administration by popular election attained considerable vogue during the nineteenth century and still has a strong grip in many states; but in many others these administrative posts, or most of them, are filled by persons whom the governor appoints.[2] This is particularly true of boards which have technical tasks to perform, such as public service commissions. In the exercise of his appointing power, however, the governor is usually subject to limitations, that is to say, his appointments are not valid until confirmed. The confirming authority is ordinarily the upper chamber of the state legislature; but in exceptional cases, as in Massachusetts, it is the governor's council.

This practice of subjecting the governor's appointments to confirmation is one that harks back to the days of im-

[1] J. M. Mathews, *Principles of American State Administration* (N. Y., 1917), ch. iv.
[2] In the case of those heads of departments whose positions are established by the constitution, however, popular election is still the general rule.

plicit confidence in the principle of checks and balances. Fearing that governors would abuse their authority, restraints were put upon it. In many cases the necessity of confirmation has proved a wholesome check upon governors who sought to repay personal or partisan obligations by giving to their supporters an anchorage upon the public pay-roll. It has availed at times to prevent governors from using their patronage as a means of building up political machines. But just as frequently, on the other hand, the power of confirmation has been used to balk a governor's plans for improving state administration by the appointment of honest and capable officials. The confirming power represents a bludgeon which a partisan state Senate can hold above the governor's head in the endeavor to force him to withhold a prospective veto or to recommend expenditures in which individual senators may be interested. Whether the several states, taken as a whole, have had more examples of wholesome obstruction or positive intimidation, whether the power of confirmation has in the totality of its exercise worked for good or ill, is hard to decide. With the right sort of governor no such check is needed; with the wrong sort it may be moderately effective, or on the other hand his ingenuity may enable him to bargain his appointments through. The outstanding defect of the present system is that it permits an evasion of responsibility for appointments. In municipal government the power of confirmation, which remained for many decades in the hands of the aldermen or the councillors, has been generally abolished, all responsibility for appointments being thereby concentrated upon the mayor. The results have been advantageous.

*Checks upon the appointing power: (a) confirmation by the Senate.*

The other common check upon the governor's appointing power is the civil service system, which exists, however, in only a minority of the states. The restrictions provided by the civil service laws, in states where such laws have been enacted, do not cover the heads of departments and other high officials of state administration. They apply to subordinate appointments only. Where there is a civil service or merit system the governor does not have discretion as regards these minor positions. They are filled by competitive examinations held under the auspices of a civil service board

*(b) civil service rules.*

or commission. These examinations are usually open only to residents of the state, and the names of those who stand highest are certified to the head of the department in which the position is to be filled.

<small>The principles of the civil service system.</small>

The civil service system in state appointments has proved a noteworthy improvement over the traditional method of distributing paid offices among the party stalwarts as a reward for political services. It has closed the door to one of the most pernicious traditions in American political life, that of degrading the public service to a plane of indolence, inefficiency, and arrogance in order that the obligations of party leaders may be defrayed from the taxes of the people. It is a system based upon the principle that merit alone should be the passport to public as to private employment, and that political or personal favoritism should not outweigh ability, character, and experience in determining the choice of the state's employees. With these ideals most people are nowadays in agreement. Their difference of opinion arises in connection with the mechanism to be used in putting these sound principles into practice.

<small>The discrepancy between its ideals and its actual achievements.</small>

Between the ideals and the achievements of the civil service system there is, no doubt, a considerable disparity. With the best of aims and endeavors the civil service authorities in the various states have had to use such machinery of selection as they could lay their hands upon. Written and oral examinations have been their chief reliance, supplemented of course by information secured in other ways as to the merits of candidates. But formal examinations, as those who have much to do with them know, are very fallible instruments for eliciting sure information concerning the general merits of candidates. They are poor tests of such qualities as initiative, industry, honesty, tact, patience, resourcefulness, and they are not always dependable tests of intelligence; yet these are qualities which spell success in public as in private employ. The general tendency of the civil service system, in its actual workings-out, has been to draw into the public service a sluggish stream of men and women who have diligently prepared for the examinations and who pass them for that reason rather than by reason of their native ability. It has not raised the efficiency of public service to that of private employment.

The civil service system would bring better and more enduring results if its principles and methods were carried further. Merit should determine not only appointments but promotions. Thus far, however, it has had relatively little to do with the latter, and hence the chief incentive to hard work, after a man or woman has entered the lower ranks of the public service, is altogether lacking. Here again, however, one encounters the practical difficulty of sorting out real merit by any inflexible mechanism. Promotions continue to be made at the discretion of the governor or the heads of departments. *Promotions.*

With the power of appointment goes the power to suspend or to remove state officials. Authority to suspend an official from office appertains to governors in most of the states, but governors do not, as a rule, have any free power to dismiss even those officials whom they themselves appoint. Charges must usually be filed, hearings given, and in many states the concurrence of the upper chamber of the state legislature is required. Here, again, the restriction has often availed to forestall arbitrary and unjust removals, but quite as often it has served to keep in office men of political influence whose malfeasance or negligence amply warranted dismissal. When officials are appointed under civil service rules, moreover, they may be removed only by compliance with such formalities as the laws prescribe. These usually afford adequate protection against dismissal save for reasons of actual misconduct or gross inefficiency. *Removals.*

The power to pardon offenders who have been convicted in the state courts is frequently one of the governor's prerogatives.[1] In England the power of pardoning offences had been from earliest times a prerogative of the crown, and in the state constitutions which were framed immediately after the Revolution this authority was vested in the governor alone, or in the governor and his council where there was a council. In most of the states at the present day the power of pardoning as respects all convictions made by state courts *2. The power of pardon.*

[1] *Bulletin* No. 4 of the Massachusetts Constitutional Convention, entitled "The Pardoning Power" (Boston, 1917).

rests with the governor alone. Usually, however, this power does not cover convictions arising from impeachment or penalties imposed for treason. In some of the remaining states the governor's power of pardon is circumscribed by the necessity of acting in conjunction with a Board of Pardons or with some other body. In a few states the power is given entirely to a board of this sort, the governor being sometimes a member of it. One reason for this is the fear that otherwise the pardoning power might be used by a governor for personal or political ends. Some governors, indeed, have used it too freely and at times unwisely. In only one state, Connecticut, is the pardoning power vested with the legislature.

3. Military powers

The military powers of the state governor are not as extensive as they used to be. The governor is nominally the commander-in-chief of the state militia or national guard. His functions, however, are determined by law, and for the most part they are actually performed by an adjutant-general or some similar officer. As commander-in-chief of the militia the governor may appoint officers unless the constitution directs differently, or the legislature makes some other provision, as it often does. Each state has a body of laws relating to the organization of its militia, and these laws, like all other laws, are for the governor to carry out according to their tenor. When the state militia is mustered into the national service, the governor ceases to have anything to do with it. Usually the state constitution and laws authorize the governor to call out the militia in time of riot or other civil disorder. This may be and commonly is done on the request of the mayor or other executive authority of the municipality in which the disturbance has arisen, but governors as a rule have the right to act upon their own initiative as well. When the aid of federal troops is required by any state to quell internal violence, the governor calls upon the President of the United States for this assistance, provided the state legislature is not in session. If it be in session, the legislature by resolution makes the request.

The governor has become by tradition the recognized medium of official intercourse between his own state and the federal authorities. While no specific constitutional obligations are imposed upon the chief state executives in the way of assisting the national government to perform any of its functions, the practice is to call upon them for such help when occasions arise. During the Civil War the President called upon the northern governors to assist in the calling out and organization of the Union forces, and they promptly responded. In the work of raising the national army during the European War the governors were asked to recommend persons for service upon the various draft boards, and in all cases complied readily. The governor is also the channel of official communication between his own state and other states. His functions in relation to the extradition of fugitives from justice have been already referred to.[1] When one state desires to sue another in the Supreme Court, a statute authorizing the suit is usually passed by the legislature; but the governor is regarded as having authority, on his own initiative, to institute any such suit for the protection of his state.

4. Functions in relation to the federal government and to other states.

Finally, the governor is charged with a general supervision over the enforcement of the laws and the conduct of the state's administrative affairs. Just how much actual authority he can exercise in this capacity depends in part upon the personality of the governor and in part upon the nature of his legal relations with other state officials. A dominating personality in the governor's chair, if he have public opinion as an ally, will often compel all other state officials to help carry out his policy, no matter how independent of his actual control they may be. Yet the governor's executive supremacy is in most states far from being so complete as is that of the President in national affairs. It is here, more than at any other point, that the analogy between the two positions fails to hold. The President appoints all the heads of federal departments and can remove them at will. His control over them is unquestioned and his responsibility for their actions is not to be evaded. But the heads of state departments are not in most cases chosen by the governor and cannot be removed from office by him. His influence over their actions can only be indirect and imperfect, nor can entire responsibility for the conduct

5. The general oversight of state administration.

Functions in this sphere compared with those of the President.

[1] Above, p. 403.

of state administration be properly allotted to him, although public opinion too often puts the blame upon him when things go wrong. Heads of state departments not infrequently set themselves out to thwart the governor's plans; they intrigue with the legislature against him and at times openly defy his instructions. Nothing of that sort is encountered at Washington.

<small>Changes in the prestige and powers of the office during the nineteenth century.</small>

Surveying the office of governor in its development and present status, one may say that it has considerably increased its powers but not its prestige in the last century and a quarter. In the early days of the Union the post was one of great dignity and honor, not outranked in the public mind by membership in the federal cabinet or in the national Senate. Yet the influence of the governor upon legislation, his patronage in appointments, and his power as a party leader were all of them far less extensive at that time than they are to-day. During the nineteenth century the actual powers of the state governor have everywhere been steadily increased, but this has not, curiously enough, enabled the glory and dignity of the office to be maintained. On the contrary, any governor would nowadays regard election to the national Senate or appointment to the federal cabinet as a real promotion. Indeed a term of service in the governor's chair has come to be regarded as a prelude to the senatorial aspirations. The status of a governor in the public imagination is not now much higher than that of the mayor of a large city.

The office of governor is a difficult one to fill with marked success. Men who occupy the post are expected by public opinion to achieve results which, owing to their restricted control over the other officials of state administration, are entirely beyond their powers. Few governors of recent years have come out of office richer in reputation than when they went in. Occupancy of a governor's chair, nevertheless, has sometimes placed men in line for the presidency. Rutherford B. Hayes of Ohio, Grover Cleveland and Theodore Roosevelt of New York, and Woodrow Wilson of New Jersey afford four notable examples of this during the past forty years.

# CHAPTER XXXI

## STATE ADMINISTRATION

AT the first establishment of state government in America there were, in addition to the governor and the lieutenant-governor, a small number of state administrative officials, notably a secretary, a treasurer, and an attorney-general. Frequently these officials, with some additional elective members, formed a governor's council, an institution which still survives in a few states of the Union.[1] The officers had the general duties which their titles indicate. The secretary kept the official records, the treasurer served as custodian of the public funds, and the attorney-general prosecuted suits in the name of the state. Almost invariably they were elected by the people and hence were not accountable to the governor. *The original administrative officers.*

By and by other officials were added to the list and chosen in the same way, an auditor or comptroller, a superintendent of education, a commissioner of labor, and so on, each at the head of his respective department. Then, likewise, with growth in population and with the consequent development of both social and economic problems still other administrative departments were established, sometimes headed by a single state official, sometimes by a board of three, five, or more members. This development, which has led to an almost complete disintegration of state administrative functions, is largely the product of the last thirty or forty years. In all the larger states these officials and boards have multiplied to formidable proportions, and in some of them the total number of state administrative departments has now reached sixty, eighty, and even one hundred. *Their multiplication in recent years.*

[1] In Massachusetts, Maine, New Hampshire, and North Carolina.

*Reasons for this development:*
*1. the stricter regulation of business.*

The changing relation between government and business has been in the main responsible for this elaboration of administrative machinery.[1] The era of laissez-faire, of official non-interference, has been rapidly passing away. Banks, other financial institutions, insurance companies, railroad, express, telegraph, telephone, lighting, street railway, and other public service corporations have been brought within the provisions of regulatory laws. Laws relating to the conditions and hours of labor, especially for women and children, laws relating to sanitation in industrial establishments, laws providing for workmen's compensation, for minimum wage scales in certain employments, for the adjustment of labor disputes, for the care of immigrant workers, for the protection of wage-earners against loan-office extortion, — all this legislation has been crowding its way to a place upon the statute books during the past generation. But the mere enactment of these regulatory statutes would avail little, and might readily work more harm than good if their enforcement were not committed to some administrative authority charged with that function and empowered also to provide that measure of flexibility which all regulatory laws ought to have. Hence the creation of boards, commissions, and departments.

*Why regulation increases administrative machinery.*

These boards serve a dual purpose. First, they see to it that the detailed and often intricate provisions of present-day regulatory laws are carried into effect; they receive complaints and adjust them; they prosecute violations. Second, they provide the legislature, when it undertakes any new step in the way of regulating business, with a repository of administrative power. It is impossible to incorporate in any law a specific provision for every case that may arise. Far better, it has been found by experience, is the plan of stating the general principles with as much detail as is convenient, and leaving their specific application to men appointed for the purpose. In a word, the strict insistence upon a government of laws alone has given way under

---

[1] The best book on this subject is J. M. Mathews, *Principles of American State Administration* (N. Y., 1917). The legal aspects of state administration are fully discussed in F. J. Goodnow, *Principles of the Administrative Law of the United States* (N. Y., 1905).

the pressure placed upon the state authorities by the kaleidoscopic needs of modern business. The human touch is needed to make regulations both effective and just.

2. the expansion of state service in other fields.

It is not in the sphere of business alone that the regulating arm of the state has been growing more energetic with the lapse of time. The state of to-day is trying to give, and is giving, a far greater modicum of service in all departments of the common life than ever before. Care for the public safety, for the health of the community, for the poor, the handicapped, and the defective, for public comfort and recreation, for the preservation of natural resources — all these have added to the volume of the law and to the intricacy of the administrative mechanism. One need only glance over the list of departments, boards, and commissions in any state to have well impressed upon his mind the comprehensiveness, variety, and importance of the functions which the American commonwealth now endeavors to perform for its people.

Present departments of state administration:

These various departments may perhaps best be classified by grouping them according to the functions which they share in exercising. First, there are various officials and boards having to do with general administration. Within the category of departments which, along with the governor, share in the work of general state administration are those of the secretary of state, the treasurer, the auditor, the attorney-general, the elections board, and the civil service commission, each of which departments performs functions designated in part only by its title. The secretary of state not only keeps the official records, but is intrusted with many other functions such as the distribution of public documents, the custody of the state seal, and sometimes with various duties relating to elections. The treasurer is not only the custodian of the revenues, but pays out the money when called upon to do so by the proper authority. He also issues bonds when the state borrows funds. The auditor or comptroller must approve every bill before the treasurer will pay it; he also checks up the treasurer's books and reports regularly to the legislature. The attorney-general is the chief prosecuting officer of the state, but he also acts as legal adviser to the governor and to all other state

1. General administrative departments.

Their functions.

officials. In some states he has a certain degree of supervision over the work of district prosecuting attorneys. Election boards, where they exist, control the machinery of polling, but usually do this through local election officials. When there is a civil service commission, it supervises the administration of the laws relating to the merit system of appointments, holds the competitive examinations, and protects the public service against the evils of patronage. This does not exhaust the list, moreover, of departments which have to do with general administrative matters. In many states there are other officials and boards of this character.

2. Public health and sanitation.

A second group of state departments includes all those which have to do with sanitation and public health protection. Nearly every state in the Union has a department of health and sometimes other officials or boards whose duty it is to carry out the provisions of laws relating to the collection of vital statistics, the prevention of disease, and the general protection of the public against epidemics. Usually this department has some degree of supervision over the work of local health boards or officials. The laws and regulations relating to the protection of the public health have become numerous and complicated in all the more populous states; they cover a host of matters, such as the registration of births and deaths, the reporting of contagious diseases, disinfection, and quarantine, the disposal of sewage and garbage, the protection of water supplies, the inspection of food, especially of meats and milk, the abatement of nuisances, and the amelioration of unsanitary conditions in shops and dwellings. The drift towards central supervision in public health administration has been strong during recent years. Individual communities are no longer left to make and apply their own capricious regulations in this vital field.

3. The regulation of public utilities.

For many decades it was the policy of the states to let public service companies of all sorts go unregulated except in so far as general regulations could be prescribed by law. Administrative machinery for enforcing even these general regulations was entirely lacking save that in a few cases the work was intrusted in a perfunctory way to the secretary of state. The result was that many large corporations, particularly those engaged in furnishing gas, electricity, or transportation, abused their freedom from official regulation, and by various extortions or discriminations eventually forced the states to come upon them with an iron hand. Hence there has been, during the last thirty years, a marked growth in the number of state officials and boards having to do with corporate and public utility supervision. Within this category are found commissioners of corporations, insurance commissioners, railroad commissioners, and public service commissions. In practically all the states regulating bodies of this sort now exist. Their functions are so manifold that anything akin to a complete summary of them would be impossible here. Some of these boards are endowed with large powers to hear complaints and adjust them, to make rules on their own initiative, to pass upon the reasonableness of rates and conditions of service, to compel the submission of financial reports, and to enforce compliance with their orders. Others have varying degrees of lesser authority, and some have powers of an investigating and advisory character only. Everywhere, however, the powers of such administrative officials and boards are expanding and becoming yearly more effective. Their work constitutes a highly important phase of state government and plays a considerable part in the interaction of state politics.

Two branches of corporate activity which have become subject to increasingly strict supervision in recent years are banking and insurance. To insure sound financial methods in both these fields of business the various state legislatures have passed elaborate laws, and to insure that these laws shall be strictly carried into effect many of them have established departments of banking and insurance. These departments are in charge of commissioners who have power to examine the books of all insurance companies and banks which do business under state charters, to audit their accounts, to make sure that their investments are in legal securities, to insist upon adequate allowances for depreciation, and in general to insist upon conservative financial management.

4. The regulation of banking and insurance.

During the last few years some of the states have been

extending their supervisory activities to the business of selling bonds and shares as well as to banking and insurance. The rules of supervision are embodied in the so-called "blue-sky laws" and usually provide that no stocks or bonds may be offered for sale to the public until adequate information concerning the tangible assets behind them has been laid before the bank commissioner and a permit obtained from him.[1] The issuing of this permit does not mean that the bonds or stock of a corporation are recommended to the people for investment or that the state vouches for the solvency of the companies concerned. It is merely an indication that the flotations have been found to be non-fraudulent.

5. The regulation of industrial and mercantile affairs.

More recent than the development of state supervision over public utilities, banks, and insurance corporations is the growth of state regulations as applied to ordinary industry and trade. Twenty years ago there was little or none of this; to-day there is a great deal, and it is rapidly increasing. It is an indication of the transition from an individualist to a social viewpoint in the attitude of public authority toward private business: a transition which is not peculiar to America alone. Old doctrines of strict non-interference have been jettisoned; the state no longer concedes the right of the manufacturer or the merchant to do as he pleases in the conduct of his own business, particularly as regards the hours and conditions of labor. Concerning the justice and expediency of this growing official intervention in the affairs of private business there are widely divergent opinions; but as to the fact that the limits of state interference are being rapidly broadened there can be no dispute. State commissioners and boards with functions in this new domain of regulation are springing into existence all over the country. Most conspicuous among them are commissioners of labor or labor boards whose duty it is to investigate industrial conditions, to enforce the laws relating to the employment of women and children, to see that factories are regularly

[1] The term originated in Kansas, where the first law of this sort was enacted in 1911. The implication was that many mining, gas, oil, and land companies were issuing bonds and shares upon assets no more tangible than the blue sky.

inspected as to their sanitary arrangements and their proper equipment with safety devices, to eliminate the evils of sweatshop production, and in many cases to mediate in disputes between employers and employees. In a few states this last named function is intrusted to a special state board of arbitration or conciliation. Provision for the compulsory arbitration of labor controversies does not yet exist, however, in any of the states.

The passing of workmen's compensation laws in many states, moreover, has necessitated the establishment of boards for the detailed administration of these statutes, usually called <u>industrial accident commissions</u> or workmen's compensation boards. The principle at the basis of these compensation laws is that when an employee is injured in the course of his work, from whatever cause, the burden should not be placed wholly upon himself, or upon his family, or even upon the employer; it should be included in the cost of production and thus borne by the entire consuming public.[1] Employers are therefore either compelled outright, or allowed under conditions which are almost compulsory, to insure their workmen against the industrial accidents which inevitably occur in every occupation. Presumably they set down the cost of this insurance as one of their regular expense items, like taxes or fire insurance or the replacement of machinery. It is the function of the workmen's compensation board to supervise the working out of this general policy, to determine in the first instance all disputed questions between the insurer and the injured workman, and to make a prudent disposition of the compensation awarded.

The constitutionality of workmen's compensation laws, in that they virtually require an employer to insure his employees against the results of their own negligence, has been attacked in the courts. In a famous decision, rendered in 1913, the New York Court of Appeals declared that this requirement constituted "a deprivation of liberty and

<sub>Workmen's compensation laws and their administration.</sub>

<sub>Their constitutionality.</sub>

---

[1] The common law gives the workman redress only when the accident is due to the fault or negligence of his employer. It gives no redress when the injury can be shown to be due to his own negligence or to the negligence of a fellow-workman.

property under the federal and state constitutions" not justifiable as a reasonable exercise of the police power.[1] This decision drew forth much popular criticism, and an amendment was accordingly added to the New York constitution expressly permitting the legislature to enact a compulsory compensation law. In other states the constitutionality of such legislation is now pretty well established.

<small>Minimum wage laws.</small>
Minimum wage laws have also been passed in some states, and such action usually adds another to the list of state commissions. The function of this department is to investigate the rates of wages paid to women and minors in factories or stores and to recommend, in some cases to compel, the payment of a minimum weekly wage. The doctrine at the basis of this system is that society as a whole cannot safely or economically permit large bodies of women and children to be employed at rates which are well below the point of decent subsistence; if such conditions are tolerated, the ultimate cost to the community in crime, poverty, disease, and immorality will be high. To permit such a situation, it is urged, is to allow grasping employers the privilege of thrusting upon society as a whole a burden which their own expense budgets ought to bear. Where women and children are overworked and underpaid (and by the same token, underfed), the community as a whole will ultimately suffer. That is an inexorable law of social evolution. Better it is, therefore, that the community should pay its way year by year in higher prices for the goods which women and children make, than that a social canker should be tolerated in the name either of higher business profits or of lower living costs.

<small>Practical difficulties connected with their administration.</small>
In their actual application, however, minimum wage laws are not without objectionable features. Even-handed justice to both the employer and the wage-earner is doubly essential in this field of administration, yet it is in practice difficult to secure a board of men or women who will relegate their own personal sympathies to the background and give no advantage to either side. Too often the doctrine that the administration of a law should be placed in sympathetic

[1] *Ives* vs. *South Buffalo Railway Co.*, 201 N. Y. 271.

hands has resulted in the establishment of boards whose members assume the rôle of crusaders with a mission not merely to protect the weak against industrial injustice but to compel the general readjustment of wage scales. It is to be remembered, moreover, that under the conditions of to-day, the family rather than the individual is the unit which should be fairly viewed in determining whether income is below the subsistence point. When a minimum wage is fixed for certain industries in one state and no such action has been taken in other states, again, the cost of production is likely to be so increased in the former that its products are at a disadvantage in competition with those of the latter. These various objections, however, are not fundamental.

Programmes of social insurance which are now under discussion in various states will inevitably require, if adopted in whole or in part, the establishment of additional administrative departments. Proposals for health insurance, old-age pensions, and for insurance against unemployment are now being considered with varying degrees of seriousness, and the time is not distant when some or all of them will be carried into effect. The principle upon which these proposals rest is the one already indicated, namely, that society should take better care of its workers by protecting them, at the cost of the whole community, against the inevitable vicissitudes of modern economic life. The individualist policy in industry puts upon the worker the necessity of protecting himself against the hardships which result from overwork, underpayment, accident, sickness, and old age. The worker's failure to do this adequately has not only impaired the efficiency of industry, but has put a huge burden on society in the end. The contention is that the state should take over the responsibility for this protection, relieving the community from the ultimate cost by making it pay its way as it goes. Many practical difficulties are sure to arise, however, in the application of this principle.

*The pending programmes of social insurance.*

The problem of the poor is still with us, which means that every state has a department under some name or other assigned to their interests. Commonly it is called the state board of charities. As a rule, the state does not directly undertake the relief of poverty, but intrusts this function

6. *The administration of charities and corrections.*

to counties, cities, towns or villages. The duty of the state department of charities is to supervise and in some measure to coördinate the work of those local poor-relief authorities. Likewise this department may have oversight of the institutions maintained for the care or instruction of the insane, the blind, the deaf and dumb, or the handicapped in other ways, or this work may be intrusted to separate authorities. Preferably it is handled separately. The general supervision of state prisons and reformatories is also a function which requires a department of its own; it may be headed by a single prison commissioner or it may be intrusted to a board. Both in charitable and correctional administration the drift is toward a more humane and enlightened application of the laws. The decentralization of administrative machinery represents in part an endeavor to meet demands in that direction.

7. The supervision of public property and natural resources.
Every state possesses valuable assets in land, roads, and buildings; some of them have also harbors, forests, mines, and fisheries. Various departments are given supervisory functions in relation to these natural resources. Among the several states there is the greatest variation in the names and the duties of the commissioners or boards which have to do with all such matters. Massachusetts, for example, has a board of agriculture, a department of animal industry, a state forest commission, a commission on fisheries and game, a commission on harbors and public lands, and a highway commission, or six boards in all. Throughout the greater part of the nineteenth century the natural resources of the country seemed so inexhaustible that they were allowed to be wasted ruthlessly for the profit of individuals but to the ultimate detriment of the whole people. Of late, however, conservation has come to be looked upon as not only desirable but necessary. This policy, as applied to forests, fish, and game, has directed itself to the work not only of protection but of restoration. In the case of harbors, lands, waterways, roads, the problem has been that of improving natural resources and turning them to better account. The encouragement of agriculture in its various branches has also obtained greater attention from the states as well as from the nation during recent years.

The department of education is almost everywhere one of the most important among agencies of state administration. It was not always so. In earlier days education was left almost wholly to the cities, towns, and rural areas to be regulated by local school boards according to their own ideas of educational efficiency. Even yet the local school board is in immediate control and in many cases its discretion is still unrestricted; but steadily the state is everywhere taking over a coördinating and supervising jurisdiction. Every state to-day has a department of education or of public instruction under an executive head, commonly called the superintendent of education or instruction. Many of them have state boards of education as well, and some have special authorities for the supervision of the state university or for the other public institutions of higher education. The functions of an education department vary with the degree of centralized control which the state authorities have assumed. In no two states are they alike. In some the department outlines the programme of school studies, chooses the text-books, apportions state funds to local schools, prescribes the qualifications of teachers, appoints school superintendents and settles nearly all the details of educational policy; in others it has much more limited powers; and in others, again, its functions are little more than advisory. On the whole, however, the tide has set towards centralization, towards giving the state departments more power and leaving less discretion to the local school boards.

8. The supervision of public education.

The laws relating to the assessment of property for taxation and to the methods of taxing this property have everywhere become so involved and technical that new administrative agencies for interpreting and applying their provisions have had to be created. State boards of assessment or of equalization, state tax commissioners, and various allied authorities now figure upon the list of departments in many of the states. There was a time when virtually complete dependence for public revenue was placed upon property taxes. Such taxes were easy to assess and when imposed could not be evaded. But with the increase of "intangible" property in its varied forms, mortgages, stocks, bonds, franchise-values, and bank deposits, the task of

9. Assessment and taxation.

making this form of wealth contribute its just share of the public revenue presented a much more difficult problem. Intangible property, when left to be assessed and taxed by the local authorities, often escapes taxation altogether. Taxes on the profits of corporations, on franchise values, and on inheritances also present practical difficulties in the way of local assessment. So the states, in many instances, have provided the municipalities with assistance; in others they have taken the levying of some taxes directly into their own hands. State tax commissions or commissioners now exist in more than half the states, with constantly increasing powers for the assessment of property for purposes of taxation, both local and state, and for the collection of corporation, business, inheritance, and income taxes, and other revenues.[1]

10. Regulation of the professions.
In nearly all the states there are various boards whose business it is to issue certificates for the practice of different professions or trades. There are boards of medical and dental examiners, boards of examiners in pharmacy, and in some states boards for the licensing of stationary engineers, plumbers, chauffeurs, nurses, and so on. In some states the courts are charged with the duty of examining candidates for admission to the practice of law; in others this is handled by a board of bar examiners. The general rules concerning eligibility for license to practice these various professions and trades are made by the legislature; but the boards conduct the examinations and grant the certificates. They have also, in most cases, authority to hear charges made against any licensed practitioner and to suspend or revoke certificates. The expense of maintaining these licensing boards is usually defrayed by the fees which applicants are required to pay.

11. Supervision of military affairs.
All the original state constitutions paid particular attention to the organization and control of the militia. It was taken for granted that the military forces of each state would be largely within its own jurisdiction, even though the federal constitution gave to the national government certain authority in time of peace and complete powers in time of war. The federal laws of the last few years have

[1] H. L. Lutz, *The State Tax Commission* (Cambridge, Mass., 1918).

greatly reduced the freedom which the several states have traditionally possessed with reference to their national guard establishments; nevertheless, all the states continue to maintain departments of military affairs. Usually the head of this department is the adjutant-general, appointed by the governor in his capacity of commander-in-chief. Associated with him is a quartermaster-general, a surgeon-general, and sometimes an armory board. Or each of these officials may be, as in Massachusetts, the head of a separate department.

In addition to all the foregoing there are various miscellaneous departments which look after the odds and ends of state administration. Each state has its quota of them, but the example of Massachusetts will suffice to indicate what some of them are. In that commonwealth there are an art commission, a homestead commission, a commissioner of public records, a comptroller of county accounts, a commissioner of state aid and pensions, a board of boiler rules, a fire prevention commissioner, a board of appeal on fire insurance rates, a commissioner of weights and measures, a commissioner of statistics, and a dozen other departments in charge of commissioners or boards of trustees. Nor does this latter include the numerous *ad hoc* bodies, that is, boards created to exercise functions of a temporary nature such as the building of a state capitol or the consolidation of the state laws or the taking of a census. Such boards go out of existence when their work is finished. Taking the entire category of officials and boards, whether permanent or temporary, the number is surprisingly large. Each department, moreover, has its own sphere of duty and is independent of the others. There is usually no coördinating pressure except such as the governor may be able to apply.

12. Miscellaneous.

This somewhat detailed enumeration of state departments has been undertaken in order to emphasize two features of state administration: first, the scope and variety of its tasks, and second, the decentralized machinery with which these functions are performed. Far more frequently than any agencies of the national government these numerous boards and officials regulate, supervise, and circumscribe the daily

Outstanding features of state administration.

life of the citizen. This fact is not appreciated by the average man, who is prone to look upon the state as merely exercising an inconsiderable residuum of governmental authority, the bulk of which is possessed by the nation on the one hand and by the municipalities on the other. That is far from being the case. The state is the real centre of public administration in the United States.

It is well that the top-heaviness, the disintegration, and the absurd clumsiness of state administrative machinery should be impressed upon every student of American government. At the present rate of increase some of the states will soon have as many boards as there are problems to be solved. A state board grows by what it feeds upon. When a new administrative department is established, its officials recognize that it must justify its creation and its continuance by finding enough work to do. Having found more work it asks more power, more money, more clerical assistance. In a few years it becomes a far more portentous affair than any one anticipated when its work began.

*Reaction against the increase of state boards.*

This tangled web of commissioners and boards, wholly unplanned in development or coördination, represents an endeavor to cope with the new and urgent problems which rapid growth in population and in the complexity of urban life have thrown upon the public authorities. But it embodies a method of administration which cannot be expanded indefinitely. The maze of interlocking jurisdictions and of isolated centres of authority will break down of its own sheer weight. Some states have already reached the point where they are seriously considering the best method of integrating this surfeit of officials and commissions. One or two states, as will be indicated later, have already made substantial progress in this direction.

*A practical difficulty in the way of efficient state administration.*

The shortcomings of state administration, as one may so easily observe them at the present day, are not wholly due, however, to the multiplication of isolated departments or to the lack of coöperation among them. Something is attributable to the difficulty which the departments encounter in obtaining capable helpers. In the service of these various departments are a huge number of subordinate officials and employees. In New York state there are more than eighteen thousand of them. Positions on the payroll of the state are everywhere eagerly sought, chiefly because the remuneration is better, the discipline less strict, the hours of work fewer per day, and the holidays more frequent than in private employment for service of the same quality. Yet the return which the state receives for its generosity as an employer is proverbially small.

The lack of a comprehensive and genuine merit system, covering not only appointments but promotions, is chiefly to blame for all this. State administration does not in America, as in Europe, offer a career comparable in attractiveness with the regular professions. It does not secure its recruits from among the ambitious and capable, but to a large extent from among those who are satisfied to give no more than the worth of their wages and who on that account have failed to make headway in private vocations. The fault concerns itself, therefore, not only with systems but with men. There are too many departments; they are too often badly organized; they are rarely in any proper articulation with one another; and last, but by no means least, they are everywhere provided with employees who display far less skill, intelligence, initiative, and industry than is to be found in the service of ordinary business concerns.

*The handicap of inferior service.*

The state is undertaking a programme of business regulation on a huge scale. Yet the officials and employees to whom it commits the actual administration of this programme are for the most part men who could make no conspicuous success in managing any form of business for themselves.

## CHAPTER XXXII

### STATE FINANCE

**Development of state financial systems.**

THE states of the Union began their history with financial methods which were simple and uniform. They did not, at the outset, attempt to do much in the way of public services. They required very little money, and they got most of it from the same sources. But as time went on and administrative functions were extended the need for more money appeared. New ways of obtaining it and of spending it were developed, until to-day the various systems of state finance are neither simple nor in any degree alike.

**The scope of public finance.**

Public finance, whether in nation, state, or city, is usually considered under three main heads: revenue, expenditure, and debt.[1] But each of these headings suggests various subdivisions. Under the head of revenue is necessarily included a discussion of the various sources from which a public authority obtains money to carry on its work, whether from taxes on property or from the granting of privileges, from fees, from the sale of public lands, and so on. Likewise, there are questions as to the mechanism by which the taxes are levied, the system of assessment, the classification of property for taxation, and the practice of exempting certain forms of property from taxation altogether. Under the general head of expenditure various important questions also arise. Who may appropriate money and under what restrictions? How and by whom is the budget made, if there is a budget? What checks are there upon extravagance or dishonesty in expenditures? Finally, a

[1] H. C. Adams, *The Science of Finance* (N. Y., 1898); C. F. Bastable, *Public Finance* (3d ed., N. Y., 1903); W. M. Daniels, *The Elements of Public Finance* (N. Y., 1899); and C. C. Plehn, *Introduction to Public Finance* (3d ed., N. Y., 1915), are some of the best-known books in this field.

consideration of state debts brings forward such matters as constitutional limitations upon indebtedness, the methods of borrowing, and the nature of the arrangements made for the payment of public debts as they mature.

Of the entire revenue obtained by the several American states at the present time the larger part comes from taxes on real and personal property, usually but not always in the form known as the "general property tax." This is a tax levied at a uniform rate upon the assessed value of real property, which includes lands and buildings, and upon personal property such as merchandise, bonds, stocks, and mortgages. Taxes on property may be levied by the state directly, or they may be imposed by the county, city, or town, and then turned over in part to the state treasury. {Sources of state revenue.} {The general property tax.}

Most of the states formerly maintained in their constitutions a provision that all taxes on property should be general or proportional; in other words that all property of whatsoever kind, if taxed at all, should be taxed at a uniform rate. This provision was part and parcel of a political philosophy which insisted upon the strict equality of all men before the law. That dogma was interpreted so rigidly in the early years of American history that public opinion regarded the taxing of one form of property at a different rate from another as an act of discrimination and fundamental injustice. The natural equality of men extended, it was assumed, not only to their persons but to their property. In these earlier days, moreover, property consisted for the most part of tangible things: lands, buildings, merchandise, and slaves. Securities or intangibles, such as mortgages, bonds, and stocks, did not form a large factor in the total wealth of the community. {Restrictions on the classification of property for taxation.}

In recent years this situation has altogether changed. The idea that taxation should regard first of all the inalienable rights of the individual has been supplanted by the doctrine that it should make the general good of the whole people its foremost care. Moreover, the growth of intangible wealth during the last half century has been enormous. It now forms the major element in the national opulence. Its distribution among the people has become so unequal that the imposition of taxes at a uniform rate no longer serves the ends of social justice. Hence it is commonly {Removal of such restrictions.}

believed that a more equitable distribution of public burdens can be made by classifying property into various forms and by levying a different rate upon each. Many of the states now permit this to be done, but the requirement as to uniformity still remains in about one-third of them.

*The taxing of intangible property.* Entirely apart from any theory of social justice in taxation there is also the practical consideration that when a state or city attempts to tax both tangible and intangible property at the same rate, a large portion of the latter escapes taxation altogether and the former is forced to bear a disproportionate share of the burden. Lands and buildings, machinery and merchandise, cattle and grain, are in sight to be levied upon; they cannot be spirited out of view. But intangible wealth does not parade itself to be taxed, and unless the owner, either voluntarily or by compulsion, comes forward with a declaration of its value it is difficult to list it for taxation at all. Bonds and stocks are stowed away in safety-deposit boxes. It is mainly for this reason that in one state after another during recent years the practice of separating tangible from intangible property and of levying a much lower rate upon the latter has been adopted. This lower rate is either placed directly upon the value of intangible property or it is levied upon the income derived therefrom. In either case there is usually a legal requirement that every owner, trustee, or recipient of income (with certain exceptions) must file a sworn declaration as a basis for a true assessment. Only in this way has it proved practicable to make wealth in the form of securities pay its due contribution to the public income. When taxed at the same rate as tangible property a large part of it will evade taxation at all hazards, even if it be necessary to remove it outside the taxing jurisdiction of the state altogether.

*What the states may tax.* States have the right to tax all tangible property situated within their borders no matter to whom it belongs. The only exception is property belonging to the United States. But they have no legal right to tax tangible property outside their own limits, even though the owner resides within. Intangibles may be taxed either where the owner resides or where the securities are kept. The usual plan, in accordance with the principle *mobilia sequuntur personam*, is to levy the taxes upon the intangibles where the owner has his domicile or legal residence. Income derived from property in other states is also taxable where the recipient resides and not at its source. No state or subdivision of a state may tax any intangible property in the form of bonds or other obligations of the United States, nor may it tax any tangible property such as lands, fortifications, buildings, or equipment belonging to the federal government. This was made clear, it will be remembered, in the case of McCulloch vs. Maryland. But the instrumentalities of interstate commerce, such as stations, wharves, telegraph lines, although their operations are under federal control, may be taxed as property by any state so far as they happen to be within its boundaries.

The levying of taxes is always preceded by a formal step known as the assessment. In nearly all the states outside New England this assessment or recording of property valuation is made by county officials. The same lists are then used as the basis of state and county and municipal taxes. Usually some higher authority, often called a board of equalization, has power to review these assessments, to hear appeals from the action of the assessors, and to adjust or equalize where necessary. In any event the assessments are revised from time to time, sometimes every year, but for purposes of state and county taxation not usually more often than once in every three or five years. Ostensibly all property is assessed either at its fair market value or at a designated percentage of that appraisal as provided in the tax laws. In Illinois, for example, the stipulated percentage is one-third of the actual value. Throughout the country the work of assessing is rather poorly performed because the assessors are usually elective officials with no special training for the function of estimating property values correctly. Much of what they do is mere guesswork. *The process of assessment.*

While many states place their chief reliance upon the taxation of property, either at uniform or classified rates, all of them have other taxes and some derive a large part of their entire income from these other sources. The inheritance tax is one of them. It is levied upon inherited property and the rate of taxation commonly rises with the distance at *Other state taxes.* *The inheritance tax.*

which the heirs stand in point of blood relationship. Occasionally, moreover, it is progressive in rate according to the value of the estate. Small inheritances are usually exempt.

*Taxes on incomes. Corporation taxes.* Taxes on the income of individuals and on the income of corporations are also levied in several states. Corporations, especially railroads, street railways, lighting, telegraph, and telephone companies, banks, and insurance organizations are being more and more placed in special categories and taxed accordingly. In some states they contribute large amounts each year to the public income. *Poll taxes.* Poll taxes do not yield a great deal, as a rule, for the individual tax is small and a large percentage of it frequently remains uncollected. Some states have abolished it altogether.

*Revenues from sources other than taxation.* Other sources of state revenue are the license fees exacted from certain forms of business. The proceeds from liquor licenses have hitherto formed the largest item among these. As a rule, the state turns back a part of whatever money it may derive from these licenses, usually the larger part, to the municipalities. License fees are also collected from some other forms of business, occasionally by the state but more often by the local authorities. Fees of various sorts come into the state treasury from many quarters, fees paid by corporations when organized, by lawyers when admitted to practice, by owners of automobiles and by others too numerous to mention.

*State expenditures.* When money comes into the state treasury it can be paid out again in only one way, that is under authority of an appropriation duly made by the legislature. The appropriation may be specific, designating a certain sum for a certain purpose, or it may be general and continuing, as for example when it authorizes a state department to expend such amounts as it may receive in fees. Most of a state's income is appropriated annually or biennially upon estimates of necessary or desirable expenditure submitted to the legislature by the governor or the heads of departments, but appropriations are also made on the initiative of the legislature itself.

It is a general rule of American state government, whether written or unwritten, that measures which involve the expenditure of money shall originate in the lower chamber of the legislature. The upper chamber may, however, amend or reject such measures. But in none of the states, with one exception, is there anything approaching the English practice which restricts the initiative in appropriations to members of the executive department.[1] Any citizen may father a proposal to spend the state's money, and he usually finds no difficulty in getting some member of the legislature to introduce it for him. The authority to propose outlays is not in America an executive prerogative as it is in countries where the doctrine of coördinate governmental powers prevails. Hence there are proposals of expenditure from all quarters, each one making its own bid for adoption. That is one reason why the states spend so much.

*Appropriation bills originate in the lower chamber.*

The process by which a state's total expenditure for any year is authorized may be summarized as follows: shortly after the legislature convenes it is the custom of the various administrative departments (for example, the attorney-general's office, the state board of charities, the state board of education and so on) to transmit to the legislature either directly or through some designated officer their estimate of what each requires. These estimates are referred to the various committees of the legislature and may also go to some general committee on appropriations or finance by which they are reported back to the legislature either with or without changes. Then in the form of appropriation bills they pass the legislature like other measures. The estimates rarely come before the legislature all at once. They straggle in at various stages of the session. Meanwhile, a throng of bills carrying appropriations or providing new revenues are brought forward by members of the legislature on their own responsibility, and although many of these fail to advance very far, there are always some which work their way to enactment. Until the session comes to an end, therefore, no one can tell just what the total revenue or expenditure is going to be. Thus the prime essential of a sound financial system, accurate knowledge of income and outgo, is lacking in most of the states. To express it in another way, less than one-third of the states have what

*How appropriations are usually made.*

[1] See above, p. 306.

is known to students of public finance as a budget system.[1]

*Types of budget systems:*
*1. The legislative budget.*

There are at least three different ways of framing a state budget. First, there is the "legislative budget" system, which is still used by a number of states. Under this plan the estimates of revenue and expenditure for the fiscal year are transmitted by the various executive departments to some committee of the legislature, usually the committee on ways and means. There the various items are scrutinized, altered as may be deemed advisable, embodied in one large appropriation bill, and reported in revised form to the state House of Representatives, where it goes through the regular procedure. The distinguishing feature of this system is that the framing of the budget is entirely in the legislature's hands. Executive officials have no direct part in it.

*2. The joint budget.*

In half a dozen states or so, including New York and Wisconsin, the work of preparing the budget is intrusted to a board or committee which is usually made up of certain administrative officials (such as the state comptroller, tax commissioner, and sometimes the governor), together with the chairmen of the appropriation committees in the two branches of the state legislature. The idea embodied in this plan, which may be called the "joint budget" system, is that both the legislative and executive branches of the government should be represented in the making of financial proposals because the plans will be broader, more accurate, and more acceptable to all concerned when they are prepared by joint counsel than when made wholly by either organ of government alone. As to the exact composition of this joint body there is considerable variation among the half dozen states which have adopted the plan, but the principle is the same, namely, that the legislature should have a share, though not an exclusive share, in preparing the state budget.

The third plan of budget-making, which is used in seven or eight states, including Ohio, New Jersey, and Maryland,

[1] On budgets and budget-making methods, see S. Gale Lowrie, *The Budget* (Madison, 1912); E. E. Agger, *The Budget in the American Commonwealths* (N. Y., 1907); and *Bulletin No. 2* of the Massachusetts Constitutional Convention entitled "State Budget Systems" (Boston, 1917); and W. F. Willoughby, *The Movement for Budgetary Reform in the States* (N. Y., 1918).

is commonly known as the "executive budget" system. Under this arrangement the function of preparing a tentative budget of estimated revenue and expenditure is intrusted to the governor alone. The various financial officers transmit to him their estimates of probable income, and the administrative departments send in a statement of what money they desire for carrying on their work. To these the governor, after making such changes as he desires, adds his own proposals, whether they concern new revenues or new outlays. Then the whole budget is laid before the legislature for its consideration.

<small>3. The executive budget.</small>

In all these states except Maryland the legislature retains full power to amend or reject the budget whether prepared by its own committee, or by a joint body, or by the governor alone. It may increase, reduce, strike out, or insert any item. In Maryland, by a constitutional amendment adopted during 1916, the legislature is restricted to the power of reducing or striking out items only; it cannot insert or increase. The idea is to concentrate upon the governor the sole responsibility for all increases in state expenditure. The Maryland legislature is not, however, deprived of all initiative in matters of state finance. On any matter not included in the governor's budget the legislature may make, upon its own initiative, supplementary appropriations, but only under a special and rather difficult procedure which the constitution provides.

<small>Budget powers of legislatures.</small>

<small>The Maryland system.</small>

There has been much discussion as to which of these budget-making plans is likely to give the best results. Is the work of budget-making primarily a legislative or an executive function? In England, where the fruits of long experience are available, the entire initiative in all financial matters rests with the executive, the ministry. But the ministry, although constituting the executive, is nevertheless a great standing committee of parliament, all its members having seats in parliament. For its continued existence the ministry is dependent upon the will of that body. It is therefore quite defensible to argue that England has a legislative budget system, since parliament, through a body made up of its own members, controls the entire budget-making power from start to finish. In the United States, however, owing

<small>Relative merits of different budget plans.</small>

to the divorce of executive from legislative power, there is no way in which the function of budget-making can be given entirely to one branch of the government without excluding the other. Hence, the rather cumbrous and not altogether promising experiment with joint budget-framing boards. The tendency in the states is towards vesting the budget-making power in the governor alone. This is because the plan insures concentration of responsibility and in the long run is apt to prove the most effective method of keeping expenditures within bounds.

*The absence of budgets in most of the states.* In most of the states the continued waste of public money is not occasioned by the use of one rather than the other of the foregoing budgetary systems, but by the fact that they have no budgets at all. Administrative officials go directly and individually to the legislature for their appropriations, and they usually get what money they ask for, provided they are influential enough politically. Members of the legislature spend their time and energies in trading and bargaining their votes on different appropriations, each striving to muster support for the things in which their own districts are concerned. The interests of reasonable economy demand that responsibility for proposals of increased expenditure shall be lodged somewhere. At present, in two-thirds of the states, it is located nowhere. It rests neither with the governor nor with the legislature. It is the right and privilege of any official, of any member of the legislature, and indeed of any citizen, to set the wheels in motion towards new expenditures. Proposals to spend money come forward every year by the thousand. Their chance of adoption is not proportioned to their merits, but rather to the political influences behind them.

*The executive type of budget is proving the most popular.* The governor represents the state as a whole, and the general direction of financial policy may on that account be appropriately committed to him. But this policy, if consistently followed, would disturb the traditional balance of power in state government. Analogous action in city government has made the mayor a much more powerful officer than he used to be. It is altogether probable, judging from municipal experience, that a budget system like that of Maryland, if generally adopted by the states, would in time greatly weaken the authority of the legislature in matters of financial policy and lead to executive supremacy in that field. Such an outcome, however, would not necessarily be unfortunate, and there are indications that the evolution of state government is steadily working towards it.

State expenditures have risen at a rapid rate during the past generation, more rapidly than the increase of population or the growth of property values. During the decade 1906–1916 they more than doubled, and in the last-named year amounted to more than four hundred million dollars. Only a small part of this increase has been due to the rising cost of services and materials; in larger measure it is merely an indication that the several states are taking on new functions without having learned to perform either new or old functions economically. Scarcely a legislative session passes in any of the states without some new activity being undertaken, whether in education, in the care of the poor, in the regulation of industry, in protecting the public health, in building state roads, in humanizing the prison system, and what not. All these new services cost money, very little at the outset, perhaps, but more and more as they get under way. Hence state expenditures keep growing in spite of the spasmodic endeavors of governors and legislatures to keep them down. It is difficult to make the revenues keep pace. The problem of making both ends meet has become, accordingly, the most difficult problem of American state government. It is not being satisfactorily solved. Many of the states, although their annual reports may not show it, are regularly spending more than they take in. That is one reason for the growing burden of state indebtedness.

The states, like the nation, have power to borrow money and are unrestricted in the exercise of this power by any provision of the national constitution except that they may not "emit bills of credit," that is to say, they may not issue paper money. But many of the state constitutions set forth limitations upon the borrowing power.[1] These constitutional "debt limits" are of several sorts. In some

*The rapid increase of state expenditures.*

*Reasons therefor.*

*State debts, and debt limits.*

---

[1] Horace Secrist, *An Economic Analysis of the Constitutional Restrictions upon Public Indebtedness in the United States* (Madison, 1914).

470 THE GOVERNMENT OF THE UNITED STATES

states a definite sum is fixed, above which indebtedness must not be incurred except for special purposes, or, in some instances, except with the express assent of the people obtained at a referendum. In other states no definite sum is fixed in the constitution, but the purposes for which debts may be incurred are carefully specified, and borrowing for other purposes is not permitted except when certain onerous formalities have been complied with. A few states fix the limit of indebtedness at a certain percentage of the total assessed value of taxable property. Only four of the forty-eight states have no constitutional debt limits at all. In the remaining forty-four the limitations are of the widest variety in character, scope, and stringency. At the one extreme is Louisiana, which permits no borrowing at all except for the purpose of repelling invasion or suppressing insurrection; at the other is Massachusetts, which has allowed its legislature [1] to borrow as much as it pleased.

*Is the present debt burden excessive?*

Naturally there is a great variation in the amounts of indebtedness which the several states are carrying. This is not altogether due to the presence or absence of constitutional checks upon the borrowing power, but is in part accounted for by the wide difference in what the several states undertake to do for their citizens. No one of the forty-eight states is entirely without debt, although a few of them have no net debt; in other words, their sinking-fund assets are sufficient to cover all obligations as they mature. Others have debts of moderate but steadily expanding dimensions, while not a few are paying interest each year on many millions of bonds. The net debt of New York state is more than one hundred and twenty-five millions. Massachusetts and California come next, with less than a quarter of that sum. In estimating the burden which a debt imposes upon any state it is usual to express it in terms of so much per head of population. On that basis the burden is nowhere excessive. The net debt of New York is only about thirteen dollars per capita; that of California, less than ten dollars. The national debt of the United States, expressed in per capita terms, is many times as much.

The states borrow money, when they have occasion to do

[1] In November, 1918, Massachusetts established a debt limit.

so, by the issue of bonds. These bonds run from ten to fifty years or even longer in some cases. A generation or two ago it was the almost invariable custom to issue bonds with no special provision for having funds in hand to pay them at maturity. Consequently when the bonds fell due in twenty or fifty years thereafter, there was no easy way of making payment except by re-borrowing. Sometimes this could be effected at some saving by the issue of new bonds bearing a lower rate of interest than the old. Paying off old bonds by issuing new ones at a lower rate of interest, as has been mentioned, is commonly known as refunding. But in recent years it has become the practice, although there are still many departures from it, to provide a sinking-fund whenever an issue of bonds is made. This is a fund into which is paid every year out of current income a sum sufficient to enable the bonds to be redeemed when they mature.

*Methods of borrowing, and of providing for repayment.*

*1. The sinking-fund system.*

The sinking-fund method of providing for the ultimate liquidation of state debts is of course far better than no provision at all, yet in actual practice it has shown serious defects. The necessary annual contributions to the fund are sometimes omitted for one reason or another, usually because of urgent demands from other quarters. Money is sometimes taken from the fund to meet a temporary emergency and then is not replaced. The sinking-funds are occasionally invested without due care and lost. When a state invests its sinking-funds, it takes the same risk as a private individual. Because of losses in the past the laws now restrict the investment of sinking-funds in such way as to reduce the element of risk to a minimum. But in any case the sinking-fund places a large amount of money and securities in the custody of a few officials who are usually chosen by popular vote, the state treasurer or a board of sinking-fund commissioners. The temptation to deposit the funds in favored banks or in other ways to use them for political or personal ends is sometimes too strong to be resisted. Hence it often happens, for one reason or another, that sinking-funds do not contain enough money when the time comes to use them in extinguishing the state's obligations.

*Defects of this plan.*

A better plan of borrowing is to serialize the dates of

2. The serial bond system.

maturity in such way that one or more bonds will come due for payment each year. This serial bond plan obviates entirely the need of creating sinking-funds. A definite proportion of the debt is regularly extinguished each year by applying from current revenue what would go into the sinking-fund, more or less. Many cities now use the serial plan, and a few of the states have adopted it with highly satisfactory results. Between the ultimate cost of the two plans there is no great difference, provided each is carried out exactly as planned. But in actual practice the serial plan almost invariably works out to be the cheaper method of borrowing, for it entails no long holding-over and investing of money with the attendant dangers of loss.[1]

Some general considerations.

It has been the custom in some states to look upon all public debts as evils to be scrupulously avoided. In others the idea seems to be that nothing should be paid for out of current income if by any way it can be provided for by loan, and thus passed on to a future generation. Neither policy is sound. When money is needed for public works of enduring character, such as a state capitol or a system of canals or of state highways, borrowing is a legitimate and even an equitable way of obtaining it. It is neither just nor expedient that the taxpayers of to-day should be forced either to bear the whole burden or go without. The cost of capital improvements may fairly be pro-rated over the years in which they are destined to render service to the public. On the other hand, future generations will have their own sufficient burdens and ought not to be unduly hampered by legacies of debt from the past.

[1] *Bulletin No. 21* of the Massachusetts Constitutional Convention, entitled "Methods of Public Borrowing, Sinking Funds *vs.* Serial Bonds" (Boston, 1917), and references therein given.

# CHAPTER XXXIII

### STATE PARTIES AND PRACTICAL POLITICS

IN its party organization as well as in its frame of government each state of the Union is an independent unit. The states control all such matters as the suffrage, the methods of nomination, the settlement of electoral disputes, and even the mechanism of the parties themselves. The system of party committees, the methods of raising and spending party funds, and many other essentials of party organization are determined by the state laws. In matters affecting the machinery and work of its political parties each state has complete self-government. There are national party committees, as has been seen, but they do not control the state organizations. This aspect of state self-government, to wit, party independence, has not always received the emphasis it deserves, but it is important because the party system, as Lord Bryce once remarked, is the power which sets and keeps in motion the wheels and pistons of representative government. *[Theoretical autonomy of state parties.]*

Since each state is independent as regards the organization and machinery of its political parties, it is quite conceivable that each might develop and maintain a different system from the others, that each might have its own set of political parties based upon state issues and in no way connected with party organization in other states. But that is not what has happened. The same party divisions exist in all the states, and these divisions are not determined by state issues. Interest in questions of national policy has overshadowed, on the whole, popular interest in matters with which the individual states have to deal, and the consequence is that the great lines of political cleavage run their course right through the nation from end to end. Party lines in *[But state and national parties have become identified.]*

the nation and in the states have become for all practical purposes identical, and it is national issues that determine them.

*With a few temporary exceptions.* To this general rule, there are, no doubt, some exceptions. A political party may prove itself, in any state, stronger or weaker in national than in state campaigns. But when this occurs it is usually due to some abnormal circumstance such as the injection of a non-partisan issue, or to dissensions within one of the organizations, or to some other factor which causes a partial breakdown of the regular party lines for the time being. In the normal course of events the strength of a political party is approximately the same in state and national affairs, although there is for the most part no relation whatever between the political issues in the two fields of government.

*Reasons for this identification of state and national parties.* The reason for this identification of state and national party lines is to be found in the fact that during the first twenty-five years after the formation of the Union many national questions of great importance forced themselves to the front, while political affairs within the states commanded very little public interest. These national issues ranged the people into two great political parties. As it was not possible without a tremendous expenditure of energy to create and keep in operation two separate sets of party divisions, one based on momentous national issues and the other on commonplace questions of state government, the natural result ensued, namely, that the greater division engulfed the smaller. The national parties during the opening years of the nineteenth century did not wipe out the state organizations, but merely swallowed them.[1] This situation, once created, has not proved easy to change. There have been times during the past hundred years when local issues in various states have taken the uppermost place in the minds of the electorate; but no permanent shattering of the established party lines has resulted. Party divisions, when once established, are hard to realign.

It is tacitly assumed that men select their party affiliations of their own free will and accord. As a rule they do nothing

[1] For the history of party rivalries in this period see Henry Jones Ford, *The Rise and Growth of American Politics* (N. Y., 1911).

of the sort. The great majority, as has already been said, inherit their party allegiance or have it determined for them by their early environment. The most important factor in determining whether a young man on becoming a voter will identify himself with one party or another is the political allegiance of his parents. Probably ninety per cent of the young men who reach voting age every year in the United States take their political beliefs, as they take their religion, in accordance with the influence of parentage and environment.[1] Hence a state may remain overwhelmingly in the control of one political party through successive generations although the issues have changed again and again. Party lines may be originally determined by issues; but they are perpetuated by inheritance.

The influence of heredity on party affiliations.

Not only are party lines identical in all the states, but the frame of party organization and the methods of party activity are much the same everywhere. The central organ of the party in the state is a state committee. This is made up of committeemen chosen directly or indirectly by the party voters in the various districts of the state, one or more from each district. The districts used for this purpose vary from state to state, and indeed different parties within the same state may not use the same districts for the selection of committeemen.

Organization of state parties: 1. The state committee.

In New York, for example, the Republican state central committee is made up of one delegate chosen to represent each of the forty-three congressional districts of the state.[2]

(a) In New York.

---

[1] This statement is not based on mere conjecture. Each year for many years I have taken a poll of my classes at Harvard in order to ascertain what proportion of the students intend to affiliate with the same political party as their parents. Save for a temporary lapse during the Progressive schism of 1912–1915 the proportion has uniformly proved to be 90 % or more. These young men, all of them nearing the age at which they will become voters, have been drawn from every part of the country, from every social class, and from all the political parties. The disposition to political independence is probably more marked among college men than it is throughout the country at large, so that the influence of heredity upon political allegiance would in all probability prove to be greater there if it could be accurately measured. In my inquiries, which have included many hundreds of young men, I have been able to find no greater departure from parental influence in politics than in religion.

[2] These forty-three select at large one additional committeeman to represent the colored voters of the state.

The Democratic state committee, on the other hand, consists of fifty-one members, one from each senatorial district. In both cases the committeemen are chosen, not by party voters, but by the delegates sent by the district to the party convention, a body which will be described presently.

(b) In Massachusetts and other states.

In Massachusetts the senatorial district is used by both political parties in the election of state committeemen. Here, however, the choice is not made by delegates to the convention but by the party voters at the polls. Other states use still different methods, but in general the committee is selected to represent districts, with possibly some committeemen at large, and its members are either chosen by the state convention or elected by the party voters. Each party, it need scarcely be added, has its own state committee.

Functions of the state committee.

What are the functions of these state committees? In general they see that the local party organizations both in the cities and in the rural districts are kept alive, and that they attend to such matters as the registration of the party voters and the proper distribution of local patronage. In a word it is the function of a state committee to keep the whole party machine in repair and in running order. Between election campaigns the committee does not meet very often; its functions during these periods of political quiescence are exercised usually by the committee's chairman, or secretary, or both. The only questions likely to be of interest to the individual members of the committee in this interval are those which relate to appointments. When the time for an election draws near, however, the committee limbers up and makes the party's campaign plans, often determining when and where the party convention shall be held, and how funds shall be raised. Sometimes it quietly hand-picks its own slate of candidates. It matters little whether the actual nominations are to be made by the convention or by means of a primary election; in either case the state committee is likely to make the preliminary selections, and under normal conditions its action will be ratified. During the campaign the committee serves as a general board of strategy, arranging for the chief speakers, soliciting contributions and apportioning the available money for expenses, preparing and issuing the campaign literature, and so on. Most of the actual work is done by the chairman or the secretary of the committee in coöperation with the local party committees all over the state, but the committee itself usually decides all questions of campaign policy.[1]

While the chairman of the state committee is nominally the head of his party organization in the state, he is not always the real leader or party boss. He may be such, it is true, but more often he is a pliant figurehead who is given the chairmanship at the behest of someone else who desires to exercise the real authority without having the spotlight of publicity thrown upon him. The secretary is usually a paid official, an energetic worker with a capacity for handling details. The state committee also has its treasurer, upon whom devolves the duty of helping to raise the campaign funds, paying the expenses, and finding some way to liquidate the inevitable deficit after the election is over. This last problem, it need scarcely be added, is less difficult when the party wins than when it loses. A victorious party, with preferment and patronage in its gift, rarely lacks good angels.

*Its chairman.*

Mention has been made of the party convention. Ordinarily each party holds a convention some time prior to the state election. The members represent the party voters in the various municipalities or districts of the state. They may be chosen by districts, by towns, by wards, or by some other type of local unit. The selection, however, may be made directly by the party voters, as in Massachusetts, or in an indirect manner, as in New York. Ordinarily a party convention will contain a hundred or more delegates. When the convention meets, it chooses its own chairman and proceeds to business. Each party, of course, has its own separate convention.

*The state party convention.*

Until a decade or two ago, the party convention nominated all the candidates, drew up the party platform, and even selected the state committee. The nominating function it has now lost in many of the states. Where the primary

*Its work.*

[1] This topic and indeed all the other matters outlined in the present chapter are much more fully dealt with in P. Orman Ray's *Introduction to Political Parties and Practical Politics* (2d ed., N. Y., 1917).

system of nomination is in vogue the convention no longer selects the candidates but leaves this work to the party voters. The convention's chief work is to draw up the party platform. This is usually done by a committee appointed for the purpose. As a matter of practice, however, some of the party leaders usually agree upon the main "planks" of the platform beforehand, so that the work of the committee is merely that of putting them together for adoption by the convention.

*The party platform in state campaigns.* Each of the parties issues a state platform at the outset of the campaign. These platforms purport to be declarations of what the party stands for in the coming state election, but they usually contain expressions of the party's attitude on national questions as well. Like the national party platforms they are sometimes evasive and tend to make a specialty of platitudes. A portion of the platform is always devoted to a criticism of what the opposing party has done or has failed to do. Then come intimations of how the party itself proposes to hasten the millennium. Interwoven with these things, occasionally, are expressions of opinion upon various matters of foreign policy, with which the state has no concern. These declarations are of course quite innocuous and merely inserted to humor some section of the voters. That is why the New York party platforms are solicitous for the Jews in Russia, while those of Massachusetts contain a perennial declaration in favor of Irish home rule. On some points, of course, the pledges of a party platform are specific, but the more definite the provisions the greater are the chances of future embarrassment in case the party changes front.

*The local party committees.* The work of both the state central committee and the party convention is of a general nature. These bodies plan and supervise. The real burden and heat of the day are borne by the local committees and the ancillary organizations which exist in every senatorial or assembly district, in every county, town, or township, in every city, and indeed in every ward of a city. Where the party is thoroughly organized this committee system extends even to the voting precincts, the smallest electoral unit of all. It is to these committees that the party leaders look for the proper registration of the voters, the canvassing, the holding of local rallies, the providing of conveyances for voters on election day, and the mustering of a full party vote at the polls. These committees are chosen in all sorts of ways, but their functions are much the same everywhere. Their members are active party workers. The precinct or ward committee is no place for slackers. State conventions and committees may provide the platform, the candidates, and the funds, but the active work among the voters must be done by local organizations. It is upon them, accordingly, that victory in a close campaign usually depends. The proof of good state leadership is to be found in the efficiency of these local bodies.

In addition to the local committees there are various ancillary or independent party associations, particularly in the cities. These usually take the name of leagues or clubs, and their main purpose is political although they may have some social activities as well, especially in the intervals between election campaigns. Groups of voters belonging to a party organize themselves together, secure a hall or other headquarters and make it their place of rendezvous. Usually there is a recognized leader as the moving spirit of the organization, and the members make up his personal following.

The reasons for the existence of such organizations are in part practical and in part psychological. Not all the party workers can be given places on the local committees. The clubs or leagues afford opportunities for many others who are ready to help in an unofficial capacity. Moreover, these associations can do things which a regular party committee might hesitate to do. The activities and expenditures of the regular committees must be conducted strictly according to law, but the clubs are not so closely hampered in their operations. The party may welcome their help, but it can also disclaim responsibility for the acts of voluntary and non-official groups over which its leaders have theoretically no control. The party's war chest often contributes to the expenses of these clubs, however, and they are an integral part of the political machine. These are practical considerations. As a matter of psychology, moreover, men like to be among their fellows when there is excitement and particularly when the spirit of victory is in the air. Impersonal loyalty to a political party does not satisfy the more ardent partisans, and the clubs provide the opportunity for making this allegiance more personal.

*The machine.*

The active workers in these conventions, central and local committees, clubs, the leaders, and bosses, together make up the party machine. It is appropriately so called because its various parts are smoothly geared together, and possibly also because it constantly needs financial lubrication.

*A purely American institution.*

Political machines exist in America only.[1] There are party organizations in other countries, but they are not called machines and do not deserve the name, for they possess no such smooth articulation nor are they held so well under central control as are the political machines of the American states. Yet the development of the machine in America is not an accident. Various conditions and circumstances have contributed to its upbuilding.

*Why it has evolved in the United States.*
*1. Frequency of elections.*

Among these causes one of the most important is the frequency of elections, due to the fact that so many officials of state government are elective and hold their posts for short terms. In no other country do elections come so often. No sooner do the echoes of one campaign die away than the preliminaries begin to be arranged for the next. The result is that those who look after the party's interests have time for little else. A fraternity of professional politicians is the logical outcome. The professional politician is more in evidence among Americans than among Europeans for the simple reason that Americans provide far more for him to do. If political campaigns were four or six years apart, as they

---

[1] The terms "party organization" and "party machine" are often used synonymously, but strictly speaking the *organization* includes all the members of the party while the *machine* includes the active workers only. A *machine* exists, therefore, only when the organization is highly efficient and has a considerable number of well-disciplined workers. The term "machine" is also used, sometimes, to designate the personal organization of a particular leader within the party. The machine may thus be the party organization as a whole, or only a part of it, or it may have no direct connection with the regular organization at all. It can be defined perhaps as a thoroughly organized hierarchy of party workers supporting either a leader or a cause. On its evolution and methods, see Samuel P. Orth, *The Boss and the Machine* (New Haven, 1919).

are on the other side of the Atlantic, it would not be so easy to keep party organizations in full working trim from election to election. But when voters are called to the polls at least every year for some form of election and sometimes (if the primary be included) even twice or three times a year, the political leaders are never accorded a long vacation. The American political machine would rust in other countries.

The vice of patronage has also had its part in creating the machine. Patronage is of two sorts, offices and favors. The distribution of offices under the spoils system, by which party heelers are rewarded with lucrative appointments, has been a natural incentive to political diligence. State and local committeemen, organizers of clubs and rallies, and those who pull door-bells as canvassers, do not give days and weeks to their work from motives of pure patriotism. They are, for the most part, seekers after the loaves and fishes which they hope to see distributed when the time comes. The spoils system has provided one means of rewarding them.

2. The nourishment of patronage.

Its various forms.

But there is another form of patronage, and although it has had less prominence in public discussion it is even more influential in its contribution to the vitality of the machine. This form of patronage includes the controlling of legislation so that party leaders or their friends may be financially benefited. It includes also the awarding of contracts for public works and the bestowal of favors in a multitude of other ways. It is not from those who aspire to places on the public payroll that all the money which keeps the machine in operation is usually obtained. It comes from public service corporations, or if corporations are prohibited by law from contributing to party funds, it is supplied by individuals who are known to be in touch with them. It comes from contractors, from those who have supplies which they desire at some favorable opportunity to sell to the state or the city, from the liquor dealers who seek to fortify their trade against hostile legislation, and from a variety of other sources where the quest for public favors is the mainspring of private generosity. The national party organizations derive a goodly proportion of their funds in small or moderate contributions from the rank and file of the voters; but the state organizations secure relatively less from that source. The machine, in a word, flourishes because the system of practical politics which exists in most of the states provides the sinews of war in the form of patronage. Civil service reform has done something to minimize this evil, and strict laws relating to the competitive awarding of contracts have also helped in some measure. Yet valiant party service and free-handed contributions to the party chest continue to be recognized as the surest passports to official favor.

3. Other factors which have helped the growth of political machines.

Other factors have also, no doubt, contributed to the evolution of political machines in America. The presence of newly naturalized citizens in large numbers, particularly in some of the eastern states, has been an incentive to thorough organization. Assiduous party propaganda counts for much with these voters who have not, like the native-born, inherited a predilection towards one or other of the regular parties. The long ballot with its party columns and its consequent premium on voting a straight ticket has also played into the hands of the machine. The apathy and docility of the rank and file of the voters, which is probably more pronounced in the United States than in most other countries, may also be a contributing factor. The political machine exists because conditions of environment have been favorable to it.

America's most conspicuous machine: Tammany Hall.

By common consent the most efficient party machine in the country is the organization known as Tammany Hall.[1] It is the local organization of the Democratic party for New York County (which includes only a portion of New York City); but it exercises a considerable influence upon the party's organization in New York state as a whole. Originating in the eighteenth century as a benevolent and fraternal association, it was first known as the Society of St. Tammany. Soon, however, the organization became strongly partisan and anti-Federalist. Aaron Burr was its first prominent leader, and he managed to make it a tower

[1] This is, of course, the name of the headquarters; but it is popularly used to personify the organization itself. A full account of the organization may be found in Gustavus Myers, *History of Tammany Hall* (2d ed., N. Y., 1917).

of strength to the Republican party of his day. When the old Republican party went to pieces and the Jacksonian Democrats obtained their long lease of power, Tammany became a Democratic-Republican organization and it still bears this official title, although it has of course no affiliations with the Republican party of to-day. It has become so famous the world over and is so conspicuous for its machine-like operations, if not for its political ideals, that a sketch of its organization and methods may well be included here. *Its origin and early history.*

The jurisdiction of Tammany extends over the thirty entire assembly districts and one-half assembly district which are included within New York County.[1] In each of these assembly districts the Democratic voters choose at an annual primary a district general committee, the membership of which varies according to the number of voters. The choice is made by election precincts, each precinct choosing its quota of committeemen. This district general committee is the chief party organ in the assembly district.[2] *Its present structure.*

*1. The district general committees.*

Its chairman, chosen by itself, is the directing figure in its operations. He appoints in every election district or precinct a district captain who is the official agent of the party in the precinct and is responsible for the showing which it makes on election day. He assigns the party workers in his precinct to their various tasks, as canvassers, watchers at the polls, challengers, or messengers. Each captain receives from the county committee's treasurer a sum of money to cover the expenses of this work, but is not paid for his own services. These captains form the staff which carries out the instructions of the district central *2. The district chairman.*

---

[1] These are the districts which elect assemblymen to the state legislature at Albany.

[2] The district central committee appoints from outside its own membership an auxiliary committee to assist it in its general activities, likewise several sub-committees from among its own members. Each district also has its clubs, usually bearing the name of some past or present district leader. These clubs maintain their headquarters the year around. From time to time they provide smokers, banquets, picnics, and so on for members and their friends. At Christmas and on other occasions they also make gifts of food, clothing, shoes or fuel to the poor of the district. But when an election campaign draws near, the activities of these clubs are wholly political.

committee. They are an active body and much of Tammany's strength depends upon their work.¹

3. The district leader or district boss.

But the district chairman, who appoints these captains, is not the district leader, so-called. The latter, who is also chosen by the district general committee, is the district's representative on the executive of the county committee; in addition he makes the various recommendations for appointments to office, apportions whatever patronage may be allotted to his district, and exercises a considerable influence over the selection of the party's candidates. In the practical aspects of political activity the district leader is a much more important personage than the district chairman.

4. The county committee and its executive committee.

For the whole county there is the county or general committee made up of all the members of the thirty district central committees sitting together. On paper it is a very large body, numbering several thousand members; but as it holds no regular meetings this unwieldiness is no obstacle. All its business is done by an executive committee made up of the thirty district leaders, together with some ex-officio members.² This committee chooses its own chairman; but he is not the county leader, or boss of Tammany Hall.

5. The county leader or boss of Tammany.

The latter is informally elected by the high lights of the party, whether district leaders or not, and technically is only an ordinary member of the executive committee. But he is by general acquiescence the dominating figure in that body, and his advice, whether on matters of policy or methods, is regularly followed.

Why he is a true boss.

The head of Tammany Hall is thus a party boss in the true sense of the term, a man who exercises large political powers without holding any official position or incurring any official responsibility. Leader and boss are often used as interchangeable words in the vernacular of practical politics, but it is not accurate to employ them in that way. A leader has a position which is clearly defined by law or by the rules of the organization. He has definite duties and a

---

¹ All the precinct captains in each assembly district meet from time to time to discuss plans and to insure thorough coöperation as regards both aims and methods.

² This executive committee appoints the various standing committees which also act, within their special fields, on behalf of the dormant county committee.

direct responsibility which he cannot conceal. His acts are performed in the open. A boss, on the other hand, while he may be a party official, does not derive his power from that fact. His authority comes through informal and undefined channels; he uses his machine for personal as well as party ends; and he does not owe any real responsibility to the rank and file of the voters.

In methods also, as well as in responsibility, leadership and bossism are different. "The difference between a boss and a leader," as Theodore Roosevelt once remarked, "is that a leader leads and a boss drives. The difference is that a leader holds his place by firing the conscience and appealing to the reason of his followers, while a boss holds his place by corrupt and underhand manipulation. The difference is that a leader works in the light of day while the boss derives the greater part of his power from deeds done under cover of darkness."[1] Every area of party organization has its leader or recognized head; but not every such area has a boss. Where it has both, the two may or may not be the same person.

Many denunciations have been showered upon bosses and bossism; but both are logical products of political conditions which have existed in most American states and cities until recent years, and which still continue in some of them. Discipline helps to win elections as well as battles, and good discipline cannot be maintained except by lodging vast final powers in the hands of a shrewd, active, and experienced commander-in-chief. The man who is best fitted to organize the party cohorts, to drive them forward at top speed, to dole out the funds where they will do most good, and to provide whatever strategy the campaign may demand is not always the one whom the party cares to put on a pedestal as its official leader. Far better it is, in such cases, to have someone of irreproachable record and demeanor in the post of technical leadership, while informally leaving the real power to some Warwick behind the throne. There will be bosses in American politics so long as government by

*Bosses and leaders distinguished:*
*1. in responsibility.*

*2. in methods.*

*The political circumstances which have encouraged bossism in America.*

---

[1] Speech at the New York State Convention, September, 1910, quoted by P. Orman Ray, *Political Parties and Practical Politics* (2d ed. N. Y., 1917), pp. 456–457.

patronage, the spoils system, the multiplicity of elective offices, the long ballot, the frequency of polling, the lobby, the policy of legislation by trade and bargaining, the gerrymander, and a dozen other iniquities combine to place at a disadvantage the leader who insists upon fair and open methods of electoral combat.

*Where does bossism find its most fertile soil?*

There has never been a national boss in the United States, at any rate, not since Andrew Jackson's day, and the chief reason is that the methods of national organization and political campaigning do not lend themselves readily to bossism. In some states, for the same reason, there are no bosses. In others, where the tone of politics is more sordid, the boss is a well-established institution. Bossism has flourished particularly in the large cities, where party methods have sometimes descended to the lowest plane of all. The standards of political morality, in short, determine whether leadership or bossism shall dominate the activities of parties.

*Qualities a boss must have.*

A successful boss must be possessed of personal qualifications. He must be firm in purpose, aggressive, and courageous. He must not be arrogant and dictatorial in dealing with his followers, but patient, tactful and abounding in resource when there are difficulties to be surmounted or animosities to be ironed out. He must be a shrewd judge of men, able to detect variations in the pulse of public opinion, and never caught napping when opportunity is before his eyes. He must have a vigorous physique, able to stand hard work and to enjoy it. Habits of dissipation will bring a boss to grief in short order. He must have a zest for doing favors, thus placing voters and their friends under obligations to him. His motives may be in all cases selfish or sordid, but that matters little. In time of trouble it is deeds and not motives that count with those whom the boss befriends. Finally, he must know the tricks of his trade and have no ingrowing conscience to hamper his freedom in applying them. Bosses who continue in power over long periods are for the most part men whose natural gifts would readily bring them success in other vocations. They cling to politics for the love of it, and very few, despite a popular impression to the contrary, make money out of it.

The cure for bossism is in the eradication of the things

which have brought it into being. The reduction in the number of elective offices, the use of the short ballot, the extension of the merit system to all subordinate appointments and to all promotions, the simplification of nominating and election machinery, the practice of requiring all campaign contributions and expenditures to be made public, the placing of all public contracts on an open-competition basis, the purchase of all supplies by public tender, the extermination of lobbying in legislatures, the extension of social service facilities in the crowded sections of large cities, and the encouragement of civic education — these reforms have helped and are helping to rid the states of boss politics. Such riddance, moreover, is in the highest degree desirable, for no political system can be really democratic so long as it suffers any man to exercise large political powers without formal authority or responsibility. The boss system transforms free government into autocracy. It is far-reaching in its ramifications and insidious in its effects. *The remedies for boss rule.*

A clear distinction should be made, however, between these excrescences upon the party system and the system itself. Too often the merits of party organization are wholly disregarded. Its lapses are made the theme of sermons and editorials which advocate the ruthless harrying of all party organizations. That is like urging the abolition of bank notes because they are sometimes counterfeited, or of newspapers because some of them print libels. The founders of the nation had an aversion to party politics, as well they might, for party struggles were associated in their imagination with the old factional conflicts of the Greek and Roman republics, of Guelphs and Ghibellines in the Middle Ages, and of Cavaliers and Roundheads in seventeenth century England. These were party struggles in which bloodshed, conspiracy and banishment figured as part of the day's work. But the history of nations during the last hundred years has shown that party contests can be conducted fairly, on clear-cut issues, and without personal malice. It has proved, moreover, that real democracy can nowhere exist without party organization. These lessons, as President Lowell has said, represent the greatest single contribution of the nineteenth century to the art of free government. *Ridding the land of bosses does not mean the abolition or weakening of the party system.*

# CHAPTER XXXIV

## THE STATE COURTS

**Relation of the state to the federal courts.**

IN addition to the federal courts already described, every state of the Union has a system of state courts established under the provisions of its own constitution and laws. Between these state courts and the federal courts there are many marked similarities of organization and procedure, but two essential differences are to be noted. One is that in most of the states the judges are elected by the people, whereas there are no elective judges in any federal courts. The other difference has to do with the range of jurisdiction possessed by the two sets of tribunals. The matters with which the federal courts may deal are explicitly defined in the constitution of the United States. The federal courts possess such branches of jurisdiction as are there enumerated, and no more. The state courts, on the other hand, are vested with all remaining judicial authority. The result is that the state courts exercise authority over a far wider range, and handle a far larger proportion of the total litigation of the country, than do the federal courts.

**Early history of state courts.**

The state courts, in their organization and procedure, are an inheritance from the colonial period, but their evolution has been considerably influenced by the principle of separation of powers. The administration of justice in the colonies was not always kept distinct from the making and the execution of the laws. The governor and his advisers sometimes served as the supreme court of the colony. After the winning of independence the various colonial courts were transformed into state tribunals without great alteration, and it was not until a half century after the Revolution that radical departures from the traditional English forms of organization began.

These changes, which involved more particularly a democratization of the courts, were due to the influence of the new states, particularly during the Jacksonian era. They were part and parcel of the frontier influence upon American government during the second quarter of the nineteenth century. Pioneer communities want certainty, promptness, simplicity, cheapness, and a certain propinquity to popular sentiment in the administration of justice. These needs directly controlled the development of judicial institutions in the pioneer states and indirectly affected judicial institutions in all the states.[1] They led to the supplanting of appointive by elective judges, the establishing of regular local courts in place of circuit tribunals which came only at intervals to each locality, and the simplification of procedure.

*Their democratization during the nineteenth century.*

This frontier influence was naturally least effective in the older states, particularly in New England, where it was not felt to any appreciable degree. Other currents and cross-currents of judicial reorganization have also surged from time to time during the past fifty years, but not with equal strength in all the states. The several states have developed differences in the character and distribution of their populations, likewise in the complexity of the problems with which their courts have to deal. Some have become great industrial conglomerations, with the need for a greater refinement of jurisprudence, for more learned and capable judges, and for a higher degree of specialization in the structure of their courts. They have developed their judicial systems accordingly. Others remain agricultural areas, with the relative simplicity of rural life, and hence have no such need for so high a degree of expertness or professionalism in their judiciary. They can and do proceed upon the principle that every man is competent to be his own lawyer and every lawyer fit to be a judge, a doctrine which would soon bring chaos in states where legal relations are more intricate.

*The adjustment of state courts to community needs.*

Hence it is that no two states have judicial systems exactly alike in organization or in procedure. Each has adapted its method of selecting judges, its rules of procedure,

[1] A. N. Holcombe, *State Government in the United States* (N. Y., 1916), p. 347.

and its judicial guarantees to what it assumes to be its own particular requirements. Yet the influence of the federal bill of rights upon the state constitutions has been such that practically all the latter impose upon the state courts the same general restrictions for the protection of the individual. The organization and procedure of the federal courts have also had a powerful influence on the states. Hence the variation in essentials among the judicial systems of the various states is not so great as it undoubtedly would have been without these two unifying factors.

The judiciary in every state now comprises at least three sets of courts, sometimes more.[1] First there are local courts, presided over in most cases by justices of the peace, municipal justices, or similar officers who are chosen by popular election in all but a very few states. Everywhere the jurisdiction of these local courts is limited to civil and criminal cases of relatively minor importance. Frequently, however, the local justice conducts the preliminary hearings where serious criminal charges have been made and determines whether or not the accused shall be held for trial by a higher court. These local courts are not provided with juries; their procedure is of a summary character, and their work usually leaves much room for improvement. As a rule the justices of the peace have had no training in the law and their administration of justice is proverbially crude. It has the saving grace, however, that if the justice does not know the law he knows the suitors, and his decisions are probably not far wide of the eternal equities. Nevertheless, the faulty work of these lowest courts and the frequency with which one can successfully appeal from their decisions have contributed to the congestion of business in the higher state tribunals.

Next come a higher range of courts, frequently known as county courts, which hear appeals from the decisions of the local justices and which also have original jurisdiction over a considerable range of cases, both civil and criminal. In some states these county courts, after the old English fashion, are given certain functions of an administrative character,

---

[1] S. E. Baldwin, *The American Judiciary* (N. Y., 1908), especially ch. viii, and A. N. Holcombe, *State Government* (N. Y., 1916), ch. xi.

including the supervision of county prisons, the maintenance of county roads, and various matters relating to poor relief. A county court is presided over by a judge who is in most states elected by popular vote. As a rule provision is made for trial by jury in these courts. In some states, especially in New England, there are no regular county courts of this sort. Their place is taken by sessions of the Superior Court which are held at stated times in each county.

The Superior Court, as it is called in Massachusetts and some other states, or District Court as it is frequently called in western states, has authority to hear cases both at law and in equity on appeal from the lower tribunals and also has practically unlimited jurisdiction in all higher civil and criminal cases. Invariably these courts are empowered to try cases with the assistance of a jury. Their decisions are ordinarily final so far as the facts of a controversy are concerned. The judges of these intermediate courts, whether district or superior tribunals, are in most states elected by popular vote; in a few states they are appointed by the governor.

*and other intermediate courts.*

Finally, each state has a tribunal of last resort, usually called the Supreme Court, but sometimes the Court of Errors, or the Court of Appeals.[1] It has original jurisdiction in only a few matters; most controversies come before it by way of appeal from decisions of tribunals below. Moreover, it deals, in the main, with questions of law, not questions of fact. The state Supreme Court includes from five to fifteen judges (the number is fixed by law), who are either elected for considerable terms, or appointed by the governor, or in rare cases chosen by the legislature. Everywhere this highest state court has the last word in litigation except in those relatively few cases where, because the controversy raises some substantial point involving the federal constitution or the federal laws, the matter may be carried, by the issue of a writ of error, to the Supreme Court of the United States.

*3. The highest state courts.*

---

[1] The nomenclature in New York State is confusing. The Supreme Court of that state does not have final jurisdiction. Final authority is given to the Court of Appeals.

**The supremacy of the state courts in their own sphere.**

There is an impression in the popular mind that all state courts are subordinate to all federal courts, that the lowest court in the federal system is superior to the highest state court. To students of government it should be superfluous to mention that such impression is altogether wrong. Each set of courts is independent, each has its own field of jurisdiction and within that field cannot be interfered with by the other. Most cases which originate in the state courts reach their final determination there. Not one in a thousand among them ever reaches the federal Supreme Court.

Whether a case is brought before a state or a federal court in the first instance depends wholly upon the nature of the case itself. If it concerns matters or persons within state jurisdiction, the state courts handle it; if it concerns matters or persons within federal authority, it goes before the federal courts. If the suit is commenced in either, and in the course of the trial it becomes apparent that it should have been entered in the other, it can be removed to the latter. But if a controversy is properly within the jurisdiction of the state courts it can go no farther than the highest state tribunal unless the Supreme Court of the United States obtains appellate cognizance of it by writ of error. No such writ of error, to take a case on appeal from the highest state court to the highest federal court, will be issued "unless it appears affirmatively that not only was a federal question presented for decision to the highest court of the state having jurisdiction, but that its decision was necessary to the determination of the cause, and that it was actually decided, or that the judgment as rendered could not have been given without deciding it."[1] In the vast majority of instances this condition, which is the essential of appeals to the federal Supreme Court, cannot be met, and there is consequently no chance of an appeal.

**Relative infrequency of federal interference with state decisions.**

The Supreme Court of the United States has not been free-handed in its interference with the decisions of the highest state tribunals. It has repeatedly declared that in controversies affecting the interpretation of a state law the decision of the highest court in that state is ordinarily to be regarded as final and will not be set aside. It concedes,

[1] *De Saussure* vs. *Gaillard*, 127 U. S. 216.

therefore, as a matter of deference to state sovereignty, that those who proceed in the state courts must accept whatever interpretation of the state laws these tribunals may finally give. When the highest state court, moreover, passes upon any question as to whether a state law is or is not repugnant to the federal constitution and decides that the law is on that ground unconstitutional, the Supreme Court of the United States has not been empowered until within the last few years to review such decision. Now, however, the Supreme Court of the United States may hear appeals concerning the constitutionality of state laws in relation to the federal constitution, no matter what the decision of the highest state court may have been.[1] When state laws are declared unconstitutional, however, it is usually by the state courts and because of their repugnance to the constitution of the state, not to that of the nation.

In addition to its regular tribunals every state has certain courts of a special character. Among these are probate or surrogate's courts for the settlement of questions relating to wills and inheritances, although in some states there are no special courts for these matters, the work being done by the regular county courts. In a few states there is a tribunal known as the Land Court, which has to do with the investigation and registration of land titles. *Special courts.*

In nearly all the state courts it is the practice to select judges in one of two ways, by election or by appointment. Election is the method used in the great majority of the states, that is to say, by thirty-eight states in all. Of the remaining ten states, six leave the selection of their judges, *The method of selecting judges.*

[1] The Judiciary Act of 1789, with its various amendments, gives the Supreme Court of the United States authority to reëxamine, reverse, or affirm the final judgment or decree of any highest state court: (1) wherever there is drawn in question the validity of a statute or treaty of the United States and where the decision was against its validity; (2) wherever the validity of a state law is attacked as repugnant to the constitution, statutes, or treaties of the United States; and (3) wherever there is drawn in question the interpretation of any clause in the federal constitution, or of any federal law or treaty, and where the decision of the state court has been adverse to the claim set up thereunder. These are the only conditions under which the Supreme Court of the United States can review a decision of the highest tribunal in any state. For a further discussion of this matter see F. N. Judson, *The Judiciary and the People* (New Haven, 1913), pp. 114–115 and *passim*.

## 494   THE GOVERNMENT OF THE UNITED STATES

so far as the higher courts are concerned, to the governor.[1] They provide, however, various requirements as to the confirmation of those whom the governor may appoint. In four states the judges of the higher courts are chosen by the legislature.[2]

**The terms of judges.**

The term for which judges are chosen varies from life to a few years. In Massachusetts, for example, judges of all courts, whether higher or lower, are appointed by the governor with the consent of his council and usually hold office until they die or resign. In Pennsylvania the judges of the Supreme Court are elected by the people for twenty-one years, in New York for fourteen years, and in Illinois for six years. In Vermont they are chosen by the legislature for two years only. Many states make a distinction between the judges of the higher and the lower courts, giving the former longer terms.

**The system of electing judges: its extension.**

Much may be said both for and against the practice of choosing judges by popular election. Before the Revolution the judges were appointed by the crown through the governor in all the colonies except in Rhode Island and Connecticut, where they were chosen by the assembly. The early state constitutions for the most part followed this latter precedent and intrusted to the legislature the function of choosing the judges, although in some cases it was left with the governor. In only one of the original thirteen states, Georgia, were judges chosen by popular vote.[3] This elective method made no considerable progress for many years after the Union was established, but the Jacksonian democracy gave it great impetus and it thereafter continued to spread, particularly through the new states of the West. To-day there are no appointive judges west of the Alleghanies except in the single state of Mississippi. In only five states outside New England are the judges of the state Supreme Court chosen otherwise than by popular election.

The reasons which dictated resort to popular election of judges were both sentimental and practical. The fixed

[1] Delaware, New Jersey, Massachusetts, New Hampshire, Maine, and Mississippi.
[2] Rhode Island, Vermont, South Carolina, and Virginia.
[3] F. N. Judson (*The Judiciary and the People*, New Haven, 1913, p. 160) declares that none of the states had elective judges in 1789.

notion that no branch of the government should exist outside the realm of direct popular control is one which must always be reckoned with in ultra-democratic communities. People are apt to reason that they should directly control not only the making and administration of their own laws but the interpretation of these laws as well. The tide of popular opinion set strongly in that direction during the middle period of American constitutional history and has continued without greatly diminished force down to the present day.

*Reasons for its adoption. 1. The logic of popular sovereignty.*

More practical reasons for the change from appointive to elective judges were to be found in the partisanship and chicanery which too often marked the selection of judges by legislatures in the early part of the nineteenth century. By dint of political manipulation and appeals to party allegiance men of doubtful integrity were frequently elevated to judicial positions. Hence the demand for the popular election of judges was in part a protest against the way in which legislatures were abusing their trust, just as in latter days and for much the same reasons public opinion insisted upon the popular election of United States senators in place of their appointment by state legislatures.

*2. Defects of legislative selection.*

Nor does the plan of letting the governor choose the judges prove to be free from serious objection. Judicial appointments made under that plan often go as the reward of party service to men who are not properly qualified. Appointment by governors has not, on the whole, worked out so unsatisfactorily as selection by legislatures, but it does not to-day commend itself to many of the states. Popular election has obtained the upper hand.

*3. Poor appointments often made by governors.*

But in actual operation, as experience proves, the people do not really choose their judges. How, indeed, can a body of a hundred thousand voters obtain the knowledge necessary to insure the placing of legal knowledge, sound judgment, and integrity on the state bench? The answer is, that the people do not have such knowledge and do not presume to have it. In many states there is a tradition that a judge, when once elected, shall be retained in office so long as his conduct is at all satisfactory. This means, then, that vacancies on the bench occur, for the most part, only when a judge dies or resigns. When vacancies come in this way,

*How the system of elective judges has worked out.*

the governor is usually given the right to make an appointment until the next election, and this appointee is likely at that time to be a candidate with the chances much in his favor. Many elective judges, therefore, really owe their election to a governor's temporary appointment.

If it happens, on the other hand, that a judge retires upon the expiry of his elective term, the choice among aspirants for his place is almost invariably made, in the first instance, either by the prominent lawyers of the state or by the political leaders. The voters merely choose as between rival candidates thus presented to them. Whichever way they decide they merely approve one or other of the preliminary selections made by the leading lawyers or politicians. Other candidates, supported neither by the bar associations nor by political parties, have ordinarily no chance of being elected. Under the system of nominations by convention the political leaders did their work openly and with a certain sense of responsibility; under the plan of nomination by direct primaries they merely do it less openly and without responsibility.

Wherever judges are chosen by popular election there is almost always a *de facto* appointing power. Whether the system of election works out well or otherwise depends upon where this *de facto* power resides and how wisely it is used. There is no great difference in the quality of judges obtained in Massachusetts by governor's appointment and in Wisconsin by popular election. This is because the lawyers, through their bar associations, have a considerable influence in both.[1] The system of elective judges works best where the legal fraternity has the greatest practical weight in making the preliminary selections; it works badly where the nominations are dictated by the political leaders.

Closely connected with the question of appointing judges is the method of removing them from the bench. Judges of the federal courts may be removed in one way only, that is, by impeachment. Judges of state courts may be removed by impeachment also, but some of the states provide two

[1] There is an illuminating discussion of this matter, showing the relation between *de jure* election and *de facto* appointment, in Bulletin No. IV A, of the American Judicature Society.

other methods of removal, namely, by address, or by recall.

Removal by impeachment is an available method in all the states without exception. The process involves the filing of charges by the lower chamber and a trial before the upper chamber of the legislature. Conviction usually requires a two-thirds vote. Removals have frequently been accomplished in this way, but the total number is not large.

Removal "by address" is not a usual method of ousting a state judge from office although it is provided for in several states. It has its prototype in a procedure which has long existed in England and which was there devised as a means of protecting the judges against arbitrary removal by the crown. As established in various American states it permits the governor to remove a judge from office in compliance with an "address" or formal request of the legislature. As a rule, a two-thirds vote of both Houses of the legislature is necessary, but not always. In Massachusetts, for example, a mere majority suffices. It is not ordinarily required that specific charges be filed or that anything like a trial, as in an impeachment, shall be conducted; but it is customary to reduce the complaints against a judge to written form and to give him some sort of hearing thereon, either before a committee of the legislature or before the governor. The governor, moreover, is not bound to act in response to an address for removal unless he chooses to do so. There is a marked difference, accordingly, between a removal by impeachment and a removal by address. The former is a judicial proceeding and is carried out with due regard to the forms of law and the rights of the accused. The latter is an *ex parte* legislative process with the final decision resting in the governor's hands. Another difference is that a conviction by impeachment may disqualify from office for the future, whereas a removal by address does not.

2. by address.

A third method of removing judges exists in a few states, namely, by means of the recall.[1] This device is elsewhere explained with respect to the executive and legislative branches of state government; its machinery and workings

3. by recall.

[1] Oregon, California, Arizona, Colorado, and Nevada.

are much the same when applied to the judiciary.[1] A petition signed by a designated number of voters is presented asking for the recall of a judge from office. The question is put upon the ballot, and if the popular verdict is adverse, the judge steps down.

*Reputed merits and defects of the recall as applied to the judiciary.*

The reputed merit of the plan is that it serves to keep the interpretation and enforcement of the laws in harmony with public sentiment. The judge sits with the sword of Damocles over his head, being thus reminded that he is the servant and not the master of the people. On the other hand the objections commonly urged against the recall of administrative officials apply with even greater force in the case of judges. The courts should be free from the momentary onsets of prejudice or passion. Courage and independence, freedom from the taint of political partiality, are essentials of a good judiciary. It is argued that the recall will place a premium on pusillanimity, making the bench no longer a rock of defence against the abuse of political power, but a reed shaken by every gust of sentiment or prejudice. Much will depend, of course, upon the tradition which the recall develops. If wisely and conservatively used, the recall offers no greater menace to the independence of the judges than does the plan of removal by address. The latter might easily become a weapon of shameless intimidation, but has nowhere done so. Potential dangers, it ought to be remembered, are often not realized in the actual practice of free government.

*The recall of judicial decisions.*

The recall of judicial decisions has been adopted in one state only, Colorado. When the Supreme Court of that state declares any law to be unconstitutional, a stated number of voters may petition to have a popular referendum on the question of enforcing the law despite the court's decision. The popular verdict, whatever it is, will then prevail. The power of recalling judicial decisions, it should be noted, does not apply to all judgments, but only to those which deny the constitutionality of laws. The arrangement merely embodies a poor method of doing what could be quite as easily accomplished in a less offensive way, namely, by amending the state constitution so as to bring the par-

[1] Below, pp. 518–521.

ticular law within bounds. It is ordinarily no more difficult to amend a state constitution than to order the enforcement of an unconstitutional law, a popular majority being the chief requirement in either case.

Many state laws are held unconstitutional because they violate the provisions of the national constitution. The highest state courts are to that extent, therefore, guardians of the private rights which are guaranteed by that document. To provide that decisions of this sort shall be subject to recall by popular vote in any state is virtually to permit the local annulment of the national constitution, thus reviving the doctrine of nullification in a new and very obnoxious form. The movement for the recall of judicial decisions seems to have derived its impetus from certain unpopular decisions rendered by state courts in affirmation of claims to federal right, and is not directed solely against the alleged misinterpretation of state constitutions by state courts. *A proposal of popular nullification.*

As state courts administer both law and equity, the burden of litigation which is placed upon them is very great. Practically the whole domain of private law comes within state jurisdiction. This includes the civil rights of the individual, the law of property, of contracts, of torts and of personal relations. Within the cognizance of the states, moreover, is the great field of criminal law and the great bodies of law which have been developed in relation to corporate business, state banking, insurance, and exchange. Under the propulsive influence of modern social and economic activity the volume of state law has been increasing at an enormous rate. More laws mean more lawsuits, and more lawsuits mean more courts, although this elementary truism of political science is not always appreciated by law-makers. The courts in many of the states are not able to keep up with their work. In some cases their dockets are filled for many months and even for years ahead. *The scope of the laws which state courts administer.*

The cumbrous formalities of judicial procedure, relics of older days when litigation was associated with wealth and leisure, have also had their share in accentuating the congestion of business in the courts. Constitutions and laws have been so regardful of the individual's rights that they have *The archaic nature of judicial procedure.*

given to every suitor an undue liberty to stay proceedings, to take exceptions, to move in arrest of judgment, and to make appeal. These rights, in many cases, are transformed into privileges of obstruction and delay. They restrain the judges from doing many things which judges are permitted to do in all other countries and which, if allowed here, would greatly expedite the administration of justice. Many of the laws relating to judicial procedure, ostensibly in the interest of justice, actually operate to withhold from the citizen the first essential of justice, which has been so recognized since the days of Magna Carta, namely, that it "shall not be delayed to any man." This technical and superlegalistic spirit has sometimes made the courthouses fit the undergraduate's definition of them as "places where justice is dispensed with."

*The methods of judicial reform.*

*Where reform should begin.*

The thing most urgently needed to make the administration of justice in the state courts more satisfactory is not a change in the manner of selecting judges, or in the method of removing them. Judicial reform should begin with the fountains of state justice, which are the state constitutions. To be effective, it must also reach into the halls of legislation and secure an improvement in the standards of law-making.

*A word as to lawyers.*

The whole system of procedure needs radical overhauling, and this reconstruction would have come long ago were it not that the removal of legal complexities would leave less work for lawyers to do. Lawyers form a large element in legislatures, and they are not usually partisans of judicial reform. Yet despite their conservatism in matters affecting their own profession, lawyers form an element of the greatest value in legislative bodies. Their influence is almost always on the side of justice and moderation. They realize, as the layman usually does not, that if the laws are unjust in their provisions no court can wring justice out of them. American legislatures without lawyers would make a far worse showing, popular notions to the contrary notwithstanding.

# CHAPTER XXXV

## DIRECT LEGISLATION AND THE RECALL

THE movement for direct legislation by the people through the use of the initiative and referendum has made substantial headway among the states during the last twenty years. Its progress is, perhaps, the most striking political phenomenon of the present generation. It indicates, on the one hand, a widespread spirit of popular dissatisfaction with the workings of strictly representative government, and on the other hand, a growing confidence in the ultimate political capacity of the voters themselves. In nearly half the states the voters have taken directly into their own hands the right to propose and to enact laws without the intervention of the legislature. The legislature remains, of course, the normal agency of law-making; but where the legislature is unresponsive to any call for legislation the people may, by their petitions and their votes, put the desired law into effect.

*The most striking political phenomenon of our day.*

The mechanism of direct legislation consists of two political instruments known as the initiative and the referendum.[1]

---

[1] The literature relating to the initiative and referendum has become most voluminous during the past dozen years. Among the various discussions of the subject from every point of view the following may be mentioned as the more useful: E. P. Oberholtzer, *The Initiative, Referendum and Recall in America* (N. Y., 1911); D. F. Wilcox, *Government by All the People, or The Initiative, Referendum and Recall as Instruments of Democracy* (N. Y., 1912); C. S. Lobingier, *The People's Law* (N. Y., 1909); A. L. Lowell, *Public Opinion and Popular Government* (N. Y., 1914); C. A. Beard and B. E. Schultz, *Documents on the State-wide Initiative, Referendum and Recall* (N. Y., 1912); and J. D. Barnett, *The Operation of the Initiative, Referendum, and Recall in Oregon* (N. Y., 1915). The most compact and most informing of all monographs on the subject, however, is *The Initiative and Referendum* (Boston, 1917), printed as Bulletin No. 6, for the Massachusetts Constitutional Convention of 1917-1918.

## 502 THE GOVERNMENT OF THE UNITED STATES

**The initiative defined.**

The initiative is a device by which any person or group of persons may draft a proposed law or amendment to the state constitution, and by securing in its behalf a designated number of signatures may require that the proposed law or constitutional amendment be submitted to the voters at the polls; and if it is approved by a majority it goes into effect. In some cases the requirement is that the proposal, having been duly signed by a sufficient number of voters, shall go first to the legislature and not before the people at the polls unless the legislature, after due opportunity, fails to accept it. The first plan is known as the direct initiative; the second as the indirect initiative.

**The referendum defined.**

The referendum, on the other hand, is an arrangement whereby any measure already proposed and passed by a legislature may, under certain circumstances, be withheld from going into force until the people have had an opportunity to express their opinion on it. The circumstances under which withholding is necessary are various. Under

**Different types of referendum.**

the *optional* referendum the legislature may or may not submit a measure to the people as it sees fit. Under the *compulsory* referendum a measure must be so submitted whenever a designated number of voters by petition request that this be done. As ordinarily used the term referendum applies to this compulsory arrangement, namely, submission whenever required by petition. A distinction may also be drawn between the *constitutional* referendum, which is the compulsory referendum applied to proposed constitutional amendments only, and the *statutory* referendum, which applies to proposed laws only, and not to constitutional changes.

**Interworking of the two.**

The initiative and the referendum logically go together and supplement each other. The initiative is a positive instrument of legislation; it can be used to set the wheels in motion. The referendum, on the other hand, is negative in its operation; it gives the people a potential veto upon laws enacted by the legislature. It permits the voters to have the last say as to whether any particular law shall go into effect or not.

Notwithstanding a popular impression to the contrary, direct legislation by the people is not new in principle or in practice. The initiative and the referendum are merely new names for very old institutions. The Athenian democracy used both of them, although in a somewhat crude form. It employed them in determining questions of war and peace, or in actually adjudging the guilt or innocence of accused persons. Socrates was condemned to death by what we would nowadays call a bill of attainder enacted through the agencies of direct legislation. The so-called democracy of all ancient peoples was of the direct rather than of the representative type. Those who have read Tacitus will remember his description of the way in which the primitive Saxons, progenitors of the English race, regulated their public affairs by the will of the tribesmen expressed in an assembly of the adult males. Nor does one have to go back ten or twelve centuries in order to pick up the precedents. The cantons of Switzerland have used the initiative and referendum in one form or another for many generations. The two Bonapartist emperors of the French were ardent believers in having great questions of public policy determined by *plebiscites*, which they usually manipulated, however, to their own profit. Before the middle of the seventeenth century the colony of Massachusetts employed methods of proposing and enacting laws which were to all intents similar to the direct legislation methods of to-day.[1] Among the earliest American state constitutions, several expressly reserved to the people the right "to give instructions to their representatives" in the legislature. The doctrine, therefore, that the people should have the right to take the first step in law-making, or the last step, or both, is not new. What is relatively novel in the direct legislation of to-day is the somewhat intricate machinery whereby the will of the people is given its power of expression. This, however, is only because states which include many hundred thousands of voters cannot pursue the simple procedure which served Athens, or a Saxon tribe, or a Swiss canton, or a Puritan colony.

*Direct legislation is no novelty.*

*But its present-day mechanism is new.*

The first American state to adopt the initiative and referendum as regular instruments for the making of laws was South Dakota. In a general way it copied the system

[1] See the examples cited in the *Bulletin* on *The Initiative and Referendum* (Boston, 1917), pp. 8–10.

504    THE GOVERNMENT OF THE UNITED STATES

*Spread of the system in the American states.*

used by the cantons of the Swiss Republic. Other states followed soon after, Utah in 1900, Oregon in 1902 and so on.[1] To-day about half the states have provided for direct legislation in some form or other. In the early stages of the movement its progress was entirely in the western states, and even yet its main strength lies west of the Mississippi. Maine, Ohio, Michigan, Massachusetts and Maryland are as yet the only converts in the eastern half of the country. As movements of such fundamental importance go, however, its spread has been astonishingly rapid.

*Reasons for this spread:*

How is this remarkable progress of direct legislation in the states of the Union to be accounted for? There has been no such development in other great countries having representative systems of government, such as Great Britain and France. Two reasons may be assigned, and perhaps more. On the one hand the popularity of the initiative and referendum is clearly indicative of a declining confidence in the judgment and integrity of legislators. As regards the caliber and capacity of the men elected to serve in them, state legislatures are not what they used to be.

*1. the decline of public confidence in legislatures.*

The reasons for this decline in quality, which is everywhere apparent to the naked eye, are manifold. They include such factors as the selection of representatives from small, gerrymandered districts, the complicated methods of nomination, the encroachment of the state constitutions upon legislative freedom, and many others which have been already dilated upon. Legislatures, moreover, have been lacking in leadership, and by reason of this handicap have conspicuously failed to do their work in a businesslike way. This lack of leadership has developed irresponsibility, spinelessness, procrastination, and the other shortcomings which have given the legislatures a popular reputation for fickleness and incapacity. At any rate, the unsatisfactory results of representative law-making in many states has led

[1] The full list is as follows: South Dakota, 1898; Utah, 1900; Oregon, 1902; Nevada (referendum only), 1905; Montana, 1906; Oklahoma, 1907; Maine, 1908; Missouri, 1908; Arkansas, 1910; Colorado, 1910; Arizona, 1911; New Mexico (referendum only), 1911; California, 1911; Nebraska, 1912; Washington, 1912; Idaho, 1912; Ohio, 1912; Nevada (adds initiative), 1912; Michigan, 1913; North Dakota, 1914; Mississippi, 1914; Maryland (referendum only), 1915; Massachusetts, 1918.

to the conviction that the people themselves could not do much worse and might do a great deal better. It may be taken as axiomatic in a democracy that when things go badly the populace will not hasten to place the blame on its own shoulders. It is the habit of the electorate to take for granted its own infallibility. When the representatives of the people give any just ground for criticism, accordingly, the popular remedy is not the adoption of some measures designed to get better representatives by giving them more responsibility, but rather to take away from the wicked and slothful servant even that which he hath.

Another reason for the spread of direct legislation is to be found in the readiness of the average legislator to subordinate the public interest to his own political ambitions. On many questions which come before legislatures the chief desire of many members is to escape the dilemma of taking one side or the other. The senator or assemblyman whose first care is for his own reëlection finds himself likely to lose some votes in his district no matter which way he votes on these questions. What more natural, therefore, than that he should welcome an easy way out of his personal difficulties by "putting the matter directly up to the people." Hence it is that in many states the legislatures of their own volition and in evasion of their own responsibility have fallen into the practice of referring matters to the people, not because the voters could be trusted to settle them more wisely, but because supine members preferred that means of avoiding duties which they were elected to perform. The people, of course, soon learned to relish the compliment involved in this constant reference of difficult problems to their omniscience for decision. Having found their task both easy and interesting, the voters quite naturally declare themselves ready to perform it on a more comprehensive scale.

*2. the readiness of legislatures to evade their responsibility.*

Direct legislation requires considerable formalities. No states have exactly the same requirements, although there is a similarity in essentials. The mode of initiating a proposed law is everywhere by petition; the method of enacting it (if the legislature does not act in the meantime) is by popular vote. Between the starting of a petition,

*The mechanism of direct legislation.*

however, and the ultimate decision of the people at the polls there is a considerable intervening procedure which will be summarized in the next few paragraphs.

1. the initiative petition.

The first step in the exercise of the popular initiative is the framing of a proposed law or constitutional amendment. This may be done by any one; but it is usually undertaken by some organization. A proposed measure relating to labor, or agriculture, or prohibition, or woman suffrage, for example, is customarily initiated by bodies which represent such interests or movements. Then comes the quest for signatures. From five to ten per cent of the qualified voters is the usual requirement where a law is proposed; a higher percentage (from eight to fifteen or even twenty per cent) is ordinarily required if the proposal is for a constitutional amendment. In some cases, however, the percentage is the same for both. If, accordingly, there are a half million qualified voters in the state, the number of required signatures will be from twenty-five thousand to fifty thousand according to the percentage stipulated. Each state has its own rule on this point, but a substantial number of signatures is everywhere essential, at any rate, a number large enough to show that there is some degree of popular demand for the measure.

2. the submission of proposals at the polls.

When a petition has obtained the requisite number of signatures it is submitted to some designated state official, usually the secretary of state, who checks the names and if he finds them sufficient makes out a certificate to that effect. Occasionally there is provision for the filing of additional signatures in case those on the original petition prove insufficient. Then the measure is placed (usually in abbreviated form or by its title only) upon the ballot at the next regular state election, or at a special election. As many measures may be placed on the ballot as are properly petitioned for, and the legislature may submit its own measures in addition. If two conflicting proposals appear on the ballot and both are approved by the voters, it is usually provided that the one receiving the highest number of affirmative votes shall become effective. Ordinarily a majority of the votes recorded upon the measure is sufficient to pass it; but in a few states it is provided that at least a designated percentage of the total vote shall be cast on the question, otherwise the proposal is not to be regarded as having been accepted by the people.

To inform the voters upon the questions submitted to them publicity pamphlets are in some states prepared and distributed before the polling. In California this pamphlet contains the text of the measures which are to be voted upon, together with the arguments for and against each proposal, these arguments being prepared by persons who are designated for the purpose from among the supporters and opponents respectively by the presiding officer of the senate. A copy of this pamphlet is mailed to every voter in the state. While the expense of this publicity work is considerable and a great many of the pamphlets are thrown away without being read, the plan undoubtedly aids in informing the voters and stimulates interest in the question submitted.[1] *Publicity for these measures.*

When a measure has been adopted by the people at the polls, it cannot ordinarily be amended or repealed by any action of the legislature. No measure referred to the people and adopted by them, moreover, can be vetoed by the governor. If a proposal is rejected by the people, it may usually be brought forward by another petition the next year; but this liberty has been found to result in the too frequent submission of the same question, and a few states have made provision that a rejected measure may not be brought forward for at least three years unless a much larger than the customary number of signatures is secured. *Resubmission of measures.*

Generally speaking, the compulsory referendum follows the same general lines so far as concerns the securing and certifying of signatures. The petition in this case does not propose a new law, but merely asks that some measure passed by the legislature be submitted to the voters before being put into effect. The question is then placed on the ballot; and if a majority of the voters indorse the measure it becomes effective; but if a majority vote adversely, it becomes as invalid as if the legislature had never enacted it. *How the referendum works.*

[1] In California, during the years 1908–1915 when no publicity pamphlets were issued, the average vote upon measures submitted was 43% of the total attendance at the polls; in 1916, with the publicity pamphlet in use, it was 79%. *Bulletin* on *The Initiative and Referendum* (Boston, 1917), p. 37.

**Emergency measures.**

The requirement that a measure passed by the legislature shall not go into force for a certain period (usually ninety days), so that opportunity may be given for filing petitions against it, might become a serious obstacle in case of emergency, as for example, in the event of war, or civil strife, or a financial panic. To meet this eventuality it is usually provided that emergency measures, that is to say "measures immediately necessary for the preservation of the public peace, health, and safety," may be put into force by the legislature at once. To guard against the abuse of this privilege it is required that the existence of an emergency shall be explicitly stated in the preamble of the measure, and that no emergency law shall be passed except by a two-thirds vote of both chambers in the legislature. In spite of these safeguards, however, the emergency privilege is frequently abused.

**Summary.**

In states which have the initiative and referendum, therefore, questions may be placed upon the ballot in any one of three different ways. First, the legislature may of its own accord refer a measure to the voters for their decision. Second, an initiative petition may be presented bearing the requisite number of signatures asking that any proposed measure be placed upon the ballot either without going to the legislature at all or because the legislature has declined to pass it. Third, a law may have passed the legislature but by reason of formal protest embodied in a petition may be withheld from going into force until submitted to the people. By one or other of these ways a considerable batch of questions is every year submitted to the voters of the various states.

**The merits and defects of direct legislation.**

As to the merits and defects of the initiative and referendum there are wide differences of opinion. Although direct legislation in its present form has been used in the United States for only twenty years or thereabouts, it has nevertheless received during this period a trial on a sufficiently broad scale and under sufficiently varied conditions to warrant a fair survey of its achievements and shortcomings. As a result of this experience a substantial body of facts and figures has become available, but close observers hold diverse views as to what these facts and figures really disclose. No question of present-day political discussion, indeed, affords ground for wider, yet thoroughly sincere, divergences of conviction than the question whether direct legislation actually helps or hinders the efficient workings of a representative democracy.

Chief among the reputed merits of the initiative and referendum is the claim that it does not supplant but supplements, improves, and renders more democratic the traditional machinery of representative government. It is argued that the policy of making the laws exclusively through the medium of a legislature has not measured up to reasonable expectations. Conditions which have existed in many American states, and which continue in some of them, afford proof that legislatures are not always inspired by considerations of public interest alone, but are influenced by sectional, partisan, class, and even by private motives to a considerable extent. This is hardly the place to particularize among legislatures, but the pressure of sinister influences upon the course of law-making has been far stronger than the average citizen realizes. Even those who are firmly opposed to the use of the initiative and referendum have frankly admitted this too frequent subordination of the public welfare to the arrogant demands of invisible interests.[1] Laws have been enacted and bills have been defeated year after year in some state legislatures for no other reason than because the railroads, the liquor interests, the banks, the labor leaders, or the political bosses have given the word. In this matter, it is quite true, there has been a considerable difference between state legislatures. Some have been consistently under the thumb of special interests. Others have shown the influence of lobbying to a relatively slight degree. All have been more or less touched by the taint, however, as any legislator of experience can testify.

In view of the arrangements under which state legislators have been chosen and of the handicaps under which they have tried to perform their work it is not at all surprising

*Reputed merits of direct legislation:*

1. prevents the domination of law-making by special interests.

---

[1] See, for example, the speech of the Hon. Elihu Root on "Invisible Government" in the New York Constitutional Convention of 1915, reprinted in his *Political Addresses* (Cambridge, 1916).

that the results have failed to satisfy. The methods of nominating and electing members of the legislature have played largely into the hands of sinister interests. They have tended to befog the voters, to make politics a profession, and to encourage the professional politician; they have made election to the legislature such an expensive process that candidates are tempted to form alliances with those who are able and willing to contribute generously to their campaign funds. The system of nomination by party primaries, the long ballot, the use of party designations on the ballot, and the frequency of elections have all helped to lower the general integrity of legislative bodies. These defects in the system of representative legislation could undoubtedly be eradicated by the process of one reform after another, but reform by steady evolution is a slow method, whereas the initiative and referendum are heralded as providing a means by which all can be set right at once. And public opinion seems to prefer the brand of reform that comes in full doses.

*Why special interests have had an advantage in the past.*

Again, it is argued that the system of direct legislation possesses an educational value. By means of the initiative the political instincts and abilities of the individual are encouraged; men are inspired to formulate political ideas and policies of their own and to press these upon the public attention with a reasonable hope that they may ultimately accomplish something. Under the system of law-making by legislatures alone, we are told, the public welfare suffers not alone from the assaults of the special interests but from public apathy as well. The individual citizen is not encouraged to do his own thinking on public matters; his representative is paid to do it for him. Under the system of direct legislation, on the other hand, the voter is virtually compelled to inform himself upon public questions. He cannot depute that task to any one else. He is showered with publicity pamphlets and other data; he is confronted with discussions in the newspapers; he has the pros and cons of measures thrust before him at every turn until "he cannot chuse but hear." Eternal vigilance on the citizen's part, not merely on the part of his representatives, is the price of liberty. It is of the essence of democracy

*2. affords an incentive to political education.*

that the whole people shall bear their own public responsibilities and shall not deposit them permanently upon the shoulders of a few representatives.

Between what the people want, and what the people get, there is in some American states a considerable gap. The voters have sometimes sought to obtain what they want by changing their representatives, but only to find that candidates from both political parties are amenable to the same underhand influence. To be truly representative of the electorate a government must be readily responsive to public opinion, and to be responsive it must have the machinery of close contact. Where there is no opportunity for legislation by direct methods the legislators sometimes ignore public opinion and sometimes act in wilful disregard of it. The growth of popular interest in public affairs is stunted by the fact that this is so. Men will not produce new ideas or urge the adoption of new ideas unless there is some hope of carrying them to fruition. Political thought and discussion can best be stimulated by giving ideas the opportunity of materializing into constitutions, policies, and laws. In a word, the way to get voters interested in measures is to ask for their opinions on measures, not merely for their opinions on men. The way to educate the voter in matters of government is to submit things to him in person and not merely to some one who happens to be his official spokesman.

3. makes government truly responsive to public opinion.

A legislator represents only the majority of the voters in his district. He does not represent either the wishes or the opinions of the minority. Hence it is that under the system of representative lawmaking a considerable fraction of the voters are not represented at all. True, these voters may also be in the minority when measures are submitted directly; but they will at least feel in such case that they are being given a real voice in the determination of public policy.

4. gives the plain man an interest in his government.

John Stuart Mill once remarked that "the magic of property turns sand into gold." The voter will soon be roused from indifference if he can be shown that the government is his property and belongs to no one else. The initiative and referendum afford regularly an overt demonstration of the right which the people possess in their own public affairs and impose upon them a corresponding responsibility. They bring home to every voter's mind the realization that he is a sovereign in fact as in name. Or, to express it in legal phraseology, the interest of the legislator in government is fiduciary only; that of the people is proprietary. Hence, it is claimed, the system of direct lawmaking will eliminate in large degree that public apathy which has been the ultimate source of many political abuses, by inspiring the serious and public discussion of all important measures.

5. general.   There are other arguments in favor of the initiative and referendum, but they are for the most part auxiliary to the ones just outlined. Representative lawmaking has not been satisfactory in American states, and to a large fraction of the voters experience has demonstrated that without a thorough reconstruction of the whole American political system it cannot be made anything different, for it is in large part due to the principle of checks and balances which has compelled legislatures to undertake the making of laws without leadership or real responsibility. Direct legislation cuts right through this principle, restores to the people their sovereignty in all branches of government, makes their fiat binding on all, whether legislators, governors, or courts, and thus "rolls away the stone from the sepulchre of real democracy." That, at any rate, is what its partisans claim for it.

Reputed defects of direct legislation:
1. breaks down the distinction between constituent and lawmaking authority.

But there is quite as much to be said on the other side. First, it is urged that if the system of direct legislation is applied on the same basis to both constitutions and laws, it breaks down the traditional distinction between these two branches of jurisprudence. For a long time American states have been governed on the theory that constitutions are the embodiment of fundamental principles, that they guarantee the inalienable rights of the citizen (whether he be among the majority or among the minority), and that they should not be changed at every rash expression of popular caprice. Laws, on the other hand, have been regarded as possessing no such fundamental character, and hence have not been placed beyond the reach of easy change. The initiative and referendum arrangements now in vogue in such states as

Oregon and California sweep away this distinction. Constitutions and laws can be changed by the people in precisely the same way; the provisions of the one are no more fundamental than those of the other. Minorities have no rights as against the wishes of the majority as expressed on the ballot.

That doctrine upsets a recognized presupposition of all free government, namely, that certain rights such as freedom of religious belief, equality before the law, and security in person and property, are the impregnable rights of the whole people and are not within the power of a mere majority to alter or deny. "Government by majority," as one writer puts it, " is merely a convenient means of conducting public affairs, where and in so far as there is a basis of general agreement deeper and more persistent than the variations of public opinion; but as soon as a really fundamental point is touched, as soon as a primary instinct, whether of self-preservation or of justice, begins to be seriously and continuously outraged, the democratic convention [*i.e.* basis of government] gives way. No minority, for example, even in a compact modern state, either would or ought to submit to a decision of the majority to prohibit the exercise of their religion." [1]

*Importance of this objection.*

There has been much loose talk on the subject of "government by public opinion." It has been assumed in some quarters that government by the selfish desires of a bare majority is entitled to that appellation. Yet desires and opinions are two quite different things, nor is the general sentiment of any community always ascertainable by merely counting heads.[2] The intrinsic character of the issues, the actuating motives, the intensity of the contending beliefs, all count for something; or should do so, in measuring public opinion. If fifty-one per cent of the voters, for example, made up entirely of those who own no property, should adopt a constitutional amendment confiscating without compensation all the property of the other forty-nine per

*What public opinion is.*

---

[1] G. Lowes Dickinson, *The Development of Parliament during the Nineteenth Century*, pp. 161-162.

[2] For a full discussion of this topic see President Lowell's *Public Opinion and Popular Government* (N. Y., 1913), especially chs. i–iii.

cent, would that be an act of government by public opinion or of government by organized selfishness? Would such action be consistent with the usual conception of democracy as a system of government for the people, by the people, and of the people? Or would it not be necessary to redefine democracy as a scheme of government under which "they may take who have the power, and they may keep who can"? "It cannot be too often repeated," as President Hadley has said, "that those opinions which a man is prepared to maintain at another's cost, but not at his own, count for little in forming the general sentiment of a community, or in producing any effective public movement."[1]

2. tends to break down the quality of legislatures.

The system of direct legislation, according to its opponents, is incompatible with the representative type of government; its adoption will not supplement but must eventually supplant representative law-making; it will deprive legislators of power and responsibility, and thus make the position of representative even less attractive to men of adequate quality and character than it is at present. This is an objection which cannot be lightly brushed aside, for the institutional history of all democratic countries lends it support. Indeed, if there is any principle which American political experience seems to substantiate it is the doctrine that a sure way to deteriorate the membership of any representative body is to reduce its powers and its responsibility. When the choice of inferior representatives does not bring any serious penalty upon the voters in the way of bad laws, high taxes, and general inefficiency, it has become a truism that inferior men will be chosen.

It is always easy to choose inferior men, for they are the ones who put themselves forward. They are ready to neglect their own personal affairs, ready to promise much, ready to do favors. Men of the right type have to be drawn into political life at personal sacrifice, and they cannot be induced to make this sacrifice in order to accept public posts which do not offer real opportunities of service. Hence it has been found that when the authority of any representative body is reduced to the point where it can do little harm (and by

[1] *The Education of the American Citizen* (New Haven, 1910), p. 27.

the same token, little good) the quality of its membership trends downward. The history of city councils in the United States during several decades gave an interesting exemplification of this. If the resort to direct legislation on any large scale would not result in filling the legislatures with poorer representatives of the people, then the political annals of America have been teaching a false lesson. The gains through direct legislation may more than offset this loss, it is true, but to maintain that state legislatures will continue under the new arrangements to turn out work of as good or even better quality is to disregard practical experience for pure empiricism.

Attention is frequently called to the great gulf which lies between what the system of direct legislation purports to do and what it actually does. It purports to obtain a popular verdict on measures, to establish lawmaking by a majority of the electorate. In actual practice, however, measures are usually adopted or rejected by a decided minority of the voters. Not more than 80 per cent of the voters appear at the polls in regular elections, as a rule, and of these only from 70 per cent to 85 per cent vote on any particular question, the remainder confining their attention to the candidates. Thus it is that no more than 60 per cent of the registered voters usually pass upon any proposed measure, and a majority of these, in other words 31 per cent of the whole electorate, is sufficient for a decision. Constitutions are changed and laws enacted more often by one-quarter or one-third of the whole electorate than by a larger percentage. So that the "rule of the majority" becomes in fact the rule of a majority among those who are sufficiently interested in a matter to come to the polls and record their verdict upon it.  <small>3. while professing to give government by majority it establishes in fact a system of minority rule.</small>

Who are the ones thus sufficiently interested? Who circulate and sign the initiative petitions for the various questions which go upon the ballot? Are they drawn from the general rank and file of the voters, or are they mainly those who have some strong personal interest at stake? These queries are of importance, for if the twenty, thirty, or forty per cent of the voters who form a sufficient majority to carry a measure are a fair sample of the whole body of the  <small>4. promotes the power of organized self-interest.</small>

voters, their action may still be reasonably regarded as reflecting the general will. But in most cases they are not a fair sample. The ease or difficulty with which signatures to an initiative petition can be gathered depends in large degree upon what the petition asks for. If it is a matter affecting the interests of labor the requisite names are not hard to obtain. Passing the lists around at meetings of labor organizations will accomplish the work. Commercial organizations, churches, granges, and agricultural associations all have the same facility in any matter which affects their particular interests. A movement that has the support of wealth can pay canvassers to get signatures. But where measures are desired in the interest of the ordinary citizen who has no particular organization looking out for him, the work of getting questions on the ballot by means of several thousand signatures is not likely to be undertaken at all. Legislation for the ordinary citizen, under the initiative and referendum, is nobody's business.

So it is also at the polls. The elements among the voters to whom a question appeals as a matter of personal or class interest will go to the polls and vote upon it. Those who stay away from the polls are for the most part the ones whose personal interests are not affected. The rule of the majority gives way, accordingly, to legislation by a minority which embodies the strength of organized self-interest.

5. does not promote independence of thought or effort.

It is taken for granted by its supporters that the system of direct legislation will transfer to the unorganized and independent elements among the people those advantages which have hitherto been monopolized by the great political parties or by the vested economic interests. American political history does not afford any ground for such assumption. Measures without organized support have the same chance of winning at the polls as candidates similarly situated; and it has been all-too-often demonstrated that the customary place of the independent candidate with unorganized support is at the bottom of the list when the votes are counted. Is it reasonable to hope that by virtue of any mere change in the mechanism of legislation an unorganized majority of the people, actuated by unselfish motives, can regularly triumph at the polls over a well organized minority, backed by ample funds and spurred on by all the zeal that self-interest can supply?

The experience in various American states with the machinery of direct legislation during the last dozen years answers that question. The power in law-making has not been taken from the organized part of the electorate but merely transferred from one set of organizations to another. For guidance upon the merits of the questions upon his ballot, as well as upon the claims of candidates, the voter still turns to his political party, to his business associates in a chamber of commerce, to his labor union, or to whatever other organization he may be affiliated with. These bodies officially indorse some measures and oppose others. The chances of a measure's success depend, to a large extent, upon the number and strength of the organizations supporting it. The real voting is done, not by the voters who have taken the time to study each one of many questions and to form unbiased opinions thereon, but by leaders and counsellors whose advice on such matters the voters in large groups are habituated to follow. Direct legislation does not, in practice, reduce the premium which is placed on organization under the strictly representative system of government.

The referendum is at best a call for the yeas and nays, not for a full expression of opinion. It assumes that every voter is ready and able to give an unqualified yes or no to any question of public policy. The truth is, however, that the man who is prepared to give categorical answers is usually the one who gives no thought to the questions. The process of law-making by legislatures affords opportunity for compromises, for conciliating opposition by concessions which do not affect the groundwork of measures, and for reaching agreements by the procedure of give and take. The initiative and referendum have no such flexibility of operation. Every voter must be wholly for or wholly against a measure. His vocabulary of opinion is limited to two words. That fact precludes all need of study on his part. It makes easy the policy of following some leader's counsel or some organization's advice.

6. is limited by its categorical nature.

In balancing these various arguments for and against direct legislation much depends upon an individual's own

**The balance of advantage.**

temperament and point of view. Some men are politically impatient, disdainful of traditions, oblivious to the lessons of history, and intolerant of the scientific attitude in public affairs. Others are conservative in habits of mind, their eyes so firmly fixed on the past that they fail either to interpret the present or to discern its portents for the future, wedded to obsolete tenets of individualism, and obtaining their political nourishment from a diet of musty formulas. Between these two extremes, prefigured by the radical and the reactionary, there is every type of mind. The facts as to the working of the initiative and referendum in America, while themselves incontrovertible, are thus subjected to a wide variety of interpretation. There are no impartial authorities on this subject, for the only ones who remain impartial are those who know too little about it to be authorities.

**The recall.**

The recall is not a necessary accompaniment of the initiative and referendum, but in many cases all three have been adopted simultaneously, and in discussions of popular government they are commonly linked together. The recall may be defined as a process by which any elective officer, whose services are unsatisfactory to those who have elected him, may be removed from office by them before the expiration of his term. In principle this is not a novelty in American political history, being at least as old as 1780, for in that year the constitution of Massachusetts made provision that delegates to the Congress at Philadelphia might be "recalled at any time . . . and others chosen . . . in their stead."[1] This provision was evidently copied from the Articles of Confederation, which expressly reserved to each state the power to "recall its delegates, or any of them, at any time. . . ." In the constitution of the United States, however, no provision for the recall of senators or representatives was incorporated, although there was some protest against this omission. The idea of choosing officers for short, but definite terms, without the opportunity of removing them otherwise than by impeachment, gained general acceptance after 1787 in all branches

**Early provisions for it in American history.**

---

[1] *Constitution of Massachusetts*, ch. iv. The provision still stands unrepealed and unaltered, although it is, of course, inoperative.

of American government and continued throughout the nineteenth century.

The recrudescence of the recall, this time in a somewhat different form, has been a feature of American politics during the past twenty years. Its adoption was proposed in the closing years of the nineteenth century, but it was not until 1903 that any such adoption took place. In that year the city of Los Angeles made provision in its charter for the use of the recall in its municipal government. Five years later the state of Oregon made provision for its application to all state officers, and since 1908 the recall has spread to nine other states of the Union.[1] *Its revival in a different form.*

The purposes of the recall are twofold. First, it is designed to give the people a means of removing from public office any elective official who may have proved unworthy of their continued confidence. For gross malfeasance an official may always be removed by impeachment; but impeachment is a clumsy and slow method. Impeachment cannot well be employed, moreover, except in flagrant cases. The recall may be used for any cause whatsoever, and it is an expeditious method of removal. Second, the existence of the people's right to recall a public officer at any time is said to operate as a wholesome reminder of preëlection promises and thus to keep every official alert to the proper performance of his duties. *Objects of the recall.*

The initial procedure in recalling any official is the filing of a petition. Any voter may do this. This petition assigns reasons for the requested removal, but the reasons need not be very definite. Petitions must bear a designated number of signatures, each representing a qualified voter, but the number of signatures differs from state to state. Ordinarily the requirement is at least 25 per cent of the registered voters or of the vote cast at the last preceding *The recall procedure: 1. the petition.*

---

[1] The other nine states are California, Arizona, Idaho, Colorado, Nevada, Washington, Michigan, Kansas, and Louisiana. In Idaho, however, the provision remains inoperative because the legislature has not passed the necessary laws to put the constitutional provision into effect. The best brief treatise on the recall of elective officers is that contained in *Bulletin No. 26*, prepared for the Massachusetts Constitutional Convention (Boston, 1917). This Bulletin contains a selected bibliography.

election. Some designated state officer counts the signatures and compares them with the names on the voters' rolls. Realizing, however, that an official should not be subjected to the possibility of recall before he has had time to show what he can do, it is usually stipulated that no recall petition shall be received until at least six months after his installation in office. In the case of members of the legislature, this period of immunity is not customarily accorded, for that would enable them to finish a legislative session before being subject to removal.

*2. the official's reply.*  When a recall petition is presented, the official against whom it is directed must at once be notified. He has a right to make a reply, and this reply is in some cases required to be printed on the ballot when the question of his removal goes before the people. He may, on the other hand, resign his office without choosing to fight the issue at the polls.

*3. the recall election.*  Within a designated time after a petition has been filed, a recall election is held. The interval is usually from one to three months. The ballot at this election may contain a statement of the grounds alleged for the removal, and also the official's reply thereto. It is usually provided, however, that neither of these statements shall contain more than two hundred words. The ballot also indicates the name of the official whose removal is sought and the names of such candidates as may have been nominated in opposition to him. In some states, Oregon for example, an official is deemed to be recalled if he fails to obtain a plurality of votes over these opposing candidates. In other states, as in California, the question of recalling the officer, yes or no, is put first on the ballot, and it is only when a majority of the voters answer this question in the affirmative that the counting of the votes cast for the various candidates is proceeded with. When an official successfully defends himself against an attempt to bring about his recall, it is sometimes provided that he shall be reimbursed from the public treasury for his necessary expenses in connection with the recall election.

*No state officials yet recalled.*  Although the state-wide recall has been in existence for ten years, no state official has yet been removed by this procedure. It is a fair inference from this fact that there are practical obstacles to its frequent use and that the recall will not, in all likelihood, be employed as an everyday means of getting men ousted from office.

A good deal has been said and written as to the reputed merits and dangers of the recall, as applied to state government, but these discussions rest upon no solid ground of actual experiments. The recall has obvious possibilities for good if rightly used, and equally obvious possibilities for harm if employed vindictively. But so long as it remains unused altogether we have no way of knowing which of these possibilities is apt to be realized.

*Merits and dangers of the recall.*

## CHAPTER XXXVI

### THE RECONSTRUCTION OF STATE GOVERNMENT

*State government has been less satisfactory than is commonly realized.*

SURVEYING American state government as a whole, what are its most obvious defects and by what steps may they be remedied? There is a widespread but not at all well-founded impression that state government in the United States has been tolerably satisfactory. One reason for this, no doubt, may be found in the fact that municipal government was for many decades a far more conspicuous failure and hence engrossed the attention of reformers. The weakness of state government, moreover, has been to some extent screened and retrieved by the relative excellence of the federal system. By the steady expansion of its authority the national government has taken over and has administered with comparative efficiency many functions which, had they been left to the states, would undoubtedly have been handled so unskilfully as to bring theptitudes of state government into a far bolder relief.

*Reasons for this situation.*

The shortcomings of state government are due in part to faulty organization. This is not to imply, however, that the thirteen original states framed their constitutions unwisely. They began with a frame of government which was not unsuited to the needs of pioneer communities in the closing decades of the eighteenth century. The chief and almost the only function of a state government in those days was to make laws. The original states adopted a mechanism which was well suited to the performance of that function. But the making of laws has long since ceased to be the chief work of the state. Administration in all its branches, particularly in its application to social, economic, and humanitarian activities, has grown to huge proportions and now quite overshadows all else.

Yet the states continue to attempt the proper performance of the new tasks with the old machinery. They are trying to carry forward huge administrative and business enterprises with appliances which were designed for the making of laws and for the general safeguarding of popular liberties. It is the ancient fault of putting new wine into old bottles. The traditional mechanism has been patched up, added to, and otherwise tinkered with, so that it has not entirely broken down under the new load; but in no state has it been entirely overhauled and reconstructed.

*State functions have outgrown the old machinery.*

The tinkering process has been carried on mainly by means of constitutional revision and amendment. Compared with the organic instrument of the nation the state constitutions are easy to change. In some states, indeed, the process of altering the constitution has become so simple that the temptation to incessant alteration is very strong, too strong to be resisted. The state constitution in such cases becomes an ephemeral affair, without any essentially fundamental character, and without the halo which should surround a supreme law.

*The essentials of a satisfactory reconstruction:*
*1. fewer constitutional provisions especially in the way of limitations.*

Back in the middle of the nineteenth century a customer once asked a Paris bookseller for a copy of the French Constitution. "We do not deal in periodical literature," the bookseller replied. American state constitutions have gone into this periodical class. Details of governmental organization, even to the salaries of officials, clutter up their pages. Limitations of every conceivable sort are crowded into these documents until the legislature, the governor, the administrative departments, and even the courts find themselves without sufficient elbow room for the satisfactory performance of their respective duties. The demand for changes in this or that detail is incessant. The reconstruction of state government must begin, accordingly, with the state constitution itself.

Constitution-makers should return to an appreciation of the true purpose and the proper scope of a constitution, which is to set forth the basic principles of government, not to provide a code of laws. There is no need for the relentless piling on of limitations. Neither the liberty of the individual nor the welfare of the community demands it. The limi-

*The need of a return to first principles in constitution-making.*

tations which stand in the federal constitution are relatively few, yet who will say that the rights of the citizen are not fully guarded there? Who will assert that the states, with their constitutions a hundred pages long, have more effectively precluded the abuse of legislative, executive, or judicial power?

*2. less reverence for the formula of division of powers.*

The time has come, moreover, for a resurvey of the doctrine of checks and balances in its practical workings. During the second half of the nineteenth century it was accounted a political heresy to question the infallibility of this dogma. It was hailed as the very corner-stone of American democracy. To get rid of it seemed an impossibility. As well might one move to repeal the law of gravitation. To-day, however, this attitude is visibly changing. Montesquieu's aphorism that "power must be a check to power" has been repudiated entirely in the reconstructed charters of several hundred American cities, and is now being rudely assailed as an obstacle to the efficient government in some of the states as well. Not alone political philosophers but men of long experience in the actual work of state administration have in some cases concluded, on due reflection, that the triple division of governmental powers is a delusion and a snare.

*Merits and defects of this formula in its practical application.*

A government organized upon the principle of checks and balances derives both strength and weakness therefrom. Division of powers makes for safety. It provides the ship of state with water-tight compartments. When one compartment floods, the others hold firm, keeping the craft afloat and on its course. So long as the balance of powers is preserved, no one branch of government can arrogate to itself any dangerous excess of authority. But on the other hand, the system of tripartite supremacy means that there can be no full concentration of responsibility for what is done, that the public interest is likely to suffer whenever the three departments fail to work in harmony, and that the community as a whole can have no effective public leadership.

Is it well that these three great essentials of good government, responsibility, harmony, and leadership, should be sacrificed for the assurance of safety? In the case of the federal government that question might well be answered affirmatively, for its establishment represented a novel and precarious experiment. The states were asked to give over great powers and they were wise in taking no chance that a despotic exercise of this vast authority should some day dissipate all that the Revolution had won. The land had not shaken off an hereditary despotism in order that it might establish an elective one in its stead. Safety first was therefore an appropriate rule in the planning of the national government. But whether it ought to be given anything like so much weight to-day is quite another question.

There is no likelihood, however, that any successful assault can be made upon the principle of checks and balances so far as the federal government is concerned. That would involve the entire rewriting of the national constitution, which is something that the present generation will probably never live to see. It is a good deal easier to pick flaws in the constitution of the United States than it is to get even a small body of men to agree upon a substitute.

But in the case of the state governments the situation is in all respects different. The great advantage of divided governmental powers, which is that it provides an assurance against despotism, counts for far less in the states than in the nation. The national constitution guarantees to every state "a republican form of government," which means that the whole strength of the Union is available to protect the people of each state from any gross infringement of their liberties. So long as a system of free government is maintained in the nation as a whole, the danger of despotism in any state is purely fanciful. The chief argument in favor of division of powers in state government thus falls to the ground. *In state government the merits disappear.*

On the other hand the disadvantages of the divided system are far greater in state than in national government. Administration bulks relatively larger among state functions and includes matters of a far greater variety. The party system, moreover, which has served to provide an extra-legal coördinating force in national affairs has not succeeded in doing so to the same degree at the state capitals. Finally, *And the defects are magnified.*

the states have pressed the principle of checks and balances to an extreme length, establishing a division of powers not only as between the legislative, executive and judicial organs of government but even within the executive branch itself. In the national system the President remains the supreme administrative authority, sharing his powers with no one else. But the state governor, as has been shown, occupies no such position. Administrative authority in most of the states is so hopelessly disintegrated that it may fairly be said to portray a system of checks and balances run riot.

*The logical conclusion.* It would appear, therefore, that division of powers is not needed by the states in the interest of safety, that it is the mainspring of clouded responsibility and the absence of vigorous leadership in state government, that it has been blindly carried to an extreme in the decentralizing of executive power, and that it should give place to some plan of concentrated authority.

*But if the division of powers be abandoned, what then? The two alternatives:* But by what type of organization might the present system be replaced? Two courses are open. The legislative branch of state government might be restored to a position of supremacy and given full control of the executive, or the powers of the executive can be concentrated and increased until the legislature becomes a wholly secondary organ. On the face of it the former alternative would seem to be not only more in harmony with American traditions and temperament, but in keeping with the practice of responsible government in other countries. Nevertheless the development of American state government during the past thirty or forty years has been altogether in the other direction. The legislatures have been sinking to a secondary place in the control of public policy. Constitutional conventions have been steadily circumscribing their sphere of influence *(a) legislative supremacy.* while the progress of the executive branch to greater prestige and power has gone forward unchecked. Notwithstanding its disintegration the executive branch of state government is nearly everywhere the more vigorous, the more influential and the more secure in public confidence to-day. It is altogether unlikely that this movement can be halted and a march begun in the opposite direction. Whatever the logic of the situation one must face the obvious fact that a distrust in the capacity and in the integrity of legislatures is one of the most deep-seated of American political convictions. Being founded upon abundant reason, moreover, this conviction is not likely to pass away. No scheme of reconstruction, therefore, is likely to gain much popular support if it is postulated upon that principle of legislative supremacy which is frankly accorded recognition in most other countries. *Hardly a practical plan at present.*

The other alternative, that of elevating the executive branch of state government to a place where it will be in law as in fact the dominant arm, would in the end produce an anachronism of political science. Yet the general use of direct legislation, the adoption of executive budget systems, the extension of the governor's veto power, and the consolidation of boards and commissions, are all manifestations of waning confidence in legislatures and waxing trust in the executive. It is in recognition of this fact that various schemes for the reduction of the legislature to a single chamber and for making that chamber a mere legislative commission have been materializing in recent years. *(b) executive supremacy. The drift is in that direction.*

The most radical of these proposals is that made by the governor of Kansas in 1913. He suggested that the executive organization of the state be left without any change, but that the double-chambered legislature be abolished. In its place it was proposed to establish an elective commission made up of sixteen members, two from each of the eight congressional districts of the state with terms of four or six years, the governor to be an *ex officio* member of this body and to preside at its sessions. The function assigned to the commission was to be that of lawmaking only, and it was argued that the proper performance of this task would take up the entire time of its members every working day in the year. Accordingly the commissioners were to be amply paid. *Some concrete proposals: (a) the Kansas plan.*

This Kansas plan found its inspiration, of course, in the commission form of government which many cities have adopted with highly advantageous results during the past dozen years. But it goes only half the distance covered by the latter in that it leaves the executive branch of state government wholly outside the commission's sphere of *A halfway and illogical proposal.*

authority. Commission government as applied to cities involves not only the reconstruction of the municipal legislature but the complete telescoping of both legislative and executive organs into a single authority. The Kansas plan, being a halfway measure, did not command the general favor of reformers, and needless to say it was not cordially received by the legislature which the scheme proposed to abolish. It is significant, however, that any such suggestion should be seriously put forward by a man of experience in high state office. Twenty years ago a project of this sort would have been ridiculed as preposterous and irrational.

*(b) the Oregon plan.*

Rather less radical in the way of legislative reconstruction is the plan which was brought forward by the People's Power League in Oregon some years ago, but the essentials of which were defeated by the people at the polls. The most conspicuous feature of the Oregon plan was the proposal to abolish the two-house legislature in favor of a single chamber made up of sixty members, with provision for minority representation. In connection with this abolition of the bicameral system it was proposed to increase greatly the strength and influence of the executive. The governor was to be intrusted with the appointment of all heads of departments, other high officials and boards. He and his cabinet (made up of the chief state officials) were to have seats in the one-house legislature. He was to have the sole power to initiate all measures for the spending of money but no longer to have the right of veto in any matter. The Oregon plan, accordingly, while less radical than the Kansas proposal so far as legislative reconstruction is concerned, provided for a much more drastic change in the position and powers of the executive. As a whole it was never submitted to the people for their approval, but various parts of it, including the proposal for a single chamber, were placed upon the ballot and defeated.

*Public opinion not yet ready for a radical overhauling of state framework.*

In none of the states does public opinion seem to be ready for any drastic alteration in the organization of the legislature or for any great and sudden curtailment of its powers, although minor changes in both directions are being made year by year. The real initiative in legislation is gradually passing into executive hands, chiefly because the people are looking more and more to the governor for aggressive leadership in the formulation and carrying through of public policy. Governors on the whole have been less susceptible than legislatures to the control of political bosses and more ready to assume full responsibility. They have more promptly sensed the drift of popular sentiment and have been more responsive to it.

Without any organic changes there are ways in which the work of legislatures may be improved and their prestige with the people restored. One agency of improvement, as several states have discovered, is a bureau of legislative reference with facilities for giving expert assistance in the drafting of laws. Legislatures are judged by the products which they turn out, and these have hitherto left much to be desired. The proper drafting of a law is not merely a matter of clearness in phraseology. It involves a thorough knowledge of the conditions to which the law is to apply; in many cases it also necessitates a careful study of laws already enacted in the same field so that there may be no unintentional conflict; and always it demands a full appreciation of whatever constitutional restrictions there may be. In the drafting of a law it is almost always possible to obtain profitable guidance from the experience of other states both as to what should be provided and what left out. The work is technical to a far greater degree than legislators have realized, and it ought to be intrusted to professional hands. The legislative reference and bill-drafting bureau is therefore an institution which should be provided for in all the states, not merely in some of them. *How legislation may be improved without reconstructing legislatures.*

More essential to good government than any readjustment of the relations between governor and legislature, however, is the reorganization of the machinery by which the vast and varied administrative work of the state is now carried on. This machinery, as has been shown, is extensive and intricate, consisting of departments, boards and officials by the score. It has been built up without plan or set purpose. In scarcely a state of the Union does the scheme of administrative organization conform to the simplest requirements of unity and coöperation. It embraces merely a heterogeneous group of disjointed authorities, with the lines of responsi- *3. the consolidation of administrative agencies.*

bility running in all directions, with powers which are ill defined and functions which overlie, and with no means of working in unison. The situation in New York State is perhaps worse in degree but not widely different in nature from that which exists elsewhere. There, as a distinguished student of statecraft remarked a few years ago, "anybody can see one hundred and fifty-two outlying administrative agencies, big and little, lying around loose, accountable to nobody, spending all the money they can get, and violating every principle of economy, of efficiency, and of the proper transaction of business."[1]

**Proposals and progress in this direction during recent years.**
The simplification of state administrative machinery has been earnestly urged by governors in all parts of the country during the last few years. Their annual messages have had more to say on this than on any other topic except the War and its problems. Legislatures have been responsive to the extent of having the question studied by special commissions or committees, but there the matter has usually ended. One reason for this is to be found in the fact that projects of administrative reform usually require changes in the state constitution. These constitutions have grown to be so all-embracing that they have literally stereotyped the number, the method of selection, the tenure, the powers, and sometimes even the salaries of the various boards and officials. In such cases the governor and the legislature, even when they agree, are powerless to do any considerable overhauling.

**The obstacles which have been encountered:**

**(a) constitutional barriers.**

**(b) opposition of state officials.**
But even where constitutional obstacles do not stand in the way the legislatures have been slow to act. Opposition to any radical consolidation of the existing administrative departments comes chiefly from the officials of these departments themselves, a considerable proportion of whom are or have been prominent party leaders. Their influence with the legislature, when they oppose reform unitedly, is very great, and in most of the states it has proved to be the chief practical hindrance to administrative reconstruction. The wholesale consolidation of departments and boards has been proposed in a score of states, but in only one or two of them

---

[1] Speech of the Hon. Elihu Root in the New York Constitutional Convention of 1915.

has it been accomplished. Illinois and New Jersey are the states where the progress towards the simplification and the general improvement of the administrative mechanism has been most conspicuous. Other states, however, are certain to follow in their wake, for the situation is plainly in need of reform.

The reconstruction of state government must not, however, confine itself to official machinery alone. The party system, whether legally so recognized or not, is a factor of high importance in the actual workings of state government and should not be left outside the reckonings of reform. Much criticism has been bestowed upon the system of party organization, but not all of it has been deserved. Some reformers complain that the party organizations are dominated by bosses who pay no attention to the demands of public opinion; others make it their grievance that party leaders truckle to every popular whim and are too spineless to stand up for their own conceptions of sound public policy. Both these complaints can scarcely be well founded.

<small>4. less hostility to the party system.</small>

The chief shortcomings of party organization, as a matter of fact, do not arise from the perverseness of leaders, whether despots or demagogues, but from the fact that the laws of the land have been inclined either to ignore the existence and influence of parties altogether or else to treat party organizations in a wholly suspicious or hostile spirit. Lawmakers have not appreciated the fact that parties must exist in a democracy and that the only choice is between compelling them to be helpful and permitting them to develop abuses. No phase of American state government has had so little earnest study as the party system. The tendency has been to look upon party politics as the soiled dove among public activities, something to be spoken of only in terms of apology or denunciation. "It is much easier," as President Lowell has pointed out, "to bring a railing accusation against men or institutions than to ascertain how far they are a natural product of the conditions in which they exist. To the scientific mind every phenomenon is a fact that has a cause, and it is wise to seek that cause when attempting to change the fact. The need of scientific

<small>Party organizations have not been fairly treated or properly understood.</small>

investigation is as great in the case of parties as of any other phenomenon in politics."[1]

*Some results of this unfriendly attitude.*

One great result of this failure to appreciate the real function and the potential usefulness of parties is the practically complete failure of the various attempts which have been made to impair their influence. Twenty or thirty years ago the Australian ballot was welcomed as a device which would shatter the grip of the party organization upon the voter and restore him to a position of independence. But this ballot has not broken down the strength of party organizations in any appreciable degree. Somewhat later, the direct primary took its turn in public favor as the instrument which would really break the chains of partisan bondage. This new method of nominating public officers has demonstrated some features of superiority over the old caucus or convention system; but it has signally failed to attain its main objective. It has increased the number of pollings and by so doing has helped to fatigue the electorate to a point where public interest is more deficient than it was before. The party leaders control the nominations as securely as ever, the only difference being that they can now disclaim all responsibility for the outcome.

*Party organizations should be encouraged, not ignored or repressed.*

The time has come, therefore, to make a truce with partyism, to take it into camp as an ally, not an enemy, of responsible government, to recognize, legalize, and sympathetically regulate it. In the reconstruction of state government the aim, so far as party functions are concerned, should not be to destroy but to fulfil. Constitutions and laws should lend their assistance to the upbuilding of strong political parties with regularized organizations. These organizations should be recognized as integral factors in actual government and dealt with accordingly. They should be given such measure of friendly consideration with respect to their proper and necessary functions as is accorded the courts. Constitutions and laws should be no more ruthlessly hostile to the one than to the other. They should recognize that parties need leaders and ought to be provided with a rightful way of choosing them. These posts of leadership should be dignified in keeping with the real power which

[1] *Public Opinion and Popular Government* (N. Y., 1913), p. 101.

they represent, and no longer treated as representing a species of political usurpation. It is time to recognize, moreover, that party organizations need money, and that they should be provided with convenient and lawful means of obtaining it. The need, in a word, is for less repression and more encouragement. One obvious way to keep party organizations from going wrong is to make it more easy for them to go right.

Another field of state government in which a considerable reorganization has become essential is that of finance. If the states are to keep taking on new functions and particularly if they embark upon comprehensive programmes of social insurance, as they are altogether likely to do, they must have far more money to spend. This means that new and lucrative sources of revenue must be sought and found. Between the levies of the national government on the one hand and those of the municipalities on the other, the field of taxation which the states may readily exploit is not a wide one, hence the task of finding new sources of revenue which can be utilized without economic or social injustice is one of the most difficult that confronts the states to-day. It is here more than in any other field of reconstruction that there is need for the highest grade of expert leadership. Following the dictates of class prejudice, or seizing in haphazard fashion upon any source of revenue which looks attractive at the moment, are not the right steps to a sound and permanent financial policy. When legislators pass from the domain of politics to that of economics, there is an especial reason for moving circumspectly; yet opportunism and favoritism rather than careful planning or expert counsel have too often been the determining factors in the discovery of new state revenues.

*5. integration of financial policy.*

Finally, no programme of reconstruction will assure improvement in the quality of state government if it begins and ends in changes of mechanism alone. There can be no considerable regeneration if the fundamental factor in all democratic government, the voter himself, is left out of the reckoning. The patent medicines of politics, including the initiative and referendum, the recall, direct primaries, short ballots, proportional representation, civil service, administrative

*6. the better enlightenment of the electorate.*

consolidations, segregated budgets, woman suffrage — and all the rest — may be useful so far as they go; but no one of them or all of them put together will ever make a real democracy out of an ignorant, indifferent, or unthinking electorate. So long as the masses of the voters remain befogged as to the real issues at stake, so long as the mechanism of the state remains unintelligible to them, just so long will they be altogether likely to have "unpopular" government, which has been well defined as "a government of the few, by the few, and for the few, at the expense and against the wish of the many." [1]

*The mere reconstruction of machinery will not avail.*

The maintenance of oligarchic government does not involve the open and avowed placing of power in the hands of a class. Power, when avowedly vested in the masses, may stealthily gravitate into a few hands, indeed its inveterate tendency is to do so unless the utmost vigilance is exercised. The inclination of all government is towards tyranny, whether it be tyranny of one, or of the few, or of a majority. That is a law of political science and human nature. A clear appreciation of that axiom was the greatest asset the framers of the federal constitution possessed. According to their lights they set up various barriers to what they regarded as an inevitable tendency, and these safeguards have helped greatly, even if they have not proved altogether adequate. No purely mechanical devices, however, will fully avail to prevent the perversion of democracy into oligarchy on the one hand or mobocracy on the other. Such assurance can be provided only by the political education of the voters. This work has been the last and least among the functions of the state; it ought to be the first and most important.

The greatest merit of democratic government is not its efficiency or its cheapness, but its possibilities in the way of contenting, unifying, and educating the people. When such a government fails to utilize these possibilities, it cuts away the chief justification of its existence.

[1] Albert M. Kales, *Unpopular Government in the United States* (Chicago, 1914), p. 7.

# CHAPTER XXXVII

### THE HISTORY OF LOCAL GOVERNMENT

"MUNICIPAL institutions," says De Tocqueville, "constitute the strength of free nations." History has demonstrated the truth of this assertion. It was in the areas of local government that representative institutions first developed. Local democracy arose in the English township, borough, and shire long before the government of the nation became free even in form. It was in these local areas that men first became familiar with the principles of civil liberty, and it was there that they obtained their first lessons in free government as a practical art. *The genesis of local self-government.*

When Englishmen first came to America, their own local institutions had been in existence for at least seven centuries and had thus become an integral part of the national life. The spirit of these institutions, and to a large extent the form as well, they brought with them. The environment of the new land differed much, however, from that of the old, hence there was need of adapting the ancient township and county institutions to the demands of frontier communities. This the colonial ancestors of America did, the alterations being rather considerable in some parts of the country but much less extensive in others. Three types of local government were soon evolved, all of them derivations from the ancient institutions of England.[1] *The English parentage of American local institutions.*

In the New England colonies the town was the unit of local government upon which, for reasons of practical expediency, the main emphasis was laid, although counties

---

[1] For a full survey of this development see John A. Fairlie, *Local Government in Cities, Towns and Villages* (New York, 1906), chs. i, ii; and G. E. Howard, *Local Constitutional History of the United States* (N. Y., 1889).

were also organized on the English model. Some historians have endeavored to see in this accenting of town organization a renaissance of the old Teutonic *landesgemeinde* or community of freemen. But there was no conscious imitation of any mediæval practice. The settlers who came to the New England colonies gravitated into compact communities. They did this because their farms were relatively small, because the dangers from hostile Indians could be better avoided in that way, and because the untamed wilderness was at best a lonesome place in the long winters when there was very little work to do. Having congregated their dwellings together it was quite natural that the democratic spirit of Puritanism, which permeated the political as well as the religious belief of these colonists, should assert itself and find ready expression in a form of town government in which all freemen might share.

The government of the New England town was vested, therefore, in a town meeting, which at the outset consisted of all the adult male inhabitants. This meeting, which was held several times a year, elected its own moderator or presiding officer, levied the local taxes, provided for all expenditures, passed whatever by-laws were needed, made provision for roads and bridges, for schools, and for the care of the poor. The town was the local unit for the organization of the colonial militia and also for election of representatives in the colonial assembly. Its organization and functions were thus not unlike those of the open vestry or parish meeting in England.[1]

In the earliest colonial days the town meeting was called at frequent intervals, but as the communities grew in size this was found to be inconvenient. Consequently the townsmen adopted the plan of appointing, at the annual town meeting, a board of selectmen or executive committee whose function it was to carry out the decisions of the town meeting in the intervals between sessions. The board consisted of never less than three nor more than thirteen townsmen, elected for a single year, and unpaid. Their duties, at first very loosely defined, became in time more clearly marked out. They took immediate charge of such administrative

[1] See also below, pp. 561-564.

work as there was to do. The town had some other officials, also, such as assessors, surveyors of roads, and constables, all elected in town meeting. This town type of local government predominated in all the New England colonies.

In the southern colonies a different type prevailed. There the county became the chief unit of local administration. Its officers, including a county lieutenant, a sheriff, and several justices of the peace, were appointed by the governor; there was no general meeting of all the citizens to vote the taxes or to determine matters of local policy. The voters of the county, that is to say, those citizens who held property or were otherwise qualified to vote, elected the county's representatives in the colonial assembly. It was just as logical, however, that the county type of local government should have developed in the South as that the town type should have predominated in New England. In the southern colonies there were large plantations with relatively few settlers occupying a considerable area. The homes of the planters were scattered at distances one from another, and there was no such social or religious homogeneity as that which characterized the population of New England. Almost everywhere throughout the colonial South the management of local affairs drifted into the hands of the plantation-owners, who formed a close corporation. The chief organ of county government was the county court, which, as in England, combined administrative with judicial functions. For example, it had charge of the building and repair of roads and bridges. This county court was made up of justices of the peace, and its sessions were held four times a year.

2. The southern colonies.

The county type.

There were parishes also in the southern colonies, notably in Virginia, each parish being a civil as well as a religious district. The management of its affairs was in the hands of a vestry, a body of twelve parishioners. These vestrymen were at first chosen by the people of the parish, but in time the vestry became a self-perpetuating body, filling all vacancies in its own membership as they occurred. The county soon dwarfed the parish to a very subordinate position.

In the middle colonies, particularly in New York and Pennsylvania, there was a mixed type of local government;

**3. The middle colonies.**

**The mixed type.**

in other words, a combination of county and town administration. After the evacuation of the New Netherland by the Dutch the English divided the colony into counties each with a county court. The county did not, however, become as strong as in the southern colonies, and the administrative functions of the county courts were in time taken over, for the most part, by the elective county supervisors. Towns and townships were also established in the middle colonies, especially in New York, and they became important areas of local government although by no means so dominating as in New England.

**The colonial borough.**

Another unit of local government in nearly all the colonies except those of New England was the borough. In England a borough was a community which had received a charter from the crown; in America it was a community chartered by the governor as the crown's representative. Various colonial towns received such charters and thereby became boroughs, among them New York and Albany in 1686, Philadelphia in 1691, Annapolis in 1696, Richmond in 1742, and Trenton, the last, in 1742. There were about twenty boroughs in all. None of them were in the New England colonies, for there the system of town government was regarded as sufficient and satisfactory even for the largest colonial communities such as Boston, Salem, and New Haven.[1] When a town became a borough, it received a new scheme of administration, modelled upon the prevailing system of borough government in England. Thenceforth it had its mayor, aldermen, and common councillors. The mayor was in some cases appointed by the governor; more often he was elected by the aldermen and councillors together. The voters or freemen of the borough chose the councillors, and the latter, in turn, named the aldermen; but all sat in the same borough council, — mayor, aldermen, and councillors together. This borough system, as will be shown later, was the genesis of the American plan of city government.

The system of local government before the Revolution, despite its considerable variations in different parts of the

[1] Two borough charters were granted in New England, but no borough governments were actually established.

land, was regarded by the colonists as satisfactory. It was especially so in New England, and in the other areas no serious outcry was ever raised against it. Oppression in local government was not one of the causes of the Revolution. The colonists everywhere had as much control over their local affairs as had Englishmen at home; in New England they had a great deal more. A large part of the local organization which existed in colonial days was carried over into the new order after the Revolution, and some portion of it has remained to this day. The New England system of town government, for example, has come into the twentieth century without substantial change. *Satisfactory nature of local government in the colonial era.*

The Revolution did not, therefore, bring about any general reconstruction of local government, nor did it set in motion any appreciable progress toward uniformity. New England retained its town organization intact; Virginia retained the county system without any change whatsoever. In the other states there were some alterations, chiefly in the way of making the county officials elective, either by the people or by the state legislature. Direct election by the people did not at once commend itself on any general scale, and where that plan was adopted the suffrage remained for the most part in the hands of freeholders or taxpayers. Such changes as the Revolution effected in local government, however, were in the direction of increased local control. *General effect of the Revolution upon local institutions.*

In the closing years of the eighteenth century and during the first decade of the nineteenth, the great western regions began to be settled and organized. To these territories the local institutions of the older states were transplanted. In moving westward they followed roughly the parallels of latitude.[1] In other words, the new states of Kentucky and Tennessee took their local institutions from Virginia and the other states of the older South, while Indiana and Ohio adopted systems of local government similar in main outlines to that of Pennsylvania. Mississippi and Alabama were influenced by Georgia. In the Northwest Territory the influence of New England was discernible in the establishment of town meetings, although these meetings developed *Development of local institutions during the period from the Revolution to 1820.*

[1] J. A. Fairlie, *Ibid.*, p. 35.

no important function except that of electing the local officials.

**Influence of the frontier states.**

But although the new states derived their types of local government from the older communities they were inclined to develop them more rapidly along democratic lines. The principle of popular election in the case of county and town officials received greater emphasis. In consequence of this the original diversity of local government was not only maintained but intensified. By 1820 there were not only three general types of local government in the various states, but numerous modifications of these three types representing all degrees of progress towards complete local autonomy.

**Developments between 1820 and the Civil War.**

It was about this time, 1820, that the movement towards the direct popular election of all local officials began to gain an irresistible momentum. During the next twenty years the elective plan made great headway, not only in the frontier states but in New England, New York, and Pennsylvania. In Virginia, however, and in a few other states which followed the lead of the Old Dominion, the appointment of county officers continued to be the rule. The policy of appointment as applied to officials of local government proved to be a lost cause, for the practice of popular election commended itself to one after another of the new states as territories west of the Mississippi were organized into commonwealths. The democratic wave which marked the Jacksonian era, moreover, swept the elective principle into acceptance almost everywhere, while the widening of the suffrage placed the control of local elections in the hands of the whole people and not of the taxpayers alone.

**Fairlie's summary of the situation in 1860.**

Thus by the time the Civil War began, the main features of present-day local government throughout the United States had become well established.[1] "Throughout the country," as Professor Fairlie has shown, "the states were divided into counties, each with a considerable number of elective offices, but with important differences in the organization of the fiscal authority. Everywhere, too, the county was subdivided into smaller districts; but these varied in importance from the New England town, through the township of the Middle West, to the election and judicial pre-

[1] J. A. Fairlie, *Ibid.*, pp. 47–48.

cincts in the South. The basis of suffrage for local elections was the same as for state elections, and had been steadily expanding during the half-century before 1860, until the general system was one where every free white male citizen could vote."

During the fifty years or more which have elapsed since the conclusion of the Civil War there have been many changes in the local systems of the various states, but few of them are of vital importance. To some extent the southern states have divided their counties into townships or other minor districts, but nowhere in these states has a vigorous town or township organization been developed as in the North. In several of the southern states, moreover, there has been a tendency to expand the sphere of state control over local institutions. This has been aimed, in part at least, to secure the more efficient maintenance of law and order, the better administration of justice, and greater provision for education in those counties where there is a large negro population. Officials of local government are now for the most part directly elected in the southern states; but the suffrage in local as in state elections is confined almost entirely to white male citizens. The Fourteenth and Fifteenth amendments to the national constitution guaranteed that there should be no political discrimination in any of the states on account of "race, color, or previous condition of servitude," but this guarantee has proved as ineffective at local as at state or national elections.

*Changes in local government since the Civil War.*

1. In the southern states.

In the northern and western states there has been no great or steady extension of state control over the areas of local government except in the case of the cities. The county, particularly in the states west of the Mississippi, has been developing to a position of greater importance during the last half century, while the townships, owing to the growing practice of incorporating villages, towns, and special districts within their borders, as will be explained presently, have hardly held their own. In areas which are sparsely settled it is natural that the county should be first established as the main unit of local government, but as population increases in density and a subdivision of local

2. In the North and West.

functions becomes essential the logical step is to develop smaller divisions whether in the form of townships, towns, or incorporated cities.

<small>The confusion of local government names.</small>

The terminology of local government in the United States is very confusing. The New England town, for example, has its geographical analogy in the township of the Mississippi valley states. It is not necessarily an urban or thickly settled area. It may have thirty or forty thousand inhabitants crowded closely together, or it may have only a few hundred scattered over many square miles. The town, in other parts of the country, is usually an incorporated urban community, covering only a part of a township and immune from township government. So with cities. In some states this designation is reserved for the largest urban communities, with populations of ten thousand or even more. In others any area of local government, even though its population be only a few hundred, may be incorporated as a city. The distinction between city, town, and village, taking the United States as a whole, is not one of size or population or importance, but merely one of legal status.

<small>The growth of incorporated areas.</small>

The practice of incorporating not only villages, boroughs, towns and cities, but school districts, police districts, fire districts and sanitary districts as well, has been another feature of development during the last decades. When any portion of a township, county or other rural area becomes more thickly settled than the rest, its inhabitants make request for some special public services in the way of fire protection, police, schools, water supply, or sanitation. Accordingly, the small area in which they live is often incorporated by law into a district for one or other of these special purposes. The district becomes a corporation with power to borrow money and to raise taxes in connection with the special purpose for which it is incorporated; its inhabitants being usually given the right to elect trustees or other officers of local administration with carefully limited jurisdiction. As population becomes more congested in all the states, therefore, the township becomes less important as an area of local government because one portion of it after another is virtually given independence in whole or in part by a charter of incorporation.

Decentralization in the framework of local government continues to be the rule throughout the country, although it is more pronounced in some states than in others. Save in a very few cases, and these are in the southern states, no attempt has been made to place the appointment of county, town, or township officers in the hands of the state authorities, thus removing them from the direct control of the people concerned. The forms of local autonomy are almost everywhere preserved. This is a matter, moreover, upon which the communities have strong sentiments. State interference with the *selection* of local officers is everywhere vigorously resented.

<small>The forms of local self-government have been preserved.</small>

But state supervision over the *work* of these officials does not provoke so much local antagonism, and it has been developing steadily in recent years although not at the same rate of progress in all the states. It began with school administration, for two reasons. First, it became generally recognized many years ago that the system of free public education, being so vital to the general welfare of the whole state, could not be safely left to the voluntary and capricious action of towns, villages, or townships. Compulsory education laws were passed by the states and state authorities were created to see that these laws were carried out. Second, the local communities receive from the state, in most cases, large annual subsidies or grants for the support of their schools. The policy of state financial aid carries with it, of course, the right of the state to see that these contributions are not misapplied or wasted, a right which is capable of expansion to a point where it virtually permits the state to control the general policy of the local school authorities. At any rate, the centralizing movement obtained its first foothold in the realm of local education.

<small>But state control of local activities has been increased.</small>

<small>The starting point: Education.</small>

From that point of vantage it has spread to other fields of local activity, public health, poor relief, the assessment of property for taxation, and the enforcement of the law. In all these matters it is not difficult to demonstrate that a policy of strict non-intervention may be detrimental to the general interest. When each county, town, or township is permitted to make and enforce, or to leave unenforced, whatever rules for the preservation of the public health its

<small>State supervision in other fields.</small>

own officials may decide upon, it is altogether likely that one community will be made to suffer for the negligence or ignorance of its neighbors. It should not be within the power of any county, town, or township to decide whether or not it will quarantine cases of infectious disease. The public health can be effectively protected only when all communities are uniformly vigilant, and to insure this situation there must be some general supervisory authority. So with various other matters which at first glance may seem to be functions of strictly local administration but appear upon careful analysis to be things which intimately concern the people of the state as a whole. The guiding hand of state authority is being therefore applied to local administration in many of its branches, and the end of this development is not yet in sight. It is in the cities, however, rather than in the rural areas, that the progress of centralized supervision has been most marked, and it is there, as will be seen later, that the protest against this movement, the cry for local home rule, has become most vociferous.

*More local self-government in the United States than in European countries.*

Yet with all this widening of central supervision over local government, the counties, towns, and townships of the United States have on the whole a larger measure of autonomy than have their prototypes in European countries. Centralization in England has gone much further during the last half century, although even there the officials of local government retain far greater freedom from national supervision than has been left to the local authorities in any country of continental Europe.

*The merits and defects of local autonomy.*

Home rule in counties or townships, as in cities, has its merits and defects, both of which are too obvious to need much elucidation. It fosters local initiative, encourages the trying of experiments which may prove worthy of general adoption, allows each local community to adapt its own administration to its own needs, and tends to develop a wholesome spirit of local rivalry in good works. Local independence begets local responsibility. On the other hand, local home rule too often becomes another name for local misrule, and the sins of one remiss community are visited upon its neighbors. The right of the individual community to do as it pleases, spend its own money as it may see fit, and be a law unto itself is surely no greater than that of the individual citizen. The limits of liberty in each case are set by the rights of others. That is the fundamental consideration to be borne in mind when dealing with the problem of local self-government.

# CHAPTER XXXVIII

### COUNTY GOVERNMENT

The county as a geographical area.

EVERY state of the Union, with the single exception of Louisiana, is divided into counties.[1] In these forty-seven states there are nearly three thousand of them. They are of all sizes and density. The largest is San Bernardino County in California which takes in more than 20,000 square miles; the most populous are New York County in which the downtown portion of New York City is located, and Cook County, Illinois, which includes Chicago.[2] For the most part the county is a firmly established geographical area, and its boundaries are rarely changed in the older states. In the newer states the counties were mapped out in the first instance on a large scale, hence they are frequently divided as population increases. In the long run, however, the tendency is to make the county a fixed and permanent division of the state.

The creation of counties.

As a general rule the creation of new counties is within the powers of the state legislature, but in many of the states there are numerous constitutional provisions which limit the legislature's authority by providing that new counties

[1] In Louisiana the parish is the equivalent of the county in the other states.

[2] The smallest county in point of area is Bristol County, R. I., which contains about twenty-five square miles; the smallest in population is Cochran County, Texas, which had 65 inhabitants in 1910. "Comparing the American county in area and population with the districts in European countries most nearly similar it will be seen that the former is a less important administrative division. English counties average nearly a thousand square miles in area, and (omitting the large cities which for administrative purposes are considered as separate counties), 300,000 population. French departments average over 2000 square miles in area and 400,000 population. Prussian provinces average over 100,000 miles in area and nearly 2,000,000 population, and even the circles (*Kreise*), although smaller in area (averaging about 300 square miles), have an average population of over 50,000." John A. Fairlie, *Local Government in Counties, Towns, and Villages* (N. Y., 1906), p. 62.

may be established or the boundaries of existing counties changed only with the consent of the voters concerned. The state legislature likewise has power to determine the form of county government, the location of the county seat, and the powers of the various county officials. This it has usually done not by enacting a general county code but by innumerable special laws which have created much confusion and conflict of authority. It is for this reason that the constitutions of many states have set up numerous limitations upon the legislature's discretion in dealing with county affairs. In some it is stipulated that the government of counties must be provided for by a general statute and not by special laws. In a few, in California, for example, the inhabitants of counties are permitted to determine their own form of county government through the framing of a county charter by a board of freeholders and the adoption of the charter by vote of the people. Ultimate approval of the county charter by the state legislature is required, but this is not likely to be denied. Los Angeles County in 1912 adopted a new charter in this way, greatly simplifying and improving its frame of government. *Legislative control of counties and county "home rule."*

Counties are commonly spoken of as public quasi-corporations, which implies that they are corporate bodies in a sense but do not possess the full rights and powers of municipal corporations such as cities or incorporated towns. They are the agents of the state in the performance of its political, administrative, and judicial functions; they may sue and be sued, may make contracts, raise taxes, borrow money, and own property, so that they are public corporations to all general intents and purposes. *Legal status of the county.*

A county, however, has no inherent right of self-government. Save in so far as it is protected by the provisions of the state constitution it is the creature of the state legislature; hence its authority and functions can be enlarged, determined, diminished, or even abrogated at the will of that body.[1]

Counties are established to serve as political, adminis-

---

[1] For a discussion of the legal aspects of county government, see Eugene McQuillin, *A Treatise on the Law of Municipal Corporations* (6 vols., Chicago, 1913), i, pp. 428–488.

*General functions of the county as an area of local government, political, administrative, and judicial.*

trative, and judicial districts. They are political divisions because in most of the states the county is the unit upon which representation in the state legislatures is based, each county electing one or more senators and also its quota of assemblymen or representatives. Not infrequently, too, it serves as a unit for the determination of certain questions of public policy, as for example, in the matter of local option on the question of prohibiting the sale of intoxicants, each county being allowed in many states to determine this matter for itself. As an administrative district, however, it is more important. Practically everywhere it is an area of financial administration. The taxes are in many states assessed, levied, and collected by county officers, a part of the proceeds being turned over to the state, a part in some cases to the towns or townships within the county, and the remainder retained for county purposes. Nearly everywhere, again, the county is given considerable authority with reference to the construction and repair of main highways and bridges. Occasionally it has the duty of providing other public works as well. Poor relief, including the providing of poorhouses, is in most states a county function. Particularly in the southern states the system of elementary school administration is organized on a county basis. To some extent it is a primary unit for the enforcement of law and order through its sheriff and its deputy sheriffs, especially in the sparsely settled regions; and finally it is in some parts of the country the recognized unit for the organization of the state militia. The administrative functions of the county are therefore varied and extensive, much more so, however, in some states than in others. But the chief function of the county is to serve, not as a political or administrative area of government, but as a judicial district. It is in practically every state a district for the administration of civil and criminal justice, usually also for the registry of deeds and the probating of wills, and almost invariably for the maintenance of courthouses and institutions of correction. In the judicial systems of the several states the county court and its various officers form an important part.[1]

[1] See H. S. Gilbertson, *County Government* (N. Y., 1917).

The centre of county government is the county seat or capital. The selection is made by the legislature when the county is first established, and the legislature may remove it to some other city or town at any later time, but in many of the states the constitution forbids this unless the voters of the county approve the change. The county seat is the location of the county courthouse, the offices of the county board, and often the other county offices as well.[1]  *The county seat.*

The chief administrative organ of the county in all the states but two is a county board.[2] Members of this board are usually known as commissioners or supervisors. They differ greatly in number and in method of selection from state to state. In New England the boards are small, usually consisting of three members. They are elected by the voters of the county at large except in Connecticut, where they are appointed by the state legislature. In other eastern states, such as New York and New Jersey, the board is a much larger body, including from fifteen to twenty-five members or even more. The members, usually known as supervisors, are not chosen by the voters of the county at large, but are sent as representatives by the townships and cities included in the county. In this case the representation is not according to population, for each community, however small, has at least one representative. This method of constituting the county board is also followed in some states of the Middle West, including Michigan and Wisconsin. Still another plan is found in Pennsylvania and in various states throughout the West, including Ohio, Indiana, Minnesota, Nebraska, Kansas, and the Dakotas. Here the board is small, with from three to seven members; but the choice of members is not made by the voters at large as in New England or by municipalities as in New York. The counties in these last-named western states are divided into districts and each district elects one or more supervisors. In the southern states there is a great variety of practice. The board is usually a small body, but its members are  *The county board. Its organization.*

---

[1] Occasionally a county has two county seats, each with a courthouse and other county offices.

[2] The exceptions are Louisiana, which has parish boards but no counties, and Rhode Island, which has counties but no boards.

sometimes elected at large and sometimes by districts. Finally in the states of the Pacific slope and Rocky Mountain areas the preference has been for a small board, usually of three members, but there is no uniformity in the method of selecting these three commissioners.

**Diversity in organization of the boards.**  It is commonly said that county boards may be divided into two general classes: first, the small board of three or more members elected at large for the whole county or from large districts; and second, the representative board composed ordinarily of one member elected from each township within the county. It is added, usually, that the first type prevails in New England, in the South, in the Middle West and in the Pacific states, while the latter is to be found in New York, New Jersey, Michigan, and a few other states.[1] This generalization, however, is true only in the rough. There are many compromises between these two types, and some states do not conform in any essential respect to either. There is almost as much variety in county government as in city government throughout the United States.

**The functions of county boards:**  The functions of the county board are established by law. Some states have general laws on the subject, but in most of them the duties of county commissioners or supervisors are set forth in a long succession of separate and unrelated special acts of the legislature which sometimes apply to one county and not to others. Taking the boards as a whole, however, their functions may be grouped under six general heads: financial, highways and bridges, other public works, poor relief, elections, and miscellaneous.

**1. Financial.**  Most county boards have the right to levy county taxes and to make appropriations for expenditure. There are some exceptions to this, however, notably in Massachusetts, where the appropriations are made by the legislature (usually on the recommendation of the county commissioners), and in New Hampshire and Connecticut, where the legislature retains the function both of determining the county tax **Taxation and appropriations.** rate and of making the appropriations. In most of the other states, where the county board both makes the appropriations and spends them, there is a fusion of two

[1] C. A. Beard, *American Government and Politics* (N. Y., 1916), pp. 639–640.

powers which are usually kept separate in government. In the national government, Congress makes the appropriations, and the executive has the function of applying the money to the purposes designated. In the states, again, the legislatures appropriate and the executive spends. So in the cities (except those under the commission form of government), the council votes the budget, while the mayor and the heads of departments disburse the funds. But in county government throughout the larger part of the country the same board, of three or seven or fifteen members as the case may be, lays the taxes, votes the appropriations, and then proceeds to spend the money thus appropriated. This has been criticised as an unsafe policy and in practice it has encouraged extravagance, although it does not appear to have done so on any large scale.

*The fusion of appropriating and spending powers.*

In addition to the function of levying county taxes, making appropriations, and supervising expenditures the county board, as a rule, has other financial duties. From time to time, either by general or special law, the board is given authority to borrow money on the county's credit, either with or without the necessity of first securing the approval of the voters. Ordinarily the county board has no general power to borrow but must obtain special legislative authority in each case. Borrowing powers are frequently obtained in this way for the building of roads, bridges, and county buildings. The county board, again, sometimes serves as a tribunal of appeal from the assessments made by local assessors or as a board of equalization for making the proper adjustments in assessments among different municipalities.

*Other financial functions.*

In many states all the important highways are either state or county roads. The towns and townships are responsible for the minor thoroughfares only. Nearly everywhere the county board has authority to lay out, to construct, and to repair the various rural highways which may be designated as county roads; but there are great differences among the states in the extent to which this authority is exercised. In some, such as Ohio, Indiana, and California, county roads are numerous; in Massachusetts they are very few. Main bridges, especially those which

*2. Roads and bridges.*

connect two cities, or towns, or townships, are also commonly built and maintained by the county authorities. The money for these enterprises, whether roads or bridges, is obtained partly by taxation and partly by borrowing.

3. Other public works.

Various other public works are provided by the county board, particularly the courthouse, the county jail, the house of correction, and the registry of deeds (wherever this is needed). Such buildings are often erected on an expensive scale, far more so than a county requires or can well afford. The management of these buildings, their supervision, repair, and upkeep is also a function of the board. In states here and there the county officials have been given other public enterprises to carry through, such as the construction of irrigation works, the abolition of grade railway-crossings, or the building of levees, dikes, and drains. In general, when a project concerns all the municipalities in the county, or several of them, the county board is the natural authority to have charge of it.

4. Poor relief.

Poor relief in the great majority of the states is primarily a county rather than a local function. The chief exceptions are the New England states where local responsibility in matters of poor relief still remains extensive. Over the greater part of the country the county poorhouse and county farm are well-known institutions. Persons who need public assistance are sent to these institutions from all the towns or townships of the county. County hospitals exist in a few of the states. Institutions for the care of the insane are usually provided by the state, not by the county. Expenditures for the relief of the poor have had a relatively large place in county budgets, but these expenditures have not been, for the most part, administered in an enlightened or humane way. The general policy has been merely to build a poorhouse and to put paupers into it, supporting them there at whatever may happen to be the cost. There has been relatively little attention to the problem of helping the poor to help themselves, thus reducing the burden of poor relief by measures designed to prevent pauperism. For this the county officials are not mainly to blame. The states have lent little encouragement to those who do otherwise than follow the methods of a hundred years ago. In most

American counties the system of poor relief remains exactly as it was when the county was first established. There has been far less progress in the methods of public charity than in the methods of road-building.

County boards have various duties with reference to elections, although here again the New England states provide conspicuous exceptions to the general rule. Throughout the South and the West the county board has immediate charge of election machinery; it designates the polling places, appoints the poll officials, provides the ballots, and canvasses the returns. It sometimes also selects the jury panels from the voters' lists. The county, as has been already mentioned, is the prevailing unit for the selection of senators and representatives in the state legislature. *5. Elections.*

Finally, the county board has miscellaneous powers. It appoints some county officers, although in most counties these officials (such as the sheriff, the county prosecuting attorney, the registrar of deeds, the county treasurer, and county clerk) are elected by the voters. In the counties of the southern states and to some extent in the central and western states as well, the boards grant the liquor licenses; but the spread of prohibition during the past decade has greatly diminished the importance of this authority. Occasionally they issue charters of incorporation for smaller companies. Odds and ends of jurisdiction go to the county boards here and there; for example, the extermination of noxious animals, the regulation of schools for truants, the licensing of pedlers, and so on. *6. Miscellaneous.*

It will be seen that the county board, as the chief organ of county administration, gathers to itself a considerable variety of functions. They are in part legislative, since the levying of taxes and the making of appropriations are legislative functions. But they are in larger part administrative, as has been indicated. In a few cases the county board has some judicial duties as well, and sometimes, as in West Virginia and Missouri, it is officially listed as a court. County boards cannot, therefore, be placed exclusively in the legislative, executive, or judicial division of government, and they are among the very few American political institutions of which that can be said. *Some of the county board's work.*

*The county as a judicial area.*

While the county board has, occasionally, some minor judicial functions, it is not that fact which makes the county an important area of judicial administration. It is rather the existence of the county court, an institution which exists in almost all the states.

*The county court.*

These county courts are not always constituted in the same way. In about sixteen of the states each county has its own judge and court. In a few others there are separate judges and courts for a few populous counties only. Most of the states do not have a judge for each county, but group the counties into judicial districts with one judge for each district. This judge then goes on a circuit, holding sessions at the courthouse of each county in succession. The judges are in most cases elected by the voters of the counties or districts, as the case may be, but they are ranked as state officials and form an integral part of the state judiciary.

*Its jurisdiction.*

The jurisdiction of the county court usually extends to the hearing of appeals from local courts presided over by justices of the peace, with original cognizance of criminal cases and of civil controversies where the amount at issue does not exceed a certain sum. But the powers of these courts differ so greatly among the states that no general rule can be laid down. The probating of wills and the administration of estates is also, as a rule, a function of the county court, or of a branch of it.

*Other county officials:*

In addition to the county board and the judge of the county court there are some other officials of county administration. The most important, at any rate the oldest of these offices, is that of sheriff. "Every county has a sheriff; and the office may be called the constituent office of the county."[1]

*(a) the sheriff.*

The name is an abbreviation of the old Saxon shire-reeve, which antedates the Norman conquest of England. During the middle period of English history the sheriff was the right arm of the crown in the counties, the keeper of the king's peace, and the enforcer of the common law. These functions, in a general way, the sheriff of an American county has inherited. He is the chief conservator of law and order and the executive agent of the county court. The office of sheriff is everywhere

[1] Fairlie, *Ibid.*, p. 106.

elective save in Rhode Island. There the legislature chooses the sheriffs. The sheriff is usually empowered to appoint deputies who assist him in keeping the peace, attending court sessions, making arrests, serving court papers, and so forth. Both sheriffs and their deputies are sometimes paid fixed salaries; but more often their remuneration comes from fees. In populous counties these fees make the sheriff's office a very lucrative one. In rural counties, on the other hand, the compensation is small and the duties are often onerous, particularly in unruly parts of the land. In such areas the security of life and property depends to a considerable extent upon the alertness, honesty, and courage of the sheriff. This is particularly true in time of serious disorder or riot, when the sheriff may not only summon his deputies for assistance, but may raise the *posse comitatus* by sending out a general call for help to the citizens, and in the last resort may obtain the aid of the state militia.

The sheriff, in addition to his functions as guardian of the peace within the county, is also the chief executive officer of the county court. It is through his office that the judgments of the court are carried out. He is the keeper of the county jail and has the custody of all prisoners there. He looks after the comfort of juries while the court is in session. He or his deputies serve subpœnas upon witnesses, or seize property in satisfaction of judgment; or place writs of attachment upon property, or perform whatever other duties the court may request. {His collateral function: executive officer of the court.}

The coroner is another important county officer. His duty is to hold an inquest whenever a death takes place under circumstances which excite suspicion of crime. To assist him at the inquest the coroner usually calls together a jury of citizens, who hear the evidence and render a verdict. If the jury finds grounds for believing that a crime has been committed, it may so declare in its verdict, whereupon the coroner may usually issue an order for the arrest of the person accused. But neither the coroner nor his jury finally determines any question of guilt or innocence. That function is left to the regular courts. {(b) the coroner. His duties.}

In the United States coroners are almost always elected.

**Unsatisfactory character of inquests in general.**

To perform their duties efficiently they should be either physicians or lawyers, but often they are neither. Their juries, moreover, are selected by summoning anybody who happens to be near at hand. On the whole, therefore, coroner's inquests have not contributed greatly to the discovery of crimes or to the apprehension of offenders. Still the whole process is not so deserving of derision, perhaps, as Shakespeare in *Hamlet* makes it out to be.[1] The office of county coroner has a long and interesting history behind it, and one might hesitate to see it generally abolished, yet the procedure is not well adapted to conditions of to-day. Massachusetts for over forty years has gotten along very well without coroners, having provided for the appointment of medical examiners who make investigations without the aid of improvised juries and report the results, if necessary, to the regular prosecuting officials for action.

**(c) the prosecuting attorney.**

The regular prosecuting official of the county is an attorney whose office bears various designations.[2] Usually he is elected by the people of the county or district. His chief duty is that of conducting prosecutions in the name and on behalf of the state. He prepares the evidence for presentation to the grand jury and advises the jurymen as to whether there is sufficient ground for an indictment. If an indictment is found, the prosecuting attorney is responsible for the proper handling of the case when it is brought before the trial jury. These officials have considerable discretion in the way of discontinuing prosecutions, either by entering a *nolle prosequi* or by asking that a case be placed on file.[3] The court's approval is sometimes necessary for such action, but more often the prosecuting attorney takes the whole responsibility. In a few states, including Michigan, Wisconsin, and Minnesota, the requirement of grand jury action in all but the most serious criminal cases has been

---

[1] Act 5, Scene 1.

[2] Prosecuting attorney or state's attorney or district attorney or county attorney or county solicitor.

[3] A *nolle prosequi* is entered when the prosecuting attorney feels that there is no occasion for pressing an indictment to trial. Such action is popularly termed "nol prossing" an indictment. Placing an indictment on file involves an indefinite postponement of the prosecution, and while it does not preclude a trial at some future date, this rarely takes place.

abolished. Proceedings are begun by an information, which is a sworn declaration made by the prosecuting attorney to the effect that there is sufficient ground for placing an accused person on trial.

Other county officers are the treasurer, who receives the revenue and makes all payments out of the county funds, the auditor, who inspects the accounts and prepares from time to time a statement of the county's financial condition for presentation to the county board; the assessors, who appraise property for taxation; the clerk of the county court, who looks after the judicial records; the registrar of deeds or recorder, and the county superintendent of schools. Not all counties have this entire set of officials. In Massachusetts, for example, there are no county auditors, assessors, or school superintendents. Nearly everywhere these various officials are elective, although some of them are in a few states appointed by the county board. It is generally admitted that there are too many elective county officers and the result has been the selection of inferior men. The voter's interest is centred upon the candidates for state office on the one hand and for municipal office on the other. The county, coming in between, gets little of his attention. The consequence is that county nominations and elections have been proverbially dominated by small rings of professional politicians. There has been less genuine political independence in the counties than in the other areas of government.

(*d*) the treasurer, auditor, assessor, clerk, registrar, etc.

County government, taking the country as a whole, has not been conspicuously bad, but it has been far from what it ought to be. Corruption and political dishonesty has not been so prevalent as in the cities. But mediocrity in office, unprogressiveness in policy, a failure to get full value for expenditures, favoritism in appointments and in the award of contracts, lack of popular interest in county affairs — these things have characterized county administration in most of the states. The situation has been tolerated because the need of reform in other quarters appeared to be more pressing. Now that both state and municipal governments have been improved the tide of reform is directing itself towards county affairs.

Actual workings of county government.

The reconstruction of county government will involve

558    THE GOVERNMENT OF THE UNITED STATES

The need of county reconstruction.

1. County should have a chief executive.

2. Fewer elective offices.

three changes of far-reaching importance in the present system. First among the needs of county government to-day is the better organization of county executive work. As matters now stand there is no county official corresponding to the president, governor, and mayor in national, state, and municipal government. Executive responsibility is scattered, some of it devolving upon the county board, and the remainder accruing to the various county officers, each of whom is independent of the others. "Either the sheriff should again become the chief executive of the county, transferring his ministerial functions to an under-sheriff, or some other officer should become chief executive, and the sheriff be confined to his ministerial duties as court bailiff."[1] Probably the latter alternative would be the more practical as it would be difficult to separate the office of sheriff from its police and judicial duties. The vesting of executive power in an elective county president, with powers somewhat analogous to those of a mayor, might prove to be a better solution of the problem. At any rate the need of executive centralization will appear most clearly to any one who studies the actual workings of county government.

The concentration of responsibility for the management of county business will entail a reduction in the number of elective offices. There is no good reason why treasurers, auditors, recorders, and clerks should be appointed in cities and elected in counties. The elective principle, when applied to these positions, means an undue lengthening of the ballot with a consequent flagging of public interest in the claims of individual candidates. With a dozen or more county officials to be elected at large the average voter will not inform himself of particular qualifications but will be guided entirely by party designations. The party leaders, appreciating this lack of popular interest and information, place in nomination for the county offices men who would not be put forward for positions in the state or municipal government. That is why the county has been aptly called "the jungle of American politics." It is the region where the voter finds the greatest difficulty in threading his way.

[1] Fairlie, *Ibid.*, p. 112.

The practice of electing these purely administrative officers of county government has, moreover, encouraged frequent changes in posts where experience is valuable and where permanence ought to be encouraged. Too often a county treasurer, auditor, or registrar has no sooner acquired familiarity with the duties of his office than he is supplanted by some other party worker whose turn has come to enjoy the emoluments. County officers whose functions are purely ministerial and who have no responsibility for the shaping of policy ought to be made appointive. The power of appointment might well be given to the county board or to an elective chief executive, such as has been suggested in a preceding paragraph.

Civil service reform has as yet made scarcely a ripple upon the face of county politics, yet selection by merit is a principle which ought to be applied to subordinate positions in the service of the county as in that of the city, state, or nation. Clerks in courthouses, keepers in jails, attendants in poorhouses, foremen in road-construction are almost everywhere chosen by a strict application of the spoils system. The progress of civil service in other fields, moreover, has tended to make the county service a last refuge for the incompetent. The march of the merit system has been impeded there by the machine-like organization and overwhelming political influence of the "county rings" whose concerted pressure upon the state legislature is difficult to overpower. But the wedge has been inserted and the salient will be widened in time. 3. Civil service reform should be applied to counties.

Special problems of county government arise whenever a large city spreads itself over all or a great portion of the county area. This is the situation, for example, in Cook County which contains Chicago, in Suffolk County which shelters Boston, in Philadelphia County which includes Philadelphia, and so on. In some such cases, as in San Francisco, Philadelphia, and Boston, the same body acts as a city council and county board combined. In other instances there are two separate bodies with powers which interlock, sometimes overlap, and are frequently ill-defined. The special problems of metropolitan counties.

# CHAPTER XXXIX

## TOWNS, TOWNSHIPS, AND VILLAGES

**The various areas of local government in the several states.**

FOR purposes of local government counties are usually divided into towns, districts, or townships, but whenever any portion of a county becomes urban in character through the growth of population it is commonly organized as an incorporated village, town, borough, or city. The practice and the terminology are very different in various parts of the country, so that any clear and accurate presentation of local government throughout the United States is a task of considerable difficulty. All that can be attempted in this chapter, therefore, is to set forth the general principles according to which local administration is carried on and to describe in a summary way the organization of the more important units of local government, particularly the New England town and the western township.

**Relation of local to state government.**

Local government in the United States, it need hardly be explained, is exclusively a matter of state control. The national government has nothing to do with it. Each state has full power to devise its own system of town, township, district, or borough government, and to modify this system at will. But although each state is supreme as respects its own form and functions of local government, the state legislatures are not always given a wholly free hand in such matters. The state constitutions contain many limiting provisions which guarantee to the local units their existence and the possession of various privileges. And as constitutions are revised, the tendency is to insert more of these restrictive provisions. Nevertheless, the towns, townships, villages, and other communities are largely under the legislature's control. Acts of the legislature provide what officers a community shall have, how they shall be chosen, and what their duties shall be. Such acts are usually of a general character applying to all local areas of the same legal character, that is, to towns or townships as a class; but special laws applying to individual communities are also common except in states where they are forbidden by constitutional provision.

Among the various areas of local government the New England town is one of the oldest and in every respect the most interesting. The town is not always, as the name would ordinarily imply, a thickly settled community. Some New England towns, it is true, are towns in the generally accepted sense, or places with populations running into the thousands. Most of them, however, are what would elsewhere be called townships, that is to say, agricultural regions covering twenty or thirty square miles. They differ from the western townships in that they are not of regular shape or uniform area, having been laid out in early days according to no fixed system of survey. They are as diverse in population, moreover, as in size or shape. One Massachusetts town has a population of nearly forty thousand; another has less than four hundred. In Maine, Vermont, and Connecticut a few villages or boroughs have been incorporated within the limits of the towns; but in general this practice has not been pursued. A town remains intact until its people secure incorporation as a city.

<small>The New England town.</small>

The New England town does not possess a charter of incorporation, yet it has practically all the rights and privileges of a municipal corporation. Originally the towns derived their powers from the common law, but since the Revolution it has been well-settled legal doctrine that they can claim no powers except such as "have been expressly conferred by statute or which are necessary for conducting municipal affairs."[1] The idea that towns have inherent and inalienable rights because they are in many cases older than the states is widely held by town officers in New England; but it is without any legal basis. The New England town is as completely under the thumb of the state legislature as is the western township or any other area of local government.

<small>Its legal status.</small>

To some extent the powers now possessed by the towns

[1] *Bloomfield* vs. *Charter Oak Bank*, 121 U. S. 129.

*General powers of towns.*

have been conferred by a general law dealing with town government; but special statutes have also, from time to time, added new privileges or functions. To-day the New England town has substantially all the authority which a city charter conveys. It may sue and be sued, make contracts, levy taxes, borrow money, and own property. It may by ordinances or by-laws provide for the protection of life and property, the public health and public morals. It has the usual powers of a municipal corporation to build and maintain streets and sewers, to provide water supply, public lighting, police and fire protection, parks and public buildings. It is required to establish schools, and it may maintain a hospital, a public library, and a market. Poor relief is also a town function in New England. The town, in fact, provides many services which in other parts of the country are among the functions of counties.

*The town meeting.*

The chief organ of town government in New England is the town meeting. An annual town meeting is usually held in May, with special meetings whenever necessary, but not more than two or three special meetings are commonly called during the year. Every voter of the town is entitled to attend the annual and the special town meetings, both of which convene in the town hall. As a rule, however, not more than half of them do attend, and the percentage is frequently much smaller. The town meeting selects its own presiding officer, who is known as the moderator, but this honor customarily goes year after year to some prominent citizen.[1]

*Their organization and functions.*

Town meetings are called with considerable formality, and their procedure is strictly regulated by law and tradition. The call is in the form of a warrant issued by the selectmen to the constables of the town commanding them "to notify and warn" the townsmen and to "make due return" of their having done so. The warrant specifies item by item the matters which are to be brought before the meeting and no other business can be considered. At the annual meeting the various town officers are elected for the year, a poll being

---

[1] It is the highest honor that the townsmen can bestow and is appreciated accordingly. Even governors and United States senators do not disdain to serve as moderators at the annual meetings in their home towns.

opened for this purpose whenever there is a contest. Usually this polling takes place in the morning, the afternoon being devoted to a business session in which the appropriations are voted and all matters of general town policy settled. In the more populous towns, however, the polling often continues throughout the day, with the business session in the evening. When the warrant contains many items, it is impossible to finish the entire docket of business at a single session, in which case the meeting is adjourned to a subsequent afternoon or evening, and still further adjourned if necessary.

In the smaller rural towns the occasion of the annual town meeting has always been and still is a neighborhood holiday. The debate, particularly upon matters which the world would not regard as of momentous importance, is often spirited and piquant, with no dearth of humor and an occasional flare-up of personalities. It is a picturesque gathering, this annual meeting in a small New England town, with its copious flow of homely oratory, its insistence upon settling even the smallest details by common voice, its prodigious emission of tobacco smoke, and the general retail of local gossip which takes place around the doors. In the larger towns things are quite different. There the business of the town meeting is for the most part cut and dried beforehand; a few active politicians monopolize the debate, and the large amount of business necessitates the strict application of parliamentary rules. In some of these larger towns, moreover, it has become the practice to have the moderator appoint a committee, usually of fifteen or more townsmen, which makes recommendations to the town meeting on all matters in the warrant, and these recommendations are usually adopted. *How the system works: 1. in smaller towns. 2. in larger towns.*

The town meeting ceases to be a satisfactory organ of local government when the population of the town exceeds five or six thousand. When that point is reached, a reasonably full attendance of the voters becomes impractical and the control of the town policy passes into the hands of whatever element happens to be the stronger or more aggressive politically. For this reason many towns, on reaching an unwieldy size, apply for incorporation as cities. Some *Recent changes in the town meeting.*

others, however, have been reluctant to give up local institutions which have served so long, and hence continue a scheme of government which no longer suits their needs. Others, again, have attempted to modify the town meeting without actually abolishing it, but these halfway measures do not seem to be proving altogether successful.[1] There is, in fact, no practical halting place between direct and representative government. A town meeting must represent one or other of these types; it cannot well embody both. A "limited" town meeting, accordingly, is not a town meeting at all, but merely a camouflaged town council of unwieldy size.

The selectmen.

In the earliest days of seaboard settlement the town meeting was the sole organ of town government. But it was soon found necessary to have officials who would carry the decisions of the town meeting into effect and who would also deal with minor matters in the intervals between the meetings. Hence developed the practice of choosing at the annual town meeting a committee of the townsmen, usually three or five in number, known as the selectmen.[2] Originally these selectmen were chosen for one year only, and that practice is generally continued, except in Massachusetts, where the term is three years in many of the towns, one selectman retiring annually. But in any event re-elections are common, and a selectman who is willing to serve is frequently continued in office for ten or a dozen years.

Their functions.

The selectmen form, as it were, the executive committee of the town meeting. They have no legislative authority, pass no by-laws, levy no taxes, borrow no money, and make no appropriations. All these things require action by the town meeting. Nor do the selectmen appoint the town officers. Even their administrative functions, although multifarious, are of a subsidiary character. They prepare the warrants for the annual or special meetings; they grant

[1] In 1916 the town of Brookline, Massachusetts, with a population of about 35,000, was permitted by a special act of the Massachusetts legislature to adopt a system of "limited town meetings." The town is now divided into precincts, each of which elects a quota of representatives.

[2] In Rhode Island this body is not known as the board of selectmen but as the town council.

licenses under the authority of the state laws; they lay out highways and sewers for acceptance by the town meeting; they make the arrangements for state and local elections, and they have immediate charge of town property. They usually award the contracts for public work, and all bills against the town for work or services must be approved by them before being paid. Schools are in charge of a school committee elected at the annual town meeting. The selectmen may serve as overseers of the poor or as assessors or as the town board of health; but in towns of any considerable size these functions are intrusted to separate boards, the members of which are also chosen at the annual town meeting. The New England town does not, therefore, possess a centralized executive authority. The selectmen share executive functions with various boards and officials who are not under their control.

The number and nature of these boards and officials depend upon the size of the town. Most of the towns have a school committee or board of school trustees, a board of health, and a board of overseers of the poor. A large town may also have a water board, a library board, and a board of park commissioners. In Massachusetts each town has a town planning board with advisory functions only. As for administrative officials, every town has its town clerk, who is perhaps the most important among local officers. Many functions are devolved upon him by state law, such as the issuing of marriage licenses, the registration of births and deaths, the transmission of various reports to the state authorities, and in some states the recording of deeds and mortgages. In addition the town clerk is the keeper of the local records and the general factotum of the selectmen. He is elected by the town meeting, receives a salary, and is usually continued in office as long as he does his work satisfactorily. Each town also has its assessors, its town treasurer, its constables, and often a considerable list of minor officials, such as poundkeepers, fence viewers, sealers of weights and measures, and so on. These officers are usually chosen by the town meeting, but in some towns the selectmen appoint to the minor posts. In four of the New England states the justices of the peace are elected by the

*Other town boards and officials.*

townsmen;[1] in the other two they are appointed by the governor.

<small>Why so many officials?</small>

One reason for this multiplication of administrative boards and officials, even in towns which have relatively small populations, may be found in the fact that most town officers serve without pay. If the work were concentrated in a few hands, there would be a demand for remuneration. In the smaller communities this plan of administration by scattered and unpaid agencies serves well enough and has the merit of cheapness; but in the larger towns, where there is much public business to be done, it falls far short of the requirements and has had to be in part abandoned. These places, as a rule, are now putting paid officials in charge of the more important services.

Inertia and the influence of long-standing custom also count for much in the perpetuation of the present system. The various boards and minor offices provide places for a large number of prominent townsmen; indeed it is a rare individual who can live in any small New England town for many years without being named to some official post, be it only that of constable, fence viewer, field-driver, or hog-reeve.[2] It is not that the craving for public office is greater in New England than elsewhere, but the continuance of these minor posts entails no expense and the townsmen see no urgent reason for abolishing them. There is need, however, for a considerable reduction in the number of elective town officers, and a movement in this direction is already under way. The adoption of the commission form of government by cities has had its indirect influence upon public sentiment in many of the larger New England towns.

New England town government has three centuries of good tradition behind it and enjoys a splendid reputation, which, however, is not wholly deserved. Those who are not in close touch with the actual facts of the situation imagine that

---

[1] Connecticut, New Hampshire, Vermont, and Rhode Island. In Rhode Island some justices are also appointed by the governor. Only in the first three states have the justices any judicial authority.

[2] In some towns it is the custom at each annual town meeting to elect to this last-named office all the young men who have been married during the year. This honor is assumed to represent the community's wedding gift.

these towns are miniature republics, left to handle their own local affairs in their own way, free from legislative interference, and governing themselves admirably by the device of a mass meeting. That is a pretty picture, no doubt, but far from being a true likeness.

*Erroneous notions concerning New England town government.*

The New England town has in reality no more home-rule than the New England city. It is buffeted in all directions by the action of the state legislature; and scarcely a year ever passes without new duties being thrown by the state upon town officers. The New England town has a form of government which serves well enough for a very small community where there are no important public services to be provided, where the people are all or nearly all of native stock, and where every one knows his neighbors. But in its application to places of several thousand inhabitants, and particularly to industrial towns which have a considerable proportion of foreign-born voters, it has no marked merits except those of age and good historical association. In point of actual accomplishment, it is no better than the newer forms of local government which exist in other parts of the country.

Towns and townships, as areas of local government, exist in the great group of northern and central states from New York and Pennsylvania to Nebraska and the Dakotas. In the older of these states the towns are of irregular shape and vary considerably in size; but in the newer states the territory is mapped out into uniform blocks, six miles square, and these areas are usually called townships. The surveying was done when these regions were territories under the jurisdiction of Congress, hence the divisions are sometimes called congressional townships. In some of the states, both old and new, the town meeting is an institution of local government, but nowhere outside of New England has it developed much vitality, and its chief function is that of electing the town or township officers.[1] In other states there is no town or township meeting, the work of local

*Towns and townships in the northern and central states.*

---

[1] The chief reason for this, no doubt, is the purely artificial nature of the township. It has no social homogeneity or local self-consciousness like the New England town. By incorporation, moreover, the thickly settled portions of townships are usually organized as cities or villages, thus breaking into the original unit.

**The organs of town and township government.**

administration being wholly carried on by officers elected at the polls. In a few cases, moreover, the counties have not been divided into towns or townships at all.

The administrative work of town or township government is carried on either by a board of trustees or by a single officer known as the supervisor.[1] Where the board system prevails there are different ways of constituting the board, although its members are always elected by the voters. The powers of the board also vary from state to state. So it is with the single supervisor, an elective official, whose functions are more extensive in some of the states than in others. Towns and townships also have their clerks, treasurers, assessors, constables, highway overseers, justices of the peace, and other local officials, all or most of them elected.

**The incorporated municipalities, villages, and boroughs.**

Township government has been greatly weakened by the practice of incorporating as a separate municipality any portion of the township which becomes urban in character. Nearly all the states now make provision by general law for the organization of these thickly settled areas under the name of villages, boroughs, incorporated towns, or cities. The usual course is for the inhabitants to present a petition to some designated officer, who submits the question of incorporation to a vote of the people, and if they decide affirmatively, the petition is granted. The region is thereupon incorporated as a village, borough, town, or city, as the case may be. Usually there is a minimum requirement as to population: from two hundred to three hundred in the case of a village, from two thousand to twelve thousand where the petition is for incorporation as a city.

When a region is thus incorporated, it passes from the jurisdiction of the township officers and sets up its own local government. In the case of a village this government commonly consists of a board of trustees or a council with from three to nine elected members, together with a chief executive officer, called a mayor or village president, who is either chosen

---

[1] The former plan is followed in Pennsylvania, Ohio, Iowa, Minnesota, North Dakota, and South Dakota; the latter in New York, Michigan, Illinois, and Wisconsin. In the last-named state the official is called the town chairman. In Indiana, Missouri, Kansas, and Oklahoma he is called the township trustee. John A. Fairlie, *Local Government in Counties, Towns, and Villages* (N. Y., 1906), p. 175.

by the trustees or by the village voters. In the case of a borough, an incorporated town, or a city, the organization is along somewhat the same lines; but the governmental mechanism is more elaborate. The general laws of each state provide what powers these local governments shall exercise, but they generally include the making of by-laws, the management of streets, water supply, sanitation, police, fire protection, and public recreation. Taking the United States as a whole, there are more than ten thousand of these small incorporated municipalities. They differ so widely in size, population, form of government, and functions that no general description will hold strictly true in relation to all or even to any large number of them.

In the southern states the county remains the dominant area of local government. There are no towns as in New England, and only in scattered regions any system of organized township government. Instead of townships the counties usually have districts for such purposes as the management of schools, the building of highways, the holding of elections, and the administration of justice. These districts are not corporate entities, like towns or townships; they have no taxing power and they exist for certain designated purposes only. In some southern states they are called magisterial districts; in others the name township is used, although the term is misleading. Delaware keeps the historic English "hundred," a shire division which in Anglo-Saxon times contributed one hundred warriors to the feudal array. These various districts have their elective officers whose powers are fixed by law.

*The county divisions in southern states.*

The vitality of local government in the southern states ceases with the county, the city, and in some cases the incorporated village. This is an interesting phenomenon in the American political system, and there must be a reason for it. There are, indeed, several reasons. One of them is historical, the system of great plantations and slavery before the Civil War. In those days even a considerable tract of territory contained very few voters, for the slave had no political rights. The planters controlled local affairs, and the county was none too large for their public activity. There were no public schools; there was very little public road-building, and no public poor relief was required because each planter looked

*Why areas of local government have not developed in the South.*

after the people of his own estate. There was, therefore, little or no need for community administration.

With the abolition of slavery some development of township or village government might have been expected, but several factors stood in the way. The slaves were set free, but as matters turned out, they were not destined to become voters except for a short time during the era of reconstruction. Their descendants, who form a large element in the rural population of the South, are for the most part without political power. The systematic organization of townships would only serve to make negro disfranchisement more conspicuous and perhaps more difficult to defend. A town meeting attended by negroes in almost any southern state would be unthinkable. Such a meeting, if restricted to whites, on the other hand, would have a slim attendance in some rural areas of the South. After the Civil War some townships, commonly known as reconstruction townships, were established in various southern states, and the new colored voters at once took control of them. The experience of these few years is one which the white citizens of the South have not forgotten. When the opportunity came, they abolished the reconstruction townships, and there has since been no serious thought of reëstablishing them. In a word, neither historical, ethnic, nor geographic considerations have favored the growth of local self-government as applied to small areas in this region of the country.

The county divisions in states of the Far West. Finally, in the far western states, the system of county divisions, commonly known as precincts, is more or less general. It is also a common practice to divide the county into school districts, judicial districts, and road districts, each for the purpose indicated by its name and each with elective officers. The county in these sections is the all-important unit. When its authorities cannot conveniently carry out all the work that needs to be done, a division into districts is made for single functions. Population in these states is even yet too sparse to warrant the general establishment of organized townships. In none of them is the density more than a dozen persons to the square mile, and in some it is not more than half that figure. Townships, if created, would have on the average only fifty or sixty voters, not enough to form a local electorate. Wherever the population is compact, incorporated villages or cities have been created; but for the rest of the territory the county or its special divisions are adequate. Not improbably, however, as these regions become more thickly settled, the organized civil township of the central states will find its way to the Pacific slope.

# CHAPTER XL

## THE AMERICAN CITY

*A century of city growth.*

THE development of large urban communities, or cities, has been the most striking social phenomenon of the past ten decades. England, a hundred years ago, was the only country in which the inhabitants of cities formed any considerable fraction of the national population, and even there it was less than forty per cent. The United States, in 1820, contained only about a dozen places with populations exceeding eight thousand, and taking these as a whole they contained less than five per cent of the country's total. In 1920, unless all the indications are misleading, the number of such communities will be nearly a thousand and they will contain nearly forty-five per cent of the American people.[1] The movement of the people from county to town has thus assumed huge proportions, especially in recent years, and its strength shows as yet no signs of abating.

[1] The following table shows the development of urban centres in the United States by ten-year periods:

| Year | Number of Places with More than 8,000 | Total Population Included Therein | Percentage of National Population Included |
|---|---|---|---|
| 1820 | 13 | 475,135 | 4.9 |
| 1830 | 26 | 864,509 | 6.7 |
| 1840 | 44 | 1,453,994 | 8.5 |
| 1850 | 85 | 2,897,586 | 12.5 |
| 1860 | 141 | 5,072,256 | 16.1 |
| 1870 | 226 | 8,071,875 | 20.9 |
| 1880 | 291 | 11,450,894 | 22.8 |
| 1890 | 449 | 18,327,987 | 29.1 |
| 1900 | 556 | 25,142,978 | 33.1 |
| 1910 | 778 | 35,726,720 | 38.8 |

Various factors have contributed to this extraordinary development of urban communities.[1] Improvements in agriculture, for one thing, have released men from the soil, permitting great increases in the production of foodstuffs without a corresponding increase in the amount of labor required. This has permitted and even encouraged the exodus of young men and women from the rural areas. Industrial causes, too, have been of great importance: the rise and extension of the factory system with its never satiated demand for labor in the cities and towns. "God made the country, and man made the town," Cowper tells us, and that is true in a very literal sense; for man devised the means of utilizing steam power, and steam power has revolutionized the order of human life in civilized lands.

Factories congregate in cities, mainly in large cities, and where the factories are there will the laborers be gathered together. Commerce also has had its place as a contributing cause of city growth. Nearly all the great centres of population in both the Old World and the New are situated on navigable waters. It is hardly a mere accident that the American cities of two hundred thousand people or more which are not situated upon navigable waters can be counted on the fingers of one hand. Railroad transportation, furthermore, has helped to build up the large communities, making it easy to get raw materials and to market the products of manufacture. The flood of alien immigration during the fifty years between the close of the Civil War and the opening of the great European conflict directed itself chiefly to the cities for various reasons. And these are only the outstanding causes. Political factors, such as the choice of a place as the state capital or county seat, have contributed to the upbuilding of some cities; educational advantages have helped as many more. Improvements in sanitation, in housing methods, and in public recreation have made the city a better place for men to live in. Its call has become irresistible.

There are more cities in the United States than in any other country. Among the dozen largest cities of the

*Reasons for the rapid growth of American cities.*

[1] A. F. Weber, *The Growth of Cities in the Nineteenth Century* (N. Y., 1899).

## 574   THE GOVERNMENT OF THE UNITED STATES

*Effects of urban expansion.*

world, five at least are American. At the present time there are ten American cities with populations exceeding half a million and twenty-five with populations above a quarter of a million. More than a hundred cities in the United States have over 60,000 people. The nation is becoming urbanized at a rapid rate, so much so that the United States can no longer be called a rural land. In another decade or two the urban section of the population, in all likelihood, will have gained the mastery.

This is a fact of great social significance, for the influence of cities upon the national life is much greater than their numerical strength in the census figures would imply. It is the cities that supply the leaders in all branches of activity: political, social, and economic. Through their newspapers, through the various organizations which centre there, and through their leadership in every form of propaganda it is the cities that mould the public opinion of the nation to a large degree. No country can change from a rural to an urban land without some transformation in its political temperament, its social complexity, and in the nature of its economic problems.

*The city as a social unit.*

Many things differentiate the city from the rural area. The occupations of its people are highly diversified, so that no bond of common vocation and economic interest holds them together as is the case with agricultural communities. Division of labor in industry and commerce is carried to its zenith in the large urban centres, and extreme specialization in any field of activity usually narrows the horizons of men. It develops a personal expertness in doing some one thing, with a dependence upon others for everything else. "If disorder occurs in a city, it is to be put down by a professional police force; if a fire breaks out, it is to be extinguished, again, by a professional fire service; if contagious disease appears, it is to be dealt with, again, by a professional health department."[1] The city-dweller looks for professional guidance in philanthropy, in recreation, even in politics. The whole tendency of city life is towards docility and the extinction of independence in thought and

*Traits of its population.*

*The attitude of docility.*

[1] F. J. Goodnow, *City Government in the United States* (N. Y., 1904), p. 14.

action. Men who are born and grow up in large communities do not realize the workings of this psychological influence, but its pressure is incessant.

Paradoxical though it may seem, the city nevertheless tends to be radical in its attitude toward political and economic issues. Its restive frame of mind does not betray, however, the radicalism of independence but of self-interest. This is because the city is the habitat of great propertyless elements and lacks the stabilizing influence of widely distributed private ownership. In Boston not one in five families own their homes; in New York not one in eight. In the rural districts of the United States, on the other hand, more than half the adult male population can claim the ownership of land. The great disparity in income and wealth which may be found within the bounds of the city is also an incentive to restiveness on the part of the less well-to-do. Class antagonisms develop, therefore, more readily in cities than in regions where worldly possessions are more evenly distributed, and where each man's earnings do not differ greatly from those of his neighbor. *Radicalism in cities: its causes.*

The presence of large foreign-born elements in American cities is another factor which has tended to promote political docility, social unrest, and a readiness to depart from established traditions in government or law. In the nation as a whole only thirteen per cent of the population is of foreign birth;[1] but in the cities the ratio is much higher. Rarely is it less than twenty-five per cent and it sometimes exceeds fifty. Many of the largest cities are veritable melting-pots for the assimilation of aliens drawn from the ends of the earth. It is said of New York City, and doubtless with truth, that it contains "more Irishmen than Dublin, more Italians than Padua, more Germans than Potsdam, and more Jews than Jerusalem." The immigrant brings with him no knowledge of American political traditions. His eyes are on the present and future, not on the past. If he tries to enter into the spirit of existing American institutions, he finds almost insuperable obstacles in the way, his lack of education, his difficulties in mastering the new language, *The alien element in American cities.*

[1] This does not include, of course, *native-born persons of foreign parentage.*

the dearth of leisure, and the various other forces which inevitably cast him into the company of other immigrants like himself. All too soon he learns to think as they do, to be exploited by contractors and politicians as they are, to shape his attitude upon political and industrial questions in accordance with the only sources of information which are open to him.

All too soon after an immigrant passes the Statue of Liberty he is likely to be disillusioned. He came to America as to a land of promise, of political liberty, of social equality, and of economic fraternity. What he usually finds is hard labor at two dollars a day, a two-room home in a tenement, a foreman who bullies him at work, a walking-delegate who tells him to strike, and a politician who dictates how he shall vote. It is hard for the new arrival to discern the principles of liberty, equality, and fraternity in all this. Thus disillusioned and exploited the immigrant often becomes a malcontent and quite naturally becomes the prey of demagogues who use him solely for their own advantage.

*Why immigrants concentrate in urban centres.* Why do immigrants concentrate in the cities, particularly in the large cities? It is not merely because they land there, for Chicago and St. Louis, Bridgeport and Gary, Milwaukee and Schenectady, all have large infusions of foreign-born although they are not ports of entry. The real reasons are partly social and partly economic. The immigrant goes where he can be with others of his own tongue, hence whenever a colony of Italians, Greeks, Poles, Lithuanians, Armenians, or any other alien race gets a foothold in any American community, it is sure to be steadily augmented by new arrivals. But the economic magnetism of the city is even stronger. The great majority of these immigrants come to America to work, and it is in the city that jobs, particularly of the unskilled sort, can be most readily found. The factories and shops of the large industrial centres furnish an almost unlimited demand for alien labor. The largest single industry in New York City, for example, is the manufacture of "ready-to-wear" clothing, and this industry employs foreign-born labor almost entirely. Some immigrants, it is true, go to the agricultural, mining, and lumber regions of the country; but the industrial communities get by far the larger share. It is upon the cities, accordingly, that the burden of Americanizing the alien has been chiefly placed, and a heavy burden it is. At times it has looked as though the outcome might be the un-Americanizing of the city rather than the Americanization of these great alien groups. At any rate their presence has profoundly affected the city's social structure, its attitude upon public questions, its political ideals, and its part in the national life.

In many other respects a city differs from a rural unit of equal population. It has a higher birth-rate, a higher death-rate and a far higher ratio in the statistics of crime. It has relatively fewer illiterates, strange to say, despite its larger proportion of aliens. This is a tribute to the far more accessible educational advantages in the way of evening schools, for example, which the cities provide. The people of the city earn more per capita, spend more, and save more than those of rural sections. They preserve, as military statistics show, an equality with the rural population in point of good physique and the absence of serious bodily defects.[1] Other differences which cannot be statistically compared there must be in plenty. They are plain enough to any observant eye. The city populations are more volatile, less dependent upon the associations of home and church, more influenced by things of the moment and less by tradition, more ardent in their championship of new doctrines, and generally accounted to have more initiative. The city, however, is a place where extremes meet. Wealth and poverty, culture and ignorance, virtue and vice, are there brought into close proximity. The city of to-day is responsible for most of what is good, and for most of what is bad, in our national life and ideals. *Other urban traits.*

The genesis of city government in the United States may be found in the chartered boroughs of the colonial period. New York, in 1686, was the first American community to receive a borough charter, but Albany became similarly *Periods in American municipal development:*

[1] In the physical examinations of more than three million men between the ages of twenty-one and thirty-one in connection with the raising of the national army, there was no appreciable difference in the percentages of rejections on physical grounds between those who came from urban and those who came from rural areas.

2 P

**1. The colonial era.**

incorporated a few months later. In due course nearly a score of other places got their charters as boroughs, including Philadelphia, Annapolis, Norfolk, Richmond, and Trenton. All the active chartered boroughs were in the southern and middle colonies. There were none in New England, where the town system of local government met all local needs. The borough charters were in all cases granted by the colonial governor, and in a general way they were modelled upon those of English municipal corporations at the time.

**Borough organization in the colonies.**

The government of the colonial city or borough was in the hands of a borough council, made up of a mayor, aldermen, and councillors, all sitting together. In most cases the councillors were chosen by the people, and so were the aldermen; but the mayor was usually appointed by the governor of the colony. There were some other borough officers, such as the treasurer and recorder, but the administrative work of the colonial borough did not amount to much. Very little was provided for the citizens in the way of municipal services. Paved streets and sidewalks were rare; there was no public water supply or sanitation, no public lighting to speak of, no professional police or fire protection service, and no arrangements for public recreation. Poor relief to some extent, public schools in some boroughs, the administration of local justice and the making of some by-laws constituted the main functions of borough government in colonial times.

**2. From the Revolution to about 1820.**

The Revolution made some changes both in the form and spirit of these municipal institutions, although the general structure continued for the most part unaltered. Charters were now granted, not by the governor, but by the state legislature. The disposition in colonial times had been to treat the boroughs as close corporations after the prevailing tendency in the mother country. After the Revolution this idea was wholly abandoned; the suffrage was gradually widened, and the local officers were made more directly accountable to the whole body of the citizens. The formation of the new national government also had its influence upon the cities. When new borough charters were framed there was a conscious imitation of the federal system with its arrangement of checks and balances. The borough council during the early years of the nineteenth century became a double chamber, with its two branches known usually as the board of aldermen and the common council.[1] In New England the prevailing theory was that the alderman would perpetuate the selectmen of the town system, while the common council would be the successor of the town meeting. The practice of choosing the mayor by popular vote also came into existence and in time supplanted the method of appointment by either the governor or the borough council. In general the system of borough government, or city government as it was now more commonly called, became a reproduction in miniature of the national and state organizations. The principle of division of powers thus gained a general acceptance in all three fields of American government.

City growth was slow during the thirty or forty years next following the winning of independence. New York, the largest American city in 1820, had somewhat more than 100,000 people; Philadelphia, the second, had about half that number; and Boston, the third, was still a town of less than forty thousand. City government, however, was steadily increasing the scope and variety of its functions. More attention was now being given to streets, sanitation, lighting, fire protection, education, and the preservation of order. This devolved more work upon the city councils, which accordingly began the practice of intrusting the direct supervision of the various services to its own committees. {Characteristics of this period.}

From about 1820 to the Civil War municipal growth went forward at an increased pace, and with this increase in size new problems came to the front. The system of administration by committees of the council proved quite unsatisfactory in the larger communities, resulting in mismanagement and waste. Hence arose the policy of intrusting the management of public works, water supply, and similar {3. From 1820 to the Civil War.}

---

[1] The terms "aldermen" and "common council" carry back to the Anglo-Norman period of English history. Œldor-men were Saxon officials before the Conqueror came to England; the communal council (common council) or council or the commune was a Norman transplantation. The communal council remains the chief organ in French city government to-day.

technical services to boards of officials specially chosen for the purpose and wholly independent of the council. Likewise, as a further check upon the council's activities, the mayor was in many cities given the power of veto, and occasionally was empowered to appoint the various administrative boards and officials. In a word, the council began to lose its hold upon administrative affairs, and the development of a strong municipal executive commenced. This shifting of power was hastened to some extent by the decline in the quality of municipal councils which has usually been attributed to the influx of aliens during the mid-century period, but which really began before the tide of immigration set in. The spoils system of the Jacksonian era, which found its way into municipal government, did much to demoralize the city councils by placing patronage in the hands of councillors and by making party subservience the prerequisite of all municipal office-holding. The seeds of later corruption and extravagance were planted in all the larger municipalities before 1850.

The growth of state interference in city affairs. State interference in municipal affairs, as a result, became more frequent, especially during the decade 1850–1860. The lax enforcement of state laws in the larger centres of population, the freedom with which cities were spending and borrowing money, the inefficiency and wastefulness which characterized the administration of various departments, all combined to encourage state investigation of local affairs and state intervention. Cities began to lose what modicum of home rule they had. State laws stepped in to circumscribe the powers of city councils and city officials, taking away some of their discretion and increasing their legal responsibility. In a few cases, where municipal misgovernment had seemingly become incurable, the state authorities took matters out of the city's hands altogether. In New York City, for instance, the state took over the local police administration in 1857 and did not give it back until 1870. State interference in municipal affairs did not have its origin in any theory of state supremacy but in the sordid facts of urban misrule. The cities themselves, in most cases, invoked it by their perversions of democracy and their gross abuse of the freedom which had been allowed them. But once this habit of interventions began, it was hard to check, and in succeeding years it became in its own turn an abuse as serious as that which it originally set out to cure.

The third period in American municipal history extended from the close of the Civil War to the end of the nineteenth century. It began rather inauspiciously because the tide of immigration which had ceased to flow during the war years now set in again with redoubled force, with the result that the cities grew more rapidly than ever before. Industry and commerce also expanded, and optimism was the keynote everywhere. As was only natural under such conditions the cities spent money with a free hand, discounting the future as optimists are wont to do. Taxes soared, debts ran far into the millions in all the larger communities. Much of this money was spent without proper planning, much of it went to contractors who scamped their work, and in some cities not a little went into the pockets of local politicians. These were the days of the Tweed Ring in New York, the Gas Ring in Philadelphia, and of less notorious plunder-bunds in other cities. The spoils system, during the seventies and early eighties, seemed to be triumphant everywhere. It flaunted its vicious doctrines with all the truculence of a despot, and helped to make the city, in the words of Lord Bryce, "the one conspicuous failure of American government."

4. From the Civil War to about 1900.

During these years there were spasms of reform. One of them ousted the Tweed Ring in New York and secured the insertion of new safeguards in the city charter. In other cities these reform movements succeeded in transferring more power to the mayor and in making him somewhat more directly responsible for the administrative functions of city government. Civil service reform, moreover, having gained large recognition in national administration during Grover Cleveland's first term as President, presently began to make its influence felt in the cities as well. But in no city of the country was there any successful reconstruction of the entire system of municipal organization. It was taken for granted that the trouble did not lie with the machinery of city government but with the men who were running it. Reform campaigns, accordingly, were undertaken chiefly for the

The failure of reform movements in this period.

purpose of replacing one set of officials with another. But when they succeeded (as they did occasionally), little of permanent value was achieved. A few new provisions went into the city charter; the tax rate was lowered a notch or two; some spoilsmen were shaken from their grip on the city payroll, and then the reform administration would go out of office with profuse excuses for not having been able to accomplish more.

5. The period since 1900.

Municipal reform did not make much genuine progress in the United States until the opening years of the twentieth century. About that time it entered a new cycle by directing its assaults not merely against incompetent or corrupt office-holders, but against the system which permitted and even encouraged dishonest men to gain control of the city's affairs. Public opinion began to realize that efficient municipal administration is not merely a matter of men, but of laws and institutions as well. Beginning with the Galveston experiment of 1901 the first two decades of the twentieth century have accordingly witnessed the reorganization of American city government on a scale which would have been considered out of the question a generation ago. The doctrine of checks and balances has in many cases been swept away; the mechanism of city government has been everywhere simplified by the elimination of superfluous officials and boards; the commission and city-manager plans, home-rule charters, the initiative, referendum, and recall, the short ballot, stringent laws against corrupt practices, the direct primary and nomination by petition, the abolition of party designations, — these and many other changes have made the American municipal system very different from what it was in 1900.

The basis of city government — the city charter.

The basis of city government, and the medium through which any radical changes in organization must be made, is the city charter. This document, in a way, is the constitution of the municipality. It provides what officials a city shall have, how they shall be chosen, what functions they shall perform, and what powers they may exercise.

Methods of granting charters.

City charters always emanate from the state legislature, which, however, may be restricted by the provisions of the state constitution as to the manner in which such charters shall be granted. Different states pursue various methods in this matter, but in general there are five principal methods of framing and granting a city charter. These may be designated as the general, classified, special, home-rule, and optional charter systems.

The general charter system was common in several states a quarter of a century ago, but is now being abandoned. It was the outcome of a popular conviction that legislatures ought to treat all cities alike, giving no one city a more favorable charter than others. A provision was frequently inserted in the state constitution, therefore, forbidding the legislature to charter cities by special law or to give to any city powers which are not given to all.[1] The only alternative in such cases was for the legislature to enact one general charter or municipal code applying to all the cities of the state, whether large or small.

1. The general charter system.

The great defect of the general charter system is its rigidity. Not all cities are alike in size, population, characteristics, problems, or requirements. A seaport city, for instance, may need a harbor board with powers to regulate the anchoring-places of ships; but to require for the sake of general uniformity that inland cities of the state shall also have harbor authorities and anchorage regulations is a palpable absurdity. Under the general charter plan, as it formerly existed in Ohio, for example, it was found that a scheme of government which had to be fitted to both big and little cities proved satisfactory to neither.

Its defects.

Other states, realizing the undesirability of requiring absolute uniformity in city charters, have provided in their constitutions that cities shall be grouped into classes according to their respective populations and that the legislature shall grant similar charters to all cities within the same class. This allows more leeway, while at the same time preventing any discrimination in favor of, or against, a particular city. Grouping cities according to their population, however, is at best a purely artificial method of classification, for municipalities which stand close together in the census figures may be wholly unlike in the texture

2. The classified charter plan.

---

[1] See the bulletin on *Municipal Home Rule* prepared for the Massachusetts Constitutional Convention (Boston, 1917), p. 7.

of their populations, in their resources, their problems, and their administrative requirements. As cities grow, moreover, they pass from one class to another, thus coming under a new charter régime whether they desire to change the existing system or not.

**3. Special charter system.** Many states, again, have continued the original method of granting city charters, commonly known as the special charter system. Under this plan each city is dealt with as a separate problem and each gets whatever form of charter the legislature chooses to give it. All may get the same charter, or each may get a different one, the latter being the usual course. On its face, this system has much in its **Its merits and defects.** favor. It has the virtue of adaptability, enabling the legislature to frame each city's charter with an eye single to that city's needs, giving it such officials as may be required and such powers as seem necessary. But in practice it has merely thrown the door wide open to partisan discrimination and to factious interference in matters of purely local concern. To help the dominant political party, or to serve some other selfish interest, legislatures have frequently altered city charters against the will of the citizens, treating these documents as though they were entitled to no more permanence or security than any ordinary law. Where there is no barrier to the passing of special charter laws, the legislatures of some states have not hesitated to interfere with the conduct of routine business in cities, raising the salaries of favored officials, reinstating dismissed municipal officers, altering the boundaries of wards, awarding holidays to municipal employees, and so on, all such actions being dictated by purely political motives. The special charter system has thus been grossly abused, so much so that the demand for municipal home-rule has become insistent over large sections of the country.

**4. The home-rule charters.** The home-rule charter system was devised, accordingly, to protect cities against the over-activity of meddlesome legislatures. It has gained in popularity during the last couple of decades and is now established in twelve states of the Union.[1] As its name implies, it is a plan whereby

[1] These states are Missouri, California, Washington, Minnesota, Colorado, Oregon, Oklahoma, Michigan, Arizona, Nebraska, Ohio, and Texas.

cities make their own charters just as states make their own constitutions. In this connection it should be made clear, however, that cities which do not see fit to frame their own charters remain under the provisions of the general or special laws as before.

The methods of framing home-rule charters differ somewhat in the various states, but in all of them except Oregon the drafting of the document is intrusted to a body of citizens commonly known as a board of freeholders or charter commission.[1] The members of this board are in all cases elected, except in Minnesota, where they are appointed by the district court. When the board has completed its work, the charter is submitted to the people of the city and if it is approved by them at the polls, it goes into effect without further approval in most of the states.[2] {Methods of framing them.}

In actual practice, however, the home-rule system does not give as much local freedom as this brief description of it might indicate.[3] The cities, in making their own charters, are allowed entire liberty, to be sure, in matters of purely local concern. But what are matters of strictly local concern? The line of demarcation between matters of local interest on the one hand and of state interest on the other is not firmly fixed; but the sphere of the state is ever widening, and it already includes a host of things such as assessment, taxation, elections, police, licenses, education, public health, poor-relief, which on their face might be deemed to be matters of municipal jurisdiction. The provisions of home-rule charters must keep within the bounds of the general state laws on these and many other matters. Municipal home-rule does not mean, therefore, that each city can set up a little rock-ribbed republic, but merely that it may choose for itself the general outlines of its own government and that it shall be free from state interference within {Limitations of the home-rule system.}

---

[1] In Oregon a charter may be drafted by any body of citizens and submitted to the people by an initiative petition.

[2] In Arizona and Oklahoma, however, it goes first to the governor, who may withhold his signature if he finds the charter in conflict with the state constitution or laws. In California it goes to the legislature, which may accept or reject, but may not alter it.

[3] For an exhaustive discussion of the subject, see H. L. McBain, *The Law and the Practice of Municipal Home Rule* (N. Y., 1916).

that rather limited realm which is usually designated as the field of "strictly municipal affairs."

*Its merits.* But notwithstanding these limitations the home-rule charter system has some tangible advantages. It relieves the legislature from having to do with a multitude of local matters at every session, thus affording more opportunity for the due consideration of state-wide problems. Under the special charter system it has been found that municipal affairs frequently consume from one-fourth to one-third of a legislature's time. The home-rule system helps to divorce state from municipal politics, and it has also proved an agency of political education, encouraging the voters of the city to take an active interest in the form and functions of their local government. But its greatest advantage lies in the fact that under the home-rule plan a city gets whatever sort of charter its people desire, provided, of course, that their desires do not run counter to the general interest of the state as a whole.

*5. The optional charter system.* The fifth method of granting city charters is known as the alternative or optional charter system. It is a compromise between the general charter plan at the one extreme, and municipal home-rule at the other. Under this arrangement the state legislature provides several standard charters, any one of which a city may adopt by popular vote. The *New York.* optional charter law passed by the New York legislature in 1913 provided seven different forms of local government and allowed any city of the state except the three largest (New York, Buffalo, and Rochester) to choose whichever one *Massachusetts.* of these plans it might desire. The Massachusetts optional charter law of 1915 provides four options, namely, city government by a mayor and small council, by a mayor and a large council, by a commission, and by a city manager. Optional charter laws have also been enacted in North Carolina, Virginia, and some other states. The merit of this plan is that it gives flexibility to the charter system, allowing each city a reasonable range of choice, without opening the door to such rash experiments as the home-rule plan has sometimes encouraged. These optional charters are fitted to the general state laws so that there can be no conflict. The system, on the whole, seems to have the largest number of real advantages without countervailing drawbacks.

City charters, like state constitutions, are becoming more prolix and unwieldy as time goes on. The earliest extant charter of London, granted by William the Conqueror in 1066, contains about sixty words. The present charter of New York City makes up a volume of nearly one thousand closely printed pages. All manner of minor details are being provided for in charters, when they should properly be left to be dealt with by ordinances of the city council. American city charters, on the whole, have been poorly drawn, and they have consequently been the basis of much litigation.

## CHAPTER XLI

### MUNICIPAL ORGANIZATION

Types of municipal organization in the United States:
1. The mayor-and-council plan.

THE type of city government which developed in the United States during the nineteenth century and which still prevails as the most common form is the mayor-and-council plan. Under this scheme of local government the corporate powers and functions of the municipality are divided among a mayor, a number of administrative boards or officials, and a city council. In other words, this plan follows in its general outlines the frame of federal and state government. Until after 1900 the mayor-and-council plan was virtually the only type of municipal government existing in any part of the United States.

2. The commission plan.

But in 1901 a commission system of city government was established in Galveston, Texas, and since that date this arrangement has found adoption in many municipalities. The essential feature of the commission type, as will be more fully explained in another chapter, is the vesting of all the corporate powers and functions of the city in the hands of a commission made up of five persons elected by the voters. This body combines within its jurisdiction both legislative and administrative authority, thus discarding the doctrine of formal checks and balances.

3. The city-manager plan.

Finally, during the past half-dozen years the city-manager plan of municipal government has come into existence. It may be defined as a scheme by which all such corporate powers and functions of the municipality as have to do with the determination of policy and the general direction of local affairs are intrusted to a small council or commission elected by the voters at large, while the strictly administrative functions of municipal government are placed in the hands of a professional, well-paid officer, known as the city-manager, who is chosen by the council for his proficiency as an administrator. The fundamental principle of this plan is a separation of legislative from administrative functions, but without any division of ultimate power or responsibility.

The first of these three plans, the mayor-and-council, or federal executive type, is to be found in all the largest cities of the country, that is to say in all those which have populations exceeding 500,000. It prevails likewise in all American cities of over 200,000 with about a half-dozen exceptions. Taking the fifty most important municipalities of the United States, the mayor-and-council organization is retained in all but twelve. Despite the spread of the other plans, therefore, it must still be regarded as the prevailing type of municipal government. Its mechanism includes, as has been said, a mayor, a staff of administrative boards or officials or both, and a city council of either one or two chambers.[1] *Prevalence of the mayor-and-council form.*

The mayor is everywhere chosen by direct popular vote. Nominations, as a rule, are made at a primary, and the election is by secret ballot, usually with party designations thereon. To be eligible for election a candidate must in all cases be a qualified voter, and in some cases additional residence requirements are imposed. It is not necessary that a candidate for the mayoralty shall have previously held any other office or have had any experience in municipal government, but in practice the candidates are almost invariably men who have been prominent in national, state or local politics. The mayor's term is either two or four years in most cities, the former being customary in nearly all but the largest ones. Usually a mayor may be chosen for a second term; but in a few cities, including Philadelphia and Boston, this is not permitted. The office carries a salary which varies from one thousand dollars in some of the smallest cities to fifteen thousand in New York. *The mayor.*

The authority of the mayor usually includes the right to advise the city council by message or communication, to *His powers.*

[1] For a further discussion of the various matters dealt with in the following pages of this chapter, the reader may be referred to the author's volume on *The Government of American Cities* (2d ed., N. Y., 1916), and to the references there indicated.

veto ordinances, to appoint most of the higher city officials, to exercise various powers in relation to municipal finance, and to perform some miscellaneous functions.

(a) advisory.
According to the abstractions of the mayor-and-council type of municipal government the mayor has no active share in legislation, that is, in the making of city ordinances. Legislation is assumed to be the function of the city council. But the mayor, as a rule, is empowered to recommend legislative action on the part of the council and also to veto any ordinance which may meet with his disapproval, so that his actual influence over the course of municipal legislation is often considerable. Recommendations to the city council are sent by messages or written communications which are read by the council's clerk and then referred to the appropriate committees. Whether they will be adopted depends to a large extent upon the political relations which exist between the two departments of the city's government. The mayor is usually a local party leader, and if his party controls a majority in the city council, the chances of favorable action by the latter are naturally much greater than when the political situation is reversed.

(b) the veto.
Most city charters provide that any ordinance or resolution which passes the city council shall be sent to the mayor for his approval. If the mayor approves the measure, he signs it; if he does not approve he may return it unsigned within a designated number of days, usually five, seven, or ten, with a communication stating his reasons for disapproval. The council may then pass the ordinance over the mayor's disapproval or veto by a two-thirds vote.[1] If it does not do so, the measure remains inoperative. There is also, in most cases, a provision that if the mayor neither signs nor returns a proposed ordinance within the prescribed time, it becomes valid without his signature. The analogy between the veto power in federal and in municipal government is thus plainly to be recognized.

The qualified veto, however, has not proved a satisfactory institution in local government. Occasionally it has enabled a courageous mayor to check extravagance and to prevent

[1] In Baltimore the requirement is a three-fourths vote; in Philadelphia, three-fifths; and in San Francisco, seven-ninths.

the imprudent granting of franchises; but more often it has been employed to further a mayor's own political or personal interests quite regardless of the general welfare. The exercise of the veto power has been far more frequent in the cities than in the nation or the states, so much so that it has enabled the mayor in many cities to become the real dictator of local policy without having the full responsibility therefor. In its origin and by its design the veto was intended to be an emergency weapon in cases where drastic interference with the normal course of legislation seemed to be clearly justified by obvious considerations of public interest. Its employment on all and sundry occasions as a means of enforcing the personal wishes of the executive is a perversion of the veto's true place in the American scheme of government.

Merits and defects of the veto.

The higher officials of city administration, such as the treasurer, comptroller, city solicitor, police commissioner, superintendent of streets, likewise the members of the various boards and commissions, are in some cases chosen by popular vote. In a few instances, again, they are selected by the city council, but most commonly their appointment is now intrusted to the mayor. The tendency to concentrate the appointing power in the mayor's hands has been increasing in recent years. In many cities, however, there still exists the requirement that appointments made by the mayor to these higher administrative positions must have the concurrence of the city council (or the upper branch of that body) before they become valid.[1] This requirement of aldermanic confirmation is another example of the influence of the federal analogy in local government and forms part of the municipal system of checks and balances. Its advantages, however, are seriously open to question, for while the plan has at times availed to prevent the making of improper appointments it has more often served to divide the responsibility for inefficiency in municipal office between the mayor and the council to such an extent that the people are able to hold neither of them to account. It has become a prolific source of political legerdemain and imposture. Some of the larger cities, New York for example, have abolished the

(c) appointments.

[1] In Boston the approval of the state civil service commission is required.

system of council confirmation with results which have proved to be distinctly advantageous.

(d) removals. The mayor, as a rule, may remove appointive city officials, but his discretion here is also in most cases limited. Sometimes the concurrence of the council is necessary in such removals. Where the appointments have been made under civil service rules, moreover, various formalities in the way of filing definite charges and holding a public investigation must usually be complied with before an officer's removal can be effected. Suspensions, however, may usually be made by the mayor on his own authority.

(e) financial powers. Another group of mayoral powers relate to the city's financial administration. These powers differ greatly in extent from city to city, but the tendency everywhere is towards their enlargement. In some cities the mayor is given the sole right to initiate proposals of expenditure, the council being allowed to reduce any item in the mayor's list of estimates but not to increase or to insert new items. Boston affords a good example of this system whereby the entire responsibility for all increases in municipal expenditure rests upon the mayor alone. In New York City this responsibility is not imposed upon the mayor alone, but is devolved upon a body known as the Board of Estimate and Apportionment, of which the mayor is an influential member.[1] In Chicago, on the other hand, the initiative in matters of expenditure continues to be vested in the city council. On the whole it seems desirable that the function of preparing the city's annual budget should be deputed to the mayor, thus locating the responsibility where it cannot be evaded. A budget made by a city council is nothing but a means of dividing the city's money in accordance with the interplay of ward politics.

(f) miscellaneous. Some miscellaneous powers usually pertain to the mayor's office. He has the right to investigate the work of the municipal departments; sometimes his approval is required whenever contracts for public works are let; and not infre-

[1] This body is composed of eight members in all, namely, the mayor, the comptroller, the president of the board of aldermen, and the presidents of the five boroughs: Manhattan, Brooklyn, The Bronx, Richmond, and Queens. Sixteen votes are distributed among these eight members, the mayor having three votes.

quently he has the powers of a justice of the peace or local magistrate. The mayor represents the city on all occasions of ceremony and ranks as the first citizen of the community. Social duties, which are of infinite variety, take a large share of his time and energy, so much so that personal attention to the details of his official work has become exceedingly difficult in the larger cities.

In addition to its mayor a city which maintains the mayor-and-council system of government has various officials and boards in charge of its administrative departments, such as police, fire protection, highways, water supply, and public health. Originally the management of these departments was in charge of the city council's committees (as it is in English cities at the present day); but during the nineteenth century American municipalities broke away from this plan and committed the work of departmental administration to separate boards or individual officials. For a time the board system was the more popular, partly because of local prejudice against giving too much power to any one official, and partly because a board of three or five members gave an opportunity for having both political parties represented on it. But the bi-partisan board rarely proved to be an efficient or smooth-working body, and in many cases it has been supplanted by a single commissioner. The board system has some distinct merits when applied to such departments as poor relief, schools, city planning, or public libraries where deliberation and discussion are desirable. But in its application to some other city departments, police, fire protection, and health, where quickness of decision and firmness in action are essential, the board system is unsuitable and has given way in many cities to the plan of administration by a single head.

2. The heads of city departments.

Evolution of this system.

The officials in charge of the various city departments, whether members of boards or individual commissioners, are either elected by the people, chosen by the city council, or appointed by the mayor. Popular election was at one time the customary method, but it is now used in a few cases only. The council still chooses some of the higher officials in most cities, particularly the city clerk. But appointment by the mayor has become the prevailing plan. The merit

How department heads are chosen.

2 Q

system applies only to subordinate officials; in no American city are the heads of departments chosen by civil service competition. The nearest approach to it is in Boston, where the mayor's appointments to the headships of departments require the formal approval of the state civil service authorities as to their general qualifications by education, training, or experience.

<small>Should civil service rules be extended to the highest municipal offices?</small>

The selection of the higher as well as the lower officials of city administration by civil service competition has sometimes been proposed, but there are serious objections in the way. Heads of departments should not only have familiarity with the work which is to be placed in their charge, but personal qualities such as tact, ability to work with others, and a due deference to public opinion. Competitive tests may determine an official's expertness and technical knowledge, but they do not and cannot put to the proof the possession of these other qualities. Experts in all fields of human endeavor tend to be dogmatic and impersonal, while public administration is an intensely practical and personal matter, whether it be in the field of police, public health, education, poor relief, or recreation. No administrator who hopes to be successful can nonchalantly brush human nature aside and deal only with the cold canons of technique and efficiency. A disregard of that simple principle, which is as old as democracy itself, has brought many a municipal expert to grief. Work that is technical in its nature, whether in public or in private administration, should be put into the hands of trained men; but the determination of public policy must reckon not only with professional theories, but with the pragmatism of the public mind. The science of municipal government is in large part the science of managing cantankerous men and women. For of such is the kingdom of democracy.

<small>State intervention in city administration.</small>

Occasionally the state has intervened and taken into its own hands the appointment of certain higher officials in the larger cities. In Boston, Baltimore, and St. Louis, for example, the municipal police is in charge of state-appointed officials. There is always a strong local prejudice against this policy, however, and it is rigidly forbidden by the constitutions of a good many states. State appointment of municipal officials is more defensible in the case of the police department than any other, for inefficiency and corruption there results in the non-enforcement or discriminatory enforcement of the state laws. Such interference with municipal home rule is, in most cases, however, of doubtful expediency.

The other important branch of the municipal organization is the city council. Originally it was the chief and in fact the only governing organ of the city, but it has parted with many of its earlier functions and is now in most cities the less important branch of local government. The council may consist of one or two chambers. In the latter case the upper chamber is usually known as the board of aldermen and the lower chamber is called the common council. The members of both are elected, ordinarily for terms of from one to four years, and either by wards or by the voters at large or by some combination of these two plans. Nominations are usually made by means of a primary. In a few cities there are no formal nominations and the election takes place by means of a preferential ballot.

3. The city council.

Its organization.

Much has been said and written about the relative merits of the single and double chamber system in the organization of municipal councils. The bicameral plan has been defended as affording a protection against hasty and unwise action, against subservience to any sinister interest, and against the complete control of the city's legislative machinery by one political party. On the other hand it is contended that the single-chamber plan enables the city to get better councilmen, and that it permits business to be done more promptly, with far less opportunity for wirepulling. With the greatly curtailed powers of the council there is no longer any need for such an elaborate checking apparatus as the bicameral system provides. At any rate the double chamber is rapidly becoming obsolete in city government. One city after another has abandoned it, so that at the present day it is the exception rather than the rule.

The single and double chamber systems.

The relative merits of the ward and at-large methods of electing councillors have also been the theme of much controversy. The ward system is the older plan and at one

**Ward and general ticket systems of election.**

time was practically universal. But it was regarded as responsible for the mediocre quality of the men chosen to city councils, especially in the large municipalities, and for the zeal with which every councillor sought to obtain favors for his own district without any allegiance to the interests of the city as a whole. The ward system has accordingly been supplanted in many cities by the plan of election at large. The practical difficulty with this latter method, however, is that some districts of the city are likely to be left unrepresented altogether. Moreover, if elections are conducted on a party basis, as is almost invariably the case, the majority party will elect its entire slate of candidates, leaving the minority with no councilmen at all. To overcome these practical objections some cities have adopted a combination of the two plans, electing one councillor from each ward and also a designated number at large. If a city has nine wards and a council of fifteen members, for example, each voter marks his ballot for seven members, one to represent his own ward and six to be chosen at large. This plan assures some geographical representation and some measure of minority representation as well.

City councils hold regular meetings, usually once a week, and are usually empowered to select their own presiding officer. They also make their own rules of procedure, which are similar to those used in state legislatures, although much less elaborate. Most of a city council's work is done by committees whose members are appointed by the presiding officer. These committees examine into the various matters which come before the council and make recommendations, which may or may not be accepted.

**Functions of the city council. (a) the enacting of ordinances.**

Chief among the functions of a city council is that of making ordinances or local laws. These ordinances relate to a wide variety of matters, the protection of life and property, traffic in the streets, sanitation, health, housing, weights and measures, bill-boards, places of amusement, and so on. They must not, however, be inconsistent with the provisions of the city charter or any other state law. Ordinances must be enacted with due regard for the prescribed formalities and must in most cases receive the

MUNICIPAL ORGANIZATION 597

approval of the mayor before going into effect. But once properly enacted they have the force of law and are enforceable by the regular courts.

Municipal ordinances must fulfil certain conditions, however, or the courts will hold them invalid. For one thing they must be reasonable and not oppressive in character. There is, of course, no general test of reasonableness, but the courts have now set up a sufficient number of precedents to serve as a guide. Ordinances, again, must not be discriminatory in their application. They must not single out individuals or groups of persons for special restriction while permitting others of the same sort to be immune. Finally, municipal ordinances must not unduly restrain freedom of trade, freedom of contract, or the other established rights of the citizen. Considerations of public safety, health, and morals are paramount, however, and the freedom of the individual may always be restrained where these considerations require it; but factious or undue restraint will not be tolerated. On the whole, however, the courts have been lenient in these matters, giving the ordinance the benefit of any doubt, where doubt exists. *Legal limitations on the ordinance power.*

City councils also possess various powers in relation to local finance. No taxes can be levied, no appropriations made, and no money borrowed except with the council's approval. It is true that the nature of the taxes is determined by the state laws, but the city council by ordinance fixes the rate. The list of appropriations, too, is often prepared by the mayor or by a board of estimate, but no appropriation becomes effective until the city council has given its approval. And in the matter of municipal borrowing the council determines the amount, the term of the loan, and the rate of interest to be paid. The hands of the council are often tied, however, by the facts of the situation. In appropriations, for example, there are many items over which the council has no real discretion. Interest on the municipal debt, expenditures which are made compulsory by state law, the cost of maintaining city property — these must be provided for in any case. So, too, the expense of maintaining the schools, the police and fire departments, and the sanitary system cannot be reduced below a certain *(b) financial authority.*

*Limitations as to taxation and appropriations.*

point. The discretionary power of the council with respect to expenditures is not nearly so large, therefore, as is commonly imagined. The same is true of the tax-rate, which is nothing but the quotient obtained by dividing the proposed net expenditure into the total assessed valuation of taxable property. City councils, by a rigid paring of appropriations, can reduce the tax-rate a trifle, but rarely can any considerable reduction be made without crippling the administrative departments.

*Limitations upon the borrowing power.*

Most cities, again, are not permitted to borrow beyond a certain point. They are subject to debt limits fixed by the state constitution or by state law. These limits are usually set by designating a certain percentage of the assessed valuation as the maximum of municipal indebtedness. In New York, for example, a city may incur indebtedness up to ten per cent of the assessed value of the real estate within its borders, but no more. Unless municipal financing is carefully done a city soon reaches its debt limit, and thereafter can borrow no more unless there are increases in the assessed valuation.

*(c) powers in relation to franchise.*

In most cities the council retains the power to grant franchises or privileges to public service corporations such as lighting, telephone, and street railway companies. In former times it had complete authority over such matters, but grossly abused its trust. Franchises of great value were given for long periods, and sometimes in perpetuity, without securing the city any compensation. Bribery and the crack of the party whip rather than business sense and honesty too often determined whether a company's gas mains or car tracks should have the free use of a city's streets forever. The states accordingly have stepped in and by their laws now restrict the council's discretion, providing as a rule that no franchise may be granted for more than a certain term of years and that companies which receive such privileges shall be subject to public regulation.

*(d) miscellaneous powers.*

Finally, a city council possesses some powers of a miscellaneous nature which cannot be readily classified. They include such matters as authorizing the purchase of land for public buildings, deciding the location and naming of new streets, the approval of certain important contracts, the fixing of water rates, and the acceptance or rejection of permissive state legislation, in other words, of laws which are passed by the legislature with a provision that they will go into effect in any city whenever the city council accepts them.

This brief survey of the council's powers may indicate that they are of considerable scope, but they are not nearly so important as they used to be. The principle of division of powers, as applied to city government, has resulted in transferring the major share of authority to the mayor and to the heads of departments. The council remains the chief legislative organ of the city; but municipal government is not largely a matter of legislation. It is for the most part administration, a matter of managing public services and carrying on routine work. In local government the function of making laws is far outweighed in scope, importance, and influence by the function of carrying them into effect. The trend of municipal development in the mayor-and-council cities, therefore, is towards a subordination of the legislative to the administrative branch of the government. The same trend has been already noted in the state affairs, but it is much more pronounced in the cities. The situation stands out in sharp contrast with that existing in European countries. There the city council has everywhere retained its position of supremacy.

*Place of the city council in American government.*

In addition to the mayor, the heads of departments, and the members of the city council, the work of municipal government requires a large staff of superintendents, foremen, clerks, and other employees. Cities everywhere are large employers of both skilled and unskilled labor. If one adds together all the school teachers, policemen, firemen, library officials, clerks in the city hall, street cleaners, and other workers, the total is far larger than the ordinary citizen realizes. In New York City these employees make up an army nearly seventy-five thousand strong. The task of organizing these large corps of employees, recruiting their ranks, getting rid of the incompetent, and making the rest give a hundred cents' worth of service for a dollar's worth of salary — that is the most persistently difficult task which mayors and city councils have to perform.

4. *The city employees.*

Three factors have contributed to accentuate the difficulty of this problem. First and most important is the habitual

Why they have not reached a high plane of efficiency.

selection of officials and employees on purely political or personal grounds without reference to individual competence. Wherever civil service regulations have not been adopted, the spoils system flourishes; and even with civil service rules on the statute book the spoilsman often manages to gain his ends. A second factor is the customary absence of any well-defined system of promotion as a reward for efficiency. Promotions in the municipal service have scarcely any relation to individual merit. Political influence counts for a great deal more in the majority of cases. Employees, moreover, are regularly carried upon the list of active workers after they have become too old or too indolent to give any fair return for their wages. The chief incentive to diligence is thus taken away. Finally, there is the lax disciplinary organization of the various city departments and the absence of direct personal responsibility for the proper performance of duty. Subordinate officials who have close friends among political leaders often do as they please, disregarding the instructions of department heads. The slack discipline of municipal service is proverbial. Municipal employees are voters, of course, and in a position to exert strong pressure upon the mayor and upon the members of the city council. That is the fundamental explanation of the trouble and the chief reason why the situation is so difficult to remedy.

Their popular reputation not wholly deserved.

Inefficiency in the municipal service has not been as gross or as widespread, however, as the literature of reform sometimes implies. In every city there is a large body of employees who earnestly try to give the public the worth of their wages. But the people of the city see or hear little of this class. The officials and employees who give the municipal service its infelicitous reputation for indolence are the ones who can so often be seen in public places during business hours. They are a minority, no doubt, but their actions stamp upon the public imagination its general conception of city employment. This public attitude in its turn reacts unfavorably upon all those who are really trying to do their work faithfully and deprives the service of that *esprit de corps* which is essential to the best results.

The city is able to tolerate among its employees a measure of incompetence and carelessness which would be fatal to private enterprise because it does not have to bear the strain of competition. The taxpayers must bear the cost, whatever it is. The city, moreover, is in most cases not liable in damages for the incompetence or negligence of its officials and employers, another feature in which it differs from the ordinary business corporation. So far as the city is engaged in the performance of strictly governmental functions, such as police and fire protection, the safeguarding of the public health, and the promotion of education, it is not liable for any injuries which may be directly due to the incompetence of its employees in these departments. The citizen in such cases has no effective redress. A private corporation, on the other hand, is ordinarily liable for the torts of its agents or employees whenever any damage is done by them within the scope of their employment, and that fact affords an obvious incentive to the maintenance of efficiency. When a city engages in any non-governmental or business enterprise, such as the operation of a municipal lighting plant or a municipal street railway, it assumes the same legal liabilities for the acts of its employees as are imposed upon private companies; but these enterprises form but a small part of a city's entire administrative work. *Cities are not legally liable for the results of incompetence of their employees.*

The chief defect of the mayor-and-council type of city government, surveying it as a whole, has been its emphasis upon the formula of checks and balances. This has disintegrated authority and engendered friction between the two branches of local government. The endeavor to model the political organization of the city upon that of the federal government was unwise in its day, and has proved to be unfortunate in its consequences. It has resulted in placing upon the majority of American cities a governmental mechanism which is adapted to the making of laws. But what the city needs is a governmental mechanism adapted to the work of doing business as business is done in the world of to-day, awarding contracts, buying supplies, hiring labor, and getting results without wasting money. *The chief defect of the American municipal system.*

# CHAPTER XLII

## MUNICIPAL ADMINISTRATION

*The various branches of municipal administration.*

THE administrative functions of a modern city are both numerous and varied, but they may be arranged into several groups of activities which are closely related in their general nature.[1] The commission form of government assumes that five groups are enough to include all branches of municipal business, but in the larger cities this never proves to be the case unless unrelated functions are crowded into the same group or department. The extent and variety of a city's administrative activities depend in part upon its size, and in part, again, upon the measure of real service which it affords to its citizens. No fixed rule can safely be laid down in matters of this sort.

*1. Public safety. What it includes:*
*(a) police.*

Public safety, the safeguarding of life and property, is an administrative function in all organized communities. It includes primarily the two rather closely associated departments of police and fire protection. Modern police organization began in 1829 with the enactment of Sir Robert Peel's famous statute for reorganizing the police administration of London. This statute swept away the old watch and ward system of day-constables and night-watchmen, replacing it with a body of professional, uniformed police officers. The results were so advantageous that other English cities adopted the plan, and it was eventually copied by American municipalities as well. To-day the work of policing is intrusted in all urban communities to officers who devote their entire time to the service. The system of part-time constables remains in small towns and rural areas only.

[1] This chapter is, in the main, a very brief condensation of the discussion contained in the author's *Principles and Methods of Municipal Administration* (N. Y., 1916).

## MUNICIPAL ADMINISTRATION

In large American cities the police force is in charge of a board or a single commissioner, the latter being the more common plan.[1] He is usually appointed by the mayor; but in three large cities the heads of the police department are appointed by the state authorities.[2] In those cities which have adopted the commission type of government the police and fire departments are invariably combined under a commissioner of public safety, and this plan is also followed in some cities which retain the mayor-and-council form. In smaller and medium-sized communities this combination has some important advantages, but in large centres each department is of sufficient importance to have its own head. The commissioner or superintendent is in immediate charge of the entire force and supervises its work from headquarters. In the large cities he is assisted by a headquarters staff, each member of which holds a high rank (such as that of deputy commissioner, or superintendent, or inspector) and has jurisdiction over some assigned branch of police activity.

*Police control.*

For purposes of police administration a city is usually divided into districts or precincts with a police station in each. The members of the police force are graded in semi-military fashion into various ranks: captains, lieutenants, sergeants, patrolmen, and sometimes reservemen. The captains are in charge of stations, the lieutenants taking command when captains are absent. The sergeants do deskwork in the stations or perform inspectorial functions. The patrolmen perform the active function of enforcing the laws and maintaining order. Various members of the force are detailed to special duties as traffic officers, or detectives, or attendants at the courts. In round figures there are about twenty police officers for every ten thousand people in all large communities.

*Police organization.*

Whether police administration will be honest, efficient, and humane depends in large measure upon the patrolmen. The method of selecting these officers is accordingly a matter of prime importance. Forty or fifty years ago it was the invariable custom to let political and personal influence

*Essentials of good police organization.*

---

[1] Sometimes called superintendent, marshal, or chief.
[2] St. Louis, Boston, and Baltimore.

dictate both appointments and promotions, but to-day in a great many cities the police department has been brought under civil service rules. Likewise it was the practice to set patrolmen at work without any preliminary training, but the largest cities nowadays maintain regular training schools in which the essentials of a police officer's duty are taught. The smaller cities will no doubt make some similar provision in time.

*European and American police compared.* European and American police systems have frequently been compared to the disadvantage of the latter. The almost entire absence of police scandals in English and continental cities has been contrasted with their all-too-frequent recurrence in the cities of the United States. It should be borne in mind, however, that the problem of satisfactory police administration is a much more complicated and difficult one in America than it is on the other side of the Atlantic. In European cities the populations are homogeneous, and almost wholly native-born; in the majority of large American municipalities there are great elements of alien inhabitants with no uniform traditions of personal liberty. European police, moreover, have wider powers and are not restricted to the same extent by constitutional provisions relating to the inalienable rights of the citizen.

In the countries of Continental Europe, again, the police officers are recruited from among those who have had military service and who, accordingly, have served a period of probation under strict discipline. American cities, on the other hand, select their patrolmen from any branch of civil life with no real opportunity to test a man's amenability to discipline, or his regularity of habits or his resourcefulness in emergencies until after he has been appointed. Finally, the temptations to corruption have been much more plentiful in American cities, particularly in the large ones, than they are abroad. Strict laws relating to the liquor traffic, gambling, and the social evil have been enacted by state legislatures and turned over to the police of the large cities for enforcement. In many cases these laws are more rigid than the sentiment of the city itself would dictate. They are passed by legislatures in which representatives of the rural districts predominate. It is obviously difficult to secure the strict enforcement of laws which the people of any community do not as a whole support, and it is in such cases that police organizations have most frequently succumbed to sinister influence. The situation once led a well-known New York attorney to suggest that the city should have two sets of restrictive laws, one made by its own people for actual enforcement, and the other to embalm the moral yearnings of up-state prudery. The enforcement of laws relating to the liquor traffic and to sex morality present no serious problem in Europe, because not only are the rules more lenient but they are made by the cities for themselves.

Looking at police administration in its broader aspects, there are some fundamental differences between Anglo-American and Continental European conceptions of police functions. The English theory and its American derivative look upon the function of a police department as almost wholly repressive in its nature. The work of police officers is to prevent violations of the criminal laws. In the countries of Continental Europe, on the contrary, the concept of the police function is much broader. There the work of police officers includes many constructive activities such as the civil registration of the population, the censorship of the press, the granting of licenses, the inspection of buildings during construction, the control of societies, and many similar phases of jurisdiction which in America either do not exist at all or are intrusted to authorities outside the police department. The work of the European police organizations thus affords greater scope for initiative and makes a greater demand upon the versatility of its personnel. An organization which is altogether or even largely repressive in its activities, such as is the police department of the American city, cannot as readily acquire prestige or develop a vigorously progressive spirit in its ranks. *The concept of police functions*

Americans, like Englishmen, have always viewed with a resentful eye any proposed extension of police jurisdiction. That, no doubt, is a by-product of the general antipathy to military rule, and indeed to government by any class of professionals. Hence when the laws are passed to prevent overcrowding in tenements, or for the protection of workers *The American antipathy to the extension of police duties* in factories, or for the inspection of food, or for a score of other social welfare purposes, their enforcement is not usually committed to the regular police, but to inspectors who are appointed for each particular purpose and who are attached to the tenement-house department or the labor bureau or the health service as the case may be. The specialized enforcement of technical laws is not, therefore, made a part of the ordinary police jurisdiction. This policy, while much may be said in its favor, has reacted rather disadvantageously upon the latter by confining the police function in America, as it has not been confined in Continental Europe, to a rather narrow range of repressive, non-technical, and for the most part, unpopular duties.

*Recent improvements.* Nevertheless the general tone of police administration in American cities is far better than it was a generation ago. This is due in part to better methods of organization, particularly to the abolition of the bipartisan police board and the concentration of authority in a single police commissioner. In larger measure, however, it has resulted from improved methods of recruiting and training the force, better pay, and greater security of tenure. Police officers are no longer in most of the large cities appointed, promoted, reduced in rank or dismissed at the behest of ward politicians. Much still remains to be done before this branch of municipal administration is in all respects as satisfactory as it ought to be, but the progress of the past twenty years gives ample ground for optimism.

*Police courts.* The maintenance of law and order in cities depends not only upon the efficiency of the police, however, but upon the honesty and fairness of the local courts. The magistrates or judges of these municipal courts are usually elected, and too often their attitude towards the strict enforcement of the law is influenced by political considerations. It is sometimes argued that the practice of electing these judges of city courts is advantageous because it secures men who know and understand the conditions under which the people live and who can on that account administer the laws more justly. But on the other hand the elective system has its manifest dangers in the way of political chicanery and boss domination. Some large cities, therefore, have provided that the judges of the municipal courts shall be appointed by the mayor.[1]

Another branch of public-safety service is the protection of life and property against destruction by fire. This includes two separate functions, namely, fire-prevention and fire-fighting. Until recent years very little attention was bestowed upon the former, while so much was given to the latter that American fire-fighting organizations became easily the best in the world. The annual wastage by fire loss in the United States is appalling. In the cities alone it is over one hundred million dollars every year; in the rural districts it is even larger. The chief reasons, of course, are the high percentage of inflammable wooden structures, the laxity of the laws relating to fire hazards, and that most conspicuous of American traits, the readiness to take chances. *(b) fire protection.*

The science of fire-prevention, which has made noteworthy progress in recent years, is concerned primarily with four remedial measures. First, there is the fixing of what are commonly known as fire-limits, that is to say, regions in which inflammable buildings are not to be erected. These areas usually include the business sections of cities. Second, the cities have tried to eliminate by the provisions of ordinances relating to buildings, those structural features which experience has shown to be fire-spreading agencies, such as the combustible party wall in apartment houses, the wooden-shingle roof, the unprotected elevator-well, and the inflammable connection which so often exists between the cellars and the first floors of tenements.[2] Third, the science of fire-prevention has been applied to the reduction of risk, in special structures such as theatres, factories, department stores, and schools by the enforcement of rules adapted to the needs of each type. Frequent inspections to insure compliance with these regulations are made by the fire-prevention authorities. And, finally, there is the campaign of popular education which aims to make people realize that *The science of fire-prevention: what it includes.*

---

[1] Some notable progress in the way of establishing children's courts for the trial of juvenile offenders and night courts for the speedy determination of minor accusations has been made in the larger American cities during the past two decades.

[2] About one-quarter of all tenement house fires originate in the cellars.

ignorance and carelessness are the chief factors in causing unintended fires to start. Wooden walls and shingled roofs do not cause fires to begin, but merely enable them to make rapid headway. Fires break out, in most cases, as the direct outcome of human negligence.

*How fire-prevention rules are enforced.*
The work of enforcing fire-prevention rules is usually intrusted to special state or city authorities. In the latter case the fire-prevention bureau is a branch of the municipal fire department. As yet the staff of officials is too small in most cities to insure the frequent and thorough inspections which are essential to a rigid enforcement of the fire-prevention laws. Fire-prevention ought, indeed, to be a state rather than a municipal function, for if one city applies strict rules while its neighbors refrain from so doing, the general conflagration hazard will still exist and there will be inter-city friction over the matter as well. Some commonwealths, including Pennsylvania and Massachusetts, have already taken hold of fire-prevention as a state enterprise.

*The fire departments.*
The fire-fighting service or fire department in nearly all American cities is in charge of a commissioner or chief who is usually appointed by the mayor. The officers and men under his control are organized into companies on a semi-military plan, and one company is assigned to each fire-district or precinct of the city with a fire-station as its headquarters. In most of the larger cities firemen are appointed under civil service rules, and a few cities have training-schools for the new men. American fire-brigades have been brought to a high plane of tactical efficiency, much higher than those of European cities. The reason is that the need for quick and effective work, because of conflagration risks, is greater here than there.

**2. Public works.**
Public works, including the construction and management of highways, bridges, sewers, and municipal buildings, present a somewhat related group of problems which engage the attention of a separate department and sometimes of more than one department.

*(a) street planning.*
The streets are a city's most valuable asset, and occupy from one-quarter to one-third of its entire area. To provide and maintain a satisfactory system of urban highways

involves at least a half dozen different municipal tasks. First, there is the proper planning of streets, a matter of great importance, because highways can never be made to give their maximum service to the community if badly planned at the outset. There are two general types of street plan: the rectangular or chessboard scheme, which prevails in nearly all cities, and the radial plan, which has found more general favor in European municipalities. The former endeavors to make all highways straight and to have them cross each other at right angles; the latter uses diagonal or winding thoroughfares which radiate from designated centres. Each plan has its merits, and to some extent these meritorious features can be combined. As to the width of streets the general practice has been to make highways uniform or nearly uniform without due regard to the extent and nature of the traffic which they are expected to bear. Of late years, however, new streets have had their widths determined, not by any rule-of-thumb method, but by paying strict regard to the probable needs of traffic. Good street planning is not merely a matter of making the highways both straight and wide, as so many western American communities imagine. Streets have to be paved, cleaned, and lighted, every inch of them, so that every unnecessary foot of street space represents a continuing source of municipal wastefulness.

Then there is the problem of good surfacing. Cities have experimented with every variety of street paving, including granite-blocks, bricks, wooden blocks, concrete, asphalt, and its related materials, and the various types of macadam. On one thing the authorities are now agreed, namely, that there is no best form of pavement for streets of every sort. One type is best for heavy-traffic thoroughfares, another for residential streets, and still another for boulevards or parkways. One type is durable but expensive; another costs less, and is easier to keep clean, but does not last so long. The selection of a street pavement should be made in accordance with the volume and nature of traffic, the general character of the highway, whether business or residential, and the probable future development of the neighborhood. These matters can be readily worked out by

(b) street paving.

2 R

highway engineers. Too often, however, the selection is made in obedience to the superficial caprice of neighboring property owners or to the influence of politician-contractors who have some patented brand of pavement to sell.

3. Sanitation.

The congestion of factories, shops, and dwellings in urban areas makes the problem of waste disposal, including rubbish, garbage, and sewage, one of great importance. Sewage, or polluted water waste, is the most constantly dangerous of them all. There are ordinarily from one hundred and fifty to two hundred gallons of it to be disposed of daily for every head of population. Many plans of sewage disposal are in use by American cities. Some municipalities merely discharge untreated sewage into the sea. Others carry it to reservoirs, tanks, or basins, where the solids are allowed to settle and form a sludge, the effluent being run off into the sea or some neighboring waterway. The settling process is sometimes hastened by the use of chemicals. Other systems of sewage disposal such as intermittent sand filtration and oxidization by the use of slag contact-beds are in use by a few cities. The broad-irrigation or sewage farm plan of disposal, which is used in some notable instances abroad, has found little favor in America. No one of these systems can be designated as the best under all circumstances. Local conditions differ greatly from city to city and each case requires special study.

4. Public health.

No branch of municipal activity has made more conspicuous progress during recent years than the care for the public health. This, in turn, has been the result of the notable advance in the sciences of preventive medicine and public hygiene. The old boards of health, with their haphazard methods, have in many cities given way to highly trained health commissioners who are assisted by skilled specialists, each devoting his energies to some particular aspect of the general problem. The work of a municipal health department includes the collection and interpretation of vital statistics as a means of determining the health status of the community. Relatively few people realize that prompt and accurate reports relating to diseases and deaths form the groundwork of efficient health administration. Public health work also includes the quarantining of infec-

MUNICIPAL ADMINISTRATION    611

tious diseases, the inspection of the milk supply, the control of every agency by which disease may be spread, and a multitude of other functions. Nearly every state also maintains a health department, which assists the city officials when necessary and exercises a general supervision over their work.

The city's hospitals fall naturally within the jurisdiction of the health department although they are sometimes administered independently. A general hospital does not nowadays suffice for the needs of any large group of population. A separate hospital for contagious cases and a special sanitarium for the treatment of tuberculosis are also necessary, and many of the more progressive cities have provided such institutions. Hospitals.

Measured by the amount of money spent upon it, education is the most important of all municipal functions. Because of this the public schools are usually placed under the supervision of a separate board or committee, the members of which are in most cities elected directly by the people but in some are appointed by the mayor. In general these boards have three different groups of functions to perform. First, they provide the school buildings and keep them in order. Second, they have duties of a business nature, such as the purchase of fuel and supplies, the buying of school books, and the management of school finances. In some cities the school taxes are assessed and collected under the direction of the board itself; but in the majority of them the funds for the support of the schools are obtained in part from the general city revenues and in part from the state. Finally, these school boards have the duty of appointing the superintendent, engaging and promoting teachers, determining salaries, approving changes in the school curricula and settling all questions of educational policy. These functions, when taken together, are of far-reaching influence for good or ill. From one-fourth to one-third of a city's entire annual revenue, on the average, is spent upon its schools. 5. Education.

In every part of the United States the local schools are to some extent under state supervision, but the nature and strictness of this oversight differ greatly from state to state. State control of municipal schools.

In some of them the local school board has little discretion except in minor matters; in others it retains a large amount of independence. Between these extremes there are all gradations of freedom and restriction, but the strictness of state oversight is roughly proportioned to the relative amounts which the various states contribute to the cities and towns for the support of their schools. The general tendency, moreover, is toward greater centralization in order that school administration may be made more nearly uniform. Central control of local schools is exercised through a state board, or a state superintendent of education, or both.

*The widening sphere of public education.* To a greater extent than in most other city departments the school authorities have been called upon for many new public services during recent years. Evening schools, part-time schools, continuation schools, special classes for handicapped or defective children, the medical and dental inspection of pupils, vocational guidance, and the use of schools as neighborhood centres in evening hours — these indicate only a few of the more important services which large communities now call upon their school authorities to provide in addition to the regular work of ordinary education. During recent years, moreover, the establishment of public playgrounds and the supervision of play have in many cities become additional responsibilities. Supervised play, out of school hours, is now recognized as an integral part of a city's educational system.

*6. Public library administration.* The public library is potentially a far more effective agency of public education than most American cities have hitherto made it. In many municipalities it is merely a depository of books, a considerable portion of which are ephemeral works of fiction. For the most part the library authorities have not assumed an aggressive leadership in moulding the literary tastes of its clientele or in actively developing among the people of the city the habit of reading books. Library boards have usually been made up of reputable and well-intentioned citizens who give their services without pay, but who have no special competence in educational matters and who have for the most part failed to perceive the true relation between a public library and the masses of the people. A closer coördination between library and school administration would doubtless have beneficial results, for it is from the public schools that the future patrons of the library should be recruited. At any rate boards of education throughout the country have expanded their service to the whole people at a rate which has left library administration far behind. Public libraries in American cities have been administered honestly, with fair intelligence, but with little or no imagination and almost entirely without any spirit of aggressive service.

In all large centres there are several branches of administration which have to do particularly with the welfare of the people in the city's congested districts. Poor-relief is a municipal function in some states, but in others it is a function of county government. Everywhere, however, a large part of the work is left to voluntary and private philanthropy. Public responsibility for the care of the poor has not been assumed on a large scale in America as it has been in the various countries of Europe. 7. Poor-relief.

Nor, again, has the proper housing of the people had the same amount of attention except perhaps in the largest cities. New York City first began the rigorous regulation of tenement houses in 1902, and its example has since been followed by many other urban centres in the United States. Tenement house regulation aims to eliminate unsanitary conditions, fire-traps, and overcrowding. The last of these is the most difficult of all to prevent. Housing rules have not been adequately enforced, however, because of the legal difficulties which often stand in the way of drastic interference with private property and also because a sufficient corps of inspectors is rarely provided. Political or personal favoritism has often operated, also, as a barrier to the rigid enforcement of the rules. 8. Housing of the people.

Cities have long since provided parks and other open spaces for the use of the people, but it is only of late years that more positive measures have been taken in the way of facilitating public recreation. The older conception of municipal functions went no further than the essentials of community life. It recognized the right and duty of the city to provide for the public safety and convenience, but did not 9. Public recreation.

regard measures for the public amusement as being within the sphere of the governing powers. This provision, it was assumed, might better be left to voluntary organizations. But the old conception has been steadily broadening, and American government in all its branches has become more paternal during the present generation. To provide and maintain public baths and beaches, to pay for band concerts out of municipal funds, to place municipal gymnasiums in different parts of the city, and even to run municipal dance halls — public money is now being provided for all of these things in some of the larger American cities. Along with this has developed a stricter regulation of private amusement places, the censorship of motion-picture shows, and the subjecting of almost all other places of recreation to more rigid license requirements. A much greater expansion of municipal recreation facilities is likely to take place in the years to come.

10. The regulation of public utilities.

(a) water-supply.

The provision or the regulation of public utilities are important functions of all cities. Water supply is the oldest and in many respects the most essential of these. A few American cities still leave this service to be provided by private companies, but in the great majority it is owned and operated by the municipality. The work is usually intrusted to a board of three or five members, who are elected in some of the smaller cities but appointed in nearly all the larger ones. Their functions are twofold: first to secure and maintain an adequate and safe source of supply; second, to provide for its distribution to the institutions, factories, shops, and homes of the city. In many cases a safe and adequate supply can be found within a reasonable distance of the city; in others, the water must be brought a long way or must either be purified by filtration or chemically treated to make it safe. Large groups of population make heavy demands upon water-supply, averaging about one hundred gallons per capita every day in the year. A city of one hundred thousand, therefore, will have a daily requirement of ten million gallons. In its relation to public health the city's water-supply is manifestly of supreme consequence, and that is the chief reason for taking it directly under public control.

MUNICIPAL ADMINISTRATION        615

Other important public utilities operating within the limits (b) other franchised of the city are steam railroads, electric lighting plants, gas utilities. plants, telephone systems, and electric railways. Steam railroads are wholly under national or state regulation and the city authorities have relatively little to do with them. Lighting plants, whether gas or electric, operate under what are known as franchises or grants of privileges made by the municipalities, usually for a stated term of years and always subject to a variety of conditions. Street railways are in the same category, although the franchise term is usually longer. State constitutions and laws have everywhere imposed street limitations upon the powers and duties of cities in the matter of granting these franchises, and the regulation of all public utilities has passed largely into the hands of the state authorities.

Nearly every state now maintains one or more boards whose function it is to supervise the enforcement of franchise conditions, to require adequate service, to hear complaints from customers or patrons, and in some cases to regulate the rates, tolls, or fares which may be charged. The regulation of all public utilities may now be looked upon as a state rather than a municipal function. This is, on the whole, as it ought to be, for the companies usually operate in more than a single municipality, and if each city undertook its own regulating, there would be no end of friction and diversity with the consequent demoralization of the service.

A public utility is a natural monopoly. No ultimate good can come from the maintenance of competitive telephone or street railway services, for example. These corporations occupy a field in which competition means duplication of facilities, public inconvenience, and a far higher cost of rendering the service in the end. Two practical alternatives, and only two, are open to a city. It may give a complete monopoly to some one telephone company, street railway company, or gas company with a defined area and then trust to public regulation for the protection of the public interest. Or it may acquire the service and operate it under direct municipal control.

This latter alternative, municipal ownership and oper-

11. Municipal ownership.
ation of public utilities, has made considerable progress in the United States although by no means so much as in European countries. Municipal ownership of water-supply has had the greatest development everywhere. Among sixty-five American cities having populations of 100,000 and upward, all but half a dozen have municipalized their water-supply services. This is chiefly because water-supply, unlike lighting or transportation, is intimately related to the public health and to the hygienic welfare of congested regions. Electric lighting ranks next in the spread of municipal ownership. There are nearly six thousand electric lighting plants in American municipalities, large and small, of which number more than a fourth are in public hands. Gas lighting, on the other hand, has had no such development. There are only about thirty municipal gas plants in the entire country, as compared with about fourteen hundred in private ownership. Of the cities having over 30,000 population only five own and operate their gas-lighting facilities.[1] One large city, Philadelphia, owns its gas plant, but has intrusted its operation to a private company. In the matter of street railways the cities of the United States have had even less experience with the policy of municipal ownership. San Francisco is the only large city that has taken over any considerable part of its street railway system, although a few other municipalities own and operate a few miles of trackage.

Its merits and defects.
Such experience with municipal ownership as American cities have had appears to indicate that wages and hours of labor for employees are such as to increase the costs of operation; that the quality of the service rendered is not better than under regulated private ownership; that under public ownership an additional burden is usually placed on the taxpayers and that political considerations rather than business principles determine many important questions of operating policy. On the other hand, municipal ownership assures some protection against the avaricious practices which have been more than common under private operation, such as the inflation of capital stock, the payment of extravagant salaries

[1] Richmond, Va.; Wheeling, W. Va.; Duluth, Minn.; Holyoke, Mass., and Hamilton, O.

for managerial and legal services, and the arbitrary treatment of the employees. The question as to which policy is the better cannot be answered in general terms. It can only be determined with reference to a particular city and a particular form of public service.

# CHAPTER XLIII

## COMMISSION AND CITY MANAGER GOVERNMENT

THE most significant feature of American municipal development during the last twenty years has been the organic reconstruction of government in several hundred cities. This has been accomplished by throwing overboard the older form of municipal organization, with its division of powers among mayor, boards, and council, and putting either the commission or city manager system in its stead. This striking upheaval in local government represents a political renaissance of no meagre importance. It has embodied both a protest and a policy, a protest against the old régime in city administration and a policy which aims to secure greater directness of responsibility from men in public office.[1]

*The beginning of the Commission movement.* The beginnings of this renaissance were the direct result of a local disaster, the tidal inundation which partly destroyed the city of Galveston, Texas, in 1900. Prior to this time, Galveston had ranked as one of the worst-governed urban communities in the whole country. Under the old system of jurisdiction by a mayor, various elective officials, and a board of aldermen, its municipal history managed to afford illustrations of almost every vice in local government. The city debt was allowed to mount steadily, and borrowing to pay current expenses was not uncommon. City departments were managed wastefully. Professional politicians were put into places of honor and profit in the city's service. The accounts were kept in

[1] The best-known works on this subject are E. S. Bradford, *Commission Government in American Cities* (N. Y., 1911); Henry Bruère, *The New City Government* (N. Y., 1912); Ford H. MacGregor, *City Government by Commission* (Madison, 1911); and C. R. Woodruff, *City Government by Commission* (N. Y., 1911).

## COMMISSION AND CITY MANAGER GOVERNMENT 619

such a way that few could understand what the financial situation was at any time. The tax rate was high, and the citizens got poor service in return for generous expenditures.

Affairs were in this condition when, in September, 1900, a tidal wave swept in from the Gulf, destroyed about one-third of the city, and put the municipal authorities face to face with the problem of reconstruction. Before the disaster the city's financial condition was precarious; now its bonds dropped in value, and it was apparent that funds for the work of putting the city on its feet could not be borrowed except at exorbitant rates of interest. It happened that much of the real estate in Galveston was held by a comparatively small number of citizens. Some of these, accordingly, went to the legislature of the state of Texas and virtually asked that the city be put into receivership. They requested that the old city government be swept away, root and branch, and that for some years, at any rate, all the powers formally vested in the mayor, aldermen, and subsidiary organs of city government be given to a commission of business men. This drastic action they urged as a means of saving the city from involvement in grave financial difficulties, if not from actual bankruptcy. Acceding to their request, the legislature passed an act empowering the governor of Texas to appoint three of the five commissioners, and providing that the other two be elected by the voters of Galveston.[1] A year or two after they had taken office, however, a constitutional difficulty arose. In a matter which came before the courts it was held that the appointment of city officers by the state authorities was contrary to a provision in the Texas constitution; whereupon the legislature amended its act by providing that all five members of the Galveston commission should be chosen by popular vote.[2] The same three commissioners who had been holding office under the governor's appointment forthwith stood for election, and were elected by the voters.

As thus amended in 1903, the Galveston charter provides for the popular election, every two years, of five commis-

*The Galveston plan.*

*Its essential features.*

---
[1] Special Laws of Texas, 1901, ch. 12.
[2] *Ibid.*, 1903, ch. 37.

sioners, one of them to be entitled the mayor-president, and all to be chosen at large. The mayor-president is the presiding chairman at all meetings of the commission, but otherwise he has no special powers. The commission, by majority vote, enacts all ordinances and passes all appropriations, the mayor-president voting like his fellow-commissioners. It further supervises the enforcement of its own by-laws and regulates the expenditure of its own appropriations. Likewise it handles all awards of contracts for public works. In a word, it exercises all the powers formerly vested in the mayor, board of aldermen, and other officials, acting either singly or in concurrence. The commissioners, by majority vote, apportion among themselves the headships of the four administrative departments into which the business of the city is grouped; namely, the departments of finance and revenue, water and sewerage, police and fire protection, and streets and public property. The mayor-president is not assigned to the head of any one department, but is supposed to exercise a coördinating supervision over them all. Each of the commissioners is thus directly responsible for the routine direction of one important branch of the city's business. Appointments of permanent officials in each department are not made by the commissioner who is in direct charge, but by vote of the whole commission. Minor appointments are, however, left to the commissioner in whose department they may happen to fall.

*Success of the experiment.*

The Galveston plan was not intended to be a permanent system of government for the city. Its prime object was to enable Galveston to tide over a difficult emergency. Prepared somewhat hastily, with very little experience to serve as a guide, it vested in the hands of a small body of men more extensive final powers than most cities would care to give away; but the lapse of a few years demonstrated the great merits of the new system. The people's civic spirit was aroused, the business of the city recovered rapidly, and in a remarkably short time the place was again on its feet, financially and otherwise. Then developed the conviction that commission government was a good form to maintain permanently. The other cities of Texas, noting conditions under the new charter in Galveston, came forward and asked the legislature for similar legislation; and in the course of a few years the new plan of local government was authorized for use by general act in all the cities of the state.

This development naturally attracted attention in other parts of the country, and the reform organizations of various northern cities began to discuss the possibility of applying the scheme to the solution of their own municipal problems. The first municipality outside of Texas to accept the plan was Des Moines, the capital city of Iowa. In 1907 the Iowa legislature passed an act permitting any city of the state having a population of more than 25,000 to adopt a commission type of government; and forthwith the citizens of Des Moines, by whom the act had originally been brought forward and urged, took advantage of the new provision.

*The plan spreads northward.*

The Des Moines plan of government by commission is simply a new edition of the Galveston plan, similar in outline, but embodying some novel features. In brief, it provides for a commission consisting of a mayor and four councillors, all elected at large for a two-year term by the voters of the city. To this body is intrusted all the powers hitherto vested in the mayor, city council, board of public works, park commissioners, boards of police and fire commissioners, board of waterworks trustees, board of library trustees, solicitor, assessor, treasurer, auditor, city engineer, and all other administrative boards or officers. Under the Des Moines plan the business of the city is grouped into five departments; namely, public affairs, accounts and finances, public safety, streets and public improvements, and parks and public property. By the terms of the charter the commissioner who is elected mayor of the city becomes head of the department of public affairs; each of the other commissioners is put at the head of one of the other departments by majority vote of the commission, or council, as the body is called in Iowa. All officers and employees of the various departments are appointed by the council, which also has authority to choose a board of three civil service commissioners to administer, under its direction,

*Adopted by Des Moines with new features added.*

the state laws relating to the civil service. Most of the city officers come within the scope of these laws.

<small>Nature of these new features.</small> Thus far the system diverges but very slightly from the Galveston plan. The chief difference lies in the fact that the Des Moines scheme incorporates what are commonly termed the newer agencies of American democracy; namely, the initiative, referendum, and recall. The initiative is the right of 25 per cent of the qualified voters of the city to present to the council by petition any proper by-law or resolution, and to require, if such be not passed by the council, that it be submitted without alteration to the voters by referendum. If at such referendum it receives a majority of votes, it becomes effective. Or if the council should pass, of its own volition, any such measure (except an emergency measure), it cannot go into effect until ten days after its passage. Meanwhile, if a petition protesting against such by-law, signed by 25 per cent of the voters of the city, is presented to the council, it is incumbent on that body to reconsider the matter. If the by-law is not entirely repealed, it must then be submitted to the voters for their acceptance or rejection. The vote takes place at a regular election, if there is one within six months; otherwise at a special election held for the purpose. If indorsed at the polls, the measure becomes effective at once; if rejected by the voters, it becomes inoperative. The recall provision permits the voters to remove from office any member of the council at any time after three months' tenure in office. Petitions for recall or removal must be signed by at least 20 per cent of the voters, and the question of recalling, or in other words forthwith ending the term of a councillor, is put before them at a special election.

Since its adoption in Des Moines the spread of the revised commission system has been rapid. During the next ten years a great many cities, scattered about in forty-three states, abolished the old system and established the new one.[1] Some of these were large cities, but in general the

---

[1] The only states which do not have any cities with the commission form of government are Delaware, Indiana, New Hampshire, Rhode Island, and Vermont. The most important cities now having commis-

commission plan seemed to appeal more strongly to the smaller urban centres.

A list of cities that have the system at the present day would contain the names of more than three hundred municipalities. Six are cities with populations exceeding 200,000 (including Buffalo and New Orleans); fourteen are cities with populations of 100,000 or over. The others, ranging from a few thousand upwards, are scattered in all parts of the United States from the Atlantic to the Pacific and from the Canadian to the Mexican border.

What have these cities gained as a result of the change? In its actual working the new system has shown itself possessed of many advantages.[1] Of these the most striking one, of course, arises from the fact that the plan puts an end to that intolerable scattering of powers, duties, and responsibilities which the old type of city government promoted to the point of absurdity. By enabling public attention to focus itself upon a narrow and well-defined area, it allows the scrutiny which voters apply to the conduct of their representatives to be real, and not, as heretofore, merely perfunctory. The system does not guarantee that a city's administration shall be always free from good ground for criticism — no system can do that; but it does guarantee that when the administration is faulty there shall be definite shoulders upon which to lay the blame. Under the commission plan the responsibility cannot be bandied back and forth in shuttlecock fashion from mayor to council and from the council to some administrative board or officer. Issues cannot be clouded by shifty deals among several authorities. In thus eliminating a chaos

*Merits of commission government:*

*1. Fixing responsibility.*

---

sion government are as follows: Birmingham, Ala.; Berkeley and Oakland, Cal.; Des Moines, Ia.; Kansas City and Wichita, Kan.; New Orleans, La.; Lowell, Mass.; St. Paul, Minn.; Omaha, Neb.; Jersey City and Trenton, N. J.; Buffalo, N. Y.; Oklahoma City, Okla.; Portland, Ore.; Harrisburg and Reading, Pa.; Memphis, Tenn.; Dallas, Houston, and San Antonio, Texas; Salt Lake City, Utah; Spokane and Tacoma, Wash.

[1] The summary of merits and defects, as given in the next few pages, is based upon the views expressed six or seven years ago by the author in his *Government of American Cities*, and which a close observation of commission government during the interval has not in any way caused him to change.

of checks and balances, another name for which is friction, confusion, and irresponsibility, the new framework removes from the government of American cities a feature which, to say the least, has in practice been unprofitable from first to last.

2. Facilitates the handling of business.

Advocates of city government by commission have been in the habit of saying that their plan would give cities a business administration. They pointed out that a city's affairs are of the nature of business, not of government. Go through the records of a council-meeting and catalogue the items that can be classed as legislation; the list will be very short indeed. By far the greater part of a council's proceedings have to do with matters of routine administration, which differ slightly, if at all, from the ordinary operations of any large business concern.

Now no business organization could reasonably hope to keep itself out of insolvency if it had to do its work with any such clumsy and complicated machinery as that which most American cities have had imposed upon them. What would be thought of a business corporation that intrusted the conduct of its affairs to a twin board of directors (one board representing the stockholders at large and the other representing them by districts), and gave to an independently chosen manager some sort of veto power over them, besides subjecting his appointments to their concurrence? It is, of course, quite true that a city is something more than a profit-seeking business enterprise. The affairs of the municipality cannot be conducted in defiance of public opinion, or even in disregard of it; but responsiveness to popular sentiment is not necessarily incompatible with sound methods of public administration.

3. Helps to eliminate friction.

The system of government by commission has enabled the authorities of the city to conduct business more promptly and with less friction. There may be wisdom in a multitude of councillors, but the history of those municipalities which maintain large deliberative bodies seems to warrant the impression that this collective wisdom is not of very high grade. Unwieldy councils have been put upon American cities under the delusion that democracy somehow associates itself with unwieldiness. There is a notion in the minds of all democracies, and it is as deep-seated as it is illusive, that a body cannot be representative unless it is large to the pitch of uselessness for any effective action. Even deliberative bodies, however, reach a point of diminishing returns, and American municipal experience seems to show that this point is not fixed very high. Large city councils in the United States have everywhere been found to be ill adapted to the work which they are expected to do. To say that they display greater regard for the interests of the people, or more conservative judgment in the handling of questions of policy, than do small councils of five, seven, or nine men is to disregard the undeniable facts of the situation. The history of large councils, whether in New York, Philadelphia, Boston, or in smaller cities, is little more than a record of political manœuvring and factional intriguery, with a mastery of nothing but the art of wasting time and money. A council of some half dozen men offers at least the possibility of despatch in the handling of city affairs; for its small size removes an incentive to fruitless debate, and affords little opportunity for resort to subterfuges in procedure.

But the chief merit urged in behalf of the commission plan is not that it concentrates responsibility and permits the application of business methods to the conduct of a city's affairs, important as these things are. In the last analysis, municipal administration is as much a question of men as of measures. Efficiency in city administration may be assisted by one form of local government or retarded by another, but in the long run it is not less a question of personnel than political framework. Much depends, accordingly, upon whether the commission form of government does or does not install better men in the city's posts of power and responsibility.

4. Induces better men to serve the city.

In the early days of the commission propaganda it was argued that the new plan could not fail to secure a higher grade of councilmen or commissioners. "Concentrate power, it was said, and you will get men worthy to exercise it." But nearly twenty years' experience with the commission form of government has not, on the whole, borne out this prediction. The fact is that the great majority

Has it actually done so?

2 s

626    THE GOVERNMENT OF THE UNITED STATES

of those who have been elected commissioners under the new plan are men who held some public office under the old. What has actually happened is not the drawing of new men into the municipal service, but the retention of the best among the old groups and the giving to them a better chance to achieve satisfactory results. It is, at any rate, the testimony of those who have served under the old plan and the new that the latter gives greater opportunity and greater incentive; and it is the experience of those cities which have been under commission arrangements for several years that, whatever may have been the effect upon the personnel of the administration, the change has had a salutary influence upon the whole tone of municipal affairs.

5. Reduces the tax rates
Perhaps the most convincing evidence that cities derive advantages from the new form of government is that gathered by the United States Bureau of the Census and published by it in 1916. The figures relate to rates of taxation, expenditures, and loans in various cities both before and after the adoption of the commission plan. Likewise there is a comparison of annual financial statements from typical cities, some with the new form of government and some with the old. The figures leave no doubt that the new plan has had a favorable reaction on tax rates and borrowing.[1] Nor do the statistics tell the whole story. The

[1] U. S. Bureau of the Census. *Comparative Financial Statistics of Cities under Council and Commission Government* (Washington, 1916).

The eight mayor-and-council cities which were chosen for comparison were Indianapolis, Indiana (259,820); Hartford, Connecticut (107,521); Youngstown, Ohio (100,593); Troy, New York (77,560); Peoria, Illinois (70,006); Little Rock, Arkansas (53,811); Davenport, Iowa (46,537); and Charlotte, North Carolina (38,263), representing a total population in 1915 of 754,111, or an average of 94,000 each. The eight commission-governed cities were Birmingham, Alabama (164,165); Lowell, Massachusetts (111,004); Salt Lake City, Utah (109,736); Des Moines, Iowa (97,304); Pueblo, Colorado (51,218); Topeka, Kansas (47,102); Montgomery, Alabama (42,154); and Austin, Texas (33,218), with a total population of 655,901, or an average of 82,000 for each city.

A comparison of tax levies in the two groups of cities for 1915 shows that the average per capita levy of property taxes for the eight mayor cities was $16.36 as against $12.31 in the commission-governed cities, or a difference of $4.05 in favor of the cities under government by commission.

improvement in the general tone and temper of municipal government is something which counts for much, even though it cannot be set down on a balance sheet.

But even though the financial results seem favorable, there are those who continue their objection to the commission plan upon political grounds. According to these opponents, it is based upon a wrong principle and proposes a dangerous policy; and it is accordingly branded as oligarchical, undemocratic, and un-American. But to urge that because a governing body is small it must inevitably prove to be bureaucratic in its methods and unresponsive in its attitude, is merely to afford a typical illustration of politicians' logic. Whether a public official or a body of officials will become oligarchical in temper depends not upon mere numbers, but upon the directness of the control which the voters are able to exercise over those whom they put into office. And effectiveness of control hinges largely upon such matters as the concentration of responsibility for official acts, an adequate degree of publicity, and the elimination of such features as national party designations attached to the names of candidates on the municipal ballots, a practice which has always served in the United States to confuse the issues presented to the voters at the polls. In fact, it might almost be laid down as an axiom deducible from American municipal experience that the smaller an elective body the more thorough its accountability to the electorate.

*Objections to the plan:*

1. "Takes the government of the city away from the people."

Commission government, we are told by those who have been and are still opposing it, is inadequately representative; five men, chosen at large, cannot represent the varied interests, political, geographical, racial, and economic, in any large municipality. If it be true that in the conduct of his local affairs a voter cannot be adequately represented except by one of his own neighborhood, race, religion, politics, and business interests, then his criticism is entirely reasonable. But is this not the *reductio ad absurdum* of the representative principle? Would not a recognition of this doctrine absolutely preclude all chance of securing a municipal administration loyal to the best interests of the city as a whole? It has been frequently proved in the United States

2. Is not adequately representative.

that a single official, like the President of the nation or the governor of a state or the mayor of a city, may more truly represent popular opinion than does a whole Congress or state legislature or municipal council. Popular sentiment is not difficult to ascertain when a public officer takes the trouble to ascertain it. Five men can do it as easily as fifty, and they are much more likely to try.

"The smaller the council, the more easily can it be reached and corrupted." In other words, it is easier for crooked politicians or professional lobbyists to corrupt or coerce five councillors than fifty. There is safety in numbers. But the flaw in this line of argument is its assumption. It assumes that sinister influences exert themselves directly upon the councillors one by one, and hence that, where a large council exists, the forces of corruption or coercion must deal with a large body of men. That this is not the case, however, every one who has had anything to do with municipal politics knows very well. Large councils in this country have been, for the most part, made up of men who owed their nomination and election to political leaders to whom the councillors have been under permanent obligations, and from whom they have taken their orders. A few bosses, sometimes a single boss, can control a majority of the council, and can deliver the necessary votes to any proposition when the proper incentive appears. Politicians or contractors who wish to get what they are not entitled to have do not approach the council through its members one by one. They have always dealt with the middleman; that is to say, with the political leader, who controls the votes of the councilmen. Accordingly, they have had to do with perhaps five men, not with fifty, and, what is more, with five men who have power without responsibility, who were not invested with authority by the voters, and are consequently not accountable to them for the abuse of it. Under commission government, on the contrary, a favor-seeking private interest has had to deal not with a few middlemen, who have the votes of others to deliver, but with five men who are free to act as they think best and who act with the eyes of the voters upon them.

Objection is raised against commission government on

the ground that it puts into the hands of a single small body of men the power both to appropriate and to spend public money. Such an arrangement, it is said, and said truly, violates an established principle of American government, which demands that in the interests of economy and honesty these two powers should be lodged in separate hands. It commits to a single board of five men the power of fixing the annual tax rate, of appropriating the revenues to the different departments, and of supervising the detailed expenditure of the funds so apportioned. Unorthodox as this arrangement may appear to be, however, it is not necessarily objectionable on that account. Many novel features have come into American governmental methods within comparatively recent years, and all have had to meet the cry that they involved departure from the time-honored way of doing things in this country. Moreover, the fusion of appropriating and spending powers in the organization of city government is not unprecedented. This very principle is at the foundation of the English municipal system; and, as the world knows, it has proved in operation neither a source of corruption nor an incentive to extravagance. Furthermore, those American cities which have had the commission form of government for nearly a dozen years find nothing objectionable in this blending of the two powers; on the contrary, their experience with it seems to indicate that it possesses some important advantages over the old plan of separation. It inspires greater care in making the estimates and promotes greater success in keeping within them when made. Commissions have unquestionably not proved to be less capable of handling expenditures than were the various executive boards and officials that formerly had charge of such work.

3. Abolishes the safeguard of checks and balances.

A much more substantial objection to the commission plan arises from the fact that it practically abolishes the office of mayor, that it does not provide an apex for the pyramid of local administration. Now, the mayoralty is a post that has established a fair tradition in America, and there is a rational function for it to perform. It stands in the public imagination as the one municipal office in which all administrative responsibility can be centralized.

4. It places the administrative power in too many hands.

To lodge all such power and responsibility in the hands of five men is better than to put it in the hands of fifty; but to place most of it in the hands of one man, duly surrounded by the necessary safeguards, is better still. The commission plan achieves at best a five-headed unification of responsibility; it leaves room for friction on a three-to-two basis; it affords ample scope for wasted energy and for the management of the city's business in such way as to serve personal or political ambitions. This is not a mere possibility of the system, for many commission-governed cities are finding it to be a disappointing reality. Jealousy among the five commissioners has often led to friction and working at cross-purposes. There has been too much evidence of a disposition to "play politics"; that is to say, too much readiness on the part of the individual commissioner to popularize himself with his constituents even when by so doing the general interests of the city are likely to suffer.

5. Its failure to make use of experts.

But even more serious as a defect of the commission plan, as shown by its years of experience, is its failure to make full use of expert service in handling the regular work of the city. The commissioner who, on election, takes charge of some special branch of the city's business (such as police and fire protection, or water and light) is a layman, unskilled in the problems of his new department. But he draws a good salary from the city, and naturally desires to make at least a pretence of earning it. The consequence is that he becomes too busy with the matters which are under his direction, often hampering the skilled efforts of the permanent officials such as the chief of police or fire chief or head of the water service, ordering things about as political motives or as a desire to secure his own reëlection may dictate. The result is that these officials disclaim responsibility, often lose enthusiasm, or sometimes resign and are replaced by more pliable subordinates.

Now the commission plan did not at its inception contemplate that development. It assumed that the five commissioners, not being experts themselves, would be guided by expert advice. But in the great majority of commission-governed cities (that is to say, cities with 50,000 population or less) there is hardly room for two well-paid men at or near the head of each division of work. The taxpayers do not feel like paying a commissioner of public safety an annual salary of $2500 or more, and also providing full-salaried officials at the head of the police and fire protection services. The tendency has been, with political motives in play, to pay the commissioners more and the officials less. The result is that in many cases the professional's part in administration has been curtailed, while the elective commissioner, although not qualified by training to do so, has assumed technical functions.

It is with a view to improving the commission plan and particularly to securing a greater concentration of administrative responsibility that the city-manager scheme has more recently been devised. The city-manager arrangement does not embody a new scheme of local government, but merely a variation of the commission system, designed to secure a more effective concentration of administrative functions in the hands of a professional well-paid expert, removing from the elective commissioners the power to interfere with the details of municipal business. The first large city to experiment along this line was Dayton, Ohio, where the new arrangement went into effect on January 1, 1914. Since that date the example has been followed by many other municipalities, and additions to this list are being rapidly made at the present time. *The city-manager plan.* *Its origin.*

According to the Dayton plan an elective commission of five members controls all branches of the city's affairs, legislative and administrative, except the schools, which are under a separate board. The members of the commission are chosen by popular vote for a four-year term, but are subject to recall by an adverse vote at any time after six months of service. The commission, by majority action, enacts the ordinances and fixes the tax rate. It also votes the appropriations and may create or abolish city departments. But it does not directly have anything to do with the actual management of the various departments, nor does it immediately supervise the work of the officials. These responsibilities it delegates to a high official with the title of city-manager, appointed by the commission to hold office during its pleasure and paid a good salary. *Its essential features.*

**Functions of the city manager.**

Now as to the city manager's duties. They are fourfold. First of all, in an advisory capacity he attends all meetings of the commission, with the right to be heard and to make recommendations, but not to vote. Secondly, he is the enforcer of all ordinances. In the third place he appoints all other city officials and employees, subject, however, to the civil service regulations, and may suspend or dismiss any of them for proper cause. In this connection he assigns to each official the sphere of work to be done. And, finally, he prepares the annual estimates, submitting them to the commission for action; and he is the general supervisor of all the work done in the various departments and offices, having charge of contracts, the purchase of supplies, and so forth, the details being handled by his subordinates. He is, in a word, the general manager of the corporation.

Since 1914 the city manager plan, or some variation of it, has been established in about ninety American cities. Only two of these, Dayton and Grand Rapids, are places of over 100,000 population; but the list includes a dozen cities of 25,000 or over. Naturally enough the plan has proved most popular in the smaller communities.

**Is the plan a success?**

So far as one may judge from four or five years' experience, the city managership forms a highly valuable, if not an indispensable, adjunct to the commission plan of government. It strengthens the latter at its weakest point by insuring a high grade of professional skill at the apex of the city's administrative service. As for the future, much will depend upon two things: in the first place whether cities find it possible to get the right sort of men for managerial positions, and in the second place whether the position can be kept out of the vicious circle of political patronage. The latter danger is the more likely to be encountered, and indeed it has already made its appearance. Some municipalities are already insisting that the city manager shall be "a local man" and that he shall be paid a very moderate salary. If that policy becomes general, the whole plan will be rendered ineffective.

**Preferential voting.**

The commission system and the city manager plan have brought with them, in some municipalities, a change of election methods. Preferential voting, in a number of cities, has replaced the method of straight balloting. Under the so-called Australian ballot system, as used in the United States, each voter designates his first choice only. An inevitable result of this system is that the candidate who stands highest at the poll (in cases where there are several candidates for the same office) may have received a considerable minority of the total votes cast. In such instances the person elected does not genuinely represent the wishes of the majority. The preferential system of voting permits each voter to designate not only his first, but his second and third choices as well. If any candidate receives a clear majority of first choices, he is declared elected without any counting of second choices. But if no one obtains such majority, the second choices are added to the first choices and a further computation made to ascertain whether any candidate thereby secures a majority. In like manner the third choices are resorted to if necessary. Preferential voting has been adopted and used with satisfactory results in many American cities during the last ten years.[1]

Preferential voting should be distinguished from proportional representation, which is another electoral method brought into use during the past decade. Various schemes for securing the proportional representation of all factions among the voters have been under discussion by students of government for a half century or more, but none of them has had a fair trial in any American community until a few years ago when Ashtabula, Ohio, inaugurated one of these plans in connection with the workings of its commission-manager government. The details of the Ashtabula scheme seem at the first glance to be rather complicated, but in its actual operation the plan has thus far presented no great difficulties to the voters. The ballot used is something like that employed under the preferential system, but the method of counting the votes is altogether different. By dividing the total number of votes cast by

*Proportional representation.*

[1] The details of the plan differ somewhat in different cities. For a discussion of the workings and merits of the system see the *Bulletin* on *Preferential Voting*, prepared for the Massachusetts Constitutional Convention, 1917, and the references there given.

the number of offices to be filled, a quota is established. If any candidate is found to have received a number of first choices equal to this quota, or above it, he is declared elected. If he have a surplus of first choices above the quota, this surplus is distributed to other candidates in accordance with the second choices indicated. On each count, moreover, the lowest candidate drops out and his votes are distributed, similarly, among those who remain. This procedure is continued until enough persons have been declared elected to fill the available offices.

This, of course, is only one among various systems of proportional representation. There are at least a half dozen others.[1] But the purpose is in all cases the same, namely, to give each fraction of the electorate its due share of representation. Under the system of election which prevails in general throughout the United States no representation is accorded to any party except the two leading parties. The chief objection to proportional representation is its seeming complexity when presented to the average man. It looks pedantic and intricate. In its actual application, however, no scheme of proportional representation yet used in any country has proved too complicated for the voters to comprehend.

Conclusion. A word in conclusion. America has not yet reached a final solution of those problems of municipal government which seemed to constitute during the latter half of the nineteenth century the most vexing of all the problems of the Republic. But at any rate notable progress has been made. Old theories have been discarded; obsolete political mechanism has been relegated to the scrap heap. New theories and institutions are being given a new trial. With this has come an awakened interest in municipal affairs, and things which were not intelligible to the electorate because of the elaboration of municipal checks and balances have become intelligible now.

But before the average American city becomes a model

---

[1] The best known book on this subject is J. R. Commons, *Proportional Representation* (N. Y., 1907). References to recent publications dealing with the various plans may be found in the Massachusetts Constitutional Convention's *Bulletin* on *Proportional Representation* (Boston, 1917).

of efficiency and thrift, a great deal more remains to be done. Rings and bosses will still get control of cities from time to time as they managed to do in days gone by. But such victories of the enemy do not now spell disaster. Frenchmen said of the Bourbon Restoration in 1814 that it brought back the old dynasty but not the old régime. So, too, the stalwarts of Tammany and of similar organizations throughout the land may occasionally come back to a fleeting lease of power, but the public indifference which once gave them a strangle-hold on the municipal treasury is gone, and gone forever.

# INDEX

Academy of Political Science, *Proceedings*, 434 n.
Adams, H. C., *Public Debts*, 234 n; *Science of Finance*, 460 n.
Adams, John, *Works*, 48 n.
Address, removal of state judges by, 497.
Administration, national and the Cabinet, 126–145; in the states, 443–459; in cities, 602–617.
Agger, E. E., *Budget in American Commonwealths*, 466 n.
Agriculture, federal Department of, 138.
Alaska, government, 137, 377; delegates to National Convention, 334.
Albany Congress, 10.
Aldermen. *See* City Council.
Amendments, to the Constitution, 67–69; first ten, 67–68, 352–356; Eleventh, 68, 347–348; Twelfth, 68, 91; Fourteenth, 72–73, 243, 398–400; Fifteenth, 79–80; Seventeenth, 151–152; Sixteenth, 226; to state constitutions, 412.
*American Historical Review*, 28 n.
American Judicature Society, *Bulletin*, 496 n.
*American Year Book*, 274 n.
Ames, H. V., "Proposed Amendments to the Constitution," 69 n.
Andrews, C. M., *Colonial Self-Government*, 3 n.
Annapolis Convention, 24–25.
Appointments, by the President, 106–110; confirmation by Senate, 163–164; recess, 164; by state governors, 438–441, 495–496; by mayors, 591–592; of city officials, 593–595.
Appropriation bills, customary origin in House of Representatives, 66; share of Treasury Department in, 133–134; of Senate in, 173–174; passage through Congress, 302–309. *See also* Finance.
Army, control of President over, 121; under War Department, 136; of the United States, 266–268.
Articles of Confederation, adoption, 13; constitutional importance, 14–15;

general provisions, 15; powers of Congress under, 15–16; ratification, 16–17; weaknesses, 20–23; accomplishments, 23–24.
Articles of War, 269–270.
Ashtabula, Ohio, proportional representation in, 633–634.
Attainder, bill of, 169, 288–289, 396.

Baldwin, S. E., *American Judiciary*, 355, 490 n.
Ballot, in congressional elections, 184; need for shorter, 482; in preferential voting, 632–633; in proportional representation, 633–634.
Banking system, national, connection with Treasury Department, 134–135; in general, 233–248; history of, 234–239; defects, 239–240; Federal Reserve, 240–241; of the states, 449–450.
Bankruptcy, power of Congress over, 277–278.
Barnett, J. D., *Initiative, Referendum and Recall in Oregon*, 501 n.
Bastable, C. F., *Public Finance*, 460 n.
Beard, C. A., *Economic Interpretation of the Constitution*, 41 n; *Supreme Court and the Constitution*, 53 n, 362 n; *American Government and Politics*, 550 n.
Beard, C. A., and Schultz, B. E., *Documents on State-wide Initiative, Referendum and Recall*, 501 n.
Bicameral legislature, adoption of, in Congress, 146–147; merits and defects, in states, 416–418; in cities, 595.
Bicknell, Edward, *Territorial Acquisitions of the United States*, 372 n.
Bill of Rights, as first ten amendments, 67–68; rights of citizens secured by, 84–85; limitations on judicial procedure, 352–356; in original state constitutions, 406–407.
Bills, passage of, by agreement of Senate and House, 174–175; in House of Representatives, 201–206; in state legislatures, 425–428. *See also* Money bills, Veto power.

637

## 638 INDEX

Bimetallism, conflict over, 278–279.
Blackstone's *Commentaries on the Laws of England*, 349 n.
Blaine-Cleveland presidential campaign, 98.
*Bloomfield* v. *Charter Oak Bank*, 561.
*Boln* v. *Nebraska*, 394.
Bonds, federal, types of, 241–243; refunding, 243–244; in states, 471–472.
Borgeaud, C., *Adoption and Amendment of Constitutions*, 405 n.
Boroughs, in the colonies, 538, 578.
Borrowing, power of, under the Confederation, 15, 21; of Congress, 233–245; methods of, federal, 241–243; in states, 469–472; in cities, 598.
Bosses, political, 484–487.
Boston Budget Commission, *Report*, 309 n.
Bradford, E. S., *Commission Government*, 618 n.
Brannan, Henry, *Treatise on Fourteenth Amendment*, 399 n.
*Brown* v. *Maryland*, 249 n.
Bruère, Henry, *New City Government*, 618 n.
Bryce, James, *American Commonwealth*, 96, 307, 342, 361–362; on veto power, 119; on Chief Justice Marshall, 361–362.
Budget system, lack of, in federal government, 309–310; in states, 466–469.
Bullock, C. J., *Finances of the United States, 1775–1789*, 21 n.
Burke, Edmund, on form of government, 70; on duty of representatives, 186; on political parties, 322.

Cabinet, and national administration, 126–145; compared with English Cabinet, 126–127, 144–145; attitude of Constitutional Convention towards, 127–128; offices established by Congress, 128; qualifications and appointment, 128–129; powers and functions, 129–139; relation to Congress, 142–144.
*Cableman* v. *Peoria R. R. Co.*, 346 n.
*Calder* v. *Bull*, 289 n.
Calhoun, J. C., *State Papers on Nullification*, 211 n; *Disquisition on Government*, 392.
*California* v. *Central Pacific R. R. Co.*, 283.
Carpenter, W. S., *Judicial Tenure*, 371 n.
Carson, H. L., *History of the Supreme Court*, 357 n.
Catterall, R. C. H., *Second Bank of the United States*, 238 n.
Caucus, in the Senate, 156–157; beginnings of, 330–331; legislative, 331–332; congressional, 332–333; as means of nominating in states, 418.
Chamberlin, F., *Philippine Problem*, 383 n.
*Champion* v. *Ames*, 250 n.
Channing, Edward, *History of the United States*, 2 n, 17 n, 318.
Charities and corrections, administration of, in states, 453–454; in counties, 552; in cities, 663.
Charters, city, methods of granting, 583–587.
Child-labor, under Department of Interior, 139; control of Congress over, 250.
*Chisholm* v. *Georgia*, 347 n, 360 n.
Circuit Court of Appeals, 370.
Cities, growth of, 572–577; periods of development, 577–582; granting of charters to, 582–587; organization, 588–601; administration, 602–617; commission and city-manager government in, 618–635.
Citizens, rights of, 71–87; who are, 71–78; by birth, 73–74; by naturalization, 74–78; status of Porto Ricans and Filipinos as, 75, 374–375; privileges and immunities, 78–83; corporations as, 84; duties, 85–87; in connection with voting, 178–179.
City Council, organization, 595–596; functions, 596–599; place of, in American government, 599.
City-manager plan of city government, 631–632.
Civil Service Commission, 108, 141.
Civil service system, in national government, 108–109; in the states, 439–441; need for, to offset political machines, 481–482; need for, in counties, 559; lack of, in appointing department heads, in cities, 593–594; in appointment of city employees, 599–600.
Cleveland, Grover, *Presidential Problems*, 105 n.
Coinage and currency, supervision by Treasury Department, 135; control of Congress, 278–280; kinds in United States, 280; counterfeiting, 281.
Coke, Sir Edward, *Institutes*, 291 n.
Collins, C. W., *Fourteenth Amendment and the States*, 399 n.
Colonies, the Thirteen, government of, 2–13.
Commerce, federal Department of, 138.
Commerce, power of Congress to regulate, under the Confederation, 21–22, 246–247; under the Constitution,

### INDEX

246–264; what commerce is, 248–251; interstate, 256–264.
Commission government, in cities, beginnings of, 618–619; Galveston plan, 619–621; in Des Moines, 621–623; merits, 623–627; defects, 627–631; improvements effected by city-manager plan, 631–632; changes caused by, in election methods, 632–634.
Committee, National, of political parties, 334–338.
Committee of the Whole, in House of Representatives, 200, 205.
Committee on Rules, in House of Representatives, 197–198, 204.
Committees, in the Senate, 153–154; in House of Representatives, 197–198, 199–203; of Conference, 205–206; in connection with appropriations, 303–306; in political parties, 334–338, 475–477, 483–484; in constitutional conventions, 410; in state legislatures, 423–424, 426–427.
Commons, J. R., *Proportional Representation*, 634 n.
Compromises, in connection with framing the Constitution, 33–35.
Confirmation, of appointments, federal, 65, 106–108, 163–164; in states, 439.
Congress, powers under Confederation, 15–16, 20–23, 209–210; adjournment and special sessions, 112; relation of Cabinet to, 142–144; members may not be impeached, 170; power of, in general, 208–218; to tax, 219–232; to borrow, 233–245; to regulate commerce, 246–264; of war, 265–276; over naturalization and bankruptcy, 277–278; over coinage and currency, 278–280; over weights and measures, 280–281; over post offices, 281–283; to grant patents, 283–284; to establish subordinate courts, 284–285; as to the high seas, 285–286; over the capital, 286; implied, 286; limitations on, 288–298; as a legislative body, 299–302; inefficiency in public finance, 302–311; controlled by parties, 340–341; control over procedure of federal courts, 352–356; control over territories, 374–375.
Constitution, and its makers, 26–43; its framing, 27–36; ratification, 36–43; as supreme law of the land, 44–56; a grant of powers, 45–47; division of powers in, 47–52; doctrine of judicial supremacy in, 52–53; limitations on, 53–54; few innovations of, 54–56; comparison with English constitution, 57–59; development of, 57–70; by law, 59–60; by judicial interpretation, 60–64; by usage, 64–67; by amendment, 67–69; results of, 69–70; limitations on powers of state legislatures, 421.
Constitutions, state, original, 17–19, 404–407; framing, ratification, and amendment of later, 408–412; interpretation of, 412–414; limitations on powers of state legislatures, 421–422; need for changes in, 523–524.
Continental Congresses, 11–12.
Contract, freedom of, 292–293; impairment of, 397–398.
Convention, Constitutional, of 1787, proposal for, 25; organization and members, 27–31; work, 31–36; ratification, 36–43.
Conventions, National, 93–95; nominating, 333, 418; constitutional, in states, 409–412; party, in states, 477–478.
Cooley, T. M., *Constitutional Limitations*, 296 n, 353 n.
Coroner, 555–556.
Corwin, E. S., *President's Control of Foreign Relations*, 111 n; *Doctrine of Judicial Review*, 362 n.
Cotton, J. P., Jr., ed., *Constitutional Decisions of John Marshall*, 238 n, 361 n.
County courts, 490–491, 554.
County, government of, in the colonies, 537–539; in 1860, 540–541; what the county is, 546–547; its functions, 547–548; its administration, 549–550; financial duties, 550–551; administrative functions, 551–553; judicial functions, 553–554; its various officials, 554–557; need for reconstruction, 558–559; effect on other local areas, in South and in Far West, 569–571.
Courtesy, senatorial, 65, 106–108.
Court of Claims, 371.
Court of Customs Appeals, 371.
Coxe, Brinton, *Judicial Power and Unconstitutional Legislation*, 362 n.
Crandall, S. B., *Treaties, Their Making and Enforcement*, 164 n.
Cuba, relation to the United States, 383.
*Cummings* v. *Missouri*, 289 n.
Curtis, B. R., *Jurisdiction, Practice and Peculiar Jurisprudence of the Courts*, 345 n.

Dallinger, F. W., *Nominations for Elective Office*, 93 n.
Daniels, W. M., *Elements of Public Finance*, 460 n.

Dartmouth College v. Woodward, 292, 361 n, 397.
Davis, Jefferson, *Rise and Fall of the Confederate Government*, 212 n.
Dayton, Ohio, city-manager plan in, 631–632.
Dealey, J. Q., *Growth of American State Constitutions*, 405 n.
Debt, national, 233–245; state, 469–472.
Declaration of Independence, 13.
Delegation of power, legislative and administrative, 296–298; in a federal republic, to nation and to subordinate communities, 391.
Democratic Party, in 1789 (or Anti-Federalist), 314–315; in 1800 (or Republican), 316–318; history since 1828, 318–321; connection with Tammany Hall, 482.
Departments, federal, heads of, 129–131; their work, 131–140.
De Saussure v. Gaillard, 492.
Des Moines, commission government in, 621–623.
Dewey, D. R., *Financial History of the United States*, 227 n.
Dicey, A. V., *Law of the Constitution*, 46 n, 57.
Dickinson, G. L., *Development of Parliament*, 513.
Dickinson, J. M., *Special Report on the Philippines*, 383 n.
Direct legislation, 501–521; definition, 502; not a novelty, 503; reasons for its spread, 504–505; mechanism, 505–508; merits and defects, 508–518; the recall, 518–521.
District attorney, federal, 370.
District Courts, 370–371.
District of Columbia, control of Congress over, 286; delegates to National Convention, 334; history and government, 384–388.
Division of powers, in first state constitutions, 18, 406; in the Constitution, 47–52; Montesquieu's views on, 47–51; not disturbed by development of the Constitution, 69–70; in relation to Senate's special functions, 162–163; merits and defects in state government, 524–526; possible alternatives for, 526–528.
Dodd, W. F., *Government of the District of Columbia*, 384 n; *Revision and Amendment of State Constitutions*, 405 n.
Dodds, H. W., *Procedure in State Legislatures*, 424 n.
Dougherty, J. H., *Electoral System of the United States*, 93 n.

Dred Scott v. Sandford, 72, 365.
Due process of law, 291–294.

Education, supervision of, in states, 455, 543; in cities, 611–613.
Edwards, G. J., *The Grand Jury*, 353 n.
Efficiency, federal Bureau of, 141.
Election, of the President, 64, 89–96; disputes over, 90–92, 318; of Senators, 147–152; of Representatives, 182–185; frequency of, and party machines, 480–481; of judges, 494–496; after a recall, 520; supervision of counties over, 553; need for reform of, in counties, 558–559; effect of commission government on methods of, 632–634.
Electorate, effect of direct legislation on, 510–511; need of greater enlightenment of, 533–534. See also Suffrage.
Electors, of the President, 89–93, 95–96.
Elliott, Edward, *Biographical Story of the Constitution*, 27 n.
Eminent domain, 294–295.
England, control over the American colonies, 5–8; constitution, 57–58; cabinet in, compared with American, 126–127, 144–145; debates in parliament compared with Senate, 155–156; residence qualification of members of parliament, 185; comparison of House of Commons with House of Representatives, 206–207, 300–302; history of common law in, 349; origin of equity in, 351.
Equity. See Law.
Evans, L. B., *Leading Cases on American Constitutional Law*, 62 n; *Writings of Washington*, 313 n.
Executive. See President, Senate, Governor, Mayor.
Executive orders, 114–115.
*Ex parte Bollman*, 290 n.
*Ex parte Jackson*, 282 n.
*Ex parte Merryman*, 365 n.
Exports, prohibition of tax on, 222–223.
*Ex post facto* laws, 289, 396.
Extradition, 402–403.

Fairlie, J. A., *National Administration*, 127 n, 132 n; 'Veto Power of the State Governor,' 437 n; *Local Government in Cities, Towns, and Villages*, 535 n, 539 n, 540–541, 546 n, 554 n, 558, 568 n.
Farrand, Max, *Records of the Federal Convention of 1787*, 27 n; *Framing of the Constitution*, 27 n.

## INDEX

Federal courts, power of Congress over subordinate, 284–285; constitutional securities for fair trial by, 353–356; Supreme, 357–369; subordinate, 369–371. See also Judiciary, Supreme Court.
Federal government, powers of, 45–47; democracy of, under development of the Constitution, 70; need for strong judiciary, 342; place of states in, 389–403.
Federal Reserve Board, 240–241.
Federal Trade Commission, 140, 259–260.
*Federalist, The*, 48 *n*, 66 *n*, 116 *n*, 146, 147, 148, 164, 169, 222 *n*, 246, 273, 308, 311, 312 *n*, 344, 390; as letters of "Publius," 39; value of, 39–40.
Federalist party, 314–317.
Federation, of the colonies, 9–13.
*Field v. Clark*, 297 *n*.
Finance, national, part of Treasury Department in, 133–134; congressional methods regarding, 302–311; state, 460–472; municipal, 592, 597–598. See also State finance.
Finley, J. H., and Sanderson, J. F., *American Executive and Executive Methods*, 433 *n*, 435 *n*.
Fire protection and prevention, in cities, 607–608.
Fish, C. R., *Civil Service and the Patronage*, 110 *n*.
Fisher, S. G., *Evolution of the Constitution*, 55 *n*.
Fiske, John, on the gerrymander, 183 *n*.
Flack, H. E., *Adoption of Fourteenth Amendment*, 398 *n*.
Follett, M. R., *Speaker of the House of Representatives*, 193 *n*.
Ford, H. J., *Rise and Growth of American Politics*, 158 *n*, 315 *n*, 474 *n*; *Cost of our National Government*, 303 *n*.
Ford, P. L., *Pamphlets on the Constitution*, 38 *n*; *The Federalist*, 40 *n*.
Foreign affairs, power of President in, 111–112; in relation to State Department, 132–133; in connection with Senate, 164–168.
Foster, Roger, *Commentaries on the Constitution*, 44 *n*, 168 *n*, 209 *n*.
Franklin, Benjamin, at Albany Congress, 10; at Constitutional Convention, 29, 30, 37.

Gaffey, F. G., "Suffrage Limitations at the South," 80 *n*.
Galveston, commission government in, 582, 618–621.
Garner, J. W., *Introduction to Political Science*, 393 *n*; "Executive Participation in Legislation," 434 *n*.
Gerrymander, 183.
*Gibbons v. Ogden*, 210, 248–249, 361 *n*.
Gilbertson, H. S., *County Government*, 548 *n*.
Glenn, G., *Army and the Law*, 271 *n*.
*Gompers v. United States*, 366.
Goodnow, F. J., *Politics and Administration*, 340 *n*; *Principles of Administrative Law*, 446 *n*; *City Government*, 574.
Governor, colonial, 6; in first state constitutions, 17–18; as stepping-stone to presidency, 101; history of office, 431–432; salary, 432; election, 432; removal, 432–433; powers and status, 433–444; share in budget-making, 466–469; proposed reconstruction of office, 527–529.
Greene, E. B., *Provincial America*, 3 *n*; *Provincial Governor*, 6 *n*, 431 *n*.
Guam, 138, 383.

Hadley, A. T., *Education of the American Citizen*, 514 *n*.
*Hagood v. Southern*, 348 *n*.
Haines, C. G., *American Doctrine of Judicial Supremacy*, 52 *n*, 362 *n*.
Haines, Lynn, *Your Congress*, 341.
Hamilton, Alexander, at Annapolis Convention, 24–25; at Constitutional Convention, 28, 29–37; in *The Federalist*, 39–40; on terms of Senators, 148; as Secretary of the Treasury, 233–235, 245; *Report on Manufactures*, 252; on the judiciary, 344; on sovereignty of the states, 392 *n*.
Hare, J. I. C., *American Constitutional Law*, 44 *n*.
Harrison, Benjamin, *This Country of Ours*, 105 *n*.
Hart, A. B., *National Ideals Historically Traced*, 55 *n*, 210 *n*. See also McLaughlin, A. C.
Hatch, L. C., *Administration of the American Revolutionary Army*, 20 *n*.
Hawaii, status of citizens, 74; government, 137, 376–377; delegates to National Convention, 334, to Congress, 377.
Hayes-Tilden controversy, 91–92.
Haynes, G. H., *Election of Senators*, 148 *n*.
*Hepburn v. Griswold*, 368 *n*.
Hinds, A. C., *Precedents of the House of Representatives*, 192 *n*.
Hinsdale, B. A., *Old Northwest*, 372 *n*.

2 T

# 642　INDEX

Hinsdale, M. L., *History of the President's Cabinet*, 127 n.
Hoar, R. S., *Constitutional Conventions*, 405 n.
Holcombe, A. N., *State Government*, 421 n, 433 n, 489 n, 490 n.
Holdsworth, J. T., *First Bank of the United States*, 236 n.
Holmes, O. W., *The Common Law*, 350 n.
Home rule, in cities, 584–586.
Hosmer, J. K., *History of the Louisiana Purchase*, 374 n.
Housing, in cities, 613.
Houston, D. J., *Nullification in South Carolina*, 211 n.
Houston v. Moore, 344 n.
Howard, G. E., *Local Constitutional History*, 535 n.
Hughes, R. M., *Handbook of Jurisdiction and Procedure*, 345 n.
Hunt, Gaillard, *Department of State*, 133 n; "Locating the Capital," 385 n.
Hurtado v. California, 293 n.
Hylton v. United States, 224 n.

Immigration, under direction of Department of Labor, 139; control of Congress over, 255–256; effect of, on cities, 575–576.
Impeachment, of President, 124–125; power of Senate over, 168; of House of Representatives over, 171; origin and procedure, 168–172; instances, 172–173; of state governors, 432–433; of state judges, 496–497.
Implied powers, of Congress, under the Constitution, 62–63, 213–215, 286.
Incorporation, of areas for local government, 542, 568–569.
Initiative. See Direct legislation.
*In re Debs*, 122 n.
*Insular Cases*, 375 n.
Insurance, regulation of, in states, 449; social, 453.
Interior, federal Department of, 137.
Interpretation, judicial, of the Constitution, 60–64; in states, 412–414.
Interstate Commerce Commission, 140, 256–259.
*Irvine v. Marshall*, 346 n.
*Ives v. South Buffalo Ry. Co.*, 452 n.

Jackson, Andrew, as President, 100; inaugurates spoils system, 109; use of veto, 117; relation to Cabinet, 130 n; attitude towards national bank, 238; effect of election as President on political parties, 318–319.
Jameson, J. A., *Constitutional Conventions*, 405 n.

Jay, John, in *The Federalist*, 39–40; as Chief Justice, 359–360.
Jefferson, Thomas, election of, as President, 90–91, 96 n; messages to Congress, 113; on the powers of Congress, 209; as leader of Democratic party, in 1800, 316–317.
Jenks, J. W., *Principles of Politics*, 186 n.
Jones, C. L., *Statute Law Making*, 428 n.
Judiciary, colonial, 8; doctrine of supremacy of, in the Constitution, 52–53, 342–343; connection with naturalization, 75–77; immunity of Executive from, 124–125; necessity for, in the government, 343–344; sphere of, 345–349; law and equity administered by, 349–352; procedure, 352–356. See also Federal Courts, State Courts, Supreme Court.
Judson, F. N., *Judiciary and the People*, 493 n, 494 n.
Jury, grand, 353; petty, 353–355.
Justice, federal Department of, 137–138.

Kales, A. M., *Unpopular Government*, 534.
Kansas, plan for reconstruction of state government in, 527–528.
*Knox v. Lee*, 368 n.

Labor, federal Department of, 139.
Laughlin, J. L., *History of Bimetallism in the United States*, 279 n.
Law, development of Constitution by, 59–60; military, 270; martial, 270–272; and equity, of the United States, 349–352.
Learned, H. B., *The President's Cabinet*, 127 n.
Legal tender, issue over, 279–280.
*Legal Tender Cases*, 279 n.
Legislation, powers of the President in connection with, 112–121; of the Senate, 173–175; of the House, 201–206; of Congress, 208–218; delegation of power regarding, 296; merits and shortcomings of Congress in, 299–311; of state legislatures, 428–430.
Legislatures, colonial, 6–8; state, organization of, 415–418; nomination, 418–419; election, 419–420; salaries, 420; sessions, 420; powers, 421–422; procedure, 422; officers and committees, 422–423; enactment of laws, 425; share in budget-making, 466–468; in relation to direct legislation, 504–505, 514–515; proposed reconstruction, 526–529; control over counties, 547. See also Congress.
*Leisy v. Hardin*, 262 n.

L'Enfant, Pierre-Charles, work in planning Washington, 385.
Lewis, Lawrence, *History of the Bank of North America*, 235 n.
Libby, O. S., *Geographical Distribution of the Vote on the Federal Constitution*, 41 n.
Libraries, public, administration of, in cities, 612–613.
Library of Congress, 141–142.
Lieber, F., *Civil Liberty and Self-Government*, 353 n.
Lien, A. J., *Privileges and Immunities of Citizens*, 73 n.
Limitations, constitutional theory of, 53–54; on the powers of Congress, 288–298; on the states, under the Constitution, 396–403.
Lobingier, C. S., *People's Law*, 405 n, 501 n.
Local government, history of, in the colonies, 8–9, 535–539, 577–578; development since the Revolution, 539–541; control of state over, 541–545; in counties, 546–559; in towns, townships, and villages, 560–571; in cities, 572–635.
Lodge, H. C., ed., *Works of Alexander Hamilton*, 235 n.
Lowell, A. L., *Public Opinion and Popular Government*, 326–327, 328, 501 n, 513 n, 531–532.
Lowrie, S. G., *The Budget*, 466 n.
Luther v. Borden, 365 n.
Lutz, H. L., *State Tax Commissions*, 456 n.

McBain, H. L., *Law and Practice of Municipal Home Rule*, 585 n.
McCall, S. W., *Business of Congress*, 189 n, 192 n.
McClain, Emlin, *Constitutional Law*, 45 n, 263 n; *Selection of Cases on Constitutional Law*, 62 n.
McConachie, L. G., *Congressional Committees*, 199 n.
McCray v. U. S., 250 n.
McCulloch v. *Maryland*, 214 n, 219 n, 236–237, 361 n, 392.
McDonagh, Michael, *Speaker of the House*, 193 n.
MacDonald, William, *Select Charters, 1606–1775*, 4 n; *Select Documents, 1776–1861*, 15 n, 372 n.
McGehee, L. P., *Due Process of Law under the Federal Constitution*, 292 n.
MacGregor, F. H., *City Government by Commission*, 618 n.
McKinley, A. E., *Suffrage Franchise in the Thirteen Colonies*, 6 n, 180 n.

McLaughlin, A. C., *Confederation and the Constitution*, 15 n, 247 n; *Courts, Constitution, and Parties*, 362 n.
McLaughlin, A. C., and Hart, A. B., ed., *Cyclopedia of American Government*, 45 n, 173 n, 179 n.
McQuillin, Eugene, *Law of Municipal Corporations*, 547 n.
Machine, the, in political parties, 480–487.
Macy, Jesse, *Party Organization and Machinery*, 330 n, 337 n.
Madison, James, at Constitutional Convention, 29–30, 37; in *The Federalist*, 39–40; on division of powers, 47, 51; on national bank, 235 n; on state executive, 435–436 n.
Marbury v. Madison, 361 n.
Marshal, in federal District Courts, 370.
Marshall, John, on the delegation of powers, 210; on implied powers, 213–214; on power to tax, 219; on the power to charter banks, 236–238; as Chief Justice, 360–365.
Maryland, budget system in, 467.
Mason, E. C., *Veto Power*, 118 n.
Massachusetts, constitution, 404, 406; enactment of laws in, 425–428; organization of state parties in, 476; optional charter system for cities in, 586.
Massachusetts Constitutional Convention, *Bulletins*, 411 n, 416 n, 441 n, 466 n, 472 n, 501 n, 519 n, 583 n, 633 n, 634 n.
Mathews, J. M., *American State Administration*, 433 n, 438 n, 446 n.
Mayor, election, qualifications, and salary, 589; powers, 589–593.
Merriam, C. S., *Primary Elections*, 418 n.
Meyer, E. C., *Nominating Systems*, 93 n.
Michael, W. H., *History of the Department of State*, 133 n.
Militia, control of Congress over, 272–275; supervision of states over, 456–457.
Minimum wage laws, in states, 452–453.
Minor v. Happersett, 79 n, 395.
Mississippi R. R. Co. v. Wheeler, 84 n.
Montesquieu, on the division of powers, 47–49; *The Spirit of Laws*, 48 n, 55 n.
Moore, J. B., *Extradition and Interstate Rendition*, 402 n.
Moran, T. F., *American Presidents*, 100 n.

Morris, Gouverneur, in revision of Constitution, 31, 36.
Municipal administration, branches of, police, 602–607; fire protection, 607–608; public works, 608–610; sanitation, 610; public health, 610–611; education, 611–612; libraries, 612–613; poor relief, 613; housing, 613; recreation, 613–614; regulation of public utilities, 614–617.
Municipal government, in the Philippines, 382–383; in the United States, types of, 588–589; mayor, 589–593; heads of departments, 593–595; city council, 595–599; city employees, 599–600; inefficiency of, 600–601.
Municipal ownership, 615–617.
Munro, W. B., *Government of American Cities*, 589 *n*, 623 *n*; *Municipal Administration*, 602 *n*.
Myers, Gustavus, *History of Tammany Hall*, 482 *n*.

Naturalization, by statute or treaty, 74–75; by judicial process, 75–77; strictness of laws for, 77; rights conferred by, 78; power of Congress over, 277.
Navy, federal Department of the, 138; history of the, 269.
*Neely* v. *Henkel*, 365.
Negro suffrage, 79–80.
*Nereide, The*, 352.
New England Confederation of 1643, 9–10.
New England. See Colonies.
New York Constitutional Convention, *Index Digest of State Constitutions*, 405 *n*; speech of Elihu Root at, 509 *n*, 530.
New York, organization of state parties in, 475–476; optional charter system for cities in, 586.
Nomination, of candidates for President, 93–95; of presidential electors, 95; of Congressmen, 183–184; by caucus, 330–333; in conventions, 333–334.
*Northern Securities Co.* v. *U. S.*, 260.
Nullification, and secession, 211–213.

Oberholtzer, E. P., *Initiative, Referendum, and Recall*, 501 *n*.
Oleomargarine case, 250 *n*.
Ordinances, powers of city council to enact, 596–597; limitations on, 597.
Oregon, plan for reconstruction of state government in, 528.
Original Package Case, 262–263.
Origins, English and colonial, 1–13.

Orth, S. P., *Boss and the Machine*, 480 *n*.
Ostrogorski, M., *Democracy and Political Parties*, 330 *n*; *Democracy and the Party System*, 330 *n*, 331 *n*.

*Pacific R. R. Co.* v. *Soule*, 224 *n*.
Panama Canal Zone, 136, 383.
Pardons, power of granting, by the President, 110; by state governors, 441–442.
Parties, political, and the Constitution, 65–66; National Conventions of, 93; leadership of, by President, 123–124, by Speaker of the House, 198–199, by state governors, 434–435; influence in Senate, 156–157; strict allegiance to, in Congress, 301–302, in states, 474–475; history, in national government, 312–322; definition, 322; functions, 323–327; two-party system in, 328–329; organization and methods, 330–341, in states, 475–479; abstention of Supreme Court from, 364–365; activities in states, 473–474; machines, 480–485; bosses, 485–487; relation to better state government, 531–533.
Patents, control of Congress over, 283–284, 283 *n*.
Paterson plan, 32.
*Pensacola Tel. Co.* v. *W. U. Tel. Co.*, 248 *n*.
Philippine Islands, status of citizens, 75, 375; government, 136, 379–383; delegates to National Convention, 334, to Congress, 381.
Phillips, J. B., *Educational Qualifications of Voters*, 80 *n*.
Pierce, William, as secretary of the Constitutional Convention, 28 *n*.
Platform, party, adoption of, by National Convention, 334–335; by state conventions, 478.
Plehn, C. C., *Public Finance*, 460 *n*.
Police, administration of, in cities, 602–607.
Police court, 606–607.
Police power, of states, in relation to interstate trade, 262.
*Pollock* v. *Farmers' Loan and Trust Co.*, 225 *n*.
Pomeroy, J. N., *Constitutional Law of the United States*, 281 *n*.
Poor relief. See Charities.
Porto Rico, status of citizens, 75, 375; government, 136, 377–379; delegates to National Convention, 334, to Congress, 379.
Postal power, of Congress, 281–283.
Postmaster General, 137.

## INDEX

Preferential voting, 632-633.
Presidency, history of, 100-102; succession to, 103-104.
President, discussion of, at Constitutional Convention, 35-36, 88-89; election of, 64, 69, 89-96; appointments of, 65, 106-110; reëlection, 66; messages, 67, 112-113; inauguration, 96; choice of a, 97-100; salary, 103; constitutional qualifications, 104; powers and functions, 105-125; as party leader, 113-114, 123-124; veto power, 115-121; relation to the courts, 124-125; relation to Cabinet, 129-131; influence in appropriations, 306; nomination of candidates for, 334.
Primary, presidential, 102-103; direct, 418-419.
Privileges and immunities, of citizens, 78-83; not extended to corporations, 84; of Senators, 157; protected by Fourteenth Amendment, 398-399.
Progressive party, 320.
Prohibition party, 321-322.
Proportional representation, 633-634.
Prosecuting attorney, 556-557.
Protection, equal, of the laws, as provided by Constitution, 399-400.
*Public Clearing House* v. *Coyne*, 282 n.
Public health and sanitation, administration of, national, 135; in states, 448; in cities, 610-611.
Public utilities, regulation of, in states, 448-449; in cities, 614-617; granting of franchises for, in cities, 598; municipal ownership of, 615-617.
Public works, national, supervision of, by War Department, 135-136; administration of, by counties, 551-552; in cities, 608-610.

Qualifications, for office. *See* several offices. For voting, *see* Suffrage.

Randolph plan, 31-32.
Ray, P. O., *Political Parties and Practical Politics*, 330 n, 335, 477 n, 485 n.
Recall, of state governors, 433; of state judges, 497-498; of judicial decisions, 498-499; in general, 518-521.
Recreation, public, in cities, 613-614.
Referendum. *See* Direct legislation.
Reform, of state government, 522-534; in city government, 581-582.
Registration of voters, 180.
Reinsch, P. S., *American Legislatures and Legislative Methods*, 421 n, 425.
Removal, by the President, 108-109; of state governors, 432-433; of state officials, 441; of state judges, 496-498; by mayors, 592.
Representation, basis of, in Congress, 147; in Senate, 152; in House of Representatives, 176-177, 181-182; redistricting for, 182-183.
Representatives, House of, originates money bills, 66; power over treaties, 167; composition, 176-190; original conception, 176-177; elections for, 177-184; qualifications of members, 184-186; proper function of representatives, 186; sessions, 187; term, 187-188; debates, 188-190; organization and methods, 191-207; rules, 191-192; Speaker, 192-199; committees, 199-203; procedure, 203-206; comparison with House of Commons, 206-207; influence on financial policy, 308; delegates from territories in, 377, 379, 381.
Republican form of government, guarantees to states for, 394-395.
Republican party, history of, 318-321.
Residence requirement, for candidates in American legislatures, 184-185.
Restraint of trade, 260-263.
Robinson, J. H., *Original and Derived Features of the Constitution*, 55 n.
Rogers, Lindsay, *Postal Power of Congress*, 282 n.
Roosevelt, Theodore, *Autobiography*, 105 n.
Root, Elihu, *Political Addresses*, 509 n; at New York Constitutional Convention, 530.
Rose, J. C., "Negro Suffrage," 80 n.
Rowe, L. S., *United States and Porto Rico*, 378 n.
Royce, Josiah, *Philosophy of Loyalty*, 192 n.
Russell, E. B., *Review of American Colonial Legislation*, 7 n.

Salary. *See* several offices.
Salmon, Lucy M., "Appointing Power of the President," 108 n.
Samoa, 383.
*Santa Clara Co.* v. *Southern Pacific Co.*, 399 n.
Scott, W. A., *Repudiation of State Debts*, 243 n.
Secrist, Horace, *Constitutional Restrictions upon Public Indebtedness*, 469 n.
Seligman, E. R. A., *Shifting and Incidence of Taxation*, 220 n; *Income Tax*, 226 n.
Senate, confirmation of presidential appointments, 65, 106-108, 163-164; in connection with treaties, 111-112,

164–168; organization, 146–161; original conception of, 147–149; sessions, 152–153; committees, 153–154; debates, 154–156; place in American history, 157–160; special functions, 163–173; trial of impeachments, 168–172; legislative functions, 173–175; influence on financial policy, 307–308.

Separation of powers. *See* Division of powers.

*Sere* v. *Pilot*, 374 n.

Sheriff, 554–555.

Sherman Anti-Trust Act, 260–262.

Simpson, Alex., Jr., *Federal Impeachments*, 171 n.

*Slaughter House Cases*, 83 n, 398.

Smith, Adam, *Wealth of Nations*, 220 n.

Socialist party, 322.

South Carolina, nullification and secession in, 211–212.

Sovereignty, in the United States, 392–394.

Speaker, of House of Representatives, origin, 192; office in England, 192–193; development in America, 193–194; choice of, 194; powers of, 194–199.

Spoils system, 109–110.

*Springer* v. *United States*, 225 n.

Stamp Act Congress, 11.

Stanwood, Edward, *History of the Presidency*, 89 n, 317 n.

*Stare decisis*, doctrine of, as followed by Supreme Court, 368–369.

State administration, 443–459; increase of officials in, 445–447; general, 447–448; public health, 448; public utilities, 448–449; banking and insurance, 449–450; industrial affairs, 450–453; charities and corrections, 453–454; public property, 454; education, 455; assessment and taxation, 455–456; regulation of professions, 456; military affairs, 456–457; miscellaneous, 457; results of, 457–459; need for consolidation, 529–531.

State courts, relation to federal, 488; history, 488–490; organization, 490–491; supremacy, 491–493; judges, 493–498; interpretation of laws, 498–499; procedure and its reform, 499–500.

State, federal Department of, 132–133.

State finance, scope of, 460–461; revenues, 461–464; expenditures, 464–469; debt, 469–472; need for change in policy, 533.

States, early constitutions, 17–19; powers of, under the Constitution, 46; woman suffrage in, 81 n; influence in choice of President, 98–99; suffrage in, 178–180; general powers under the Constitution, 209–213; taxation of instrumentalities of, by Congress, 226–227; taxation of national banks by, 237; control over interstate commerce, 262–263; treason in, 291; due process of law in, 293; suability, 347–348; jurisdiction of federal courts over, 347–349; place of, in the nation, 389–403; federal guarantees to, 395–396; prohibitions on, 400–403; constitutions, 404–414; legislatures, 415–430; governors, 431–444; administrative officers, 445–459; finance, 460–472; parties and practical politics, 473–487; courts, 488–500; direct legislation and recall, 501–521; reconstruction of government in, 522–534; supervision over local governments, 541–545; interference in city affairs, 580–581.

Stevens, C. E., *Sources of the Constitution*, 55 n.

Story, Joseph, *Commentaries on the Constitution*, 44 n, 345 n; as Associate Justice, 367.

Streets, administration of, in cities, planning, 608–609; paving, 609–610.

Suffrage, colonial, 6; widening of, under English and American constitutions, 58–59; relation to citizenship, 78–82; negro, 79–80; woman, 80–82; at congressional elections, 177–178; extension of, 178–180; in Hawaii, 376; in Porto Rico, 379; in the Philippines, 381.

Supreme Court, provision for, in Constitution, 52–53; its power to declare laws unconstitutional, 59, 362–364; interpretation of Constitution by, 60–64; its working, 357–359; its history, 359–367; official reports, 359 n; precedents followed by, 367–369; decisions as to control over territories, 375.

Swayze, F. J., "Judicial Construction of the Fourteenth Amendment," 399 n.

Taft, W. H., *Our Chief Magistrate and His Powers*, 105 n, 117 n, 237 n; *Special Report on the Philippines*, 383 n.

Tammany Hall, 482–485.

Taney, Roger B., as Chief Justice, 365.

Tariff, the, 251–254; Commission, 140–141, 254–255; as a party issue, 319–320.

## INDEX

Taussig, F. W., *Tariff History*, 252 *n*; *Silver Situation*, 279 *n*.
*Tax Collector* v. *Day*, 227 *n*.
Taxation, power of, in the colonies, 7, 8; under Articles of Confederation, 15–16, 20–21; under the Constitution, by Congress, 219–232; by states, 461–464; by counties, 550–551; in cities, 597–598.
Taxes, definition, 219–220; essentials, 220; classification, 220–221; limitations on levy by Congress, 221–227; direct, 224–225; income, 225–226, 464; corporation, 226, 264; war, 228–229; collection of, 231–232; general property, 461; classification of property for, 461–462; on intangible property, 462; assessment for, 463; inheritance, 463–464; poll, 464.
Territories, government of, 136, 137, 372–388.
*Texas* v. *White*, 366.
Thayer, J. B., *Cases in Constitutional Law*, 62 *n*; *John Marshall*, 362 *n*; *American Doctrine of Constitutional Law*, 362.
Thompson, C. S., *Rise and Fall of the Congressional Caucus*, 333 *n*.
Thorpe, F. N., *Federal and State Constitutions*, 405 *n*.
Tiedeman, C. G., *Unwritten Constitution*, 64 *n*.
Tocqueville, Alexis de, *Democracy in America*, 158–159 *n*.
Towns, government of, in the colonies, 536–537; relation to state government, 560–561; in New England, 561–567; town meeting, 562–564; selectmen and officials, 564–566; criticism of, 566–567; in north and central states, 567–569; in South, 569–570; in Far West, 570–571.
Treason, 289–291.
Treasury, federal Department of, 133–135; relation to estimates in appropriations, 303.
Treaties, power over, of President, 111–112; of Senate, 164–167; of House of Representatives, 167; and secret diplomacy, 167–168.
Tucker, J. R., *Constitution of the United States*, 44 *n*.
*Twining* v. *New Jersey*, 291.

Unconstitutionality, of laws, federal, 59, 362–364; state, 498–499.
United States, "Report on Citizenship of the United States," 74 *n*; Tenure of Office Act, 109 *n*; National Banking Act of 1913, 238–239; Federal Reserve Act, 240; National Defence Act of 1916, 267 *n*, 274 *n*; *Manual for Courts-Martial*, 271 *n*; *Report of the President's Commission on Economy and Efficiency*, 309 *n*; Judiciary Act of 1789, 343, 369, 493 *n*; Foraker Act, 378; Philippine Civil Government Act, 380; *Comparative Financial Statistics of Cities under Council and Commission Government*, 626 *n*.
*United States* v. *Knight*, 249 *n*, 260 *n*.

Van Dyne, F., *Citizenship of the United States*, 74 *n*.
*Veazie Bank* v. *Fenno*, 224 *n*.
Veto power, of colonial governors, 7; of President, 115–119; frequency of use by, 117–118; pocket, 118–119, in states, 436–437; merits and defects of, 119; limitations on, 120–121; of state governors, 435–438; of mayors, 590–591.
Vice-President, election of, 89–96; succession to presidency, 103–104; purpose of office, 104; qualifications for, 104; in the Senate, 152–153; in impeachments, 172; nomination of candidates for, 334.
Virgin Islands, 138, 383.

War, federal Department of, 135–136.
War, powers in relation to, under the Confederation, 22–23; exercised by the President, 121–122; of Congress, 265–276; of state governors, 442.
Washington, city of. See District of Columbia.
Washington, George, on defects of the Confederation, 22, 23; presiding at Constitutional Convention, 29; attitude toward political parties, 313–315.
Weber, A. F., *Growth of Cities*, 573 *n*.
Webster, Daniel, on due process of law, 292.
*Western Union Tel. Co.* v. *Call Publishing Co.*, 352 *n*.
Whig party, 318–319.
Wilcox, D. F., *Government by All the People*, 501 *n*.
Willoughby, W. F., *Territories and Dependencies*, 373–374, 383 *n*.
Willoughby, W. W., *Constitutional Law of the United States*, 44 *n*, 209 *n*, 288 *n*, 345 *n*; *Constitutional Law*, 44 *n*; *Supreme Court*, 357 *n*; *American Constitutional System*, 370 *n*.
Wilson Act, 263.
Wilson, Woodrow, *Constitutional Govern-*

ment, 100 n, 102 n, 105 n, 124 n, 160–161, 363; *Congressional Government*, 430.

Wise, J. S., *Treatise on American Citizenship*, 74 n.

Woodburn, J. A., *The American Republic*, 198 n, 218 n; *Political Parties*, 315 n.

Woodruff, C. R., *City Government by Commission*, 618 n.

Woman suffrage, 80–82.

Worcester, D. C., *The Philippines*, 383 n.

Workmen's compensation laws, in states, 451–452.

*Yick Wo* v. *Hopkins*, 400.

Printed in the United States of America.

DARTMOUTH COLLEGE

3 3311 01466 0262